The Letter to the Galatians

THE NEW INTERNATIONAL COMMENTARY
ON THE
NEW TESTAMENT

General Editors

NED B. STONEHOUSE
(1946–1962)

F. F. BRUCE
(1962–1990)

GORDON D. FEE
(1990–2012)

JOEL B. GREEN
(2013–)

The Letter to the
GALATIANS

David A. deSilva

William B. Eerdmans Publishing Company
Grand Rapids, Michigan

Wm. B. Eerdmans Publishing Co.
4035 Park East Court SE, Grand Rapids, Michigan 49546
www.eerdmans.com

© 2018 David A. deSilva
Published 2018
Printed in the United States of America

27 26 25 24 23 22 21   3 4 5 6 7 8 9 10

ISBN 978-0-8028-3055-5

Library of Congress Cataloging-in-Publication Data

Names: DeSilva, David Arthur, author.
Title: The letter to the Galatians / David A. deSilva.
Description: Grand Rapids : Eerdmans Publishing Co., 2018. |
    Series: The new international commentary on the New Testament |
    Includes bibliographical references and index.
Identifiers: LCCN 2017060965 | ISBN 9780802830555 (hardcover : alk. paper)
Subjects: LCSH: Bible. Galatians—Commentaries.
Classification: LCC BS2685.53 .D475 2018 | DDC 227/.4077—dc23
    LC record available at https://lccn.loc.gov/2017060965s

To Daniel G. Reid

lifelong scholar and facilitator
of scholarship in the service of faith,
with gratitude

Contents

List of Excursuses   xi

General Editor's Preface   xiii

Author's Preface   xv

Abbreviations   xix

Bibliography   xxv

INTRODUCTION

   I. AUTHORSHIP   1

  II. PAUL'S MINISTRY IN GALATIA   3

 III. THE PASTORAL CHALLENGE IN GALATIA   7

 IV. THE "GOOD NEWS" ACCORDING TO THE RIVAL TEACHERS   16

    A. The Case for Circumcision   17

    B. Torah as the Way to Perfection   19

    C. Whom Should the Galatians Trust?   22

  V. WHO WERE THE GALATIAN CHRISTIANS?   26

 VI. GALATIANS IN ROMAN GEOGRAPHY AND PAULINE
     CHRONOLOGY   28

    A. The Data within Galatians   29

    B. Acts and Galatians   33

    C. Was Paul Addressing Churches in *North* or in *South* Galatia?   39

    D. Paul's Visits to Jerusalem in Galatians and Acts   48

 VII. THE DATE OF GALATIANS   58

CONTENTS

VIII. GALATIANS AS PERSUASIVE COMMUNICATION   91

     A. Galatians as Ancient Letter   91

     B. Paul's Goals for Galatians and Its Rhetorical Genre   94

     C. Appeals to Ethos, Pathos, and Logos in Galatians   97

     D. The Strategic Arrangement of Galatians   102

IX. WAS GALATIANS EFFECTIVE?   107

TEXT AND COMMENTARY

    I. PAUL'S OPENING GREETING (1:1–5)   111

    II. PAUL ANNOUNCES THE PRESENTING PROBLEM (1:6–10)   122

    III. STRATEGIC RECOLLECTIONS (1:11–2:21)   136

     A. The Divine Source of Paul's Dramatic Transformation and Gospel (1:11–17)   137

     B. Paul's First Visit to Jerusalem and Work in Syria and Cilicia (1:18–24)   158

     C. Paul's Second Visit to Jerusalem (2:1–10)   169

     D. The Confrontation in Antioch (2:11–14)   192

     E. The Coherence of Paul's Position (2:15–21)   212

    IV. ARGUMENTS AGAINST ADOPTING TORAH OBSERVANCE (3:1–4:11)   263

     A. Proof from Experience: The Galatians' Reception of the Spirit (3:1–6)   264

     B. Proof from Abraham's Precedent (3:7–9)   278

     C. Deductive Proof from the Scriptures (3:10–14)   285

     D. Proof from Analogy: Testamentary Law (3:15–18)   305

     E. Why, Then, the Torah? (3:19–22)   313

     F. Proof from Analogy: Coming of Age in the Household, Part 1 (3:23–29)   324

     G. Proof from Analogy: Coming of Age in the Household, Part 2 (4:1–7)   343

     H. Rebuke Based on Argument from Analogy (4:8–11)   362

    V. A RELATIONAL APPEAL (4:12–20)   376

    VI. A SCRIPTURAL COUP DE GRÂCE (4:21–31)   390

Contents

VII. Paul's Principal Advice (5:1–12)   407

   A. Paul's Recommended Course of Action (5:1–6)   408

   B. A Strategic Resumption of Appeals to Ethos (5:7–12)   431

VIII. Spirit-Empowered Righteousness (5:13–6:10)   443

   A. The Spirit's Sufficiency to Nurture Righteousness (5:13–26)   443

   B. Practical Advice for Walking in the Spirit (6:1–10)   478

IX. Paul's Parting Shots and Affirmations (6:11–18)   500

Index of Subjects   519

Index of Authors   522

Index of Scripture and Other Ancient Texts   528

List of Excursuses

PAUL, RHETORIC, AND LETTER-WRITING IN ANTIQUITY — 62

PAUL'S ENCOUNTER WITH THE RESURRECTED JESUS AND PAUL'S PARADIGM SHIFT — 149

JAMES, THE BROTHER OF THE LORD — 161

EATING WITH GENTILES — 198

WHAT DOES PAUL MEAN BY "SEEKING TO BE JUSTIFIED" AND "BEING JUSTIFIED"? — 216

WHAT DOES PAUL MEAN BY "WORKS OF THE LAW"? — 224

WHAT DOES PAUL MEAN BY "FAITH" QUALIFIED BY "JESUS CHRIST"? — 229

A CONTEXTUAL UNDERSTANDING OF GRACE — 254

PRONOUNS, PEOPLE GROUPS, AND THE PLAN OF GOD IN GALATIANS 3–4 — 296

WHAT ARE THE "ELEMENTARY PRINCIPLES" (*STOICHEIA*), AND IN WHAT SENSE ARE THEY "OF THE WORLD" (*TOU KOSMOU*)? — 348

GALATIANS AND THE IMPERIAL CULT — 368

INDICATIVE AND IMPERATIVE IN PAUL — 473

General Editor's Preface

As Acts tells the story, the Lord choreographed an encounter between Philip and an Ethiopian eunuch on the road from Jerusalem to Gaza. This Ethiopian, who had a copy of at least some of the Scriptures, was reading from the prophet Isaiah. Hearing him read, Philip inquired, "Are you really grasping the significance of what you are reading?" The Ethiopian responded, "How can I, unless someone guides me?" The result was that Philip shared the good news about Jesus with him, and the Ethiopian was baptized as a new Christ-follower (Acts 8:26–40).

It is difficult to imagine a more pressing mandate for the work of a commentary than this: to come alongside readers of Scripture in order to lead them so that they can grasp the significance of what they read—and to do so in ways that are not only informative but transformative. This has been and remains the aim of the New International Commentary on the New Testament. The interpretive work on display in this volume—and, indeed, in this commentary series—can find no better raison d'être and serve no better ambition.

What distinguishes such a commentary?

First and foremost, we are concerned with the text of Scripture. It does not mean that we are not concerned with the history of scholarship and scholarly debate. It means, rather, that we strive to provide a commentary on the text and not on the scholarly debate. It means that the centerpiece of our work is a readable guide for readers of these texts, with references to critical issues and literature, as well as interaction with them, all found in our plentiful footnotes. Nor does it mean that we eschew certain critical methods or require that each contributor follow a certain approach. Rather, we take up whatever methods and pursue whatever approaches assist our work of making plain the significance of these texts.

Second, we self-consciously locate ourselves as Christ-followers who read Scripture in the service of the church and its mission in the world. Reading in the service of the church does not guarantee a particular kind of interpretation—say, one that is supportive of the church in all times and places or that merely parrots what the church wants to say. The history of interpretation demonstrates that, at times, the Scriptures speak a needed prophetic word of challenge, calling the church back to its vocation as the church. And at other times, the Scriptures speak a word of encouragement, reminding the church of its identity as a people who follow a crucified Messiah and serve a God who will vindicate God's ways and God's people.

We also recognize that, although the Scriptures are best read and understood through prayerful study and in the context of the church's worship, our reading of them cannot be separated from the world that the church engages in mission. C. S. Lewis rightly noted that what we see is determined in part by where we are standing, and the world in which we stand presses us with questions that cannot help but inform our interpretive work.

It is not enough to talk about what God *once said*, for we need to hear again and again what the Spirit, through the Scriptures, *is now saying* to the church. Accordingly, we inquire into the theological significance of what we read, and into how this message might take root in the lives of God's people.

Finally, the New International Commentary on the New Testament is written above all for pastors, teachers, and students. That is, our work is located in that place between the more critical commentaries, with their lines of untranslated Greek and Aramaic and Latin, and the homiletical commentaries that seek to work out how a text might speak to congregations. Our hope is that those preparing to teach and preach God's word will find in these pages the guide they need, and that those learning the work of exegesis will find here an exemplar worth emulating.

JOEL B. GREEN

Author's Preface

Writing a commentary on Galatians has been a daunting task. First, there is the mundane cause for apprehension—the overwhelming amount of secondary literature on Galatians, compounded by the fact that one cannot engage the conversations about Galatians without also delving into the even more overwhelmingly vast secondary literature on Paul. The second and more important challenge is the inherently rich contribution Galatians makes to Christian thought and practice, on the one hand, and on the other, the theological investment that readers bring to Galatians. And the theological issues that Galatians raises, or that are brought to Galatians, are both foundational and legion.

In this commentary I have attempted to give a coherent accounting of Galatians as a piece of strategically crafted communication addressing the immediate pastoral challenge facing Paul's converts in Galatia *and* the underlying questions that gave rise to the situation in which Paul desperately seeks to intervene. Paul's communication is thoroughly theological, with the result that I have also attempted to give a coherent exposition of the theological argument and underpinnings of Galatians. I do not present these facets of my commentary as a theology of *Paul*, but simply as a theology of *Galatians*. Nevertheless, I do present the latter as an indispensable step toward the former.

In particular, I find in Paul's response to the situation in Galatia the following theological convictions and interests: (1) Paul—like the rival teachers and like the Galatians themselves—is deeply interested in the God-given means to attaining righteousness, which all parties would agree to be prerequisite to acquittal on the last day. (2) Paul—unlike the rival teachers—lays great emphasis on the importance of the Holy Spirit (essentially the promised inheritance that Christ died to secure for Jew and gentile alike) as that means. (3) The "faith" that Paul regards as the response to God that leads to acquittal is far more than a "belief that." It is a reliance upon Jesus and upon what Jesus has gained for his own at such great cost to himself, namely, the Holy Spirit;

it is a single-hearted and consistent investment of oneself in the life that the Holy Spirit seeks to bring about within and among the believers, which is nothing less than Christ living in and through them. It is a faith that invests itself in loving action and that, consequently, leads to righteousness, all by the Spirit's guiding and empowering intervention. I find, in other words, that Paul's understanding of how God has graciously intervened in the lives of human beings so as to rectify all that has gone amiss defies segmentation into the customary—but, to Paul, foreign—categories of justification, sanctification, and regeneration. I have labored under the constant awareness of Paul's fearsome pronouncement upon those who proclaim a gospel other than the one he proclaimed with the single goal of seeking to prove a faithful expositor of *Paul's* understanding of the good news of God's intervention, and not that of any particular post-Pauline theological school.

I have had significant help and support along the way. First, of course, is the aforementioned bevy of scholars who have devoted considerable effort to the investigation of Galatians, many of whom have directly and positively contributed to my understanding of the letter. A glance at the index of modern authors will quickly identify those who have been most influential. True to the goals of this commentary series, I have kept direct engagement with these scholars out of the main text, though I have made ample use of the footnotes to record not only my debts but also my reasons for not accepting many of the suggestions that others have made. Despite the percentage of each page dedicated to such notes, there are also many scholars of Paul in general and Galatians in particular whose names and works are absent therefrom. I ask them not to count this omission a slight but a necessity, given the impossibility, in the present age, of taking adequate account of every available article or book.

I am grateful to the trustees, administration, and faculty of Ashland Theological Seminary for their collective support of my scholarly pursuits. I enjoyed two study leaves, the fruit of which contributed materially to this commentary. The first was supported jointly by the Lilly Foundation, which granted me a faculty fellowship for 2010–11, and Ashland Seminary, which granted me a year's leave to take advantage of the same. It was during this year that I produced *Global Readings: A Sri Lankan Commentary on Paul's Letter to the Galatians* (Eugene, OR: Cascade, 2011), a work that allowed me to come to preliminary decisions about questions of introduction concerning, and the meaning of, Galatians, as well as explore the challenge of Galatians from a distinctly different social location. I am also grateful to Wipf & Stock for their kind permission to freely incorporate material, significantly leavened, into the present commentary. The second study leave allowed me to attend to the completion of the initial draft of the present commentary. My seminary's support of research is not limited, however, to formal study leaves: it is enjoyed constantly in the spaces between preparing for classes or attending to the administrative work of faculty, and I am grateful to Ashland for its commitment not only to the classroom but to the whole vocation of the theological educator. Another manifestation of this support is the freedom we have to offer electives in areas of our research, and I am grateful to the several groups of students with whom I have studied Galatians over the years in courses that were seedbeds for the reading presented here.

I wish also to express gratitude to the churches I have served as organist and choir director during these years of researching and writing on Galatians, among other projects—Christ United Methodist Church in Ashland, Ohio, and, more recently, Port Charlotte United Methodist Church in Port Charlotte, Florida. Aside from providing me with a venue for doing something else that I greatly love, these congregations and their pastoral staffs have both proven to be supportive communities of faith and shown what support they could offer for my vocation as a scholar (from providing me with congenial office space, to allowing me generous time away, to not requiring me to attend most weekly staff meetings).

It has been over a decade since Gordon Fee entrusted to me the task of a replacement volume on Galatians. It is humbling to "replace" the work of so esteemed a scholar as Ronald Fung, but also a great privilege to be allowed to give voice to my own reading of Galatians in such a venue, and I am grateful for his confidence. To the extent that I have remained true to the goals of the series, thanks are due to Joel Green, to whom the series has since been entrusted. This is not the first endeavor in which I have enjoyed support, encouragement, and critical feedback from Joel, and I am grateful for his reception of and contributions to this commentary. I am also grateful to the copyeditor of this volume, Craig A. Noll, for his diligence, meticulousness, and collegiality. My wife, Donna Jean, our sons who give us so much cause to be proud, and my parents have continued to provide a stable source of love and encouragement that should never be taken for granted.

Finally, it is with deep gratitude and respect that I dedicate this commentary to Daniel G. Reid, senior editor at InterVarsity Press, who has been a constant encouragement to me and an important partner in publishing. If I have enjoyed the privilege of having a voice in theological education—now, in multiple languages across the world—it is only because he saw potential in me when I was still quite green and enthusiastically supported (and received) my work. As I consider his work and the resources that have taken shape under his guidance (most impressively, the eight-volume IVP Dictionary series), I begin to realize that the contribution of an editor to scholarship can outweigh, in so many ways, the contribution of any number of authors. Thank you, Dan, for your selfless service and for your friendship.

Transfiguration
Sunday, 2017

Abbreviations

AB	Anchor Bible
ABD	*Anchor Bible Dictionary.* Edited by David Noel Freedman. 6 vols. New York: Doubleday, 1992
ABR	*Australian Biblical Review*
AcBib	Academia Biblica
ACCS: NT	Ancient Christianity Commentary on Scripture: New Testament
AGJU	Arbeiten zur Geschichte des antiken Judentums und des Urchristentums
al	*alii* (i.e., some additional manuscripts not specifically listed)
AnBib	Analecta Biblica
ANRW	*Aufstieg und Niedergang der römischen Welt: Geschichte und Kultur Roms im Spiegel der neueren Forschung.* Pt. 2, *Principat.* Edited by Hildegard Temporini and Wolfgang Haase. Berlin: de Gruyter, 1972–
ANTC	Abingdon New Testament Commentaries
APOT	*The Apocrypha and Pseudepigrapha of the Old Testament.* Edited by Robert H. Charles. 2 vols. Oxford: Clarendon, 1911–13
AUSS	*Andrews University Seminary Studies*
BBR	*Bulletin for Biblical Research*
BECNT	Baker Exegetical Commentary on the New Testament
BETL	Bibliotheca Ephemeridum Theologicarum Lovaniensium
BEvT	Beiträge zur evangelischen Theologie
Bib	*Biblica*
BibInt	Biblical Interpretation Series
BJRL	*Bulletin of the John Rylands University Library of Manchester*
BJS	Brown Judaic Studies
BR	Biblical Research
BRev	*Bible Review*
BSac	*Bibliotheca Sacra*

BZ	*Biblische Zeitschrift*
BZAW	Beihefte zur Zeitschrift für die alttestamentliche Wissenschaft
BZNW	Beihefte zur Zeitschrift für die neutestamentliche Wissenschaft
CBQ	*Catholic Biblical Quarterly*
CC	Continental Commentary
CEB	Common English Bible
Chm	*Churchman*
CRINT	Compendia Rerum Iudaicarum ad Novum Testamentum
CTJ	*Calvin Theological Journal*
CTR	*Criswell Theological Review*
CurBR	*Currents in Biblical Research*
CurTM	*Currents in Theology and Mission*
EBib	*Études bibliques*
EgT	*Église et théologie*
ESV	English Standard Version
ETL	*Ephemerides theologicae lovanienses*
EvQ	*Evangelical Quarterly*
EvT	*Evangelische Theologie*
ExAud	*Ex Auditu*
ExpTim	*Expository Times*
FoiVie	*Foi et Vie*
FRLANT	Forschungen zur Religion und Literatur des Alten und Neuen Testaments
GTA	Göttinger theologische Arbeiten
GW	God's Word: Today's Bible Translation That Says What It Means
HCSB	Holman Christian Standard Bible
HNT	Handbuch zum Neuen Testament
HThKNT	Herders Theologischer Kommentar zum Neuen Testament
HTR	*Harvard Theological Review*
HTS	Harvard Theological Studies
HUCA	*Hebrew Union College Annual*
IBS	*Irish Biblical Studies*
ICC	International Critical Commentary
IGR	*Inscriptiones Graecae ad res romanas pertinentes.* Vol. 4. Edited by G. Lafaye. Paris: Leroux, 1927.
Int	*Interpretation*
JBL	*Journal of Biblical Literature*
JES	*Journal of Ecumenical Studies*
JETS	*Journal of the Evangelical Theological Society*
JGRChJ	*Journal of Greco-Roman Christianity and Judaism*
JQR	*Jewish Quarterly Review*
JRS	*Journal of Roman Studies*

JSJ	*Journal for the Study of Judaism in the Persian, Hellenistic, and Roman Periods*
JSNT	*Journal for the Study of the New Testament*
JSNTSup	Journal for the Study of the New Testament Supplement Series
JSOT	*Journal for the Study of the Old Testament*
JSOTSup	Journal for the Study of the Old Testament Supplement Series
JTS	*Journal of Theological Studies*
KD	*Kerygma und Dogma*
KEK	Kritisch-exegetischer Kommentar über das Neue Testament (Meyer-Kommentar)
KJV	King James Version
LCL	Loeb Classical Library
LN	Johannes Louw and Eugene A. Nida, eds. *Greek-English Lexicon of the New Testament Based on Semantic Domains*. 2nd ed. 2 vols. New York: United Bible Societies, 1989
LNTS	The Library of New Testament Studies
LS	*Louvain Studies*
LSJ	Henry George Liddell, Robert Scott, and Henry Stuart Jones. *A Greek-English Lexicon*. 9th ed. Oxford: Clarendon, 1996
LSJA	Henry George Liddell and Robert Scott. *A Lexicon Abridged from Liddell and Scott's Greek-English Lexicon*. Oxford: Clarendon, 1871
LXX	Septuagint (the Greek Old Testament)
MilS	*Milltown Studies*
MS(S)	manuscript(s)
NA	Nestle-Aland *Novum Testamentum Graece*
NAB	New American Bible
NAC	New American Commentary
NASB	New American Standard Bible
NEB	New English Bible
Neot	*Neotestamentica*
NET	New English Translation
NIB	*The New Interpreter's Bible*. Edited by Leander E. Keck. 12 vols. Nashville: Abingdon, 1994–2004
NICNT	New International Commentary on the New Testament
NICOT	New International Commentary on the Old Testament
NIDB	*New Interpreter's Dictionary of the Bible*. Edited by Katharine Doob. 5 vols. Nashville: Abingdon, 2006–9
NIGTC	New International Greek Testament Commentary
NIV	New International Version
NJB	New Jerusalem Bible
NKJV	New King James Version

NLT	New Living Translation
NovT	*Novum Testamentum*
NovTSup	Supplements to Novum Testamentum
NPNF[1]	*Nicene and Post-Nicene Fathers,* Series 1
NRSV	New Revised Standard Version
NTAbh	Neutestamentliche Abhandlungen
NTL	New Testament Library
NTOA	Novum Testamentum et Orbis Antiquus
NTS	*New Testament Studies*
OTP	*Old Testament Pseudepigrapha.* Edited by James H. Charlesworth. 2 vols. New York: Doubleday, 1983–85
PG	Patrologia Graeca [= Patrologiae Cursus Completus: Series Graeca]. Edited by Jacques-Paul Migne. 162 vols. Paris, 1857–86
pm	*permulti* (i.e., attested by many manuscripts within the Majority Text family, when that witness is divided)
Presb	*Presbyterion*
ProEccl	*Pro Ecclesia*
PRSt	*Perspectives in Religious Studies*
PSB	*Princeton Seminary Bulletin*
RB	*Revue biblique*
RelSRev	*Religious Studies Review*
RSV	Revised Standard Version
RTR	*Reformed Theological Review*
SBL	Society of Biblical Literature
SBLDS	Society of Biblical Literature Dissertation Series
SBLSP	Society of Biblical Literature Seminar Papers
SBLStBL	Society of Biblical Literature Studies in Biblical Literature
SBM	Stuttgarter biblische Monographien
SBT	Studies in Biblical Theology
SE IV	*Studia Evangelica IV* (= TU 102 [1968])
SEÅ	*Svensk exegetisk årsbok*
SIG[2]	*Sylloge Inscriptionum Graecarum.* Edited by William Dittenberger. 3 vols. Rev. ed. Leipzig: S. Hirzel, 1898–1901
SJT	*Scottish Journal of Theology*
SNTSMS	Society for New Testament Studies Monograph Series
SP	Sacra Pagina
SPCK	Society for the Promotion of Christian Knowledge
ST	*Studia Theologica*
SUNT	Studien zur Umwelt des Neuen Testaments
SwJT	*Southwest Journal of Theology*
TDNT	*Theological Dictionary of the New Testament.* Edited by Gerhard

	Kittel and Gerhard Friedrich. Translated by Geoffrey W. Bromiley. 10 vols. Grand Rapids: Eerdmans, 1964–76
TF	Theologische Forschung
Them	*Themelios*
THKNT	Theologischer Handkommentar zum Neuen Testament
TJ	*Trinity Journal*
TLB	The Living Bible
TLZ	*Theologische Literaturzeitung*
TU	Texte und Untersuchungen
TynBul	*Tyndale Bulletin*
UBS	United Bible Societies
WA	Martin Luther. *Werke. Kritische Gesamtausgabe* (Weimarer Ausgabe). 121 vols. Weimar: Böhlau et al., 1883–2009
WBC	Word Biblical Commentary
WTJ	*Westminster Theological Journal*
WUNT	Wissenschaftliche Untersuchungen zum Neuen Testament
WW	*Word and World*
ZNW	*Zeitschrift für die neutestamentliche Wissenschaft und die Kunde der älteren Kirche*
ZTK	*Zeitschrift für Theologie und Kirche*

Bibliography

I. COMMENTARIES

These commentaries are cited by last name, volume number where appropriate, and page.

Becker, Jürgen. *Der Brief an die Galater.* Göttingen: Vandenhoeck & Ruprecht, 1976.

Betz, Hans Dieter. *Galatians.* Hermeneia. Philadelphia: Fortress, 1979.

Bligh, John. *Galatians: A Discussion of St. Paul's Epistle.* London: St. Paul Publications, 1969.

Bonnard, Pierre. *L'Epître de Saint Paul aux Galates.* Neuchâtel: Delachaux & Niestle, 1972.

Borse, Udo. *Der Brief an die Galater.* Regensburg: Pustet, 1984.

Bray, Gerald L., ed. *Galatians, Ephesians.* Reformed Commentary on Scripture: New Testament 10. Downers Grove, IL: InterVarsity Academic, 2011.

Bring, R. *Commentary on Galatians.* Philadelphia: Muhlenberg, 1961.

Bruce, F. F. *The Epistle to the Galatians.* NIGTC. Grand Rapids: Eerdmans, 1982.

Burton, Ernest de Witt. *A Critical and Exegetical Commentary on the Epistle to the Galatians.* ICC. New York: Scribners, 1920.

Cousar, Charles B. *Galatians.* Atlanta: Knox, 1982.

Das, A. Andrew. *Galatians.* St. Louis: Concordia, 2014.

deBoer, Martinus C. *Galatians.* NTL. Louisville: Westminster John Knox, 2010.

Duncan, George S. *The Epistle of Paul to the Galatians.* New York: Harper & Brothers, 1934.

Dunn, James D. G. *The Epistle to the Galatians.* Peabody, MA: Hendrickson, 1993.

Ebeling, Gerhard. *The Truth of the Gospel: An Exposition of Galatians.* Philadelphia: Fortress, 1985.

Eckey, W. *Der Galaterbrief: Ein Kommentar.* Neukirchen-Vluyn: Neukirchener Verlag, 2010.

Edwards, M. J. *Galatians, Ephesians, Philippians.* ACCS: NT 8. Downers Grove, IL: InterVarsity Press, 1999.

Esler, Philip F. *Galatians.* London: Routledge, 1998.

Fee, Gordon D. *Galatians.* Pentecostal Commentary Series. Dorset, UK: Deo, 2007.

Fung, Ronald Y. K. *The Epistle to the Galatians.* NICNT. Grand Rapids: Eerdmans, 1988.

Garlington, Don. *An Exposition of Galatians: A Reading from the New Perspective.* 3rd ed. Eugene, OR: Wipf & Stock, 2007.

George, Timothy. *Galatians.* NAC. Nashville: Broadman & Holman, 1994.

Guthrie, Donald. *Galatians.* New Century Bible Commentary. Grand Rapids: Eerdmans, 1973.

Hansen, G. Walter. *Galatians.* InterVarsity Press New Testament Commentaries. Downers Grove, IL: InterVarsity Press, 1994.

Hays, Richard B. "The Letter to the Galatians: Introduction, Commentary, and Reflections." Pages 181–348 in *NIB* 11. Nashville: Abingdon, 2000.

Jervis, Ann B. *Galatians.* Grand Rapids: Baker Books, 2011.

John Chrysostom. "Commentary on Paul's Letter to the Galatians." PG 61:611–82. Cited by English translation in *NPNF*[1] 13:1–48.

Lagrange, Marie-Joseph. *Saint Paul Epître aux Galates.* 2nd ed. EBib. Paris: Gabalda, 1950.

Lietzmann, Hans. *An die Galater.* HNT 10. 4th ed. Tübingen: Mohr Siebeck, 1971.

Lightfoot, Joseph B. *St. Paul's Epistle to the Galatians.* 10th ed. London: Macmillan, 1890.

Longenecker, Richard N. *Galatians.* WBC. Dallas: Word, 1990.

Lührmann, Dieter. *Galatians.* Minneapolis: Fortress, 1992. Translation of *Der Brief an die Galater.* Zürich: Theologischer Verlag, 1988.

Luther, Martin. *A Commentary on St. Paul's Epistle to the Galatians* (1535). Translated by P. S. Watson. London: James Clarke, 1953.

Martyn, J. Louis. *Galatians.* AB 33A. Garden City, NY: Doubleday, 1997.

Matera, Frank J. *Galatians.* SP. Collegeville, MN: Liturgical Press, 1992.

McKnight, Scot. *Galatians.* New International Version Application Commentary. Grand Rapids: Zondervan, 1995.

Moo, Douglas J. *Galatians.* BECNT. Grand Rapids: Baker Academic, 2013.

Mussner, Franz. *Der Galaterbrief.* 5th ed. HThKNT. Freiburg: Herder, 1988.

Ngewa, S. *Galatians.* Africa Bible Commentary Series. Nairobi: Hippo, 2010.

Oakes, Peter. *Galatians.* Paideia Commentaries. Grand Rapids: Eerdmans, 2015.

Oepke, Albrecht. *Der Brief des Paulus an die Galater.* 3rd ed. THKNT. Berlin: Evangelische Verlagsanstalt, 1973.

Ramsay, William. *A Historical Commentary on St. Paul's Epistle to the Galatians.* 2nd ed. London: Hodder & Stoughton, 1900.

Ridderbos, H. N. *The Epistle of Paul to the Churches of Galatia.* Translated by H. Zylstra. NICNT. Grand Rapids: Eerdmans, 1953.

Rohde, J. *Der Brief des Paulus an die Galater.* THKNT 9. Berlin: Evangelische Verlagsanstalt, 1989.

Schlier, Heinrich. *Der Brief an die Galater.* 13th ed. KEK 7. Göttingen: Vandenhoeck & Ruprecht, 1965.

Schreiner, Thomas. *Galatians.* Zondervan Exegetical Commentary on the New Testament. Grand Rapids: Zondervan, 2010.

Sieffert, Friedrich. *Der Brief an die Galater.* Göttingen: Vandenhoeck & Ruprecht, 1899.

Vouga, François. *An die Galater.* HNT. Tübingen: Mohr Siebeck, 1998.

Williams, Sam K. *Galatians.* ANTC. Nashville: Abingdon, 1997.

Witherington, Ben, III. *Grace in Galatia: A Commentary on Paul's Letter to the Galatians.* Grand Rapids: Eerdmans, 1998.

Zahn, T. *Der Brief des Paulus an die Galater.* Leipzig: Deichert, 1905.

II. ANCIENT SOURCES

Anaximenes. *Rhetoric to Alexander.* See under Aristotle.

Aristotle. *Problems, Volume 2: Books 20–38. Rhetoric to Alexander.* Edited and translated by Robert Mayhew and David C. Mirhady. LCL 317. Cambridge, MA: Harvard University Press, 2011.

Cicero. *Ad Herennium.* Translated by H. Caplan. LCL 403. Cambridge, MA: Harvard University Press, 1954.

———. *Letters to His Friends.* Translated by D. R. Shackleton Bailey. LCL 230. Cambridge, MA: Harvard University Press, 2001.

Dio Chrysostom. *Discourses 31–36.* Translated by J. W. Cohoon and H. Lamar Crosby. LCL 358. Cambridge, MA: Harvard University Press, 1940.

Diogenes Laertius. *Lives of Eminent Philosophers, Volume I: Books 1–5.* Translated by R. D. Hicks. LCL 184. Cambridge, MA: Harvard University Press, 1925.

Josephus. *Jewish Antiquities, Volume V: Books 12–13.* Translated by Ralph Marcus. LCL 365. Cambridge, MA: Harvard University Press, 1943.

———. *The Life. Against Apion.* Translated by H. St. J. Thackeray. LCL 186. Cambridge, MA: Harvard University Press, 1926.

Nicolaus of Damascus. *Life of Augustus: A Historical Commentary Embodying a Translation.* Translated by Clayton M. Hall. Menasha, WI: George Banta Publishing, 1923.

Philo. *On the Confusion of Tongues. On the Migration of Abraham. Who Is the Heir of Divine Things? On Mating with the Preliminary Studies.* Translated by F. H. Colson and G. H. Whitaker. LCL 261. Cambridge, MA: Harvard University Press, 1932.

———. *On the Decalogue. On the Special Laws, Books 1–3.* Translated by F. H. Colson. LCL 320. Cambridge, MA: Harvard University Press, 1937.

———. *The Works of Philo.* Translated by C. D. Yonge. New, updated ed. Peabody, MA: Hendrickson, 1993.

Pseudo-Cicero. *Ad Herennium.* See under Cicero.

Quintilian. *Institutio Oratoria* [The Orator's Education]. *Books 1–3.* Translated by H. E. Butler. LCL 124. Cambridge, MA: Harvard University Press, 1920.

Seneca. *Moral Essays, Volume I: De Providentia. De Constantia. De Ira. De Clementia.* Translated by John W. Basore. LCL 214. Cambridge, MA: Harvard University Press, 1928.

———. *Moral Essays, Volume II: De Consolatione ad Marciam. De Vita Beata. De Otio. De Tranquillitate Animi. De Brevitate Vitae. De Consolatione ad Polybium. De Consolatione ad Helviam.* Translated by John W. Basore. LCL 254. Cambridge, MA: Harvard University Press, 1932.

———. *Moral Essays. Volume III: De Beneficiis* [*On Benefits*]. Translated by John W. Basore. LCL 310. Cambridge, MA: Harvard University Press, 1935.

Strabo. *Geography.* Translated by Horace Leonard Jones. 8 vols. LCL. Cambridge, MA: Harvard University Press, 1923–32.

III. GENERAL BIBLIOGRAPHY

Achtemeier, P. J. "An Elusive Unity: Paul, Acts, and the Early Church." *CBQ* 48 (1986): 1–26.

Alexander, Loveday. "Chronology of Paul." Pages 115–23 in *Dictionary of Paul and His Letters.* Edited by Gerald F. Hawthorne, Ralph P. Martin, and Daniel G. Reid. Downers Grove, IL: InterVarsity Press, 1995.

Allison, Dale C. "The Pauline Epistles and the Synoptic Gospels: The Pattern of the Parallels." *NTS* 28 (1982): 1–32.

———. "Peter and Cephas: One and the Same." *JBL* 111 (1992): 489–95.

Anderson, R. Dean. *Ancient Rhetorical Theory and Paul.* Rev. ed. Contributions to Biblical Exegesis and Theology 18. Leuven: Peeters, 1998.

APOT. See Charles.

Armitage, D. J. "An Exploration of Conditional Clause Exegesis with Reference to Galatians 1,8–9." *Bib* 88 (2007): 365–92.

Arnold, Clinton E. "'I Am Astonished That You Are So Quickly Turning Away!' (Gal 1.6): Paul and Anatolian Folk Belief." *NTS* 51 (2005): 429–49.

———. "Returning to the Domain of the Powers: *Stoicheia* as Evil Spirits in Galatians 4:3, 9." *NovT* 38 (1996): 55–76.

Aune, David E. *The New Testament in Its Literary Environment.* Philadelphia: Westminster, 1987.

———. "The Use and Abuse of the Enthymeme in New Testament Scholarship." *NTS* 49 (2003): 299–320.

Aus, R. D. "Three Pillars and Three Patriarchs: A Proposal concerning Gal 2:9." *ZNW* 70 (1979): 252–61.

Avemarie, Friedrich. "Erwählung und Vergeltung: Zur optionalen Struktur rabbinischer Soteriologie." *NTS* 45 (1999): 108–26.

———. "Paul and the Claim of the Law according to the Scripture: Leviticus 18:5 in Galatians 3:12 and Romans 10:5." Pages 125–48 in *The Beginnings of Christianity: A Collection of Articles.* Edited by Jack Pastor and Menachem Mor. Jerusalem: Yad Ben-Zvi Press, 2005.

Baarda, T. Tί ἔτι διώκομαι in Gal 5:11: Apodosis or Parenthesis?" *NovT* 34 (1992): 250–56.

Baasland, Ernst. "Persecution: A Neglected Feature in the Letter to the Galatians." *ST* 38 (1984): 135–50.

Bachmann, Michael. *Anti-Judaism in Galatians? Exegetical Studies on a Polemical Letter and on Paul's Theology.* Translated by Robert L. Brawley. Grand Rapids: Eerdmans, 2008.

———. "The Church and the Israel of God: On the Meaning and Ecclesiastical Relevance of the Benediction at the End of Galatians." Pages 101–23 in *Anti-Judaism in Galatians? Exegetical Studies on a Polemical Letter and on Paul's Theology.* Grand Rapids: Eerdmans, 2008.

———. "4QMMT und Galaterbrief, מעשׂי התורה und ΕΡΓΑ ΝΟΜΟΥ." *ZNW* 89 (1998): 91–113.

———. "Gal 1,9: 'Wie wir schon früher gesagt haben, so sage ich jetzt erneut.'" *BZ* 47 (2003): 112–15.

———. *Sünder oder Übertreter: Studien zur Argumentation in Gal 2,15ff.* WUNT 2/59. Tübingen: Mohr Siebeck, 1992.

BAGD. See Bauer et al.

Bammel, E. "Galater 1,23." *ZNW* 59 (1968): 108–12.

———. "Gottes διαθήκη (Gal. iii.15–17) und das jüdische Rechtsdenken." *NTS* 6 (1959/60): 313–19.

Bandstra, A. J. *The Law and the Elements of the World: An Exegetical Study in Aspects of Paul's Teaching.* Kampen: Kok, 1964.

Banks, Robert. *Paul's Idea of Community: The Early House Churches in Their Historical Setting.* Peabody, MA: Hendricksen, 1994.

Barclay, John M. G. "Mirror-Reading a Polemical Letter: Galatians as a Test Case." *JSNT* 31 (1987): 73–93.

———. *Obeying the Truth: Paul's Ethics in Galatia.* Minneapolis: Fortress, 1991.

———. "Paul among Diaspora Jews." *JSNT* 60 (1995): 89–120.

———. *Paul and the Gift.* Grand Rapids: Eerdmans, 2015.

———. "Paul, the Gift, and the Battle over Gentile Circumcision: Revisiting the Logic of Galatians." *ABR* 58 (2010): 36–56.

Barclay, William. *Flesh and Spirit: An Examination of Gal 5:19–23*. London: SCM, 1962.

Barnett, P. "Galatians and Earliest Christianity." *RTR* 59 (2000): 112–29.

———. *Paul: Missionary of Jesus*. Grand Rapids: Eerdmans, 2008.

Barnikol, E. *Der nichtpaulinische Ursprung des Parallelismus der Apostel Paulus und Petrus (Galater 2:7–9)*. Keil: Mühlau, 1931.

Barr, J. "'Abba' Isn't 'Daddy.'" *JTS* 39 (1988): 28–47.

Barrett, C. K. "The Allegory of Abraham, Sarah, and Hagar in the Argument of Galatians." Pages 1–16 in *Rechtfertigung: Festschrift für Ernst Käsemann zum 70. Geburtstag*. Edited by J. Friedrich et al. Tübingen: Mohr Siebeck, 1976.

———. *A Critical and Exegetical Commentary on the Acts of the Apostles*. 2 vols. ICC. Edinburgh: T&T Clark, 1998.

———. *Essays on Paul*. Philadelphia: Westminster, 1982.

———. *Freedom and Obligation*. London: SPCK, 1985.

———. *The New Testament Background: Selected Documents*. Rev. ed. New York: Harper & Row, 1973.

———. "Paul and the 'Pillar' Apostles." Pages 1–19 in *Studia Paulina in honorem Jr. de Zwaan*. Edited by J. N. Sevenster and W. C. van Unnik. Haarlem: Bohn, 1953.

———. *The Second Epistle to the Corinthians*. London: Harper & Row, 1973.

Barth, Markus. "Jew and Gentile: The Social Character of Justification in Paul." *JES* 5 (1968): 241–67.

———. "The Kerygma of Galatians." *Int* 21 (1967): 131–46.

Bassler, J. M. *Divine Impartiality*. Atlanta: Scholars Press, 1982.

———. "Divine Impartiality in Paul's Letter to the Romans." *NovT* 26 (1984): 43–58.

———. *Navigating Paul: An Introduction to Key Theological Concepts*. Louisville: Westminster John Knox, 2007.

Bauckham, Richard. "Barnabas in Galatians." *JSNT* 2 (1979): 61–71.

———. "James and the Jerusalem Church." Pages 415–80 in *The Book of Acts in Its Palestinian Setting*. Edited by R. Bauckham. The Book of Acts in Its First-Century Setting. Grand Rapids: Eerdmans, 1995.

———. "James, Peter, and the Gentiles." Pages 91–142 in *The Missions of James, Peter, and Paul: Tensions in Early Christianity*. Edited by B. Chilton and C. Evans. Leiden: Brill, 2004.

———. *Jude and the Relatives of Jesus in the Early Church*. Edinburgh: T&T Clark, 1990.

Bauer, Walter, William F. Arndt, and F. Wilbur Gingrich. *A Greek-English Lexicon of the New Testament and Other Early Christian Literature*. Translated and adapted by W. F. Arndt and F. W. Gingrich. 2nd ed. revised and augmented by F. W. Gingrich and F. W. Danker. Chicago: University of Chicago Press, 1979.

Bauernfeind, O. "ἀσέλγεια." *TDNT* 1:490.

Baugh, S. M. "Galatians 5:1–6 and Personal Obligation: Reflections on Paul and the Law." Pages 259–82 in *The Law Is Not of Faith: Essays on Works and Grace in the Mosaic Covenant*. Edited by B. Estelle, J. Fesko, and D. VanDrunen. Phillipsburg, NJ: P&R, 2009.

Baumert, N., and J. Meissner. "Nomos bei Paulus." Pages 9–245 in *Nomos und andere Vorarbeiten zur Reihe Paulus neu gelesen*. Edited by N. Baumert. Würzburg: Echter, 2010.

BDAG. See Danker et al.

Beale, G. K. "The Old Testament Background of Paul's Reference to 'the Fruit of the Spirit' in Galatians 5:22." *BBR* 15 (2005): 1–38.

———. "Peace and Mercy upon the Israel of God: The Old Testament Background of Galatians 6,16b." *Bib* 80 (1999): 204–23.

Beasley-Murray, G. R. *Baptism in the New Testament*. Grand Rapids: Eerdmans, 1962.

Becker, Jürgen. *Paul: Apostle to the Gentiles*. Louisville: Westminster John Knox Press, 1993.

Beilby, James K., and Paul R. Eddy, eds. *Justification: Five Views*. Downers Grove, IL: InterVarsity Press, 2011.

Beker, Johan C. *Paul the Apostle: The Triumph of God in Life and Thought*. Philadelphia: Fortress, 1980.

Belleville, Linda L. "'Under Law': Structural Analysis and the Pauline Concept of Law in Galatians 3.21–4.11." *JSNT* 26 (1986): 53–78.

Berger, Peter L. *Invitation to Sociology: A Humanistic Perspective*. New York: Anchor, 1963.

———. *The Sacred Canopy: Elements of a Sociological Theory of Religion*. New York: Doubleday, 1967.

Bergmeier, R. *Gerechtigkeit, Gesetz und Glaube bei Paulus: Der judenchristliche Heidenapostel im Streit um das Gesetz und seine Werke*. Biblisch-theologische Studien 115. Neukirchen-Vluyn: Neukirchener Theologie, 2010.

———. "Vom Tun der Tora." Pages 161–81 in *Lutherische und neue Paulusperspektive: Beiträge zu einem Schlüsselproblem der gegenwärtigen exegetischen Diskussion*. Edited by M. Bachmann and J. Woyke. WUNT 182. Tübingen: Mohr Siebeck, 2005.

Betz, Hans D. "The Literary Composition and Function of Paul's Letter to the Galatians." *NTS* 21 (1974–75): 353–79.

———. "Spirit, Freedom, and Law: Paul's Message to the Galatian Churches." *SEÅ* 39 (1974): 145–60.

Biguzzi, G. "Ephesus, Its Artemision, Its Temple to the Flavian Emperors, and Idolatry in Revelation." *NovT* 40 (1998): 276–90.

Billings, J. Todd. *Calvin, Participation, and the Gift: The Activity of Believers in Union with Christ.* Changing Paradigms in Historical and Systematic Theology. Oxford: Oxford University Press, 2007.

Bird, Michael F. "Justification as Forensic Declaration and Covenant Membership: A Via Media between Reformed and Revisionist Readings of Paul." *TynBul* 57 (2006): 109–30.

———. "Reassessing a Rhetorical Approach to Paul's Letters." *ExpTim* 119.8 (2008): 374–79.

———. *The Saving Righteousness of God: Studies on Paul, Justification, and the New Perspective.* Milton Keynes: Paternoster, 2007.

Bird, Michael F., and Preston Sprinkle, eds. *The Faith of Jesus Christ: Exegetical, Biblical, and Theological Studies.* Peabody, MA: Hendrickson, 2009.

Blanton, Thomas. "The Benefactor's Account-Book: The Rhetoric of Gift Reciprocation according to Seneca and Paul." *NTS* 59 (2013): 396–414.

Blass, F., and A. Debrunner. *A Greek Grammar of the New Testament and Other Early Christian Literature.* Translated and revised by Robert W. Funk. Chicago: University of Chicago Press, 1961.

Blinzler, Josef. "Lexikalisches zu dem Terminus *ta stoicheia tou kosmou.*" Pages 427–43 in *Studiorum Paulinorum Congressus Internationalis Catholicus, 1961.* Vol. 2. AnBib 18. Rome: Pontifical Biblical Institute, 1963.

Blocher, H. "Justification of the Ungodly (*Sola Fide*): Theological Reflections." Pages 465–500 in *The Paradoxes of Paul.* Vol. 2 of *Justification and Variegated Nomism.* Edited by D. A. Carson, P. T. O'Brien, and M. A. Seifrid. WUNT 2/181. Tübingen: Mohr Siebeck, 2004.

Blommerde, A. C. M. "Is There an Ellipsis between Galatians 2,3 and 2,4?" *Bib* 56 (1975): 100–102.

Bockmuehl, M. *Jewish Law in Gentile Churches: Halakah and the Beginning of Christian Public Ethics.* Edinburgh: T&T Clark, 2000.

Boers, Hendrikus. *The Justification of the Gentiles: Paul's Letters to the Romans and the Galatians.* Peabody, MA: Hendrickson, 1994.

———. "We Who Are by Inheritance Jews, Not from the Gentiles, Sinners." *JBL* 111 (1992): 273–81.

Bonner, Stanley F. *Education in Ancient Rome from the Elder Cato to the Younger Pliny.* Berkeley and Los Angeles: University of California Press, 1977.

Borgen, Peder. *Early Christianity and Hellenistic Judaism.* London: T&T Clark, 2000.

———. "Paul Preaches Circumcision and Pleases Men." Pages 37–46 in *Paul and Paulinism: Essays in Honor of C. K. Barrett.* Edited by M. D. Hooker and S. G. Wilson. London: SPCK, 1982.

———. *Philo, John, and Paul: New Perspectives on Judaism and Early Christianity.* BJS 131. Leiden: Brill, 1987.

———. "Some Hebrew and Pagan Features in Philo's and Paul's Interpretation of Hagar and Ishmael." Pages 151–64 in *New Testament and Hellenistic Judaism*. Edited by P. Borgen and S. Giversen. Aarhus: Aarhus University Press, 1995.

Bornkamm, Gunther. *Paul*. New York: Harper & Row, 1971.

———. "The Revelation of Christ to Paul on the Damascus Road and Paul's Doctrine of Justification and Reconciliation." Pages 90–103 in *Reconciliation and Hope*. Edited by R. Banks. Exeter: Paternoster, 1974.

Bouttier, M. "Complexio Oppositorum: Sur les formules de I Cor 12:13; Gal 3:26–8; Col 3:10, 11." *NTS* 23 (1976): 1–19.

Bovon, François. "Une formal prépaulinienne dans l'Epître aux Galates (Gal 1.4–5)." Pages 91–107 in *Paganisme, Judaïsme, Christianisme*. Edited by A. Benoit et al. Paris: de Boccard, 1978.

Boyarin, Daniel. *A Radical Jew: Paul and the Politics of Identity*. Berkeley: University of California Press, 1994.

Boyer, James L. "A Classification of Imperatives: A Statistical Study." *Grace Theological Journal* 8 (1987): 35–54.

———. "Second Class Conditions in New Testament Greek." *Grace Theological Journal* 3 (1982): 81–88.

Brandenburger, E. *Fleisch und Geist*. Neukirchen-Vluyn: Neukirchener Verlag, 1968.

Braswell, J. P. "'The Blessing of Abraham' versus 'The Curse of the Law': Another Look at Gal 3:10–13." *WTJ* 53 (1991): 73–91.

Brawley, Robert L. "Contextuality, Intertextuality, and the Hendiadic Relationship of Promise and Law in Galatians." *ZNW* 93 (2002): 99–119.

———. "Meta-Ethics and the Role of Works of Law in Galatians." Pages 135–59 in *Lutherische und neue Perspektive: Beiträge zu einem Schlüsselproblem der gegenwärtigen exegetischen Diskussion*. Edited by M. Bachmann. Tübingen: Mohr Siebeck, 2005.

Braxton, Brad R. *No Longer Slaves: Galatians and African American Experience*. Collegeville, MN: Liturgical Press, 2002.

Bray, Gerald L., ed. *Ambrosiaster: Commentaries on Galatians–Philemon*. Ancient Christian Texts. Downers Grove, IL: IVP Academic, 2009.

Brehm, H. A. "Paul's Relationship with the Jerusalem Apostles in Galatians 1 and 2." *SwJT* 37 (1994): 11–16.

Breytenbach, Cilliers. *Paulus und Barnabas in der Provinz Galatien: Studien zu Apostelgeschichte 13f.; 16,6; 18,23 und den Adressaten des Galaterbriefes*. Leiden: Brill, 1996.

———. "Versöhnung, Stellvertretung und Sühne." *NTS* 39 (1993): 59–79.

Bring, R. *Christus und das Gesetz: Die Bedeutung des Gesetzes des Alten Testaments nach Paulus und sein Glauben an Christus*. Leiden: Brill, 1969.

Brinsmead, B. H. *Galatians—Dialogical Response to Opponents*. SBLDS 65. Chico, CA: Scholars Press, 1982.

Briones, David. "Paul's Intentional 'Thankless Thanks' in Philippians 4.10–20." *JSNT* 34 (2011): 47–69.

Brown, Raymond E. "Not Jewish Christianity and Gentile Christianity but Types of Jewish/Gentile Christianity." *CBQ* 45 (1983): 74–79.

Bruce, F. F. "The Curse of the Law." Pages 27–36 in *Paul and Paulinism: Essays in Honor of C. K. Barrett.* Edited by M. D. Hooker and S. G. Wilson. London: SPCK, 1982.

———. "Galatian Problems." Pt. 2: "North or South Galatia?" *BJRL* 52 (1970): 243–66.

———. *Paul: Apostle of the Heart Set Free.* Grand Rapids: Eerdmans, 1977.

Bryant, Robert A. *The Risen Crucified Christ in Galatians.* SBLDS 185. Atlanta: SBL, 2001.

Buck, C. H. "The Date of Galatians." *JBL* 70 (1951): 113–22.

Bultmann, Rudolf. "Das Problem der Ethik bei Paulus." *ZNW* 23 (1924): 123–40.

———. *Theology of the New Testament.* 2 vols. New York: Scribner's, 1951–55.

Burchard, C. "Noch ein Versuch zu Galater 3,19 und 20." Pages 184–202 in *Studien zur Theologie, Sprache und Umwelt des Neuen Testaments.* Edited by D. Sänger. Tübingen: Mohr Siebeck, 1998.

———. "Zu Galater 4,1–11." Pages 41–58 in Das *Urchristentum in seiner literarischen Geschichte: Festschrift für Jürgen Becker zum 65. Geburtstag.* Edited by U. Mell and U. B. Müller. Berlin: de Gruyter, 1999.

Burke, Trevor J. *Adoption into God's Family: Exploring a Pauline Metaphor.* New Studies in Biblical Theology 22. Downers Grove, IL: InterVarsity Press, 2006.

Burkitt, F. C. *Christian Beginnings.* London: University of London Press, 1924.

Burton, Ernest de Witt. *Syntax of the Moods and Tenses of New Testament Greek.* 3rd ed. Chicago: University of Chicago Press, 1898.

Byrne, Brendan. *"Sons of God"—"Seed of Abraham": A Study of the Idea of the Sonship of God of All Christians in Paul against the Jewish Background.* Rome: Pontifical Biblical Institute, 1979.

Byron, John. *Slavery Metaphors in Early Judaism and Pauline Christianity.* Tübingen: Mohr Siebeck, 2003.

Caird, G. B. *Principalities and Powers.* Oxford: Oxford University Press, 1956.

Calder, W. M. "Adoption and Inheritance in Galatia." *JTS* 31 (1930): 372–74.

Callan, Terence. "The Background of the Apostolic Decree (Acts 15:20, 29; 21:25)." *CBQ* 55 (1993): 284–97.

———. "Pauline Midrash: The Exegetical Background of Gal 3:19b." *JBL* 99 (1980): 549–67.

Callaway, M. C. "The Mistress and the Maid: Midrashic Traditions behind Galatians 4:21–31." *Radical Religion* 2 (1975): 94–101.

Calvert-Koyzis, N. *Paul, Monotheism, and the People of God: The Significance of*

Abraham Traditions for Early Judaism and Christianity. JSNTSup 273. London: T&T Clark, 2004.

Calvin, John. *The Epistles of Paul the Apostle to the Galatians, Ephesians, Philippians, and Colossians.* Grand Rapids: Eerdmans, 1965.

Campbell, Constantine. *Verbal Aspect and Non-indicative Verbs: Further Soundings in the Greek of the New Testament.* Studies in Biblical Greek 15. New York: Peter Lang, 2008.

Campbell, Douglas A. *The Deliverance of God: An Apocalyptic Reading of Justification in Paul.* Grand Rapids: Eerdmans, 2009.

———. "False Presuppositions in the πίστις Χριστοῦ Debate: A Response to Brian Dodd." *JBL* 116 (1997): 713–19.

———. "Galatians 5.11: Evidence of an Early Law-Observant Mission by Paul?" *NTS* 57 (2011): 325–47.

———. "The Meaning of πίστις and νόμος in Paul: A Linguistic and Structural Perspective." *JBL* 111 (1992): 91–103.

———. *The Quest for Paul's Gospel: A Suggested Strategy.* London: T&T Clark, 2005.

———. *The Rhetoric of Righteousness in Romans 3.21–26.* JSNTSup 65. Sheffield: JSOT Press, 1992.

———. "Romans 1:17—a *Crux Interpretum* for the πίστις Χριστοῦ Debate." *JBL* 113 (1994): 265–85.

Campbell, R. A. "'Against Such Things There Is No Law'? Galatians 5:23b Again." *ExpTim* 107 (1996): 271–72.

Campbell, Thomas H. "Paul's 'Missionary Journeys' as Reflected in His Letters." *JBL* 74 (1955): 80–87.

Caneday, A. "The Faithfulness of Jesus Christ as a Theme in Paul's Theology in Galatians." Pages 185–205 in *The Faith of Jesus Christ: Exegetical, Biblical, and Theological Studies.* Edited by M. F. Bird and P. M. Sprinkle. Peabody, MA: Hendrickson, 2009.

———. "'Redeemed from the Curse of the Law': The Use of Deut 21:22–23 in Gal 3:13." *TJ* 10 (1989): 185–209.

Caragounis, Chrys C. *The Development of Greek and the New Testament: Morphology, Syntax, Phonology, and Textual Transmission.* Grand Rapids: Baker Academic, 2006.

Carson, D. A. "Pauline Inconsistency: Reflections on 1 Corinthians 9:19–23 and Galatians 2:11–14." *Chm* 100 (1986): 6–45.

Carson, D. A., P. T. O'Brien, and M. A. Seifrid, eds. *The Complexities of Second Temple Judaism.* Vol. 1 of *Justification and Variegated Nomism.* Tübingen: Mohr Siebeck, 2001.

Catchpole, David R. "Paul, James, and the Apostolic Decree." *NTS* 23 (1977): 428–44.

Cavallin, H. C. C. "'The Righteous Shall Live by Faith': A Decisive Argument for the Traditional Interpretation." *ST* 32 (1978): 33–43.

Chapman, D. W. *Ancient Jewish and Christian Perceptions of Crucifixion.* WUNT 2/244. Tübingen: Mohr Siebeck, 2008.

Charles, J. D. "Virtue and Vice Lists." Pages 1252–57 in *Dictionary of New Testament Background.* Edited by Craig A. Evans and Stanley E. Porter. Downers Grove, IL: InterVarsity Press, 2000.

Charles, R. H., ed. *The Apocrypha and Pseudepigrapha of the Old Testament.* Oxford: Clarendon, 1913.

Charlesworth, James H., ed. *Apocalyptic Literature and Testaments.* Vol. 1 of *The Old Testament Pseudepigrapha.* Garden City, NY: Doubleday, 1983.

———. *Expansions of the "Old Testament" and Legends, Wisdom and Philosophical Literature, Prayers, Psalms, and Odes, Fragments of Lost Judeo-Hellenistic Works.* Vol. 2 of *The Old Testament Pseudepigrapha.* Garden City, NY: Doubleday, 1985.

Chester, A. *Messiah and Exaltation: Jewish Messianic and Visionary Traditions and New Testament Christology.* WUNT 207. Tübingen: Mohr Siebeck, 2007.

Chester, S. J. "It Is No Longer I Who Live: Justification by Faith and Participation in Christ in Martin Luther's Exegesis of Galatians." *NTS* 55 (2009): 315–37.

———. "Paul and the Galatian Believers." Pages 63–78 in *The Blackwell Companion to Paul.* Edited by S. Westerholm. Chichester: Wiley-Blackwell, 2011.

———. "When the Old Was New: Reformation Perspectives on Galatians 2:16." *ExpTim* 119 (2008): 320–29.

Chibici-Revneanu, N. "Leben im Gesetz: Die paulinische Interpretation von Lev 18:5 (Gal 3:12; Röm 10:5)." *NovT* 50 (2008): 105–19.

Chilton, B. "Galatians 6:15: A Call to Freedom before God." *ExpTim* 89 (1978): 311–13.

Choi, Hung-Sik. "ΠΙΣΤΙΣ in Galatians 5:5–6: Neglected Evidence for the Faithfulness of Christ." *JBL* 124 (2005): 467–90.

Ciampa, Roy E. "Abraham and Empire in Galatians." Pages 153–68 in *Perspectives on Our Father Abraham: Essays in Honor of Marvin R. Wilson.* Edited by S. A. Hunt. Grand Rapids: Eerdmans, 2010.

———. *The Presence and Function of Scripture in Galatians 1 and 2.* WUNT 2/102. Tübingen: Mohr Siebeck, 1998.

Cimok, Fatih. *Journeys of Paul: From Tarsus "to the Ends of the Earth."* Istanbul: A Turizm Yayınları, 2004.

Classen, C. J. "Paul's Epistles and Ancient Greek and Roman Rhetoric." Pages 95–113 in *The Galatians Debate: Contemporary Issues in Rhetorical and Historical Interpretation.* Edited by Mark D. Nanos. Peabody, MA: Hendrickson, 2002.

———. *Rhetorical Criticism of the New Testament.* Tübingen: Mohr Siebeck, 2000.

Cohen, S. J. D. "Crossing the Boundary and Becoming a Jew." *HTR* 82 (1989): 13–33.

Collins, Adela Yarbo. *Mark: A Commentary.* Hermeneia. Minneapolis: Fortress, 2007.

Collins, C. John. "Galatians 3:16: What Kind of Exegete Was Paul?" *TynBul* 54 (2003): 75–86.

———. "A Syntactical Note (Genesis 3:15): Is the Woman's Seed Singular or Plural?" *TynBul* 48 (1997): 139–48.

Comfort, Philip W. *New Testament Text and Translation Commentary.* Carol Stream, IL: Tyndale House, 2008.

Conzelman, Hans. *Acts of the Apostles.* Philadelphia: Fortress, 1987.

———. *Gentiles, Jews, Christians: Polemics and Apologetics in the Greco-Roman Era.* Translated by M. Eugene Boring. Minneapolis: Fortress, 1992.

Cook, David. "The Prescript as Programme in Galatians." *JTS* 42 (1992): 511–19.

Coppins, W. *The Interpretation of Freedom in the Letters of Paul.* WUNT 261. Tübingen: Mohr Siebeck, 2009.

Corley, Bruce. "Interpreting Paul's Conversion: Then and Now." Pages 1–17 in *The Road from Damascus: The Impact of Paul's Conversion on His Life, Thought, and Ministry.* Edited by R. N. Longenecker. Grand Rapids: Eerdmans, 1997.

———. "Reasoning 'By Faith': Whys and Wherefores of the Law in Galatians." *SwJT* 37 (1991): 17–22.

Cosgrove, C. H. "Arguing like a Mere Human Being: Galatians 3:15–18 in Rhetorical Perspective." *NTS* 34 (1988): 536–49.

———. *The Cross and the Spirit.* Macon, GA: Mercer University Press, 1988.

———. "Justification in Paul: A Linguistic and Theological Reflection." *JBL* 106 (1987): 653–70.

———. "The Mosaic Law Teaches Faith: A Study in Galatians 3." *WTJ* 41 (1978): 146–64.

Cranfield, C. E. B. *Introduction and Commentary on Romans I–VIII.* Vol. 1 of *A Critical and Exegetical Commentary on the Epistle to the Romans.* ICC. Edinburgh: T&T Clark, 1975.

———. *On Romans and Other New Testament Essays.* Edinburgh: T&T Clark, 1998.

———. "St. Paul and the Law." *SJT* 17 (1964): 43–68.

———. "'The Works of the Law' in the Epistle to the Romans." *JSNT* 43 (1991): 89–101.

Cranford, M. "The Possibility of Perfect Obedience: Paul and an Implied Promise in Galatians 3:10 and 5:3." *NovT* 36 (1994): 242–58.

Crossan, John D. "Roman Imperial Theology." Pages 59–73 in *In the Shadow of Empire.* Edited by Richard Horsley. Louisville: Westminster John Knox Press, 2008.

Cullmann, Oscar. *Peter: Disciple, Apostle, Martyr: A Historical and Theological Essay.* Translated by Floyd V. Filson. New York: Westminster, 1953.

Culy, Martin M. "The Clue Is in the Case: Distinguishing Adjectival and Adverbial Participles." *PRSt* 30 (2003): 441–53.

———. "Double Case Constructions in Koine Greek." *JGRChJ* 6 (2009): 82–106.

Cummins, S. A. *Paul and the Crucified Christ: Maccabean Martyrdom and Galatians 1 and 2.* SNTSMS 114. Cambridge: Cambridge University Press, 2001.

Cuss, Dominique. *Imperial Cult and Honorary Terms in the New Testament.* Fribourg: University Press, 1974.

Daalen, D. H. van. "'Faith' according to Paul." *ExpTim* (1975): 83–85.

Dahl, Nils A. "Der Name Israel." Pt. 1: "Zur Auslegung von Gal 6,16." *Judaica* 6 (1950): 151–70.

———. "Paul's Letter to the Galatians: Epistolary Genre, Content, and Structure." Pages 117–42 in *The Galatians Debate: Contemporary Issues in Rhetorical and Historical Interpretation.* Edited by Mark D. Nanos. Peabody, MA: Hendrickson, 2002.

Dalton, W. J. "The Meaning of 'We' in Galatians." *ABR* 38 (1990): 33–44.

Danker, Frederick W. *Benefactor: Epigraphic Study of a Graeco-Roman and New Testament Semantic Field.* St. Louis: Clayton Publishing House, 1982.

Danker, Frederick W., Walter Bauer, William F. Arndt, and F. Wilbur Gingrich. *A Greek-English Lexicon of the New Testament and Other Early Christian Literature.* Revised and edited by Frederick W. Danker. 3rd ed. Chicago: University of Chicago Press, 2000.

Das, A. Andrew. "Another Look at ἐὰν μή in Galatians 2:16." *JBL* 119 (2000): 529–39.

———. "Oneness in Christ: The *Nexus Indivulsus* between Justification and Sanctification in Paul's Letter to the Galatians." *Concordia Journal* 21 (1995): 173–86.

———. *Paul and the Jews.* Peabody, MA: Hendrickson, 2003.

———. "Paul and the Law: Pressure Points in the Debate." Pages 99–116 in *Paul Unbound: Other Perspectives on the Apostle.* Edited by M. D. Given. Peabody, MA: Hendrickson, 2010.

———. *Paul and the Stories of Israel: Grand Thematic Narratives in Galatians.* Minneapolis: Fortress, 2016.

———. "Paul and Works of Obedience in Second Temple Judaism: Romans 4:4–5 as a 'New Perspective' Case Study." *CBQ* 71 (2009): 795–812.

———. *Paul, the Law, and the Covenant.* Peabody, MA: Hendrickson, 2001.

———. *Solving the Romans Debate.* Minneapolis: Fortress, 2007.

Daube, David. "Rabbinic Methods of Interpretation and Hellenistic Rhetoric." *HUCA* 22 (1949): 239–64.

Dautzenberg, G. "'Da ist nicht männlich und weiblich': Zur Interpretation von Gal 3:28." *Kairós* 24 (1982): 181–206.

Davies, W. D. *Paul and Rabbinic Judaism*. London: SPCK, 1955.

————. "Paul and the Dead Sea Scrolls: Flesh and Spirit." Pages 157–82 in *The Scrolls and the New Testament*. Edited by Krister Stendahl. New York: Harper, 1957.

————. "Paul and the People of Israel." *NTS* 24 (1977): 4–39.

————. *The Setting of the Sermon on the Mount*. Cambridge: Cambridge University Press, 1963.

Davis, Anne. "Allegorically Speaking in Galatians 4:21–5:1." *BBR* 14 (2004): 161–74.

Davis, Basil S. *Christ as Devotio: The Argument of Galatians 3:1–14*. Lanham, MD: University Press of America, 2002.

————. "The Meaning of προεγράφη in the Context of Galatians 3.1." *NTS* 45 (1999): 213–29.

Debanné, Marc J. *Enthymemes in the Letters of Paul*. LNTS 303. London: T&T Clark, 2006.

deBoer, Martinus C. "The Meaning of the Phrase τὰ στοιχεῖα τοῦ κόσμου in Galatians." *NTS* 53 (2007): 204–24.

————. "Paul's Quotation of Isaiah 54.1 in Galatians 4.27." *NTS* 50 (2004): 370–89.

————. "Paul's Use and Interpretation of a Justification Tradition in Galatians 2.15–21." *JSNT* 28 (2005): 189–216.

Deidun, T. J. *New Covenant Morality in Paul*. AnBib 89. Rome: Pontifical Biblical Institute, 1981.

Deissmann, Adolf. *Light from the Ancient East: The New Testament Illustrated by Recently Discovered Texts of the Greco-Roman World*. Translated by L. R. M. Strachan. London: Hodder & Stoughton, 1909.

————. *Paul: A Study in Social and Religious History*. New York: Harper & Brothers, 1957.

Dennison, William D. "Indicative and Imperative: The Basic Structure of Pauline Ethics." *CTJ* 14 (1979): 55–78.

deSilva, David A. *Despising Shame: Honor Discourse and Community Maintenance in the Epistle to the Hebrews*. Rev. ed. SBLStBL 21. Atlanta: SBL, 2008.

————. *The Epistle to the Hebrews in Social-Scientific Perspective*. Eugene, OR: Cascade, 2012.

————. "Exchanging Favor for Wrath: Apostasy in Hebrews and Patron-Client Relations." *JBL* 115 (1996): 91–116.

————. *4 Maccabees*. Guides to the Apocrypha and Pseudepigrapha. Sheffield: Sheffield Academic Press, 1998.

————. *4 Maccabees: Introduction and Commentary on the Greek Text of Codex Sinaiticus*. Leiden: Brill, 2006.

————. *Galatians: A Handbook on the Greek Text*. Baylor Handbooks on the Greek New Testament. Waco, TX: Baylor University Press, 2014.

————. *Global Readings: A Sri Lankan Commentary on Paul's Letter to the Galatians.* Eugene, OR: Cascade, 2011.

————. "Grace, the Law, and Justification in *4 Ezra* and the Pauline Letters: A Dialogue." *JSNT* 37 (2014): 25–49.

————. *Honor, Patronage, Kinship, and Purity: Unlocking New Testament Culture.* Downers Grove, IL: InterVarsity Press, 2000.

————. "How Greek Was the Author of 'Hebrews'?" Pages 629–50 in *Christian Origins and Greco-Roman Culture: Early Christianity in Its Hellenistic Context.* Edited by Stanley Porter and Andrew Pitts. Vol. 1. Leiden: Brill, 2012.

————. *Introducing the Apocrypha: Message, Context, and Significance.* Grand Rapids: Baker Academic, 2002.

————. *An Introduction to the New Testament: Contexts, Methods, and Ministry Formation.* Downers Grove, IL: InterVarsity Press, 2004.

————. *The Jewish Teachers of Jesus, James, and Jude: What Earliest Christianity Learned from the Apocrypha and Pseudepigrapha.* New York: Oxford University Press, 2012.

————. *The Letter to the Hebrews in Social-scientific Perspective.* Eugene, OR: Cascade Books, 2012.

————. "Meeting the Exigency of a Complex Rhetorical Situation: Paul's Strategy in 2 Corinthians 1 through 7." *AUSS* 34 (1996): 5–22.

————. *Perseverance in Gratitude: A Socio-rhetorical Commentary on the Epistle "to the Hebrews."* Grand Rapids: Eerdmans, 2000.

————. *Seeing Things John's Way: The Rhetoric of the Book of Revelation.* Louisville: Westminster John Knox, 2009.

————. "The Strategic Arousal of Emotions in the Apocalypse of John." *NTS* 54 (2008): 90–114.

————. *Transformation: The Heart of Paul's Gospel.* Bellingham, WA: Lexham Press, 2014.

————. *Unholy Allegiances: Heeding Revelation's Warning.* Peabody, MA: Hendrickson, 2013.

————. "Using the Master's Tools to Shore Up Our House: A Postcolonial Analysis of *4 Maccabees*." *JBL* 127 (2007): 99–127.

————. "'We Are Debtors': Grace and Obligation in Paul and Seneca." Pages 150–78 in *Paul and Seneca in Dialogue.* Edited by Joseph Dodson and David Briones. Leiden: Brill, 2016.

————. "Why Did God Choose Abraham?" *BRev* 16 (2000): 16–21, 42–44.

————. "X Marks the Spot? A Critique of the Use of Chiasm in Macro-Structural Analyses of Revelation." *JSNT* 30 (2008): 343–71.

Dibelius, Martin. *From Tradition to Gospel.* London: Nicholson & Watson, 1934.

Dibelius, Martin, and Heinrich Greeven. *James.* Hermeneia. Philadelphia: Fortress, 1975.

Dillenberger, J., ed. *Martin Luther: Selections from His Writings*. Garden City, NY: Doubleday, 1961.

Di Mattei, Steven. "Paul's Allegory of the Two Covenants (Gal 4.21–31) in Light of First-Century Hellenistic Rhetoric and Jewish Hermeneutics." *NTS* 52 (2006): 102–22.

Dodd, Brian J. "Christ's Slave, People Pleasers, and Galatians 1.10." *NTS* 42 (1996): 90–104.

———. *Paul's Paradigmatic "I": Personal Example as Literary Strategy*. Sheffield: Sheffield Academic Press, 1999.

Dodd, C. H. *The Apostolic Preaching and Its Developments*. London: Hodder & Stoughton, 1937.

———. "*Ennomos Christou.*" Pages 134–48 in *More New Testament Studies*. Manchester: Manchester University Press, 1968.

Donaldson, T. L. "The 'Curse of the Law' and the Inclusion of the Gentiles: Galatians 3.13–14." *NTS* 32 (1986): 94–112.

———. *Judaism and the Gentiles: Jewish Patterns of Universalism (to 135 CE)*. Waco, TX: Baylor University Press, 2007.

———. *Paul and the Gentiles: Mapping the Apostle's Convictional World*. Minneapolis: Fortress, 1997.

———. "Zealot and Convert: The Origin of Paul's Christ-Torah Antithesis." *CBQ* 51 (1989): 655–82.

Donfried, Karl P. "Justification and the Last Judgment in Paul." *ZNW* 67 (1976): 90–110.

Doty, W. G. *Letters in Primitive Christianity*. Philadelphia: Fortress, 1973.

Downs, D. J. *The Offering of the Gentiles: Paul's Collection for Jerusalem in Its Chronological, Cultural, and Cultic Contexts*. WUNT 2/248. Tübingen, Mohr Siebeck, 2008.

Drane, John. *Paul, Libertine or Legalist?* London: SPCK, 1975.

Dülmen, A. van. *Die Theologie des Gesetzes bei Paulus*. SBM 5. Stuttgart: Katholisches Bibelwerk, 1968.

Dumbrell, W. "Abraham and the Abrahamic Covenant in Galatians 3:1–14." Pages 19–31 in *The Gospel to the Nations: Perspectives on Paul's Mission: In Honour of P. T. O'Brien*. Edited by P. Bolt and M. Thompson. Downers Grove, IL: InterVarsity Press, 2000.

———. "Justification in Paul: A Covenantal Perspective." *RTR* 51 (1992): 91–101.

Dunn, J. D. G. *Baptism in the Holy Spirit*. SBT 15. London: SCM, 1970.

———. *Beginning from Jerusalem*. Vol. 2 of *Christianity in the Making*. Grand Rapids: Eerdmans, 2009.

———. *Christology in the Making: A New Testament Inquiry into the Origins of the Doctrine of the Incarnation*. 2nd ed. Grand Rapids: Eerdmans, 1996.

———. *Did the First Christians Worship Jesus? The New Testament Evidence*. Louisville: Westminster John Knox, 2010.

————. "Echoes of Intra-Jewish Polemic in Paul's Letter to the Galatians." *JBL* 113 (1993): 459–77.

————. "Ἐκ Πίστεως: A Key to the Meaning of πίστις Χριστοῦ." Pages 351–66 in *The Word Leaps the Gap: Essays on Scripture and Theology in Honor of Richard B. Hays.* Edited by J. R. Wagner, K. C. Rowe, and K. Grieb. Grand Rapids: Eerdmans, 2008.

————. "Faith, Faithfulness." Pages 407–23 in *The New Interpreter's Dictionary of the Bible,* vol. 2: *D–H.* Edited by K. D. Sakenfeld. Nashville: Abingdon, 2007.

————. "4QMMT and Galatians." *NTS* 43 (1997): 147–53.

————. "The Incident at Antioch (Gal 2:11–18)." *JSNT* 18 (1983): 3–57.

————. *Jesus, Paul, and the Law: Studies in Mark and Galatians.* Louisville: Westminster John Knox, 1990.

————. "The Justice of God." *JTS,* n.s., 43 (1992): 1–22.

————. "'A Light to the Gentiles,' or 'The End of the Law'? The Significance of the Damascus Road Christophany for Paul." Pages 89–107 in *Jesus, Paul, and the Law.* Louisville: Westminster John Knox Press, 1990.

————. "The New Perspective on Paul." Pages 183–214 in *Jesus, Paul, and the Law.* Louisville: Westminster John Knox Press, 1990.

————. *The New Perspective on Paul: Collected Essays.* WUNT 185. Tübingen: Mohr Siebeck, 2005.

————. *The New Perspective on Paul: Collected Essays.* Rev. ed. Grand Rapids: Eerdmans, 2008.

————. "Once More, πίστις Χριστοῦ." Pages 730–44 in SBLSP 30. Atlanta: Scholars Press, 1991. Also published as pages 61–81 in *Looking Back, Pressing On.* Vol. 4 of *Pauline Theology.* Edited by E. E. Johnson and D. M. Hay. Atlanta: Scholars Press, 1997.

————. *Paul and the Mosaic Law.* Tübingen: Mohr Siebeck, 1996.

————. "Paul's Understanding of the Death of Jesus as Sacrifice." Pages 35–56 in *Sacrifice and Redemption: Durham Essays in Theology.* Edited by S. W. Sykes. Cambridge: Cambridge University Press, 1991.

————. "The Relationship between Paul and Jerusalem according to Galatians 1 and 2." *NTS* 28 (1982): 461–78.

————. *Romans 1–8* and *Romans 9–16.* WBC 38A and B. Dallas: Word, 1988.

————. "Son of God." Pages 587–93 in *The Encyclopedia of the Historical Jesus.* Edited by Craig A. Evans. London: Routledge, 2008.

————. "The Theology of Galatians: The Issue of Covenantal Nomism." Pages 125–46 in *Thessalonians, Philippians, Galatians, Philemon.* Vol. 1 of *Pauline Theology.* Edited by J. M. Bassler. Minneapolis: Fortress, 1991.

————. *The Theology of Paul's Letter to the Galatians.* Cambridge: Cambridge University Press, 1993.

————. *The Theology of Paul the Apostle.* Grand Rapids: Eerdmans, 1998.

———. *Unity and Diversity in the New Testament.* 2nd ed. London: SCM, 1990 (1977).

———. "Was Paul against the Law? The Law in Galatians and Romans: A Test-Case of Text in Context." Pages 455–75 in *Texts and Contexts: Biblical Texts in Their Textual and Situational Contexts.* Edited by T. Fornberg and D. Hellholm. Oslo: Scandinavian University Press, 1995.

———. "What Was the Issue between Paul and 'Those of the Circumcision'?" Pages 295–312 in *Paulus und das antike Judentum.* Edited by Martin Hengel and U. Heckel. Tübingen: Mohr Siebeck, 1991.

———. "Works of the Law and the Curse of the Law (Gal 3.10–14)." *NTS* 31 (1985): 523–42.

———. "Yet Once More—'The Works of the Law': A Response." *JSNT* 46 (1992): 99–117.

Dupont, Jacques. "The Conversion of Paul and Its Influence on His Understanding of Salvation by Faith." Pages 176–94 in *Apostolic History and the Gospel.* Edited by Ward W. Gasque and Ralph P. Martin. Grand Rapids: Eerdmans, 1970.

du Toit, A. "Alienation and Re-identification as Pragmatic Strategies in Galatians." Pages 149–69 in *Focusing on Paul: Persuasion and Theological Design in Romans and Galatians.* Edited by C. Breytenbach and D. S. du Toit. BZNW 151. Berlin: de Gruyter, 2007.

Dzino, Danijel. *Illyricum in Roman Politics, 229 BC–AD 68.* Canbridge: Cambridge University Press, 2010.

Easter, Matthew C. "The *Pistis Christou* Debate: Main Arguments and Responses in Summary." *CurBR* 9 (2010): 33–47.

Eastman, Susan G. "'Cast Out the Slave Woman and Her Son': The Dynamics of Exclusion and Inclusion in Galatians 4.30." *JSNT* 28 (2006): 309–36.

———. "The Evil Eye and the Curse of the Law: Galatians 3.1 Revisited." *JSNT* 83 (2001): 69–87.

———. *Recovering Paul's Mother Tongue: Language and Theology in Galatians.* Grand Rapids: Eerdmans, 2007.

Easton, B. S. "New Testament Ethical Lists." *JBL* 51 (1932): 1–12.

Eckert, J. *Die urchristliche Verkündigung im Streit zwischen Paulus und seinen Gegnern nach dem Galaterbrief.* Regensburg: Pustet, 1971.

Eckstein, Hans-Joachim. *Verheissung und Gesetz: Eine exegetische Untersuchung zu Galater 2,15–4,7.* WUNT 86. Tübingen: Mohr Siebeck, 1996.

Edelstein, Ludwig. *The Hippocratic Oath: Text, Translation, and Interpretation.* Baltimore: Johns Hopkins Press, 1943.

Ehrman, B. D. "Cephas and Peter." *JBL* 109 (1990): 463–74.

Eisenbaum, P. *Paul Was Not a Christian: The Original Message of a Misunderstood Apostle.* New York: HarperOne, 2009.

Elliott, J. H. "Paul, Galatians, and the Evil Eye." *CurTM* 17 (1990): 262–73.

Elliott, Mark A. *The Survivors of Israel: A Reconsideration of the Theology of Pre-Christian Judaism*. Grand Rapids: Eerdmans, 2000.

Elliott, M. W. "Πίστις Χριστοῦ in the Church Fathers and Beyond." Pages 277–89 in *The Faith of Jesus Christ: Exegetical, Biblical, and Theological Studies*. Edited by M. F. Bird and P. M. Sprinkle. Peabody, MA: Hendrickson, 2009.

Elliott, Neil. *Liberating Paul: The Justice of God and the Politics of the Apostle*. Minneapolis: Fortress, 1994.

Elliott, Susan. "Choose Your Mother, Choose Your Master: Galatians 4:21–5:1 in the Shadow of the Anatolian Mother of the Gods." *JBL* 118 (1999): 661–83.

———. *Cutting Too Close for Comfort: Paul's Letter to the Galatians in Its Anatolian Cultic Context*. JSNTSup 248. London: T&T Clark, 2003.

Ellis, E. Earle. "The Circumcision Party and the Early Christian Mission." Pages 390–99 in *SE IV*. Edited by F. L. Cross. TU 102. Berlin: Akademie, 1968.

———. *Paul's Use of the Old Testament*. Grand Rapids: Baker, 1957.

———. *Prophecy and Hermeneutic in Early Christianity: New Testament Essays*. Grand Rapids: Eerdmans, 1978.

Elmer, I. J. *Paul, Jerusalem, and the Judaizers: The Galatians Crisis in Its Broadest Historical Context*. WUNT 2/258. Tübingen: Mohr Siebeck, 2009.

Engberg-Pedersen, Troels. "Galatians in Romans 5–8 and Paul's Construction of the Identity of Christ Believers." Pages 477–505 in *Texts and Contexts: Biblical Texts in Their Textual and Situational Contexts*. Edited by T. Fornberg and D. Hellholm. Oslo: Scandinavian University Press, 1995.

———. "Gift-Giving and Friendship: Seneca and Paul in Romans 1–8 on the Logic of God's Χάρις and Its Human Response." *HTR* 101 (2008): 15–44.

———. "Paul, Virtues, and Vices." Pages 608–33 in *Paul in the Greco-Roman World*. Edited by J. Paul Sampley. Harrisburg: Trinity Press International, 2003.

———. *Paul and the Stoics*. Louisville: Westminster John Knox, 2000.

———, ed. *Paul in His Hellenistic Context*. Minneapolis: Fortress, 1995.

Esler, Philip F. "Making and Breaking an Agreement Mediterranean Style: A New Reading of Galatians 2:1–14." *BibInt* 3 (1995): 285–314.

Evans, C. A. "Paul and 'Works of the Law' Language in Late Antiquity." Pages 201–26 in *Paul and His Opponents*. Edited by S. E. Porter. Pauline Studies 2. Leiden: Brill, 2005.

Fairweather, Janet. "The Epistle to the Galatians and Classical Rhetoric." Pts. 1–2 and 3. *TynBul* 45 (1994): 1–38 and 213–43.

Faith of Jesus Christ[1]. See under Hays, *The Faith of Jesus Christ* (1983).

Faith of Jesus Christ[2]. See under Hays, *The Faith of Jesus Christ* (2002).

Farmer, W. R. "James the Lord's Brother, according to Paul." Pages 133–53 in *James the Just and Christian Origins*. Edited by B. D. Chilton and C. A. Evans. NovTSup 98. Leiden: Brill, 1999.

Fee, Gordon D. *God's Empowering Presence: The Holy Spirit in the Letters of Paul.* Peabody, MA: Hendrickson, 1994.

———. *Pauline Christology: An Exegetical-Theological Study.* Peabody, MA: Hendrickson, 2007.

Feldman, Louis H. *Jew and Gentile in the Ancient World.* Princeton: Princeton University Press, 1993.

Feldman, Louis H., and Meyer Reinhold, eds. *Jewish Life and Thought among Greeks and Romans: Primary Readings.* Minneapolis: Fortress, 1996.

Feuillet, A. "Loi de Dieu, loi du Christ et loi de l'Esprit d'après les epîtres pauliniennes: Les rapports de ces trois avec la loi Mosaique." *NovT* 22 (1980): 29–63.

Fitzmyer, Joseph A. "Crucifixion in Ancient Palestine, Qumran Literature, and the New Testament." *CBQ* 40 (1978): 493–513.

———. "Justification by Faith in Pauline Thought: A Catholic View." Pages 77–94 in *Rereading Paul Together: Protestant and Catholic Perspectives on Justification.* Edited by D. E. Aune. Grand Rapids: Eerdmans, 2006.

———. "Paul's Jewish Background and the Deeds of the Law." Pages 18–35 in *According to Paul: Studies in the Theology of the Apostle.* New York: Paulist, 1993.

———. *To Advance the Gospel.* New York: Crossroad, 1981.

Foakes-Jackson, F. J., and Kirsopp Lake, eds. *The Acts of the Apostles.* Part 1 of *The Beginnings of Christianity.* 5 vols. London: Macmillan, 1922.

Forbes, Chris. "Pauline Demonology and/or Cosmology? Principalities, Powers, and the Elements of the World in Their Hellenistic Contexts." *JSNT* 85 (2002): 51–73.

———. "Paul's Principalities and Powers: Demythologizing Apocalyptic?" *JSNT* 82 (2001): 61–88.

Foster, Paul. "The First Contribution to the πίστις Χριστοῦ Debate: A Study of Ephesians 3.12." *JSNT* 85 (2002): 75–96.

Fredricksen, Paula. "Judaism, the Circumcision of the Gentiles, and Apocalyptic Hope: Another Look at Galatians 1 and 2." *JTS*, n.s., 42 (1991): 532–64.

Frey, Jörg. "The Relevance of the Roman Imperial Cult for the Book of Revelation." Pages 231–55 in *The New Testament and Early Christian Literature in Greco-Roman Context: Studies in Honor of David E. Aune.* Edited by John Fotopoulos. Leiden: Brill, 2006.

Friedrich, J., et al., eds. *Rechtfertigung: Festschrift für Ernst Käsemann.* Tübingen: Mohr Siebeck, 1976.

Friesen, Steven. *Imperial Cults and the Apocalypse of John: Reading Revelation in the Ruins.* Oxford: Oxford University Press, 2001.

———. *Twice Neokoros: Ephesus, Asia and the Cult of the Flavian Imperial Family.* Leiden: Brill, 1993.

Fuller, Daniel P. "Paul and 'the Works of the Law.'" *WTJ* 38 (1975–76): 28–42.

Furnish, Victor P. *The Love Command in the New Testament*. London: SCM, 1973.

———. *Second Corinthians*. AB 32A. New York: Doubleday, 1984.

———. *Theology and Ethics in Paul*. Nashville: Abingdon, 1968.

Gaffin, Richard B., Jr. *"By Faith, Not by Sight": Paul and the Order of Salvation*. Waynesboro, GA: Paternoster, 2006.

Gager, J. G. *The Origins of Anti-Semitism: Attitudes towards Judaism in Pagan and Christian Antiquity*. New York: Oxford University Press, 1983.

Gardiner, E. N. *Greek Athletic Sports and Festivals*. Oxford: Clarendon, 1955.

Garlington, Don. "'Even We Have Believed': Galatians 2:15–16 Revisited." *CTR* 7 (2009): 3–28.

———. *Faith, Obedience, and Perseverance: Aspects of Paul's Letter to the Romans*. WUNT 2/79. Tübingen: Mohr Siebeck, 1994.

———. "Paul's 'Partisan ἐκ' and the Question of Justification in Galatians." *JBL* 127 (2008): 567–89.

———. "Role Reversal and Paul's Use of Scripture in Galatians 3.10–13." *JSNT* 65 (1997): 85–121.

———. *Studies in the New Perspective on Paul: Essays and Reviews*. Eugene, OR: Wipf & Stock, 2008.

Gaston, Lloyd. *Paul and the Torah*. Vancouver: University of British Columbia Press, 1987.

Gathercole, S. J. "The Doctrine of Justification in Paul and Beyond: Some Proposals." Pages 219–41 in *Justification in Perspective: Historical Developments and Contemporary Challenges*. Edited by B. L. McCormack. Grand Rapids: Baker Academic, 2006.

———. "Justified by Faith, Justified by His Blood: The Evidence of Romans 3:21–4:25." Pages 147–84 in *The Paradoxes of Paul*. Vol. 2 of *Justification and Variegated Nomism*. Edited by D. A. Carson, P. T. O'Brien, and M. A. Seifrid. WUNT 2/181. Tübingen: Mohr Siebeck, 2004.

———. "A Law unto Themselves: The Gentiles in Romans 2.14–15 Revisited." *JSNT* 24 (2002): 27–49.

———. "The Petrine and Pauline *Sola Fide* in Galatians 2." Pages 309–27 in *Lutherische und neue Paulusperspektive*. Edited by M. Bachmann. Tübingen: Mohr Siebeck, 2005.

———. "Torah, Life, and Salvation: Leviticus 18:5 in Early Judaism and the New Testament." Pages 126–45 in *From Prophecy to Testament: The Function of the Old Testament in the New*. Edited by C. A. Evans. Peabody, MA: Hendrickson, 2004.

Gaventa, Beverly R. *From Darkness to Light*. Philadelphia: Fortress, 1986.

———. "Galatians 1 and 2: Autobiography as Paradigm." *NovT* 28 (1986): 309–26.

———. "The Maternity of Paul: An Exegetical Study of Gal 4:19." Pages 189–201 in *The Conversation Continues: Studies in Paul and John in Honor of J. Louis*

Martyn. Edited by R. T. Fortna and B. R. Gaventa. Nashville: Abingdon, 1990.

———. *Our Mother St. Paul*. Louisville: Westminster John Knox, 2007.

———. "Our Mother St. Paul: Toward the Recovery of a Neglected Theme." *PSB* 17 (1996): 29–44.

———. "The Singularity of the Gospel: A Reading of Galatians." Pages 147–59 in *Thessalonians, Philippians, Galatians, Philemon*. Vol. 1 of *Pauline Theology*. Edited by J. M. Bassler. Minneapolis: Fortress, 1991.

Georgi, Dieter. *Remembering the Poor: The History of Paul's Collection for Jerusalem*. Nashville: Abingdon, 1992. ET of *Die Geschichte der Kollekte des Paulus für Jerusalem*. TF 38. Hamburg: Evangelischer Verlag, 1965.

Gese, H. "τὸ δὲ Ἁγὰρ Σινᾶ ὄρος ἐστὶν ἐν τῇ Ἀραβίᾳ (Gal 4,25)." Pages 59–72 in *Vom Sinai zum Zion: Alttestamentliche Beiträge zur biblischen Theologie*. BEvT 64. Munich: Kaiser, 1974.

Gignac, A. "Citation de Lévitique 18,5 en Romains 10,5 et Galates 3,12: Deux lectures différentes des rapports Christ-Torah?" *EgT* 25 (1994): 367–403.

Gignilliat, M. "Paul, Allegory, and the Plain Sense of Scripture: Galatians 4:21–31." *Journal of Theological Interpretation* 2 (2008): 135–46.

Gill, Christopher, Norman Postlethwaite, and Richard Seaford, eds. *Reciprocity in Ancient Greece*. Oxford: Oxford University Press, 1998.

Goddard, A. J., and S. A. Cummins. "Ill or Ill-Treated? Conflict and Persecution as the Context of Paul's Original Ministry in Galatia (Galatians 4.12–20)." *JSNT* 52 (1993): 93–126.

Goldin, J. "Not by Means of an Angel and Not by Means of a Messenger." Pages 412–24 in *Religions in Antiquity*. Edited by Jacob Neusner. Numen Supplements 14. Leiden: Brill, 1968.

Goldingay, J., and D. F. Payne. *A Critical and Exegetical Commentary on Isaiah 40–55*. 2 vols. ICC. London: T&T Clark, 2006.

Gombis, Timothy B. "The 'Transgressor' and the 'Curse of the Law': The Logic of Paul's Argument in Galatians 2–3." *NTS* 53 (2007): 81–93.

Goodenough, E. R., and A. T. Kraabel. "Paul and the Hellenization of Christianity." Pages 23–68 in *Religions in Antiquity*. Edited by J. Neusner. Leiden: Brill, 1968.

Goodman, M. "Jewish Proselytizing in the First Century." Pages 53–78 in *The Jews among Pagans and Christians in the Roman Empire*. Edited by Judith Lieu, J. North, and Tessa Rajak. London: Routledge, 1992.

Goppelt, L. *Typos: The Typological Interpretation of the Old Testament in the New*. Grand Rapids: Eerdmans, 1982.

Gordon, T. David. "Abraham and Sinai Contrasted in Galatians 3:6–14." Pages 240–58 in *The Law Is Not of Faith: Essays on Works and Grace in the Mosaic Covenant*. Edited by B. D. Estelle, J. V. Fesko, and D. VanDrunen. Phillipsburg, NJ: P&R, 2009.

———. "A Note on παιδαγωγός in Galatians 3.24–25." *NTS* 35 (1989): 150–54.

———. "The Problem at Galatia." *Int* 41 (1987): 32–43.

Gorman, M. J. *Apostle of the Crucified Lord: A Theological Introduction to Paul and His Letters.* Grand Rapids: Eerdmans, 2004.

———. *Inhabiting the Cruciform God: Kenosis, Justification, and Theosis in Paul's Narrative Soteriology.* Grand Rapids: Eerdmans, 2009.

Grant, Robert M. "Jewish Christianity in Antioch in the Second Century." *RelSRev* 60 (1972): 97–108.

———. "Neither Male nor Female." *BR* 37 (1997): 5–14.

Grässer, E. "Das eine Evangelium: Hermeneutische Erwägungen zu Gal 1,6–10." *ZTK* 66 (1969): 306–44.

Griffin, Miriam. "*De Beneficiis* and Roman Society." *JRS* 93 (2003): 92–113.

Grüneberg, K. N. *Abraham, Blessing, and the Nations: A Philological and Exegetical Study of Genesis 12:3 in Its Narrative Context.* BZAW 332. Berlin: de Gruyter, 2003.

Gundry, Robert H. "Grace, Works, and Staying Saved in Paul." *Bib* 66 (1985): 1–38.

Guthrie, W. C. K. *A History of Greek Philosophy.* 2 vols. Cambridge: Cambridge University Press, 1965.

Güttgemanns, E. *Der leidende Apostel und sein Herr: Studien zur paulinischen Christologie.* Göttingen: Vandenhoeck & Ruprecht, 1966.

Haacker, K. "Paulus und das Judentum im Galaterbrief." Pages 95–111 in *Gottes Augapfel: Beiträge zur Erneuerung des Verhältnisses von Christen und Juden.* Edited by E. Brocke and J. Seim. Neukirchen-Vluyn: Neukirchener Verlag, 1986.

Haenchen, Ernst. *Acts of the Apostles.* Translated by R. McL. Wilson. Philadelphia: Westminster Press, 1971.

———. "The Book of Acts as Source Material for the History of Early Christianity." Pages 258–78 in *Studies in Luke-Acts.* Edited by Leander E. Keck and J. Louis Martyn. Nashville: Abingdon, 1966.

Hafemann, Scott. "'Because of Weakness' (Galatians 4:13): The Role of Suffering in the Mission of Paul." Pages 131–46 in *The Gospel to the Nations: Perspectives on Paul's Mission, in Honour of P. T. O'Brien.* Edited by P. Bolt and M. Thompson. Downers Grove, IL: InterVarsity Press, 2000.

———. "Paul and the Exile of Israel in Galatians 3–4." Pages 329–71 in *Exile: Old Testament, Jewish, and Christian Conceptions.* Edited by J. M. Scott. Leiden: Brill, 1997.

———. *Paul, Moses, and the History of Israel.* Tübingen: Mohr Siebeck, 1995.

———. "The Role of Suffering in the Mission of Paul." Pages 165–84 in *The Mission of the Early Church to Jews and Gentiles.* Edited by J. Adna and H. Qvalbein. Tübingen: Mohr Siebeck, 2000.

Hagner, Donald A. "Paul and Judaism: Testing the New Perspective." Pages 75–

105 in *Revisiting Paul's Doctrine of Justification: A Challenge to the New Perspective* by Peter Stuhlmacher. Downers Grove, IL: InterVarsity Press, 2001.

Hahn, F. "Genesis 15:6 im Neuen Testament." Pages 90–107 in *Probleme Biblischer Theologie: Gerhard von Rad zum 70. Geburtstag*. Edited by H. W. Wolff. Munich: Kaiser, 1971.

Hahn, Scott W. "Covenant, Oath, and the Aqedah: Διαθήκη in Galatians 3:15–18." *CBQ* 67 (2005): 79–100.

———. *Kinship by Covenant: A Canonical Approach to the Fulfillment of God's Saving Promises*. New Haven: Yale University Press, 2009.

Hall, Robert G. "Arguing like An Apocalypse: Galatians and an Ancient Topos outside the Greco-Roman Rhetorical Tradition." *NTS* 42 (1996): 434–53.

———. "The Rhetorical Outline for Galatians: A Reconsideration." *JBL* 106 (1987): 277–87.

Hamerton-Kelly, R. G. *Sacred Violence: Paul's Hermeneutic of the Cross*. Minneapolis: Fortress, 1992.

Hamilton, V. P. *The Book of Genesis: Chapters 1–17*. NICOT. Grand Rapids: Eerdmans, 1990.

Hansen, B. *All of You Are One: The Social Vision of Galatians 3.28, 1 Corinthians 12.13, and Colossians 3.11*. LNTS 409. London: T&T Clark, 2010.

Hansen, G. Walter. *Abraham in Galatians: Epistolary and Rhetorical Contexts*. Sheffield: Sheffield Academic Press, 1989.

Hanson, A. T. *Studies in Paul's Technique and Theology*. London: SPCK, 1974.

Hanson, R. P. C. *Allegory and Event*. London: SCM Press, 1959.

Hardin, Justin K. *Galatians and the Imperial Cult: A Critical Analysis of the First-Century Social Context of Paul's Letter*. WUNT 2/237. Tübingen: Mohr Siebeck, 2008.

Harland, P. A. "Familial Dimensions of Group Identity: 'Brothers' (ΑΔΕΛΦΟΙ) in Associations of the Greek East." *JBL* 124 (2005): 491–513.

Harmon, M. *She Must and Shall Go Free: Paul's Isaianic Gospel in Galatians*. BZNW 168. Berlin: de Gruyter, 2010.

Harnack, Adolf von. *The Acts of the Apostles*. Translated by J. R. Wilkinson. New York: G. P. Putnam's Sons, 1909.

Harris, M. J. *Prepositions and Theology in the Greek New Testament*. Grand Rapids: Zondervan, 2012.

———. *Slave of Christ: A New Testament Metaphor for Total Devotion to Christ*. New Studies in Biblical Theology 8. Downers Grove, IL: InterVarsity Press, 1999.

Harrison, James R. *Paul's Language of Grace in Its Graeco-Roman Context*. WUNT 2/172. Tübingen: Mohr Siebeck, 2003.

Harrisville, Roy A. "Before πίστις Χριστοῦ: The Objective Genitive as Good Greek." *NovT* 48 (2006): 353–58.

———. *The Figure of Abraham in the Epistles of St. Paul*. San Francisco: Mellen University Research Press, 1992.

———. "ΠΙΣΤΙΣ ΧΡΙΣΤΟΥ: Witness of the Fathers." *NovT* 36 (1994): 233–41.

Hartman, Lars. "Galatians 3:25–4:11 as Part of a Theological Argument on a Practical Issue." Pages 127–58 in *The Truth of the Gospel (Galatians 1:11–4:11)*. Edited by J. Lambrecht. Rome: Benedictina, 1993.

Hawthorne, G. F., R. P. Martin, and D. G. Reid, eds. *Dictionary of Paul and His Letters*. Downers Grove, IL: InterVarsity Press, 1993.

Hay, David M. "Pistis as 'Ground of Faith' in Hellenized Judaism and Paul." *JBL* 108 (1989): 461–76.

Hays, Richard B. "Apocalyptic Hermeneutics: Habakkuk Proclaims 'The Righteous One.'" Pages 119–42 in *The Conversion of the Imagination: Paul as Interpreter of Israel's Scripture*. Grand Rapids: Eerdmans, 2005.

———. "Christology and Ethics in Galatians: The Law of Christ." *CBQ* 49 (1987): 268–90.

———. *Echoes of Scripture in the Letters of Paul*. New Haven: Yale University Press, 1989.

———. *The Faith of Jesus Christ: An Investigation of the Narrative Substructure of Galatians 3:1–4:11*. SBLDS 56. Chico, CA: Scholars Press, 1983.

———. *The Faith of Jesus Christ: The Narrative Substructure of Galatians 3:1–4:11*. Rev. ed. Grand Rapids: Eerdmans, 2002.

———. "Justification." Pages 3:112–33 in *Anchor Bible Dictionary*. Edited by David N. Freedman. New York: Doubleday, 1992.

———. "*Pistis* and Pauline Christology: What Is at Stake?" Pages 714–29 in SBLSP 30. Atlanta: Scholars Press, 1991. Also published as pages 35–60 in *Looking Back, Pressing On*. Vol. 4 of *Pauline Theology*. Edited by Elizabeth E. Johnson and David M. Hay. Atlanta: Scholars Press, 1997.

Heckel, U. *Der Segen im Neuen Testament*. WUNT 2/150. Tübingen: Mohr Siebeck, 2002.

Heiligenthal, R. "Soziologische Implikationen der paulinischen Rechtfertigungslehre im Galaterbrief am Beispiel der 'Werke des Gesetzes.'" *Kairos* 26 (1984): 38–53.

Heliso, D. *Pistis and the Righteous One: A Study of Romans 1:17 against the Background of Scripture and Second Temple Jewish Literature*. WUNT 235. Tübingen: Mohr Siebeck, 2007.

Hemer, Colin J. "Acts and Galatians Reconsidered." *Them* 2 (1977): 81–88.

———. "The Adjective 'Phrygia.'" *JTS* 27 (1976): 122–26.

———. "Observations on Pauline Chronology." Pages 3–18 in *Pauline Studies: Essays Presented to F. F. Bruce*. Edited by Donald A. Hagner and Murray J. Harris. Exeter: Paternoster, 1980.

Hemer, Colin J., and Conrad H. Gempf. *The Book of Acts in the Setting of Hellenistic History*. WUNT 2/49. Tübingen: Mohr Siebeck, 1989.

1

Hengel, Martin. *Acts and the History of Earliest Christianity.* Translated by John Bowden. London: SCM Press, 1979.

———. "The Attitude of Paul to the Law in the Unknown Years between Damascus and Antioch." Pages 25–51 in *Paul and the Mosaic Law.* Edited by James D. G. Dunn. Grand Rapids: Eerdmans, 1996.

———. *Crucifixion in the Ancient World and the Folly of the Message of the Cross.* Translated by J. Bowden. Philadelphia: Fortress, 1977.

———. *The Hellenization of Judaea in the First Century after Christ.* London: SCM, 1989.

———. *Jews, Greeks, Barbarians.* Philadelphia: Fortress, 1980.

———. *Judaism and Hellenism.* 2 vols. Philadelphia: Fortress, 1974.

———. *The Pre-Christian Paul.* Valley Forge, PA: Trinity Press International, 1991.

———. *The Son of God: The Origin of Christology and the History of Jewish-Hellenistic Religion.* Translated by John Bowden. Philadelphia: Fortress, 1976.

———. *The Zealots: Investigations into the Jewish Freedom Movement in the Period from Herod I until 70 AD.* Edinburgh: T&T Clark, 1961.

Hengel, Martin, and Anna Maria Schwemer. *Paul between Damascus and Antioch: The Unknown Years.* Louisville: Westminster John Knox Press, 1997.

Henten, Jan Willem van. *The Maccabean Martyrs as Saviours of the Jewish People.* Leiden: Brill, 1997.

Hester, James D. "The Rhetorical Structure of Galatians 1:11–2:14." *JBL* 103 (1984): 223–44.

Hietanen, Mika. *Paul's Argumentation in Galatians: A Pragma-Dialectical Analysis.* LNTS 344. London: T&T Clark, 2007.

Hill, C. G. *Hellenists and Hebrews: Reappraising Division within the Earliest Church.* Minneapolis: Fortress, 1991.

Hodge, J. *If Sons, Then Heirs: A Study of Kinship and Ethnicity in the Letters of Paul.* New York: Oxford University Press, 2007.

Hoenig, Sidney B. "Circumcision: The Covenant of Abraham." *JQR*, n.s., 53 (1962–63): 322–34.

Hofius, Otfried. "Gal 1:18 ἱστορῆσαι Κηφᾶν." *ZNW* 75 (1984): 73–85.

———. "Das Gesetz Mose und das Gesetz Christi." *ZTK* 80 (1983): 262–86.

———. *Paulusstudien I.* WUNT 51. Tübingen: Mohr Siebeck, 1989.

———. "'Werke des Gesetzes': Untersuchungen zu der paulinischen und johanneischen Theologie und Literatur." Pages 271–310 in *Paulus and Johannes: Exegetische Studien zur paulinischen und johanneischen Theologie und Literatur.* Edited by D. Sänger and U. Mell. WUNT 198. Tübingen: Mohr Siebeck, 2006.

Holl, K. "Der Kirchenbegriff des Paulus in seinem Verhältnis zu dem der Urgemeinde." Pages 44–67 in *Gesammelte Aufsätze zur Kirchengeschichte*. Vol. 2. Tübingen: Mohr Siebeck, 1928.

Holmberg, Bengt. *Paul and Power: The Structure of Authority in the Primitive Church as Reflected in the Pauline Epistles*. Philadelphia: Fortress, 1980.

———. *Sociology and the New Testament: An Appraisal*. Minneapolis: Fortress, 1990.

Hong, In-Gyu. "Being 'under the Law' in Galatians." *Evangelical Review of Theology* 26 (2002): 354–72.

———. "Does Paul Misrepresent the Jewish Law? Law and Covenant in Gal 3:1–14." *NovT* 36 (1994): 164–82.

———. *The Law in Galatians*. JSNTSup 81. Sheffield: Sheffield Academic Press, 1993.

Hooker, Morna D. *From Adam to Christ. Essays on Paul*. Cambridge: Cambridge University Press, 1990.

———. "ΠΙΣΤΙΣ ΧΡΙΣΤΟΥ." *NTS* 35 (1989): 321–42.

Horton, M. S. *Covenant and Salvation: Union with Christ*. Louisville: Westminster John Knox, 2007.

Houlden, J. L. "A Response to James D. G. Dunn." *JSNT* 18 (1983): 58–67.

Hove, Richard W. *Equality in Christ? Galatians 3:28 and the Gender Dispute*. Wheaton, IL: Crossway, 1999.

Howard, George. *Crisis in Galatia*. Cambridge: Cambridge University Press, 1979.

———. "'The Faith of Christ.'" *ExpTim* 85 (1973–74): 212–14.

———. *Paul: Crisis in Galatia; A Study in Early Christian Theology*. 2nd ed. SNTSMS 35. Cambridge: Cambridge University Press, 1990.

Hubbard, M. B. *New Creation in Paul's Letters and Thought*. SNTSMS 119. Cambridge: Cambridge University Press, 2002.

Hübner, Hans. "Der Galaterbrief und das Verhältnis von der antiker Rhetorik und Epistolographie." *TLZ* 109 (1984): 241–50.

———. "Das Ganze und das eine Gesetz: Zum Problemkreis Paulus und die Stoa." *KD* 21 (1975): 239–56.

———. *Law in Paul's Thought*. Translated by James C. G. Greig. Edinburgh: T&T Clark, 1984.

Hultgren, A. J. "Paul's Pre-Christian Persecutions of the Church: Their Purpose, Locale, and Nature." *JBL* 95 (1976): 97–111.

———. "The *Pistis Christou* Formulations in Paul." *NovT* 22 (1980): 248–63.

———. "The Scriptural Foundations for Paul's Mission to the Gentiles." Pages 21–44 in *Paul and His Theology*. Edited by S. E. Porter. Pauline Studies 3. Leiden: Brill, 2006.

Hunn, Debbie. "Christ versus the Law: Issues in Galatians 2:17–18." *CBQ* 72 (2010): 537–55.

———. "'Ἐὰν μή in Galatians 2:16: A Look at Greek Literature." *NovT* 49 (2007): 281–90.

————. "Habakkuk 2.4b in Its Context: How Far Off Was Paul?" *JSOT* 34 (2009): 219–39.

————. "PISTIS CHRISTOU in Galatians 2:16." *TynBul* 57.1 (2006): 23–33.

Hurtado, L. W. "The Jerusalem Collection and the Book of Galatians." *JSNT* 5 (1979): 46–62.

————. *Lord Jesus Christ: Devotion to Jesus in Earliest Christianity*. Grand Rapids: Eerdmans, 2003.

Hyldahl, N. "Gerechtigkeit durch Glauben: Historische und theologische Beobachtungen zum Galaterbrief." *NTS* 46 (2000): 425–44.

Jackson, T. R. *New Creation in Paul's Letters: A Study of the Historical and Social Setting of a Pauline Concept*. WUNT 2/272. Tübingen: Mohr Siebeck, 2010.

Jayakumar, Samuel. "Caste." Pages 1622–23 in *South Asia Bible Commentary*. Edited by Brian Wintle. Grand Rapids: Zondervan, 2015.

Jensen, Joseph. "Does *Porneia* Mean Fornication? A Critique of Bruce Malina." *NovT* 20 (1978): 161–84.

Jeremias, J. *Abba: Studien zur neutestamentlichen Theologie und Zeitgeschichte*. Göttingen: Vandenhoeck & Ruprecht, 1966.

————. *New Testament Theology: The Proclamation of Jesus*. New York: Scribner's Sons, 1971.

Jewett, Robert. "The Agitators and the Galatian Congregations." *NTS* 17 (1971): 198–212.

————. *A Chronology of Paul's Life*. Philadelphia: Fortress, 1979.

————. *Paul's Anthropological Terms: A Study of Their Use in Conflict Settings*. AGJU 10. Leiden: Brill, 1971.

————. "Paul, Shame, and Honor." Pages 551–74 in *Paul in the Greco-Roman World*. Edited by J. Paul Sampley. Harrisburg, PA: Trinity Press International, 2003.

————. *Romans*. Hermeneia. Minneapolis: Fortress, 2007.

Jobes, Karen H. "Jerusalem, Our Mother: Metalepsis and Intertextuality in Galatians 4:21–31." *WTJ* 55 (1993): 299–320.

Johnson, H. W. "The Paradigm of Abraham in Galatians 3:6–9." *TJ* 8 (1987): 179–99.

Johnson, J. F. "Paul's Argument from Experience: A Closer Look at Galatians 3:1–5." *Concordia Journal* 19 (1993): 234–37.

Johnson, Luke T. *The Letter of James*. AB 37A. New York: Doubleday, 1995.

————. "Rom 3:21–26 and the Faith of Jesus." *CBQ* 44 (1982): 77–90.

Johnson, S. L. "Paul and 'The Israel of God': An Exegetical and Eschatological Case-Study." Pages 183–94 in *Essays in Honor of J. Dwight Pentecost*. Edited by S. Toussaint and C. Dyer. Chicago: Moody Press, 1986.

Jones, F. Stanley. *"Freiheit" in den Briefen des Apostels Paulus: Eine historische, exegetische, und religionsgeschichtliche Studie*. GTA 34. Göttingen: Vandenhoeck & Ruprecht, 1987.

Joubert, Stephan. *Paul as Benefactor: Reciprocity, Strategy, and Theological Reflection in Paul's Collection.* WUNT 2/124. Tübingen: Mohr Siebeck, 2000.

———. "Religious Reciprocity in 2 Corinthians 9:6–15: Generosity and Gratitude as Legitimate Responses to the χάρις τοῦ θεοῦ." *Neot* 33.1 (1999): 79–90.

Judge, Edwin A. "Paul's Boasting in Relation to Contemporary Professional Practice." *ABR* 16 (1968): 37–50.

Jüngel, E. *Justification: The Heart of the Christian Faith; A Theological Study with Ecumenical Purpose.* Edinburgh: T&T Clark, 2001.

Kahl, Brigitte. "No Longer Male: Masculinity Struggles behind Galatians 3:28?" *JSNT* 79 (2000): 37–49.

Kaiser, W. C., Jr. "The Book of Leviticus." Pages 1:983–1191 in *The New Interpreter's Bible.* Edited by L. E. Keck et al. Nashville: Abingdon, 1994.

Käsemann, Ernst. "The Righteousness of God in Paul." Pages 168–82 in *New Testament Questions of Today.* Edited by E. Käsemann. Philadelphia: Fortress, 1969.

Keck, Leander. *Paul and His Letters.* Philadelphia: Fortress, 1979.

———. "The Poor among the Saints in Jewish Christianity and Qumran." *ZNW* 57 (1966): 54–78.

———. "The Poor among the Saints in the New Testament." *ZNW* 56 (1965): 100–129.

Keener, Craig. *Acts: An Exegetical Commentary.* 4 vols. Grand Rapids: Baker Academic, 2012–15.

———. *Miracles: The Credibility of the New Testament Accounts.* 2 vols. Grand Rapids: Baker, 2011.

Kemmer, Suzanne. *The Middle Voice.* Philadelphia: John Benjamins, 1993.

Kennedy, George. *Invention and Method: Two Rhetorical Treatises from the Hermogenic Corpus.* Atlanta: SBL, 2005.

———. *New Testament Interpretation through Rhetorical Criticism.* Chapel Hill: University of North Carolina Press, 1984.

———. *Progymnasmata: Greek Textbooks of Prose Composition and Rhetoric.* Atlanta: SBL, 2003.

Kern, Philip H. *Rhetoric in Galatians: Assessing an Approach to Paul's Epistle.* SNTSMS 101. Cambridge: Cambridge University Press, 1998.

Kertelge, K. "Freiheitsbotschaft und Liebesgebot im Galaterbrief." Pages 326–37 in *Neues Testament und Ethik: Für Rudolf Schnackenburg.* Edited by H. Merklein. Freiburg: Herder, 1989.

———. "Gesetz und Freiheit im Galaterbrief." *NTS* 30 (1984): 382–94.

Kilgallen, J. J. "The Strivings of the Flesh . . . (Galatians 5:17)." *Bib* 80 (1999): 113–14.

Kilpatrick, G. D. "Peter, Jerusalem, and Galatians 1:13–2:14." *NovT* 24 (1983): 318–26.

Kim, Seyoon. *Christ and Caesar: The Gospel and the Roman Empire in the Writings of Paul and Luke*. Grand Rapids: Eerdmans, 2008.

———. *The Origins of Paul's Gospel*. Grand Rapids: Eerdmans, 1982.

———. *Paul and the New Perspective: Second Thoughts on the Origin of Paul's Gospel*. Grand Rapids: Eerdmans, 2002.

Kirk, G. S., and J. E. Raven. *The Presocratic Philosophers: A Critical History with a Selection of Texts*. Cambridge: Cambridge University Press, 1983.

Kittel, G., and G. Friedrich. *Theological Dictionary of the New Testament*. Translated by Geoffrey W. Bromiley. 10 vols. Grand Rapids: Eerdmans, 1964–76.

Klaiber, Walter. *Der Römerbrief*. Neukirchen-Vluyn: Neukirchener Verlag, 2009.

Klauck, Hans-Josef. *Ancient Letters and the New Testament: A Guide to Context and Exegesis*. Waco, TX: Baylor University Press, 2006.

———. "Hellenistiche Rhetorik im Diasporajudenum: Das Exordium des vierten Makkabäerbuchs." *NTS* 35 (1989): 451–65.

Klawans, Jonathan. *Impurity and Sin in Ancient Judaism*. Oxford: Oxford University Press, 2000.

Klein, G. "Galater 2,6–9 und die Geschichte der Jerusalemer Urgemeinde." *ZTK* 57 (1960): 275–95.

Knox, John. *Chapters in a Life of Paul*. Rev. ed. Macon, GA: Mercer University Press, 1987.

Koch, D. A. "Barnabas, Paul und die Adressaten des Galaterbriefs." Pages 85–106 in *Das Urchristentum in seiner literarischen Geschichte: Festschrift für Jürgen Becker zum 65. Geburtstag*. Edited by U. Mell and U. B. Müller. Berlin: de Gruyter, 1999.

Köstenberger, Andreas. "The Identity of the Ἰσραὴλ τοῦ θεοῦ (Israel of God) in Galatians 6:16." *Faith and Mission* 19 (2001): 3–24.

Kraftchick, Steven. "*Ethos* and Pathos: Arguments in Galatians 5 and 6; A Rhetorical Approach." PhD diss. Emory University, 1985.

———. "Why Do the Rhetoricians Rage?" pp. 55–79 in *Text and Logos: The Humanistic Interpretation of the New Testament*. Edited by Theodore W. Jennings Jr. Atlanta: Scholars Press, 1990.

Kraybill, Nelson. *Imperial Cult and Commerce in John's Apocalypse*. JSNTSup 132. Sheffield: Sheffield Academic Press, 1996.

Kruger, M. A. "Law and Promise in Galatians." *Neot* 26 (1992): 311–27.

Kruse, C. *Paul, the Law, and Justification*. Leicester: Inter-Varsity Press, 1996.

Kuck, D. W. "Each Will Bear His Own Burden: Paul's Creative Use of an Apocalyptic Motif." *NTS* 40 (1994): 289–97.

Kuhn, H. W. "Die Bedeutung der Qumrantexte für das Verhältnis des Galaterbriefes." Pages 169–221 in *New Qumran Texts and Studies*. Edited by G. J. Brooke. Leiden: Brill, 1994.

Kümmel, W. G. *Introduction to the New Testament*. Translated by A. J. Mattill Jr. Nashville: Abingdon, 1975.

Kuula, K. *The Law, the Covenant and God's Plan*, vol. 1: *Paul's Polemical Treatment of the Law in Galatians*. Publications of the Finnish Exegetical Society 72. Göttingen: Vandenhoeck & Ruprecht, 1999.

Kuyper, L. J. "Righteousness and Salvation." *Scottish Journal of Theology* 3 (1977): 233–52.

Kwon, Yon-Gyong. *Eschatology in Galatians: Rethinking Paul's Response to the Crisis in Galatia*. WUNT 2/183. Tübingen: Mohr Siebeck, 2004.

Lake, Kirsopp. "Simon, Cephas, Peter." *HTR* 14 (1921): 95–97.

Lambrecht, Jan. "Abraham and His Offspring: A Comparison of Galatians 5,1 with 3,13." *Bib* 80 (1999): 525–36.

———. "Critical Reflections on Paul's 'Partisan ἐκ' as Recently Presented by Don Garlington." *ETL* 85 (2009): 135–41.

———. "The Line of Thought in Gal. 2.14b–21." *NTS* 24 (1977–78): 484–95.

———. "Once Again Gal 2:17–18 and 3:21." *ETL* 63 (1987): 148–53.

———. *Pauline Studies: Collected Essays by Jan Lambrecht*. BETL 115. Leuven: Leuven University Press, 1994.

———. "Paul's Reasoning in Galatians 2:11–21." Pages 53–74 in *Paul and the Mosaic Law*. Edited by J. D. G. Dunn. Tübingen: Mohr Siebeck, 1996.

———. "Transgressor by Nullifying God's Grace. A Study of Gal 2,18–21." *Bib* 72 (1991): 217–36.

Lampe, G. W. H. "The New Testament Doctrine of *Ktisis*." *SJT* 17 (1964): 457–58.

Lappenga, Benjamin. *Paul's Language of Ζῆλος: Monosemy and the Rhetoric of Identity and Practice*. BibInt 137. Leiden: Brill, 2015.

Lategan, B. "The Argumentative Situation of Galatians." *Neot* 26 (1992): 257–77.

———. "Is Paul Defending His Apostleship in Galatians? The Function of Galatians 1:11–12 and 2:19–20 in the Development of Paul's Argument." *NTS* 34 (1988): 411–30.

Leithart, Peter. "Justification as Verdict and Deliverance: A Biblical Perspective." *ProEccl* 16 (2007): 56–72.

Lemmer, H. R. "Mnemonic Reference to the Spirit as a Persuasive Tool (Gal. 3:1–6 within the Argument 3:1–4:11)." *Neot* 26 (1992): 359–88.

Lenski, Richard C. H. *The Interpretation of St. Paul's Epistles to the Galatians, to the Ephesians, and to the Philippians*. Minneapolis: Augsburg, 1961.

Levinsohn, Stephen H. *Discourse Features of New Testament Greek: A Coursebook on the Information Structure of New Testament Greek*. 2nd ed. Dallas: Summer Institute of Linguistics, 2000.

Levy, I. C. *The Letter to the Galatians*. The Bible in Medieval Tradition. Grand Rapids: Eerdmans, 2011.

Lewis, C. S. *The Four Loves*. New York: Harcourt, Brace & World, 1960.

Lichtenberger, Hermann. "Alter Bund und Neuer Bund." *NTS* 41 (1995): 400–414.

———. "The Understanding of the Torah in the Judaism of Paul's Day: A Sketch."

Pages 7–23 in *Paul and the Mosaic Torah*. Edited by James D. G. Dunn. Grand Rapids: Eerdmans, 1996.

Liddell, Henry G., Robert Scott, and Henry Jones. *A Greek-English Lexicon*. 9th ed., with revised supplement. Oxford: Clarendon, 1996.

Lieu, J. M. "Circumcision, Women, and Salvation." *NTS* 40 (1994): 358–70.

Lohmeyer, E. *Diatheke: Ein Beitrag zur Erklärung des neutestamentlichen Begriffs*. Leipzig: Hinrichs, 1913.

Longenecker, Bruce W. "*Pistis* in Rom 3:25: Neglected Evidence for the Faithfulness of Christ." *NTS* 39 (1993): 478–80.

———. *Remember the Poor: Paul, Poverty, and the Greco-Roman World*. Grand Rapids: Eerdmans, 2010.

———. "Salvation History in Galatians and the Making of a Pauline Discourse." *Journal for the Study of Paul and His Letters* 2 (2012): 65–87.

———. *The Triumph of Abraham's God: The Transformation of Identity in Galatians*. Edinburgh: T&T Clark, 1998.

———. "'Until Christ Is Formed in You': Supra-human Forces and Moral Character in Galatians." *CBQ* 61 (1999): 92–108.

Longenecker, Richard N. "Ancient Amanuenses and the Pauline Epistles." Pages 281–97 in *New Dimensions in New Testament Study*. Edited by M. C. Tenney and R. N. Longenecker. Grand Rapids: Zondervan, 1974.

———. "The Pedagogical Nature of the Law in Galatians 3:19–4:7." *JETS* 25 (1982): 53–61.

———. *The Road from Damascus: The Impact of Paul's Conversion on His Life, Thought, and Ministry*. Grand Rapids: Eerdmans, 1997.

Loubser, J. A. "The Contrast Slavery/Freedom as Persuasive Device in Galatians." *Neot* 28 (1994): 163–76.

Louw, Johannes, and Eugene A. Nida, eds. *Greek-English Lexicon of the New Testament Based on Semantic Domains*. 2 vols. New York: United Bible Societies, 1988.

Lüdemann, Gerd. *Paul, Apostle to the Gentiles. Studies in Chronology*. Philadelphia: Fortress, 1984.

Lührmann, Dieter. "Die 430 Jahre zwischen den Verheisungen und dem Gesetz (Gal 3,17)." *ZNW* 100 (1988): 420–23.

———. *Das Offenbarungsverständnis bei Paulus und in Paulinischen Gemeinden*. Neukirchen-Vluyn: Neukirchener Verlag, 1965.

———. "Pistis im Judentum." *ZNW* 64 (1973): 19–38.

———. "Tage, Monate, Jahreszeiten, Jahre (Gal 4,10)." Pages 428–45 in *Werden und Wirken des Alten Testaments*. Edited by R. Albertz et al. Göttingen: Vandenhoeck & Ruprecht, 1980.

Lull, D. J. "'The Law Was Our Pedagogue': A Study in Galatians 3:19–25." *JBL* 105 (1986): 481–98.

————. *The Spirit in Galatia: Paul's Interpretation of Pneuma as Divine Power.* SBLDS 49. Atlanta: Scholars Press, 1980.

Lütgert, Wilhelm. *Gesetz und Geist: Eine Untersuchung zur Vorgeschichte des Galaterbriefes.* Gütersloh: Mohn, 1919.

Luther, Martin. "The Freedom of a Christian." In *Three Treatises.* Translated by W. A. Lambert. Revised by Harold J. Grimm. Philadelphia: Fortress, 1970.

————. *Lectures on Galatians 1535: Chapters 1–4.* Vol. 26 of *Luther's Works.* Edited by Jaroslav Pelikan. St. Louis: Concordia, 1963.

————. *Lectures on Galatians, 1535: Chapters 5–6; Lectures on Galatians 1519: Chapters 1–6.* Vol. 27 of Luther's Works. Edited by Jaroslav Pelikan. St. Louis: Concordia, 1964.

Lutjens, Ronald. "'You Do Not Do What You Want': What Does Galatians 5:17 Really Mean?" *Presb* 16 (1990): 103–17.

Luz, Ulrich. *Das Geschichtsverständnis bei Paulus.* Munich: Kaiser, 1968.

Lyall, F. "Roman Law in the Writings of Paul—Adoption." *JBL* 88 (1969): 458–66.

————. *Slaves, Citizens, Sons: Legal Metaphors in the Epistles.* Grand Rapids: Zondervan, 1984.

Lyons, George. *Pauline Autobiography: Toward a New Understanding.* SBLDS 73. Atlanta: Scholars Press, 1985.

Machen, J. Gresham. *Machen's Notes on Galatians: Notes on Biblical Exposition and Other Aids to Interpretation of the Epistle to the Galatians from the Writings of J. Gresham Machen.* Edited by John H. Skilton. Nutley, NJ: P&R, 1977.

Malherbe, A. J. *Ancient Epistolary Theorists.* Atlanta: Scholars Press, 1988.

————. "*Mē genoito* in Diatribe and Paul." *HTR* 73 (1980): 231–40.

————. *Paul and the Popular Philosophers.* Philadelphia: Fortress, 1989.

Marcus, Joel. "The Evil Inclination in the Letters of Paul." *IBS* 8 (1986): 8–21.

————. "'Under the Law': The Background of a Pauline Expression." *CBQ* 63 (2001): 72–83.

Marrou, H. I. *A History of Education in Antiquity.* London: Sheed & Ward, 1956.

Martin, B. L. *Christ and the Law in Paul.* Leiden: Brill, 1989.

Martin, D. B. *Slavery as Salvation: The Metaphor of Slavery in Pauline Christianity.* New Haven: Yale University Press, 1990.

Martin. Ralph P. *James.* WBC 48. Nashville: Thomas Nelson, 1988.

Martin, Troy W. "The Ambiguities of a 'Baffling Expression' (Gal 4:12)." *Filologia Neotestamentaria* 12 (1999): 123–38.

————. "Apostasy to Paganism: The Rhetorical Stasis of the Galatian Controversy." *JBL* 114 (1995): 437–61.

————. "The Covenant of Circumcision (Genesis 17:9–14) and the Situational Antitheses in Galatians 3:28." *JBL* 122 (2003): 111–25.

————. "Pagan and Judeo-Christian Time-Keeping Schemes in Gal 4.10 and Col 2.16." *NTS* 42 (1996): 105–19.

―――. "Whose Flesh? What Temptation? (Galatians 4.13–14)." *JSNT* 74 (1999): 65–91.

Martyn, J. Louis. "Apocalyptic Antinomies in Paul's Letter to the Galatians." *NTS* 31 (1985): 410–24.

―――. "Christ, the Elements of the Cosmos, and the Law in Galatians." Pages 16–39 in *The Social World of the First Christians: Essays in Honor of Wayne A. Meeks*. Edited by L. M. White and O. L. Yarbrough. Minneapolis: Fortress, 1995.

―――. "A Law-Observant Mission to the Gentiles: The Background of Galatians." *SwJT* 38 (1985): 307–24.

―――. *Theological Issues in the Letters of Paul*. Edinburgh: T&T Clark, 1997.

Matera, Frank J. "The Culmination of Paul's Argument to the Galatians: Gal 5.1–6.17." *JSNT* 32 (1988): 79–91.

―――. "The Death of Christ and the Cross in Paul's Letter to the Galatians." *LS* 18 (1993): 283–96.

Mathew, Susan. *Women in the Greetings of Romans 16.1–16: A Study of Mutuality and Women's Ministry in the Letter to the Romans*. LNTS. London: Bloomsbury, 2013.

Matlock, R. Barry. "Detheologizing the ΠΙΣΤΙΣ ΧΡΙΣΤΟΥ Debate: Cautionary Remarks from a Lexical Semantic Perspective." *NovT* 42 (2000): 1–23.

―――. "'Even the Demons Believe': Paul and πίστις Χριστοῦ." *CBQ* 64 (2002): 300–318.

―――. "Helping Paul's Argument Work? The Curse of Galatians 3.10–14." Pages 154–79 in *The Torah in the New Testament: Papers Delivered at the Manchester-Lausanne Seminar of June 2008*. Edited by M. Tait and P. Oakes. London: T&T Clark, 2009.

―――. "πίστις in Galatians 3:26: Neglected Evidence for 'Faith in Christ'?" *NTS* 49 (2003): 433–39.

―――. "The Rhetoric of πίστις in Paul: Galatians 2.16, 3.22, and Philippians 3.9." *JSNT* 30 (2007): 173–203.

―――. "Saving Faith: The Rhetoric and Semantics of Πίστις in Paul." Pages 73–89 in *The Faith of Jesus Christ: Exegetical, Biblical, and Theological Studies*. Edited by Michael F. Bird and Preston M. Sprinkle. Peabody, MA: Hendrickson, 2009.

―――. *Unveiling the Apocalyptic Paul: Paul's Interpreters and the Rhetoric of Criticism*. JSNTSup 127. Sheffield: Sheffield Academic Press, 1996.

McCartney, D. *James*. BECNT. Grand Rapids: Baker Academic, 2009.

McEleney, Neil. "Conversion, Circumcision, and the Law." *NTS* 20 (1974): 319–41.

McKay, K. L. *A New Syntax of the Verb in New Testament Greek: An Aspectual Approach*. New York: Peter Lang, 1994.

McKnight, Scot. "The Ego and 'I': Galatians 2:19 in New Perspective." *WW* 20 (2000): 272–80.

————. *James*. NICNT. Grand Rapids: Eerdmans, 2011.

————. *A Light among the Gentiles: Jewish Missionary Activity in the Second Temple Period*. Minneapolis: Fortress, 1991.

McNamara, M. "'*To de (Hagar) Sina oros estin en tē Arabia*' (Gal 4:25a): Paul and Petra." *MilS* 2 (1978): 24–41.

Meeks, Wayne A. *The First Urban Christians: The Social World of the Apostle Paul*. New Haven: Yale University Press, 1983.

————. "Understanding Early Christian Ethics." *JBL* 105 (1986): 3–11.

Meeks, Wayne A., and R. L. Wilken. *Jews and Christians in Antioch*. Missoula, MT: Scholars Press, 1978.

Meier, John P. "The Brothers and Sisters of Jesus in Ecumenical Perspective." *CBQ* 54 (1992): 1–28.

————. *Mentor, Message, and Miracle*. Vol. 2 of *A Marginal Jew: Rethinking the Historical Jesus*. New York: Doubleday. 1994.

Meiser, M. *Galater*. Novum Testamentum Patristicum 9. Göttingen: Vandenhoeck & Ruprecht, 2007.

Mell, U. *Neue Schöpfung: Eine traditionsgeschichtliche und exegetische Studie zu einem soteriologischen Grundsatz paulinischer Theologie*. BZNW 56. Berlin: de Gruyter, 1989.

Mellor, R. *ΘΕΑ ΡΩΜΗ: The Worship of the Goddess Roma in the Greek World*. Hypomnemata 42. Göttingen: Vandenhoeck & Ruprecht, 1975.

Merk, O. "Der Beginn der Paränese im Galaterbrief." *ZNW* 60 (1969): 83–104.

Metzger, Bruce M. *A Textual Commentary on the Greek New Testament*. 2nd ed. Stuttgart: Deutsche Bibelgesellschaft, 2002.

————. *A Textual Commentary on the New Testament*. Rev. ed. New York: United Bible Societies, 1994.

Meyer, H. A. W. *Critical and Exegetical Handbook to the Epistle to the Galatians*. New York: Scribner, Welford & Armstrong, 1873.

Meyer, Jason. *The End of the Law: Mosaic Covenant in Pauline Theology*. NAC Studies in Bible and Theology 6. Nashville: Broadman & Holman, 2009.

Meyer, P. W. "The Holy Spirit in the Pauline Letters." *Int* 33 (1979): 3–18.

Miller, Neva F. "Appendix 2: A Theory of Deponent Verbs." Pages 423–30 in *Analytical Lexicon of the Greek New Testament*. Edited by T. Friberg, B. Friberg, and N. Miller. Grand Rapids: Baker, 2000.

Minear, P. S. "The Crucified World: The Enigma of Galatians 6,14." Pages 395–407 in *Theologia Crucis—Signum Crucis: Festschrift für Erich Dinkler zum 70. Geburtstag*. Edited by C. Andersen and G. Klein. Tübingen: Mohr Siebeck, 1979.

Mitchell, Stephen. *Anatolia: Land, Men, and Gods in Asia Minor*. Oxford: Clarendon, 1993.

————. *The Ankara District: The Inscriptions of North Galatia*. Oxford: B.A.R., 1982.

———. "Galatia." *ABD* 2:870–72.

Moffatt, J. *An Introduction to the Literature of the New Testament.* 3rd ed. Edinburgh: T&T Clark, 1918.

Mommsen, Theodor. *The Provinces of the Roman Empire.* Translated by W. P. Dickson. 2 vols. London: Macmillan, 1909.

Moo, Douglas J. "Creation and New Creation." *BBR* 20 (2010): 39–60.

———. *The Epistle to the Romans.* NICNT. Grand Rapids: Eerdmans, 1996.

———. "Justification in Galatians." Pages 160–95 in *Understanding the Times: New Testament Studies in the Twenty-First Century; Essays in Honor of D. A. Carson on the Occasion of His Sixty-Fifth Birthday.* Edited by A. Köstenberger and R. Yarbrough. Wheaton: Crossway, 2011.

———. "The Law of Christ as the Fulfillment of the Law of Moses: A Modified Lutheran View." Pages 319–76 in *The Law, the Gospel, and the Modern Christian: Five Views.* Grand Rapids: Zondervan, 1993.

———. "Law, 'Works of the Law,' and Legalism in Paul." *WTJ* 45 (1983): 73–100.

———. *The Letter of James.* Pillar New Testament Commentary. Grand Rapids: Eerdmans, 2000.

Moore-Crispin, D. R. "Galatians 4:1–9: The Use and Abuse of Parallels." *EvQ* 60 (1989): 203–23.

Morales, R. J. "The Words of the Luminaries, the Curse of the Law, and the Outpouring of the Spirit in Gal 3,10–14." *ZNW* 100 (2009): 269–77.

Morland, Kjell Arne. *The Rhetoric of the Curse in Galatians: Paul Confronts Another Gospel.* Atlanta: Scholars Press, 1995.

Motyer, A. *The Prophecy of Isaiah: An Introduction and Commentary.* Downers Grove, IL: InterVarsity Press, 1993.

Moule, C. F. D. "The Biblical Conception of 'Faith.'" *ExpTim* 68 (1957): 157, 221–22.

———. "Death 'to Sin,' 'to the Law,' and 'to the World': A Note on Certain Datives." Pages 367–75 in *Mélanges bibliques en hommage au R. P. Béda Rigaux.* Edited by A. Descamps and A. de Halleux. Gembloux: Duculot, 1970.

———. *An Idiom-Book of New Testament Greek.* Cambridge: Cambridge University Press, 1959.

———. "Obligation in the Ethic of Paul." Pages 389–406 in *Christian History and Interpretation: Studies Presented to John Knox.* Edited by W. R. Farmer et al. Cambridge: Cambridge University Press, 1967.

Moulton, J. H. *Prolegomena.* Vol. 1 of *A Grammar of New Testament Greek.* Edinburgh: T&T Clark, 1908.

Moulton, James H., and G. Milligan. *The Vocabulary of the Greek New Testament: Illustrated from the Papyri and Other Non-literary Sources.* Grand Rapids: Eerdmans, 1930.

Moxnes, Halvor. "Patron-Client Relations and the New Community in Luke-

Acts." Pages 241–68 in *The Social World of Luke-Acts*. Edited by J. H. Neyrey. Peabody, MA: Hendrickson, 1991.

Mullins, T. Y. "Formulas in New Testament Epistles." *JBL* 91 (1972): 380–90.

Munck, Johannes. *Paul and the Salvation of Mankind*. London: SCM Press, 1959.

Murphy-O'Connor, Jerome. *Keys to Galatians*. Collegeville, MN: Michael Glazier, 2012.

———. *Paul: A Critical Life*. Oxford: Clarendon, 1996.

———. "Paul and Gallio." *JBL* 112 (1993): 315–17.

———. "Paul in Arabia." *CBQ* 55 (1993): 732–37.

———. "Pauline Missions before the Jerusalem Conference." *RB* 89 (1982): 71–91.

———. "To Run in Vain (Gal 2:2)." *RB* 197 (2000): 383–89.

———. "The Unwritten Law of Christ (Gal 6:2)." *RB* 119 (2012): 213–31.

Nanos, Mark, ed. *The Galatians Debate: Contemporary Issues in Rhetorical and Historical Interpretation*. Peabody, MA: Hendrickson, 2002.

———. "Intruding 'Spies' and 'Pseudo-brethren': The Jewish Intra-group Politics of Paul's Jerusalem Meeting (Gal 2:1–10)." Pages 59–97 in *Paul and His Opponents*. Edited by S. E. Porter. Leiden: Brill, 2005.

———. *The Irony of Galatians: Paul's Letter in First-Century Context*. Minneapolis: Fortress, 2002.

———. *The Mystery of Romans: The Jewish Context of Paul's Letter*. Minneapolis: Fortress, 1996.

———. "Paul and Judaism: Why Not Paul's Judaism?" Pages 117–60 in *Paul Unbound: Other Perspectives on the Apostle*. Edited by M. D. Given. Peabody, MA: Hendrickson, 2010.

———. "What Was at Stake in Peter's 'Eating with Gentiles' at Antioch?" Pages 282–318 in *The Galatians Debate: Contemporary Issues in Rhetorical and Historical Interpretation*. Edited by Mark Nanos. Peabody, MA: Hendrickson, 2002.

Newman, C. C. *Paul's Glory-Christology: Tradition and Rhetoric*. NovTSup 69. Leiden: Brill, 1992.

New Perspective. See under Dunn, *The New Perspective on Paul: Collected Essays*. Rev. ed. (2008).

Neyrey, J. H. "Bewitched in Galatia: Paul and Cultural Anthropology." *CBQ* 50 (1988): 73–100.

Nickle, Keith F. *The Collection: A Study in Paul's Strategy*. London: SCM, 1966.

Niebuhr, K.-W. *Heidenapostel aus Israel: Die jüdische Identität des Paulus nach ihrer Darstellung in seinen Briefen*. WUNT 2/62. Tübingen: Mohr Siebeck, 1992.

Nock, A. D. *Conversion: The Old and New in Religion from Alexander the Great to Augustine of Hippo*. London: Oxford University Press, 1933.

———. *St. Paul*. London: Butterworth, 1938.

Nolland, John. "Uncircumcised Proselytes?" *JSJ* 12 (1981): 173–94.

Noth, M. "For All Who Rely on Works of the Law Are under a Curse." Pages 118–31 in *The Laws in the Pentateuch and Other Essays*. Edinburgh: Oliver & Boyd, 1966.

Oakes, Peter. *Reading Romans in Pompeii: Paul's Letter at Ground Level*. Minneapolis: Fortress, 2009.

O'Brien, Kelli S. "The Curse of the Law (Galatians 3.13): Crucifixion, Persecution, and Deuteronomy 21.22–23." *JSNT* 29 (2006): 55–76.

O'Brien, Peter T. *Commentary on Philippians*. NIGTC. Grand Rapids: Eerdmans, 1991.

———. "Was Paul a Covenantal Nomist?" Pages 249–96 in *The Paradoxes of Paul*. Vol. 2 of *Justification and Variegated Nomism*. Edited by D. A. Carson, Peter T. O'Brien, and Mark A. Seifrid. WUNT 2/181. Grand Rapids: Baker, 2004.

———. "Was Paul Converted?" Pages 361–91 in *The Paradoxes of Paul*. Vol. 2 of *Justification and Variegated Nomism*. Edited by D. A. Carson, Peter T. O'Brien, and Mark A. Seifrid. WUNT 2/181. Grand Rapids: Baker, 2004.

Olbricht, Thomas H. "An Aristotelian Rhetorical Analysis of 1 Thessalonians." Pages 216–36 in *Greeks, Romans, and Christians: Essays in Honor of Abraham F. Malherbe*. Edited by D. L. Balch, E. Ferguson, and W. A. Meeks. Minneapolis: Fortress, 1990.

Olson, S. N. "Pauline Expressions of Confidence in His Addressees." *CBQ* 47 (1985): 282–95.

O'Neill, J. C. *The Recovery of Paul's Letter to the Galatians*. London: SPCK, 1972.

Oropeza, B. J. "The Expectation of Grace: Paul on Benefaction and the Corinthians' Ingratitude (2 Cor 6:1)." *BBR* 24.2 (2014): 207–26.

Owen, Paul L. "The 'Works of the Law' in Romans and Galatians: A New Defense of the Subjective Genitive." *JBL* 126 (2007): 553–77.

Painter, John. *Just James: The Brother of Jesus in History and Tradition*. Minneapolis: Fortress, 1999.

Patte, Daniel, ed. *The Global Bible Commentary*. Nashville: Abingdon, 2004.

Pennington, Jonathan T. "Deponency in Koine Greek: The Grammatical Question and the Lexicographical Dilemma." *Trinity Journal* 24 (2003): 55–76.

Perelman, Chaim. *The Realm of Rhetoric*. Translated by William Kluback. Notre Dame, IN: University of Notre Dame Press, 1990.

Perelman, Chaim, and Lucie Olbrechts-Tyteca. *The New Rhetoric: A Treatise on Argumentation*. Notre Dame, IN: University of Notre Dame Press, 1971.

Perriman, A. C. "The Rhetorical Strategy of Galatians 4:21–5:1." *EvQ* 65 (1993): 27–42.

Pervo, Richard. *Dating Acts: Between the Evangelists and the Apologists*. Santa Rosa, CA: Polebridge, 2006.

Phillips, Thomas E. *Paul, His Letters, and Acts*. Library of Pauline Studies. Peabody, MA: Hendrickson, 2009.

Piper, John. *The Future of Justification: A Response to N. T. Wright*. Wheaton, IL: Crossway Books, 2007.

Plumer, Eric. *Augustine's Commentary on Galatians: Introduction, Text, Translation, and Notes*. Oxford: Oxford University Press, 2003.

Pollmann, I. *Gesetzeskritische Motive im Judentum und die Gesetzeskritik des Paulus*. NTOA/SUNT 98. Göttingen: Vandenhoeck & Ruprecht, 2012.

Porter, S. E., and S. A. Adams, eds. *Paul and the Ancient Letter Form*. Leiden: Brill, 2011.

Porter, S. E., and A. W. Pitts. "Πίστις with a Preposition and Genitive Modifier: Lexical, Semantic, and Syntactic Considerations in the Πίστις Χριστοῦ Discussion." Pages 33–53 in *The Faith of Jesus Christ: Exegetical, Biblical, and Theological Studies*. Edited by M. F. Bird and P. M. Sprinkle. Peabody, MA: Hendrickson, 2009.

Porter, Stanley. *Idioms of the Greek New Testament*. Biblical Language: Greek 2. Sheffield: Sheffield Academic Press, 1992.

———. "Paul of Tarsus and His Letters." Pages 533–85 in *Handbook of Classical Rhetoric in the Hellenistic Period, 330 BC–AD 400*. Edited by Stanley E. Porter. Leiden: Brill, 2001.

———. "The Theoretical Justification for Application of Rhetorical Categories to Pauline Epistolary Literature." Pages 100–122 in *Rhetoric and the New Testament: Essays from the 1992 Heidelberg Conference*. Edited by Stanley E. Porter and Thomas H. Olbricht. Sheffield: JSOT Press, 1993.

———. *Verbal Aspect in the Greek of the New Testament, with Reference to Tense and Mood*. New York: Peter Lang, 1989.

Price, S. R. F. *Rituals and Power: The Roman Imperial Cult in Asia Minor*. Cambridge: Cambridge University Press, 1984.

Przybylski, Benno. *Righteousness in Matthew and His World of Thought*. Cambridge: Cambridge University Press, 2004.

Qimron, Elisha. *Discoveries in the Judean Desert X (Cave 4)*, vol. 5: Miqṣat Maʿaśe Ha-Torah. Oxford: Oxford University Press, 1994.

Rabens, Volker. *Holy Spirit and Ethics: Transformation and Empowering for Religious-Ethical Life*. WUNT 2/283. Tübingen: Mohr Siebeck, 2010.

———. "'Indicative and Imperative' as the Substructure of Paul's Theology-and-Ethics in Galatians?" Pages 285–305 in *Galatians and Christian Theology*. Edited by Mark W. Elliott, Scott J. Hafemann, N. T. Wright, and John Frederick. Grand Rapids: Baker Academic, 2014.

Rad, G. von. "Die Anrechnung des Glaubens zur Gerechtigkeit." *TLZ* 76 (1951): 129–32.

Rainbow, Paul A. *The Way of Salvation: The Role of Christian Obedience in Justification*. Waynesboro, GA: Paternoster, 2005.

Räisänen, Heiki. "Galatians 2.16 and Paul's Break with Judaism." *NTS* 31 (1985): 543–53.

———. *Jesus, Paul, and Torah: Collected Essays*. Sheffield: Sheffield Academic Press, 1992.

———. "Legalism and Salvation by the Law: Paul's Portrayal of the Jewish Religion as a Historical and Theological Theme." Pages 63–83 in *Die Paulinische Literatur und Theologie*. Edited by S. Pedersen. Aarhus: Forlaget Aros, 1980.

———. *Paul and the Law*. Tübingen: Mohr Siebeck, 1983.

Ramachandra, Vinoth. *Subverting Global Myths: Theology and the Public Issues Shaping Our World*. Downers Grove, IL: InterVarsity Press, 2008.

Ramsay, William. *Historical Geography of Asia Minor*. London: John Murray, 1890.

———. *St. Paul the Traveller and Roman Citizen*. 14th ed. London: Hodder & Stoughton, 1920.

———. *The Teaching of Paul in Terms of the Present Day*. London: Hodder & Stoughton, 1913.

Reed, J. T. "The Epistle." Pages 171–93 in *Handbook of Classical Rhetoric in the Hellenistic Period, 330 BC–AD 400*. Edited by Stanley E. Porter. Leiden: Brill, 1997.

———. "Using Ancient Rhetorical Categories to Interpret Paul's Letters: A Question of Genre." Pages 292–324 in *Rhetoric and the New Testament: Essays from the 1992 Heidelberg Conference*. Edited by S. Porter and T. H. Olbricht. JSNTSup 90. Sheffield: JSOT, 1993.

Refoulé, F. "Date de l'Épître aux Galates." *RB* 95 (1988): 161–83.

Reicke, Bo. "Der geschichtliche Hintergrund des Apostelkonzils und der Antiochia-Episode, Gal 2,1–14." Pages 172–87 in *Studia Paulina in honorem Johannis de Zwaan septuagenarii*. Edited by J. N. Sevenster and W. C. van Unnik. Haarlem: Bohn, 1953.

———. "The Law and This World according to Paul. Some Thoughts concerning Gal 4.1–11." *JBL* 70 (1951): 259–76.

Reumann, J. *Creation and New Creation: The Past, Present, and Future of God's Creative Activity*. Minneapolis: Augsburg, 1973.

———. *Righteousness in the New Testament: "Justification" in the United States Lutheran–Roman Catholic Dialogue*. Philadelphia: Fortress, 1982.

Richards, E. Randolph. *Paul and First-Century Letter Writing: Secretaries, Composition, and Collection*. Downers Grove, IL: InterVarsity Press, 2004.

———. *The Secretary in the Letters of Paul*. WUNT 2/42. Tübingen: Mohr/Siebeck, 1991.

Richardson, P. *Israel in the Apostolic Church*. SNTSMS 10. Cambridge: Cambridge University Press, 1969.

———. "Pauline Inconsistency: 1 Cor 9:19–23 and Gal 2:11–14." *NTS* 26 (1980): 347–61.

Riches, John. *Galatians through the Centuries.* Blackwell Bible Commentaries. Oxford: Blackwell, 2008.

Ridderbos, H. N. *Paul: An Outline of His Theology.* Grand Rapids: Eerdmans, 1975.

Riddle, Donald W. "The Cephas-Peter Problem and a Possible Solution." *JBL* 59 (1940): 169–80.

Riesner, Rainer. *Paul's Early Period: Chronology, Mission Strategy, Theology.* Translated by Doug Stott. Grand Rapids: Eerdmans, 1998.

Robbins, Vernon K. *Exploring the Texture of Texts: A Guide to Socio-rhetorical Interpretation.* Valley Forge, PA: Trinity Press International, 1996.

———. *The Invention of Christian Discourse.* Vol. 1. Dorset, UK: Deo, 2010.

———. *The Tapestry of Early Christian Discourse: Rhetoric, Society, Ideology.* London: Routledge, 1996.

Robertson, A. T. *A Grammar of the Greek New Testament in the Light of Historical Research.* Nashville: Broadman, 1934.

Robertson, C. K. *Barnabas vs. Paul: To Encourage or Confront?* Nashville: Abingdon, 2015.

Robertson, O. P. *The Books of Nahum, Habakkuk, and Zephaniah.* NICOT. Grand Rapids: Eerdmans, 1990.

———. "Genesis 15:6: New Covenant Exposition of an Old Covenant Text." *WTJ* 42 (1980): 259–89.

Robinson, D. W. B. "The Circumcision of Titus, and Paul's 'Liberty.'" *ABR* 12 (1964): 24–42.

———. "Distinction between Jewish and Gentile Believers in Galatians." *ABR* 13 (1965): 29–48.

———. "'Faith of Jesus Christ'—a New Testament Debate." *RTR* 29 (1970): 71–81.

Robinson, J. A. T. *Redating the New Testament.* London: SCM, 1976.

Roetzel, Calvin. *The Letters of Paul: Conversations in Context.* 2nd ed. Atlanta: John Knox Press, 1985.

Roo, J. C. R. *Works of the Law at Qumran and in Paul.* New Testament Monographs 13. Sheffield: Sheffield Phoenix, 2007.

Ropes, James H. *The Singular Problem of the Epistle to the Galatians.* HTS 14. Cambridge, MA: Harvard University Press, 1929.

Rosner, B. "'Known by God': The Meaning and Value of a Neglected Biblical Concept." *TynBul* 59 (2008): 207–30.

Rowlingson, Donald T. "The Jerusalem Conference and Jesus' Nazareth Visit: A Study in Pauline Chronology." *JBL* 71 (1952): 69–74.

Royalty, Robert. "The Rhetoric of Revelation." Pages 596–617 in SBLSP 36. Atlanta: Scholars Press, 1997.

Runge, Steven E. *Discourse Grammar of the Greek New Testament: A Practical Introduction for Teaching and Exegesis.* Peabody, MA: Hendrickson, 2010.

Rusam, D. "Neue Belege zu dem *stoicheia tou kosmou* (Gal 4,3.9; Kol 2,8.20)." *ZNW* 83 (1992): 119–25.

Russell, W. B. *The Flesh/Spirit Conflict in Galatians*. Lanham, MD: University Press of America, 1997.

———. "Rhetorical Analysis of the Book of Galatians." Pts. 1 and 2. *BSac* 150 (1993): 341–58 and 416–39.

Saller, Richard P. *Personal Patronage under the Early Empire*. Cambridge: Cambridge University Press, 1982.

Sampley, Paul. "'Before God, I Do Not Lie' (Gal. i. 20): Paul's Self-Defense in the Light of Roman Legal Praxis." *NTS* 23 (1976–77): 477–82.

———. "Romans and Galatians: Comparison and Contrast." Pages 315–39 in *Understanding the Word: Essays in Honour of Bernhard W. Anderson*. Edited by J. T. Butler, E. W. Conrad, and B. C. Ollenburger. JSOTSup 37. Sheffield: JSOT Press, 1985.

Sand, A. *Der Begriff "Fleisch" in den paulinischen Hauptbriefen*. Regensburg: Pustet, 1967.

Sanders, E. P. "Jewish Association with Gentiles and Gal 2:11–14." Pages 170–88 in *The Conversation Continues: Studies in Paul and John in Honor of J. Louis Martyn*. Edited by R. T. Fortna and B. R. Gaventa. Nashville: Abingdon, 1990.

———. *Jewish Law from Jesus to the Mishnah*. London: SCM, 1960.

———. *Judaism: Practice and Belief; 63 BCE–66 CE*. Philadelphia: Trinity Press International, 1992.

———. *Paul*. New York: Oxford, 1991.

———. *Paul and Palestinian Judaism*. Philadelphia: Fortress, 1977.

———. *Paul, the Law, and the Jewish People*. Philadelphia: Fortress, 1983.

Sanders, J. T. "Paul's 'Autobiographical' Statements in Galatians 1–2." *JBL* 85 (1966): 335–43.

Sandnes, K. O. *Paul—One of the Prophets? A Contribution to the Apostle's Self-Understanding*. WUNT 43. Tübingen: Mohr Siebeck, 1991.

Sänger, D. *Die Verkündigung des Gekreuzigten und Israel: Studien zum Verhältnis von Kirche und Israel bei Paulus und im frühen Christentum*. WUNT 2/75. Tübingen: Mohr Siebeck, 1994.

Savage, Timothy B. *Power through Weakness: Paul's Understanding of the Christian Ministry in 2 Corinthians*. SNTSMS 86. Cambridge: Cambridge University Press, 1996.

Schäfer, P. "Die Torah der messianischen Zeit." *ZNW* 65 (1974): 27–42.

Schäfer, R. *Paulus bis zum Apostelkonzil: Ein Beitrag zur Einleitung in den Galaterbrief, zur Geschichte der Jesusbewegung und zur Pauluschronologie*. WUNT 179. Tübingen: Mohr Siebeck, 2004.

Schechter, Solomon. *Aspects of Rabbinic Theology*. New York: Schocken, 1961 (1909).

Schellenberg, Ryan. *Rethinking Paul's Rhetorical Education: Comparative Rhetoric and 2 Corinthians 10–13*. Atlanta: SBL, 2013.

Schewe, S. *Der Galater Zurückgewinnen: Paulinische Strategien in Galater 5 und 6.* FRLANT 208. Göttingen: Vandenhoeck & Ruprecht, 2004.

Schlatter, A. *The Theology of the Apostles: The Development of New Testament Theology.* Grand Rapids: Baker, 1998.

Schmid, H. H. *Gerechtigkeit als Weltordnung: Hintergrund und Geschichte der alttestamentlichen Gerechtigkeitsbegriffes.* Beiträge zur historischen Theologie 40. Tübingen: Mohr Siebeck, 1968.

———. "Gerechtigkeit und Glaube: Genesis 15,1–6 und sein biblisch-theologischer Kontext." *EvT* 40 (1980): 396–420.

Schmidt, A. "Das Missionsdekret in Galater 2.7–8 als Vereinbarung vom ersten Besuch Pauli in Jerusalem." *NTS* 38 (1992): 149–52.

Schmithals, Walter. "Die Häretiker in Galatien." *ZNW* 47 (1956): 25–67.

———. *Paul and the Gnostics.* Nashville: Abingdon, 1971.

Schnabel, E. J. *Paul and the Early Church.* Vol. 2 of *Early Christian Mission.* Downers Grove, IL: InterVarsity Press, 2004.

Schnelle, U. *Apostle Paul: His Life and Theology.* Grand Rapids: Baker Academic, 2005.

———. *Gerechtigkeit und Christusgegenwart.* Göttingen: Vandenhoeck & Ruprecht, 1983.

———. *Theology of the New Testament.* Grand Rapids: Baker Academic, 2009.

Schoeps, H. J. *Paul: The Theology of the Apostle in the Light of Jewish Religious History.* Translated by Harold Knight. Philadelphia: Westminster, 1961.

Schrage, W. "Probleme paulinischer Ethik anhand von Gal 5,25–6,10." Pages 155–94 in *La foi agissant par l'amour (Galates 4,12–6,16).* Edited by A. Vanhoye. Rome: Abbaye de S. Paul, 1996.

Schreiner, Thomas. "Did Paul Believe in Justification by Works? Another Look at Romans 2." *BBR* 3 (1993): 131–58.

———. *Faith Alone: The Doctrine of Justification.* Grand Rapids: Zondervan, 2015.

———. "Is Perfect Obedience to the Law Posssible? A Re-examination of Galatians 3:10." *JETS* 27 (1984): 151–60.

———. *The Law and Its Fulfillment: A Pauline Theology of Law.* Grand Rapids: Baker, 1993.

———. *New Testament Theology: Magnifying God in Christ.* Grand Rapids: Baker, 2008.

———. "Paul and Perfect Obedience to the Law: An Evaluation of the View of E. P. Sanders." *WTJ* 47 (1985): 245–78.

———. *Romans.* BECNT. Grand Rapids: Baker, 1998.

———. "'Works of Law' in Paul." *NovT* 33 (1991): 217–44.

Schrenk, Gottlob. "*Dikē* etc." *TDNT* 2:182–225.

———. "Was bedeutet 'Israel Gottes'?" *Judaica* 5 (1949): 81–94.

Schürmann, H. "'Das Gesetz des Christus' (Gal 6,2): Jesu Verhalten und Wort als letztgültige sittliche Norm nach Paulus." Pages 282–300 in *Neues Testament und Kirche*. Edited by J. Gnilka. Freiburg im Breisgau: Herder, 1974.

Schüssler-Fiorenza, E. "Neither Male nor Female: Gal 3:28—Alternative Vision and Pauline Modification." Pages 205–41 in *In Memory of Her*. New York: Crossroad, 1984.

Schütz, J. H. *Paul and the Anatomy of Apostolic Authority*. Cambridge: Cambridge University Press, 1975.

Schwank, B. "Neue Funde in Nabatäerstädten und ihre Bedeutung für die neutestamentliche Exegese." *NTS* 29 (1983): 429–35.

Schweizer, Eduard. "Dying and Rising with Christ." *NTS* 14 (1967–68): 1–14.

———. "Slaves of the Elements and Worshipers of Angels: Gal 4:3, 9 and Col 2:8, 18, 20." *JBL* 107 (1988): 455–68.

———. "Was meinen wir eigentlich, wenn wir sagen 'Gott sandte seinen Sohn . . .'?" *NTS* 37 (1991): 204–24.

Scott, I. W. "Common Ground? The Role of Galatians 2:16 in Paul's Argument." *NTS* 53 (2007): 425–35.

———. *Implicit Epistemology in the Letters of Paul: Story, Experience, and the Spirit*. WUNT 205. Tübingen: Mohr Siebeck, 2006.

Scott, James M. *Adoption as Sons of God: An Exegetical Investigation into the Background of* huiothesia *in the Pauline Corpus*. WUNT 48. Tübingen: Mohr Siebeck, 1992.

———. "'For as Many as Are of Works of the Law Are under a Curse' (Galatians 3:10)." Pages 187–221 in *Paul and the Scriptures of Israel*. Edited by J. A. Sanders and C. A. Evans. Sheffield: JSOT, 1993.

———. *Paul and the Nations: The Old Testament and Jewish Background of Paul's Mission to the Nations, with Special Reference to the Destination of Galatians*. Tübingen: Mohr Siebeck, 1995.

———. "Paul's Use of Deuteronomistic Tradition." *JBL* 112 (1993): 645–65.

Scott, K. *The Imperial Cult under the Flavians*. Stuttgart: Kohlhammer, 1936.

Segal, Alan. *Paul the Convert: The Apostolate and Apostasy of Saul the Pharisee*. New Haven: Yale University Press, 1990.

Seifrid, Mark A. *Christ Our Righteousness: Paul's Theology of Justification*. Downers Grove, IL: InterVarsity Press, 2000.

———. "The Faith of Christ." Pages 129–46 in *The Faith of Jesus Christ: Exegetical, Biblical, and Theological Studies*. Edited by M. F. Bird and P. M. Sprinkle. Peabody, MA: Hendrickson, 2009.

———. *Justification by Faith: The Origin and Development of a Central Pauline Theme*. Leiden: Brill, 1992.

———. "Paul, Luther, and Justification in Gal 2:15–21." *WTJ* 65 (2003): 215–30.

———. "Paul's Use of Righteousness Language against Its Hellenistic Background." Pages 39–74 in *The Paradoxes of Paul*. Vol. 2 of *Justification and*

Variegated Nomism. Edited by D. A. Carson, P. T. O'Brien, and M. A. Seifrid. WUNT 2/181. Tübingen: Mohr Siebeck, 2004.

———. "Righteousness Language in the Hebrew Scriptures and Early Judaism." Pages 415–42 in *The Complexities of Second Temple Judaism*. Vol. 1 of *Justification and Variegated Nomism*. Edited by D. A. Carson, P. T. O'Brien, and M. A. Seifrid. Tübingen: Mohr Siebeck, 2001.

Shauf, S. "Galatians 2:20 in Context." *NTS* 52 (2006): 86–101.

Siker, J. S. *Disinheriting the Jews: Abraham in Early Christian Literature*. Louisville: Westminster John Knox, 1990.

Silva, Moisés. "Faith versus Works of Law in Galatians." Pages 217–48 in *The Paradoxes of Paul*. Vol. 2 of *Justification and Variegated Nomism*. Edited by D. A. Carson, P. T. O'Brien, and M. A. Seifrid. WUNT 2/181. Tübingen: Mohr Siebeck, 2004.

———. "Galatians." Pages 785–812 in *Commentary on the New Testament Use of the Old Testament*. Edited by G. K. Beale and D. A. Carson. Grand Rapids: Baker, 2007.

———. *Interpreting Galatians: Explorations in Exegetical Method*. 2nd ed. Grand Rapids: Baker Academic, 2001.

Slingerland, Dixon. "Acts 18:1–8, the Gallio Inscription, and Absolute Pauline Chronology." *JBL* 110 (1991): 439–49.

Smiles, Vincent M. "The Blessing of Israel and 'the Curse of the Law': A Study of Galatians 3:10–14." *Studies in Christian-Jewish Relations* 3 (2008): 1–17.

———. *The Gospel and the Law in Galatia: Paul's Response to Jewish-Christian Separatism and the Threat of Galatian Apostasy*. Collegeville, MN: Liturgical Press, 1998.

Smit, Joop. "The Letter of Paul to the Galatians: A Deliberative Speech." *NTS* 35 (1989): 1–26.

Smith, C. C. "Ἐκκλεῖσαι in Galatians 4:17: The Motif of the Excluded Lover as a Metaphor of Manipulation." *CBQ* 58 (1996): 480–99.

Smyth, Herbert Weir. *Greek Grammar*. Cambridge, MA: Harvard University Press, 1956.

Snodgrass, Klyne. "Justification by Grace—to the Doers: An Analysis of the Place of Romans 2 in the Theology of Paul." *NTS* 32 (1986): 72–93.

———. "Spheres of Influence: A Possible Solution to the Problem of Paul and the Law." *JSNT* 32 (1988): 93–113.

Snyman, A. H. "Modes of Persuasion in Galatians 6:7–10." *Neot* 26 (1992): 475–84.

Spicq, Ceslaus. *Theological Lexicon of the New Testament*. Translated by James D. Ernest. Peabody, MA: Hendrickson, 1994.

Sprinkle, Preston. *Law and Life: The Interpretation of Leviticus 18:5 in Early Judaism and Paul*. WUNT 2/241. Tübingen: Mohr Siebeck, 2008.

———. "πίστις Χριστοῦ as an Eschatological Event." Pages 165–84 in *The Faith *of Jesus Christ: Exegetical, Biblical, and Theological Studies.* Edited by Michael F. Bird and Preston M. Sprinkle. Peabody, MA: Hendrickson, 2009.

————. "Why Can't 'the One Who Does These Things Live by Them'? The Use of Leviticus 18:5 in Galatians 3:12." Pages 126–37 in *Exegetical Studies.* Vol. 2 of *Early Christian Literature and Intertextuality.* Edited by C. A. Evans and H. D. Zacharias. London: T&T Clark, 2009.

Stacey, D. *The Pauline View of Man: In Relation to Its Judaic and Hellenistic Background.* London: Macmillan, 1956.

Stamps, Dennis L. "Rhetorical Criticism of the New Testament: Ancient and Modern Evaluations of Argumentation." Pages 129–51 in *Approaches to New Testament Studies.* Edited by Stanley E. Porter and David Tombs. Sheffield: Sheffield Academic Press, 1995.

Standaert, B. "La rhétorique antique et l'épître aux Galates." *FoiVie* 84 (1985): 33–40.

Stanley, Christopher D. *Arguing with Scripture: The Rhetoric of Quotations in the Letters of Paul.* London: T&T Clark, 2004.

————. *Paul and the Language of Scripture: Citation Techniques in the Pauline Epistles and Contemporary Literature.* SNTSMS 74. Cambridge: Cambridge University Press, 1992.

————. "'Under a Curse': A Fresh Reading of Galatians 3.10–14." *NTS* 36 (1990): 481–511.

Stanton, Graham. "The Law of Moses and the Law of Christ: Galatians 3.1–6.2." Pages 99–116 in *Paul and the Mosaic Law.* Edited by J. D. G. Dunn. Tübingen: Mohr Siebeck, 1996.

————. "Review of *Abraham in Galatians: Epistolary and Rhetorical Contexts.*" *JTS* 43 (1992): 614–15.

Stein, Robert H. "The Relationship of Galatians 2:1–10 and Acts 15:1–35: Two Neglected Arguments." *JETS* 17 (1974): 239–42.

Stendahl, Krister. *Paul among Jews and Gentiles and Other Essays.* Philadelphia: Fortress, 1977.

Stirewalt, M. L. *Studies in Ancient Greek Epistolography.* Atlanta: Scholars Press, 1993.

Stowers, Stanley K. *Letter Writing in Greco-Roman Antiquity.* Philadelphia: Westminster, 1986.

————. "Paul and Self-Mastery." Pages 524–50 in *Paul in the Greco-Roman World.* Edited by J. Paul Sampley. Harrisburg, PA: Trinity Press International, 2003.

————. *A Rereading of Romans: Justice, Jews, and Gentiles.* New Haven: Yale University Press, 1994.

Strelan, J. "Burden-Bearing and the Law of Christ: A Re-examination of Galatians 6:2." *JBL* 94 (1975): 266–76.

Stuhlmacher, Peter. "The Apostle Paul's View of Righteousness." Pages 68–93 in

Reconciliation, Law, and Righteousness: Essays in Biblical Theology. Philadelphia: Fortress, 1986.

———. *Biblische Theologie des Neuen Testaments.* 3rd ed. Göttingen: Vandenhoeck & Ruprecht, 2005.

———. "The End of the Law: On the Origin and Beginnings of Pauline Theology." Pages 134–54 in *Reconciliation, Law, and Righteousness: Essays in Biblical Theology.* Philadelphia: Fortress, 1986.

———. "Erwägungen zum ontologischen Charakter der *kainē ktisis* bei Paulus." *EvT* 27 (1967): 1–35.

———. *Gerechtigkeit Gottes bei Paulus.* FRLANT 87. Göttingen: Vandenhoeck & Ruprecht, 1965.

———. "The Pauline Gospel." Pages 149–72 in *The Gospel and the Gospels.* Ed. P. Stuhlmacher. Grand Rapids: Eerdmans, 1991.

———. *Das Paulinische Evangelium.* Göttingen: Vandenhoeck & Ruprecht, 1968.

———. *Revisiting Paul's Doctrine of Justification: A Challenge to the New Perspective.* With an essay by Donald A. Hagner. Downers Grove, IL: InterVarsity Press, 2001.

Stuhlmueller, C. *Creative Redemption in Deutero-Isaiah.* Rome: Pontifical Biblical Institute, 1970.

Suggs, M. J. "Concerning the Date of Paul's Macedonian Ministry." *NovT* 4 (1960): 60–68.

Suh, M. K. W. "'It Has Been Brought to Completion': Leviticus 19:18 as Christological Witness in Galatians 5:14." *Journal for the Study of Paul and His Letters* 2 (2012): 115–32.

Suhl, A. "Der Beginn der Selbständigen Mission des Paulus." *NTS* 38 (1992): 430–47.

———. "Der Galaterbrief—Situation und Argumentation." *ANRW* II.25.4 (1987): 3067–134.

Sumney, Jerry L. *Identifying Paul's Opponents: The Question of Method in 2 Corinthians.* JSNTSup 40. Sheffield: Sheffield Academic Press, 1990.

Tabor, James D. *The Jesus Dynasty: The Hidden History of Jesus, His Royal Family, and the Birth of Christianity.* New York: Simon & Schuster, 2006.

Talbert, Charles H. "Again: Paul's Visits to Jerusalem." *NovT* 9 (1967): 26–40.

———. "Freedom and Law in Galatians." *ExAud* 2 (1995): 17–28.

———. *Reading Luke-Acts in Its Mediterranean Milieu.* NovTSup 107. Leiden: Brill, 2003.

Tannehill, R. *Dying and Rising with Christ: A Study in Pauline Theology.* BZNW 32. Berlin: Töpelmann, 1967.

Taubenschlag, R. *The Law of Greco-Roman Egypt in Light of the Papyri.* New York: Herald Square, 1948.

Taylor, Bernard A. "Deponency and Greek Lexicography." Pages 167–76 in *Bib-*

lical Greek Language and Lexicography: Essays in Honor of Frederick W. Danker. Edited by B. A. Taylor et al. Grand Rapids: Eerdmans, 2004.

Taylor, G. M. "The Function of *Pistis Christou* in Galatians." *JBL* 85 (1966): 58–76.

Taylor, Lily R. *The Divinity of the Roman Emperor*. Middletown, CT: American Philological Association, 1931.

Taylor, N. *Paul, Antioch, and Jerusalem. A Study in Relationships and Authority in Earliest Christianity*. Sheffield: JSOT, 1992.

TDNT. See Kittel and Friedrich.

Theissen, Gerd. *The Social Setting of Pauline Christianity: Essays on Corinth*. Philadelphia: Fortress, 1982.

Thielman, Frank. *From Plight to Solution: A Jewish Framework for Understanding Paul's View of the Law in Galatians and Romans*. Leiden: Brill, 1989.

———. *Paul and the Law*. Downers Grove, IL: InterVarsity Press, 1994.

Thompson, J. W. *Moral Formation according to Paul: The Context and Coherence of Pauline Ethics*. Grand Rapids: Baker Academic, 2011.

Thompson, Michael. *Clothed with Christ: The Example and Teaching of Jesus in Romans 12.1–15.13*. JSNTSup 59. Sheffield: JSOT Press, 1991.

Thurén, L. *Derhetorizing Paul: A Dynamic Perspective on Pauline Theology and the Law*. WUNT 124. Tübingen: Mohr Siebeck, 2000.

Thüsing, W. *Per Christum in Deum: Studien zum Verhältnis von Christozentrik und Theozentrik in den paulinischen Hauptbriefen*. NTAbh 1. Münster: Aschendorff, 1965.

Titrud, Kermit. "The Function of καί in the Greek New Testament and an Application to 2 Peter." Pages 240–70 in *Linguistics and New Testament Interpretation: Essays on Discourse Analysis*. Edited by D. A. Black. Dallas: Summer Institute of Linguistics, 1992.

Tolmie, D. François. *Persuading the Galatians: A Text-Centred Rhetorical Analysis of a Pauline Letter*. WUNT 2/190. Tübingen: Mohr Siebeck, 2005.

Tomson, Peter J. *Paul and the Jewish Law: Halakah in the Letters of the Apostle to the Gentiles*. CRINT 3/1. Minneapolis: Fortress, 1990.

Treier, D. J. "Typology." Pages 823–27 in *Dictionary for the Theological Interpretation of the Bible*. Edited by K. J. Vanhoozer. Grand Rapids: Baker Academic, 2005.

Turner, Nigel. *Grammatical Insights into the New Testament*. Edinburgh: T&T Clark, 1965.

———. *Syntax*. Vol. 3 of *A Grammar of New Testament Greek*. Edinburgh: T&T Clark, 1963.

Tyson, J. B. "'Works of the Law' in Galatians." *JBL* 92 (1973): 423–31.

Ulrichs, K. F. *Christusglaube: Studien zum Syntagma* πίστις Χριστοῦ *und zum paulinischen Verständnis von Glaube und Rechtfertigung*. WUNT 227. Tübingen: Mohr Siebeck, 2007.

Vainio, Olli-Pekka. *Justification and Participation in Christ: The Development of Justification from Luther to the Formula of Concord*. Leiden: Brill, 2008.

Vanhoye, A. "Pensée théologique et qualité rhétorique en Galates 3,1–14." Pages 91–114 in *The Truth of the Gospel (Galatians 1:1–4:11)*. Edited by J. Lambrecht. Rome: Benedictina, 1993.

VanLandingham, Chris. *Judgment and Justification in Early Judaism and the Apostle Paul*. Peabody, MA: Hendrickson, 2006.

Vermes, Geza. *The Complete Dead Sea Scrolls in English*. New York: Penguin, 1998.

Verseput, D. J. "Paul's Gentile Mission and the Jewish Christian Community." *NTS* 39 (1993): 36–58.

Vickers, B. *Jesus' Blood and Righteousness: Paul's Theology of Imputation*. Wheaton, IL: Crossway, 2006.

Vielhauer, Philip. "Gesetzesdienst und Stoicheiadienst im Galaterbrief." Pages 543–55 in *Rechtfertigung: Festschrift für Ernst Käsemann zum 70. Geburtstag*. Edited by J. Friedrich et al. Tübingen: Mohr Siebeck, 1976.

Vollenweider, S. *Freiheit als neue Schöpfung: Eine Untersuchung zur Eleutheria bei Paulus und in seiner Umwelt*. FRLANT 147. Göttingen: Vandenhoeck & Ruprecht, 1989.

Voorst, R. E. "Why Is There No Thanksgiving Period in Galatians? An Assessment of an Exegetical Commonplace." *JBL* 129 (2010): 153–72.

Vos, J. S. "Die hermeneutische Antinomie bei Paulus (Galater 3:11–12, Römer 10:5–10)." *NTS* 38 (1992): 254–70.

———. "Paul's Argumentation in Galatians 1–2." *HTR* 87 (1994): 1–16.

Vouga, François. "Zur rhetorischen Gattung des Galaterbriefes." *ZNW* 79 (1988): 291–92.

Wakefield, Andrew H. *Where to Live: The Hermeneutical Significance of Paul's Citations from Scripture in Galatians 3:1–14*. AcBib 14. Atlanta: SBL, 2003.

Walker, William O., Jr. "Translation and Interpretation of Ἐὰν Μή in Galatians 2:16." *JBL* 116 (1997): 515–20.

Wallace, Daniel B. "Galatians 3.19–20: A *Crux Interpretum* for Paul's View of the Law." *WTJ* 52 (1990): 225–45.

———. *Greek Grammar beyond the Basics: An Exegetical Syntax of the New Testament*. Grand Rapids: Zondervan, 1996.

Wallace-Hadrill, Andrew, ed. *Patronage in Ancient Society*. London: Routledge, 1989.

Wallis, Ian G. *The Faith of Jesus Christ in Early Christian Traditions*. SNTSMS 84. Cambridge: Cambridge University Press, 1995.

Walter, N. "Christusglaube und Heidnische Religiosität in Paulinischen Gemeinden." *NTS* 25 (1979): 422–42.

———. "Paulus und die Gegner des Christusevangeliums in Galatien." Pages 351–56 in *L'Apôtre Paul*. Edited by A. Vanhoye. Leuven: Leuven University Press, 1986.

Wan, Sze-Kar. "Abraham and the Promise of Spirit: Points of Convergence between Philo and Paul." Pages 209–20 in *Things Revealed: Studies in Early Jewish and Christian Literature in Honor of Michael E. Stone*. Edited by E. G. Chazon, D. Satran, and R. A. Clements. Leiden: Brill, 2004.

Waters, G. *The End of Deuteronomy in the Epistles of Paul*. WUNT 221. Tübingen: Mohr Siebeck, 2006.

Watson, Duane F. *The Rhetoric of the New Testament: A Bibliographical Survey*. Dorset, UK: Deo, 2006.

Watson, Francis. "By Faith (of Christ): An Exegetical Dilemma and Its Scriptural Solution." Pages 147–63 in *The Faith of Jesus Christ: Exegetical, Biblical, and Theological Studies*. Edited by M. F. Bird and P. M. Sprinkle. Peabody, MA: Hendrickson, 2009.

———. *Paul and the Hermeneutics of Faith*. London: T&T Clark, 2004.

———. *Paul, Judaism, and the Gentiles*. Cambridge: Cambridge University Press, 1986.

———. *Paul, Judaism, and the Gentiles: Beyond the New Perspective*. Rev. ed. Grand Rapids: Eerdmans, 2007.

Watson, N. M. "Justified by Faith, Judged by Works—an Antinomy?" *NTS* 29 (1983): 209–21.

Weima, J. A. D. "Gal. 6:11–18: A Hermeneutical Key to the Galatian Letter." *CTJ* 28 (1993): 90–107.

———. *Neglected Endings: The Significance of Pauline Letter Closings*. JSNTSup 101. Sheffield: Sheffield Academic Press, 1994.

———. "What Does Aristotle Have to Do with Paul? An Evaluation of Rhetorical Criticism." *CTJ* 32 (1997): 458–68.

Wengst, Klaus. *Pax Romana and the Peace of Jesus Christ*. Philadelphia: Fortress, 1987.

Wenham, David. *Paul: Follower of Jesus or Founder of Christianity?* Grand Rapids: Eerdmans, 1995.

Wenham, G. J. *The Book of Leviticus*. NICOT. Grand Rapids: Eerdmans, 1979.

———. *Genesis 1–15*. WBC 1. Nashville: Nelson, 1987.

Wesley, John. *The Works of John Wesley*. Edited by Thomas Jackson. New York: Emory & Waugh, 1931.

Wessels, G. F. "The Call to Responsible Freedom in Paul's Persuasive Strategy: Gal 5:13–6:10." *Neot* 26 (1992): 475–84.

Westerholm, Stephen. *Israel's Law and the Church's Faith: Paul and His Recent Interpreters*. Grand Rapids: Eerdmans, 1988.

———. *Justification Reconsidered: Rethinking a Pauline Theme*. Grand Rapids: Eerdmans, 2013.

———. "Letter and Spirit: The Foundation of Pauline Ethics." *NTS* 30 (1984): 229–48.

———. "On Fulfilling the Whole Law (Gal 5.14)." *SEÅ* 51–52 (1986–87): 229–37.

———. *Perspectives Old and New on Paul: The "Lutheran" Paul and His Critics.* Grand Rapids: Eerdmans, 2004.

———. *Preface to the Study of Paul.* Grand Rapids: Eerdmans, 1997.

Westermann, C. *Genesis 12–36.* Translated by John J. Scullion. CC. Minneapolis: Fortress, 1995.

White, C. Dale. *Making a Just Peace: Human Rights and Domination Systems.* Nashville: Abingdon, 1998.

White, John L. *The Form and Function of the Body of the Greek Letter: A Study of the Letter-Body in the Non-literary Papyri and in Paul the Apostle.* Missoula, MT: Scholars Press, 1972.

———. "Introductory Formulae in the Body of the Pauline Letter." *JBL* 90 (1971): 91–97.

Wilckens, Ulrich. "Die Bekehrung des Paulus also religionsgeschichtliches Problem." *ZTK* 56 (1959): 273–93.

———. *Rechtfertigung als Freiheit.* Neukirchen-Vluyn: Neukirchener Verlag, 1974.

———. "Zur Entwicklung des paulinischen Gesetzesverständnis." *NTS* 28 (1982): 154–90.

Wilcox, Max. "The Promise of the 'Seed' in the New Testament and Targumim." *JSNT* 5 (1979): 2–20.

———. "'Upon a Tree'—Deut 21:23 in the New Testament." *JBL* 96 (1977): 85–99.

Wilk, F. *Die Bedeutung des Jesajabuches für Paulus.* FRLANT 179. Göttingen: Vandenhoeck & Ruprecht, 1998.

Williams, Jarvis J. *Christ Died for Our Sins: Representation and Substitution in Romans and Their Jewish Martyrological Background.* Eugene, OR: Pickwick Publications, 2015.

———. *Maccabean Martyr Traditions in Paul's Theology of Atonement.* Eugene, OR: Wipf & Stock, 2010.

Williams, Sam K. "Again Pistis Christou." *CBQ* 49 (1987): 431–47.

———. "The Hearing of Faith: ΑΚΩΗ ΠΙΣΤΕΩΣ in Galatians 3." *NTS* 35 (1989): 82–93.

———. *Jesus' Death as Saving Event.* Missoula, MT: Scholars Press, 1975.

———. "Justification and the Spirit in Galatians." *JSNT* 29 (1987): 91–100.

———. "Promise in Galatians: A Reading of Paul's Reading of Scripture." *JBL* 107 (1988): 709–20.

Willitts, Joel. "Context Matters: Paul's Use of Leviticus 18:5 in Galatians 3:12." *TynBul* 54 (2003): 105–22.

———. "Isa 54,1 and Gal 4,24b–27: Reading Genesis in Light of Isaiah." *ZNW* 96 (2005): 188–210.

Wilson, Todd A. *The Curse of the Law and the Crisis in Galatia: Reassessing the Purpose of Galatians.* WUNT 2/225. Tübingen: Mohr Siebeck, 2007.

———. "The Law of Christ and the Law of Moses: Reflections on a Recent Trend in Interpretation." *CurBR* 5 (2006): 123–44.

———. "'Under Law' in Galatians: A Pauline Theological Abbreviation." *JTS* 56 (2005): 362–92.

———. "Wilderness Apostasy and Paul's Portrayal of the Crisis in Galatians." *NTS* 50 (2004): 550–71.

Winger, Michael. "Act One: Paul Arrives in Galatia." *NTS* 48 (2002): 548–67.

———. *By What Law? The Meaning of Nomos in the Letters of Paul.* SBLDS 128. Atlanta: Scholars Press, 1992.

———. "The Law of Christ." *NTS* 46 (2000): 537–46.

Wink, Walter. *Engaging the Powers: Discernment and Resistance in a World of Domination.* Minneapolis: Fortress, 1992.

———. *Naming the Powers: The Language of Power in the New Testament.* Minneapolis: Fortress, 1984.

———. *Unmasking the Powers: The Invisible Forces That Determine Human Existence.* Minneapolis: Fortress, 1986.

Winter, Bruce W. *Divine Honours for the Caesars: The First Christians' Response.* Grand Rapids: Eerdmans, 2015.

———. "The Imperial Cult and Early Christians in Roman Galatia (Acts XIII 13–50 and Gal VI 11–18)." Pages 67–75 in *Actes du 1er Congrès International sur Antioche de Pisidie.* Edited by T. Drew-Bear, M. Tashalan, and C. M. Thomas. Lyon: Kocaeli, 2002.

———. "Is Paul among the Sophists?" *RTR* 53 (1994): 28–38.

———. *Seeking the Welfare of the City: Christians as Benefactors and Citizens.* Grand Rapids: Eerdmans, 1994.

Wischmeyer, O. "ΦΥΣΙΣ und ΚΤΙΣΙΣ bei Paulus: Die paulinische Rede von Schöpfung und Natur." *ZTK* 93 (1996): 352–75.

Wisdom, Jeffrey R. *Blessing for the Nations and the Curse of the Law: Paul's Citation of Genesis and Deuteronomy in Gal 3.8–10.* WUNT 2/133. Tübingen: Mohr Siebeck, 2001.

Witherington, Ben, III. *The Acts of the Apostles: A Socio-rhetorical Commentary.* Grand Rapids: Eerdmans, 1998.

———. "The Influence of Galatians on Hebrews." *NTS* 37 (1991): 146–52.

———. *New Testament History: A Narrative Account.* Grand Rapids: Baker, 2001.

———. *The Paul Quest: The Renewed Search for the Jew of Tarsus.* Downers Grove, IL: InterVarsity Press, 1998.

———. *Paul's Narrative Thought World.* Louisville: Westminster John Knox Press, 1994.

———. "Rite and Rights for Women—Galatians 3:28." *NTS* 27 (1980): 593–604.

———. *What Have They Done with Jesus? Beyond Strange Theories and Bad History.* New York: Harper One, 2006.

Witulski, T. *Die Adressaten des Galaterbriefes: Untersuchungen zur Gemeinde von Antiochia ad Pisidiam.* Göttingen: Vandenhoeck & Ruprecht, 2000.

Wright, Benjamin G., III. *The Letter of Aristeas.* Berlin: de Gruyter, 2015.

Wright, D. F. "Justification in Augustine." Pages 55–72 in *Justification in Perspective: Historical Developments and Contemporary Challenges.* Edited by B. L. McCormack. Grand Rapids: Baker Academic, 2006.

Wright, N. T. *The Climax of the Covenant: Christ and the Law in Pauline Theology.* Edinburgh: T&T Clark, 1991.

———. *Justification: God's Plan and Paul's Vision.* Downers Grove, IL: InterVarsity Press, 2009.

———. "Justification: Yesterday, Today, and Forever." *JETS* 51 (2011): 49–64.

———. "The Letter to the Galatians: Exegesis and Theology." Pages 205–36 in *Between Two Horizons: Spanning New Testament Studies and Systematic Theology.* Edited by J. B. Green and M. Turner. Grand Rapids: Eerdmans, 2000.

———. "The Letter to the Romans: Introduction, Commentary, and Reflections." Pages 393–770 in *NIB* 10. Nashville: Abingdon, 2002.

———. *Paul and His Recent Interpreters.* Minneapolis: Fortress, 2015.

———. "Paul, Arabia, and Elijah (Galatians 1:17)." *JBL* 115 (1996): 683–92.

———. *Pauline Perspectives: Essays on Paul, 1978–2003.* Minneapolis: Fortress, 2013.

———. *Paul in Fresh Perspective.* Minneapolis: Fortress, 2005.

———. *The Resurrection of the Son of God.* Minneapolis: Fortress, 2003.

———. *What Saint Paul Really Said.* Grand Rapids: Eerdmans, 1997.

Yinger, K. L. *Paul, Judaism, and Judgment according to Deeds.* SNTSMS 105. Cambridge: Cambridge University Press, 1999.

Young, N. H. "*Paidagogos*: The Social Setting of a Pauline Metaphor." *NovT* 29 (1987): 150–76.

———. "Pronominal Shifts in Paul's Argument to the Galatians." Pages 205–15 in *Ancient History in a Modern University.* Vol. 2 in *Early Christianity in Late Antiquity and Beyond.* Edited by T. W. Hillard, R. A. Kearsley, C. E. V. Nixon, and A. M. Nobbs. Grand Rapids: Eerdmans, 1998.

———. "Who's Cursed—and Why? (Galatians 3.10–14)." *JBL* 117 (1998): 79–92.

Young, Richard A. *Intermediate New Testament Greek: A Linguistic and Exegetical Approach.* Nashville: Broadman & Holman, 1994.

Zanker, Paul. *The Power of Images in the Age of Augustus.* Ann Arbor: University of Michigan Press, 1988.

Zerwick, Maximilian. *Biblical Greek, Illustrated by Examples.* Translated by J. Smith. Scripta Pontificii Instituti Biblici 114. Rome: Pontifical Biblical Institute, 1963.

Ziesler, J. A. *The Meaning of Righteousness in Paul: A Linguistic and Theological Inquiry.* SNTSMS 20. Cambridge: Cambridge University Press, 1972.

————. *Pauline Christology*. Oxford: Oxford University Press, 1991.

Zimmerman, Clayton. *The Pastoral Narcissus: A Study of the First Idyll of Theocritus*. London: Rowman & Littlefield, 1994.

Zimmerman, Ruben. "The 'Implicit Ethics' of New Testament Writings: A Draft on a New Methodology in Analysing New Testament Ethics." *Neot* 43 (2009): 398–422.

————. "Jenseits von Indikativ und Imperativ: Zur 'impliziten Ethik' des Paulus am Beispiel des 1. Korinterbriefs." *TLZ* (2007): 260–84.

Zuntz, G. *The Text of the Epistles: A Disquisition upon the Corpus Paulinum*. London: Oxford University Press, 1953.

Introduction

I. AUTHORSHIP

While the authorship of several letters attributed to Paul (particularly 2 Thessalonians, Ephesians, Colossians, and the Pastoral Epistles) continues to be disputed, no one seriously challenges Paul's authorship of this letter to the Galatian Christians.[1] It has all the hallmarks of being shaped by a specific and unrepeatable situation in the ministry of Paul and in the life of his congregations and offers a response thoroughly conditioned by that situation. It does not have the appearance of trying to reclaim an apostle's voice and authority to address later problems in the church or to provide generally useful theological or practical guidance. The author's personality and passion shine through to a degree that is unmatched among Paul's letters, save perhaps for 2 Corinthians, but not in a way that could ever be the result of a pious fiction. Galatians shows us Paul "under fire," long before he became so widely a revered figure that any early Christian would find it useful or advantageous to write fictitiously under Paul's name.

This widespread affirmation of Pauline authorship makes Galatians an especially important source both for the biographical study of Paul and his ministry and, to a slightly lesser extent, for the study of the history of the early church, particularly as this history took shape around the question of how to incorporate gentile believers into the predominantly Jewish Jesus movement. Because Galatians is written firsthand by one of the major players in that history, it tends (rightly) to be privileged as a historical source over Acts of the Apostles when it comes to reconstructing the complexities of that history. Nevertheless, as the commentary proper will emphasize, we cannot lose sight of the fact that Paul selectively shares and shapes the episodes he tells of his

---

1. Betz, 1. A brief review of the few attempts to challenge Pauline authorship can be found in Burton, lxix–lxxi.

own story and the church's story with a view to achieving certain goals in the Galatian situation. That is to say, the purpose behind every autobiographical statement in Galatians, every narrative of an earlier event in Galatians, is not to provide material for later historians and biographers of Paul, but to win the debate in Galatia and bring these congregations back around to looking to Paul for the way toward the "truth of the gospel" (2:5, 14).[2]

The title "To the Galatians" was added only after Paul's letters began to be collected and the need arose to distinguish between different letters in a single codex or scroll. Scribes tended to assign short titles on the basis of the named recipients.[3] Scribes could not resist the temptation to expand these titles with more information than they actually possessed. Thus several manuscripts and families entitle this book "To the Galatians written from Rome."[4] That Paul wrote this letter from Rome, however, is highly unlikely on any modern theory of the letter's dating and the location of the addressees (whether in North or South Galatia).

Did Paul have the help of a secretary in the process of composing Galatians? It is possible to read Paul's command to the readers "See with what large-sized letters I wrote to you" (6:11) as signaling a *change* in handwriting at that point, with the implication being that Gal 1:1–6:10 was dictated by Paul to a coworker or even to a hired scribe functioning as a secretary.[5] This imperative is, however, not nearly as clear and unambiguous a signal of the practice of a secretary handing off the stylus to Paul to write a personal greeting or conclusion as we find in others of Paul's letters (see esp. the explicit attention to Paul's authenticating signature in 1 Cor 16:21; Col 4:18; 2 Thess 3:17; also the personal greetings from the Christian scribe Tertius in Rom 16:22).[6] It is a mistake to assume too quickly that Paul *always* wrote through someone else's hand, and Galatians may well have been written out by Paul in its entirety.[7]

---

2. Here and throughout this commentary, all translations from Galatians and other biblical texts are my own, unless otherwise noted (in which case, the source of the English version quoted appears after the reference).

3. The letter bears the simple subscription πρὸς Γαλάτας in ℵ A B* C; πρὸς Γαλάτας ἐπληρώθη in D; ἐτελέσθη ἐπιστολὴ πρὸς Γαλάτας in F G.

4. B^c K P 𝔐; similarly L. See Metzger, *Textual Commentary*, 531.

5. So Longenecker, lix–lxi; Betz, *Galatians*, 1; Richards, *Paul and First-Century Letter Writing*, 81; Das, 67, 630–33. John Chrysostom (45–46), by contrast, understood Gal 6:11 to imply that Paul wrote the entire letter in his own hand.

6. Ironically, the authorship of two of the three letters in which an "authenticating" signature appears is disputed. See the evaluation of the arguments in deSilva, *Introduction to the New Testament*, 539–43, 696–701.

7. See commentary on 6:11.

II. PAUL'S MINISTRY IN GALATIA

The Roman province of Galatia covered a vast territory during Paul's active ministry. It included the central portion of what is now Turkey, the principal cities being Ancyra, Pessinus, and Tavium, stretching north to the Paphlagonian mountains (abutting the provinces of Bithynia and Pontus). It also reached far to the south to include the regions often referred to as Lycaonia, Pisidia, and part of Phrygia, and thus the important cities of Pisidian Antioch, Iconium, Lystra, and Derbe. The northern region of Roman provincial Galatia was the historic home of the Celtic people who originally migrated to this area, while the southern region was joined to the northern region under the Roman Republic to form a single administrative unit. Which of these regions was home to the congregations to which Paul sent this letter remains a much-debated issue, to which we will return later.

Paul himself gives us no details about the precise geographic location of the addressees. It is only when Galatians is read within the framework of Paul's mission work in Acts that this question can even be raised, let alone answered. What Paul *does* tell us about his founding visit to the congregations addressed by Galatians is quite different from anything we read in Acts. "You know that I first proclaimed the message of good news to you on account of bodily illness, and you neither scorned nor rejected the trial you endured in my flesh, but rather you received me as an angel from God, even as Christ Jesus" (Gal 4:13–14).

According to his own account, Paul appears to have evangelized in the city or cities to which he now writes because an illness prevented him from moving ahead to the destination he himself had in mind. Paul offers an example here of a truly positive and Spirit-led response to the frustrations of being hindered in one's plans, seeking out God's purposes in the midst of otherwise inopportune circumstances. The fact that he himself was afflicted by illness could have been expected to arouse scorn for his message. After all, how could a person who clearly was not experiencing the divine favor of good physical health proclaim the ready availability of divine favor in Christ? Those brought up in Greek culture, moreover, came to expect a good show from public speakers. Manner of presentation, physical grace, poise, and vocal quality were all as important as what was said. Those who lacked these qualities could provoke ridicule rather than gain an attentive hearing. Against all such expectations, however, the Galatians received Paul warmly and embraced both him and his message. Paul also recalls for them how they experienced the reality of God's presence and power through the manifestations of God's Holy Spirit in their midst—a power invading their own lives as well—in conjunction with Paul's preaching (Gal 3:1–5).

3

What was Paul's message in Galatia? Paul identifies the central feature of his gospel here, as in Corinth, as "Christ crucified" (Gal 3:1; 1 Cor 2:2). This formula would have required some unpacking, especially for the gentiles among his audience in Galatia. Jesus as the "Christ," or "Messiah," was a foreign concept, and crucifixion was a sign of utter degradation. Greek culture, however, could envision a divine being suffering excruciating torments, and doing so specifically on behalf of humanity. The myth of Prometheus, for example, typifies this pattern (see the well-developed version of this story in Aeschylus, *Prometheus Bound*). Zeus, the king of the gods, was angry at humankind and planned to destroy them. Prometheus, a Titan, sought to save humankind by equipping them with the starting point of all technology—fire, stolen from the gods. His reward was to be chained to a rocky peak and to be visited every day by an eagle, which tore into his abdomen to eat his liver. (Prometheus was immortal, so his liver grew back every night.)

Jews among Paul's audience were also familiar with pious Jewish men and women suffering torture and death with the aim of restoring God's favor toward the larger, disobedient people. Second Maccabees tells the story of the attempt to reshape Jerusalem after the fashion of a Greek city under Antiochus IV, which the author interprets as an act of apostasy from the covenant led by the very priestly elite charged with preserving the covenant. The reform devolves quickly into repression of Torah observance and enforced apostasy. At this point the author introduces an aged priest, seven brothers, and the mother of the seven who willingly—even willfully—refuse to eat a mouthful of pork (a sign of their acquiescence to forsaking the covenant), dying under the most grievous tortures (see 2 Macc 6:18–8:5) as a result. These martyrs are presented as offering their obedience unto death on behalf of the larger nation, asking God to spend the remainder of his wrath upon them and allow their obedience to restore his favor toward the nation. Thus the youngest brother declares: "I, like my brothers, give up body and life for the laws of our ancestors, appealing to God to show mercy soon to our nation and by trials and plagues to make you confess that he alone is God, and through me and my brothers to bring to an end the wrath of the Almighty that has justly fallen on our whole nation" (7:37–38 NRSV). According to the narrator, their obedience unto death is indeed effective. Immediately following, Judas Maccabeus and his army experience their first victories, "for the wrath of the Lord had turned to mercy" (8:5 NRSV).[8]

---

8. The self-offering of the martyrs to God on behalf of the nation is even more highly developed in 4 Maccabees, a Hellenistic Jewish text originating in the northeastern regions of the Mediterranean. Thus Eleazar prays as he stands on the threshold of death, "God, you know that I could have saved myself; instead, I am being burned and tortured to death for the sake of your law. Have mercy on your people. Make our punishment sufficient for their

The gospel of "Christ crucified" is the good news about the rescue that Jesus's offering of himself brought to human beings and about the change it produced in their relationship with God. Throughout Galatians, Paul refers to Jesus as one who, in death, "gave himself on behalf of our sins" (Gal 1:4), who "loved me and gave himself up for me" (2:20), who "rescues" believers "from the present, evil age" (1:4). The condensed formulas that Paul uses here suggest that Paul had spoken of these topics at much greater length before and could assume the Galatians' familiarity with these concepts from his earlier visit. Paul presented Christ's crucifixion in terms of a benefactor who poured himself out completely in order to bring benefit to his clients. This terminology of "giving oneself," or "pouring oneself out," is attested in Greek and Latin inscriptions honoring benefactors as the apex of generosity.[9] The shameful death of the cross was thus transformed into a noble act of supreme generosity and beneficence. Giving himself "for our sins" (1:4), Jesus presented his extreme and complete obedience to God as a representative act on behalf of the many who were disobedient and unmindful of God. In this way, his death—the outcome of his perfect obedience—removed the obstacles, the sins against and affronts to God, which stood in the way of humanity experiencing God's favor rather than God's sentence.

Paul's claim that Jesus died in order to "rescue us from this present evil age" (1:4) recalls the apocalyptic framework of his earlier preaching in Galatia. According to this framework, this world and its history are a temporary phenomenon, one in which God's justice and rewards for the righteous cannot fully be manifested. The death and resurrection of the Messiah signaled, for Paul, the beginning of the end of this current age and the imminence of the "coming age," a better, eternal age in which God's purposes are completely fulfilled and God's people enjoy their full reward. The good news, then, was that Christ's death brought rescue from this age and its fate at God's judgment so that those who were rescued could enjoy the benefits of living with God in the age to come.

The way to share in the benefits of the Messiah's self-giving death and resurrected life was by "faith," trusting in the effectiveness of his death on

---

sake. Purify them with my blood, and take my life in exchange for theirs" (6:27–29 CEB); toward the close of his discourse, the author comments: "The tyrant was punished, and the homeland purified—they having become, as it were, a ransom for the sin of our nation. And through the blood of those devout ones and their death as an atoning sacrifice, divine Providence preserved Israel that previously had been mistreated" (17:21–22 NRSV). See further deSilva, *4 Maccabees: Introduction and Commentary*, 137–41. On the importance of these martyrs as a potential background to Jesus's understanding of his own death, see deSilva, *Jewish Teachers*, 158–74; on their importance as a background to Paul's understanding of Jesus's death, see Williams, *Maccabean Martyr Traditions*.

9. See the discussion in Danker, *Benefactor*, 321–23, 363–66, 417–35.

behalf of others and in his ability to connect people with God. Those who are "of faith" trust that Jesus is a competent patron, able to procure the favor of the ultimate Patron, God. They trust that the provisions they receive by virtue of their association with Christ—most notably, the Holy Spirit—are sufficient to bring them where God wants them to be. Included within this "faith" are uncompromising loyalty to Jesus and obedience to him ("faithfulness"). The response of loyalty and gratitude toward Christ and the God he makes known would require a complementary turning away from every idol and all involvement in the worship of the no-gods that they represent. This step was fundamental to the gentiles' response to the gospel (as in 1 Thess 1:9–10), and Paul would have had a wealth of anti-idolatry polemic at his disposal from the writings of the Jewish Scriptures (e.g., Ps 115:1–8; Isa 44:8–21; Jer 10:1–12) and Hellenistic-era Jews (e.g., the Epistle of Jeremiah and the Wisdom of Solomon). Moreover, Greek and Roman philosophers had long emphasized the essential oneness of God, who was worshiped imperfectly in the many partial guises and inadequate representations of traditional Greco-Roman religion. Paul could connect this philosophical view with his own understanding that the one God of the Jews was also the one God of the gentiles. His cosmopolitan approach would certainly have been more attractive than the traditional Jewish appeal, which stressed the ethnic particularity of the one God and the way of life by which one could please him.

Reception of the good news meant also a transformation of life. Paul writes in Galatians that "the works of the flesh are clearly evident: sexual immorality, impurity, shameless debauchery, idolatry, drug-induced spells, enmities, strife, jealousy, wrathful outbursts, rivalries, divisions, factions, envying, drunken bouts, gluttonous parties, and other things like these. Concerning these things I tell you in advance, *just as I warned you before*: Those practicing such things will not inherit the kingdom of God" (5:19–21). Paul presents this moral teaching—the imperative of leaving behind a life impelled by self-centered impulses—as something the Galatians should recognize from Paul's earlier communications, the most likely occasion being a visit with them in person (whether his initial evangelization visit or a second, follow-up visit). The moral imperative that accompanies the proclamation of what Christ has done to offer human beings a fresh start with God is a constant theme of Paul's writing. Its prominence in Romans (see esp. Rom 6:1–7:6; 8:1–14; 12:1–13:14), which is essentially Paul's presentation of the message that he preaches (shared at least in part in an attempt to gain the Roman Christian congregations' support for his ongoing missionary endeavors), suggests that it was prominent as well in his missionary preaching prior to that point. Paul's preaching in Thessalonica also included an explicit moral component, which he recalls in 1 Thess 4:1–7 (see esp. 4:2: "For you know what directives we gave to you through the Lord Jesus").

The indisputable sign for Paul that Jesus's work was sufficient and effective on the Galatians' behalf is the Galatians' reception of the Holy Spirit. When these Jews and gentiles responded with trust to the message Paul brought about Christ crucified, God manifested himself, pouring out the Holy Spirit upon them (Gal 3:1–5). This experience of the Holy Spirit is a common feature of the Pauline mission (see also 1 Cor 2:1–5 and Heb 2:1–4).[10] Having experienced this divine power in their midst, the Galatians would have been quite aware that a decisive change had occurred in them and in their relationship with God, and that they had in fact received the Spirit of God. Paul reminds his converts of this experience, since he believes that it should have been enough to show them that God had made them part of God's family. The gentile converts among them were no longer unclean, no longer outside the people of promise, since God himself had decisively accepted them into his household.

III. THE PASTORAL CHALLENGE IN GALATIA

Paul's undisguised shock at what he has learned about his converts in Galatia since leaving them (1:6) suggests that he parted from them under the conviction that his work there rested on a firm foundation. What happened to shake that foundation in the months that followed his visit? We have only Paul's passionate response to the situation in Galatia as a witness to the situation itself, and we must exercise some caution as we attempt to see the situation through the mirror Paul holds up to the same.[11]

---

10. Although not written by Paul, Hebrews appears to have originated within the circle of Pauline churches, as the anonymous author works to coordinate his own travels with the movements of Timothy, a well-known figure from the Pauline team (Heb 13:23; see deSilva, *Perseverance in Gratitude*, 23–27). Hebrews 2:1–4 thus provides a witness from another member of Paul's team to the clear experience of divine authentication that accompanied Paul's preaching and the birth of the congregations that were a part of his mission.

11. A helpful theoretical discussion of this process of careful historical reconstruction of a situation from one party's response to the situation is Barclay, "Mirror-Reading." Barclay identifies four common methodological missteps in attempts to reconstruct the situation behind a letter: (1) undue selectivity (basing a theory on a few choice statements but failing to make sense of the reconstruction in light of the whole text); (2) overinterpretation (proceeding as if every positive statement is a response to an opponent's or the congregation's denial, or every denial a rebuttal of an opponent's claim; similarly treating every command as a sign that the hearers are doing something different and every prohibition as a sign that the hearers are engaged in the prohibited activity); (3) mishandling polemics (failing to account for the inevitable distortions that will occur when an author is trying to draw people away from heeding other voices, presenting these speakers in the worst possible light, ascribing

New teachers have appeared on the scene, saying some new things about the "good news" of Christ. They would most likely have identified themselves as *Christian* teachers, something reflected also in Paul's admission that they are proclaiming some variation on the gospel (1:6), which he quickly denies the status of being "gospel" at all (1:7).[12] The Galatian Christians, moreover, appear to be giving them a careful and attentive hearing, even standing on the verge of being persuaded by them (1:6; 5:1). Paul does not say much about the specific message of these rival teachers. He does indicate that persuading the gentile converts to receive circumcision was a notable feature of their message (explicitly in 5:2; 6:12–13; indirectly in 5:11–12), probably as a means of securing their place in the family of Abraham, the line of promise (3:6–29), and as a means of combating the power of the flesh (indirectly, 5:13–6:10) and thus experiencing freedom from its power over them so that they can make progress in their new life of godliness (3:3). Their influence coincides with the Galatians' adoption of some of the calendrical observances prescribed in the Torah, the Jewish law (4:10).[13] Paul's language suggests that the Galatians' attraction to these Torah-prescribed observances (alongside a much broader adoption of a Torah-observant practice) and to taking the final plunge of circumcision lay in the rival teachers' promise that aligning oneself with the commandments of the Torah was the surest path to aligning oneself with God's standards and thus being "justified" before God ("being deemed to be righteous" or "brought into line with God's righteous demands by means of the law," 5:4).[14]

---

to them the worst possible motives); and (4) latching onto particular words as if these automatically indicated the presence of opponents for whom these words were key terms (like taking the appearance of γνῶσις, "knowledge," or πνευματικός, "spiritual," as indications of the presence of Gnostic teachers). Such methodological missteps can be minimized, Barclay argues, by weighing several criteria when sifting through a letter for indications of the situation behind it or the opposing positions addressed. These would include (1) the *type of utterance* (assertions, denials, commands, and prohibitions) and the degree to which it may be a reflection of the situation addressed; (2) *tone* (is the author's tone urgent? emphatic? casual?); (3) *frequency* (does the author return frequently to this topic, or mention it only once in passing?); (4) *clarity* (do we really understand the passage we are reading, or is it too unclear or ambiguous to be of real help in getting behind the situation?); (5) *unfamiliarity* (the presence of atypical vocabulary or themes might signal a feature of the particular situation or position to which the author responds); (6) *consistency* (with a preference for a single front of opposition); and (7) *historical plausibility* (are the rival teachers reconstructed known or seen anywhere else in contemporaneous literature? Is the situation plausible?). See also the methodological refinements in Sumney, *Identifying Paul's Opponents*, 75–120.

12. So also Betz, 7; Brinsmead, *Galatians*, 86.

13. This verse is sometimes taken to reflect reversion to a *pagan* religious calendar; see commentary on 4:8–11 for further discussion.

14. So also Betz, 6–7.

Paul never names these rival teachers or suggests where they came from.[15] He refers to them only as "agitators" or "troublemakers" (1:7; 5:10b, 12), clearly not welcoming their intrusion or their interpretation of the gospel. This does not mean that Paul lacks firsthand information about them and who they are.[16] Rather, referring to one's opponents only in vague ways was a standard feature of classical rhetoric, as if naming them specifically or taking too close or too detailed an interest in them would be to show them more respect than they merit. Paul likens their influence to the "evil eye," the magical calling down of a curse upon someone out of envy (often translated as "bewitching" the Galatians, 3:1). He speaks of them as ill-mannered athletes who have "cut in" on the lane of the Galatian Christians, tripping them up as they ran (5:7). Paul suggests that the motives of these new teachers are far from pure. They pretend, he alleges, to have the Galatian Christians' best interests at heart, but they are really trying to deprive the Galatians of their place in Christ so that the Galatians will instead become dependent upon the teachers (4:17). They are too cowardly to endure the opposition that preaching the truth of the gospel arouses. Instead, they are trying to escape persecution themselves (from their fellow Jews) by making the Galatian Christians adopt Jewish practices, hence making the Christian movement and its message more acceptable to non-Christian Jews (6:12). They are not even fully committed to all the practices of the Torah themselves but are trying to use the Galatian Christians as an opportunity to enhance their own reputation (6:13). The mercilessness of Paul's assaults on these rival teachers' credibility (4:17; 6:12–13) may well reflect the degree to which their message appealed to Paul's converts. Paul's goals for his communication are clear: he wants his converts to reject outright the course of action that the rival teachers have

---

15. Indeed, it is not *essential* that the rival teachers have come from outside Galatia. They may themselves have been resident in its cities, belonging to a different group of Jewish Christ-followers, perhaps planted as a result of converted Jewish pilgrims returning home from Jerusalem prior to Paul's mission, who then react against Paul's mission to the area. This seems to me a less plausible scenario, however, than the scenario in which they come from Jewish Christian congregations closer to the epicenter of the movement.

16. Against the inference of Witherington, 23. Much depends also on how Paul was informed about the emerging situation in Galatia. Martyn, 14, highlights the importance of the "catechetical instructors" (6:6), local leaders appointed perhaps personally by Paul to continue the nurture of the congregations in the Pauline gospel, the Pauline interpretation of the Jewish Scriptures, and so forth. These leaders would have been the likeliest candidates for traveling to Paul with news of developments in Galatia, as well as returning from Paul to the congregations to read Paul's response in the assemblies. The author of Acts also speaks of Paul appointing elders in the congregations that he had planted in southern Galatia on his return journey to Syrian Antioch as a means of consolidating and preserving his work in those cities (14:21–23), which corroborates Martyn's suggestion.

proposed (5:1) and to expel these rivals before they can do any more damage to his converts' theology or practice (4:30; 5:8–9).

Despite Paul's hostile presentation of these teachers, the fact that Paul needs to write Galatians at all testifies to the fact that these rival teachers had a persuasive message to which many among Paul's converts were giving a ready hearing. Paul did not leave Galatia having anticipated and answered all the questions that would arise for the Galatians about their new life in Christ and their relationship to prominent aspects of God's historic dealings with his people. While we can only speculate about what some of these questions were, there is a high probability that most if not all gentiles who had come to faith in this Jewish Messiah would have had to ask such questions as the following at some point in their faith journey: (1) If the Torah is a God-given law for God's historic people, are we obliged to follow it or any part of it? It seems to dominate all of God's dealings with God's people from Moses to Malachi. Should we give it more attention, if we really want to be sure that we are right with God? (2) If we really have God's Spirit, why do we still struggle so much with temptation and fall so often into sin? How do we even know what is sin versus what is legitimate pleasure or a just course of action? Not everyone following the Spirit agrees on the answers to such questions, so perhaps it is not enough just to have the Spirit, if we want to really know what God expects of us.[17] These were precisely the sorts of questions that the rival teachers were poised to answer, and answer persuasively. If the Galatian converts were not already asking these questions, the rival teachers could certainly have introduced them and impressed upon the Galatian Christians the importance of finding reliable answers to them.

Who, then, are these rival teachers? Paul gives every indication that they are representatives of another Christian mission, led by Jewish Christians, presenting Torah observance as a necessary part of responding to God's favor offered in Jesus Christ.[18] These missionaries sought to keep the new

---

17. Betz, 8, similarly focuses on the likely dissonance in the converts' experience of being "in the Spirit" while also still liable to their lower drives as a problem for which Paul had not adequately prepared them, but for which "Paul's opposition had concrete help to offer."

18. There is near consensus on this point. See, for example, Lightfoot, 27, 52–53; Burton, liv–lv; Ridderbos, 15–16; Bligh, 17–35; Guthrie, 10–11; Betz, 7; Bruce, 25–27, 31–32; Barclay, "Mirror-Reading," 88–89; Fung, 7–9; Longenecker, lxxxviii–xcvi; Matera, 7–11; Dunn, 9–11; Martyn, 18, 117–26; Witherington, 23–25; deBoer, 50–61; Schreiner, 47–49, 51–52; Das, 10–14; Moo, 19–20.

Johannes Munck (*Paul and the Salvation of Mankind*, 87–89) had argued that the "Judaizers" were actually gentile Christians from within Paul's churches (see also Segal, *Paul the Convert*, 208–9). Paul distinguishes clearly, however, between his converts who are succumbing to bad influences (whom he addresses in the second person) and those who are exerting this bad influence (of whom he speaks in the third person). He shows no interest

Christian movement firmly anchored within the historic covenant between God and Israel. The activity of this kind of mission is reflected in Acts 15:1–4, which tells of Jewish Christians from Judea coming to Antioch, the home base of Paul and Barnabas's mission, seeking to impose circumcision and Torah observance on the converts there.[19] Galatians suggests that such missionaries were active beyond Antioch as well. Paul refers briefly to this rival mission again in Phil 3:2–21, presenting them as a foil for Paul's own model of discipleship.[20]

---

in addressing the influencers or in winning them back to some position they might have originally held, were they themselves among Paul's converts in Galatia. The way Paul speaks of these rival teachers is thus more consonant with the view that they have come into the congregations from the outside rather than the view that they are insiders who have gone wrong (Bruce, 25; see also Dunn, *Theology of Paul's Letter to the Galatians*, 8; Das, 3–4).

More recently, Mark Nanos proposed that the rival teachers are non-Christian Jews reaching out to gentile Christians (*Irony of Galatians*, 284–316; see, earlier, Foakes-Jackson and Lake, *Beginnings of Christianity*, 5:215). According to Nanos, both Jewish and gentile Christians in Galatia were still attending worship in the local synagogue, with the non-Christian Jews urging their gentile (Christian) "guests" and "visitors," whom they were commending for their desire to be "righteous," to take the necessary step of circumcision so as to separate themselves from the pagan world to which they still belonged (*Irony*, 317–18). Nanos believes that these gentile Christians would still regard circumcision and full inclusion into the Jewish people as complementary to their faith in Jesus (227). Paul, however, presents the situation as one in which a rival "gospel" is being proclaimed, not a term he would have used if the source of the troublesome teaching was the synagogue. While other events are indeed proclaimed by gentiles and Jews as "good news," Christian authors use the singular noun form to name their distinctive "message of good news," whereas almost all non-Christian authors use the plural form (Das, 10–13). The sole exception, in Josephus (*Jewish War* 2.420), has nothing to do with any divine message of deliverance, but rather with how the corrupt governor Florus received the report that a revolt was beginning to erupt in Judea. If, moreover, the pressure were coming from non-Christian Jews, it also seems that Paul could have used their lack of belief in Jesus to his advantage in creating distance between them and his converts. Paul gives evidence, on the contrary, of assuming trust in Christ as a basic starting point shared with those with whom he debates (reading 2:15–16 as addressing not only Peter in retrospect, but also the position of the rivals, pointing out the inconsistencies in their position). The phenomenon of early (Jewish) Christians wrestling with the implications of the Christ event for the ongoing observance of Torah and for Jewish-gentile relations within the churches is well attested beyond the immediate situation in Galatians and, thus, quite plausible here.

19. Bruce, 55, regards the situation in Galatia to have been very close in time and kind to the situation described in Acts 15:1–2. Dunn, 14, suggests that the teachers were probably themselves Antiochene Jewish Christians seeking to clean up after Paul in the churches that fell within the authority and under the auspices of the church in Antioch (thus including the South Galatian churches, which were founded by Antiochene missionaries Paul and Barnabas).

20. More complicated theories about Paul having to fight on two separate fronts in

Despite Paul's allegations about the rival teachers' motives being self-serving and cowardly (4:17; 6:12–13), their primary motivation was probably theologically grounded. They sought to preserve the integrity of the covenant and to set the work of Jesus the Messiah within the context of this covenant, which was spelled out in the law of Moses. Jesus was indeed still the one who brought light to the gentiles, initiating the gathering in of the nations at the end of this age, but Jesus and his agents would accomplish this work by bringing the gentiles fully into the Jewish people through circumcising them and getting them to take upon themselves the "yoke of Torah," at least to a certain extent.[21] These rival teachers were also concerned about the unity of

---

Galatia formerly enjoyed some popularity. Wilhelm Lütgert (*Gesetz und Geist*) and James H. Ropes (*Singular Problem*) thought that the congregations were afflicted both by Judaizers who had come from outside and by "libertines" who believed that Christian freedom meant freedom from all (or many) traditional moral restraints. Paul wrote Galatians to urge the former to embrace Christian freedom and to warn the latter not to misuse or abuse it. Richard Longenecker (xcix) also thinks that Gal 5:21 signals a problem of libertinism: "I warn you, *as I did before*, that those who live like this will not inherit the kingdom of God" (5:21; emphasis and translation his). In either form, this theory would represent an excess of mirror-reading. Paul's instructions about Christian ethics need not imply a wanton neglect of morality among the Galatian Christians.

The theory of Walter Schmithals ("Die Häretiker in Galatien" and *Paul and the Gnostics*, 13–64) that Paul is combating the influence of Jewish Christian Gnostics also relies on excessive mirror-reading of Paul's rather casual use of terminology in Galatians that might also have meaning within (later) Gnosticism, such as the concept of "perfection" in 3:3, but that makes perfect sense in context apart from any Gnostic connotations. Bruce (25) rightly counters that "Gnosticism has really to be read into the teaching of these people as reflected in Paul's attack on them before it can be read out of it."

21. The degree of Torah observance that these teachers urged upon the Galatian Christians is a matter of some debate. There are hints in Paul's letter that the Galatians may not have been made aware by the rival teachers of just what they were getting themselves into. "I bear witness again to every man who undergoes circumcision that he is obligated to perform the whole law" (5:3). If the rival teachers were espousing complete Torah observance, how would this solemn declaration be "news" to the Galatians? Paul also explicitly claims that the rival teachers "do not themselves keep the law" but are only collecting trophies from the gentile Christians to bolster their own esteem in other circles (6:13). Paul, however, does speak of the Galatians as those who are seeking to align themselves with God's righteousness on the basis of "law" (4:21; 5:2) and not merely on the basis of circumcision, so a minimalist understanding of the Torah observance being urged is also excluded. Das (6–7) cogently argues that circumcision was not akin to dipping one's toe in the pool of Torah—rather, it was the plunge into a Torah-observant lifestyle, the mark of conversion to the Jewish way of life.

One possibility here that does not appear to have received much attention in the history of the question is that the rival teachers, regarding Jesus's sacrifice as the sufficient act of atonement between humans (both Jews and gentiles) and the one God, understood the cultic law laid down in the Torah—the prescriptions for sin offerings, sacrifices of atonement, even thank offerings—to have been rendered obsolete by Jesus's once-for-all offering of himself. At

the church. Like Paul, they sought to enable Jew and gentile to come together in Christ in one worshiping body, the one body of the redeemed. Unlike Paul, they believed it was essential that the gentiles, and not the Jews, alter their behavior to make that fellowship possible. This particular issue appears to stand at the heart of the dispute in Antioch related by Paul in Gal 2:11–14.

The rival teachers acted out of their own zeal for the Torah and their commitment to keep God's people distinct from all the other peoples of the earth, as required by the Holiness Code of Leviticus. Luke relates a particular rumor about Paul that was, he claims, running rampant in Jerusalem, to the effect that Paul was leading Jews to abandon the Torah and forsake the covenant (Acts 21:20–21). Such a rumor was not entirely inaccurate. Paul claims to have become a Jew to Jews and gentile to gentiles (1 Cor 9:19–23). He flouted deeply cherished taboos held by at least some Second Temple Jews concerning table fellowship with gentiles by eating at the same table with his uncircumcised gentile converts, perhaps even eating food improper for Jews (1 Cor 10:25–30). He encouraged his Jewish coworkers (such as Barnabas, before his "course correction" in Antioch; Gal 2:11–14) to do the same for the sake of the mission and the gospel, setting aside those restrictions within Torah designed to keep Jews from freely associating with gentiles, and hence being polluted by those contacts. Moreover, he encouraged his Jewish converts to do the same with regard to his gentile converts, to "welcome one another as Christ welcomed you" (Rom 15:7), and to regard the keeping of kosher laws or special observances of Sabbaths and other days as matters of personal choice (Rom 14:1–6).[22] Paul might well have been seen to promote willful neglect of, if not apostasy from, the covenant in his demolition of the palisades that *God* erected to keep his holy people separate from the nations.[23]

---

the core of Paul's dissuasive argument, however, is the claim that taking on Torah now as the means of aligning oneself with God's righteousness and arriving at the goal of "life" means a complete repudiation of the grace shown by God in Christ, cutting one off from the benefits of the latter (2:20–21; 5:2–4). Thus, if one seeks righteousness by means of Torah, one also must return to seeking forgiveness for sins by the means prescribed by Torah, since "Christ will be of no benefit to you" (5:2). One can no longer seek shelter at the foot of the cross. The *whole* law thus means more than the rival teachers have communicated, being ignorant themselves of the incompatibility of Torah and Christ (thus they too are unduly selective in their Torah observance and not doing "the whole law").

22. Even though Romans is itself considerably later, such texts clearly reflect Paul's position already in the practice of the Antiochene church prior to the Antioch incident and in the letter to the Galatians.

23. There were no doubt a wide variety of convictions and practices concerning table fellowship with gentiles among first-century Jews. A number of texts, however, stemming from a variety of provenances and settings identify separation from the gentiles (and their negative theological and ethical influence) as a major goal of Torah's legislation concerning clean and unclean foods, to the extent that Torah itself came, in some circles, to be under-

For Jewish Christians convinced of the eternal validity of the Torah and the covenant it sustained, Paul's teaching and practice on this point would be unacceptable.[24] Indeed, Paul would be seen to be endangering the Jewish people as a whole by loosening *Jewish* Christians' commitment to observe the boundary-maintaining laws of Torah faithfully and rigorously. After all, the God who enforced the covenant promised all the curses of Deut 27–28 upon the nation of Israel if they should neglect and transgress the covenant, walking in the ways of the non-Jewish nations, a promise that had proven all too reliable throughout Israel's history.[25]

For Jewish Christians who might themselves be disposed to agree with Paul in principle, there was also the very real danger posed by more zealous, non-Christian Jews, who often reacted vigorously and violently when their fellow Jews turned away from Torah for the sake of mingling more easily with the gentiles. Zeal for the Torah had led Paul himself to persecute Jewish Christians prior to his own conversion (Gal 1:13–14, 23; Phil 3:6) and had led other non-Christian Jews to continue to apply significant pressure on Chris-

---

stood to forbid table fellowship between Jew and non-Jew. See excursus "Eating with Gentiles" on pp. 198–203 below. On the effectiveness of Torah observance vis-à-vis the restriction of social intercourse between Jews and gentiles, see deSilva, *The Apocrypha*, 95–100, and *Introducing the Apocrypha*, 315–17; Das, 223–30.

24. Paul's view of the Torah as a kind of stopgap measure between Moses and the coming of the Messiah, which he develops in Gal 3:15–25; 4:1–7, stands in stark contrast with the view of the Torah promoted, for example, by the authors of Jubilees and Testaments of the Twelve Patriarchs. In these writings, God's holy people have *always* lived in alignment with Torah, even in the patriarchal period long before the Torah was delivered at Sinai. Thus Abraham, Isaac, Jacob, and the patriarchs observed the Festival of Weeks (Jub. 6.19) and the Festival of Tabernacles (16.27–29), as it was decreed "in the heavenly tablets" (6.17; 16.28–29). Isaac teaches Levi "the law of the priesthood, of sacrifices, of whole-offerings, of first-fruits, of freewill-offerings, of peace offerings" (T. Levi 9.6–7), the requirements for ritual purification both before and after offering sacrifices, the requirements of offering only clean animals, rules for what kind of wood to use for burnt offerings, and the necessity of adding salt to sacrifices (9.9–14; on the last topic, see Lev. 2:13). In Jubilees, Abraham gives these instructions to Isaac (see 21.5–18). As there was never a time in the past, then, that the Torah did not govern the practice of God's people, it could reasonably be expected that God's holy people would *always* walk in the light of God's law. In regard to the command to observe the Feast of Tabernacles (though this could indeed have been said of every commandment), the author of Jubilees writes: "And to this there is no time limit; for it is ordained for ever concerning Israel" (16.30).

25. The Deuteronomistic History of 1 Samuel–2 Kings interprets the decline of the monarchy and eventual conquest of Israel by Assyria and Judah by Babylon in these terms, to the point of recontextualizing several of the details of the Deuteronomistic curses in the narration of Nebuchadnezzar's actions against Jerusalem and the temple. Similarly, 2 Maccabees quite explicitly interprets the history of the Hellenizing reform and its aftermath within the Deuteronomistic framework (see esp. 2 Macc 4:16–17; 5:17–20; 6:12–17; 7:30–38).

tian Jews. This kind of activity is evident, for example, from 1 Thess 2:14–16, in which Paul speaks of his converts (certainly, in light of 1:9–10, including a strong gentile representation) in Thessalonica as "imitators of the churches of God in Christ Jesus that are in Judea, for you suffered the same things from your own compatriots as they did from the Jews, who killed both the Lord Jesus and the prophets, and drove us out; they displease God and oppose everyone by hindering us from speaking to the gentiles so that they may be saved" (NRSV). Paul reflects here two levels of pressure and violence perpetrated by Torah-observant Jews on other Jews who were less observant or less overtly committed to central pillars of Jewish identity: pressure exerted upon Christian Jews in Judea, and pressure exerted upon Christian Jewish missionaries like Paul on account of his approach to the question of gentile inclusion.[26] Such expressions of zeal for the Torah and the covenant were firmly rooted in the tradition of Phinehas, who struck down an Israelite man and his Moabite lover and so won for himself the promise of perpetual priesthood and saved Israel from being destroyed by a plague for its apostasy (Num 25:1–13). It was rooted in the tradition of Mattathias and his sons at the outset of the Maccabean Revolt, as they purged Israel of the apostate and lapsed Jews from its midst and thus "turned away [God's] wrath from Israel" (1 Macc 2:15–28, 42–48; 3:6, 8). It is also evidenced in diaspora settings, as, for example, in the reaction of covenant-committed Jews to those Jews who were favorably disposed to accept a fictitious Ptolemy's offer of citizenship and enfranchisement at the cost of leaving behind the socially isolating behaviors for which the Jewish population was known (see esp. 3 Macc 2:31–33; 7:10–15, which, though fictitious, reflects real tensions and pressures).[27]

A significant movement within Jewish Christianity therefore wanted to make it clear to both non-Christian and Christian Jews that the Jesus move-

---

26. Acts provides corroborative testimony both concerning Paul's former activity as a persecutor of the Jesus movement (7:58; 8:1–4; 9:1–6, 21) and concerning the opposition of Jewish communities to figures like Stephen and Paul, whom they considered to be speaking and acting against the covenant. Particularly important is the elders' report of the reason for Jewish opposition to Paul: "You see, brother, how many thousands of believers there are among the Jews, and they are all zealous for the law. They have been told about you that you teach all the Jews living among the gentiles to forsake Moses, and that you tell them not to circumcise their children or observe the customs" (21:20–21 NRSV).

27. Robert Jewett ("Agitators and the Galatian Congregations") suggests that the rival teachers undertook their Judaizing mission specifically as a means of appeasing the growing Zealot party at home, for whom Jewish association with gentiles was highly suspect and might provoke reprisals. While he is right to take seriously the indications in Galatians that non-Christian Jews are putting significant pressure on Jewish Christians (and perhaps gentile Christians as well), "pressure from the Zealots in Judea" represents "only one possible background" (so, rightly, Borgen, "Paul Preaches Circumcision," 42).

ment was in no way a movement that promoted apostasy from the ancestral law. By reinforcing Jewish (Christian) adherence to the Torah, and all the more by bringing gentiles to the light of the law, the rival teachers could save themselves, the church in Judea, and the churches in the diaspora where non-Christian Jewish communities were strong from the intramural persecution that perceived apostasy could invite. Judaism could tolerate Messianic sects, but not the negation of its most central identity markers (like circumcision, Sabbath-obedience, and care regarding foods).

It is impossible to say, however, that the particular rival teachers Paul confronts in Galatia were primarily motivated by a desire to avoid persecution. It is equally likely that they chose their path based on their convictions concerning the eternal validity of the Torah as the way to live pleasingly before God, to have a part among God's covenant people, and thus to enter into the community of the promise. If encouraging gentile obedience to the Torah provoked strong opposition from the Roman or local gentile authorities, they might well have embraced persecution for their devotion to the Torah, in the tradition of the martyrs of the Maccabean period, whose devotion to the Torah was tested and proven through their endurance of torture to the point of death, a devotion that Jews would prove again in many different contexts (e.g., in the pogroms in Alexandria, Egypt, during the reign of Caligula, in persecutions in various Greek cities during the First Jewish War and following the Diaspora Revolt, and of course in persecutions by Christians after the church merged with imperial power).[28]

IV. THE "GOOD NEWS" ACCORDING TO THE RIVAL TEACHERS

What, then, was the "other gospel" proclaimed by the rival teachers?[29] They have left no testimony of their own, but we can reconstruct plausible elements of their message from two sources. First, Paul's response to their message surely highlights the topics and the specific positions that his rivals used when they presented their case. In order for Paul's rebuttal to be a rebuttal at all, their message would have had to include points such as (1) circumcision is the manner by which one joins the family of Abraham and becomes an heir

---

28. On the martyrs of the Hellenizing crisis, see 1 Macc 1:60–63; 2 Macc 6:10–11, 18–7:42; 4 Macc 5:1–17:1. The story of the martyrs in Alexandria—Jewish women who refused to eat pork to escape torture and death—is told in Philo, *Against Flaccus* 96.

29. See Martyn, "Law-Observant Mission," 321–23, for a similar exercise in the imaginative reconstruction of the rival teachers' message.

of the promises given to Abraham; (2) Christ's death allows both Jews and gentiles to enter together anew into the historic covenant God has made with God's people, the Torah, which is God's gift to all who would "choose life"; and (3) the Torah is God's gracious provision for us to make progress in our life in Christ and in our struggle to master the passions of the flesh and to experience freedom from their power over us.

Second, this information can be supplemented by investigating primary texts that display Jewish reflection about these topics or that advance positions similar to those Paul feels compelled to address in Galatians. Hellenistic Jews energetically sought to build bridges with Greek culture, and many of their writings have survived in which they explain the benefits and wisdom of keeping Torah and of circumcision. It is plausible that the rival teachers would have had at their disposal, if not these texts themselves, at least many well-articulated and widely attested arguments of the types found therein as resources for their own attempts to bring gentiles over to the Jewish way of life.

A. THE CASE FOR CIRCUMCISION

In the opinion of gentiles, the Jewish rite of circumcision was not one of the more admirable features of the Jewish way of life, though it was certainly the best known. It was largely regarded as a barbaric mutilation of the human form. Poseidonius (a Greek philosopher from the early first century BCE), though an admirer of Moses's theology and civil law, could explain the legislation concerning circumcision only as a later innovation among Moses's followers, part of the degeneration of Moses's enlightened vision into the superstition that Judaism had become in gentile eyes.[30] Philo, an Alexandrian Jew active in the first half of the first century CE, is well aware of such ridicule and writes to dispel such widespread prejudice (see esp. *On the Special Laws* 1.1.1-2). Apion, a trenchant gentile critic of Jewish practice who was Philo's contemporary and active in Alexandria and Rome, "derides the practice of circumcision" (Josephus, *Against Apion* 2.137; LCL). In the early years of the second century CE, the Roman writers Tacitus and Juvenal spoke of circumcision with disdain, alongside avoidance of pork and the observance of the Sabbath, as one of those strange things Jews do just to maintain their distinctiveness and distance from people of other *ethnoi*.[31] What would make

---

30. As represented in Strabo, *Geography* 16.760-61. On gentile criticism of Judaism and Jewish apologetics, see Feldman and Reinhold, *Jewish Life and Thought*, 350-95; Feldman, *Jew and Gentile*, 107-76; Conzelman, *Gentiles, Jews, Christians*, 45-133. A brief synthesis appears in deSilva, *Introduction to the New Testament*, 100-105.

31. Tacitus, *Histories* 5.5.1-2; Juvenal, *Satires* 14.98-106.

circumcision suddenly so appealing, so pressing an option, for the gentile Christians in Galatia?

The Jewish Scriptures promoted circumcision as a positive and powerful ritual. Paul himself had affirmed the value of the Jewish Scriptures in his preaching, looking to these texts as essential resources for knowing the one God and for understanding the believers' place in God's family. The rival teachers were able to ground their message fully in the sacred Scriptures themselves. After all, Scripture says that the promises were given to Abraham and his children (Gen 13:15; 17:8; 24:7). And how did one become a part of the family of Abraham? How does one become an heir of the promises given to Abraham? The Scriptures are unambiguous on this point—through circumcision.

When God made the covenant with Abraham, promising him that he would be the "ancestor of a multitude of nations," God gave Abraham circumcision as the absolute, unavoidable, and essential sign of that covenant: "This is my covenant, which you shall keep, between me and you and your offspring after you: Every male among you shall be circumcised. . . . Any uncircumcised male who is not circumcised in the flesh of his foreskin shall be cut off from his people; he has broken my covenant" (Gen 17:10, 14 NRSV). Gentiles wishing to join God's people must likewise circumcise themselves, following both the command of God and the example of Abraham, the first gentile proselyte![32] The rule for the incorporation of the gentile sojourner into the life and worship of the ancient community of Israel (Exod 12:48–49) continues to be in force. Moreover, only the circumcised have any part in the heavenly Zion, the life of the age to come, for it is written:

> Awake, awake,
> put on your strength, O Zion!
> Put on your beautiful garments,
> O Jerusalem, the holy city;
> for the uncircumcised and the unclean
> shall enter you no more. (Isa 52:1 NRSV)

Likewise Ezekiel, speaking of the eschatological temple, says: "Thus says the Lord GOD: No foreigner, uncircumcised in heart and flesh, of all the foreigners who are among the people of Israel, shall enter my sanctuary" (44:9

---

32. Barclay, *Obeying the Truth*, 52–54. For early Jewish texts describing Abraham as a model gentile convert to the worship of the one God, see Apoc. Ab. 1–8; Jub. 11.15–17; Philo, *On the Virtues* 212–16. Circumcision figured prominently wherever gentiles joined themselves to the people of Israel, both in literary fiction (as in the story of Achior in Jdt 14:10) and historical report (as in Josephus, *Jewish Antiquities* 13.257–58, 318).

NRSV). The sacred oracles of God demonstrate, therefore, that circumcision is the means by which to join Abraham's family and God's people and the prerequisite to participating in the age to come.[33]

Circumcision, moreover, has great moral significance, as do all the Jewish laws and customs when viewed symbolically and observed in both mind and body. Circumcision symbolizes the cutting away of pleasures and the passions of the flesh, which lead the reason astray from its proper course, as well as an acknowledgment that the human male is not capable of producing offspring without the help of God, and therefore also a remedy for pride.[34] The rite may also be seen as a symbolic initiation into a way of life that will make for the mastery of the passions—those desires, sensations, and emotions that belong to our human nature and so often hinder us from following the dictates of virtue and righteousness.[35]

B. TORAH AS THE WAY TO PERFECTION

Circumcision is a good beginning, but it is only an initiation. God's covenant was made with Israel in the Torah, and all who hope to share in the blessings

---

33. Jewish texts from the Second Temple period make significantly grander claims concerning circumcision. For example, Jubilees speaks of circumcision as "an eternal ordinance, ordained and written on the heavenly tablets. And every one that is born, the flesh of whose foreskin is not circumcised on the eighth day, belongs not to the children of the covenant which the Lord made with Abraham, but to the children of destruction; nor is there, moreover, any sign on him that he is the Lord's, but [he is destined] to be destroyed and slain from the earth, and to be rooted out of the earth, for he has broken the covenant of the Lord our God" (15.25–26, APOT). An unnamed rabbi (making dating the tradition impossible) says of circumcision: "Circumcision is eminent, for in spite of all the pious deeds of Abraham he was not called 'perfect' until after his circumcision, as it is written, 'Walk before me and be perfect'" (m. Ned. 3.11). For further rabbinic texts on circumcision and uncircumcision, see Hoenig, "Circumcision."

34. See Philo, *On the Migration of Abraham* 89, 92; *Special Laws* 1.2.9–11; *Questions and Answers on Genesis* 3.48. For further discussion of Philo's analysis of circumcision's significance in the context of debates about the rite and proselytizing, see Borgen, *Philo, John, and Paul*, 61–71, 233–54.

35. Many Jews would not have regarded circumcision as a requirement for gentile *salvation*, which depended rather only on following a minimum number of requirements generally associated with the covenant with Noah, typically involving the avoidance of idolatry, murder, theft, incest, blasphemy, and eating the flesh of living creatures, as well as the establishment of law courts and making provision for justice (see b. Sanh. 56b; Segal, *Paul the Convert*, 194–201). There was a spectrum of views concerning how far gentiles needed to move toward becoming Jews in order to be saved, with some, but by no means all, voicing the opinion that full conversion to Judaism was in fact required (Segal, *Paul the Convert*, 217; see also Fredriksen, "Judaism, the Circumcision of Gentiles," 534–48).

of Israel and avoid the curses upon the disobedient must submit to the yoke of Torah, as it stands written, "Cursed be everyone who does not uphold the words of this law by observing them" (Deut 27:26 NRSV). It is by keeping God's "statutes and ordinances" that "one shall live" (Lev 18:5),[36] as God makes abundantly clear in his invitation:

> I have set before you today life and prosperity, death and adversity. If you obey the commandments of the LORD your God that I am commanding you today, by loving the LORD your God, walking in his ways, and observing his commandments, decrees, and ordinances, then you shall live and become numerous, and the LORD your God will bless you in the land that you are entering to possess. . . . I call heaven and earth to witness against you today that I have set before you life and death, blessings and curses. Choose life so that you and your descendants may live, loving the LORD your God, obeying him, and holding fast to him; for that means life to you and length of days. (Deut 30:15–16, 19–20)

By obeying God's commandments, one can be assured of being acquitted as righteous when God comes to judge the earth. If God will judge each person in accordance with his or her deeds,[37] how better to prepare for that day than by living in line with the works God has prescribed in God's law? When asked how one might have eternal life, did not even Jesus himself respond, "If you wish to enter into life, keep the commandments" (Matt 19:17; see also Mark 10:19)? It is therefore not for the sake of this life only that we must align ourselves with the practices laid out in the Torah.

The way of life prescribed by Torah is far from a collection of barbaric, ethnocentric rules, as some gentile critics claimed. The giving of the Torah was a supreme manifestation of divine favor.[38] For the person who is confused about how to make progress in living a God-pleasing life of virtue, as the newly converted might well be, Torah provides the God-given guide for the perplexed. Jewish defenses of the enlightened quality of the Torah focused on the virtues that a Torah-observant way of life nurtured. Philo, as we have already seen in regard to circumcision, draws out the hidden moral mean-

---

36. Paul recites Deut 27:26 and Lev 18:5 in Gal 3:10, 12, but it appears he is pushed to take account of them because they are significant pieces of the rival teachers' argument (Das, 7–8).

37. This view is a commonplace in Scripture: see Ps 62:11–12; Prov 24:12; Isa 59:18; Jer 17:10; Ezek 24:14; Eccl 12:14; Sir 16:12.

38. Dunn, 16–17. Many Second Temple Jewish authors spoke of the giving of Torah as an act of God's grace toward Israel (e.g., Sir 24:7–8, 10–12, 23; Bar 3:23–4:1, 4; 4 Macc 2:21–23; see deSilva, *Apocrypha*, 37–43). On Jewish attitudes toward the law, see Lichtenberger, "Understanding of the Torah."

ing behind the particular commands that most clearly distinguish Jews from gentiles. The author of the Letter of Aristeas, a Hellenistic Jewish text from the second century BCE, takes a similar approach.[39] For example, he explains that the dietary laws are to be understood in terms of the characteristics of the particular animals that are classified as either clean or unclean, commending the virtues of the clean animals and warning against imitation of the unclean (128–69). Vultures and eagles are unclean because they live by feeding on the dead bodies of other creatures or preying violently upon weaker animals, teaching Jews never to prey upon the weak or the vulnerable. Weasels are unclean because they conceive through their ears and give birth through their mouths (apparently ancient zoology had a few holes in its research!), teaching Jews not to participate in internalizing or passing along gossip. Animals that have split hooves and chew their cud are designated as clean, commending to Jews the virtue of distinguishing carefully between virtue and vice and setting their foot only upon the virtuous path (the split hoof) and of always meditating on virtue and righteousness ("ruminating").[40]

One particular Hellenistic Jewish defense of the value of Torah, 4 Maccabees, provides an exceptionally informative background. This book offers itself as a philosophical "demonstration" of the thesis that the mind that has been trained by following Torah is able to master the passions (4 Macc 1:1, 13–17). Rising above these passions was a central topic of Greco-Roman philosophical ethics, since the passions—whether emotions like fear or anger, sensations like pleasure or pain, or desires like greed or lust—were deemed the most potent obstacles to living a virtuous life.[41] Unchecked, the passions would clamor louder than one's reasoning faculty, derailing a person's commitment to virtue and ability to walk in line with virtue. The battle

---

39. On the provenance and date of Letter of Aristeas, see Wright, *Aristeas*, 16–30.

40. Both Philo and the author of Letter of Aristeas support obedience to the commandments themselves, alongside appreciation of their moral or philosophical lessons, such that learning the latter does not render actual obedience obsolete or optional (see esp. Philo, *Migration* 86–93. For the author of Aristeas (139, 142), it is the *literal* fulfillment that creates the sociological boundaries that protect the distinctive ideology of the Jewish *ethnos*.

41. According to the author of Letter of Aristeas, the essence of philosophy is "to deliberate well over every contingency and not to be carried away by impulses, but to ponder the injuries which are the outcome of the passions, and to perform the duties of the moment properly, with passions moderated" (256). The same author identifies the highest rule to be the ability "to rule oneself and not be carried away by passions" (221–22). On the importance of equipping reason to master (or, in the case of hardline Stoics, extirpate) the passions, see also, for example, Plato, *Phaedo* 93–94; Cicero, *Tusculan Disputations* 3.22; 4.38, 57; Plutarch, *On Moral Virtue* 1 (*Moralia* 440D), 3 (*Moralia* 442A–443D). These and other texts are discussed in deSilva, *4 Maccabees*, 52–58; and *4 Maccabees: Introduction and Commentary*, 67–78, 84–91.

against these forces became the true battle for honor, the truly noble athletic competition.

The Jewish law provides a complete exercise regimen for strengthening the rational faculty and subduing the passions. The dietary laws and prohibitions against coveting exercise one in self-control (4 Macc 1:31–2:6a); the regulations concerning debt-release and leaving the gleanings of the harvest subdue greed (2:7–9a); limits on vengeance and actions against enemies subdue the passion of enmity or hate (2:14). Torah is to be valued because it "teaches us self-control, so that we can have control over any pleasure or desire. It trains us to be brave, so that we willingly bear any suffering. It educates us about justice, so that it is always our custom to treat everyone fairly. It educates us in the godly way of life, so that we worship with due respect the only God who really exists" (5:23–24 CEB).

This is precisely the kind of argumentation that the rival teachers would have had ready at hand to use as they encountered the Galatian converts, still painfully aware of being at the mercy of their own fleshly impulses and desires.[42] The final chapters of Paul's letter (5:13–6:10) have sometimes been viewed as an afterthought, a bit of moral exhortation added to the letter once the real argument was completed. However, these chapters were an integral, essential part of his counterargument against the position of the rival teachers, who would have been readily able to present the Torah as the reliable guide to virtue and the Torah-observant life as the discipline that would develop virtue and inhibit vice that the Galatians knew they sorely needed.[43] The rival teachers presented the Torah as the best trainer in virtue, the way to perfection in terms of ethical progress, a proven discipline for mastering the "passions of the flesh." Paul, then, would have to demonstrate that the Galatians had already received all that they needed to rise above the passions and embody the virtues that God sought in God's people—in the Spirit, in which they were to learn to walk.

C. WHOM SHOULD THE GALATIANS TRUST?

Both Paul's defensiveness in Galatians and the well-established ancient rhetorical practice of attacking a rival's credibility in order to make room for one's own position make it highly likely that the Jewish Christian missionaries had

---

42. Barclay (*Obeying the Truth*, 62–65) rightly points to evidence indicating that the Galatian Christians "want to be under the law" (4:21) and are about to shoulder up again "a yoke of slavery" (5:1), hardly a danger "if the Galatians were not interested in observing the law" (63).

43. Betz, 72; Barclay, *Obeying the Truth*, 60–72.

called Paul's reliability into question on some points in the course of seeking to win the Galatian Christians over to their own position.[44] This is not to say that they came to Galatia with the *goal* of besmirching Paul or undermining his authority or that attacks on Paul constituted a *primary* element of their message or that they would necessarily have considered Paul particularly as an enemy in the area of mission.[45] However, these rival teachers would at the very least have needed to provide an answer to a basic question likely to have been posed by the Galatian believers about the difference between Paul's earlier presentation of the gospel and the new emphases they were hearing from the more recently arrived teachers: "Why did Paul not tell us any of this, and why should we trust *you* on these matters when our beloved Paul said nothing about circumcision or taking on the yoke of Torah?" The rivals' commendation of their own position over Paul's position, which would to some extent entail their commendation of their own credibility over Paul's credibility as well, would necessarily have cast Paul and his message in a less favorable light.

The question of how the rival teachers viewed themselves and their mission vis-à-vis Paul and his mission is admittedly a complex one, as we have only Paul's response to them and their *perceived* attack on his authority and work. They have been traditionally viewed as entering upon their mission specifically to *correct* Paul's gospel, cleaning up after him, as it were. Given Paul's prior history with Jewish Christians who affirmed the ongoing validity

---

44. This conclusion was reached as early as the fifth century by John Chrysostom (2). A number of scholars have argued, however, that one can understand the opening chapters of Galatians without the supposition that the rival teachers have made allegations about Paul's apostleship and character. See, for example, Lategan, "Is Paul Defending?"; Vos, "Paul's Argumentation"; Dodd, "Christ's Slave."

45. In this regard, Witherington's suggestion (25) that the rival teachers did not come *overtly* attacking Paul's apostleship is not objectionable, though it needs to be balanced against the fact that the rival teachers' advocacy of Torah observance as a vital facet of the Christian life for Jews and gentiles—and their investment in winning *Paul's* converts over to their way of thinking—implies their own questioning of the adequacy of Paul's message and thus also his reliability or credibility as a representative of the gospel.

Howard (*Crisis in Galatia*, 9) suggests even more unconventionally that the rival teachers understood themselves to be "completing" Paul's gospel and mission work by introducing Torah, even to be amicably disposed to Paul, considering him their ally in a mission equally dependent upon the Jerusalem apostles. The inordinate attention Paul gives to establishing his credibility suggests, to the contrary, that the rival teachers were *not* amicably disposed toward Paul. He raises specific topics concerning his consistency in a manner suggesting that specific suggestions to the contrary had first been made by others. Galatians 1:10 has the character of rebuttal rather than thesis statement. One says "Am I *now* catering to people?" most naturally after someone else has said "He is given to people-pleasing." See also 5:11 and commentary.

of Torah as the bedrock of covenant with God (both the old covenant of Sinai and the new covenant of Jer 31, which they would have identified as a renewal of the former covenant), this motive is plausible. Paul himself speaks of a previous confrontation with "false brothers" in Jerusalem who took issue with his mission (specifically, his noncircumcision of Titus and the "freedom" his converts enjoyed, presumably freedom from aligning their practice with the Torah's stipulations; Gal 2:3–5). Paul gives no indication that the Jerusalem apostles satisfied these "false brothers" in regard to their concerns about him and speaks only of his stubborn resistance against them and their case. Paul also gives indications in his recounting of the Antioch incident (Gal 2:11–14) of Christian Jews who were not at all happy with the degree of social interaction between uncircumcised gentile Christians and (properly) circumcised Jewish Christians that he promoted. Acts tells of a mission from Jerusalem to Antioch specifically bringing a law-observant mission to a Torah-neutral Christian community that had been in existence—and under the influence of Paul and Barnabas—for quite some time (Acts 15:1–2). There were certainly Jewish Christians "out there" who were active in lobbying for a different understanding of the gospel than Paul's and were willing to travel to promote this different understanding, regarding Paul as at least deficient in the theology and practice he promoted.

None of the aforementioned groups, however, are clearly to be identified with the rival teachers who came into Galatia, so the rival teachers' precise attitude concerning Paul must remain uncertain, except for the fact that they disagreed with him on what was, for both parties, a significant (for Paul, a deal-breaking!) point and were essentially *re*-evangelizing his converts. The addition of Torah observance could hardly be described as a friendly amendment to Paul's gospel, which they deemed inadequate in itself. Their approach to the question of Paul's authority and mission among the Galatian Christians, however, may have been quite subtle by comparison with Paul's reaction: "We are genuinely surprised that Paul failed to tell you about all of this. We can hardly imagine what his reasons were, all the more as he has promoted circumcision elsewhere."

Judging from Paul's response, their attempts to establish their greater credibility as representatives of the gospel would have plausibly included the following elements. First, the rival teachers claimed to represent the Jerusalem apostles, who supposedly supported a much stricter observance of Torah than Paul. James was well known for his piety, even among non-Christian Jews. Peter had wavered on this issue, but the rival teachers themselves might have been the first to bring up the Antioch incident (Gal 2:11–14) to prove that Peter had come to his senses and remained true to the original, Torah-observant gospel. Second, they likely claimed that Paul's authority and knowledge of the gospel—like those of the rival teachers themselves—are dependent upon the Jerusalem "pillars," as Paul's travels to Jerusalem demonstrate.[46] If Paul's message differs from the rival teachers' message, then, it is *Paul* who has been an unreliable and unfaithful messenger (contrast Gal 1–2). Third, they appear to have asserted that Paul preached circumcision in other instances, so it is a mystery why he failed to do so in Galatia as well (contrast Paul's counterclaims in Gal 5:11; 6:15). Perhaps he thought it would make his mission less successful here, so he left it out in order to make the gospel more winsome. Whatever his reasons for not preaching "the whole truth of the gospel," they were not ultimately in the Galatians' best interests. Such allegations provide the cause, the effect of which is evident throughout Galatians, namely, Paul's repeated attention to reestablishing his own credibility in the Galatians' eyes as prerequisite to influencing their ongoing formation (Gal 1:1–2:14; 4:12–20; 5:7–12; 6:11–17).[47]

The rival teachers assured the Galatians that, unlike Paul, *they* would teach the people the whole truth. Even though it involved difficulties, like the rite of circumcision, they would not keep anything back from the Galatian Christians just to win their assent. The plain sense of Scripture supported their position. The Galatians could trust these teachers to take them on the next step in their journey toward righteousness, moving them further toward their goal (the "perfection" or "completion" of the journey they began when they trusted Jesus; see Gal 3:3).

Such a reconstruction of the rival teachers' position would well account for each of the three major parts of Paul's response to the situation in Galatia—the opening portion, focusing on issues of Paul's call, confirmation of the

---

46. The attention that Paul gives to his interactions with the Jerusalem leadership (directly in 1:17–19; 2:1–10; indirectly in 1:1, 11–12) is most easily accounted for on the theory that he is not merely affirming the divine source of his gospel but also denying the role of human beings in the communication of the gospel to him and in his commissioning in the face of some affirmation to this effect made by the rival teachers. Francis Watson (*Paul, Judaism, and the Gentiles*, 60) correctly observes that "it is not necessarily true to say that Paul's opponents *criticized* him for his dependence on Jerusalem. It seems that their case against him was in two parts: they *asserted* that his authority was dependent on the Jerusalem leaders, and they *criticized* him for defying those leaders at Antioch."

47. Scholars overstate the contrary case when they attribute this supposition to "unnecessary and excessive mirror-reading" (Das, 75) or claim that "there is not a shred of evidence . . . that the 'agitators' had questioned [Paul's] authority" (Witherington, 71). Nor can we view Gal 1–2 merely as "Paul taking the offensive" (Schütz, *Anatomy of Apostolic Authority*, 127–28) against the rival teachers (though I would affirm that Paul *also* takes the offensive), for 1:11–2:14 argues precisely *defensive* points. Aside from 1:10 and 5:11 both suggesting that Paul is responding to an allegation that he at least *believes* to have been made about him, the whole narration of 1:11–2:14 (in terms of purposeful selection of events and emphasized points) is best explained as Paul setting straight a record that has to some extent been called into question.

same, and steadfastness therein (1:10–2:21); the middle portion, constituting a series of arguments against making a place now for reliance on the Torah in one's walk with God (3:1–4:21); and the closing portion, turning to focus on ethical guidance (5:13–6:10). In effect, Paul appears to be addressing three primary questions:

1. Why should the Galatians trust Paul rather than the rival teachers?
2. What are we to say about the role of Torah and circumcision in God's economy, and thus the Christian's relationship to the law given by God, in response to the "other gospel," which is no gospel?
3. If we aren't going to rely on Torah to help us progress toward righteousness before God, what do we have to guide us?

Each of these questions, and therefore every part of Galatians, can be read as integral to the challenge posed by the situation in Galatia.

V. WHO WERE THE GALATIAN CHRISTIANS?

The Christians Paul addresses were Paul's own converts, with whom he felt he had established a deeply personal connection (Gal 4:12–15). He calls them his children, in line with his tendency to use the language of parenting or nursing when referring to his relationship to people whom he has personally brought to faith in Christ (Gal 4:19; see also 1 Cor 4:14–15 and 1 Thess 2:7–8, 11–12). These might be rather recent converts, if Paul's remark of astonishment is to be read as indicating the small amount of time that has passed since their first invitation into God's favor (1:6), though other readings of this verse are certainly possible.

Gentile converts self-evidently constitute a substantial portion of the audience. It is for such people that the question of whether or not to accept circumcision would have *been* a question (rather than a fait accompli), and therefore the bulk of Paul's argumentation is most obviously directed to the gentile Christians among the congregations as he tries to persuade them that their attraction to the rite reveals a misalignment of their theology and trust. We should not, however, conclude too quickly that Jewish converts were not also a part of the congregations addressed by Paul.[48] Despite Paul's focus on

---

48. Martyn, 16, for example, remarks that Paul makes no distinction in his letter between gentile Christians, who would be contemplating circumcision, and Jewish Christians, for whom the question of whether or not to receive circumcision was rendered moot by their parents on their eighth day of life. He finds nothing said about the harmlessness of the

the imminent choices facing his gentile converts, much of what Paul says in Galatians would speak to any Jewish Christian bystanders in the congregations, giving them adequate guidance concerning how to process the fact of their own circumcision (2:15–16; 3:23–26; 4:4–7; 5:5–6; 6:15–16). A Jewish Christian would not be threatened by Paul's dire words concerning the consequences of circumcisions performed *now* (Gal 5:2–4); rather, Paul clearly regards as harmless (though also of no particular advantage) those circumcisions already performed upon the bodies of Jewish males who have since come to trust in Christ: "Neither circumcision nor uncircumcision matters, but only faith working through love" or "a new creation" (5:6; 6:15).

While the presence of Jewish Christians among the Galatian congregations cannot be positively proven, any more than their presence can be ruled out, several factors weigh in favor of their presence. First, Paul is particularly interested in creating *one* people of God out of the two peoples formerly alienated from one another by virtue of the boundary-maintaining power of the Torah. Ephesians 2:11–22 celebrates this goal as the heartbeat of Paul's mission (whether Ephesians comes from Paul's hand or that of another familiar with his mission). The church in Syrian Antioch was of vital importance in Paul's formation and early practice of evangelism, and it was a church that particularly modeled the bringing together of Jews and gentiles into one fellowship, one people, in Christ. It would be his model for his ongoing efforts west of that city. The "Antioch incident" that Paul recounts (Gal 2:11–14), moreover, represented a dangerous threat to this unity, and Paul's (over)reaction to the behavior of Peter, Barnabas, and the other Jewish Christians in that church is a measure of his passion for this unity. By withdrawing to separate tables, Peter, Barnabas, and the other Jewish Christians were only reaffirming Jewish commitment to live by Torah. It is only because Paul could not conceive of a divided church—a church of Jewish Christians and a church of gentile Christians—that he interpreted this withdrawal as an act that would "compel the gentiles to take up the Jewish way of life" (Gal 2:14b). Second, the pattern of Paul's preaching in Acts, to the extent that it reflects known Pauline practice (which is likely, since its author appears to have been a member of the Pauline

---

circumcision received by Jewish males prior to their coming to faith in Jesus. Paul explicitly speaks of the idolatrous past of his addressees (4:8–9), differentiating no one in the audience who had previously worshiped the God of Israel. Martyn, 16, uses these observations to support a North Galatian destination, on the supposition that, as far as we know, the cities there housed no Jewish population in the mid-first century CE. Martyn's observations do not, in my opinion, adequately take into account the nature of the focal problem (see also Longenecker, lxix, who considers this assumption to be "patently false"). His conclusion is just slightly less erroneous than the suggestion that there are no women among the congregations addressed by Galatians, since Paul says nothing explicitly to women comparable to the attention he gives to circumcision and the gentile Christian *men* contemplating it.

circle), consistently presents Paul beginning his mission work in a local synagogue, gathering a core of Jewish and "God-fearing" adherents (see, in regard to cities in the province of Galatia, Acts 13:43; 14:1), before moving out from there into the home of one of these early adherents to continue his outreach and his nurturing of a congregation, or simply moving on to a new location. Mixed congregations of Jewish and gentile Christians, then, would seem to be the norm in terms both of Paul's ecclesiology and of his reputed practice.

VI. GALATIANS IN ROMAN GEOGRAPHY AND PAULINE CHRONOLOGY

It is more difficult to answer the question, "*Where* were the Galatian Christians?" The geographic term "Galatia" could have been used to refer to the areas in north central Turkey where Gallic (Celtic) tribes began to settle in the third century BCE. As a major, distinctive ethnic group living in this region, these Gallic people gave their name to the area.[49] By the last decades of the first century BCE, however, it could also have been used to refer to the Roman province created by Augustus, a province that included most of the historic region of Celtic settlement in the north but was extended to south central Turkey to include the regions of Pisidia, Lycaonia, and part of Phrygia. These facts raise the question: when Paul used the terms "Galatia" (1:2) and "Galatians" (3:1), was he denoting residents of the ethnic region or members of the Roman province? If the latter, the term would allow us to understand the cities of southern Galatia (old Pisidia and Lycaonia) like Antioch, Iconium, Lystra, and Derbe, which Paul and Barnabas evangelized in the mission work narrated in Acts 13:14–14:23, as the location of the rival teachers' activity and the congregations affected.[50] If the former, Paul would almost *have* to be writing to churches in the major cities of northern Galatia

---

49. It does not appear to be the case, however, that the population was still particularly "Celtic" by the first century CE. While there is a higher percentage of Celtic names in inscriptions from the northern portion of the Roman province of Galatia than in inscriptions from the southern portion, Celtic names are significantly outnumbered by Phrygian and Greek names in both regions. See Mitchell, *Ankara District*, 377–95; Oakes, 17–18. Addressing people in either region as "Galatai" ("Celts") in an ethnic sense would be almost as inappropriate in Ancyra as in Antioch.

50. The fact that Luke himself does not refer to this region as Galatia in Acts 13–14 is not significant (against Moffatt, *Introduction*, 93). The important point is that these cities were, in fact, part of the province of Galatia and could be referred to as cities of Galatia. Whether Luke chose to do so is not determinative for the question of whether Paul would do so.

such as Ancyra, Pessinus, and Tavium, which he allegedly evangelized on the journey narrated in Acts 16:6; 18:23.

I will lay out here why I favor a South Galatian setting. The question is of some value in terms of developing a more precise picture of the place of Galatians (and its presenting situation) in the early church's process of discernment concerning the important questions of gentile inclusion and the conditions for commensality at the Lord's Supper among Jewish and gentile Christians. It is also important for one's understanding of the local context of the letter and how its presenting situation came about, as well as locating the letter in Paul's career and his developing theology. Here I will make the case for reading Galatians as perhaps Paul's earliest letter, written in the thick of the unresolved issues swirling around the question of how gentiles could become full participants alongside Jewish Christians in the assemblies of God in Christ. Scholars of considerable ability and repute, however, have weighed in favor of both the South Galatian and the North Galatian hypothesis,[51] so that one must admit that the evidence is inconclusive on either side.[52]

A. THE DATA WITHIN GALATIANS

In the majority of Paul's letters, the apostle addresses himself to Christian converts in a particular *city* (Rome, Corinth, Philippi, Thessalonica, Colossae, Ephesus), which has often proven to be of great help to scholars wishing to develop a more detailed picture of the congregation, its setting, and the correlations between the issues and challenges reflected in the letter and social, cultural, and archaeological realities.[53] It is not so evident in the case of "Ga-

---

51. On locating these churches in the northern territory of Galatia, see Lightfoot; Moffatt, *Introduction*, 83–107; Schnelle, *Apostle Paul*, 266–69. The "North Galatian hypothesis" reaches back into the patristic period, which is fully understandable, however, given that, by the mid-second century CE, the Roman province of Galatia had been reduced once again to its northern territories. Between 74 and 137 CE the territories of Lycaonia and Pisidia/Phrygia were detached from the province of Galatia and joined to other provinces, with the result that Antioch, Iconium, Lystra, and Derbe were no longer known as Galatian cities (Longenecker, lxiii). The patristic commentators on Galatians were simply reading the address in terms of their own contemporary geography (Bruce, 6). W. M. Ramsay made the classic case for locating these churches in the southern cities of Galatia in his *Historical Commentary on St. Paul's Epistle to the Galatians*; see also Hemer and Gempf, *Book of Acts*, 277–307. Longenecker (lxiii–lxxii) provides an exceptional summary of the issues involved and of the positions taken.

52. So rightly Bruce, 18; Dunn, 7.

53. Two of the most deservedly celebrated studies in this regard are Theissen, *Social Setting of Pauline Christianity,* and Meeks, *First Urban Christians*, each taking advantage of the wealth of archaeological, epigraphic, and literary data concerning Roman Corinth.

latians." The breadth of address—to multiple Christian assemblies in a given region—testifies to the broader nature of the problem confronted. The rival teachers' mission has not been confined to one city by the time Paul writes. He may write proleptically to some extent, warning assemblies that have not yet encountered the rival teachers about their mission and its dangers, but he writes as if primarily to multiple congregations that have already shown themselves receptive to the rivals' message.

Paul refers to his audience as "the churches of Galatia" in his salutation (1:2) and addresses them directly as "Galatians" (3:1). Paul's use of these terms in no way specifies the narrower territory within which the intended recipients reside, despite frequent claims to the contrary. While the terms may refer to the historic area of original Celtic migration in north central Anatolia and its residents,[54] by the time Paul writes, it may equally well refer to any part of the Roman province of Galatia, including the south central area of Paul's mission to Pisidian Antioch, Lystra, Iconium, and Derbe, irrespective of the various ethnicities represented among the people groups included therein. As early as the second century BCE, "the Phrygian origin of the larger half of the Galatian population was forgotten by ordinary people of the surrounding countries, and the whole state was thought of as Galatia and its people Galatians."[55] That is to say, the non-Celtic peoples living under the domination of the Celtic tribes that had migrated to the region came to think of themselves quite naturally as "Galatians" after a few generations. When Galatia was organized as a Roman province by Augustus and expanded to include Pisidia and Lycaonia in 25 BCE, the same would hold true.[56] Almost no one in Pisidian Antioch or Lystra living at the time of Paul's missionary work would have had a parent who would have remembered not being a part of the Galatian kingdom of Deiotarus (or his successor, Amyntas) or the Roman province of Galatia. The status of each person was that of a "provincial" as the Roman Empire designated provinces. It would be perfectly appropriate, and indeed only courteous, for a writer or orator to address a population by its provincial identity, not by its original ethnic identity or identities.[57] Hence, Paul would be following standard procedure by addressing *any* congregations within Galatia as "*Galatae*, i.e., members of the Roman empire as being members of the

---

54. Martyn, 16.

55. Ramsay, 84.

56. The cities of Antioch, Lystra, and their neighbors had in fact already been part of the kingdom of Galatia under Amyntas since at least 36 BCE (Mommsen, *Provinces*, 1:340).

57. Whether Paul ought to have called them "*foolish* Galatians" (Gal 3:1) is another matter. Against the dubious argument that calling the people of Pisidian Antioch or Lystra "Galatians" would be less preferable to them than being called "Phrygians and Lycaonians," Keener (*Acts 3:1–14:28*, 2119) rightly points out that Paul here is "hardly attending to their sensitivities."

Province Galatia."[58] More to the point, if Paul were addressing people from Antioch, Iconium, Lystra, and Derbe (i.e., people from the subregions of Phrygia and Lycaonia), no other single term besides "Galatians" would have been sufficiently inclusive for the audience.[59]

Paul provides a fair amount of historical and chronological data in this letter as well, which is best laid out on its own before being discussed in relation to Acts. From Galatians we learn that:

1. Paul formerly defined himself by his diligent observance of the Torah, claiming to have outpaced his peers in terms of bringing every aspect of his life and practice in line with Torah by means of the interpretative traditions then current among the Pharisaic school.[60] Motivated by this zeal for the Torah and the covenant, he applied pressure to Jews whose practice and convictions he deemed out of line with, or perhaps inimical to, the Mosaic covenant (1:13–14, 24).

2. Paul had a spiritual experience (which he describes as one in which God "imparted revelation," 1:15–16) that thoroughly changed his convictions concerning Jesus, the movement formed in his name, and God's relationship to God's people Israel and the gentile nations. This experience was redefining: his life prior to this experience had been "in Judaism" or "pursuing the Jewish way of life" (1:13) and was now something new.

3. Paul immediately went into "Arabia," probably meaning the more populated areas of the Nabatean kingdom, and then returned to Damascus (1:17), most likely engaging in evangelistic activity (fulfilling the commission communicated in his spiritual experience, 1:16).

4. "After three years" Paul traveled to Jerusalem to meet Peter, spending two weeks there and also seeing James the Just, Jesus's half-brother (1:18–19). He denied direct involvement in the life of Judean churches (1:22).

5. Paul then spent a significant time in the regions of Syria and of Cilicia, in the northeast corner of the Mediterranean basin, promoting the Jesus

---

58. Ramsay, 120. He points out further that, since foreigners were often associated with enemies or slaves, addressing an audience in terms of their ancient ethnic heritage rather than terms denoting inclusion within the empire would be insulting—all the more for any Roman citizens in the audience. Witherington, 4, cites several first-century inscriptions as evidence that the entire region, and not just the northern territory, was commonly called Galatia during Paul's lifetime.

59. Burton, xxix; Bruce, 16; Riesner, *Paul's Early Period*, 287; Das, 28. Hemer and Gempf (*Acts*, 289–99) and Breytenbach (*Paulus und Barnabas*, 150–51) have collected inscriptional evidence that residents in the southern cities of the province Galatia were, in fact, regularly referred to as Galatians.

60. Admittedly, this summary introduces evidence from Phil 3:5 at this point to name the party within Judaism with which Paul self-identified, but it is still firsthand testimony on Paul's part.

whose followers he once opposed (1:21), according to the report about him circulating in Judea, of which he had become aware (1:23–24).

6a. "After fourteen years" Paul went to Jerusalem again with Barnabas and Titus for a private meeting with Peter, James the Just, and John. At this meeting the Jerusalem pillars signaled their affirmation of Paul and Barnabas's work, their mutual understanding of working together in the same God-appointed and God-empowered cause, and the basic division of labor that would guide their major missionary emphases—"we to the gentiles, they to the circumcision" (2:1–2, 6–10). Paul reported that the pillars laid no conditions or obligations upon Paul and his mission, other than that he and Barnabas "continue to remember the poor" (2:10).

6b. In connection with this visit, more conservative Jewish Christians appear to have made a case to the pillars that Titus ought to have been circumcised as part of the process of assimilating him to the people of God in Christ. Paul thoroughly resisted their efforts, with the result that the pillars did not put their weight behind this recommendation (2:3–5).

7. Paul recounted an episode that transpired in Antioch, likely following his second trip to Jerusalem (since his entire narrative has been carefully sequential up to this point). He celebrated the fact that Jews and gentiles shared table fellowship together as part of the one people of God in Christ, and that Peter took part in this shared fellowship. In response to some (more conservative) Jewish Christians from Jerusalem ("from James," Paul says), however, Peter broke off this practice and ate separately from the gentile Christians, presumably with the visiting Jewish Christians. The other Jewish Christians in the Antioch congregation, including Barnabas, followed suit. Paul instigated a public confrontation on this matter (2:11–14).

8. Paul extended his evangelistic efforts to some part of the Roman province of Galatia. He attributes his work there to "a weakness of the flesh," likely an illness—one that could have caused his audience there to despise this unfavored messenger of divine favor. They did not, however, allow Paul's condition to get in the way of listening to him (4:13–14). Indeed, their response to him amounted to nothing less than devotion (4:15). Ecstatic/charismatic experience played a significant part in their conversion (3:2, 5), and they underwent baptism as a rite of initiation/incorporation into Christ (3:26–29).

9. At some point or points (where in this sequence is unspecified), Paul suffered physical violence on account of his promotion of his gospel (6:17).

10. Another group of Christ-followers, promoting observance of the law of Moses and the inclusion of gentiles in the church on the basis of their joining the Jewish *ethnos*, entered this same territory (1:8–9; 5:7–12; 6:12–13), perhaps not long after Paul's departure from the region ("so quickly turning away," 1:6).

11. Paul wrote to the Christians in Galatia to dissuade them from accepting the rival teachers' claims and recommendations, arguing that they simply needed to continue in the path on which he set them in order to arrive at the goal of "righteousness" and their inheritance.

B. ACTS AND GALATIANS

Taken by itself, Paul's letter to the Galatians does not provide enough data to answer the question of the addressees' location. And although Paul reveals more about his own story and missionary work in this letter than any other (at least in regard to seventeen years of his own activity, including some important interactions with other principal figures in the early church), even this information proves inadequate for locating Paul's work in Galatia, the arrival of a more conservative Jewish mission, and the writing of the letter itself within the framework of Paul's overall ministry with precision. For this reason, virtually every investigation of the location of the addressees of Galatians and the place of the Galatian mission and crisis in the unfolding story of the early church proceeds on the basis of two principal sources—Galatians and Acts. In part this is an almost self-evident procedure for any historian to follow, as both documents tell overlapping stories, like the books of Samuel and Kings vis-à-vis the books of Chronicles in regard to the Israelite monarchy, 1 and 2 Maccabees in regard to the Maccabean Revolt and its causes, or Suetonius and Tacitus in regard to the early Roman Empire. It is also, however, a procedure fraught with difficulties because of, at the very least, the differing perspectives, proximities to the events, and purposes of their authors.

To what degree ought this endeavor to depend upon the historical reliability of the Acts of the Apostles? What role should Luke's historical framework play in determining the historical setting of Galatians (as well as other books of the New Testament that seem to fall within Luke's narrative scope)?[61] At one far end of the spectrum of possible responses lies the position that Acts and Galatians are both completely historically reliable; they can and must be harmonized (which essentially means that Galatians is read and fitted within the framework of Acts). Such a position is normally taken because of a commitment to a high view of Scripture and a wish, therefore, to honor both texts as inerrant or infallible. Nevertheless, as with all attempts at harmonization, this approach invariably does violence to the details of the very texts whose authority and reliability its practitioners seek otherwise to affirm. At

---

61. Bruce, 17, rightly affirms that there is no necessary correlation between the South Galatian hypothesis and a high regard for the historical value of Acts, nor between the North Galatian hypothesis and a low regard for the same.

the opposite end of the spectrum lies the position that Acts and Galatians are documents written to tell "history" in such a way as supports the authors' agenda, with the result that recovery of the *actual* events lies beyond the realm of possibility. In practice, however, even the most skeptical approach tends to be more positive, privileging Paul's account as a firsthand and earlier witness to events and regarding Acts as a highly tendentious and, therefore, highly suspect resource for supplementing the historical picture (since Acts is held to reflect Luke's idealized portrait rather than the facts). Moving too far into this range of the spectrum often leads to an unwarranted dismissal of potentially valuable information in Acts. Toward the middle of the spectrum lies the position that Acts and Galatians are both generally reliable in terms of providing historical information, but they must be read and evaluated in terms of the authors' different perspectives, knowledge of events, principles of selection, and goals for shaping the story in the way that each author does. Together, each can contribute to a reliable picture of the history of the early church, but neither one presents a spotless mirror of actual events. Even here, privilege tends to be given to Galatians as a firsthand testimony to the events of which Paul speaks.

The following discussion of Galatians proceeds mainly from within the middle range of this spectrum. There are minute details in Luke's narrative that can be readily corroborated from details in Paul's earlier and firsthand accounts. For example, the movements of Paul and his team from Thessalonica to Athens and Corinth in Acts 17:1–18:5 closely follow the same movements about which Paul himself speaks in 1 Thess 1:7–8; 2:17–3:6, as do details surrounding Paul's ministry in Corinth.[62] Such correspondences bolster confidence in Luke's care in presenting such details.[63] However, we must also take seriously the differences between Luke's account of Paul's conversion and early mission and Paul's own account of the same in Galatians. Furthermore, we must acknowledge that *none* of Luke's accounts of Paul's visits to Jerusalem square absolutely with Paul's firsthand accounts of these encounters.

---

62. See the discussion of these accounts in Riesner, *Paul's Early Period*, 366–67; Keener, *Acts: Introduction and 1:1–2:47*, 244–48. Several studies have outlined in great detail the points of correspondence between Luke's account of Paul's ministry and the accounts reflected in Paul's own letters. See especially von Harnack, *Acts of the Apostles*, 264–74; Campbell, "Paul's 'Missionary Journeys,'" 81–84; Talbert, *Reading Luke-Acts*, 203–8; Keener, *Acts: Introduction and 1:1–2:47*, 237–50.

63. Harnack suggested in this regard that "the agreement which in these numerous instances exists between the Acts (chaps. i.–xiv.) and the Pauline epistles, although the latter are only incidental writings belonging to the later years of the Apostle, is so extensive and so detailed as to exclude all wild hypotheses concerning those passages of the Acts that are without attestation in those epistles" (*Acts*, 272).

The principal points of divergence between the two accounts include the following:

1. Paul insists that, immediately following his conversion, he "did not confer with flesh and blood" (Gal 1:17); rather, he went immediately into Arabia, then returned to Damascus for the remainder of a three-year period after his conversion, and only then went to Jerusalem (Gal 1:17–18). According to Luke, Paul confers immediately with Ananias and remains with the disciples in Damascus, doing so only for "some days" or, at most, "many days" before going up to Jerusalem (Acts 9:10–26).[64] There is no mention of Arabia, nor any account of a three-year intervening period.

2. According to Luke, Paul is introduced to all the apostles by Barnabas shortly after his conversion ("after many days" in Damascus, Acts 9:23) and even preaches openly in Jerusalem until being forced to flee (Acts 9:26–30); according to Paul, he met only Peter and James the Just on a two-week visit to Jerusalem a full three years after his conversion, during which he remained "unknown by face to the churches in Judea" (1:16–22).[65]

3. Luke makes no mention of a visit undertaken by Paul, Barnabas, and Titus to Jerusalem for a private meeting with Peter, James the Just, and John, one specifically involving (somehow) the question of whether Titus needed to be circumcised in order for his conversion to the one God through Christ to be valid, as well as the Jerusalem pillars' confirmation of the validity of Paul's apostolic work thus far (Gal 2:1–10). Instead, Luke tells of Paul and Barnabas going to Jerusalem to deliver funds for famine relief (Acts 11:27–30), and then going yet another time for the more widely attended "Jerusalem Conference" in response to the activity of preachers of a Torah-observant gospel for gentiles (and Jews) in Antioch (Acts 15:1–29).

---

64. Phillips (*Paul, His Letters, and Acts,* 148) suggests that Luke's account might be the more accurate here, as "it probably would have worked against Paul's rhetorical strategy to include a reference to Ananias. . . . Thus one could easily conjecture that Paul's account of his early missionary career suppressed Ananias's role in order to bolster Paul's claims to independence from the Jerusalem authorities." While Paul might indeed be the one more selectively shaping the narrative of that episode, this would be more egregious than an omission of truth. Paul affirms (under self-imposed oath, 1:20) that he did *not* immediately confer with flesh and blood after his encounter with the glorified Christ (1:17). Ethics aside, it would be a risky ploy for Paul to claim not to have immediately conferred with "flesh and blood" had Ananias (along with the disciples in Damascus) been his first tutor in the faith three days after his visionary experience (Acts 9:10–19).

65. Keener (*Acts: Introduction and 1:1–2:47,* 242) may unduly minimize the differences between Acts 9:26–30 and Gal 1:18–19. The absence of Barnabas in the latter, Paul's insistence on meeting only with Peter and James the Just, and the brevity of the visit according to Paul are significant points of divergence.

4. Luke makes no mention in Acts of the "Antioch incident" and the falling out between Paul and Peter (and Barnabas!) that looms so large in Paul's memory as he writes Galatians (Gal 2:11–14).

5. Luke makes no mention of Paul's illness in his account of Paul's activities in Galatia, whether in the southern part of the Roman province of Galatia (i.e., Pisidian Antioch, Lystra, Iconium, Derbe) or the northern part of the same (Ancyra, Pessinus, and Tavium), although this detail is prominently featured in Paul's account of this visit (Gal 4:13–14). If the visits to the Galatian territory in Acts 16 represent a new evangelization effort in the cities of northern Galatia, Luke strangely makes no mention of such activity, even omitting mention of any specific cities Paul visited.[66]

These are important discrepancies. While not disqualifying the historical framework of Acts as a resource for understanding the history leading up to the crisis in Galatia, they do suggest that we keep several principles in mind as we read Galatians alongside Acts in an attempt to locate Galatians in the life and ministry of Paul and of the early church.

First, Luke is clearly selective in what he chooses to report.[67] Even a report that is highly accurate in what it includes can create bias by virtue of what it excludes. Luke has chosen to minimize division and uncertainty within the inner circle of apostles regarding the inclusion of the gentile Christians and related issues. Luke was deeply concerned with giving his gentile Christian readers "certainty" or "security" (Luke 1:4) about their place in the people of God. It would not have suited his purposes to speak of the sharp division between Peter and Paul at Antioch over the matter, or of James's potential reservations about Jewish Christians eating with uncircumcised gentiles (Gal 2:12). Nor would it help to recall the ways

---

66. Some minor points of divergence in the midst of broad strokes of congruence would include the following. First, Acts also presents Paul as a persecutor of the Jesus movement, specifying that he was active both within Palestine and beyond (Acts 8:3; 9:1–2). In itself this information would not conflict with Paul's claim that he was unknown by face to the churches in Judea (Gal 1:22), as his activity as a persecutor was limited to Jerusalem, though Luke's later statement that Paul preached the Gospel "first to those in Damascus, then in Jerusalem and throughout the countryside of Judea, and also to the gentiles" (Acts 26:20) would conflict. Second, Luke provides a much more detailed account of Paul's encounter with the glorified Christ and of his conversion/commissioning (Acts 9:1–19; cf. the retellings with some variations in Acts 22:6–21; 26:12–20), which may reflect Paul's experience or may result from Luke's creative expansions. Third, Acts also locates Paul in "Syria and Cilicia" in the years between his first and second visits to Jerusalem, but Luke limits mention of Paul's activity entirely to the walls of two cities—his native Tarsus and then Syrian Antioch (Acts 9:30; 11:25–26). Paul gives the impression of mission work throughout the two *regions* (Gal 1:21).

67. See Keener, *Acts: Introduction and 1:1–2:47*, 194–96, however, on omission and selectivity as characteristic of ancient historiography.

in which key figures like Peter and Barnabas may have vacillated on this issue.[68]

Second, while Luke did accompany Paul and continued to be a part of the Pauline mission for some time (Col 4:14; Phlm 24; 2 Tim 4:11), he was not present for its early stages. He may not have been privy to information about the private meeting between Paul, Barnabas, Peter, James, and John. Paul speaks of this meeting only once in all his letters, and that only when absolutely pressed. Luke writes Acts after the end of the Jewish Revolt in 70 CE,

---

68. Serious problems arise specifically concerning the role of Peter in these proceedings as reported independently by Luke and by Paul. In Luke's account of Peter's mission, Peter is the one concerning whom "God made a choice that the gentiles should hear the word of the Gospel through my mouth and come to faith" (Acts 15:7). Luke refers here specifically to Peter's visit to the household of Cornelius in Caesarea Maritima (Acts 10:17–48), for which God had prepared him by means of a vision in which Peter saw clean and unclean animals side by side on a single picnic blanket and was warned by a heavenly voice: "What God has cleansed, do not consider 'common'" (Acts 10:9–16). Luke presents Peter as understanding quite clearly that this vision applied to the way gentiles and Jews are now to relate to one another after the coming of Christ and the sending of the Holy Spirit, specifically the abrogation of old rules keeping the two separate from one another in regard to social interaction (Acts 10:28–29, 34–35). Peter remains with Cornelius for several days (Acts 10:48), in apparent transgression of the taboos against staying in the homes of gentiles (10:28–29); while Luke does not specifically say at this point whether they ate at the same table, in the next scene "those of the circumcision" criticize Peter because he "went to uncircumcised people and ate with them" (11:2–3). In his response, Peter never denies the charge. *Qui tacit consentire videtur.* Peter becomes the champion for acknowledging that God makes no distinction between gentiles and Jews in Christ, since "the Holy Spirit fell upon them just as it had upon us at the beginning" (11:15).

The Cornelius episode and Peter's successful defense of his actions happen before any second visit by Paul to Jerusalem or any visit by Peter to Antioch (to be confronted by Paul). If both Luke and Paul are recounting events with *complete* accuracy, we are left to wonder how the apostle who had the visions of Acts 10:9–16 and who championed the gentile mission in Acts 11 could turn around and withdraw from the gentiles as "common" or "unclean" in Antioch (Gal 2:11–14) under the pressure of a few more rigorist Jewish Christians (of the sort that he successfully opposed and silenced in Acts 11:1–18). Affirming the historical reliability of Acts in this presentation necessitates affirming the historic unreliability of Peter.

Peter bears witness in the apostolic conference that "we trust to be saved through Christ's favor in the same manner as they [the gentiles]" (Acts 15:11), almost echoing the position Paul presents as his own in Gal 2:15–16 (which Paul at least *imagines* needing to argue about with Peter). If the visit of Gal 2:1–10 and the Jerusalem Conference are to be identified (an identification I reject), we once again face the situation of Peter reneging on his earlier—and quite public—position as he withdraws from the table in Antioch, or at least the situation of the Jerusalem Conference not dealing with the question of commensality between Jewish and gentile Christians. Given the mixed ethnic nature of the Antioch congregation and the activity of the Torah-observant mission there, it is difficult to imagine that this topic would not have been a part of the agenda for the Jerusalem Conference.

and thus well after James the Just, Paul, and Peter have been killed.[69] As Luke composed Acts, these major players (and firsthand witnesses) were no longer available to him for further investigation of the events that took place well before Luke himself appeared on the stage of this story. From another angle, James, Paul, and Peter were also therefore unavailable to correct Luke's story, reminding Luke or his readers that the process of sorting out the question of gentile inclusion was more complex and contested than Acts suggests.

Third, we should expect Luke to adhere to the standards of ancient historiography, not modern historical writing. The wholesale invention of events would be frowned upon, but there would be considerable latitude in terms of the representation of speeches and dialogue, the filling in of gaps in regard to inaccessible material,[70] and the effective ordering of material, both in terms of the shaping of discrete episodes (like Paul's work in Corinth) and in terms of the arrangement of episodes into a narrative. In regard to this last point, comparison with Luke's Gospel may be instructive. The question of the historical value of each particular unit of tradition is quite a different one from the question of the historical value of the ordering of these units and chronological indicators between units.[71] As we proceed, we will frequently appeal to these observations in our assessment of the weight that should reasonably be given to particular details and constraints in Luke's version of this history vis-à-vis those in Paul's version of the same.

The question of whether Paul addressed Christians in the older, ethnic region of North Galatia or in the cities of South Galatia and the question of how the events narrated in Gal 1–2 align with the events narrated in Acts are closely intertwined. Nevertheless, for the sake of presenting the issues and evidence as clearly and systematically as possible, we will take these questions up separately, with some inevitable cross-referencing and overlap.

---

69. It is commonplace to read that Mark, Matthew, and Luke were all written after the destruction of Jerusalem in 70 CE, which effectively brought the First Jewish Revolt to an end. This is certain, however, only in the case of Luke, who alters the wording of Jesus's predictions about the "end" (see Mark 13:14–19; Matt 24:15–21), replacing the allusive language Jesus used (e.g., the "abomination of desolation") with clear descriptions of the siege of Jerusalem of 70 CE (Luke 21:20–24), which Luke understood to be the fulfillment of Jesus's predictions. Since Luke presents Acts unambiguously as the sequel to his Gospel, it follows that Acts also was composed after 70 CE. James the Just was lynched in 62 CE; Paul and Peter are both believed to have been executed in Rome under Nero, hence before 68, and most likely before or in connection with the fire of 64.

70. Keener (*Acts: Introduction and 1:1–2:47*, 241) identifies as the "most obvious" example of this filling in "the behind-the-scenes dialogue of Festus with Agrippa and Bernice" (Acts 25:14–22). Such invention, he avers, falls within the parameters of the practice of ancient historians (e.g., for the sake of preserving narrative rather than introducing commentary).

71. See Rowlingson, "The Jerusalem Conference."

C. WAS PAUL ADDRESSING CHURCHES IN *NORTH* OR IN *SOUTH* GALATIA?

One of the commonplaces in arguments in favor of the position that Paul was addressing Christian communities in the major cities of northern Galatia (e.g., Ancyra, Pessinus, and Tavium) is the use of the terms "Galatia" and "Galatians" in both Paul and Acts. In addition to the assertion that such terms would be more appropriately used of the ethnic region of North Galatia and its inhabitants, a claim that inscriptional evidence has shown to be dubious at best, supporters of a North Galatian destination also claim that both Paul and Luke tend to use the older, ethnic designations for regions rather than Roman provincial names. Therefore, Paul and Luke are more likely referring to the northern part of the province when they speak of "Galatia" or address "Galatians" (Gal 1:2; 3:1; Acts 16:6; 18:23).[72] Acts 16:6 and 18:23 thereby record a new mission to the northern part of Galatia, with Paul's letter addressed then to the churches formed as a result of this mission.[73]

In regard to these authors' use of geographic terms, Paul actually uses the *Roman provincial* designations far more often to designate his audience

---

72. Lightfoot, 26.

73. Several arguments often presented in support of a northern destination for Galatians ought to be discarded as ambiguous or simply fallacious. One is that the mention of Paul's passing twice (allegedly) through northern Galatia (Acts 16:6; 18:23) better suits Paul's own testimony to have visited the Galatian churches more than once (τὸ πρότερον, "the former time," in Gal 4:13 implying more than one visit; Lightfoot, 46–47; Moffatt, *Introduction*, 84). Even granting this understanding of τὸ πρότερον, Acts 13:13–14:23 *also* speaks of Paul and his team passing twice through the cities in South Galatia—an initial evangelistic visit (13:13–14:20) and a follow-up, return visit to consolidate the work and appoint elders (14:21–23). The argument is thus fundamentally inconclusive, even before factoring in the ambiguity of Luke's geographic referents in 16:6 and 18:23. Another fallacious argument concerns the stereotype of the Gauls as a superstitious and fickle people (see Caesar, *Gallic War* 2.1; 4.5; 6.16; Cicero, *On Divination* 1.5; 2.36–37), which supposedly accords well with the fickle temperament of Paul's addressees (Lightfoot, 12, 21–24; rightly rejected by Moffatt, *Introduction*, 99). Stereotypes of indigenous people groups formulated by the colonizers are naturally suspect, as they almost inevitably serve to justify colonizing (and thereby "improving") these people groups. Caesar and Cicero themselves hail from a no less superstitious people (given, for example, the significant role that divination and horoscopes played in imperial policy!).

Contrariwise, a weak argument frequently presented *against* the North Galatian hypothesis is based on the fact that, in Acts 20:4, one finds two disciples from South Galatia (Gaius of Derbe and Timothy of Lystra) among Paul's companions on his trip to Jerusalem, but none from a North Galatian city. While we have here another place where *positive* evidence of North Galatian Christians is conspicuously absent, the argument carries no real *negative* weight. If the evidence were reversed (listing a Justus from Ancyra), we would of course take it as strong evidence for a North Galatian mission.

and to speak of his movements.[74] The Pauline corpus contains references to Achaia (Rom 15:26; 1 Cor 16:15; 2 Cor 1:1; 9:2; 11:10; 1 Thess 1:7–8), Asia (1 Cor 16:19; 2 Cor 1:8; 2 Tim 1:15), Crete (Titus 1:5, 12), Dalmatia (2 Tim 4:10), Illyricum (Rom 15:19),[75] Macedonia (Rom 15:26; 1 Cor 16:5; 2 Cor 1:16; 2:13; 7:5; 8:1; 9:2, 4; 11:9; Phil 4:15; 1 Thess 1:7–8; 1 Tim 1:3), and Spain (Rom 15:24). Paul may not show absolute consistency in this regard, depending on whether we understand his references to Arabia (Gal 1:17), Syria and Cilicia (Gal 1:21), and Judea (Rom 15:31; Gal 1:23; 1 Thess 2:14) as provincial or regional, but the preponderance of Pauline usage favors Roman provincial designations. This usage would suggest that his own references to "Galatia" and its inhabitants (Gal 1:2; 3:1; see also 2 Tim 4:10), whatever Luke's understanding of the designation "Galatia" (Acts 16:6; 18:23), are to the Roman province or some or any portion thereof.

Luke appears to be considerably freer in his usage, employing Roman designations of the provinces and other administrative units[76] alongside regional terms[77] and specifically ethnic terms.[78] In Acts 16:7 Luke refers to the Roman province of Bithynia side by side with the regional Mysia; in Acts 16:6 Luke refers to at least one province (Asia) and at least one region (Phrygia). This flexibility (one is tempted to call it carelessness) in regard to designations

---

74. Ramsay, 147–64, 314–21. See also Burton, xxvii; Keener, *Acts 3:1–14:28*, 2118.

75. Illyricum was a province until 10 CE (or perhaps 25 CE), after which it was subdivided into Pannonia and Dalmatia. Even if Paul uses the term anachronistically, it is still a Roman provincial designation. See Dzino, *Illyricum in Roman Politics*.

76. Achaia: 18:12, 27; 19:21; Arabia ("Arabs"): 2:11; Asia: 2:9; 6:9; 16:6; 19:10, 22, 26–27; 20:4 ("Asians"), 16, 18; 21:27; 24:19; 27:2; Bithynia: 16:7; Cappadocia: 2:9; Cilicia: 6:9; 15:23, 41; 21:39; 22:3; 23:34; 27:5; Crete: 2:11 ("Cretans"); 27:12–13, 21; Cyprus: 4:36; 11:19–20; 13:4; 21:16; 27:4; Cyrene: 2:10; 6:9; 11:20; 13:1; Egypt: 2:10; Macedonia: 16:9, 10, 12; 18:5; 19:21–22, 29; 20:1, 3; 27:2; Pontus: 2:9; Syria: 15:23, 41; 18:18; 20:3. Admittedly, a number of these terms overlap with regional designations. There are no other ways to refer to "Cyprus" or "Egypt" besides these terms, which double as provincial names and preprovincial names. For Syria and Cilicia to be joined as a single administrative unit does not seem to overturn the fact that both are still Roman provincial terms and that either could be used to indicate with greater precision the half of the linked province that the author had most in mind. Acts 2:9 is interesting insofar as Luke specifies "the parts of Libya belonging to Cyrene," thus carefully designating the narrower territory involved by reference to the Roman provincial unit.

77. Galilee: 1:11; 9:31; 10:37; Judea: 1:8; 2:14; 8:1; 9:31; 10:37, 39; 11:29; 12:19; 15:1; 21:10; Lycaonia: 14:6; Lycia: 27:5; Mysia: 16:7–8; Pamphylia: 2:10; 13:13; 14:24; 15:38; 27:5; Phoenicia: 11:19; 15:3; 21:2; Phrygia: 2:10; 16:6; 18:23; Pisidia: 13:14; 14:24; Samaria: 1:8; 8:1, 5, 14; 9:31; 15:3. I omit terms referring to regions outside of the Roman Empire, which would de facto have no possible provincial designation. Judea is a strange case insofar as the boundaries shifted frequently in the period of interest here. At the time of Pentecost, however, it did not include Samaria (which was part of the tetrarchy of Herod Antipas), with the result that it may be taken as a provincial designation in the opening chapters of Acts.

78. Israelites: 2:22; 3:12; Lycaonian (language): 14:11.

should make one cautious before making hard-and-fast claims concerning the nature of the designation "Galatia" in Acts 16:6.[79]

It is indeed curious that Luke locates Antioch, Iconium, Lystra, and Derbe using the regional names of "Pisidia" and "Lycaonia," though this is not an "inexplicable" obstacle to Luke's regarding these cities as belonging also in some sense to what he later calls Galatia.[80] Luke appears to choose whatever terms will help his readers locate the action with the greatest precision, rather than select terms with a view to anything like consistency in the type of designation. In the instances of these important sites of Pauline missionary work, the more local, more geographically precise and descriptive regional terms served Luke's aim better. In itself, this practice need not prejudice us against Luke speaking later of all or part of this southern region using "Galatia" as a provincial (and less geographically focused) term.

Fundamentally, however, the question needs to be asked afresh whether there *was* ever a Pauline mission to the cities of North Galatia—indeed, whether Luke himself intended for his readers to think that he was speaking of such a mission in Acts 16:6 and 18:23.[81] The theory that there were Christians in the cities of northern Galatia to be addressed by Paul in a letter in the first place rests on the slender evidence of the two references in Acts to "the Phrygian and Galatian territory" (16:6) and "the Galatian territory and Phrygian" (18:23) and, in particular, the reading of these verses as Luke's *extremely* brief narrative of a Pauline mission to North Galatia.[82] On this reading, "the

---

79. Keener, *Acts 15:1–23:35*, 2326.

80. Moffatt, *Introduction*, 93.

81. See also Riesner, *Paul's Early Period*, 282–86; Das, 24–26. It does seem likely that, by the time 1 Peter is written, the northern part of the province has been evangelized—along with Cappadocia, Bithynia, and Pontus. Luke says nothing about the spread of the gospel to those provinces either, a reminder to us of how little we really do know about missionary activity in the early church.

82. There is some disagreement concerning whether "the Phrygian and Galatian region" (τὴν Φρυγίαν καὶ Γαλατικὴν χώραν, Acts 16:6) refers to one region or two. Moffatt (*Introduction*, 93) had asserted that they must be understood as two regions, each referred to by its ethnic designation. Burton (xxxii), however, argues from a close observation of the grammar that this phrase designates a single region, with the singular noun χώρα ("region") being described by two proper adjectives joined by a single article, thus denoting that part of the southwestern area of the Roman province of Galatia that overlaps with regional Phrygia (so also Hemer and Gempf, *Acts*, 282–85; Riesner, *Paul's Early Period*, 285; this would be true for τὴν Γαλατικὴν χώραν καὶ Φρυγίαν, the construction in 18:23 as well, with the second proper adjective simply being stylistically deferred). If Luke had intended to speak here of two separate regions, it is striking that he did not write τὴν Φρυγίαν χώραν καὶ τὴν Γαλατικήν (still allowing for elision of a second χώραν) or τὰς Φρυγίας καὶ Γαλατικὰς χώρας, "the Phrygian and Galatian region*s*," or simply reversed the order to τὴν Γαλατικὴν χώραν καὶ τὴν Φρυγίαν ("the Galatian region and Phrygia"; the second article is important,

Phrygian and Galatian territory" is further understood as a specific way of indicating two originally independent territories by their older, ethnic designations. But it is far from clear that Luke intended such an inference to be made (or as shown above, that his use of ethnic versus provincial designations is indeed all that precise).

What contextual indicators does Luke give that he is narrating a new mission in new territory in Acts 16:6? The initial purpose for this journey is announced in 15:36: "After some days Paul said to Barnabas, 'Come, let us return and visit the believers in every city where we proclaimed the word of the Lord and see how they are doing'" (NRSV). This wording accounts well for their trip "through Syria and Cilicia, strengthening the churches" (15:41), as well as for their return to Derbe and Lystra, where we pause to meet Timothy (16:1–5). What of the churches in Iconium and Pisidian Antioch? Did Paul and Barnabas fail to visit them, or would Luke fail to think about the appropriateness of their doing so at this point in the narrative, given the prominence given to the mission in Pisidian Antioch in Acts 13:13–52? Given the reader's knowledge of these mission sites, it seems more than plausible, and perhaps even most probable, that he or she would understand 16:6 to signify Paul and Barnabas's moving on to Iconium and Antioch ("in the Galatian territory") to finish the proposed tour of established churches before moving on to new mission grounds (eventually) in Macedonia.

It is also striking that Luke gives no indication at this point that Paul engaged in new missionary work in "the Phrygian and Galatian territory," not even a brief mention of the cities in which he formed churches. This omission is especially striking insofar as it would be the only instance in Acts where new mission work would be presumed to happen in a region that Luke names without Luke drawing any attention to the fact.[83] A tour through Ancyra and Pessinus and, even more so, Tavium at this point in Luke's narrative (i.e., Acts 16:6) would also represent an extensive detour for a missionary who left Lystra intending to head for Ephesus, or even directly toward Mysia.[84] If such a journey had been undertaken, surely it would have

---

as it distinguishes Φρυγία as a second, distinct noun, whereas in the wording of Acts 18:23, τὴν Γαλατικὴν χώραν καὶ Φρυγίαν, it is likely to be construed as a deferred adjective). Even if Luke does intend to name two geographic areas, he may be joining a provincial with an older regional term (see his blending otherwise of regional alongside provincial designations in 16:6 and 16:7), aware that they are somewhat overlapping, because he finds this wording gives a more precise indication of the apostle's trajectory from Derbe toward Ephesus. Ramsay (315–16) suggests that Luke is referring to the province of Galatia when he shifts his terminology to speak of "the Galatian *region*" (τὴν . . . Γαλατικὴν χώραν) in Acts 16:6; 18:23, rather than just using the term "Galatia" (as with Lycaonia, Mysia, Pisidia, etc.).

83. Burton, xxxvii; Zahn, 16–17.

84. Witherington, 5–6. The major cities of northern Galatia "lay some 200 km NE of

merited Luke's using even just a single verse to name the places where new congregations had been planted. Indeed, the only details about mission in this journey concern the Spirit's *restraining* Paul from engaging in evangelization efforts until he crosses into Macedonia.[85]

Tracing out the movements of Paul and his team as related in Acts 16:6–9 on a map of ancient Asia Minor more readily suggests the following picture. After the Jerusalem Conference, Paul and Barnabas returned to the churches in Syria, Cilicia, and South Galatia (specifically Derbe and Lystra) to deliver the decision of the Jerusalem leadership (Acts 16:1, 4) and pass on from there to the remaining cities of "the Phrygian and Galatian region" (Acts 16:6), namely, the portion of the Roman province of Galatia associated with Pisidia and Phrygia (hence, southern Galatia), with the intention of traveling on to plant new churches in the major cities of the Roman province of Asia (on the west coast of Asia Minor). If the original goal of Paul's team was to preach in Ephesus, there is a direct route through Pisidian Antioch and thence through Phrygia (a region that sits half in the province of Galatia and half in the province of Asia) to the eastern parts of Roman Asia with their bustling cities along the Via Sebaste. The Spirit prevents them from preaching in Asia (16:6), so Paul and his team head north through Phrygia (quite possibly through the part that lies within Roman Asia) until they reach the edge of Mysia. At this point they contemplate heading northeast into the province of Bithynia but instead, under the Spirit's guidance, head directly west through the region of Mysia to the port city of Troas and embark upon the Macedonian mission.

Paul will return to these churches one more time after the mission in Macedonia and Achaia and before finally making it to Asia.[86] After visiting Caesarea, Jerusalem (presumably), and Antioch, Paul "departed, traveling through the Galatian region and [the] Phrygian [region] in order, strengthening all the disciples" (Acts 18:23). The Greek word translated here as "in order" is also often translated "from one place to the next."[87] Even if it is understood in its narrowest sense of referring to Galatia and Phrygia "in that

---

any natural route between Lystra and Mysia," let alone between Lystra and Asia (Mitchell, "Galatia," 871).

85. Keener, *Acts 15:1–23:35*, 2327.

86. One interesting consequence of such a reading (a consequence at the very least confirmed by 15:36–16:5, regardless of one's final position on 16:6) is that we begin to see Paul and his team more as church planters/pastors than as traveling evangelists who move through an area once and then move on. The picture of Paul in Acts, very much like the picture in the Epistles (esp. the Corinthian correspondence), is that of someone deeply committed to the nurture and ongoing shepherding of the churches he plants.

87. As in the ESV ("from place to place" in the NRSV), following the guidance in BDAG 490 (s.v. καθεξῆς).

order," it still accords with Paul's westward movement from Syrian Antioch to Ephesus, his next new mission field and the destination for this particular journey. The cities of southern Galatia lie directly on this route, and it makes perfect sense that Paul would visit the churches there again to check on their status and assist their progress.[88]

Affirming a North Galatian destination for the letter necessarily means affirming that Paul's mission to those churches and the trouble with the rival teachers occur after the events described in Acts 15 (since the only possible opening Luke leaves for a North Galatian mission occurs in 16:6). However, the argument does not work the other way.[89] One might readily support the correlation of the meeting recounted in Gal 2:1–10 with the Jerusalem Conference of Acts 15 while also holding that Galatians is addressed to the churches in the southern part of the province, whether Paul is understood to revisit those southern Galatian churches in Acts 16:6 and 18:23 or whether the troubles in Galatia are simply held to have been more likely to erupt in the southern portion of the province. An important point here is that Luke's use of "Galatia" does not determine (or even prejudice) Paul's use of "Galatia." If Luke does indeed use this term to distinguish the northern part of the province from the southern part, Paul could *still* have written Galatians to the Christians in Antioch, Iconium, Lystra, and Derbe—whom Paul would have equally well called "Galatians" following his typical practice—either prior to or following the Jerusalem Conference.

The primary argument in favor of the view that Paul writes to the congregations in the southern part of the province of Galatia is the fact that we have strong documentation of actual missionary activity in that area, with Acts foregrounding and providing detailed accounts of Paul and Barnabas's mission in Pisidian Antioch, Iconium, Lystra, and Derbe (Acts 13:13–14:23).[90] Such detail stands in stark contrast to the merely *potential* evidence for a North Galatian mission (reading Acts 18:23 as evidence for a mission that took place on the trip of Acts 16:6 without any mention of such a mission at

---

88. Asterius of Amasea, a fourth-century bishop, understood these terms to refer to the areas of the south of the Roman province of Galatia. See also Hemer, *Acts*, 120; Mitchell, "Galatia," 871; Witherington, 6; Das, 26.

89. Rightly, Silva, *Interpreting Galatians*, 131–32; contra Lightfoot, 326–32; Moffatt, *Introduction*, 100, who make this assertion. Silva himself holds to a South Galatian destination *and* a later date, as he finds the case for identifying the meeting of Gal 2:1–10 with Acts 15 compelling.

90. So also Das, 28. For further argumentation in favor of a South Galatian destination, see Bruce, 10–18; Bruce, "Galatian Problems"; Ridderbos, 23–31; Hemer, "Acts and Galatians," 82–85; Hemer and Gempf, *Acts*, 278–307; Riesner, *Paul's Early Period*, 286–91; Breytenbach, *Paulus und Barnabas*, 99–126.

that point).[91] The fact that Luke does not speak of these four cities as part of a larger administrative unit called "Galatia" is simply irrelevant to the question of whether Paul would do so. The fact that these cities and their inhabitants would have been part of the province of Galatia for over seventy years prior to Paul's writing his letter, that they are otherwise called Galatians in inscriptions and other literary witnesses, and that Paul's overwhelming tendency is to use Roman provincial designations for territories all renders Paul's address of these south central churches as "Galatians" natural, fitting, and plausible.[92] The situation addressed by Paul would also have a highly plausible origin: more conservative Jewish Christian missionaries, encountering the state of the church in Antioch, continued westward to extend their work of bringing the communities of the Jesus movement in line with the historic covenant of the people of God, thus entering the cities of South Galatia, where Paul's work was widely known to have flourished.[93]

---

91. William Ramsay is correct that (1) Paul's policy was to concentrate on the main Roman roads and evangelize along those routes and that (2) none of these roads led through northern Galatia, a part of the province that was not well developed until Diocletian (Ramsay, *Historical Geography*, 197–200; so also Mitchell, "Galatia," 870; Das, 28). Nevertheless, these observations themselves do not argue against the possibility of Paul taking the less well-developed paths into North Galatia—he was an evangelist, not a tourist to be thus easily dissuaded were it his (or the Spirit's) purpose (Longenecker, lxix). Evidence that he *actually* took those roads into northern Galatia is simply lacking.

92. In itself, of course, Paul's calling them Galatians does not tilt the balance between a North and a South Galatian audience one way or the other.

93. This scenario is one factor that leads Dunn (17) to favor a South Galatian setting for the epistle. In regard to the situation reflected in Paul's letter, Martyn (16) argues that Jewish-Christian missionaries would be more likely to be drawn to an area with fewer ethnic Jews (hence North Galatia) for their mission than the cities of South Galatia, with their significant Jewish communities. This argument, however, seems counterintuitive. Jewish-Christian missionaries would, like Paul, probably seek out places with an established Jewish presence if for no other reason than to be assured of hospitality in a religiously acceptable environment. Moreover, if the rival teachers are indeed at all concerned about how non-Christian Jews are viewing the Christian movement and therefore seeking to promote the full proselytization of gentiles in part out of a desire to show the Christian movement as a whole to be compatible with the Mosaic covenant rather than a threat thereto, they would gain more by doing so in an area with an established Jewish presence to witness their work of bringing the Christian movement in line with the covenant. (This is not to say that the rival teachers are indeed motivated by a cowardly desire not to be persecuted on account of "the cross of Christ," as Paul avers in Gal 6:12, but only that Paul's attribution of the motive must be situationally plausible. Preaching a Torah-free gospel where there are no or few Jews is not a risk even for cowardly preachers.) It is also difficult to believe that the rival teachers would purposefully pass by the flourishing Pauline churches in South Galatia, even if they also intended to move into North Galatia (so Das, 24; see also Riesner, *Paul's Early Period*, 286; Ridderbos, 24–25).

Considerations of Paul's coworkers—both those who are named and those not named in Galatians—tend to confirm a South Galatian destination. The prominence with which Barnabas is mentioned (Gal 2:1, 9, 13) more naturally presumes acquaintance with Barnabas on the part of the addressees. This factor would point to the churches founded jointly by Paul and Barnabas in southern Galatia (Acts 13:1–14:28), but not to any churches founded along the journey narrated in Acts 16–18 (again, *if* Acts 16:6 and 18:23 actually speak of a mission in northern Galatia), since Barnabas does not travel with Paul for long after the Jerusalem Conference (Acts 15:22, 35–41). While it is always possible that the addressees of Galatians could have learned of Barnabas indirectly (as the Corinthian Christians appear to have done; 1 Cor 9:6),[94] the emphatic character of Paul's remark that "*even* Barnabas was caught up in this play-acting" (2:13) suggests rather that Barnabas's defection should be more surprising to the audience than Peter's, thus presuming personal acquaintance with Barnabas and his previous, more inclusive vision of the Christian church.[95] The absence of any mention of Timothy also weighs in favor of an earlier date as well as a South Galatian destination. Timothy is Paul's constant missionary companion from Acts 16:1–4 (starting from Paul's third recorded visit to Lystra) through the journey to Jerusalem (Acts 20:4) and is named as a cosender in 2 Corinthians, Philippians, Colossians, 1–2 Thessalonians, and Philemon. If the letter is addressed to churches that both evangelized together, or if it was written after Paul had been working together with Timothy, it is strange that Paul never mentions Timothy, given his prominence across the Pauline corpus.[96]

Many objections raised against understanding Paul to address churches in the southern area of the province of Galatia are, upon closer examination, weak, easily answered, or dependent upon disputable presuppositions.[97]

1. A South Galatian destination "arbitrarily makes the burning question of circumcision for gentile Christians emerge in an acute shape some time before the period of Acts 15—a view for which there is no evidence in Acts

---

94. Martyn (17–18) asserts, on the contrary, that "it seems probable that that knowledge came from the Teachers," that is, from the rival mission. He does not, however, offer any argumentation in support of his claims regarding greater probability.

95. Dunn, 17; Bauckham, "Barnabas in Galatians," 61–71. The fact that Paul writes Galatians without naming Barnabas as a cosender points to the letter's having been written while the two were at odds, whether immediately following their falling out in Antioch or in the period after their second disagreement (over the value of John Mark as a traveling companion, if that is an accurate historical reflection).

96. Longenecker, lxx–lxxi.

97. I survey here those objections invoked by Moffatt (*Introduction*, 83–107), offering responses in a point-counterpoint manner; numbers in parentheses refer to Moffatt, *Introduction*.

and against which the probabilities of the situation tell heavily" (92). To the extent that Luke is writing to give gentile Christians assurance concerning their place in the covenant community of God and also to display the essential unity of early Christian leaders on this point, it is not in his interest to relate all the events prior to Acts 15:1 that might have brought the question of gentile circumcision to a boiling point. However, even within that tension Luke raises the problem of Jewish-Christian interaction with gentiles and gentile Christians as early as chapters 10 and 11. Scholars have also affirmed a South Galatian destination while understanding Paul's letter to postdate the Jerusalem Conference of Acts 15 (= Gal 2:1–10, on their view).

2. "It involves the incredible idea that Paul circumcised Timotheus (Acts 16:3) after he had written Gal 5:2" (92). This is not incredible at all. Paul regularly advocates for observance of Jewish customs or nonobservance of the same, on the basis of the individual believers' preference (Rom 14:5–6) and on the basis of what will give least offense while not violating the gospel (1 Cor 9:19–23, a very important testimony to Paul's flexibility regarding Jewish practice in either direction). Timothy's Jewish descent (on his mother's side) is also relevant to this decision. What Paul objects to in Galatians and opposes in 5:1–4 is laying the requirement of circumcision upon disciples (and particularly gentiles) as a condition of belonging to the community of promise and the family of God.

3. "If Luke had viewed Derbe, Lystra, and the rest of Paul's earlier mission field as belonging to Galatia proper, it is inexplicable why the name should not occur in Acts 13–14" (93). The determinative point is that these cities were, in fact, part of the province of Galatia and *could be* referred to as cities of Galatia. Whether *Luke* chooses to do so is by no means determinative for the question of whether *Paul* had done so in a letter written decades earlier.

4. "If the opening of the South Galatian mission is so fully described in Ac 13–14, why is there no mention of the illness which Paul specially mentions in Gal 4:13?" (99). This is indeed a point of divergence, but only a valid objection to the extent that we expect Luke to tell the story entirely in line with Paul's (much more recent) memory of the same.[98]

5. "There is not a hint in the epistle of any persecution or suffering endured by him in his evangelization of Galatia, whereas his South Galatian mission was stormy in the extreme (Acts 13–14; 2 Tim 3:11)" (99). Actually, on this point, Paul does refer to his own endurance of persecution as proof

---

98. Moffatt, *Introduction*, 99. The same response would apply to Moffatt's further objection that, according to Paul, the Galatians received him as "an angel of God, even Christ Jesus" (Gal 4:14), which is very different from receiving him as the pagan god Hermes (in Lystra, Acts 14:12).

of his credibility and the rival teachers' wish to avoid persecution as a sign of their unreliability at Gal 5:11; 6:12, 17. The "brand-marks of Christ" on Paul's body (6:17) would include any scars from wounds incurred in South Galatia.

6. "If Paul had evangelized S. Galatia prior to the Council, it is not easy to understand why he did not say so in Gal 1:21" (99). This objection assumes that Gal 2:1–10 refers to the meeting of Acts 15:6–35; it would evaporate if Gal 2:1–10 proves to connect to the events related, rather, in Acts 11:29–30 and 12:25, hence prior to his evangelization of South Galatia. I would add that a South Galatian destination is not rendered more or less probable whether one identifies the visit to Jerusalem recounted in Gal 2:1–10 with the visit depicted in Acts 11:29–30;12:25 or Acts 15.[99]

The balance of probability therefore seems to me to rest with the Christians in the cities of South Galatia as the more likely recipients of Paul's letter to "the churches in Galatia" (Gal 1:2). This determination, however, does not yet help us in placing the trouble in Galatia or Paul's response within the timeline of the story that Luke tells in Acts.

D. PAUL'S VISITS TO JERUSALEM IN GALATIANS AND ACTS

We come, then, to the question of Paul's visits to Jerusalem in Acts vis-à-vis the visits of which Paul himself speaks in Gal 1–2. Luke tells of five visits that Paul made to Jerusalem over the course of his Christian career. The first occurs shortly after his conversion/commission (Acts 9:26–30; see commentary on 1:15–16), in which Paul is introduced to the apostles by Barnabas and spends some time coming and going in their midst and preaching in Jerusalem. The second occurs in connection with relief funds taken up in Antioch for those affected by the famine in Judea, which Paul and Barnabas deliver to the elders of the church there (Acts 11:27–30; 12:25). The third occurs in response to the appearance of Jewish Christian missionaries in Antioch claiming that gentile converts must also be circumcised and observe the Torah (Acts 15:1–5), resulting in the Jerusalem Conference, at which the issue was decided: gentiles did not need to be circumcised or observe Torah. They would need only to avoid foods sacrificed to idols, fornication (of course), eating meat from animals that had been strangled (hence with the blood still in the tissues), and from all ingestion of blood (Acts 15:20, 29). A fourth visit is probably to be

---

99. If one holds that Gal 2:1–10 is to be equated with Acts 11:27–30, *and* that Paul would surely have referred to the conference of Acts 15 and its proceedings had it occurred prior to the time of his writing Galatians, *and* that the outcome of the conference was essentially as reported by Luke, then a South Galatian destination for the letter becomes the only tenable choice (working within the framework of Acts; Fung, 22–23).

inferred in Acts 18:22, where, upon Paul's return to Caesarea after his missionary work in Achaia, he "went up and greeted the church." Within Palestine, one "went up" to Jerusalem and "went down" again to wherever one's home was,[100] with the result that the mere expression "going up" from Caesarea might be heard to indicate a trip that had Jerusalem as its destination.[101] The fifth visit results in Paul's imprisonment of several years and voyage to Rome to stand trial (Acts 21:17).

In Galatians, Paul speaks only of two visits to Jerusalem. The first occurs "after three years," with Paul probably counting from the time of his conversion rather than from his return to Damascus after his stay in Arabia (Gal 1:18–20). Paul's purpose for this visit was to make Peter's acquaintance, and to this end he stayed with Peter for two weeks. He declares on oath that he saw none of the other apostles "except James, the Lord's brother." The second visit occurs "after fourteen years," counting either from Paul's conversion or from the first visit (Gal 2:1–2). The central feature of this visit, according to Paul, was a private meeting involving himself, Barnabas, Peter, James the Just, and John (Gal 2:2b) for the purpose of seeking their confirmation of how God was at work both through Peter, taking the gospel to the Jewish people, and through Paul, taking the gospel to the non-Jewish nations (Gal 2:7–9). At stake for Paul was the pillars' acknowledgment of the fundamental unity of their differently focused missions. Paul finds it also highly relevant that these three leaders did not see fit at that time to demand that Titus, Paul and Barnabas's gentile companion and coworker, be circumcised, despite pressure from "false brothers" in that direction. As far as Paul is concerned, this lack of concern by the pillars should serve as precedent enough to settle the issue now facing the Galatian gentile converts (Gal 2:3–5). According to Paul, the pillars did not seek to correct Paul's gospel or his manner of incorporating gentiles into the church at all, only urging him to "continue to remember the poor," a task already fixed in Paul's own heart (Gal 2:10).

In what ways and to what extent do these two stories mesh, and how can answering these questions help us locate Galatians in Paul's ministry?[102]

---

100. "Going up" (using forms of ἀναβαίνω) to Jerusalem: Matt 20:17, 18; Mark 10:32, 33; Luke 18:31; 19:28; John 2:13; 5:1; 7:8, 10; 11:55; 12:20; Acts 15:2; 21:12, 15; 25:1, 9; "going down" (using forms of καταβαίνω) from Jerusalem to another place: Mark 3:22; Luke 2:51; 10:30, 31; Acts 8:15, 26; 24:1, 22; 25:6, 7.

101. So also in Luke 2:42 (see also John 7:8, 10).

102. The data from Gal 1–2 and Acts 8–15 are often approached as though each passage is essentially a set of puzzle pieces that can be fitted together to form a better single picture of the first two decades of the church's story. At many points, it is difficult to suppress the impression that they are not pieces from the same puzzle at all but simply two different pictures. Nevertheless, the same tension faces every historian of a period from the distant past, so we cannot excuse ourselves from the task.

Paul and Luke give consistent testimony to Paul's former zeal for Torah, expressed in the suppression of the deviant Jesus movement, and his stunning transformation from persecutor to apostle. Both Paul and Luke agree that Paul visited Jerusalem not too long after his conversion in order to become acquainted with the leaders of the Christian movement (Gal 1:18–20; Acts 9:26–30), though they differ in the details. Most notably, Paul *swears* that he met only with Peter and James the Just (Gal 1:19–20), while Luke depicts him meeting "the apostles" more generally (Acts 9:26–27). Luke also suggests that Barnabas's mediation was required because of the apostles' fear of the persecutor, which is hardly likely, given the number of years that had, according to Paul's firsthand testimony, elapsed. These differences, however, are readily attributable to Paul's interest in recounting his early relationship with Jerusalem and Luke's greater distance from the events (possibly further hindered by the unavailability of any firsthand witnesses to Paul's first visit by the time Luke writes) and thus his freer imagining of that first visit. Both go on to speak of Paul's carrying out of his apostolic commission in the provinces of Syria and Cilicia after this initial visit.

At this point a critical question arises: are we to identify the second visit recounted by Paul in Gal 2:1–10 with the second visit mentioned by Luke (Acts 11:28–30) or with the third visit, undertaken in conjunction with the Jerusalem Conference (Acts 15:1–30)?[103] Reading Acts alongside Galatians, we see that Acts 11:28–30 occupies the same position in the narrative flow that one would assign to the conversations about which Paul writes in Gal 2:1–10.[104] Paul's narrative suggests that, prior to the visit of 2:1–10, he worked only in Syria and Cilicia. If his missionary travels were more extensive in this interim, it would have been easy for him simply to add the names of a few more prov-

---

103. These are by no means the only options, though they are the preferred ones. Knox (*Chapters in a Life of Paul*, 64–73) and Foakes-Jackson and Lake (*Beginnings of Christianity*, 5:195–212) have all suggested that Luke has heard two different accounts of what was actually a single visit but treated them as if they were accounts of separate visits. Foakes-Jackson and Lake thus identify Gal 2:1–10 with both Acts 11:28–30 and 15:6–21, while Knox identifies Gal 2:1–10 with both Acts 15:6–21 and 18:22. The former position, which the authors claim to be "the only theory which can do justice to the arguments set out by Lightfoot in favour of identifying Acts xv and Galatians ii without doing violence to the fact that Paul says that Gal. ii. was his second visit to Jerusalem" (*Beginnings*, 5:202), has been adopted and advanced by Haenchen, "Book of Acts," 271, and *Acts of the Apostles*, 400–404, 438–39.

104. Burkitt, *Christian Beginnings*, 116. In the opinion of Fung (17), this view "gives Paul's words in 2:1 their most natural sense in the context: G2 [Gal 2:1–10] was Paul's second post-conversion visit to Jerusalem, which, according to Acts, must be identified with A2 [Acts 11:27–30; 12:25]." In favor of this identification, see the fuller arguments in Ramsay, *Teaching of Paul*, 372–92; Bruce, 43–56; Fung, 16–28; Longenecker, lxxx–lxxxiii; Witherington, *Acts*, 90–97, 440–43; Schnabel, *Mission*, 988–92; Das, 40–43.

inces (or to omit specific reference to *any* particular provinces).[105] In other words, the most natural reading of Gal 1–2 alongside Acts suggests that the meeting of Gal 2:1–10 happened exactly where Luke places the visit of Acts 11:28–30—between Paul's work in Tarsus and Antioch (11:19–26) and Paul and Barnabas's mission to the cities of southern Galatia (Acts 13–14).[106] Luke's account of this second visit is, however, *significantly* different from what we read in Gal 2:1–10. Rather than speak of any meeting between Paul, Barnabas, Peter, James the Just, and John on this occasion or raising the questions of (1) the conditions of gentile inclusion or (2) the validity of Paul's commission and ministry, Luke speaks only of Paul and Barnabas delivering relief funds to the "elders" (Acts 11:27–30; 12:25).

In favor of making this identification nevertheless is Paul's evident care in relating the sum of his visits to Jerusalem and interactions with the Jerusalem church and its leadership in Gal 1:13–2:14 up to the point at which his narrative ends. Paul recounts his own story under a self-imposed oath in Gal 1–2 (1:20), which suggests that he is attempting to lay out his visits to Jerusalem and other events in his life with careful attention to chronology and completeness ("then after three years . . . ," 1:18; "then . . . ," 1:21; "then after fourteen years . . . ," 2:1), at least where his dealings with Jerusalem and the Jerusalem church powers are concerned, so as to establish certain points about his relationship to those powers (his commission and authorization came from God, not people, including the Jerusalem church leaders; his message is principally informed by his encounter with the glorified Lord and its implications, not by teaching received from other human beings; he preaches as God's envoy, not the envoy of the Jerusalem leadership).[107] Omission of an

---

105. A weakness in Knox's reconstruction of the situation is that he assumes Paul to have evangelized Macedonia and Achaia prior to meeting with the Jerusalem pillars in Gal 2:1–10, effectively postponing any conference between Paul and the Jerusalem leadership until the point in the Acts narrative where Luke relates Paul's (alleged) fourth visit to Jerusalem (Knox, *Chapters*, 57). If this were the case, however, Paul's decision to name Syria and Cilicia as his next field of mission work after Arabia, but to omit reference to Macedonia and Achaia as such a field, in Gal 1:21 lacks any plausible explanation. See also Das, 35–36; Longenecker, lxxv–lxxvii, in critique of Knox's approach.

106. The objection that this reading does not give Paul sufficient missionary experience and achievement to claim that he has been entrusted with "apostleship for the gentiles" (see Stein, "Relationship of Galatians 2:1–10," 239–42) does not take sufficient account of Paul's understanding of his calling. For him, "apostleship to the gentiles" was fixed at his experience of God's revelation of Jesus. The objection also needlessly downplays his investment in this commission in "Arabia," Syria, and Cilicia over the span of a decade (Longenecker, lxxxi).

107. Granted that one can read 1:20 as an oath taken only in regard to the details of the first visit to Jerusalem, it does not seem plausible that Paul would voluntarily invoke such an oath only then to play fast and loose with the other data. On the significance of Paul's repeated use of "then," see also Longenecker, 45; Das, 161.

entire visit, especially when he has invoked an oath about the truthfulness of his report at an earlier juncture, would seriously undermine the credibility of the remainder of his report. The argument that Paul simply considered the famine relief visit irrelevant is beside the point; he would need to have mentioned it and declared its irrelevance so as not to leave himself vulnerable to disconfirmation by the rival teachers who were still active among his churches as Galatians is read to them.[108]

Another strong impetus for making this identification is that it provides the best explanation for Paul's silence concerning the decision rendered concerning gentile circumcision in the apostolic decree (Acts 15:19–21, 23–29).[109] If, after hearing the evidence from the various parties involved, James the Just had indeed decided that gentiles would not be required to undergo circumcision as a prerequisite for joining the Jesus movement but be asked only to adopt some minimal practices characteristic of Godfearers—and if he had even issued an official letter to this effect to be circulated among the churches at least of Syria and Cilicia—it is difficult to believe that Paul would not mention this fact as the climax of his narrative.[110] In an environment in which the pillars are held in high esteem, such a document (or even oral report) would have been damning to the rival teachers' case.[111] Paul could *also* claim that

---

108. Rightly, Burton, 67–68; Foakes-Jackson and Lake, *Beginnings*, 5:200–201; Longenecker, lxxviii. If one wished to maintain that Paul did *not* omit mention of an intervening visit but still was inclined to identify Gal 2:1–10 with Acts 15, the alternative would be to admit that Luke was misinformed about a famine-relief visit occurring earlier than the Jerusalem Conference (as in Haenchen, *Acts*, 377–79).

109. Fung, 17; Bruce, 52.

110. If it is argued that Gal 2:1–10 is in fact Paul's representation of this climax (with Gal 2:11–14 as an unfortunate anticlimax), then we need to wrestle with the degree to which Luke has exaggerated his depiction of the meeting's scope, formality, and results. It is implausible that Paul would have remained silent about the decree in toto because he was unhappy with the stipulations, as an easy win against the rival teachers with the most minor concessions (concessions of the sort, moreover, that Paul would later urge making anyway for the sake of the comfort of the "weak" in the church) would be preferable to the risk of a complete loss.

111. The evident respect that the addressees had for the pillars, such that Paul has to carefully delineate his own relationship with them, also suggests that nothing like the apostolic decree of Acts 15 had already been disseminated in the name of the pillars, only then to be disregarded by both the rival teachers and the Galatian converts in regard to the question of gentile circumcision (though Ridderbos, 33, does think that a postdecree date would be in line with Paul's astonishment at what is happening in Galatia; Gal 1:6).

It is also often urged that Peter's and Barnabas's behavior in Antioch (Gal 2:1–14) is more readily understandable prior to an official decision concerning what would be required of gentiles entering the Christian community, since the ruling of the council would otherwise have given them adequate guidance concerning table fellowship with gentiles and, indeed, made it impossible for anyone coming "from James" to say otherwise (e.g., see Fung, 17; Longenecker, lxxxi; Das, 41). While one gets the distinct impression from Acts 16–28 that the

the Jerusalem church leaders "added nothing" to his own message and the practice of his churches (Gal 2:10) only prior to the apostolic decree, since this decree did specifically call for observance of four prohibitions on the part of gentile converts.[112]

The differences between Acts 11:28–30 and Gal 2:1–10 may be accounted for by the fact that Luke and any informants available to Luke as he wrote looked upon this meeting from the outside, underscoring the external fact of the visit as a famine relief project (Acts 11:27–30). The phrasing of Gal 2:10, in which the Jerusalem apostles urge Paul and Barnabas to "continue to re-member the poor," while Paul asserts that he was already eager to do this very thing, would complement the "relief fund" aspect of this visit.[113] Such a limited focus also reflects Luke's interest in simplifying the process by means of which early Christian leaders arrived at clarity on the whole issue of gentile inclu-sion, which is in keeping with his tendency to portray greater unanimity than was likely the case.[114] Paul, however, speaks of the visit as an insider, being privy to the private meeting with James, Peter, and John. While Paul is intent on demonstrating his essential independence from these Jerusalem pillars, the narration of this meeing also affords him an opportunity to assert their validation of his calling at the same time, as well as relate an anecdote about Titus, which Paul invokes as a historical judgment and quasi-legal precedent.

Holding to this position comes at the cost at least of affirming the pre-cise chronological accuracy of Acts 11:27–12:25. There is ample evidence for

---

Jerusalem Conference ironed out all the difficulties surrounding the place of gentiles within the church and issues concerning Jew-gentile interactions within that body, it remains plau-sible that the four stipulations laid upon gentiles in the decree, if the decree was a historical document, had conclusive value only for gentile inclusion, not for Jew-gentile interaction.

112. Longenecker, lxxix–lxxx; Fung, 14–15. The additional requirements would also have merited naming and explanation so that they could not be used by the opposition as support for the observance of the Torah more broadly (Das, 39).

113. Paul's choice of the *present* subjunctive form here (μνημονεύωμεν), which can indicate continued or ongoing engagement in an activity, may be significant (thus Longe-necker, lxxx–lxxxi; deSilva, *Handbook*, 34; contra Keener, *Acts 15:1–23:35*, 2197). Of course, the tense could also speak about the quality of an action not yet begun ("that we should go about mindful of the poor [in Jerusalem]" or "that we should make the [material] remem-brance of the poor a consistent part of our work").

114. Luke's treatment of Peter vis-à-vis the questions of preaching to the gentiles and the basis for and conditions of gentile inclusion in the new community is again a case in point. Peter is credited with the insight that the giving of the Spirit to gentiles on the basis of faith shows God to have accepted them in their uncircumcised state and to have considered them "clean" for association with God's self (Acts 10:45–48; 11:12, 17–18; 15:8–11), the very insight that led Paul to his own position (Gal 3:1–5; 4:6–7), behind which Peter was clearly lagging in Antioch (Gal 2:11–14). Comparing Peter's speech in Acts 15:11 with Paul's retort to Peter in Gal 2:15–16 especially brings Luke's agenda to the fore.

a famine affecting the eastern Mediterranean between 46 and 48 CE. Pliny the Elder speaks of grain prices spiking in Egypt in 45–46 CE, and Josephus speaks of relief efforts undertaken by Queen Helena of Adiabene in response to famine in Syria and Palestine under Tiberius Julius Alexander, governor of Judea from 46 to 48 CE (*Jewish Antiquities* 20.51–53).[115] However, Luke narrates Paul and Barnabas's famine relief visit as an event sandwiching an episode of persecution of core Jerusalem Christian leaders by Herod Agrippa I, who died in 44 CE. Paul and Barnabas travel prior to this episode in Acts 11:27–30 and are said to return after it in Acts 12:25. If Luke is correct to relate the famine visit as occurring prior to Herod's death (Acts 12:20–23), it occurred so early as to make it almost impossible within Paul's timeline in Gal 1–2.[116] It is entirely plausible, however, and quite in keeping with ancient historiography, that Luke has woven his narrative of the persecution under Herod Agrippa, which happened some time prior to Paul's second visit, into his account of that visit for reasons other than striving after chronological accuracy.[117] One reason for doing so might have been to introduce John Mark into the narrative (12:12) in close connection with this visit by Paul and Barnabas, since they return to Antioch taking John Mark along (12:25).

The very different pictures of the purposes and natures of Paul's visits to Jerusalem in Acts 11:27–30 and 12:25 vis-à-vis Gal 2:1–10 lead many to identify the latter narrative rather with the event described in Acts 15:6–21 because, in their opinion, "the central issue, key participants and principal arguments are so close that the two accounts must be variant versions of the same episode."[118] Barnabas, Paul, Peter, and James are all present at both meetings; a more conservative Jewish-Christian party is represented; the subject of whether or not gentile converts need to accept circumcision as part of their initiation into Christ arises in regard to both; there is an agreement reached. Alongside these similarities, however, are significant differences:

---

115. Pliny, *Natural History* 5.10 §58; 18.46 §168; Gapp, "Universal Famine"; Das, 42.

116. Salvaging Luke's timetable would require Paul to have been converted in 30 or 31, counting Paul's "three" and "fourteen years" (Gal 1:18; 2:1) as running concurrently from that conversion date, *and* a reckoning of partial years as full years within the fourteen.

117. See, for example, the varying accounts of the timing of the death of Antiochus IV Epiphanes in 1 and 2 Maccabees. In the former, this event occurs significantly later than the rededication of the Jerusalem temple (the rededication, 1 Macc 4:36–58; Antiochus's death, 6:1–16); in 2 Maccabees, the two events are concurrent, with the episode of Antiochus's death (9:1–29) being formally concluded (10:9) only after the narration of the rededication (10:1–8).

118. Dunn, 88; so also Lightfoot, 123–28; Schlier, 115–16; Ridderbos, 78–80; Stein, "Galatians 2:1–10 and Acts 15:1–35"; Betz, 81–83; D. Williams, *Acts*, 256–61; Dunn, *Beginning*, 446–50; Pervo, *Dating Acts*, 79–96; Keener, *Acts 15:1–23:35*, 2200–2202; Schnelle, *Apostle Paul*, 125; Mussner, 128–32.

1. Paul speaks of a private meeting between himself, Barnabas, the pillars, and possibly Titus. He is emphatic on this point (Gal 2:2b) and speaks of the more conservative Jewish Christians as an uninvited, intrusive party to the conversation. Luke, however, speaks of the intentional convening of a more general assembly consisting at least of "the apostles and the elders," alongside other concerned parties (Acts 15:5–7, 12–13, 22).

2. The meeting narrated in Acts is focused principally on the question of what gentile converts were required to do to be part of the new people of God formed from both Jews and gentiles.[119] The meeting narrated by Paul in Gal 2:1–10 was chiefly focused on the confirmation of Paul's calling as apostle to the gentiles and on the parameters of the two principal missions of Peter and Paul (2:7–10).[120] The particular "test case" of Titus was a secondary matter, one that appears to have arisen incidentally.

3. In Paul's account of his second visit, he and Barnabas go away with only one stipulation placed on his work, namely, that they continue to remember the poor (Gal 2:10), whereas Luke documents four stipulations being laid upon all gentile believers, including the avoidance of the ingestion of blood (e.g., left in the tissues of strangled animals) and the avoidance of meat from animals that had been sacrificed to idols, as a kind of "bare minimum" in the way of purity requirements for being part of the new people of God. More notably, the one requirement that Paul names is not among the four requirements that Luke names.

These differences are accounted for by appealing to the differing perspectives, purposes, and proximities of the narrators, with Luke crafting a picture of a grander, more formal, and decisive meeting than probably was the case. Identifying the visit of Gal 2:1–10 with the Jerusalem Conference, however, creates the problems alluded to earlier. First, either one must believe that Paul omitted a reference to a famine relief visit occurring between the visits recounted in Gal 1:18–20 and Gal 2:1–10 (as well as omitting reference to the additional territories in which he worked in between those visits), despite the appearances he gives of giving a complete accounting of his interactions with the Jerusalem church through that earlier period; or one must conclude that Luke has invented such a visit (or seriously misunderstood the "collection" visit, reflected in Rom 15:25–28, which is otherwise curiously absent from Acts). Second, Paul's silence concerning the terms of

---

119. Lightfoot (126) believes that Gal 2:1–10 gives hints of speaking about both a plenary and a private meeting. If this is true, Paul's perspective on the "plenary" meeting (as involving false brothers who surreptitiously inserted themselves where they did not belong) is strikingly different from Luke's.

120. Fung, 13; Das, 38. Schnabel (*Mission*, 987) also finds the discrepancies to be too great to allow for identification of these events.

the apostolic decree (Acts 15:22–29) becomes difficult to explain—even on the supposition that the Jerusalem Conference failed to solve the problems it addressed—unless one attributes to Luke a great deal of license in his representation of the event (though the wholesale invention of a document like the decree is not in keeping with the best practices of ancient historiography).[121]

One important consequence of identifying Gal 2:1–10 with Acts 15 is that the struggle to come to grips with gentile inclusion in the church is significantly prolonged. The confrontation in Antioch between Paul on the one hand and Peter and Barnabas on the other would show that the magnificent consensus of the Jerusalem Conference was quickly shattered, with no clear indication that a new consensus was reached during Paul's lifetime.[122] On this view, Paul becomes increasingly alienated from the principal (and original) leaders of the movement, and his sphere of influence becomes more marginalized (being eventually limited to Macedonia and Achaia). "The rehabilitation of Paul" thus becomes "one of Luke's major purposes for writing Acts," crafting a Paul who was both accepted by the Jerusalem apostles and more accepting of them and their strictures himself.[123] Of course, whether one places Gal 2:1–10 and its aftermath in Antioch prior to the Jerusalem Conference or identifies the meetings, the path to consensus through discernment remains significantly more difficult in historical reality than in the pages of Acts.

A decision between these two positions is not easy, nor (again) is one's place on the spectrum between operating with a hermeneutic of suspicion and operating with a hermeneutic of trust a reliable index of which solution one will prefer. On balance, the data seem to me to support the following narrative best. After Paul and Barnabas are active in mission work in the regions of Syria and Cilicia for quite some time, they travel to Jerusalem with the aim of meeting with Peter, James, and John to make sure that their own mission continues to be in harmony with the work of, and have the support of, the original apostles (even if Paul would not admit to being subject to their authority or direction). They do not go empty-handed but bring with them the fruits of a collection taken in Antioch for the mother church in Jerusalem and the poor in its community. Such a gesture is already more than mere almsgiving; it is a symbol of kinship and commitment, meant to provoke reciprocal feelings. The private conversation related in Gal 2:1–10 is a preliminary conversation about two missions; it achieves mutual affirmation

---

121. It would certainly not be unprecedented, as scholarly investigations of the documents quoted in 1 and 2 Maccabees have often determined, but even such inventions as one finds in these texts are fabricated on the basis of probable facts (e.g., attempts to form political alliances, the original texts of which missives came to be lost; see deSilva, *Introducing the Apocrypha*, 252–53, 269–70).

122. Phillips, *Paul, His Letters, and Acts*, 194.

123. Phillips, *Paul, His Letters, and Acts*, 195.

of the practice of these missions without yet considering the implications, for example, for table fellowship between the circumcised and the uncircumcised in a single congregation.

A group of more conservative Jewish Christians uses the opportunity of the pillars and the renegade missionaries standing together in the same space to push their agenda of requiring that gentile converts to the Christian faith undergo the same process as full proselytes to the Jewish way of life (a perfectly natural viewpoint for those who regard the Jesus movement completely as a subset of Judaism, as Paul apparently does not; Gal 1:13–14). Paul holds his ground. It is not clear whether the pillars actually made a pronouncement in this regard ("No, Titus does not need to be circumcised") or simply refrained from saying the opposite ("Titus, you need to be circumcised"). It is clear, however, that Paul understood the absence of a demand placed on Titus to accept circumcision to have settled the issue of whether or not gentile converts needed to accept circumcision and other markers of Jewish identity then and there.[124]

Paul read more into the noncompelling of Titus to be circumcised than Peter, to judge from the confrontation in Antioch. More conservative Jewish Christians arrived from Jerusalem (probably with some level of support from James himself; see commentary on 2:11–13) and began raising questions that some people at the table in the conversations of Gal 2:1–10 did not regard as having been clearly settled. The earlier agreement does not appear to have envisioned a congregation of Jewish and gentile Christians mingling—and eating—together. The pressure these visitors applied on Peter, and through him upon other Jewish Christians in Antioch, to eat at a separate table where greater attention was paid to purity regulations need not be seen as a breach of the earlier agreement, nor would Peter have thus viewed his change of practice, undertaken simply to enable Jewish Christians who feel the need to do so to remain in their social patterns, and even to accommodate to them for the sake of their comfort and consciences.

The confrontation in Antioch, and more especially the continued activity of the more conservative Jewish Christian lobbyists and missionaries

---

124. Dunn, 38, objects to identifying Gal 2:1–10 with the visit of Acts 11:28–30, since, "if . . . the issue of circumcision was resolved as decisively as Gal. ii.1–10 indicates, with the full and formal approval of the Jerusalem leadership (ii.3, 6–9) in the face of strong internal pressure to the contrary (ii.4–5), it is difficult to see how it could have become an issue once again in Acts xv. In order to preserve Luke's reliability, it seems necessary to impugn the good faith of the Jerusalem leadership." Dunn, however, seems to be assuming here—like Paul himself!—that the meeting of Gal 2:1–10 resolved more than it actually did. From the perspective of the pillars, it may have only resolved questions of two separate but equal missions, one to Jews and one to gentiles. Keener (*Acts: Introduction and 1:1–2:47*, 244) also believes that Gal 2:7–9 shows only that the "leaders agree that gentiles need not be circumcised."

whose reach extended into Syria, Cilicia, and the cities of South Galatia, lead to a more formal and inclusive meeting at which the church comes to a consensus decision—though there will continue to be dissenters and issues with implementation—about the terms under which gentiles will be included in the movement and the question of table fellowship between Jews and gentiles in the church. We cannot tell from the surviving evidence of Paul's writings the extent to which he would have been personally supportive of stipulations like avoiding the meat of strangled animals or taking care to avoid the ingestion of blood, since his letters respond only to topics that had become issues in his churches, though in his planting of churches he might indeed communicate these issues as the price of a unified vision for mission. His careful, casuistic attention to the question of how to deal with the meat from animals that had been killed in idolatrous rites could be taken as evidence of his trying to work out one detail of the apostolic decree within his churches that had become an issue.[125] Of course, his agreement that fornication was to be avoided was automatic, given his own ethical convictions (see, e.g., 1 Cor 6:12–20).

VII. THE DATE OF GALATIANS

When it comes to assigning actual dates for the events in Galatians, and indeed any events associated with the first decades of the Christian movement, we are dependent upon Luke-Acts and its synchronisms. Luke dates the beginning of John the Baptizer's ministry to a time within the fifteenth year of the reign of Tiberius, or 28–29 CE. Luke also locates several episodes in Acts by connecting them with Roman administrators: Paul and Barnabas in Cyprus during the proconsulate of Sergius Paulus (13:6–12); Paul in Corinth during the proconsulship of Lucius Junius Gallio (18:12–17); Paul in custody in Caesarea during the final two years of the prefecture of Antonius Felix and the beginning of the prefecture of Porcius Festus (23:23–26:32). The transition between these governors can be dated to 59 or 60 CE.[126] To these we could add the death of James, son of Zebedee, under Herod Agrippa I, king of Judea from 41 to 44 CE.

---

125. Longenecker, lxxx. See Rom 14:3–4, 14; 1 Cor 8:1–9; 10:25–31. Paul himself is remembered to have insisted that all foods are clean, if received with thanksgiving (1 Tim 4:3–5) and to have defended, in principle, the harmlessness of eating the meat of animals that had been sacrificed to idols, though he was clearly willing to make concessions in this regard.

126. Helen K. Bond, "Felix," *NIDB* 2:448; David C. Braund, "Felix," *ABD* 2:783.

Of special interest to New Testament chronology is the synchronism of Paul's work in Corinth with the proconsulship of Gallio. An inscription in Delphi recording the emperor Claudius's response to Gallio's report on the province of Achaia reads as follows:

> Tiberius [Claudius] Caesar Augustus Germanicus, [Pontifex maximus, in his tribunician] power [year 12, acclaimed Emperor for] the 26th time, father of the country, [consul for the 5th time, censor, sends greetings to the city of Delphi.] I have for long been zealous for the city of Delphi [and favourable to it from the] beginning, and I have always observed the cult of the [Pythian] Apollo, [but with regard to] the present stories, and those quarrels of the citizens of which [a report has been made by Lucius] Junius Gallio my friend, and [pro]consul [of Achaea]. . . .[127]

Claudius's response can be dated to between January 52 and January 53 (his twelfth year in power),[128] prior to August 52 (when he was declared *imperator* a twenty-seventh time). Gallio had therefore likely been dispatched to Achaia to begin his term in July 51 (July being the typical start of the term for provincial governors) in order to have reported on conditions in the province to Claudius in time for the latter to have issued a response to the province in mid-52.

Assuming Luke to be correct that Paul was accused before Gallio in Corinth,[129] this information would fix Paul's ministry in Corinth chronologically. This date, in turn, becomes essential for working backward and forward through the rest of the chronology of Paul's career. We do not need to assume that this event falls late in Paul's stay. Luke reports that Paul stayed in Corinth for about a year and a half (Acts 18:11), giving no clear indication of the point during that stay at which his hearing before Gallio occurred.[130] Paul could thus have begun his ministry in Corinth in spring 51, with sufficient time elapsing for him to alienate the local Jewish population prior to Gallio's arrival

---

127. Barrett, *New Testament Background*, 51–52; see the discussion of this inscription in Murphy-O'Connor, "Paul and Gallio."

128. The number twelve is inferred in the text based on the fact that Claudius was known to have been acclaimed *imperator* a twenty-second, twenty-third, and twenty-fourth time during his eleventh year (Barrett, *New Testament Background*, 52).

129. For arguments in defense of Luke's accuracy in making this claim, see Keener, *Acts 15:1–23:35*, 2760–61.

130. Luke narrates crises at the climax of each episode where possible: the confrontation with Elymas in Paphos; the incident in Philippi leading to beating, imprisonment, and hasty exit; the hearing before Gallio; and the riot in Ephesus. Luke tends to relate these as occurring at the end of Paul's stay at a given place, though in the case of Corinth he mentions that Paul stayed on for a considerable time thereafter. See also Witherington, *Acts*, 552.

around May of 51 and his early departure from office (illness prevented Gallio from completing his term), probably in the fall.[131]

Paul also provides relative chronology within his narrative in Gal 1–2. According to him, his first visit to Jerusalem occurred "after three years" (1:18), presumably counting time from his dramatic turnaround, with his second visit occurring "after" (or "at the end of") "fourteen years" (2:1). A significant question is whether Paul is counting the fourteen years also from his conversion, giving an accounting from a fixed reference point, or from the time of the first visit to Jerusalem.[132]

Identifying Gal 2:1–10 with the visit of Acts 11:28–30 raises some challenges for chronology as it pertains to the reconciliation of Galatians with the framework of Acts.[133] In order to accommodate the time spans named in Galatians along with the events named in Acts, one would need to be willing to grant at least two of the following three presuppositions:

1. Paul is counting partial years as whole years.
2. The three years and the fourteen years are concurrent, both beginning with Paul's life-changing encounter with the glorified Christ.[134]
3. The crucifixion occurred in 29 or 30 CE (and not later), with Paul's conversion occurring by 32, though there is nothing to preclude Paul's conversion happening within a year of the crucifixion.[135]

Adopting the latter two presuppositions, we could arrive at the following chronology:

29 or 30 CE: Jesus's death and resurrection
31–32: Paul's conversion

---

131. This fact is reported by Gallio's brother, Lucius Annaeus Seneca, in *Moral Essays* 104.1. Longenecker's dating (lxxxii) of the beginning of Paul's stay in Corinth to the ninth year of Claudius's reign seems arbitrarily early.

132. The fact that ἔπειτα is always used sequentially in Paul is irrelevant to this question. Granting that ἔπειτα indicates the next event in a sequence in Gal 2:1, it still does not tell us where the "fourteen years" begin. "I began teaching at Ashland Theological Seminary as an assistant professor in 1995. Then after three years I was promoted to associate professor. Then at the end of seven years I was made a full professor." Did the process take seven or ten years to complete?

133. Hemer, "Acts and Galatians," 87.

134. Robinson, *Redating*, 37; Martyn, 180–82; Das, 161–63.

135. Longenecker, lxxxiii. Hemer ("Observations on Pauline Chronology," 13) argues that the events of Acts 1–8, to the extent that they are historical, need not have occupied more than a few months—such was the vigor of the early Christian movement at its inception. See also Riesner, *Early Period*, 67–74; Keener, *Acts 3:1–14:28*, 1602–3.

32–34: Paul's first attempts at evangelism in Arabia and Damascus

35: Paul's first visit to Jerusalem

46 or 47: The famine relief visit and private meeting with the pillars[136]

47–49: Paul and Barnabas's mission to South Galatia; the Antioch incident; activity of rival missionaries in Syria, Cilicia, and southern Galatia

48 or 49: Composition of Galatians

49: Paul's third visit to Jerusalem and the Apostolic Conference

49–51: Paul's return visit to South Galatian churches to consolidate his work; mission in Macedonia and arrival in Corinth.

This is admittedly a tight schedule, and any uncertainty in the decisions involved becomes a factor against identifying Gal 2:1–10 with the visit in Acts 11:27–30 or against the chronological reliability of the Acts narrative overall.[137]

Several approaches to the question of dating Galatians relative to Paul's other letters are fundamentally flawed. One approach treats the content or theological perspective of each letter as a reliable indicator of date. Thus the strong eschatological orientation of 1 Thessalonians, contrasted with the relative lack of interest in eschatology in Galatians, suggests to some that Paul could not have written the two letters within a short span of each other, with the result that Galatians ought to be dated considerably later. This argument ignores the more fundamental issue governing the content of Paul's letters, namely, the situations of, and issues faced or raised by, the addressees of each particular letter, which will largely determine the degree to which Paul gives voice to a particular theme or topic (whether as a direct point at issue or as an ancillary topic invoked to address a principal issue).[138] Similarly, the absence of the so-called faith-works antithesis in the Corinthian and Thessalonian letters is not due to Paul's not having yet formulated it, such that Galatians and Romans should both be dated among the later of Paul's letters, but to its irrelevance to the challenges in the situations being addressed in Corinth and Thessalonica.[139] Furthermore, the fact that Galatians and Romans treat many of the same topics and are profitably read in connection with one another does not help us determine when Galatians was written.[140]

---

136. This event can be pushed forward to 47–48 CE. See Becker, *Paul: Apostle to the Gentiles*, 31; Witherington, *Paul Quest*, 314–18; Alexander, "Chronology of Paul," 122–23.

137. Phillips (*Paul, His Letters, and Acts*, 81) rightly observes that "the final question becomes whether one prefers an awkward fit that seems to support the chronological accuracy of Acts or a much more comfortable fit that calls the chronological accuracy of Acts into question." Phillips himself opts for the latter.

138. Rightly, Fung, 23.

139. Rightly, Bruce, 49.

140. Lightfoot argues that the similarities in content between Galatians and Romans

Arguments based on "tone" are even less helpful.[141] Readers of Paul cannot help but notice that Galatians and 2 Corinthians contain some of Paul's most virulent attacks regarding rival teachers and his own converts' stupidity for listening to them, as well as Paul's most defensive treatments of his own apostolic legitimacy. The shared tone, however, does not provide any solid evidence that the two letters were written in close proximity, only that Paul responded with a similar degree of intensity when he felt his own apostleship to be called into question and saw his converts shifting their loyalty to his critics. Both the tone and the content of a given epistle are matters related to the challenges and stresses of its particular situation, not to a particular period of Paul's life.

The fact that Paul's rivals in both Galatians and 2 Corinthians are Jewish Christian teachers also tells us nothing about the dating of the letters, since most early Christian leaders and teachers were in fact Jewish Christians. Moreover, Paul's rivals in Corinth do not appear to have been Judaizers per se. There is therefore no ground for trying to solve the question of the relative dating of these letters on the basis of discerning some progression in Paul's conflicts with these particular opponents, as they are likely *not* the same opponents.

EXCURSUS: PAUL, RHETORIC, AND LETTER-WRITING IN ANTIQUITY

Two important contexts for thinking about Galatians in terms both of Paul's objectives and of the text's impact upon the Christians he addresses are the contexts of letter-writing (epistolography) and rhetoric in Greco-Roman antiquity. The use of contemporary or near-contemporary oratorical practice

---

presuppose that Galatians was written shortly before Romans. John Drane, however, focusing on the theological *distance* between Galatians and Romans (as well as the Corinthian letters), could come to the opposite conclusion. He observes that Galatians is much more negative in terms of the role of Torah in the life of the believer and much more confident in the sufficiency of the Spirit than Paul is in Romans and the Corinthian letters, suggesting to him that some significant time had to elapse between the writing of Galatians and Romans (*Paul, Libertine or Legalist?*, 140–43; also Betz, 12, who favors a relatively earlier date for Galatians vis-à-vis Romans to allow for the taming of his emphasis "on the 'Spirit' without any qualification"). Keener (*Acts 15:1–23:35*, 2197) favors a later date in part because Galatians "addresses the same sorts of issues [found in Romans] and may derive from the same period in Paul's life." Discussing the same *topics*, however, is not the same as addressing the same sorts of *issues*. Gentile circumcision, the main issue in Galatians, is not an issue in Romans at all.

141. See, for example, Lightfoot, 49–55.

(rhetoric) in New Testament interpretation, however, is also highly contested.[142] The approach has invited a great deal of legitimate criticism on account of (1) the lack of consensus among rhetorical analysts of any given New Testament letter concerning the kind of rhetoric it exhibits and the role of the various parts of the discourse, and (2) the ways in which classical rhetorical theory, in the hands of its more zealous practitioners, becomes a series of templates to be imposed upon a given New Testament text and drives the results of exegesis. Some remarks here concerning the methods, excesses, criticisms, and promise of these approaches seem to me to be a necessary prelude to their employment throughout the present commentary.[143] Each of these two backgrounds merits consideration for what it can contribute to the illumination of Galatians, while pressing neither beyond what it can reasonably and reliably offer.

The reader who is not concerned about the methodological debate, however, is invited to proceed to the section entitled "Galatians as Persuasive Communication" on 91–106.

RHETORIC IN THE GRECO-ROMAN WORLD

A significant number of handbooks on the art of persuasive public speaking written during or near to the period of the composition of the New Testament texts have survived from antiquity, giving us firsthand information about what people native to that time and culture thought to be essential and useful to the task of attaining a variety of goals through argument and other kinds

---

142. The approach has nevertheless been pursued with particular energy and has resulted in an extensive body of publications. See the bibliography compiled in Duane F. Watson, *The Rhetoric of the New Testament: A Bibliographical Survey* (Dorset, UK: Deo, 2006). The intuition that classical rhetorical practice provides an appropriate background for exploring Paul's strategic invention and disposition of material is by no means novel. Although Kern (*Rhetoric and Galatians*, 258) is correct that "both Christians and their opponents found Paul to be no sophisticated author," the gifted exegete and preacher John Chrysostom, for example, analyzed Paul's material using the concepts of Greco-Roman oratory with some consistency in his own commentary on Galatians (see Fairweather, "Galatians and Classical Rhetoric," 2–22).

143. Porter, for example, justifiably demands some response to "the necessary question of what theoretical justification there is for employing the categories of classical rhetoric, especially those related to the species and arrangement, to the Pauline letters" ("Paul of Tarsus and His Letters," 565). I shall be content to offer theoretical justification for looking to the rhetorical handbooks for guidance at the levels of "invention" and "style" more than "species" and, certainly, "arrangement." Special mention is due Tolmie, *Persuading the Galatians*, a profoundly insightful analysis of the rhetoric of Galatians apart from a (direct) reliance upon classical rhetorical theory; my own analysis has greatly benefited from his work.

of appeal. The most important, because most comprehensive and detailed, would include Aristotle, *Art of Rhetoric* (fourth century BCE); Anaximenes, *Rhetoric to Alexander* (fourth century BCE); Pseudo-Cicero, *Rhetorica ad Herennium* (Rhetoric for Herennius, first century BCE); Cicero, *On Invention* and *On the Orator* (both mid-first century BCE); and Quintilian, *The Orator's Education* (late first century CE). To these can be added the earlier *progymnasmata*, textbooks offering training preliminary to the study of rhetoric, such as those by Theon of Alexandria (late first century CE) and Hermogenes of Tarsus (second century CE).[144]

Oratory was born out of the practical needs of the Greek city and the institutions required for the regulation of civic life. A city's enrolled citizens met to determine what course of action they should take on behalf of the city to meet some particular need. This setting was the home of "deliberative" rhetoric, the object of which was to discover the most advantageous course of action for the (usually immediate) future. Speakers promoting a particular course of action would try to establish that it was the *right* thing to do (i.e., that it was in keeping with the culture's core values, like courage, prudence, justice, or generosity), the *expedient* course to pursue (tending to preserve existing goods, gain other advantages, or ward off ills), a *feasible* course (the resources to undertake the course being available), an *honorable* response (embodying virtues, tending toward the praiseworthy), and the like.[145] Speakers trying to dissuade the assembly from pursuing a particular course would use the opposite topics.

A second principal setting for the development of a distinctive kind of rhetoric was the law court, where enrolled citizens (or a judge or judges) would be called upon to assess the innocence or guilt of a particular person in regard to some past action identified as a wrongdoing. This was another area of competition between speakers (a prosecutor and an advocate), with each seeking a particular judgment from the audience (the jury and/or judges) in regard to whether or not a particular person committed a particular wrong. "Judicial" or "forensic" rhetoric typically relied on the testimony of witnesses, oaths, material evidence, and logical probabilities for reconstructing the past event and assigning guilt.

---

144. The rhetorical handbooks are all available in the Loeb Classical Library. The *Progymnasmata* of Theon and Hermogenes, alongside several others, are helpfully collected in Kennedy, *Progymnasmata*; see also the texts collected in Kennedy, *Invention and Method*.

145. "One delivering an exhortation must prove that the courses to which he exhorts are just, lawful, expedient, honourable, pleasant and easily practicable; or failing this, in case the courses he is urging are disagreeable, he must show that they are feasible, and also that their adoption is unavoidable. One dissuading must apply hindrance by the opposite means" (Anaximenes, *Rhetoric to Alexander* 1421b21–27, LCL; these strategies are then more fully discussed in 1421b33–1423a12). See also Pseudo-Cicero, *Rhetorica ad Herennium* 3.2.2–3.4.9.

A third genre of rhetoric, "epideictic" or "demonstrative" oratory, was much broader in scope. In its most basic form and setting, epideictic rhetoric is connected with speeches given on civic occasions to remember and to praise the honored dead or to acknowledge exceptional benefactors, in which the goal was to lay out the virtues and achievements of the subject and win, essentially, assent from the audience concerning the virtue of the subject and the value of the qualities he, she, or they embodied (and thus the audience's ongoing commitment to those qualities as well).[146] This category also came to include speeches aimed at the demonstration of a particular thesis or proposition where, again, the goal of the speech was assent to the thesis or proposition, though one finds little discussion of this manifestation of the genre in the rhetorical handbooks.[147]

Each of these three types or species of rhetoric aligned with one of the three principal goals for a speech in one of the three principal settings for oratory in civic life. Those who turned the observation of successful rhetorical strategies into prescriptive textbooks for the composition and delivery of successful orations focused specifically on these three species in these three specific settings. The strategies used in these three genres of rhetoric were, however, by no means limited to the particular, civic settings in regard to which they are considered in the classical handbooks. Wherever some group needed to make a decision about a future course of action, deliberative strategies would be employed by those involved.[148] Questions of wrongdoing were raised not only formally in law courts but also in less formal settings, such that forensic strategies could be employed wherever one person accused another of wrongdoing, putting him or her on the defensive in the eyes of some group (whether it be a family, a circle of friends, or a voluntary association).[149]

---

146. This last point was often explicit in commemorative speeches. See Thucydides, *History*, 2.44; 4 Macc 18:1–2; Dio Chrysostom, *Discourses* 29.21.

147. The author of 4 Maccabees, however, understands both facets of his speech—the demonstration of a philosophical thesis and the praise of a group of Jewish martyrs—to represent facets of epideictic oratory, as he employs the language both of demonstration (ἐπιδείκνυσθαι, 1:1; ἀπόδειξιν, 3:19; ἀπέδειξα, 16:2) and of encomium (ἔπαινον, 1:2; ἐπαινεῖν, 1:10) when referring to his work. Anaximenes (*Rhetoric to Alexander* 1421b8–12) had identified "investigation" (ἐξεταστικόν) as one of seven subtypes of rhetoric (each of the principal three kinds having a pair of contrasting subtypes), useful either "by itself or in relation to another species."

148. Anaximenes is forthright on this point: "First let us discuss exhortation [τὰς προτροπάς] and dissuasion [τὰς ἀποτροπάς], as these are among the forms most employed *in private conversation and in public deliberation*" (*Rhetoric to Alexander* 1421b18–20; emphasis mine).

149. For this reason, I find objections to the use of rhetorical handbooks as aids in the interpretation of Pauline texts, based on the alleged distance in subject matter, venue, audience, and style between Paul's letters and classical rhetoric, unpersuasive (as in Kern,

Paul uses forensic strategies throughout 2 Cor 1 and 2, where he must acquit himself of (informal) charges about his truthfulness and sincerity, proving that he did not injure the believers by sending his painful letter rather than making a promised visit.[150] Only after Paul offered a successful defense of his changes in travel plans and his behavior otherwise could he and the church move forward in their relationship together.

Real speeches were also rarely pure in regard to exhibiting material belonging only to a single genre of rhetoric, as classical theorists themselves acknowledge.[151] Epideictic rhetoric could be incorporated into a defense speech to amplify the proven virtue and merit of the defendant before a jury in service of securing a favorable verdict. Epideictic rhetoric could be incorporated into a deliberative speech to hold up the praiseworthy memory of people who, in the past, had followed a course of action similar to the one being proposed, or to remind the audience of the dishonor that befell people who failed, in similar circumstances, to act as the speaker now urges. Forensic strategies could be employed within a deliberative speech to tear down the credibility of a rival speaker, or

---

Rhetoric and Galatians). A letter sent to urge a group of people in a house church or group of house churches to choose one course of action over another differs from an oration delivered to urge an assembly to choose one course of action over another only in accidents and particulars, not essence.

150. See deSilva, "Meeting the Exigency," 14–22. In 2 Cor 1:15–2:11 we find Paul giving a brief statement of the facts (1:15–16) in which he admits to his change in travel plans. The issue then becomes whether Paul was right to have acted as he did: "the right or wrong of the act is in question" (Pseudo-Cicero, *Rhetorica ad Herennium* 1.24). In the course of his defense of the rightness of his action, he employs several "inartificial proofs" that would have been equally at home in the courtroom—calling witnesses (in this case, God; 1:23) and making affirmations under oath (1:18, 23). He offers several reasons why his decision not to return for a second visit was not blameworthy: he compares the course he took advantageously against the alternative course (1:23; 2:1–3), arguing that it was better for both parties that he stayed away rather than making a second visit that might only increase pain and alienation; he substitutes one motive for another (2:4; see also 7:12), asserting that he sent his harsh letter not to cause pain but rather to show the depth of his love; he shifts responsibility for his action (2:5–8) to an unnamed "offender" whose actions are more directly responsible for Paul's change of travel plans. All of these strategies are reflected in discussions of forensic rhetoric, particularly of defense speeches (see Pseudo-Cicero, *Rhetorica ad Herennium* 1.24–25; Aristotle, *Rhetoric* 3.15.3). This is not to say that 2 Corinthians is a forensic *speech* or that it ought to be outlined in terms of the structure of a forensic speech—only to say that Paul uses typical forensic strategies in the context of dealing with informal charges in the course of his work as a church planter.

151. See Aristotle, *Rhetoric* 1.3.5; also Anaximenes, *Rhetoric to Alexander* 1427b31–35; Pseudo-Cicero, *Rhetorica ad Herennium* 3.8.15. A similar phenomenon appears in the discussions of types or categories of letters in the ancient theorists of epistolography, where the "mixed" type is an expected category (see Pseudo-Libanius, *Epistolary Styles*, 46, 92).

to set aside prejudice that had been aroused against oneself by "setting the record straight" (as Paul does, again, in the opening of 2 Corinthians). A nuanced rhetorical analysis even of a speech by the late-first-century orator Dio Chrysostom, let alone a letter of Paul, would not merely try to decide *that* the speech is deliberative, for example, but to discern the ways in which epideictic and forensic topics, if present, support the overarching deliberative goal.

According to the rhetorical theorists, composing and delivering a speech involved giving attention to five basic facets of the overall task: (1) invention, (2) arrangement, (3) style, (4) memory, and (5) delivery.[152] Invention involved determining the principal issues to be addressed and resolved (the *stasis*) and considering all the possible avenues of advancing one's case, laying out the proofs and appeals at the speaker's disposal. He would consider what prejudices and arguments existed against him or his case, and how to answer these obstructions.[153] He would then consider how best to arrange the material to make the strongest impression on the hearers. As a general rule, prejudice against the speaker and his case was most effectively removed up front, prejudice against opponents most usefully aroused at the end of a speech. The strongest proofs were presented at the beginning and ending of the argument, making a strong first impression and a strong denouement.[154] The orator then attended to stylistic considerations—when to use the grand style, suitable for rousing attention and emotion, when to use the plain style, suited to rational argumentation, where to use ornaments and figures of diction to dress up the way the speech falls upon the ears of the hearers. Once the text of the speech was set, the orator would memorize the speech and go on to consider how best to use his physical presence and gestures in the delivery of the speech.[155]

---

152. See, for example, Cicero, *Orator* 1.142; *Invention* 1.9.

153. Most of Aristotle's *Rhetoric* is devoted to invention (1.4–2.26). I favor the pronoun "he" in this section in part to avoid awkwardness and in part because of the reality that the practice of oratory was dominated by males. This is not to say that females never learned or employed the art or had occasion to make persuasive speeches.

154. Thus advises the author of *Rhetorica ad Herennium* 3.10.18.

155. Since we have only the texts themselves and not their performance, the material on memory and delivery plays almost no role in New Testament interpretation. It is not likely that the reader of a Pauline letter memorized the manuscript before sharing its contents, so "memory" simply would not apply. The emissary may have been coached concerning how to deliver the contents to the gathering, or have taken thought himself how to make the delivery most effective through varying vocal tone, using physical gestures, and the like, but such matters are irretrievable. Invention, arrangement, and style are the focal points of most rhetorical-critical studies; of these, the material in the rhetorical handbooks treating the first two is the most helpful in getting at the meaning of a text.

In the process of invention, orators were attentive to a variety of kinds of appeal to the hearers, and not just to rational argumentation, since people's decisions were influenced by their emotions as well as their assessment of the speaker. Rhetorical handbooks thus routinely refer to three kinds of appeals or proofs that must be woven together into the successful speech—the appeal to rational argumentation (*logos*), the emotions of the hearer (*pathos*), and the hearer's perception of the speaker and/or rival speakers (*ēthos*).[156]

The last of these factors is foundational to all the others, since without audience trust and respect, a speaker has no hope of persuading that audience: "The orator persuades by moral character when his speech is delivered in such a manner as to render him worthy of confidence.... But this confidence must be due to the speech itself, not to any preconceived idea of the speaker's character.... Moral character, so to say, constitutes the most effective means of proof" (Aristotle, *Rhetoric* 1.2.4). This observation would still hold true four hundred years later, when Quintilian compiled his compendium of wisdom and technique learned from a lifetime of successful public speaking: "But what really carries greatest weight in deliberative speeches is the authority of the speaker. For he, who would have all men trust his judgment as to what is expedient and honourable, should both possess and be regarded as possessing genuine wisdom and excellence of character" (*Education*, 3.8.12–13). These rhetorical theorists are only recording what, upon reflection, all would recognize as common sense. Speakers must have our trust and confidence if they are to persuade us to do anything; conversely, doubts about credibility prove the quickest and most effective means to undermining a particular speaker's message.

In a situation where several speakers vie for the audience's allegiance to their cause, people are more likely to accept the arguments of, and be persuaded by, the speaker whom they trust *more*. Credibility was generally created as a speaker impressed upon the hearers that he was morally upright, expert in the matters on which he spoke, and well-disposed to the hearers, such that all that he would urge would be in their best interest.[157] Any prejudice that might exist against the speaker must be eliminated before he could effectively address the subject matter of his speech.[158] By extension, speakers often found it necessary, or at least advantageous, to cast doubt on the sincerity, reliability, and good will of opposing speakers.

The wise speaker also paid attention to the emotional state of the audience, seeking to arouse those emotions that would dispose an audience more

---

156. Aristotle, *Rhetoric* 1.2.3.

157. Aristotle, *Rhetoric* 2.1.3, 5; Quintilian, *Education* 3.8.13.

158. See especially *Rhetorica ad Herennium* 1.9 on eliminating prejudice through the "subtle approach."

readily to move in the direction that the speaker wished. Aristotle recognized that people make different decisions when they are angry, calm, afraid, or confident, and that orators would frequently arouse particular emotions in the hearers to their advantage (*Rhetoric* 1.2.5; 2.1.2, 4, 8). An orator seeking a verdict of guilt would seek to rouse indignation or anger against the defendant; an orator wishing to persuade the audience to take a certain course of action would perhaps strive to make them feel confident that they could achieve the goal, or afraid or ashamed not to try, and so forth. Aristotle provides a long list of topics and situations that arouse eleven different emotions, helping the modern reader to learn sensitivity to this aspect of oratory and to detect where an author may be trying to make his audience feel pity, fear, confidence, emulation, and the like (2.2–11). Indeed, after two millennia his catalog of emotions and what prompts can evoke them remains unsurpassed.

Finally, there is the appeal to the hearer's reason. An orator will tend to establish his case by both deductive and inductive means. Deductive proofs include the syllogism and the enthymeme. Aristotle described an enthymeme as, in effect, a statement or maxim supported by a rationale, which adds the "why and wherefore" (2.21.2). Thus, the statement "No one is truly free" is a maxim. When it is joined to an explanation, it becomes an enthymeme: "No one is truly free, for he or she is the slave of either wealth or fortune" (2.21.2). Other enthymematic forms are treated by other classical rhetoricians.[159]

The orator's goal is to lead the hearer to probable conclusions from established premises (facts that the audience would take for granted and not question).[160] Syllogisms involve at least two premises and a conclusion, for example:

> All patrons deserve gratitude.
> Erastus has benefited our community.
> Therefore, we must honor Erastus.

An enthymeme typically presupposes a syllogism or at least a fuller deductive process, but does not rehearse the whole deductive process, since the orator will assume that the audience can supply the missing steps: "We ought to honor Erastus, for he has benefited our community," or "Let us honor Erastus, for all patrons deserve gratitude." Aristotle preferred the form of the

---

159. Aune ("Use and Abuse of Enthymemes") helpfully critiques a too narrow understanding of enthymeme, drawing attention to the multiple argumentative forms referred to within the category "enthymeme" across the field of classical rhetorical theory, as well as emphasizing the critical difference between logical and rhetorical syllogisms, namely, that the former required certainty, but the latter required only probability.

160. See Aristotle, *Rhetoric* 2.22; Anaximenes, *Rhetoric to Alexander* 1430a27–34.

enthymeme as less pedantic and more effective in persuading. Enthymemes are built around a variety of topics such as the possible and the impossible, opposites or contraries, the lesser and the greater, projected consequences of an action, analogy, and cause and effect.[161] The topics special to each genre of oratory also provide the raw material of enthymemes (for a deliberative speech, for example, the considerations of what is just, expedient, feasible, and honorable). The example given above employs a topic of justice (benefactors deserve gratitude).

Inductive proofs allow the audience to draw conclusions by considering examples (which can be historical precedents or fictional stories) or analogies.[162] An orator who wishes his city to declare war may tell the story of those who, in similar circumstances, forestalled disaster and achieved greatness by taking the initiative in military conflict. Recalling historical precedents was especially effective, since the audience could, in effect, see in the past the outcome of the course they are contemplating for the future.[163] Dio Chrysostom, urging his fellow citizens not to parade their internal quarrels when the new governor first arrived in their province, used analogies drawn from the animal world to support his case (the harmony shown by bees, *Discourses* 48.15–16).

Maxims, legal precedents, and authoritative texts also furnish the raw material of appeals to *logos*. Maxims or proverbs are statements of common knowledge or opinion, and so are likely to add credibility to the conclusions based on them.[164] Similarly, authoritative texts (like Homer and Hesiod for a non-Christian, or the Septuagint for Christians and diaspora Jews) lie at the core of group identity and lend their authority freely to the points derived from them. The respect accorded the ancient text, in effect, bleeds over into the new text.

Once a speaker had gathered his or her material, he or she needed to know how to marshal the various arguments and appeals effectively to achieve persuasion. Thus the arrangement of the speech receives significant attention in the classical handbooks. Judicial and deliberative speeches tended to consist of four (following Aristotle) or five (following Roman theory) sections, each section having particular functions.[165] The opening of a speech was called the exordium, and it generally sought to give a foretaste of the subject matter, put the hearers in a receptive and attentive frame of mind (Pseudo-Cicero, *Rhetorica ad Herennium* 1.4.7), and deal with issues

---

161. Aristotle provides a host of examples of such topics in *Rhetoric* 2.18–19, 23–26.

162. Aristotle, *Rhetoric* 2.20; Anaximenes, *Rhetoric to Alexander* 1429a25–28.

163. See Aristotle, *Rhetoric* 1.9.40; Anaximenes, *Rhetoric to Alexander* 1428b12–17; 1429a25–28; Quintilian, *Education* 3.8.36.

164. Aristotle, *Rhetoric* 2.21; Anaximenes, *Rhetoric to Alexander* 1430a40–b7.

165. Epideictic speeches generally followed different sorts of outlines and displayed the greatest freedom in this regard.

related to the speaker's credibility and, if applicable, the lack of credibility of opposing speakers (Aristotle, *Rhetoric* 3.14). This section would be followed, particularly in judicial speeches, by a narration of the events under dispute. This narration would present a strategically shaped and colored rehearsal of events, putting certain parties in the best possible light and certain parties in the worst light possible, depending on the specific goal of the speech. Generally the narration (or, in deliberative addresses, quite often simply the exordium) led up to a proposition, the main point to be demonstrated (whether "my client is innocent" or "war is the more advantageous course"), followed by a section presenting arguments and evidence as proof (the *probatio*) of the speech's thesis statement. This section was the heart of the speech, establishing the speaker's position as the better founded one. The speech generally closed with a "peroration," a conclusion that brought together the main points, offered a concluding exhortation, left the audience in a strategically selected emotional state, and took parting shots at the opposing speakers and their cases (Aristotle, *Rhetoric* 3.19).

EPISTOLOGRAPHY IN CLASSICAL ANTIQUITY

Handbooks on the practice of letter-writing, as well as scattered comments about this practice, have also survived from antiquity. The two most important handbooks are *Epistolary Types* of Pseudo-Demetrius (second century BCE to third century CE) and *Epistolary Styles* of Pseudo-Libanius (fourth to sixth century CE).[166] Like the handbooks on rhetoric, these two works have great value as metalevel discussions by informants close to the time, places, and culture of the authors of New Testament letters, about the practice of, purposes for, and strategies employed in letter-writing in this period.

Pseudo-Demetrius identifies twenty-one categories of letter types, which he considers to be a comprehensive catalog: "friendly, commendatory, blaming, reproachful, consoling, censorious, admonishing, threatening, vituperative, praising, advisory, supplicatory, inquiring, responding, allegorical, accounting, accusing, apologetic, congratulatory, ironic, and thankful" (*Epistolary Types*, prologue, 25–30). The overlap between letter types and species of rhetoric is noteworthy. The aims of forensic rhetoric in the courtroom can also be pursued beyond the courtroom in less formal settings, and here specifically in writing, by means of the "accusatory" and "apologetic" ("defense") letters. The aims of deliberative rhetoric in the assembly can be

---

166. The original texts and translations of these works, together with a number of excerpted reflections on letter-writing from the letters of Cicero and Seneca and from Demetrius's *On Style*, can be found in Malherbe, *Theorists*.

pursued beyond the council chamber in less formal settings, and again specifically in writing, by means of the "advisory" letter.[167] And several letter types seem to correspond to the more general aims of epideictic rhetoric, such as the "blaming" and "praising" types. These types account, however, for only a fraction of the overall catalog. Pseudo-Demetrius thus helpfully reminds exegetes, particularly those who have an affinity for rhetorical analysis, that people in antiquity (as ever since) write letters and engage in communication more generally to attain many more goals than those of concern to ancient teachers and analysts of oratory.[168] His list thus stands as an antidote to the attempt on the part of rhetorical critics to think about every New Testament letter in terms only of deliberative, forensic, or epideictic rhetoric, while still encouraging the careful consideration of these types among the wider array.[169]

---

167. Das (57) finds it significant for the relationship between rhetorical and epistolary theory that "the 'accusing' or 'apologetic' letter categories, for instance, never specify a courtroom setting (Pseudo-Demetrius, *Eloc.* 17; Pseudo-Libanius 6)." This objection confuses the particular setting naturally envisioned by the professional orator and teacher of orators with a proof of the inapplicability of typical courtroom strategies to other settings. If we are ourselves sensitive to how often what is essentially "courtroom" rhetoric enters into our domestic relationships or our professional interactions (as when an employee's conduct is examined with a view to firing or retaining), we will instantly understand how ancient forensic rhetorical strategies could have spilled over into settings beyond the courtroom where analogous situations naturally emerge and such strategies, mutatis mutandis, would become useful to the participants as they pursued their agendas in those situations. The same can be said for deliberative rhetoric. One does not have to stand in the senate chamber to find such strategies at work; rather, one can find it in committees as resolutions are pressed, faculty or staff meetings as a course of action is promoted or urged against, sales pitches of all kinds, and, yes, sermons and other forms of religious discourse. In all such expanded settings, all that is required to turn a forensic or deliberative communication into a letter is the physical absence of one of the parties involved.

168. Pseudo-Libanius goes further in identifying forty-one types, which he speaks of in terms of letter "styles." Kern (*Rhetoric and Galatians,* 21), though overly dismissive of rhetorical analysis, is nevertheless correct to affirm that "no warrant exists for equating the handbooks with the totality of first-century discursive strategies."

169. In point of fact, there was also some dispute among ancient rhetoricians concerning "whether there are three kinds [of speech] or more. . . . On what kind of oratory are we to consider ourselves to be employed when we complain, console, pacify, excite, terrify, encourage, instruct, explain obscurities, narrate, plead for mercy, thank, congratulate, reproach, abuse, describe, command, retract, express our desires and opinions, to mention no other of the many possibilities?" (Quintilian, *Education* 3.4.1–4; Butler, LCL). Granted that Quintilian is himself waxing rhetorical here, as some of the kinds of speech he names are in fact covered within the three principal genres of concern to public speakers (thus "pleading for mercy" is, in fact, a facet of forensic rhetoric, and "terrifying" is well covered as a kind of appeal to pathos that can be variously suited to different kinds of oratory), but he also bears witness to the awareness of rhetoricians that the categories of "judicial, deliberative, and demonstrative/epideictic" oratory were never considered to be comprehensive categories of human com-

Nevertheless, the reader of these handbooks will notice at once that, in comparison with surviving treatises on rhetoric, they are extremely brief. As he works through each type, Pseudo-Demetrius provides a brief description of the type and an equally brief example. The sum total of assistance that he gives concerning letters of the "advisory type" is:

> It is the advisory type when, by offering our own judgment, we exhort (someone to) something or dissuade (him) from something. For example, in the following manner:
>
> I have briefly indicated to you those things for which I am held in high esteem by my subjects. I know, therefore, that you, too, by this course of action can gain the goodwill of your obedient subjects. Yet, while you cannot make many friends, you can be fair and humane to all. For if you are such a person, you will have a good reputation and your position will be secure among the masses. (*Epistolary Types* 11)

Pseudo-Libanius, unfortunately writing at least four centuries after Paul and thus not a transparent window into first-century practice, does not offer much more help. These handbooks provide starting points for, and samples of the flavor of, each type only, but nothing more.

Readers or students of these two surviving handbooks who wished to write actual letters would have needed to turn to other resources in order to develop the content of their letters, that is, for the topics, argumentative strategies, and other kinds of material that could help them achieve their particular goals for their particular letters in their particular situations. This would be a most reasonable assumption, since those who were able to compose letters would be literate, educated people, and since, for example, the arts of dialectic (logic) and rhetoric (argument and persuasion) were absolutely foundational to Greek and Roman education in any formal setting.[170] Correspondingly, those seeking to write letters of the "friendly" type—which is often treated as the ideal of the genre—would have needed continually to draw upon their previous education in the ethics of friendship for the range

---

munication—just the principal categories required to fuel the engines of politics, justice, and civics. Klauck considers this awareness to be a "trail . . . that ultimately leads to the twenty-one or forty-one epistolary types in the letter writing handbooks" (*Ancient Letters*, 215).

170. As Klauck (*Ancient Letters*, 210) correctly observes, "Some rapprochement has also been fostered by the fact that over the centuries rhetoric developed into a primary force in education and permeated all aspects of culture, resulting in an increasing rhetorization of diverse literary genres," though "the converging lines of the oration and the letter did not actually cross in theoretical reflection until late antiquity" (e.g., in the work of Julius Victor, a rhetorician of the fourth century CE, whose *Art of Rhetoric* includes an appendix on letter-writing; see Malherbe, *Theorists*, 62–65).

of topics they would need in order to craft their letters. The authors of these epistolary handbooks were supplementing, and would surely have been understood to be supplementing, a foundation in logic and rhetoric (and other areas of the educated person's curriculum) rather than viewed as providing everything a letter-writer needed to know in their brief treatments, as if their readers would lay aside all that they had learned from other disciplines when they sat down to compose a letter.

LETTERS, SPEECHES, AND GALATIANS

Some comments made by ancient letter-writers about the distance that existed between letter-writing and oratory might at first seem to argue against applying classical rhetorical theory to Pauline letters. Cicero, a statesman from the late Roman Republic, writes to one of his friends, "How do you find me as a letter writer? Don't I deal with you in colloquial style? The fact is that one's style has to vary. A letter is one thing, a court of law or a public meeting quite another" (*Letters to His Friends* 9.21.1 [Letter 188]). Similarly, he complains elsewhere about a letter he has received that was "similar no doubt to the speeches he is said to have delivered" (10.33.2 [Letter 409]), as opposed to what one would expect in a personal letter.[171] The distinctions Cicero draws here between what is appropriate to "a court of law" versus a letter pertain, it must be noted, explicitly to matters of style, or *elocutio*, not to rhetorical invention or even strategic disposition of material.

This topic is indeed popular among writers on the art of letter-writing. Seneca (*Moral Epistles* 75.1–2), a Roman contemporary of Paul, writes concerning his epistolary style that he wishes for his letters to be

> just what my conversation would be if you and I were sitting in one another's company or taking walks together—spontaneous and easy; for my letters have nothing strained or artificial about them. If it were possible, I should prefer to show, rather than speak, my feelings. Even if I were arguing a point, I should not stamp my foot, or toss my arms about, or raise my voice; but I should leave that sort of thing to the orator, and should be content to have conveyed my feelings toward you without having either embellished them or lowered their dignity. (translation from Malherbe, *Theorists*, 29)

We also find other authors giving explicit advice limiting the use of extended periods (long, involved, artistically balanced and constructed sentences) in

---

171. Das, 58; similarly, Reed, "The Epistle," 177–78.

letter-writing, since such ornate style is better suited to public speaking and appears artificial in a letter.[172]

Cicero and Seneca, in particular, are also speaking of the style appropriate for personal letters between friends. It is significant that the quotations from Cicero on how he is writing these letters comes from the collection *Friends (Epistulae ad familiares)*. Their point is that the style of such a letter between friends should imitate the style of natural conversation between educated acquaintances rather than the more artistic, artificial, and, let it be admitted, manipulative discourse of the political, judicial, and civic arenas (see also his *Letters to Atticus* 8.14.1). It might be fine to harangue an assembly in the council chamber, but not a friend in his tablinum—and hence not in a letter to a friend that he might read in his tablinum.[173] Cicero himself distinguished, however, between private letters and public letters and the styles appropriate to each.[174] Five centuries later, Julius Victor (*Art of Rhetoric* 27) observed a similar distinction between personal letters and official letters, also stressing the difference in style appropriate to the two types. While a grand style was never recommended for letters of any kind, the more public or official communications would naturally admit of content and, to some extent, expression more akin to the public and official venues of the forum or the council chamber. The bottom line was that the content and style of a letter needed to be appropriate to the audience, the relationship between the sender and audience, and the aims that the letter sought to achieve.[175]

---

172. Pseudo-Demetrius, *On Style* 229 (Malherbe, *Theorists*, 19): "There should be a certain degree of freedom in the structure of a letter. It is absurd to build up periods, as if you were writing not a letter but a speech for the law courts"; Philostratus of Lemnos, *On Letters*, 2.257.29 (Malherbe, *Theorists*, 43): "Periods must be eliminated from letters than run to any length, for this is too rhetorically impressive for an epistle, with the exception that they may possibly be used, if there be need, at the end of what has been written, either to pull together what has been said or finally to conclude the thought."

173. See Das, 67: "Letters were intended as a substitute for actual speech (Cicero, [*To His Friends*] 12.30.1; Cicero, [*Atticus*] 8.14.1; 9.10.1; 12.53; Seneca, [*Moral Epistles*] 75.1)." Thus what would be appropriate for the *speech* to a particular audience in their situation would largely be appropriate to the letter. It is quite conceivable, therefore, that a particular audience and setting would call for a letter that would reflect something more akin to a forensic or a deliberative speech—just not a "private letter" to a friend. (The *tablinum* is the office or formal reception area in a Roman home on the far side of the atrium from the main door.)

174. *Pro Flacco* 16.37; *Friends* 15.21.4. See Malherbe, *Theorists*, 2, 12.

175. Pseudo-Libanius (*Epistolary Styles* 2; Malherbe, *Theorists*, 67) captures this point well: "A letter, then, is a kind of written conversation with someone from whom one is separated, and it fulfills a definite need. One will speak in it as though one were in the company of the absent person." If "the absent person" is a group of people facing difficult choices, the content, style, and shape of the letter will need to conform to this situation.

If rhetorical conventions of style were not applied to personal letter-writing even by such orators as Cicero, this does not mean that a great gulf therefore existed between the strategies and skills exhibited in public speaking and *all* letter-writing, particularly letters of the sort represented by Galatians. And in this regard, those who are critical of rhetorical analysis, in their efforts to distinguish letters from speeches, have generally failed to honor the distinctions between Cicero's letters to his familiars and Paul's letter to the Galatians. The motives behind these two kinds of letters highlight one very important difference. Consider the following statements from Cicero's letters to his friends (translations from Malherbe, *Theorists*):

> I have been asking myself for some time past what I had best write to you; but not only does no definite theme suggest itself, but even the conventional style of letter writing does not appeal to me. (*Friends* 4.13.1; Malherbe, 23)

> I have no doubt my daily letter must bore you, especially as I have no fresh news, nor can I find any excuse for a letter. . . . [I write anyway since] when I seem to talk with you, I have some little relief from sorrow, and, when I read a letter from you, far greater relief. (*Atticus* 8.14.1; Malherbe, 23)

> I have nothing to write. . . . I have begun to write to you something or other without any definite subject, that I may have a sort of talk with you, the only thing that gives me relief. (*Atticus* 9.10.1; Malherbe, 25)

> Though I have nothing to say, I write all the same, because I feel as though I were talking to you. (*Atticus* 12.53; Malherbe, 25)

Cicero writes even when he has no good reason to write—his only motive seemingly being to activate contact with a friend for its own sake. The kind of letter that Cicero writes and the situation from which he writes it are so far removed from the kind of letter and situation that we find with Paul's letter to the Galatians that they bear no comparison. The use of typical rhetorical strategies indeed had no place in Cicero's self-indulgent moaning to Atticus and would indeed have done nothing to advance his aims, which were merely to keep Atticus present to himself and vice versa. Paul, in contrast, writes to intervene in a pressing situation and to influence the outcome, specifically by persuading those whom he addresses to set aside a course of action they are seriously contemplating and to pursue instead the course of action upon which he had set them (though now with greater understanding).

A second important difference arises from considering the audiences. Cicero addresses a single, private individual; Paul addresses a body, an audience.[176] It was not a "private letter" or a "personal letter," but rather a "public letter," not so far distant from an "official letter," coming as it does from God's envoy to the communities formed by this envoy's activity in the execution of his divine commission. It was a letter addressed to a number of "assemblies" (*ekklēsiai*)—perhaps not a political assembly in the heart of downtown, but to political bodies of another sort nevertheless—to influence their present deliberations.[177] Indeed, Paul's letters were most likely delivered *orally* before each gathered community, probably in the context of its gathering for worship, closing the distance between letter and spoken address even further.[178] The people addressed by this letter have moreover been listening to, and have begun to be won over by, other teachers who have been making a case in favor of the converts adopting a new course of action. Paul cannot take the floor to speak in opposition to this course of action, but he sends this letter to achieve the same goals that he would have sought to achieve had been able to enter each assembly in person to make his case against the position of other, resident speakers. Paul is sending his letter into a deliberative arena as the only means by which to make his voice heard in that arena.

Galatians has more in common with the epistles of Demosthenes, an Athenian orator from the fourth century BCE, than the personal correspondence of Cicero. These epistles are not personal, private communications, but rather attempts

> to defend Demosthenes' career. They are in the form of a letter only because he is in exile *(Ep.* 1:2–4; 3:1–35)*; otherwise, they consist of self-apology and advice to the public. As letters, they lack the many epistolary formulas and the style of the "familiar" letters *(familiares)* and instead may be categorized as *negotiates*, to which Julius Victor claims the canons of rhetoric apply *(Rh.* 27)*. The prescripts take the form ΔΗΜΟΣΘΕΝΗΣ

---

176. Das (66) also calls attention to this important difference.

177. Deliberative rhetoric is suited to "political questions" or "political oratory" (Quintilian, *Education* 2.15.19, 21, 22, 33 [citing Cicero, *Invention* 1.5.6], 36; Anaximenes, *Rhetoric to Alexander* 1420a1–3; Das, 60). If we appreciate the degree to which Galatians is "political discourse" within the world of early Christian movement, we will not find unnatural Paul's use of typical deliberative strategies and other supporting rhetorical strategies.

178. Porter ("Paul of Tarsus," 540) observes that "it is somewhat surprising that more attention has not been given to delivery [the fifth area of rhetorical instruction being the effective presentation of one's speech], since these letters were almost assuredly designed to be read before a church congregation." The fact that Galatians was thus "designed" speaks directly to the applicability of rhetorical analysis to a text composed for oral delivery within a contested situation.

ΤΗΙ ΒΟΥΛΗΙ ΚΑΙ ΤΩΙ ΔΗΜΩΙ ΧΑΙΡΕΙΝ ("Demosthenes to the Council and Assembly, greetings"), setting the stage for the epistolary body in
which Demosthenes attempts to persuade his audience on a particular
subject.[179]

The parallels with Galatians are immediately striking. Here, too, a
speaker—writing a letter on account of the distance between himself and his
audience—writes to an assembly in an attempt both to reassert his own credibility and to vehemently urge them to accept his advice in the matter facing
them.[180] Its epistolary form belongs to the realm of *accident*, not *essence*.

The contents of Galatians would have pushed the boundaries of good
taste in letter-writing according to an author like Demetrius, who claimed
that "if anybody should write of logical subtleties or questions of natural history in a letter, he writes indeed, but not a letter," since "a letter is designed
to be the heart's good wishes in brief; it is the exposition of a simple subject
in simple terms" (*Style* 231; translation from Malherbe, *Theorists*, 19). Paul
certainly plunges into "logical subtleties" in regard to the interpretation of
sacred texts and theological questions. But Paul the letter-writer is no more
bound to the conventions of letter-writing, where his aims drive him beyond
those conventions, than he is to the conventions of oratory, where his aims
drive him similarly beyond those conventions.[181]

---

179. Reed, "The Epistle," 187.

180. See, similarly, Anderson, *Ancient Rhetorical Theory*, 104, on "open letters," letters
that were essentially speeches with formal epistolary prescripts and postscripts. The "Letter"
to the Hebrews certainly fits this type, even to the extent of foregoing an epistolary prescript
in favor of its sonorous, periodic opening paragraph. Galatians also belongs more to this type
than to the typical letter, if by "typical" we understand the communication between two
individuals about personal or business matters.

181. In an example of seeking to have one's cake and eat it as well, Kern suggests that
"Paul would be opposing [Aristotelian] advice if he merely appended epistolary material to
a speech," blending types of composition that were not suited to each other (*Rhetoric and
Galatians*, 148, cited approvingly in Das, *Galatians*, 60). But this same scholar also downplays
the degree to which Paul had formal rhetorical training or followed the stated rules for rhetorical composition. How can Paul, then, be held accountable to follow advice that was not
part of his education or to rules that he is elsewhere said not to concern himself about? Kern
(*Rhetoric and Galatians*, 32) also takes as his foundational premise that "letter-writing and oratory were distinct enterprises which did not merge in the classical mind," imposing another
kind of rigidity upon Paul very much like the rigidity of forcing all of Paul's material into the
classical oratorical mold. This time, however, the rigidity concerns an alleged impermeable
boundary between epistolography and oratory, between writing a letter and composing a
persuasive discourse for oral delivery. Given the situation faced by Paul, the presence of rival
speakers, his goals for the hearers, and his wish that he could deliver his discourse in person
rather than through writing (4:19–20), this boundary seems imaginary indeed.

We ought also never to forget that Paul was not primarily a writer, let alone a writer of letters. Approximately three decades of active ministry have left us only thirteen pieces of written communication bearing his name, and the authenticity of six of these is disputed. Within these letters are references to only a further three nonextant letters (1 Cor 5:9–11; 2 Cor 2:1–4; Col 4:16), with one of these references coming from a disputed letter.[182] Paul was above all else a speaker, a preacher, a teacher. His medium was primarily oral communication, and he was very often employing this medium to persuade. It is most artificial to think that he would bracket this mind-set, experience, and its accompanying strategies—that is to say, the strategies of successful public speaking—when he turned to formulating the communications he was forced by circumstances to put into writing.[183]

The near-silence in rhetorical handbooks about letter-writing and the silence in epistolary handbooks about the practice of oratory have been taken as evidence for the claim that the two realms of discourse had very little practical overlap, with the result that rhetorical theory is ill suited *tout court* to the analysis of letters.[184] It is true that Pseudo-Demetrius, for example, does not draw upon classical rhetorical theory in his discussion of the "advisory" letter, but this is hardly evidence that rhetoric did not influence the practice of letter-writing.[185] The treatment of any one type of letter in these handbooks is so slight that the writers can hardly be said to be drawing upon *anything* as they compose their brief descriptions and thumbnail sketches. But it is interesting to find Pseudo-Demetrius speaking of the two goals of the advisory letter by using the language of deliberative oratory as he introduces his examples of the subtypes: "we promote a course" and "we dissuade from a course."[186] Pseudo-Demetrius also describes the "apologetic type" as "that

---

182. I omit here the reference in 2 Thess 2:1–2 to letters *purporting* to come from Paul but which, according to the author of 2 Thessalonians, were not genuine.

183. Contra, for example, Weima, "What Has Aristotle to Do with Paul?," 463: "There is a fundamental problem in mixing the genre of a speech (oral discourse) with that of a letter (written discourse). If one takes seriously the fact that Paul wrote letters, then the most important source for understanding Paul's letters must naturally be the letter-writing practices of his day, not the rules for oral discourse." Weima exemplifies the either/or thinking that creates unnatural boundaries between spoken and written discourse.

184. See, for example, Stamps, "Rhetorical Criticism," 144–45. It is surprising not to find more weight given to the judgment of Abraham Malherbe, upon whose collection of ancient texts and translations our acquaintance with ancient epistolary theory largely depends, that "epistolary theory in antiquity belonged to the domain of the rhetoricians," even though "it was not originally part of their theoretical system . . . and it only gradually made its way into the genre" (*Theorists*, 2).

185. Contra Das, 57.

186. Pseudo-Demetrius uses the words προτρέπομεν and ἀποτρέπομεν, words closely linked to the categories of deliberative speeches (προτρέπτικον and ἀποτρέπτικον; Anax-

which adduces, with proof, arguments which contradict charges being made" (*Epistolary Types*, 18).[187] The very language calls to mind that which is of central concern to forensic rhetoric, namely, discovery of the possible proofs and arguments that might be employed to contradict the specific charges leveled against the writer of such a letter. How could the person who writes an "apologetic type" of letter, then, not draw upon his or her knowledge of forensic oratory, to the extent that he or she has such knowledge, in the process of thinking about how to achieve his or her aims for the communiqué?

Aristotle's silence about letter-writing, in contrast, can be explained by his competence in attending to his task, which was to lay out the practices of oratory that tended to be effective, and not allowing himself significant digressions into other arenas.[188] These silences do not mean that educated people in antiquity did not think, for example, about issues of trust and relationship (*ēthos*), emotion (*pathos*), and argument (*logos*) when they turned away from composing their manuscripts for memorization and public delivery and toward writing letters.[189] The major epistolary theorists are silent about rhetorical theory because they are essentially providing *catalogs* of letter types, not comprehensive instructions about prose composition. Given the brevity of their treatments, they evidently assume their readers to have already achieved competence in rhetoric, needing only additional guidance in terms of learning a greater variety of styles suited to various ends.[190] By themselves, the epistolary handbooks would be nearly useless to the person looking for strategies that would help him, for example, win back his converts from rival teachers who have called his authority into question—evidence that their authors expected letter-writers to look to other resources and cultural conventions for the actual formulation of particular letters in particular situations seeking to accomplish situation-specific goals.

---

imenes, *Rhetoric to Alexander* 1421b7–12). Furthermore, the name for the "advisory" letter (συμβουλευτικον) is the same as the name for the deliberative species of oratory.

187. Malherbe, *Theorists*, 41

188. Quintilian writes only a very short digression about letter-writing, commenting mostly on the more conversational style and looser structuring that are appropriate to this genre in contrast to oratory (*Education* 9.4.19–20).

189. Indeed, some of the sample letters in the epistolographic handbooks provide evidence to the contrary, as in Pseudo-Demetrius's sample of the "apologetic type," which shows attention to refutative strategies, as well as to issues pertinent to *ēthos* (the trustworthiness of the writer and the lack of virtue of his accusers).

190. Thus, rightly, Malherbe, *Theorists*, 4. Pseudo-Demetrius anticipates that his handbook will help his reader "surpass others . . . in professional skills" (*Epistolary Types*, prologue, 14–16; Malherbe, *Theorists*, 31), suggesting that he writes to otherwise fully educated, professionally trained letter-writers or chancery scribes.

THE JUDICIOUS USE OF CLASSICAL RHETORICAL THEORY IN NEW TESTAMENT INTERPRETATION

Classical rhetoric is indeed misapplied where the formal outlines laid out in the rhetorical handbooks are forced upon New Testament texts or where a particular text has been forced into one or another of the rhetorical species. The authors of the rhetorical handbooks were interested in preparing elite citizens for public speaking in the customary arenas of civic life. While, I would maintain, their advice could be applied far beyond these arenas to various degrees and with varying needs for innovation, the handbooks themselves are limited in scope to the kinds of communication practiced in the principal political-civic settings. It is therefore a mistake to insist that a particular New Testament text "fit" within one of these three genres (in the sense both of fitting one of *only* these three and of fitting into *only* one of these three genres)[191]—though it is not a mistake to inquire whether a particular New Testament text *might* fit within one or more of these genres. There are advisory letters of both the protreptic and apotreptic kinds; there are accusatory and apologetic letters among the types. But there are, admittedly, many other goals for epistolary communication—even beyond what one finds in either epistolary handbook (as each handbook demonstrates by including types not found in the other!). Philippians certainly contains paragraphs reflective more of the friendly and thankful epistolary types. These paragraphs may not reflect Paul's overarching goal for writing Philippians, but neither should the mixed and variegated nature of a letter like Philippians be suppressed in favor of a single label like "epideictic" or "deliberative."

The point must be conceded likewise in terms of the application of the typical structure of a classical oration to each and every Pauline letter.[192] Analysis of a New Testament letter cannot be approached with a firm conviction that one will find material therein corresponding to an exordium, *narratio*, proposition, proof section, and peroration—and of course all in that order. Where analysis proceeds on the basis of this conviction, the outcome is predictable: the outline will be "discovered" in the text. But the results of such investigations rarely agree with one another and often appear to thrust upon a segment of text a label that reflects neither the actual content of that segment nor the likely goals or contributions of that segment to

---

191. So, rightly, Aune, *Literary Environment*, 203, who cautions that "attempts to classify one or another of Paul's letters as *either* judicial *or* deliberative *or* epideictic . . . run the risk of imposing external categories on Paul and thereby obscuring the real purpose and structure of his letters."

192. A criticism justifiably leveled by Porter, "Theoretical Justification," 115–16; similarly, Porter, "Paul of Tarsus," 561.

the persuasive strategy of the whole. The schema with its constituent labels ends up distorting rather than illumining the contribution and aim of one or more of the text's parts.[193] It is probably this commitment to discovering the classical form in every Christian communiqué that, more than any other factor, has contributed to bringing the whole enterprise of rhetorical criticism into disrepute.[194]

The rhetorical handbooks, however, have great value as native informants concerning (1) the variety of obstacles that an individual might have to address in his or her quest to persuade an audience; (2) the various kinds of appeal that an individual might make, and indeed would probably *need* to make, in order to persuade an audience, and how an individual might effectively "push the right buttons" in regard to the audience's trust and emotions; (3) a wide array of argumentative topics and strategies that an individual might employ in the course of building a persuasive case; and (4) what topics and strategies are appropriate to at least six basic communicative goals. Knowledge of the content of these handbooks prepares modern readers to discern and analyze Paul's appeals to issues of trust, the hearers' emotion, and rational argumentation, as well as to identify what Paul believes to have been obstacles to persuasion and what particular aims Paul is trying to attain, at the level both of each paragraph and of the discourse as a whole (again allowing that Paul's potential range of aims in any given letter well exceeds that of the goals that were the focus of political, judicial, and civic oratory). And we do well to keep before us that the aim of applying rhetorical theory to the interpretation of Paul's letters is not "to demonstrate to what extent Paul was familiar with them, with rhetoric and/or epistolography, theory and/or practice" but, rather, "to help modern exegetes to arrive at a more thorough understanding of the letter(s)."[195]

The argument is sometimes made that, while ancient letters contain argumentation and attempts to persuade, the persuasive strategies employed are more reflective of "a type of 'universal' rhetoric prevalent at the time and still functionally found in other communicative forms today" rather than the

---

193. Kraftchick ("Why Do the Rhetoricians Rage?," 64) cautions against "a new form of parallelomania," this time in regard to the contents of the rhetorical handbooks rather than Qumran literature or Hellenistic ethical literature. Das (56) expresses similar frustration with what he calls "the labeling game" in discussions of a New Testament text's rhetorical species and arrangement.

194. So, rightly, Klauck, *Ancient Letters*, 225; see also Porter, "Paul of Tarsus and His Letters." It is unfortunate that Galatians was the first New Testament text in the modern period to receive such focused and detailed rhetorical analysis. It gave every initial appearance of fitting into the pattern of the classical oration and no doubt raised scholarly expectations of being able to go and do likewise throughout the remainder of the Pauline corpus and beyond.

195. Classen, "Paul's Epistles," 97.

strategies of the rhetorical handbooks more narrowly.[196] Let it be granted that Paul, like most other New Testament authors, does not regard himself to be *bound by or beholden to* the conventions of political and judicial oratory.[197] If we are interested, however, in the "universal rhetoric" practiced in the first-century Greco-Roman world, it makes little sense to fail to mine rhetorical handbooks—surely our most comprehensive ancient sources concerning persuasive communication—for information about these "common communicative practices" that could also, wherever advantageous to the authors, be regularly employed in letters that seek to persuade or dissuade, to exonerate or attach blame, or to praise or censure. Classical rhetorical handbooks provide firsthand accounts of a great deal of "universal rhetoric" ("universal," at least, in regard to Mediterranean discourse in antiquity), often only *superficially* particularized in Greek and Roman civic settings.[198]

---

196. Reed, "Epistle," 188. See also Weima, "What Has Aristotle to Do with Paul?," 462–63: "If one defines rhetorical criticism very broadly as the 'art of persuasion,' then it can be readily granted that Paul uses rhetoric in his letters. It is also clear that the apostle employs a variety of literary or so-called rhetorical devices that are universally practiced in the everyday use of language and that do not necessarily provide evidence for the training in and conscious use of the ancient rhetorical rules."

197. Scholars who demonstrate reserve in regard to rhetorical criticism rightly assert that "there is no compelling evidence that [Paul] employed the classical rules of Greco-Roman rhetoric in the writing of his letters" (Porter, "Theoretical Justification," 468) or that Paul "shows relatively little concern with observing certain rules set out in the standard teaching of rhetoric" (Martyn, 23).

198. As an important theoretical framework for his critique of the use of classical rhetoric in New Testament interpretation (and in regard to Galatians, in particular), Kern (*Rhetoric and Galatians*, 7–12) lays out a four-tiered schema. Tier 1 is all-encompassing as "strategic communication," which can embrace virtually anything. Tier 2 differentiates between the major media of strategic communication: painting, sculpture, the spoken word ("oratory," his word, is too narrow), one could add music. Tier 3 differentiates between subsets of each of these media by geographic/cultural location, thus: classical Ch'an rhetoric, Greco-Roman rhetoric, one could add Buddhist rhetoric, Mayan rhetoric. Tier 4 further differentiates between the species of each cultural type, thus in regard to Greco-Roman rhetoric: diatribe, market language, classroom language, handbook rhetoric, and so forth.

On the basis of this schema, Kern argues that the application of the strategies of rhetoric found in the classical handbooks to the literature of the New Testament is fundamentally flawed because it does not honor the "restriction [of handbook rhetoric] to particular venues," namely, the law court, the civic political assembly, and the encomiastic speeches of the forum (*Rhetoric and Galatians*, 17). The rules of rhetoric proper to one slice of Greco-Roman experience are inappropriately removed to the realm of another slice of the same experience.

My primary objection to Kern's enterprise is his assumption that political, judicial, and epideictic oratory were somehow hermetically sealed off from other forms of oral and written discourse as practiced in the Greco-Roman milieu. Even though he is correct that the authors of the handbooks wrote specifically to describe the rhetorical strategies used in these contexts (increasingly for the purpose of training individuals to function in those

These handbooks provide snapshots of a wide range of contemporary rhetorical techniques, approaches, and topics to which New Testament authors and audiences would potentially have been exposed; they thus open a window into an important facet of the cultural environment within which early Christian authors and teachers lived and moved and upon which they could potentially have drawn—though, in the majority of cases, drawn *indirectly* on the basis of a less formal education in the art of persuasion or on the basis of an inductively attained understanding of how effective persuasion happens. While these handbooks came to be used "prescriptively" as textbooks for aspiring orators, they are rooted in the "descriptive" work of observing the oratorical practice of their authors' times and the analytic work of simply laying out the strategies these authors observe at work in real oratory.[199] Their "insider" location (i.e., their origin within a much closer geophysical, cultural, linguistic, and temporal location to the writings of the New Testament than our own) gives classical rhetorical handbooks their value as heuristic tools for investigating the construction, argumentation, and rhe-

---

specific contexts), there is no reason to believe that the strategies described were actually restricted to those contexts in everyday life. To the contrary, the person trying to persuade a group to take some particular action will explore and potentially use any and all strategies available from whatever source to achieve that aim.

The rhetorical handbooks are a valuable inventory of persuasive strategies available to people living and seeking to persuade others in the time of Paul's mission. Indeed, we simply have no comparable resources from the period. Granted, then, that we might consider Romans to be a *logos protreptikos* in the philosophical sense of "a form of (non-handbook) rhetoric used by philosophers to win potential adherents to their system or way of life" (*Rhetoric and Galatians*, 21), do the rhetorical handbooks have nothing of value to offer us as we unpack *how* Paul seeks to win adherents to support him, his message, and his mission? *Mē genoito.* Kern appears to me to be responding to the overly restrictive and prescriptive use of the classical rhetorical handbooks in New Testament exegesis, but he goes beyond correction to throwing out the baby with the bathwater. Kern does seem to be on point, however, when he cautions us against looking to a tier 4 resource to provide information about tier 2 discourse ("universal persuasive discourse," *Rhetoric and Galatians*, 258). One would truly need to pursue a close study of persuasive strategies in multiple geographic and cultural locations before making pronouncements about "universal" rhetoric.

199. Aristotle's *Rhetoric* is essentially grounded in the observation of effective oratory and the classification of its elements, even if it takes on a prescriptive edge here and there. While it is also true that "rhetorical theory was designed to assist in the creation of speeches but not their interpretation or analysis" (Das, 56n44), if we were to analyze Cicero's courtroom speeches or Dio's political addresses, it seems that modern analysts would automatically and rightly turn to classical Latin and Greek rhetorical theorists as native, metalevel informants about rhetorical practice to assist with such analysis. I therefore do not understand the point of this objection. The *intent* of Aristotle in writing his *Rhetoric* does not preclude its utility to serve other, closely related ends.

torical impact of the New Testament writings.[200] It is essential to emphasize again the qualifier "heuristic": classical rhetorical theory is only an ally in interpretation as long as it is used to help the interpreter think through how a text is *actually* constructed, what kinds of argumentative topics and strategies it *actually* employs, or what kinds of situational challenges it is attempting to overcome. The rhetorical handbooks offer only collections of possibilities of what we might find in Galatians, not recipes for its composition.

Just as Aristotle was engaged in a task of systematic description, it is important for students of the rhetoric of early Christian literature (as of any new body of literature or discourse not included in Aristotle's sampling) to anticipate the need to extend the catalog of forms, topics, and the like, rather than regard Aristotle's (or Cicero's or Quintilian's) catalogs of rhetorical topics, emotions, enthymemes, and the like as comprehensive and therefore sufficient in themselves to account for all the details of any New Testament text.[201]

PAUL'S TRAINING IN THE ART OF PERSUASION

Using classical rhetorical theory as a tool for investigating New Testament writings does not presuppose that a particular New Testament author received formal training in rhetoric, and it certainly does not presuppose that the author in question had a copy of Aristotle's *Art of Rhetoric* or some such textbook at his side as he thought about how to address a particular pastoral challenge. It does presuppose, however, that discussions from within the ancient Greco-Roman world about how arguments are constructed, what kinds of responses particular topics typically evoked, and what contributes to successful persuasion are useful for thinking about the construction and impact of early Christian texts written within that world.

My working premise is that most early Christian authors, to the extent that they learned the "art of persuasion," learned it inductively through observing and hearing public speakers, itinerant philosophers, and even synagogue preachers in the cities in which they dwelt (whether in the cities of Judea and Galilee or in the cities of Syria and Asia Minor).[202] It is not

---

200. They also help us to avoid "the misstep of ignoring or denigrating forms of [Paul's] argument simply because they are alien to our own" (Kraftchick, "Why Do the Rhetoricians Rage?," 56–57).

201. This awareness is one of the driving factors behind the work of the Rhetoric of Religious Antiquity Group, following the pioneering work of Vernon Robbins (see esp. his *Invention of Early Christian Discourse*).

202. Some Hellenistic Jewish addresses show a remarkable knowledge of, and facility in, rhetorical convention. Fourth Maccabees, as a perhaps extreme example, reflects awareness of rhetorical genre, argumentative topics appropriate to both praise and deliberation,

necessary to establish that Paul received formal training in rhetoric to explain the degree to which he uses recognizable rhetorical strategies; rather, he may have developed a sense of the art of argumentation on the basis of his intelligence, breadth of travel, and exposure to a wide array of persuasive communications.[203] Paul might have been quite *intent* on observing with the aim of imitating and attaining greater skill throughout his formative years and beyond, when his work demanded the application of such skills. The principal presupposition behind integrating rhetorical analysis into the larger task of exegesis is not that Paul had achieved the educational level and rhetorical proficiency of a Dio Chrysostom, but rather that the metalevel discussions of practices of persuasion known to "work" in Greco-Roman antiquity can help us recognize and assess what Paul was doing as he composed a text like Galatians, through which he sought to move his congregations from where he found them to where he wanted them, whatever the origins of his facility in persuasive self-expression.

A few biblical authors, like the authors of Hebrews and Luke-Acts, however, do possess such a facility in the art of argumentation, reproduce known patterns from the progymnasmata (curricula of exercises preparing the student for advanced study in the gymnasium), and attend to matters of style and ornament to such a degree as suggests that they received at least some formal training.[204] It would be as much a mistake to assume too little formal knowledge of rhetoric as to assume too much.[205] In Paul's particular case, it is also worth *contemplating*—though the currently available data do not permit *demonstrating*—the extent to which he might indeed have enjoyed some formal training in the art of argumentation and persuasion.

---

argumentative strategies at least at the progymnastic level, prosopopoiia, vivid description, and ornament at the level both of figures of diction and of figures of speech. This text nevertheless gives every indication of having been composed for delivery to a Jewish audience in connection with a gathering of the community for a particular occasion. See deSilva, *4 Maccabees: Introduction and Commentary*, xxi–xxix and throughout; deSilva, "Using the Master's Tools," 102–5; Klauck, "Hellenistiche Rhetorik."

203. Porter, "Paul of Tarsus," 535. Classen ("Paul's Epistles," 98) also affirms the possibility of inductively learning the skills of persuasion through reading literature, experiencing applied rhetoric in the course of life, and successful imitation, giving consistently careful thought "to the best way of expressing himself." Inductive appropriation of technique would be Augustine's *preferred* method (*De Doctrina Christiana* 4.3.4–5). On this point, see also Olbricht, "An Aristotelian Rhetorical Analysis," 221; Longenecker, 112–13; Kennedy, *New Testament Interpretation*, 10; Schellenberg, *Rethinking Paul's Rhetorical Education*.

204. See deSilva, "How Greek Was the Author of 'Hebrews'?"; deSilva, *Epistle to the Hebrews in Social-Scientific Perspective*, 3–18.

205. Royalty ("Rhetoric of Revelation," 600) strikes the right balance: "We should be cautious in assuming too much formal rhetorical knowledge . . . but we should not sell them too short as uncultured and uneducated."

According to Luke, Paul was a native of Tarsus (Acts 9:11; 21:39; 22:3). When Luke's Paul claims to be "a citizen of no unimportant city" (Acts 21:39), he is engaging in considerable understatement (technically, Luke here uses the figure of speech known as litotes). Tarsus was a cultural center of the Roman province of Cilicia, concerning which the Greek geographer Strabo writes: "The people at Tarsus have devoted themselves so eagerly, not only to philosophy, but also to the whole round of education in general, that they have surpassed Athens, Alexandria, or any other place that can be named where there have been schools and lectures of philosophers. . . . Further, the city of Tarsus has all kinds of schools of rhetoric; and in general it not only has a flourishing population but also is most powerful, thus keeping up the reputation of the mother-city" (*Geography* 14.5.13). Strabo's comments date from roughly the time of Paul's boyhood. If the historical Paul enjoyed any formal education in this city, even at the primary and secondary levels, it likely would have included those subjects for which the city was renowned, notably including the art of argumentation and public speaking.[206]

Again according to Luke, Paul received at least the more advanced part of his education in Jerusalem, "at the feet of Gamaliel, educated strictly in line with the ancestral law" (Acts 22:3). Gamaliel was a respected teacher whose name is well attested, and much revered, in later rabbinic literature. Such an education would be in keeping with Paul's parents' dedication to piety, as well as to Paul's own witness to his training as a Pharisee and his intense zeal for the traditions of the elders (Phil 3:6; Gal 1:14). It does not by any stretch mean, however, that his education was entirely parochial and that he was thereby insulated from Greek influence and learning.[207]

Jerusalem itself was a cosmopolitan city connected with the Greco-Roman world, not isolated from it.[208] The city had been the focal center for hellenization—the introduction of Greek language, culture, and political organization—in Judea several centuries before (2 Macc 4:7-17). While certain elements of hellenization were staunchly resisted (particularly where it encroached upon Jewish monotheism, dedication to the way of life and values promoted by Torah, and the preservation of the temple cult), a resistance that culminated in the Maccabean Revolt,

---

206. So also Bird, "Reassessing," 378. On the place of progymnastic exercises on the cusp between secondary and tertiary education, see Marrou, *History of Education*, 238–42. Fairweather reviews Paul's use of terms proper to classical literary theory as "inescapable evidence that Paul was a conscious exponent of the techniques of classical oratory, even if an unorthodox one" ("Galatians and Classical Rhetoric," 33–36, esp. 36).

207. Contra Weima, "What Has Aristotle to Do with Paul?," 465.

208. See Hengel, *Pre-Christian Paul*, 57–61. Jewish education in Greek, including the art of argumentation, was pursued in Jerusalem at least from the time of Herod.

the hellenization of Palestine nevertheless made substantial progress during the Hellenistic period and was given renewed attention during the period of Roman domination.[209]

Many of Rabbi Gamaliel's own students were said to have been "trained in the wisdom of the Greeks."[210] In Gamaliel's school, perhaps similar to what one would have found in the Jerusalem-based school of Yeshua Ben Sira two centuries before,[211] Paul would have learned not only of Torah and its rules of application but the art of argumentation,[212] the Jewish wisdom tradition (which energetically combined Greek, Egyptian, and Jewish wisdom), and quite probably continued his study of Greek as well, given his evident facility in the language and its written expression. Fluency in Greek would have been of great importance as the means by which to communicate with and instruct Greek-speaking Jews from the diaspora residing in Palestine, visiting during pilgrimages, or encountered in a teacher's travels away from Palestine. It was also essential to political and economic success in Greek-dominated, then Roman-dominated, Judea.[213] Conversations with Jews from the diaspora would have afforded ample opportunity for Paul to learn more of Greco-Roman philosophy and ethical traditions, as would have presentations of or debates with gentile philosophers resident in Palestine. The essential skill of letter-writing

---

209. See Hengel, *Judaism and Hellenism*, 70–78; Hengel, *Jews, Greeks, Barbarians*. Particularly important in regard to Hellenistic education and rhetoric in Judea is Hengel, *Hellenization of Judaea*, 19–29. Fairweather ("Galatians and Classical Rhetoric," 24–25) is correct to affirm that "one need look no further than the Old Testament Apocrypha, the books of Maccabees in particular, to see how widely pervasive the hellenizing of Judaea and the Jewish diaspora had been for three centuries before Paul's time. And it was part and parcel of Hellenism to give rhetoric a prominent place in the educational system."

210. See Daube, "Rabbinic Methods of Interpretation and Hellenistic Rhetoric." The thesis of his article is that "the Rabbinic methods of interpretation derive from Hellenistic rhetoric. Hellenistic rhetoric is at the bottom both of the fundamental ideas, presuppositions, from which the Rabbis proceeded and of the major details of application, the manner in which these ideas were translated into practice" (240). See also Judge, "Paul's Boasting," 40.

211. A sizable sample of Ben Sira's curriculum, as it were, can be found in the apocryphal book known alternatively as Ecclesiasticus, Sirach, or the Wisdom of Ben Sira.

212. Even if this education did not include specific training in the Greek art of rhetoric, Jewish traditions of argumentation, especially as seen in the more fully developed forms of wisdom literature, would have given Paul an ample foundation upon which to keep building as he encountered and absorbed Greco-Roman rhetorical strategies in his missionary work. See deSilva, *Introducing the Apocrypha*, 169–75, on the argumentative strategies found in the Wisdom of Ben Sira and therefore available for observation and imitation.

213. An important archaeological datum in this regard concerns the language of inscriptions found in Jerusalem, dating from the early Roman period. A full third of these are written in Greek, while an additional 7 percent are carved in both Greek and a Semitic language (Hebrew or Aramaic). See Hengel, *Pre-Christian Paul*, 55, 136n258.

would not have been neglected, as Hellenistic letter-forms had been practiced in Jerusalem at least since the rise of the Hasmoneans (see 2 Macc
1:1–9; 1:10–2:18).

This comprehensive curriculum would have remained thoroughly Jewish insofar as it was rooted in the sacred history and literature of Israel (as opposed to being based on the sacred and foundational literature of the Greeks,
notably the writings of Homer and Hesiod), conducted within the framework
of a Torah-observant lifestyle (as opposed to the Greek lifestyle, nurtured
by the educational institution of the gymnasium and lyceum), and geared
toward participation in the distinctive institutions of Judea and Jewish culture
generally.[214] The compatibility of strictly following the "ancestral (Jewish)
law" with competence in Greek language, rhetoric, and philosophical ethics,
however, is widely demonstrated throughout the Hellenistic Jewish world
(e.g., by Philo of Alexandria and the authors of 4 Maccabees and the Letter
of Aristeas), and the same would have held true for the *hellenized* Jerusalem
of Paul's time.[215]

---

214. Hengel (*Pre-Christian Paul*, 38) speaks of Paul receiving a *Jewish* education in
Greek, and considers both aspects to be important. Das (61) objects that "nevertheless,
rabbinic training was not the same as a non-Jewish rhetorical education targeting civic
oratory." While it is surely a given that any formal education Paul undertook in Jerusalem
would have been thoroughly adapted to the needs, concerns, and culture of the Jewish
people (to label all of this "rabbinic" may be a bit anachronistic and misleading), why
would we imagine that only "a non-Jewish rhetorical education targeting civic oratory"
would give Paul instruction in basic argumentative strategies useful for establishing authority, building a case for a course of action, establishing guilt or innocence, and the like?
Given the range of activities for which the sages leading schools in Jerusalem prepared
their pupils, it seems reasonable that such topics would also be part of the curriculum of
a Jewish education forming religious and community leaders—leaders who would, incidentally, often need to engage in deliberation and judicial proceedings, in diplomatic and
chancery functions, and in instructing in and investigating the particularities of Torah-
shaped practice.

215. Porter provides a balanced assessment of this milieu, rightly stressing the adaptation of Hellenistic rhetoric to the interests and concerns of Jewish practitioners of the
same: "The possible influence of Greco-Roman culture, including rhetoric, on Paul even
in Palestine could have been significant. For example, besides there being various public forums where Paul could have been exposed to rhetoric, and contact between Jewish
and Greek thinking, Daube has argued convincingly that the precepts of Rabbinic exegesis were in fact derived from Greco-Roman rhetoric. Thus it may have been possible for
Paul to have received some form of rhetorical training even in Jerusalem. The nature and
kind of this education is still subject to question, however. The formal training he would
have received would probably have been as rhetoric interpreted through its adaptation by
Rabbinic thought, rather than as rhetoric strictly for civic oratorical purposes" ("Paul of
Tarsus," 535). Philo of Alexandria, admittedly not a typical Jew, affirms the value and even
necessity of the study of rhetoric and dialectic as "preliminary studies" that prepare one

Even while we stress ways in which Paul exhibits facets of the classical arts of argumentation and persuasion, there are significant ways in which Paul expressed reservations about rhetoric and relying too much on performance-based persuasion. This topic does not arise in Galatians, but Paul gives it explicit attention in 1 Corinthians. Ancient orators invested themselves not only in developing strong appeals but also in decorating their speeches to delight the ears of the hearers with many kinds of verbal ornamentation (like alliteration and word play, such as one often hears in sermons today) and in developing the use of their voice and gesture to give their speech greater impact. Paul refused, in particular, to play to these cultural norms, because he wanted the response of his hearers to be grounded fully on the life-transforming message of the cross and on the encounter with God that the proclaimed Word facilitated (1 Cor 1:17; 2:1–5) rather than on the performance of the messenger.

This observation, however, cannot be turned into a warrant for saying that Paul did not give a thought to rhetoric.[216] First, even the claim to avoid using the flashiness of presentation to awe an audience so as to focus them on the content of the message was something of a rhetorical device.[217] Second, Paul's reserve resonates with, and may even reflect awareness of, "the Greek anti-rhetorical tradition" and may thus be equally a product of educated reflection on rhetoric.[218] Paul's critical reflection upon those aspects of rhetorical practice that he would *not* weave into his proclamation of the gospel (and, by extension, into his letters) confirms his acquaintance with the larger "art of persuasion" and helps direct us more precisely where to look for his employment of the same. And despite his reservations about pursuing an

---

for the study of philosophy and virtue in his allegorical exposition of Gen 16:1–6 (*On the Preliminary Studies*, 17–19), showing in his mind, at least, the perfect consonance of Greek *paideia* and Jewish piety.

216. Contra Porter, "Theoretical Justification," 465: "Even if Paul did know or had been trained in ancient rhetoric, there is evidence that he deliberately chose not to engage in such oratory practices." This choice is true only in regard to style and delivery. It does not mean that Paul did not thoughtfully construct arguments, seek to arouse emotions, or address issues of credibility in his preaching, teaching, and letter-writing. See, more helpfully, Winter, "Is Paul among the Sophists?"; Bird, "Reassessing," 377.

217. This particular device was used by Dio Chrysostom, a celebrated late-first-century orator: "My purpose . . . was neither to elate you nor to range myself beside those who habitually sing such strains, whether orators or poets. For they are clever persons, mighty sophists, wonder-workers; but I am quite ordinary and prosaic in my utterance, though not ordinary in my theme. For though the words I speak are not great in themselves, they treat of topics of the greatest possible importance" (*Discourses* 32.39; LCL).

218. Fairweather, "Galatians and Classical Rhetoric," 37. She affirms that Paul's disparagement of πιθανολογία in Col 2:4 (if that letter is genuine) is especially poignant, since πιθανολογία is a Platonic term (see *Theaetetus* 162e).

artificial impressiveness of style, presence, and delivery, Paul's letters were nevertheless still considered "weighty and forceful," even by his detractors (2 Cor 10:10).[219]

VIII. GALATIANS AS PERSUASIVE COMMUNICATION

A. GALATIANS AS ANCIENT LETTER

Galatians presents itself unambiguously as a letter, using an expanded form of the typical letter opening wherein a sender names himself or herself, then the recipient, and opens with words like "greetings" or "peace" or "greetings and good health" (1:1–5).[220] Paul would far preferred to have been present with the Galatians to address his speech to them personally, in his own voice and embodied presence (4:20), but he is unable or unwilling to leave his present location at that precise moment, and so he sends this letter, probably in the hands of the Galatian Christian or Christians who came to him to seek his help, to achieve the same goal as he would have sought by visiting and speaking to the Galatian assemblies in person.

Letters from the Greco-Roman period employ a good number of stock expressions as markers of transition within, and indications of the goals for, the letter.[221] These formulas include:

> Opening formula ("A to B, greetings"; see 1:1–5)
> Thanksgiving ("I give thanks for . . .")
> Prayer ("above all else, I pray for your . . .")
> Expression of joy ("I rejoiced exceedingly when . . .")
> Astonishment/rebuke ("I am amazed how . . ."; see 1:6)
> Expression of grief or distress ("I am anxious because . . ."; see 4:11, 19–20)
> Reminder of past instructions ("as I have asked you before . . ."; see 3:1; 5:21)
> Disclosure of information ("I want you to know . . ." or "I would not have you unaware . . ."; see 1:11)

---

219. Bird, "Reassessing," 377.

220. See Pseudo-Libanius, *Epistolary Styles* 51 (Malherbe, *Theorists*, 75): Any letter "should begin as follows: 'So-and-so to so-and-so, greeting'. For thus all the ancients who were eminent in wisdom and eloquence appear to have done."

221. Longenecker, cv; see also Hansen, *Abraham in Galatians*, 30–31.

Request ("I beg you to . . .", "I entreat you to . . ."; see 4:12)
Use of verbs of hearing or learning ("I was grieved to hear that . . .";
    see 1:13; 3:2)
Introduction of topics ("Now about X . . .")
Notification of upcoming visit ("I hope to come to you . . .")
References to writing ("You wrote that . . ." or "I have written
    that . . ."; see 1:20; 6:11)
Use of verbs of speaking or informing ("Alexander will tell you how it
    is with us. . . .")
Use of the vocative to indicate transition ("Brother," or "Friend, I
    urge you to . . ."; see 1:11; 3:1, 15; 4:12, 19, 28, 31; 5:11, 13; 6:1, 18)
Closing formula ("I wish you good health" or the like; see 6:18).

When this inventory is applied to Galatians, there are several places
where one can observe a cluster of these formulas, suggesting that these passages indicated important transitions within the letter.[222]

1:1–3 (salutation and greeting)
1:6–13 (astonishment-rebuke formula, disclosure statements)
3:1–7 (vocative, verb of hearing/learning, disclosure statement)
4:11–20 (expression of distress, request formula, disclosure state-
    ments, travelogue and a visit wish)
4:28–5:13 (vocatives, appeal, disclosure formula, expression of
    confidence)
6:11–18 (subscription, benediction, grace wish, vocative).

These clusters, in turn, potentially suggest the following epistolary
structure, with the particular prominence of topics and formulas of rebuke
and request providing the clues to the primary letter types that Paul has combined in Galatians:

1:1–5: Salutation
1:6–4:11: Rebuke section
4:12–6:10: Request section
6:11–18: Subscription

---

222. Longenecker, cvii–cviii, following the insight of Mullins, "Formulas in New Testament Epistles," 387, to the effect that the use of one formula tends to precipitate the use
of one or more others, making these clusters especially helpful markers of transition in the
writer's thought. See also Hansen, *Abraham in Galatians*, 32.

This structure would make Galatians a letter of a "mixed type," primarily combining the "rebuke letter" and "request letter" types.[223]

While such an analysis advances the discussion of Galatians as an ancient letter, particularly in regard to the documentation of typical epistolary formulas that appear in the text as a guide to marking major transitions, it is not clear that thinking of Galatians primarily in terms of "rebuke" and "request" really illumines its contents without distorting the same.[224] Very little of Galatians appears to effect "rebuke," something limited to 1:6–9; 3:1–5; 4:8–11; and 5:7–9 (the last, notably, in the "request" section). It would be forcing the label to argue that the intervening material (1:10–2:21; 3:6–4:7) is devoted to justifying the rebuke or explaining why the Galatians deserve the rebuke.[225] Rather, these sections appear to be serving other, and largely more constructive, goals. Paul is also not making requests comparable to the requests found in letters of the request type (e.g., in many of Pliny's letters to Trajan wherein Pliny requests imperial favors for Pliny's friends and clients), even though Paul does use the language of pleading at one point ("I beseech you," 4:12).[226]

---

223. Longenecker, cix. Hansen (*Abraham in Galatians*, 34–43) collects several examples of mixed "rebuke-request" letters from among actual papyrus letters from the late Roman period. Pure types can be found in postcard-length letters from antiquity but are rare in actual correspondence of any length. It is significant that Paul's letters are much longer (and therefore more complex) than the typical ancient letter. Galatians is 9x the length of the average letter of Cicero, 2x the length of the average letter of Seneca, and many times longer than the less formal, nonliterary letters (Das, 66). Galatians is necessarily far more complex than even typical letters of mixed types. Epistolographic analysis can no more claim a totalizing place in interpretation than rhetorical criticism.

Betz (15) had asserted that Galatians be read as an example of the "apologetic letter," in keeping with his view of Galatians primarily as a specimen of judicial rhetoric, the goal of which was to persuade the Galatian Christians about the authenticity of Paul's apostleship and the reliability of his presentation of the gospel. Betz listed several texts as examples supporting the existence of such a genre (Plato, *Letters* 7; Demosthenes, *On the Crown*; Isocrates, *Antidosis*), but further inspection of these examples revealed that none presents a genuine letter. See Hanson, *Abraham in Galatians*, 25–27; Witherington, 39.

224. Such approaches to structure, however, are on much firmer methodological grounds than contrived attempts to discover, for example, macrochiastic outlines of the complete letter (as in Bligh, 37–42). On the problems with the macrochiasm as an alleged structuring device, see deSilva, "X Marks the Spot?"

225. Neither Hanson nor Longenecker gives evidence of such an error in their exegetical work.

226. Das (66) takes issue with Hansen's selectivity, as the latter worked with only twelve of the forty-three letters among the papyri featuring a form of θαυμάζω, wondering how different Hansen's results would have been if he took all of them into equal account. Graham Stanton asks in regard to the striking differences between these brief texts and the far more complex Galatians: "Will anyone who reads these twelve papyri and then reads Galatians really imagine that he is reading the same kind of literature?" ("Review of Hansen,

Rather, he is urging, advising, even commanding them in regard to courses of actions before them (5:1, 13, 16, 25).

In regard to the argumentative content of Galatians and its explicit aims (to steer the addressees away from one course of action in favor of remaining in their present course), it is much more accurately regarded as a letter of the advisory type. Paul's explanation of his calling/commission and the course of his relationship with Jerusalem and its representatives (1:11–2:14) resonates much more closely with the accounting type or, if one views Paul primarily to be defending himself against things said to diminish his authority in the Galatian situation, the apologetic type. These particular letter types, moreover, intersect much more closely with the typical goals and strategies of classical rhetorical practice.

B. PAUL'S GOALS FOR GALATIANS AND ITS RHETORICAL GENRE

The starting point in the rhetorical analysis of Galatians often concerns the question of what kind (or species) of rhetoric it exhibits. The primary goal, of course, is to understand Galatians and what Paul sought to achieve by sending this communication, not simply to determine the proper rhetorical category into which to deposit it, as if the quest for a label were the same as the quest for understanding.[227]

Perhaps because of the prominence of Paul's apparent defense against charges of people-pleasing and departing from the commission of the Jerusalem apostles, perhaps because of the prominence of treatments of judicial rhetoric in the classical handbooks, Galatians was first read as essentially an example of forensic or judicial rhetoric, with the addressees in the role of jury, Paul as the accused, and the rival teachers as the accusers.[228] Such a reading

---

Abraham in Galatians," 615). Philemon, by contrast with Galatians, might more justifiably be seen as having more in common with Pliny's letters to individuals requesting favors for friends or clients of his than with oratory, though the arguments put forward to incline Philemon to grant the favor still merit close rhetorical analysis.

227. Kraftchick, "Why Do the Rhetoricians Rage?," 56.

228. Betz, 24. Hester ("The Rhetorical Structure of Galatians 1:11–14") also treats Galatians as a specimen of judicial rhetoric. Betz (129) found it "extremely difficult" to account for Gal 3–4 in terms of the proof section of a forensic speech. This opinion did not move him, however, to reconsider his initial decision about its principal rhetorical species (and thus Paul's principal aims): "If he were not so determined to make 'apology' the basic type to which the letter must conform, would it not appear that the whole argument from 3:1 on is primarily designed not to defend Paul's position but to exhort the Galatians to abandon their new mentors?" (Meeks, "Review," 305–6).

misdiagnoses Paul's principal aims. The best way to determine what genre of rhetoric a text is likely to represent—and one must add, "if any"—is to study it first with a view to answering one fundamental question: what does the author most want the communication to achieve among his or her readers or hearers? Does the author want to promote a decision about whether or not someone's past action was right or wrong? If so, the communication as a whole is seeking a goal proper to judicial rhetoric. Does the author want to promote a decision about what course of action the recipients will take in the (possibly very near) future? If so, the communication as a whole is seeking an end proper to deliberative rhetoric. Does the author want to promote adherence to certain basic values, virtues, or principles? If so, the communication is operating in primarily epideictic modes.[229]

Paul clearly has several goals for Galatians. Paul, indeed, hoped that his letter would, in part, offer an effective defense or reassertion of his apostolic authority, rooted in what he believes to be a divine commissioning, and of the integrity of his proclamation of God's message. He clearly sought a positive verdict from his converts in this regard and, given the rhetorical situation (in which the audience has begun to be won over by other speakers), Paul reasonably understood that he needed to attend to the question of his authority and reliability as a representative of God's message. This goal, however, was a secondary one in service of another, more ultimate goal—Paul's effective intervention in the Galatians' situation to prevent their adoption of a new course of action, namely, allowing themselves to be circumcised in response to the rival teachers' urging. Galatians is fundamentally a piece of *deliberative* rhetoric, all aimed at forestalling one imminent course of action (5:1–4) in favor of another (5:16).[230] All the material in Galatians regarding Paul's sincerity and reliability (i.e., the opening chapters that appear very much to present a self-defense) and the questionable reliability of the rival teachers (found mostly at the opening and closing of the letter) serves the purposes that appeals to ethos would in any kind of speech (see below). Such material is ancillary to the rhetorical goal of the communication and not an indication of the overall rhetorical genre itself.[231]

---

229. Kraftchick ("Why Do the Rhetoricians Rage?," 57) rightly urges exegetes to focus on "Paul's means of argumentation" rather than "debate over the [rhetorical] genre of Galatians," though close analysis of Paul's address in the context of the situation in Galatia suggests that the greater part of the content of the communiqué can be explained as a well-orchestrated collection of appeals to affect the choices the Galatian Christians are about to make in the very near future, and that Paul is concerned here with what rhetoricians would have labeled a "deliberative cause."

230. So also Witherington, 27, 359; Kennedy, *New Testament Interpretation*, 144–52; Hall, "Rhetorical Outline"; Smit, "A Deliberative Speech"; Bachman, *Sünder oder Übertreter*, 156–60.

231. Contra Betz, 14–15, 24–25.

The principal topics of Gal 3:1–5:12, moreover, appeal to categories that are typical in deliberative rhetoric—the *honor* and *advantages* that have been gained in Christ, which would be lost by turning back now to Torah's regulation of the human relationship with God (3:2b–5, 13–14, 23–29; 4:8–11; 5:1–4); the *injustice* (the wrong) that would be done by looking back to Torah on this side of Christ's self-giving death (2:21); and the *lack of feasibility* inherent in the rivals' course (3:11–12, 21b) and the *feasibility* of the path advocated by Paul (5:5–6, 13–14, 16–17).[232] Such topics are typically used to move an audience to choose one course (which preserves advantages and honor) over another course.

Even 5:13–6:10, with its combination of argumentation and exhortation, plays an integral role in the argument in support of Paul's deliberative goals.[233] In this section, Paul demonstrates the viability of the course of action that he has previously advocated, and to which Paul wants the hearers to remain

---

232. Recall the list and discussion of deliberative topics in Anaximenes, *Rhetoric to Alexander* 1421b21–1423a12 above. Das (52) claims, with regard to Gal 5–6 in particular, that "Paul employs none of the typical arguments one finds in deliberative rhetoric, such as appeals based on justice, legality, or advantage." This is simply incorrect, particularly in regard to advantage or disadvantage in regard to a course of action (topics prominent in 5:1–4, 16–18, 21, 24; 6:7–10).

233. Smit's decision to regard 5:13–6:10 as a later addition to the letter because such a block of (alleged) paraenesis did not fit into the pattern of a standard deliberative oration was misguided ("A Deliberative Speech," 9). While it might not fit into the typical pattern (why should it?), it certainly supports the deliberative goal by offering a clear argument that the alternative course that Paul supports is a feasible and advantageous alternative to the course urged by the rival speakers.

Das (52) has objected that "classifying Paul's species of rhetoric in Galatians as deliberative . . . does not resolve matters either" because Paul's paraenesis seems to him too vague to qualify as a specific course of action to which Paul is urging his hearers, such as Aristotle describes as the province of deliberation (*Rhetoric* 1.3.5). Aristotle, however, does not actually assert that deliberative rhetoric must aim at "a very specific course of action" (Das, 52), but only at "a course of action." "Walk by the Spirit" (5:16) is a very clear course of action to recommend over against walking in line with the Torah, a very clear course of action against which to dissuade ("Stand fast, then, and don't submit to a yoke of slavery again," 5:1). Moreover, Das's classification of Gal 5:13–6:10 (or 5:1–6:10) as paraenesis qua "general moral instruction" fails to recognize the close connection between this section and the Galatians' situation. Paul does not merely exhort here; he demonstrates that the course of action he recommends leads to the same good ends that the rival teachers promise and that the Galatian converts desire to attain ("perfection" of the journey begun in believing, 3:3), and that Paul's preferred course does so more reliably and without the negative consequences of the rivals' preferred course of action. It does not have the absolute quality of paraenesis, as Paul offers clearly *contested* advice here (see the distinction drawn between paraenesis and advice in Pseudo-Libanius, *Epistolary Syles*, 5). Das (18) nevertheless rightly observes the importance of 5:13–6:10 for addressing the *whole* of the rival teachers' case.

committed for the future. "Walking in the Spirit" is the sufficient, God-given means of arriving at the moral transformation God seeks to effect in the lives of believers, releasing them for living beyond the power of the impulses of the "flesh," such that turning to the Torah is neither needful nor, in the end, helpful.[234] The "protreptic" argument of Gal 5:13–6:10—the positive shaping or reshaping of the Galatians' beliefs and values with a view to affecting long-term behavior, practice, and community ethos[235]—also serves to support the "apotreptic" goal of Galatians, as expressed most clearly in 5:1–4.[236] The best way to dissuade the hearers from adopting a new course of action (the course presented by the more recently arrived rival teachers) is to demonstrate that the course they are already pursuing would assuredly bring them the desired ends they are concerned to attain.

C. APPEALS TO ETHOS, PATHOS, AND LOGOS IN GALATIANS

Throughout this commentary, we will rely on ancient rhetorical theory primarily as a body of resources that shed light on how Paul strategically framed his address to his Galatian converts in order to move them to adopt a particular course of action, while rejecting another course of action being urged upon them by rival speakers. In particular, we will consider throughout how Paul may be attending to each of the three basic kinds of appeal that orators and others in the business of persuading typically incorporated, namely, ap-

---

234. On the importance of this section for establishing Paul's position, see Fee, *God's Empowering Presence*, 385; Barclay, *Obeying the Truth*. Rhetorical criticism has, in the main, helped confirm that Gal 5–6 is not some sort of general, unrelated ethical appendix to the main portion of the letter (Longenecker, 221; Witherington, 359).

235. Kraftchick ("Why Do the Rhetoricians Rage?," 63–64) describes the letter's goal as "the reorientation of the Galatians to the true understanding of the Christ event, the restructuring of the community ethic, and so, returning their loyalty to God who called the community into existence." This wording implies, it seems, both a short-term goal (exhibiting "loyalty to God" by not submitting to circumcision) and a long-term goal (effected by the broader "reorientation" and "restructuring" mentioned above), but it remains part of an appeal to the Galatian assemblies to turn away from one particular course of action in favor of pursuing another.

236. Dahl ("Paul's Letter to the Galatians," 137) thus speaks of Galatians as containing elements that fulfill the dual goals of "the symbouleutic genre of speech." Anderson (*Ancient Rhetorical Theory*, 166) objects that "in this letter Paul is better likened to a philosopher whose pupils have departed from his doctrines than to a defendant on trial, a prosecutor in court, or a politician in an assembly." This objection loses its force as soon as we understand that a philosopher could use essentially deliberative topics and strategies to win those pupils back (from the influence of other teachers!) to his teaching and to the way of life his teaching promotes.

peals to matters of character (ethos), appeals to the emotions of the hearers (pathos), and appeals to rational argumentation (logos).[237]

Appeals to ethos are essential to overcoming the rhetorical problems in Galatia as well.[238] Paul gives attention throughout the letter to the topic of his authority and his reliability as a spokesperson for God, particularly in 1:1–2:14 and 6:11–18.

- Paul expands his self-designation as the sender of the letter, emphasizing his direct authorization by God to act as an apostle of the gospel, denying that he relies on any human authorization. This topic is developed at length in Gal 1:11–2:10 (Paul's divine commission and the divine source of Paul's message: 1:11–24; 2:7–8; Paul's independence from, but nevertheless approval by, the Jerusalem church's authorities: 1:17–2:10).
- Paul concludes the opening paragraph of his letter by affirming his freedom from courting human opinion, and therefore his complete reliability as a proclaimer of truth (1:10; 4:16).
- Paul seeks to demonstrate that, though others may falter in regard to the truth of the gospel, he has always been its consistent and courageous champion (2:3–5, 11–14).
- Paul expresses his gut-wrenching concern over the Galatian Christians as a token of his deep love for and investment in them (4:19).
- Paul defends himself against the charge of inconsistency in regard to his preaching of circumcision (5:11).
- Paul points to his own scars as proof of his sincerity and reliability: he is willing to put his body where his convictions are, enduring beatings and whippings for telling the truth about what God has done in Jesus rather than adulterating the message to avoid such pain and disgrace (6:17).

---

237. See Aristotle, *Rhetoric* 1.2.3: "Now the proofs furnished by the speech are of three kinds. The first depends upon the moral character of the speaker, the second upon putting the hearer into a certain frame of mind, the third upon the speech itself, in so far as it proves or seems to prove." Even scholars who tend to be skeptical of the application of rhetorical criticism in New Testament interpretation have proven more open to thinking about the rhetoric of a Pauline letter in terms of "invention"—the ways in which Paul has appealed to these basic kinds of appeal. Thus Classen remarks: "The theory of rhetoric, . . . though developed for another area [than letter-writing], together with practical oratory, will also render service, but again within limits, that is in the areas of *inventio* ('invention') especially for the argument and *elocutio* ('style'), where there is overlapping with the theory of epistolography." This view contrasts with Classen's evaluation of *dispositio* ("structure"), concerning which "rhetorical theory may be consulted, but extreme caution is called for" ("Paul's Epistles," 112).

238. Failure to recognize this element lies behind scholarly confusion concerning its genre (i.e., Betz's conviction that the letter is primarily concerned with issues akin to those that arise in forensic rhetoric).

Conversely, Paul devotes considerable energy to creating prejudice against the rival teachers, undermining their authority and credibility:

- Paul speaks of his rivals as agitators disturbing the peace of the congregation and perverters of the gospel (1:7; see also 5:7, 10), going so far as to call down a curse upon them (1:8–9; see also 5:12, which is not far from a curse).
- Paul suggests that the rival teachers are operating out of selfish and cowardly motives, not out of a desire truly to benefit the Galatians: they are willing to put the Galatians in a subordinate position in order to derive advantage from them (4:17); and they are driven by a desire to avoid persecution (from non-Christian Jews) by making both the gospel and the Galatians themselves palatable to their fellow Jews (6:12).
- Paul avers that the rival teachers are not sincere: they promote circumcision not because they are wholly devoted to the Torah (which they themselves do not keep in all its particulars) but because emphasizing circumcision will enhance their prestige in the eyes of the larger Jewish population (they want to "boast in your flesh"; 6:13). By contrast, Paul affirms that he is free from such selfish motives as trying to make the Galatians into a trophy for himself (6:14).

Paul does not rely wholly, or perhaps even primarily, on such appeals, but he does give the issue of whom to trust significant attention as a way of ensuring that his more content-based appeals receive a receptive hearing.[239]

Appeals to pathos are admittedly more difficult to discern in a written text, but nevertheless with the aid of a working knowledge of the topics and circumstances that tended to evoke particular emotions outlined in Aristotle's *Art of Rhetoric* 2.1–11, and with a willingness to extend those topics (and even those emotions) to include others that would be more central to the context of a voluntary religious movement, we can at least formulate suggestions concerning ways in which a given paragraph might include some attempt to arouse an advantageous emotion among its addressees as part of its overall persuasive strategy.[240]

Paul does not appeal to the emotions to the extreme degree that one might find in standard classical courtroom practice, for example, where "the

---

239. Porter ("Paul of Tarsus," 573) wrote, "Whereas Galatians and Romans seem to rely heavily upon logos or reason, in 1 Thessalonians . . . Paul relies heavily upon ethos." I would not concur that such an emphasis distinguishes 1 Thessalonians from Galatians, where Paul also gives a great deal of attention to affirming his reliability and breaking down his rivals' credibility.

240. For methodological considerations pertinent to the analysis of appeals to pathos, see further deSilva, "Strategic Arousal of Emotions," 94–96.

appeal to emotion became a manipulative tool, rather than relying upon reason and character,"[241] though he certainly makes frequent appeal to the emotions of his hearers. This does not mean Paul was being manipulative, but it does mean that his letters often have persuasive force not only on the basis of what he says (logos), or how he presents himself and rival influences (ethos), but also on how he makes his addressees feel along the way. In Galatians, in particular, I will suggest that Paul is attempting to evoke the emotions of shame (in respect to themselves) and indignation (in respect to Paul's rivals) in connection with the Galatians' allowing themselves to be duped by the recently arrived teachers (1:6–9; 3:1–5; 4:8–11, 17; 5:7–12; 6:12–13), friendship in regard to Paul (2:4–5; 4:12–16, 19–20), fear in regard to the consequences of affronting God in regard to his favor in Christ (2:20–21; 5:1–4), and confidence in regard to the results of following the Spirit's leading (5:16–25; 6:15–16).

Appeals to logos, of both the deductive and inductive kind, abound in this document. Galatians contains a thick weave of argumentative texture.[242] The concentration of inferential particles and other linguistic markers of argumentation directs readers to engage the text as a tightly argued case in favor of particular positions that should lead the hearers to favor particular courses of action. The conjunction *gar*, typically used to signal that material is being offered as a rationale or other evidence in support of a preceding statement (thus often translated "for"), appears thirty-six times in this relatively brief letter (1:10, 11, 12, 13; 2:6, 8, 12, 18, 19, 21; 3:10 [2x], 18, 21, 26, 27, 28; 4:15, 22, 24, 25, 27, 30; 5:5, 6, 13, 14, 17 [2x]; 6:3, 5, 7, 9, 13, 15, 17). Causal *hoti* ("because") appears eleven times (2:11, 16 [2x]; 3:10, 11, 13; 4:6, 12, 20, 27; 6:8). *Oun* and *ara*, both of which indicate that an inference or conclusion is being drawn on the basis of preceding claims (thus usually translated "therefore"), each appears six times (*oun*, 3:5, 19, 21; 4:15; 5:1; 6:10; *ara*, 2:17, 21; 3:7, 29; 5:11; 6:10). These linguistic markers call interpreters to attend closely to the "appeals to reason" crafted by Paul in support of the position he urges. They also invite deeper exploration of the unstated premises that would make this enthymematic reasoning persuasive for author and audience, allowing for the transfer of commitment from a premise to the conclusions drawn.[243]

Simple rhetorical exercises formed a part even of later elementary education. Surviving textbooks of these *progymnasmata* show that the basic

---

241. Porter, "Paul of Tarsus," 574. His conclusion that, "nevertheless, there are a few statements by Paul that have the ring of pathos about them" is perhaps a bit of an understatement.

242. Robbins, *Tapestry*, 58–64, and *Exploring*, 21–29.

243. Kraftchick ("Why Do the Rhetoricians Rage?," 68) stresses that exegesis should account for how the arguments offered in a given text facilitate the transference of the hearers' acquiescence from shared premises to the conclusion or inference promoted by the author.

building blocks of argumentation, both inductive and deductive, were taught quite early on in a citizen's training. A basic pattern set forward in these elementary exercises is the "elaboration," which could be applied to develop argumentation in support of a saying made by a famous person or any other kind of thesis. The exercise would consist in the composition of the following elements to create a variegated demonstration of the thesis:

1. Introduction
2. Statement of the saying or proposition
3. Cause (a reason or rationale in support of the statement)
4. Contrast (argument from the contrary: "If the statement were not true, such and such would be the case. But such and such is not the case, so the statement is true.")
5. Comparison (argument from analogy)
6. Historical example
7. A judgment (relevant quotation of authority in support of the statement)
8. Concluding exhortation or restatement of thesis. (Hermogenes, *Preliminary Exercises* 3.7–8).[244]

These elements constituted the most basic and essential kinds of deductive and inductive proofs that orators would use throughout their careers.

It is not surprising, then, to find Paul employing many of these elements in support of the propositions he seeks to establish in Galatians. The above-mentioned occurrences of "for" (*gar*) and "because" (*hoti*) point to the presence of reasons and rationales. Second-class conditions (formal and effective) throughout the letter offer arguments from the "contrary" (1:10; 2:21; 3:21; 5:11). Paul uses an argument from historical precedent (the example of Abraham, 3:6–9), arguments from analogy drawn from the raising of children in an affluent household (3:23–25; 4:1–7) and from the legal practice of making a will (3:15–18), citations of popular wisdom that function as compressed arguments from analogy (e.g., proverbial sayings about yeast and about reaping what one sows in 5:9 and 6:7), and the authoritative judgments pronounced in the Scriptures at numerous points. A particularly important kind of argument in deliberative rhetoric is the argument from the consequences (i.e., of pursuing one or another course of action), a form of enthymeme that is common in Galatians (e.g., in first-class conditions: 2:17–18; 5:15, 18, 25; 6:3; otherwise, 5:2–4, 16, 21; 6:4, 8–9).[245]

---

244. Hermogenes, *Preliminary Exercises* 3.7–8; the text is in Kennedy, *Progymnasmata*, 77–78.

245. As we have already noted briefly above, Paul also employs easily recognizable topics as he develops his case, many of these being specifically appropriate to deliberative rhetoric.

While Paul does not by any means confine his rhetorical strategies, topics, and arrangement to the strategies laid out in surviving elementary textbooks and rhetorical handbooks from his period, the descriptions of the various kinds of appeal (ethos, pathos, and logos) in those handbooks often illumine Paul's argumentation and help the modern reader discern the rhetorical force of his writings paragraph by paragraph just as they would illumine an address by Cicero or Dio Chrysostom.

D. THE STRATEGIC ARRANGEMENT OF GALATIANS

Ancient epistolary handbooks give no guidance concerning a letter's structure beyond Pseudo-Libanius's prescription of the opening salutation prior to the letter's body. Neither Pseudo-Demetrius nor Pseudo-Libanius says anything about how to close a letter. Epistolary conventions related to structure (openings, transitional markers, closings) have had to be inferred based on the examination of surviving letters. There have been many attempts to discover the structure of Galatians by seeking the alignment of segments of the text with the parts of a classical speech, since classical texts on rhetoric provide ample indigenous reflections on the strategic structuring of a persuasive communication.[246] The analysis of the structure of Galatians against this

---

246. Betz (16–23) offered a thoroughgoing analysis of the structure of Galatians as a forensic address that incorporated all the major parts of the classical oration: I. Epistolary Prescript, following the conventions of the letter form (1:1–5); II. *Exordium*, which states the "cause," or issue to be addressed (1:6–11); III. *Narratio*, the "statement of the facts" that demonstrates the thesis (here, concerning Paul's apostolic authority; 1:12–2:14); IV. *Propositio*, outlining points of agreement and disagreement between Paul and his rivals (2:15–21); V. *Probatio*, laying out the proofs in support of Paul's position versus that of his rivals (3:1–4:31); VI. *Exhortatio*, laying out the practical results that should follow from Paul's position, if the proof has been successful (5:1–6:10); VII. Epistolary Postscript/Conclusion (*Peroratio*, 6:11–18). Other scholars pursued a similar approach, though based on the conviction that Galatians pursued the goals of a deliberative oration more clearly. Kennedy (*New Testament Interpretation*, 145) proposed a simpler outline (still making room for epistolary elements like Gal 1:1–5): I. Salutation (1:1–5); II. Proem/*Exordium* (1:6–10); III. Proof (1:11–5:1); IV. Exhortation (5:2–6:10); V. Epilogue (6:11–14). Hall ("Rhetorical Outline," 277–87) followed Kennedy fairly closely, though disagreeing on how best to think about the "proof" section: I. Salutation/Exordium (1:1–5); II. Proposition (1:6–9); III. Proof (1:10–6:10); IIIA. Narration (1:10–2:21); IIIB. Further Headings (3:1–6:10); IV. Epilogue (6:11–18).

Smit ("A Deliberative Speech," 1–26) offered a more detailed outline of Galatians as a deliberative speech: I. *Exordium* (1:6–12); II. *Narratio* (1:12–2:21); III. *Confirmatio* (3:1–4:11); IV. *Conclusio* (4:12–5:12), further divided into A. *Conquestio* (4:12–20); B. *Enumeratio* (4:21–5:6); C. *Indignatio* (5:7–12); V. *Amplificatio* (6:11–18). Smit has strangely woven in elements proper to a forensic speech (the *conquestio* and *indignatio* being typical elements of

theoretical background was rendered all the more natural by Paul's evident interest in using this letter to effect persuasion and the nature of the letter itself as a public one addressed to a cluster of assemblies rather than a personal one addressed to a friend.

At the same time, Paul gives no indication that he is writing with these structural conventions in mind, and we need to use them as heuristic tools rather than as absolutes. Knowledge of the basic structures of persuasive discourses that pervaded the cities of the Greco-Roman world can help us think about the "functional corollaries" between blocks of Galatians and these typical structures. We must also allow that, while Paul composes some sections in a way that more closely resembles some parts of a typical oration, he composes others in ways that are more appropriate to the different venue of persuasion, arranging the whole in the manner that suits him and his perception of how to lead his hearers from where they are to where he wants them to be.[247] Paul is not bound by any rules of oratory and not subject to scrutiny on the basis of the same rules. Neither is Paul ignorant of the political dynamics of the voluntary association known as the Christian assembly (ekklēsia), such that he would fail to avail himself of typical strategies of political (deliberative) oratory, to the extent that he finds them helpful, as he works to achieve his ends.

The opening (1:1–10) accomplishes many of the functions traditionally assigned to the exordium of a speech.[248] This is not necessarily the result

---

courtroom rhetoric aimed at the arousal of pity toward a defendant and indignation against his or her accusers, or the opposite) into his outline of Galatians as a deliberative speech. The correct perception that Paul is appealing to his hearers' emotions at this point—and, indeed, specifically to pity (or perhaps friendship and favor) and to indignation—leads to the unwarranted leap of thinking of these segments in terms of specific structural elements of classical oratory dedicated to the arousal of pity and indignation. Critics of rhetorical analysis have rightly pointed out the problem of Smit's failing to account for 5:13–6:10 within such an outline. Because he did not find a place for paraenesis, or moral instruction, in classical oratory, he decided (4, 9) that this section was a later addition to the text. What could be a clearer example of Procrustes lopping off limbs to make the corpse/corpus fit his bed? Porter ("Paul of Tarsus," 545) rightly criticized Smit for privileging the theoretical outline of a classical speech and the typical content expected in such speeches over the facts of what we actually find in Galatians. We must also beware of the other extreme, however, namely, that the presence of material that is not typical for civic discourse negates the value of thinking through the rhetorical composition and effect of Galatians tout court.

247. See, helpfully, Porter, "Paul of Tarsus," 584: "Functional correlations between the various categories of rhetoric can be found with the various parts of the Pauline letters. These functional correlations, especially in terms of arrangement and invention, provide a way forward in the study of Pauline rhetoric, since they give access to the underlying nature and purpose of argumentation, and the effect that this argumentation may have on the shape of an entire work and its defined audience."

248. On the subject of such correspondences, Classen offers some wise observa-

of Paul's composition of this section to serve as the exordium of Galatians qua address, and certainly not a signal, therefore, that those listening to this letter being read aloud ought to expect it to continue to devolve according to the form of an oration. It is, however, the result of Paul's careful attention to matters that are strategically attended to when beginning a communicative act, particularly in a contested situation.[249] Paul quickly identifies the principal problem that he will address (the Galatians are being persuaded to adopt a new course of action in order to attain God's promises; 1:6), challenges the motives and reliability of the rival teachers to whom they have been listening (1:7), and affirms his own reliability as a representative of the divine purpose, with supporting considerations and demonstrative acts (1:8–10). Of course, the formal epistolary prescript (1:1–5)—with Paul's typical departures from (or, rather, embellishments upon) that form—also functions to raise the issue of (and affirm) Paul's reliability (1:1–2a), to provide an initial assurance of good will toward the addressees in the form of the wish for grace and peace (1:3), and to foreground a topic that will figure prominently in his case against the rival teachers' message and recommendations (1:4).

This opening is followed by a lengthy narrative (1:11–2:14) that clearly has an argumentative edge to it, relevant to the situation at hand.[250] It is not, strictly speaking, a *narratio*, however, in the sense of a segment of a speech dedicated to establishing the facts of the (judicial) case that is then taken up in the proofs that follow.[251] It develops, rather, the appeal to ethos begun in 1:1–10, demonstrating Paul's divine commission, the divine communication of his understanding of the gospel, and independence of—yet nevertheless endorsement by—the authorities of the Jerusalem church. If one were to insist on using rhetorical categories, it would be better classified as part of an extended exordium, as, indeed, the rhetorically trained Reformer Philipp

---

tions: we should expect some correspondence between a well-ordered letter and a well-ordered speech ("Paul's Epistles," 105, 110); nevertheless, the presence of some formal similarities does not necessitate the discovery of formal similarities in every part and every respect. "The fact that one element (or possibly two) of the traditional ('ideal') structure seem to occur in a composition does not warrant the inference that the other parts must be discoverable there as well or that the composition as a whole conforms to such a pattern" (111). It is more important to discern how each part, each passage, functions to facilitate the attainment of Paul's goals than to affix labels derived from the rhetorical handbooks to every part.

249. As Reed, "The Epistle," 181, observes, "certain functional parallels do exist between standard epistolary arrangement and rhetorical arrangement."

250. It is probably most proper to begin this segment at 1:11, given the presence of a well-established transitional marker at this point (Γνωρίζω γὰρ ὑμῖν, "I want you to know").

251. Kennedy, *New Testament Interpretation*, 144–46.

Melanchthon observed.[252] Paul crafts this narration, however, to move through and beyond issues pertinent to his own credibility (or his rivals' lack of credibility), ending at a point where the narrative has direct bearing on the situation in Galatia. The question he poses to Peter is also one that he poses, indirectly, to the rival teachers: "How can you compel the gentiles to adopt the Jewish way of life?" (2:14).

This question allows Paul to introduce a series of propositions with some supporting rationales (2:15–21) that are germane to the overarching goal of the communication—namely, to persuade the Galatian Christians *not* to turn now to Torah observance as a means of making progress in their new relationship with God, here advanced by providing a rebuttal of the rival teachers' position. The ensuing argumentation of 3:1–4:7, then, provides arguments in support of Paul's position and in refutation of his rivals' position. It would nevertheless be problematic, however, to speak of 2:15–21 as the *propositio* of Galatians, as if the overall goal of the letter were to win assent to these statements through the argumentation that follows.[253] If there is a true "proposition" in Galatians in the sense of a thesis toward which the whole of the speech was geared, however, it would be found unexpectedly more toward the end of the address: "For freedom Christ set us free: stand fast, then, and don't submit yourselves again to a yoke of slavery" (5:1).[254] Of course, this proposition was stated implicitly as early as 1:6: "I am astonished that you are so quickly deserting" (and so forth) translates rather readily to "Don't desert the path you've been pursuing or the one who called you to take that path."

The middle portion of Galatians is a clearly defined sequence of argumentative proofs (3:1–4:11) in support of Paul's position that righteousness, or being made right with God, does not come through Torah observance but by means of the path that Christ's death opened up for those who trust (2:16, 21). Establishing a clear dividing line where proof ends and call to action begins in Galatians is difficult, and perhaps entirely artificial. Paul moves

---

252. Classen, "Paul's Epistles," 102; Marius Victorinus was of a similar opinion (Classen, "Paul's Epistles," 110).

253. Reed, "The Epistle," 181, is correct to claim, as a general point, that "to speak of the *propositio* of a letter is dubious since letters often develop more than one 'theme'—a feature of their 'conversational' nature." This comment is certainly exemplified in a text like 1 Corinthians, for example, where Paul takes up a series of issues in turn, or in Philippians, where Paul is again interested to address a variety of topics rather than a single pressing issue.

254. The importance of 5:2–6 within the argumentative structure of Galatians has been impressively documented by Hietanen (*Paul's Argumentation in Galatians*, 181–82), who concludes that the argumentative thesis of Galatians is that "the Galatians should not be circumcised" and that "the rest of the letter supports this statement." I would differ only in seeing 5:1 as far more decisively connected with 5:2–6 than with 4:21–31, a point on which Hietanen hedges.

back and forth between the two beginning at 4:12, weaving together calls to respond and further arguments in favor of the preferred response through 6:10. A personal appeal in 4:12–20 gives way to another argument in favor of breaking with the rival teachers, this time based on an allegorical reading of a series of episodes from the Sarah-Hagar story (4:21–31). This allegory prepares the way for the central apotreptic (dissuasive) appeal in 5:1, which is itself supported with (admittedly emotive) argumentation in 5:2–6. Paul then returns to more personal remarks concerning his rivals (and their impact on the addressees) and himself in 5:7–12 as a means of reinforcing his major apotreptic appeal. This material could be taken to resemble a peroration, in which appeals to ethos are again expected, but clearly Paul has not yet completed making his case.

In 5:13 he initiates a new segment, intentionally returning to the subject matter and, to some extent, the syntax and rhythms of 5:1.[255] The first subsection (5:1–12) establishes that the gift of freedom must be preserved by not adopting the course of action promoted by Paul's rivals; the second (5:13–6:10), that it must not be misused against the Giver's purposes for it, but rather used fully in line with the Giver's intentions (intentions that can be known through the leading of the Spirit). Such walking in alignment with the Spirit that God has imparted emerges, then, as the viable alternative course forward, the course of action that Paul would have the addressees continue to follow, perhaps now with richer understanding and assurance.[256]

Galatians closes, then, with a series of statements that appear to accomplish several of the goals typically associated with perorations. Again, this correlation is probably more a sign of Paul's savoir faire as he considers the parting impact he wishes to have on his converts than a conscious desire to create a peroration per se. We find the expected parting shots at opposing advisers, leaving their reliability and motives in doubt (6:12–13), parting affirmations of reliability (6:14, 17) and emotional investment or goodwill (6:11, 18) on the part of the one addressing the audience, and closing reaffirmations of key theses supporting the goal of the speech (6:15–16).

---

255. Longenecker (223–24) rightly takes this structural parallelism as an indication that 5:1 should be understood to introduce a section (5:2–12), as does its counterpart (5:13), rather than to conclude the previous section (4:21–31), contra Witherington, 321, 340.

256. Galatians 5:13–6:10 is the "positive, protreptic part," which follows upon the conclusion to the "apotreptic" portion of the letter, in which "Paul does his utmost to dissuade the recipients from submission to the law and circumcision" (Dahl, "Paul's Letter," 137).

IX. WAS GALATIANS EFFECTIVE?

Did the churches in Galatia uniformly reject the proposals of the rival teachers and send them on their way after hearing Paul's letter? Were the rival teachers, in the end, able to rebut Paul's arguments and insinuations, retaining and solidifying their hold on the congregations? The very survival of the letter and its eventual incorporation into the collection of Pauline writings might point to Paul as the victor.[257] When Paul writes to the Corinthian churches about the collection project for the poor in Judea, he tells them to do exactly as he "instructed the churches in Galatia" (1 Cor 16:1). Assuming that Galatians was, in fact, written prior to 1 Corinthians, this would probably imply that Paul had ongoing interaction with the Galatian Christians after sending his letter to them, no doubt a good sign that he had some positive response from them.

Unfortunately, the preservation of Galatians need not imply Paul's *victory* in Galatia. If even a small number of disciples in those congregations remained loyal to him, they would have preserved the letter themselves, forming new congregations loyal to Paul's gospel in that region.[258] Galatians would have still come to be treasured by Pauline Christians throughout the Mediterranean (notably the provinces of Asia, Macedonia, and Achaia), and therefore enjoyed a broader circulation and been positioned to become part of the Pauline "canon." While Paul apparently gave the Galatians instructions about participating in the collection project (1 Cor 16:1), it is striking that, when he writes to the Roman Christians about the collection, he says only that "Macedonia and Achaia were pleased to make a certain contribution for the poor among the saints in Jerusalem" (Rom 15:26). Did the Galatian churches, in the end, elect not to participate? Would such a decision signal their having broken with Paul, or at least their having taken a significant step back from partnership with Paul?[259]

---

257. Dunn, 19.

258. We might think again of Martyn's "catechetical instructors" (14) as those who might become the leaders of splinter congregations of Galatians who remain attached to Paul and his gospel.

259. Watson (*Paul, Judaism, and the Gentiles,* 58–59) mounts a strong argument that churches beyond those in Macedonia and Achaia participated in this collection, despite Rom 15:26 mentioning only the churches in these two provinces as having done so. He points to the "brothers" who act as emissaries for the churches (2 Cor 8:23; 9:3) and to "the brother renowned in the gospel through all the churches" (2 Cor 8:18), who is specifically described as an emissary chosen "by the churches" to make sure the money makes it to Jerusalem. Watson points out that these brothers can be neither Macedonian nor Achaian Christians, and so they must have been sent from yet other churches to help with this work. There are therefore good indications that other Pauline churches contributed, but it becomes a matter of speculation, then, to identify which churches beyond Macedonia and Achaia these might be.

Participation or nonparticipation in the collection notwithstanding, Luke portrays Paul enjoying ongoing relations with the churches in Galatia. After the Jerusalem Conference and thus, by our accounting, well after Paul sent his letter to the Galatians, Paul returns to the cities of South Galatia (specifically Derbe and Lystra) to deliver the decision of the Jerusalem leadership (Acts 16:1, 4). Paul and his team may indeed return to these cities once again when Paul goes through "the Galatian and Phrygian region, strengthening all the disciples" (Acts 18:23). These follow-up visits would suggest that Paul continued to have generally strong relations with at least a good portion of the congregations in Galatia, leaving open, though, the question of Paul's silence in regard to their participation in the collection. The failure of Torah-observant Christianity to flourish outside of Palestine and Syria (where the Ebionites and Nazarenes, for example, took deep root) testifies, in its own way, to Paul's ultimate victory in Galatia and throughout the diaspora Christian mission generally.[260]

---

260. DeBoer, 411.

The Letter to the
GALATIANS

Text and Commentary

I. PAUL'S OPENING GREETING (1:1–5)

[1] *Paul, an apostle not sent out from human beings nor through a human being's agency, but through Messiah Jesus and Father God, who raised him from among the dead,* [2] *and all the brothers who are with me, to the congregations of Galatia:* [3] *May generous kindness and peace be yours from God our*[a] *Father and the Lord Jesus Christ,* [4] *who gave himself for*[b] *our sins in order that he might rescue us out of the present evil age according to the will of our God and Father,* [5] *whose is the glory into the ages of ages. Amen!*

a. There is some disagreement among early witnesses concerning whether the pronoun "our" qualifies "Father" or "Lord Jesus Christ." ℵ and A support the former reading ("our Father") and are followed by the NASB, NRSV, NIV, ESV, and NLT. 𝔓⁴⁶, ⁵¹, B, D, and 𝔐 support the latter reading and are followed by the KJV, RSV, NEB, NJB, and NET. Pauline usage favors the reading "our Father and the Lord Jesus Christ" (see Rom 1:7; 1 Cor 1:3; 2 Cor 1:2; Eph 1:2; Phil 1:2; Phlm 3; contrast Eph 1:3; 2 Tim 1:2; Titus 1:4; Metzger, *Textual Commentary*, 520).

b. Both ὑπέρ (𝔓⁵¹ ℵᶜ B H 33) and περί ("for," 𝔓⁴⁶ ℵ* A D G K P Ψ 𝔐) have strong external support. The former accords more fully with Paul's typical expression (e.g., see Gal 3:13; Das, 71).

Letters in the ancient world tended to use a standard formula (1) identifying the sender and the intended recipient or recipients and (2) adding a word of greeting.[1] We find a good example of this formula in Acts 23:26: "Claudius Lysias to his Excellency the governor Felix, greetings."[2] The basic framework of

---

1. Literally *a* word: in letters composed in Greek, χαίρειν (e.g., 1 Macc 10:18; 12:6; 15:2; Acts 23:26; Jas 1:1); in letters written in Hebrew, שָׁלוֹם (*šālôm*), "peace."

2. Similar conventions still govern letter-writing in the modern Western world, where we find standard opening formulas ("Dear X" or "To whom it may concern" or "Right and Reverend Sir") and closing formulas ("With love," "Sincerely yours," "Respectfully").

this formula remains intact in all of Paul's letter openings, though he exhibits the freedom to expand and modify it in several ways. In some instances, he expands upon his own self-identification (most notably in Rom 1:1–7, where vv. 1–6 represent such an expansion). In some, he expands slightly upon the identification of the recipients (as in 1 Cor 1:2; 1 Tim 1:2a; Titus 1:4a). In his greetings, he consistently replaces the standard word "greeting" with a wish that the recipients will experience "grace" and "peace" from God. Paul effects a bit of a pun here, replacing the expected "greetings" (*chairein*) with "grace" (*charis*). The addition of the wish for "peace" recalls the typical Hebrew greeting ("shalom").

In Galatians, as in a number of his other letters, Paul's expansions contribute to fulfilling the typical goals for the opening of an address, namely, establishing credibility and sounding the keynotes of the address, though 1:6–9 will attend to these tasks more directly and forcefully.[3] Here Paul's claim that his apostleship is one that was given by divine rather than human commission, and that he is therefore an envoy of God rather than of some human authority or body, anticipates the fuller demonstration of the fact in 1:11–2:10, as well as the theme of whom to trust, which runs throughout the letter (2:11–14; 4:12–20; 5:7–12; 6:11–17). His identification of Jesus as "the one who gave himself on behalf of our sins in order that he might rescue us from this present evil age according to the will of our God and Father" succinctly presents the seeds of the Christological and soteriological themes that will germinate throughout the remainder of the letter. Particularly noteworthy are the following:

1. Jesus endured death in order to benefit us; it was an act of grace that we must honor and to which we must respond appropriately (2:19–21; 3:13–14; 4:4–5; 5:2–4).
2. This benefit consisted in rescue from the present ordering of the cosmos, with its oppressive powers and constraints, so that we might enjoy the new order that God is bringing about (3:10–14, 23–25; 4:1–11, 21–31; 5:13–26; 6:14–15).
3. This rescue was all an outworking of the good and longstanding purposes of God (3:7–9, 15–22; 4:4–5),
4. whom we now know as Father (3:26–29; 4:6–7).

1 One of the goals a speaker would seek to achieve from the outset of a speech was to establish his or her credibility, often by demonstrating his or her authority to address a particular issue and commitment to the well-being of the audience whom the speaker was trying to lead toward making a partic-

---

3. So also Betz, 37; for a fuller treatment, see Cook, "Prescript as Programme."

ular decision. Paul addresses the issue of his authority head-on and up front as he expands his self-designation as the sender of the letter. He emphasizes his direct authorization by God to act as an apostle of the gospel, denying that he relies on any human authorization: "Paul, an apostle not sent out from human beings nor through a human being's agency, but through Messiah Jesus and Father God, who raised him from among the dead."[4]

The only name by which the apostle is known in his letters is "Paul," though Acts reports that he was known as Saul up to the time of his mission to Pisidian Antioch (the transition occurs at Acts 13:9). It is clear that his change of name was not connected to his change of religious allegiance (i.e., his encounter with the glorified Christ). As he moved further into gentile lands, he may have moved away from the Hebrew name "Saul" on account of the unfortunate meaning that *saulos* has in Greek ("prancing," "waddling," or perhaps even "effeminate," "affected").[5] If Acts preserves an accurate historical memory of Paul as a Roman citizen (16:37–38; 22:25–29), as seems likely, Paul would have had three Latin names: a praenomen, a nomen (family name), and a cognomen (the name by which he would have been typically called). Paulus, rendered in Greek as *Paulos*, would have been a typical enough cognomen. Saul would then have been a fourth name, a name given to him as a member of the Jewish community and people of Israel, a kind of second cognomen within a particular circle. Given his Benjaminite heritage (Phil 3:5), it is not at all surprising that his parents would have chosen for him the name of the first king of Israel, himself a Benjaminite (1 Sam 9:1–2).

The term "apostle" refers to an envoy or delegate who is sent to carry a message or enact a commission on behalf of another.[6] The term calls immediate attention to an awareness of a sender. Paul claims this sender to be none other than the glorified Christ and the God who had previously sent the

---

4. Following the practice of the NASV and NRSV, I have introduced the phrase "not sent out" in my translation of Gal 1:1 in order to capture the verbal facet of ἀπόστολος ("sent one," "envoy"), the noun related to the verb ἀποστέλλειν ("to send"), in relation to the adverbial prepositional phrases that follow ("from human beings," "through a human being's agency").

5. LSJ 1586; LSJA, 630.

6. BDAG 122 (s.v. ἀπόστολος). The word was regularly used in the classical period in connection with shipping; "in isolated cases it refers to persons who are dispatched for a specific purpose, and the context determines the status or function expressed in such Eng. terms as 'ambassador, delegate, messenger' (Hdt. 1, 21; 5, 38)." This becomes its primary sense in the New Testament. Many people bear this title in the NT: Peter (1 Pet 1:1; 2 Pet 1:1), the Twelve (Matt 10:2; Luke 6:13; Rev 21:14), Matthias (Acts 1:26), Barnabas (Acts 14:14), Andronicus and Junia (Rom 16:7), and Epaphras (Phil 2:25). Some are called "apostles" in a qualified sense as "delegates of the churches" (as in 2 Cor 8:23) and thus differentiated from *God's* envoys or ambassadors (2 Cor 5:20). Some call themselves "apostles" but are denied this title by other Christian leaders (see 2 Cor 11:5, 13; Rev 2:2).

Christil,[7] but not before he emphatically denies that he is acting on behalf of any human sender: "not sent out from human beings nor through a human being's agency." Paul doubly underscores this correction of a possible misunderstanding (or misrepresentation) of the source of his apostleship prior to presenting the positive statement of the same.

The two phrases "not from human beings" and "not through a human being's agency" are mutually reinforcing but not entirely redundant. With the first, Paul denies that human beings are the point of origin of his apostolic mission;[8] with the second, that any human being was instrumental in sending him out on this mission. James might have commissioned other Jewish Christian teachers to go out from Jerusalem to check on daughter churches in the nearby provinces (Gal 2:12); others might be commissioned as messengers or apostles on behalf of particular churches (see 2 Cor 8:23); James and his fellow apostles might select and commission people like Judas and Silas to represent them, distributing and explaining the apostolic decree among the churches (Acts 15:22–27). Paul, however, claims that his own commission to represent God and God's Messiah in the proclamation of the gospel came directly "through Jesus Christ and the Father God" (Gal 1:1).[9] "Through Jesus Christ" stands in explicit contrast only with "through a human being," though Paul would no doubt affirm Jesus and the Father to be the source of his apostleship, as well as the agents of his commission.[10]

Ultimately, Paul is answerable, then, to God, not to the Jerusalem apostles and, if not them, *certainly* not to the rival teachers who have come to Galatia claiming, perhaps, the authority of the Jerusalem church for their own message and mission. It is highly likely, given Paul's extended treatment of his own commission and his careful delineation of his relationship with the Jerusalem apostles in Gal 1:11–2:10, that Paul is already working from the first lines of this letter to destroy prejudice aroused against him by the rival teachers.[11]

---

7. Though rare in early Christian discourse, Jesus is himself referred to as an ἀπόστολος in Heb 3:1. Jesus as one who was "sent" by God, where some form of ἀποστέλλω is used, is common (Matt 10:40; 15:24; 21:37; Mark 9:37; 12:6; Luke 4:43; 9:48; 10:16; 20:13; Acts 3:26; Gal 4:4), especially in Johannine texts (John 3:17, 34; 5:36, 38; 6:29, 57; 7:29; 8:42; 10:36; 11:42; 17:3, 8, 18, 21, 23, 25; 20:21; 1 John 4:9–10, 14).

8. On this use of ἀπό, see BDF §210. On the distinction between these two phrases, see Lagrange, 2–3.

9. There is some tension between Paul's absolute claims here and scenes such as we find in Acts 13:1–3, where—still by the leading and action of the Holy Spirit—a group of human beings are indeed instrumental, at least, in setting apart and sending out Barnabas and Paul.

10. See Burton, 5–6.

11. Some scholars cautiously remark that the first verse does not yet give a clear indication that Paul's apostleship is under attack, but that the negations merely serve to accentuate

"Christ" is not yet here conceived of as a personal name, as is evident from the fact that Paul can write "Jesus [the] Christ" or "Christ Jesus." Ancient names did not admit of such changes in the order.[12] "Christ" is best heard as a title. The process of proclaiming the gospel and giving gentile converts preliminary instruction in their new faith and its obligations would have given Paul ample opportunity to inculcate in them a new understanding of the Greek word *christos* when applied to Jesus.[13] The resurrection of Jesus from among the dead is, of course, a core conviction within the early Christian movement, but Paul may also name it here at the outset because of its implications, which his converts are in danger of forgetting as they listen to the persuasive speech of Paul's rivals. It not merely marks God's vindication of Jesus and endorsement of the way Jesus taught but also inaugurates the end times, presaging the general resurrection from the dead at the end of days. It is a decisive sign that the boundaries of the ages are even now grating against one another as one passes away and another comes into being. It sounds a death knell for the powers of the present age, which have held humanity in bondage to the "elementary principles of the world" (the *stoicheia tou kosmou*; see commentary on 4:3 and excursus on pp. 348–53), about which Paul will speak in 4:1–11 and among which he will locate the Torah itself.

2 Paul often names a coworker as a cosender of an epistle (1 Corinthians: Sosthenes; 2 Corinthians, Philippians, Colossians, Philemon: Timothy; 1 and 2 Thessalonians: Silvanus and Timothy; Romans, Ephesians, 1 and 2 Timothy, Titus: none). Uniquely here he creates a picture not just of a single teammate but of "all the brothers and sisters who are with me" standing beside Paul in solidarity, addressing their fellow Christians in Galatia. In part, this wording could be explained by the likelihood that Paul does not have a teammate at present, since Galatians may have been written in the narrow

---

the positive claim (most forcefully, Vos, "Paul's Argumentation," 3; see also Betz, 39; Matera, 41). We do not find here, however, a merely ornamental use of the rhetorical figure of antithesis (contra Vos, "Argumentation," 3): Paul will restate this claim in 1:11–12 in regard no longer to his apostolic mission but to the message that his mission proclaims—a claim that, in turn, serves as the thesis statement for the extensive narration to follow, at least through 2:10. It is better to conclude, with Tolmie, *Persuading*, 32–33, that "the abrupt and unexpected use of these words (in particular in the salutation of a letter!) implies that the issue of his apostleship was so important for him that he used the first opportunity in the letter to address it" and that, in turn, "this would only make sense if misinformation with regard to his apostleship formed part of his opponents' strategy." See also Barclay, "Mirror-Reading," 88.

12. Das, 90–91. Das himself suggests (93–94) that we hear "Christ" as an honorific along the lines of Philopator or Epiphanes or even Augustus. Honorifics could indeed be used alongside a name or in place of a name. I am not personally aware of instances where the order of a name and its honorific are routinely changed (e.g., "Epiphanes Antiochus," "Nicator Seleucus," or "Maccabaeus Judas") in ancient literature, which argues against his suggestion.

13. See Dunn, *Theology of Paul*, 198–99.

window between his falling out with Barnabas in Antioch and their reconciliation before testifying together at the Jerusalem Conference. However, it is also a rhetorically effective way to remind the Galatians that his message is not his own idiosyncratic invention, but the shared testimony of Christian community.[14]

Paul's use of kinship language at the outset of this letter is significant; it sounds a theme that will dominate Galatians. God is the "father" of this vastly extended household (1:1, 3); the believers in Christ are "sisters and brothers" (1:2) to one another, even across great distances. The Christian movement constitutes thus a global "household of faith" (6:10). Paul, like other early Christian leaders, uses the language of family to speak of the relationships between Christians throughout the evangelized world, inviting believers to accept not only a new relationship in regard to the one God (sons and daughters) but a new relationship with one another (brothers and sisters). Those who are, by birth, "outsiders" to one another in terms of blood relations are called upon to accept one another, to look out for one another, and to invest in one another as the closest of "insiders." They are called upon to give one another the gifts that accompany being siblings—cooperation, sharing of material resources and other advantages, truth-telling and faithfulness, the nurturing of harmony and unity, investing in advancing one another's interests—and to approach one another from this vantage point. As people who have been brought together into a single family, they are called upon to banish all those things that would be unseemly within a natural family—competition, looking out for one's own interests at the expense of another, manipulation and withholding truth and true intentions, and the like. So much of the ethical vision for Christian relationships and community in the New Testament can be traced directly back to the understanding that God was fashioning a new *family* out of the many, unrelated people redeemed by Christ's blood—and who are therefore now related in truth *by blood*.[15]

Paul addresses the letter to multiple congregations (*ekklēsiai*) in the region.[16] The translation "congregations" is preferred to "churches," as the latter tends to connote buildings designated for worship. The Greek refers to an assembly of people without reference to a building or place, which is more in keeping with early Christian identity and practice. It is highly likely that the recipients regularly gathered together in the larger, private homes of the wealthier members for worship, study, and prayer, as is suggested both by the patterns we find in Acts (2:46; 5:42; 18:7; 20:20), in Paul's references

---

14. Bruce, 74; Fung, 38; Tolmie, *Persuading*, 34.

15. See further deSilva, *Honor*, 157–240; Oakes, *Reading Romans*, 107–10, 119–23.

16. On the location of these "congregations of Galatia" geographically and in the ministry of Paul, see the Introduction.

to such groups meeting in private homes (Rom 16:4–5, 23; 1 Cor 16:19; Col 4:15; Phlm 2), and by the frequent extolling and mention of the virtue of hospitality, on which the early Christian movement entirely depended (Acts 16:15; Heb 13:2; 1 Pet 4:9; 3 John 5–10).[17]

3 Alongside establishing one's own credibility (and sweeping aside prejudice, as needed), the openings of addresses tended to advance three other goals: (1) announcing the principal themes that would be taken up in the speech; (2) capturing the hearers' attention, showing that the question at hand is one of importance; and (3) arousing prejudice against speakers who were trying to lead the same audience in a different direction (see Aristotle, *Rhetoric* 3.14.6–7; Anaximenes, *Rhetoric to Alexander* 1436a33–37). Galatians 1:3–4 contributes to the first of these, as Paul describes the character and the achievements of the "Lord Jesus Christ," whose "favor" or "grace" (*charis*) and peace (*eirēnē*) he wishes upon the audience.

The Greek term *charis* is especially important throughout this epistle (indeed, it appears to be centrally at stake; see 2:21; 5:2–4), as is the larger social institution of patronage and benefaction, together with the roles and responses assumed to be appropriate within "grace" relationships (see excursus "A Contextual Understanding of Grace" on pp. 254–62). Within these relationships, the word can carry any one of three basic meanings: (1) the disposition to help another, hence "favor" or "generous kindness"; (2) the "gift" or assistance given as an expression of this generosity and willingness to help; and (3) the appropriate response to such a generous disposition and gift, hence "gratitude" or "thanks."[18] The context usually makes clear which sense is being invoked, here the favorable disposition and the generosity of God and God's Messiah as the initiating benefactors, which Paul wishes for his congregations to continue to enjoy (so also at the letter's close, in 6:18).

The Greek term *eirēnē*, particularly as the representation of the Hebrew "shalom" among Hellenistic Jews, denotes a state of health and freedom from strife and peril both individually and in one's relationships, hence "peace."[19] Peace was, however, a contested idea in the Roman world. The Latin *pax* ("peace") is a term of central importance to the ideology of Roman rule, particularly the ideology by which Augustus and his successors legitimated *their* rule. In the *Res Gestae Divi Augusti* ("Things Accomplished by the Divine Augustus"), copies of which were carved in bold relief in both Pisidian Antioch and Ancyra (modern Ankara), Augustus prominently showcases "peace" among his imperial benefactions, whether the pacification of unruly provinces or the ridding of roads and seas of brigands and pirates (see esp.

---

17. See further Banks, *Paul's Idea of Community*; Oakes, *Reading Romans*, 69–126.
18. BDAG 1079; deSilva, *Honor*, 104–19.
19. BDAG 287–88.

paragraphs 12–13 and 25–26). His gifts of peace were immortalized in the "Altar of the Augustan Peace" erected on the Field of Mars in Rome, at which sacrifices were offered annually. Inscriptions in Asia celebrate Augustus as one "who has made war to cease and who will put everything in . . . order."[20] Virgil, court poet of the Augustan age, lauds Rome as "making peace the way of life for humanity" (*Aeneid* 6.851–53). Many coins minted throughout the Principate feature the personification of peace (on the reverses of coins of Tiberius, Claudius, Galba, Otho, Vespasian, and Titus, with the legend *Pax* or *Pax Augusti*), the Altar of the Augustan Peace (Nero), or the personification of Securitas (Nero, Otho)

Paul hints here that peace must come from a different source, namely, from "Father God and Lord Jesus," who will eventually usher in a new order with a new leadership (1 Thess 1:9–10). Indeed, in 1 Thess 5:3 Paul will mock the ideology of "peace and security" (both words being common Roman slogans for benefits brought by the empire) embraced by those whom God has *not* enlightened, who are therefore not prepared for the transition of global rule from the powers that be (but are passing away) to God and his Messiah.

4 Paul recalls specific manifestations of the favor of God and of God's Messiah, benefactions that his converts have already appropriated as gifts given to them. He first recalls the fact that Jesus "gave himself for the sins we committed,"[21] announcing the theme of Jesus's sacrificial generosity toward Paul and his audience that will reemerge throughout the letter (see esp. 2:19–21; 3:10–14; 4:4–5). Both Paul and his hearers would have been familiar with the virtuous hero who won or brought benefit to the people by dying "for them." This topic was commonly used to praise military leaders and common soldiers who gave up their own lives in order to bring safety or other advantages to their people. Greek tragedies celebrated the person who was willing to sacrifice himself or herself for the greater good of another or of the city or people as a whole.[22] In Jewish tradition the martyrs who had accepted death by torture rather than release from torment at the cost of breaking God's covenant were remembered as heroes who gave themselves up for their nation,

---

20. Priene Inscription, lines 36–37; Danker, *Benefactor*, 217.

21. The preposition ὑπέρ is here to be taken more in the sense of marking the cause or reason for Christ's self-giving action (BDAG 1031) than marking the entity in whose interest an action is performed. Christ died to benefit the people responsible for sinning, but not to benefit their sins. The preposition used with inanimate objects often invites translation along the lines of "to accomplish something in regard to some object," here "in order to atone for our sins" (1031). The pronoun ἡμῶν is understood here as a subjective genitive.

22. Notable examples include the title characters in Euripides's *Iphigenia at Aulis* and *Alcestis*, as well as Menoeceus in Euripides's *Phoenician Women* and Macaria in his *Heracleidae*. On this theme, as well as the broader Greco-Roman background of this paradigm, see further van Henten, *Maccabean Martyrs*, 145–50, 210–22.

since their obedience to God was accepted by God as a representative offering of obedience to the covenant on behalf of the whole people, toward whom God turned again in mercy.[23] Both traditions, but especially the Jewish martyrological tradition, highlight the theme of the righteous person who gives himself or herself for the unrighteous, to deliver the latter from some great evil.

Jesus lavished his generosity upon Paul and his audience to the utmost, to the very point of death, so committed was he to bringing benefit to them (and to all people) in line with God's plan for extending blessing to all the nations. This is the manifestation of "grace," of "generous kindness," that Paul will himself be so careful not to "set aside" by turning to other, older supports like Torah (Gal 2:19–21), to which Paul will return when he explains how people were able at last to exchange Torah's curse for Abraham's promised blessing (3:10–14). Paul fears that the Galatian converts are devaluing this beneficence and are therefore in danger of cutting themselves off from God's favor in Christ as they contemplate trusting circumcision and Torah observance to do what they doubt Christ and the Spirit can do (5:2–4).

The deliverance brought about by Jesus is not merely a temporal one, as were those won by the heroes of Greek tragedy or the Maccabean martyrs. Rather, it is an apocalyptic deliverance: Jesus "gave himself for the sins we committed in order that he might rescue us out of the present evil age."[24] According to the apocalyptic framework within which Paul understands God to be working, time and space are divided into two ages—the present age and the age to come. Although God created the heavens and the earth "good" (Gen 1:4, 10, 12, etc.), this present cosmos was corrupted by the disobedience of both angels and human beings.[25] Humanity—from the individual person to the political, economic, and religious systems maintained by the participation of countless human beings—now labors under the powers of Sin, Death, Flesh, and the

---

23. See 2 Macc 7:1–8:5; 4 Macc 6:28–30; 17:21–22. The ultimate root of this theology of martyrdom and representative offering of oneself in obedience to God is probably Isa 52:13–53:12. See further van Henten, *Maccabean Martyrs*, 85–294; deSilva, *4 Maccabees: Introduction and Commentary*, 146–49, 249–53; deSilva, *Jewish Teachers of Jesus*, 158–74; Williams, *Maccabean Martyr Traditions*; Williams, *Christ Died for Our Sins*.

24. Or perhaps "age of the present evil," understanding τοῦ ἐνεστῶτος πονηροῦ as a substantival use of an adjective (πονηροῦ) modified by an adjectival participle (ἐνεστῶτος) in attributive position, the whole functioning as a genitive of description or definition qualifying τοῦ αἰῶνος.

25. Jewish apocalypses look less to the story of the fall (Gen 3) for an explanation of evil or the fallenness of this age and more to the story of the angels who were aroused by the beauty of human females, left their proper station to have sexual relations with them, lived among humankind and taught them all manner of forbidden skills and arts, and fathered a race of giants who wrought havoc upon the earth. This story had its roots in Gen 6:1–4 but was greatly expanded in the centuries before Paul's birth. The most important and influential representation of this story is found in 1 En. 6–36.

Devil and the demonic, which corrupt human beings and turn them aside individually and communally from God's good vision for human existence.

The present age has been so corrupted that it cannot be redeemed; the best it can do is to "pass away," along with those who belong to its corruption (1 Cor 1:18; 2 Cor 2:15; 4:3; Rev 21:1, 4). Paul's understanding of his contemporary period as "the present evil age" stands again in stark contrast with the public rhetoric of a Golden Age having returned with Augustus (Virgil, *Aeneid* 6.792–93), such that the "present age" (i.e., the first century) was also "the most pleasant age for human beings."[26] This present age will give place, however, to the coming age, God's new creation, a renewal of (or a replacement for) all things, in which God's vision for humanity, community, nature, and relationship with the Divine will become reality at last. Righteousness will be at home and receive its reward; all of God's promises will be fulfilled; the suffering of this present age will be swallowed up in the righteous shepherding of God's people by God's own self and the resulting experience of wholeness and good.[27]

The resurrection of Jesus signals the inauguration of this new age, for a major feature of the age to come is that the righteous who have died are not excluded from its rewards and blessings.[28] God would raise to life again those who have died in faithfulness to God so that they too could share in the age to come. The resurrection of the *one* righteous person, Jesus, was the firstfruits of the general resurrection—God's great harvest—to follow (1 Cor 15:20–22). Paul's letters dramatically reflect his awareness of living at the seam or the grating edge of these two ages, as the one receded into oblivion and the other began to emerge (see, most dramatically, Rom 13:11–14).

The notion of living at the end of one age and the inauguration of another is foundational to Paul's argument against the continued observance of Torah and, thus, against the perpetuation of the distinction between Jew and gentile that is so much in the foreground of his dispute with the rival teachers (3:26–28; 5:6; 6:15). The death and resurrection of Jesus marks a decisive turning point in God's dealings with humanity and, indeed, the whole of God's creation, with the result that the powers that have dominated human beings have come to the end of their term (3:23–25; 4:1–5, 8–11), with Jesus liberating people from those powers and ushering them into a new era of freedom and righteousness.[29]

---

26. *SIG*[2] 364, lines 9–10.

27. See further deBoer, 31–35; Das, 86–89. Martyn (90, also 263–75) aptly highlights liberation from the present evil age and the power of sin rather than simply the forgiveness of sins as "the fundamental remedy enacted by God."

28. See further Bryant, *Risen Crucified Christ*, 144–46.

29. The phrases "the time set by the father" (4:2) and "the fullness of time" (4:4) point also to Paul's conviction that "time is up" for this age and its powers. The implications of liberation from "the present evil age" constitute a major theme of Galatians to which we will return throughout the commentary.

These acts and their implications, Paul claims, are all "in line with what our God and Father wished."[30] The connection between the divine will and Jesus's voluntary acceptance of death is underscored in the Synoptic tradition (Matt 26:42 // Luke 22:42); here, too, the "will of the God and Father" likely includes not only the end (the rescue of human beings) but the means (Jesus's giving of himself).[31]

5 Paul closes this opening paragraph with a doxology, as is appropriate for the probable liturgical setting in which it would have been read to the congregations: "whose is the glory into the ages of ages, Amen!" It is not immediately clear whether the relative pronoun refers to "our God and Father," the nearest nominal, or to Jesus Christ, the principal subject of the whole of 1:4. Paul uses similar doxologies elsewhere, in which he leaves no doubt that God is the object of the ascription of glory (Phil 4:20; Rom 11:36). A doxology at the conclusion of Romans resembles Gal 1:5 in that both Jesus and God are available as possible antecedents for a nearly identical ascription of glory headed by a relative pronoun, though that ambiguity is almost certainly to be resolved in favor of "the only wise God" (Rom 16:27).[32] It would be more in keeping with Paul's doxologies elsewhere to regard "our God and Father" as the antecedent here, though if Paul were actually pressed with the question, it is difficult to imagine him consciously making a choice between the two.

The clause could be read either as a statement ("whose is the glory") or a wish ("to whom be glory"), as the verb itself is omitted and a form in either mood could reasonably be supplied by the hearers. The word translated "glory" denotes the widespread recognition of honor, virtue, and worth, and by extension the aura ("glory" as something almost visible) that surrounds beings and persons of such honor.[33] The final prepositional phrase is commonly translated "forever and ever" or a close equivalent (NRSV, NIV, NLT, CEB), though the Greek idiom conceives of this "forever" as a sequence of "ages."[34] The "amen" is a loan word from Hebrew, a liturgical expression typically used in the later Second Temple period at the conclusion of prayers.[35] When it is translated (rather than transliterated) in the LXX, it is rendered "may it come to be," but it may also be understood as a solemn affirmation (e.g., "truly, indeed").

---

30. Understanding κατά to announce a standard and τοῦ θεοῦ καὶ πατρός as a compound subjective genitive.

31. Burton, 15; Das, 85.

32. See also 2 Cor 1:20; 4:15; Phil 1:11; 2:11; 1 Tim 1:17; only in 2 Tim 4:18 is "the Lord," typically Jesus in Pauline literature, the referent in "to whom be/whose is glory into the ages of ages."

33. See LSJ 444; BDAG 257–58; deSilva, *Despising Shame*, 231–32.

34. Prior uses of the expression can be found, inter alia, in LXX Pss 18:10; 84:4; 145:1; Dan 7:18.

35. Burton, 16.

II. PAUL ANNOUNCES THE PRESENTING PROBLEM (1:6–10)

*6 I am astounded that you all are so quickly turning aside from the one who called you in [Christ's]ᵃ generous kindness and turning toward a different message of good news—7 not that it is another message of good news, but some people are troubling you and desiring to pervert the good news about Christ. 8 But even if we ourselves or an angel from heaven should go about proclaiming*ᵇ *[to you]ᶜ as "good news" something other than what we proclaimed to you as good news, let that person be accursed! 9 As we have said before, I say again also now: If anyone proclaims to you as "good news" something other than what you received, let that person be accursed. 10 Am I now, then, trying to win over people or God? Or am I trying to accommodate people? If*ᵈ *I were still accommodating people, I would not be Christ's slave.*

a. There is early, widespread, and strong external support for Χριστοῦ ($\mathfrak{P}^{51}$ ℵ A B Ψ 𝔐 *pm*), though the word does not appear in $\mathfrak{P}^{46}$ F G, or in the early quotations of this verse from Tertullian, Cyprian, Ambrosiaster, and Victorinus. As no scribal motive can be reasonably surmised for omitting the word if it were originally present (no scribe would have regarded it to be objectionable, nor did scribes tend to introduce ambiguity), the shorter reading may be the original (as reflected in the NEB and REB), with other copyists naming the source of "favor" as they deemed appropriate (whether "Christ's," as in the aforementioned witnesses; "Jesus Christ's," as in D; or "God's," as in a few minuscules).

b. The present middle subjunctive εὐαγγελίζηται is supported in $\mathfrak{P}^{51}$ B F G K Ψ; several early witnesses (ℵ*, 2 A) have here εὐαγγελίσηται, the corresponding aorist. A decision between the two is difficult. The difference in meaning is one of aspect ("should go about proclaiming" versus "should proclaim").

c. ὑμῖν was absent in the original text of ℵ (as well as early quotations of this verse in Tertullian, Cyprian, Eusebius, and others); it is present after the verb in codex A and ℵ² and appears before the verb in $\mathfrak{P}^{51}$ and B. This evidence is best explained by the pronoun's original absence. Scribes often understood it to be implied (perhaps under the influence of the following clause) and inserted it either before or after εὐαγγελίζηται. The shorter reading implies that Paul's concern was not only with a different gospel being preached to the Galatians but with a different gospel being preached anywhere.

d. 𝔐 (hence, the KJV) inserts an additional γάρ ("For") in the protasis, but this addition is to be rejected on the basis of its absence from $\mathfrak{P}^{46}$ ℵ A B.

In Gal 1:6–9 Paul continues to attend to tasks appropriate for the opening of a speech (or, here, a public discourse written to be read aloud in the author's absence), namely, (1) announcing the principal themes that would be taken up in the speech; (2) capturing the hearers' attention, showing that the question at hand is one of importance (here, by speaking of the high stakes involved); (3) arousing prejudice against speakers who were trying to lead the same audience in a different direction; and (4) returning to the topic of his own reliability, destroying prejudice that has been previously aroused against him by the rival teachers.

After an expanded greeting formula, Paul typically opens a letter with a paragraph expressing thanksgiving[1] or benediction,[2] often including some report of the prayers Paul offers on behalf of the addressees. Here, however, he opens with an expression of shock and amazement (1:6–7) followed by the pronouncement of a curse rather than a prayer (1:8–9). The Galatians, of course, would not know that such an opening was uncommon (and, indeed, if Galatians is an early letter it would not *yet* have been uncommon), but they would immediately recognize that Paul was about to take them to task for what they have done in his absence.

Orators typically sought to render their audience well disposed and receptive, to secure their good will at the start of the discourse. A friend writing a letter to a friend would have no need of doing this, but as we have seen, Paul's situation in sitting down to write Galatians is far more like that of the orator about to address a contested issue before an audience that has begun to be won over by other speakers than that of a Cicero or Seneca addressing a lifelong friend. If Paul were to have opened with some thanksgiving or blessing or other such device at this point, he would have put himself in the position of trying to please people, speaking so as to win them over by the customary practice.[3] Instead, he opens the body of his letter in a manner that could *not* be understood as guided by such considerations, but rather that demonstrated the opposite, namely, his freedom from people-pleasing and thus his ability to be constant in standing up for God and God's interests in any given situation. The opening is thus consistent with the claim Paul will make at the end of this paragraph about his absolute integrity as one who seeks to please him who had commissioned (even conscripted!) Paul for this work.

6 Paul opens the body of his letter with the declaration "I am astonished," which appears to have been an almost formulaic way to launch into

---

1. See Rom 1:8–12; 1 Cor 1:4–9; Phil 1:3–11; Col 1:3–14; 1 Thess 1:2–10; 2 Thess 1:3–12; 2 Tim 1:3–7; Phlm 4–7.

2. See 2 Cor 1:3–7; Eph 1:3–14.

3. Vos argues that the absence of the feature of "making the readers well-disposed" means that 1:6–9 is not preparatory to the discourse, even though the features it *does* contain are well documented facets of exordia, including "summarizing the *causa*, discrediting the adversaries, blaming the audience, expressing astonishment, and frightening the judges by threats" (Vos, "Argumentation," 5; see also Betz, 44–46). Vos prefers (7) to regard 1:6–9 as the *propositio* of the address: "The true gospel is not the gospel of the opponents, but only that of Paul. . . . The thesis that for the Galatians there is no other gospel than the one proclaimed by Paul encompasses the whole content of the letter." This thesis, however, is still merely a supporting argument in favor of the ultimate proposition (stated in the form of advice): "Don't submit to circumcision and seal yourself under that other gospel (which is *no* gospel), but rather keep to the path on which I set you in the genuine gospel I proclaimed" (5:1).

a letter of rebuke in the Hellenistic-Roman world, introducing the behavior that prompts the writer's rebuke and attempt to correct the addressee:[4] "I am astounded that you all are so quickly turning aside from the one who called you in [Christ's] generous kindness toward a different message of good news." Paul has learned, perhaps from people he had left in some leadership capacity there (e.g., the instructors whom he commends in 6:6), that his converts have been listening to other teachers who have brought a message different from Paul's, and that these teachers are close to persuading them to adopt a Torah-observant lifestyle as the means of cementing their place in God's people and advancing in God-pleasing righteousness.

The rival teachers promoted Torah observance as a complement to the Galatian converts' trust in Jesus, indeed as the next step forward in their spiritual journey toward becoming full-fledged children of Abraham and their ethical journey toward a transformed life of virtue. What the rival teachers would join together, Paul radically rends asunder. For him, the course of action they are contemplating is not a complement to their faith in Jesus but an act of desertion and repudiation of their divine Benefactor, a "turning aside from the one who called you in [Christ's] generous kindness" (1:6). Paul speaks of the desertion as (potentially) underway, but not yet an accomplished fact, hence his urgent intervention.[5] Paul adds that they are considering this action "so quickly," perhaps indicating the short amount of time that has elapsed since he left them, thinking them to have been well grounded, or perhaps adding this adverbial phrase simply to increase the shame of their desertion, since the rival teachers could "so quickly" subvert their loyalty. Either way, it amplifies Paul's own sense of disapproving surprise and calls the converts' reliability even further into question.

Paul does not explicitly name "the one who called you," though almost without exception he uses this verb elsewhere to speak of God's action,[6] and so this is likely his meaning here.[7] Paul may have been the one to deliver this invitation, but his role as envoy or delegate presupposes that the invitation

---

4. Specifically involving the verb θαυμάζω, as here; see Longenecker, cv, 14; Dahl, "Paul's Letter," 118; Hansen, *Abraham in Galatians*, 28, 33–44.

5. Das, 101. The author of 2 Maccabees uses the same verb in 7:24 to speak of Antiochus's goal of "turning" the youngest brother "away from his ancestors' ways" by persuading him to agree to adopt the Greek way of life. It is also used to speak of changing alignments with philosophical schools (as in Diogenes Laertius, *Lives of Eminent Philosophers* 7.166) and conversion from one way of life to another (Josephus, *Antiquities* 20.38, of conversion to the Jewish way of life).

6. See Rom 4:17; 8:30; 9:24; 1 Cor 1:9; 7:15, 17–24; Gal 1:15; 1 Thess 2:12; 4:7; 5:24; Das, 101. Paul occasionally uses "call" with human beings as the subject (1 Cor 10:27; implied in 1 Cor 15:9), but not with the contextual sense of "summon to a salvific destiny."

7. Martyn, 109.

ultimately came from another, in this case the God whom Paul passionately affirms to have commissioned him to extend this invitation, the God whom the Galatian Christians are in the process of deserting.

Paul describes God's calling with the prepositional phrase "in grace," which is notoriously ambiguous (the ambiguity being rendered more complex if the fairly well-attested variant "in the grace *of Christ*" is in fact original). The phrase may indicate the manner of God's action ("graciously called you"), the motivation of God's action ("called you because of his favor"), or, possibly, "extension toward a goal that is understood to be within an area or condition" ("who invited you into a grace relationship").[8] Any choice between these senses would be arbitrary, all the more as the few other uses of this phrase in the Pauline literature offer little help.[9] What *is* clear is that Paul depicts God's calling as a manifestation of favor in some sense, and thus he equates the audience's reception of the rival teachers' message with a repudiation of their divine benefactor's favorable invitation, a course both ugly and dangerous.

Paul's opening is well calculated to arouse feelings of shame among the hearers. That Paul is "shocked" at their behavior indicates that they have fallen far short of his expectations. He accuses them of having proven unfaithful to ("turning away from," even "deserting") the God who invited them into a relationship of "grace," or "favor," an especially shameful response, given the emphasis throughout the letter on the immenseness of the generosity God has shown in Christ, which should arouse only the deepest loyalty and commitment on the part of the beneficiaries. As it happens, he implicitly calls their intelligence into question as well—given the nature of the "gospel" to which they are turning "so quickly."[10]

Paul first calls this new teaching "a different gospel." The term "gospel" (*euangelion*) refers to an announcement of good news, often in connection with a forthcoming act of deliverance or other change for the better that God was to bring about for God's people Israel.[11] The word is also used in connection with the accessions of the emperors Augustus and Vespasian,[12] and so perhaps is an appropriate label for the announcement of the accession of a

---

8. See BDAG 330, 329, and 327, respectively. Schlier (37), Betz (48), and Das (102) would favor hearing this expression as an invitation into the sphere or state of favor in some sense, which is certainly as good a choice as any.

9. See Rom 5:15; Col 3:16; 4:6; 2 Thess 2:16; 2 Tim 2:1.

10. Paul will challenge their intelligence directly in a forthcoming section calculated to arouse feelings of shame for not having seen through the rival teachers' arguments and held their ground better (Gal 3:1–5, esp. vv. 1, 3).

11. See the uses of the related verb form in LXX Pss 67:12; 95:2; Isa 40:9; 52:7; 61:1.

12. Of Augustus, in the Priene Inscription (see Danker, *Benefactor*, 215–18); of Vespasian, in Josephus, *War* 4.656. Non-Christian uses tend to appear in the plural; the singular is appropriated for Christian discourse (Das, 104).

new lord/Lord. It is therefore not necessary to choose one background or one set of resonances over another,[13] all the more as the Isaianic announcement of God's interventions in the history of God's people is near in kind to the laudatory announcements of the accession of one or another emperor. In Paul's gospel, the new announcement of God's interventions *is* the announcement of a new Lord, an announcement with devastating repercussions for the Roman Empire and its ideological pretensions.

Paul and the rival teachers agree on certain key points of this good news, notably God's appointment of Jesus of Nazareth as King and Lord and the invitation to respond by pledging one's loyalty and giving one's full obedience to the new Princeps.[14] They differed on the manner of this obedience (whether obedience was to be driven by the Torah or by the Spirit of Christ), which betrays the deeper difference between them concerning the place of Israel and the Jewish people in God's new order.

7 No sooner has Paul called his rivals' message "a different gospel" than he steps back to correct or clarify this statement: "not that it *is* another (message of good news), but some people are troubling you and desiring to pervert the good news about Christ." Paul uses the rhetorical figure of self-correction here, though with a view to nuancing rather than retracting his previous claim. While the distinction between the Greek words here rendered "different" and "another" has been shown not to be hard and fast,[15] the intentional juxtaposition of the two words in such close proximity, with the immediate qualification of "a different" gospel as "not another" gospel in the next clause, suggests that, in *this* instance, the distinction is important and palpable.[16] Galatians 1:6–7 exhibits a subtle logical progression as Paul first identifies the rival teachers' message as a "different" proclamation from his own and then wrests from it the distinction of being "gospel" at all alongside his proclamation. As a perversion of the true gospel, the difference disqualifies utterly. This is the point he will need to prove in order to bring the Galatian Christians back to his own understanding of the gospel and the response for which his gospel calls. Galatians 2:14–5:12 provides this demonstration of the inadequacy of the rival teachers' "gospel," while Gal 5:13–6:10 demonstrates how *Paul's* gospel includes within it all the resources

---

13. So, appropriately, Wright, *Pauline Perspectives*, 82–83.

14. "Allegiance and loyalty to Jesus, 'faith' in this full and rich sense, is not the gospel itself; it is what the gospel is designed to produce and, by the power of the spirit, does produce" (Wright, *Pauline Perspectives*, 90).

15. ἕτερον (1:6) vs. ἄλλο (1:7). Silva (*Interpreting Galatians*, 54–56) speaks of them as interchangeable (so also Martyn, 110; BDF §306.4; BDAG 399). Das (97) reads the difference as nothing more than stylistic variation.

16. So also Tolmie, *Persuading*, 40–41. Here the adjective ἄλλο probably carries the sense of "another of the same kind" (LSJ 70; Burton, 24).

the Galatians need to see God's righteousness manifested within and among them as a community.

Paul begins to create prejudice against the rival teachers by referring to them as "agitators" or "troublemakers" in the Galatians' midst and as people whose goal is to "pervert" the good news about Christ (see also Gal 5:7, 10).[17] He casts them as disturbers of the peace, the equivalent of rabble who stir up trouble among an otherwise harmonious and prospering community.[18] Paul follows the convention of not naming these rivals or opponents, referring to them only in vague—and therefore disparaging and discounting—terms (here, "some people"). Creating distance between the hearers and these rival speakers, undermining the credibility of the latter, is a major goal throughout Galatians (see esp. 4:17–18; 5:7–12; 6:12–13).

8–9 Paul's astonishment turns to righteous indignation as, with two solemn curse formulas, he calls down divine judgment upon any who turn the good news of Christ into something that it is not: "But even if we ourselves or an angel from heaven should go about proclaiming [to you] as 'good news' something other than what we proclaimed to you as good news, let that person be accursed! As we have said before, I say again also now: If anyone proclaims to you as 'good news' something other than what you received, let that person be accursed."

The word translated here "accursed" (*anathema*) is routinely used in the Septuagint, the old Greek translation of the Jewish Scriptures, to translate the Hebrew word for the "ban" that pronounced spoils of war, a captured city, or a subjugated people to be "devoted" to God—a transaction carried out by their utter destruction (e.g., see Josh 6:17–18).[19] That which is abominable in God's sight, which must therefore not remain in the company or possession of the holy people of God, comes under this ban. The object that is declared *anathema* is a danger to anyone who shelters it: "Do not bring an abhorrent thing into your house, or you will be set apart for destruction [*anathema*] like it. You must utterly detest and abhor it, for it is set apart for destruction [*anathema*]" (Deut 7:26 NRSV; see also LXX Deut 13:18; Josh 7:11–13). The stakes of *rightly* receiving the gospel are so high that Paul thinks that anyone who would interfere with this preaching and hearing of the genuine gospel of Jesus Christ (e.g., by changing the message so that people are thrown off course) merits such a sentence. The Galatians would not need to be familiar with these passages from the Torah to understand the danger of sheltering

---

17. Understanding the genitive τοῦ Χριστοῦ as a genitive of content; it may also be heard as a genitive of source ("the good news brought by Christ").

18. The present tense (imperfective aspect) of the participle οἱ ταράσσοντες suggests that these people are still in the thick of trying to influence the converts.

19. Hebrew חֵרֶם. On the term, see Morland, *Rhetoric of the Curse*, 81–96.

the accursed thing, as the Greek cultural heritage would have conveyed this information just as effectively.[20] Paul's curse is thus a none-too-subtle inducement to the Galatians to separate themselves from the rival teachers.

Paul calls down the imprecation first upon his own head and then upon the head of any angelic messenger, in the most unlikely event that he or such a figure should come to the Galatians with a message different from the one that they had first received (the message that God had confirmed by the manifestations of God's own power and gifting of the hearers with the Holy Spirit, as Paul will remind the addressees in 3:1–5).[21] The second statement of this imprecation directly implicates the rival teachers, whom Paul has already identified as proclaiming "a different gospel" (1:6) from the one that Paul had brought to the congregations, and that they had embraced, at first.[22]

When Paul repeats the imprecation in 1:9, he indicates that he repeats an earlier warning about (or to!) people who preach a different gospel: "As we said before, so now I am saying again." It is not impossible that he is referring to the immediately preceding verse (1:8), emphasizing the solemnity of his pronouncement by heightening the drama of the repetition in the moment.[23] For several reasons, it seems more likely, however, that Paul here refers to a warning he had given during one of his earlier visits to these churches (either the evangelistic visit or the second visit on his return trip, when he confirmed them in their new Christ-centered way of life).[24] First, we find a similar reference to previous warnings in Gal 5:21, which must be a reference to instructions given during a previous visit, as there is no possible antecedent within the letter itself. Second, the distinction between an admonition given "now" and an admonition "we spoke previously" seems to require more than the passing of two seconds.[25] Third, Paul uses a plural verb to refer to the previ-

---

20. Sophocles's *Oedipus Rex*, for example, is essentially a story about tracking down the accursed thing that has taken shelter in Thebes, bringing a plague upon its inhabitants. Oedipus steps forward as the city's champion once again, determined to ferret out the cause of the gods' displeasure, only to discover that it is he himself.

21. The form of the first conditional clause (a "third-class condition"), all the more as it begins with καὶ ἐάν, "*even* if," presents what follows in 1:8 as an unlikely, hypothetical event. The preposition παρά here serves as a marker of noncorrespondence, hence "contrary to, against, out of alignment with" (BDAG 758).

22. Forms of παραλαμβάνω are frequently used in connection with the reception and acceptance of traditional instruction (BDAG 768). While Paul employs a subjunctive in 1:8, here he employs an indicative, inviting "an altogether less hypothetical application" of the conditional statement to the situation at hand (Armitage, "Conditional Clause Exegesis," 383).

23. Bruce, 84. John Chrysostom (8) appears to have read the verse this way as well.

24. Schlier, 40; Longenecker, 17; Fung, 47; Das, 109; Watson, *Paul, Judaism, and the Gentiles*, 60; Tolmie, *Persuading*, 41; Bachman, "Gal 1,9."

25. Burton, 29.

ous warning ("as *we* said before"), which is distinct from his use of a singular verb referring to his current, repeated warning in 1:9 ("so now *I* am saying"), suggesting a memory of a warning given by Paul in concert with at least one coworker (Barnabas?).[26]

It is of special interest in these curses that Paul does not claim himself to be the final authority: the message that he had brought to the Galatians when he evangelized them, the message that the holy God confirmed by working wonders and sharing his Spirit with those who listened with trust, is the final authority.[27] The Galatians should hold on to what they received as people who have been well grounded in the experience of Christ's love and God's acceptance. If a new group of teachers or Paul himself or a shining angel from heaven comes along now to tell them differently, they should not be swayed from the course on which they began, on which God himself had set them (3:1-5).

10 Paul raises the topic of his credibility explicitly as he rounds out the opening of his letter with two rhetorical questions: "Am I now, then, trying to win over people or God? Or am I trying to please people? If I were still trying to please people, I would not be Christ's slave." To what is Paul responding in 1:10, which he presents as evidence for some inference?[28] The verse is not a development of, or natural advance upon, 1:1-9. In contrast, 1:11-12 is very much a natural development of that material, as Paul goes on to show that the gospel he had brought to the Galatians at first is indeed a message given to him by God, the import of which he has faithfully preserved in the face of a series of challenges (as 1:13-2:21 will explain). The material that *follows* 1:10, then, provides supporting argumentation for why no one should preach or accept a gospel different from the one Paul had brought (i.e., the claims of 1:6-9).

The interjectory nature of 1:10 and the abrupt introduction of the idea that Paul is a people-pleaser (for which the reader has had no warning or

---

26. The choice of a perfect tense (as opposed to an aorist) may be without significance, or it may be that Paul wants to stress the ongoing effects of that earlier pronouncement (e.g., "as we said before [and thus you should already know and act in line with]").

27. So, rightly, Tolmie, *Persuading*, 42. As John Chrysostom (8) remarked: "See the Apostle's wisdom; to obviate the objection that he was prompted by vainglory to applaud his own doctrine, he includes himself also in his anathema." Das (106) correctly places the emphasis on "the *message*, not the messenger(s)," but he is wrong to assert that "Paul is not defending himself." It would be truer to say "Paul is not *only* defending himself." He is deeply concerned about the integrity of the message, more so than his own standing; but he *also* defends himself and affirms his divine commission to the extent that these actions will facilitate the Galatians' trusting him and his message.

28. Paul signals this function with the inferential conjunction γάρ, rendered here "then."

preparation) suggest that Paul is responding to something extrinsic to the developing argument, namely, a criticism that his rivals have leveled against him.[29] Any such criticism need not imply undue malice on their part, but only a defense of their own position. When they arrived in Galatia urging gentiles who had already been converted to trust in Jesus also now to accept circumcision and the basic contours of a Torah-driven life, the converts would reasonably have asked, "Why didn't Paul mention any of this?" The rival teachers could readily have responded: "Paul wanted to make it easier for you to come to faith, and so adapted the message to make it more pleasing to you, to win you over the more readily. Perhaps Paul's strategy had merit, given its results here; perhaps it was a sign of an underlying weakness on his part. Either way, you converts ought to be ready now, and sufficiently grounded in God, to hear the whole truth."[30] It is just such an allegation that Paul here denies, offering evidence to that effect in 1:10.

The first half of this verse is admittedly difficult and requires careful unpacking. The second half of the verse, however, is clear and offers a better starting point for interpretation. Against the suggestion that a desire to please or accommodate people still[31] motivates Paul and constrains his preaching, he offers his radical self-awareness of being a slave of Christ as evidence to the contrary (see also 5:11; 6:17, also commentary). Although the word "slave" refers to the lowest social status in the Roman economy (the class of "living tools," as Aristotle infamously defined slaves in *Politics* 1.4 [1253b27–33]), the term takes on a more honorific sense when connected with an exalted human personage or, especially, a divine figure (e.g., "slave of God" or "slave of Christ"; see Rom 1:1; Gal 1:10; Phil 1:1; Titus 1:1; Jas 1:1; 2 Pet 1:1; Jude 1).[32] It was nobler to be a deity's slave than a slave of public opinion, and Paul here expresses the same distaste for being classed with the latter, as would any Greco-Roman philosopher.[33]

---

29. Fee, 33; Burton, 30; Tolmie, *Persuading*, 43.

30. Paul will turn this charge back on his rivals in 6:12–13.

31. The adverb "still" might suggest that Paul would admit that there was a time when winning the approval of human beings was a driving motivator, likely a desire prior to his conversion to please his Pharisaic teachers, his peers (whom he also sought to excel), his teachers, and the representatives of the covenant (e.g., the chief priests). See Martyn, 140; essentially also John Chrysostom, 9.

32. BDAG 260. Despite the tendency of many modern translations to render this word "servant" (NRSV, NIV, NLT), Paul does in fact use the word δοῦλος, "slave," in his self-identification (thus in the CEB).

33. Those who acted with a view to the opinion of others, especially the unenlightened many, were compared to people in slavery by Greco-Roman philosophers (and those influenced by them, such as Philo). Particularly poignant is the saying of Epictetus (*Discourses* 4.1) that we are the slaves of those whom we seek to please.

Several questions arise in regard to the first half of the verse. First, what kind of action is Paul naming here with the verb typically translated "persuade"? And what might Paul mean, in particular, by "persuading *God*"? Second, is Paul asking one question or two when he writes "Am I now, then, trying to win over people or God?" That is, does Paul expect a single answer ("No, Paul, you're not trying to win *anyone* over, human or divine")[34] or potentially different answers to two different halves of this first question (e.g., "No, you're not trying to win people over, but you are trying to win God over")?[35] Finally, what is the relationship of 1:10b to 1:10a? Does 1:10b restate 1:10a, such that "pleasing people" (1:10b) and "persuading people" (1:10a) are essentially synonymous? Or are the two actions significantly different?

The second half of this verse expresses Paul's clear denial of the suggestion that he is motivated by a desire to please or accommodate people, such that he either seeks their approval or, probably more to the point here, would alter the message with which he has been entrusted so as to gain a better or an easier reception among human beings. It makes the most sense to read the first half of the verse as articulating a related denial that Paul seeks to "persuade" people in the sense of "saying whatever is necessary so as to gain their support."[36] The verb essentially means "to persuade" or "win over by argument," but often it carries the negative connotations of "crowd-pleasing," "placating," even "campaigning for favor and support."[37] Coupled

---

34. So, for example, Moo, 83–84.

35. So, for example, Martyn, 136 (taking "winning God over" in the sense of "speaking so as to please God"); Lagrange, 8; Schreiner, 89; deBoer, 63. Such scholars point to 1 Thess 2:4–6, where Paul speaks "not to please people, but God who tests our hearts." The question is not, however, whether Paul seeks to please God, which he certainly does; the question is whether he has engaged in trying to persuade God rather than accept and represent God's terms without balking because of how people would respond. Conversely, Bruce (84–85) cites 2 Cor 5:11 as warrant for thinking that Paul expects an affirmative response to his first question: "Yes, Paul, you are persuading people." The root issue here, however, is not merely the activity of persuading human beings, but altering the message so as to make it more palatable, more pleasing, and thus to increase one's success and appeal.

36. Vos, "Argumentation," 9. Others have read "persuading people" (1:10a) as *not* synonymous with pleasing people (1:10b). Das (112), for example, affirms that Paul *is* trying to persuade both people (the Galatians) and God (to enforce the anathema), though the form of the question does not seem to admit of *two* positive answers.

37. So BDAG 791 (s.v. πείθω); Burton, 30–31; Fee, 33; Longenecker, 18; Schreiner, 89. Plato uses the verb in the context of speaking about the activity of popular speakers who play to the crowds with a view to winning them over, who are more interested in gaining quick assent than in the more painstaking and disciplined tasks of discovering and teaching the truth ("to persuade people," πείθειν τοὺς ἀνθρώπους, *Protagoras* 352e; "to persuade the crowds," πείθειν τὰ πλήθη, *Gorgias* 452e; Martyn, 138; deBoer, 62). On the stereotype, see Plato, *Gorgias* 462b–466a; 500c–503d; 521a–b; Demosthenes, *Exordia*

with "people-pleasing" (1:10b), Paul gives us the picture of a speaker who will say whatever is necessary to achieve his or her ends, rather than saying only what aligns with truth—and he is not *that* speaker.[38]

The sense of "persuading God" is somewhat more elusive. One possible background is that of magicians and diviners who use spells and rites to "persuade the gods to serve them" (Plato, *Republic* 364c).[39] Paul would certainly deny that this is his modus operandi. But even in its more pedestrian sense, seeking to "persuade" God stands over against uncompromising loyalty and obedience to whatever God speaks, as it represents an attempt to change the Deity's mind or standards. Paul's rivals have come with a demanding message, calling for circumcision and submission to the yoke of the Torah. It is theoretically a "hard sell." They could well have spoken of Paul as attempting a "soft sell," trying to work out in his mind a compromise that would both please the gentiles whom he was trying to win over for Christ (and get them to embrace the gospel more readily) and still be acceptable to God. Paul's gospel represented an attempt to persuade both people and God to accept a compromise—and at some level, in his rivals' estimation, Paul would have had to have believed that he had persuaded God to accept people on very different terms than God had historically set forward in the Torah.[40]

With 1:10, then, Paul sweeps aside any such suggestion, asserting that he seeks only to please the one party that commissioned him, not work out a compromise that would ingratiate him to multiple parties. He is a faithful messenger, not adulterating the message entrusted to him for the sake of an easier reception. The flow of the paragraph suggests that Paul regards his speech in 1:6–9 as providing proof of this claim. The "now" of 1:10 makes the most sense if taken as a reference to what Paul has just been doing, namely, chiding the Galatians for their lack of discernment and steadfastness and pronouncing curses upon his rivals rather than working out compromises.[41] He has made his opening statement in Gal 1:6–9 as provocative as he did *precisely* to show the Galatians that he is not timid about causing offense for the sake of preserving the truth of the gospel and making sure his converts walk in line with that truth. For the sake of this truth, Paul will not spare his hearers—something that sets him far apart from the stereotype of the unreliable

---

1.3; 9.2; 19; 26.2; 28.1; 41; 44.1; Dio Chrysostom, *Discourses* 32.11; 33.1–16 (cited in Vos, "Argumentation," 10).

38. This reading would correlate with the apparent criticism behind Gal 5:11: "Paul still preaches circumcision; why he didn't in your case is a mystery. Perhaps he was saving it for later so as to win you over to Christ first and get you secure in that as a starting point" (see also Moo, 84–85; Schreiner, 89).

39. Betz, 55.

40. Dunn, 49–51; Tolmie, *Persuading*, 43.

41. Burton, 31; Moo, 85; deBoer, 62; Schreiner, 88–89; Tolmie, *Persuading*, 44; Das, 111.

speaker as a flatterer who will tell an audience what they want to hear just to win them over.[42]

The story of his second visit to Jerusalem and of the incident at Antioch, which Paul will soon relate (2:1–14), also address this topic very directly. Paul does not alter his message in order to please others and is more than willing to confront Christian teachers who *do* put people-pleasing ahead of walking in line with the gospel (as did Peter in Antioch). Unlike his opponents (as he will assert in 6:12–13), he will not be swayed from holding to the true gospel, nor will he blunt its force because that gospel might make him unpopular or even bring him hardship. He understands that being a people-pleaser is incompatible with being a reliable servant of Christ.

Galatians 1:1–10 makes for a rhetorically effective opening. Paul captures the hearers' attention (the main goal for the typical opening of an address) by presenting their situation as one of the gravest peril, since they find themselves in danger of proving disloyal to their great Benefactor, Jesus, forcing them to be open to reconsidering the relationship between faith in Jesus and circumcision (1:6–7). Paul makes significant strides toward reestablishing his credibility as a reliable messenger of God and a strong beginning toward calling the rival teachers' credibility into question (1:1, 6–10). Perhaps most important, he reminds the hearers of the tremendous benefits Jesus has won for them at tremendous cost to himself (1:4), making them sensitive from the outset to Paul's proposals concerning how best to honor, and show gratitude for, Jesus's generous kindness—namely, moving forward with confidence in the sufficiency of the gifts he has brought to them, foremost among these being the Spirit.

In these introductory verses, Paul raises several considerations of perpetual importance for the Christian church and those who minister therein. His insistence that there is essentially *one* gospel and that deviations from this gospel are no longer "gospel" calls us to examine ever more closely the message that we embrace for ourselves and present as God's word of invitation and demand. Paul's words should be heard in the first instance as words of caution directed to *us*, not as words of condemnation for those who speak differently from us concerning this gospel.[43] In the Galatians' situation, this "other gospel" focuses on conforming gentile Christians to the traditional practices of Jews—the practices that Paul sees more now as cultural baggage from his own Jewish upbringing, the residue from his pre-Christian existence. Paul's judgment upon the rival teachers' program might lead us to be particularly keen on examining the extent to which our churches insist upon certain behaviors or practices that *we* have adopted as a meaningful

---

42. Betz, 54–56.
43. Fee, 27.

manner of expressing commitment to God as the *only* meaningful manner of expressing obedience.

Ironically, Paul's insistence on the *one* gospel works out practically in diverse expressions of obedience and in the demand for a great deal of toleration across this diversity. Christians who worship God on Saturday as the original Sabbath are affirmed for doing so to honor God, but if they insist upon this as the only valid expression of Christian worship (see esp. Rom 14:5–6), they preach another gospel. That one Christian group can point to the scriptural "proofs" for its position over against the practice of other Christian groups is no guarantee that it is the normative and therefore only way to honor God or to be genuinely Christian. It was the rival teachers, not Paul, who had Scripture more clearly and explicitly on their side in the dispute over circumcision and Torah observance. In the face of the diversity of baptismal practices observed throughout the Christian church, for another example, and of the debates over which practice is *the* practice acceptable to God, Paul would be more concerned to have us rejoice in the work of the Holy Spirit in and around each community's baptismal practice rather than approve of one group's legislation and accept its claims that people are not part of the body of Christ apart from submitting to certain rituals in certain ways.

This is not to say that Christians ought not to engage in conversations with one another about their difference in practice. We can and ought to hold up what we think to be the merits of our tradition's particular decision about a practice; we can and ought to challenge one another to make sure that we are listening to God and not to our own "flesh" in regard to some practice; we can and ought always to bear in mind our freedom to *curtail* our freedom where it would give offense, disrupt harmony, or lead another disciple to act against his or her conscience (Rom 14:13–23). But we ought to do so in a spirit of humility, readier to affirm where the Spirit has led another Christian body in a direction different from ours (and readier to reexamine our own direction) or to discern another facet of the "truth of the gospel" expressed in their practice, than to condemn the practice of that Christian body.

Paul reminds us, however, that there are boundaries around the good news, and there are ways in which Christian teachers, well-intentioned or otherwise, can cross those boundaries such that they are presenting a perversion of the good news that is therefore no longer the life-giving, life-changing message that we received from the apostles. Selective attention to the Scriptures frequently results in a body of Christians making of the good news something that it simply is not. The "prosperity gospel" is a case in point, with a few texts about God's promises of prosperity in this life and access to anything we could want through prayer, with faith becoming the core of the message, displacing a great deal of the scriptural witness. The whole counsel of Scripture speaks of God's purposes for Christians quite differently, revealing that God is *not* out to make us happy as the world measures happiness; God is out to make us more like Jesus, something that will not happen without walking in the way of self-denial, dying to our own cravings and urges, and living for what God desires to accomplish *in others* and *for others* through us. Similarly, a presentation of the gospel that focuses so fully on God's grace and the lack of any contribution on the part of an individual to arriving at God's goal for him or her ("salvation") that it leaves little room for the many texts in Scripture (not least of all Paul) that speak of the necessity of the Christ-followers' transformation and of their living the remainder of their lives "not for themselves, but for him who died and was raised on their behalf" (2 Cor 5:15) ceases to represent the gospel.[44]

Paul also draws our attention to the challenges of social dynamics where the gospel is concerned. Here, Paul is especially attuned to the danger of compromising the terms of God's invitation and the fullness of God's vision for the sake of making the same more appealing or palatable to those with whom we have to do. In Paul's mind, the problem arises not from pleasing human beings but from making this an aim that competes with pleasing God.[45] There is no virtue in being overtly *dis*pleasing to people, and Paul is elsewhere quite finely attuned to the importance of not putting any *unnecessary* obstacles in the way of people (2 Cor 6:3).[46] He is aware, however, that there are *necessary* obstacles (e.g., see Gal 5:11b), which must be allowed to remain and to provoke the necessary changes in the hearers, if they are to enter into the new creation into which God invites all people. Pleasing both God and one's congregation or neighbors or audience at the same time is a good thing, but more often a choice must be made. Paul's own example challenges us to remember that, in every encounter, in every decision, in every intervention, there is One whom we must please, there is One to whom we, as Christ's slaves, are answerable.

---

44. See further deSilva, *Transformation*.

45. Burton, 32.

46. This sensitivity is itself somewhat ironic in context, as Paul is explaining at some length in 2 Cor 2:14–7:4 and 10:1–13:13 the very real obstacle of his own apostolic presence, "bearing" as he does "the death of Christ in [his] mortal body" (4:10).

III. STRATEGIC RECOLLECTIONS (1:11–2:21)

Paul signals the beginning of a new segment of his letter with the phrase "I want you to know," a typical transition formula in Hellenistic letters.[1] This segment extends at least through 2:14, and since it is impossible to determine within 2:14–21 where Paul's report of his response to Peter ends and his fresh statement of his position for the benefit of the Galatian converts begins, it extends effectively through 2:21.

The narrative that Paul crafts in Gal 1:11–2:14 is not a dispassionate representation of the bare facts of particular episodes, although Paul does evidence a strong concern at some points with the factuality of his account (see esp. 1:20). Paul crafts these reflections with a view to restoring his credibility in the eyes of his converts and, more specifically, with a view to reestablishing for himself a higher degree of credibility than his converts are according the rival teachers. He carefully selects episodes from his past and, especially, his interactions with the Jerusalem apostles to construct a narrative that communicates the following major points:

1. Paul's commissioning and message come directly from God, and so his presentation of the gospel must be deemed more authentic and authoritative than that now preached by the rival teachers.[2]

2. His authority is not dependent upon, or derivative from, the Jerusalem apostles, and therefore he is not ultimately answerable to them or to their position.

3. Nevertheless, Paul has worked collegially with the Jerusalem apostles, and they have recognized his apostleship as valid.[3]

4. Paul is the one apostle who has all along, in the face of any and all pressures, walked "straight toward the truth of the gospel" (Gal 2:14), the truth God revealed to him and seeks to reveal through him, and so

---

1. Longenecker, cv, 22. While Γνωρίζω ("I want to make known") does not *always* signal a new section (Vos ["Argumentation," 11] points to 1 Cor 12:3 as an example), here it is joined to a vocative of direct address (ἀδελφοί, "brothers and sisters," 1:11), which is another potential signal of a new topic. Taken together, there is the greater likelihood that Paul conceived of himself starting the next step of his argument here.

2. Classen, *Rhetorical Criticism*, 25; Tolmie, *Persuading*, 47. Vos ("Argumentation," 13) correctly affirms that, "insofar as [Paul] spoke about his apostolate, he did so in order to prove the truth of his gospel against that of the opponents" but does not recognize that dispelling doubts being cast upon his reliability by the rival teachers is a necessary precursor to proving the truth of his gospel over theirs. See above on 1:10.

3. As Holmberg (*Paul and Power*, 15) rightly observes, "The dialectic between being independent of and acknowledged by Jerusalem is the keynote of this important text."

is most plausibly the best representative of the truth of the gospel in Galatia.[4]

The final point also provides evidence in support of Paul's claim that he is no people-pleaser. If he were, he might have yielded to the pressure of the "false brothers" (2:4–5) or to the pressure of the "people from James" (2:12), as did Peter and Barnabas; instead, he stood up boldly for the truth of the gospel, even if it meant standing alone.[5]

A. THE DIVINE SOURCE OF PAUL'S DRAMATIC TRANSFORMATION AND GOSPEL (1:11–17)

[11] *For[a] I want you to know, brothers and sisters, that the message of good news proclaimed by me is not one framed according to human standards.* [12] *For I didn't receive it from a human being, nor was I taught it by a human being, but I received it by means of a revelation of Jesus Christ.* [13] *For you heard concerning my conduct when formerly in Judaism that I used to persecute God's Assembly beyond all bounds and was working to destroy it,* [14] *and I was making greater progress in Judaism than many of my peers among my race, being more exceed-*

---

4. "Paul admits that he opposed Cephas, but argues that he was merely exposing the inconsistency of Cephas's behaviour, even on his own presuppositions" (Watson, *Paul, Judaism, and the Gentiles*, 60–61), and, one must add, demonstrating the consistency of his own behavior.

5. So also Vos, "Argumentation," 14. A number of scholars have suggested that the fundamental purpose of Gal 1:10–2:14 is "to provide examples to the audience of what sort of behavior to adopt or shun (shun—Paul's pre-Christian behavior, the behavior of Peter and Barnabas at Antioch, and the behavior of the false brothers; adopt—Paul's post-conversion life style and behavior and the behavior of the pillars when Paul met with them in Jerusalem and they did not compel Titus's circumcision and endorsed Paul's mission to the uncircumcised gentiles)" (Witherington, 29; see also Lyons, *Pauline Autobiography*; Gaventa, "Galatians 1 and 2"). Aside from the fact that Paul at no point draws explicit attention to the exemplary purpose of these episodes ("Don't be like Peter or Barnabas"; "Take the pillars for your example"), something he typically does when offering examples (e.g., see 1 Cor 11:1; Gal 4:12; Phil 3:17), the specific points Paul *does* establish in regard to this string of episodes all answer—and answer very well—questions *other than* "whom should we imitate?" (in contrast to Gal 4:12). These questions would include (1) "What is the source of Paul's commissioning and message, and therefore his authority to speak on behalf of God?" (2) "What is the nature of Paul's relationship with the Jerusalem pillars?" and (3) "Who has shown the greatest consistency in regard to the 'truth of the gospel,' and what is required of gentiles to become part of God's people in Christ?" Paul's narrative thus principally affirms the ultimate reliability of Paul's gospel vis-à-vis the "other gospel." Against reading 1:11–2:14 as offering moral paradigms, see also Vos, "Argumentation," 15; Barclay, "Mirror-Reading," 93; Lategan, "Is Paul Defending?," 423–24.

ingly an enthusiast for my ancestral traditions. 15 *But when it pleased the one [or the God]*[b] *who set me apart from the time I was in my mother's womb and who called me through his generous kindness* 16 *to reveal his Son in me, in order that I should proclaim the good news about him among the nations, it wasn't with flesh-and-blood humans that I went to confer immediately,* 17 *nor did I go up*[c] *to Jerusalem to those who were apostles prior to me, but I went away, rather, into Arabia, and I returned again to Damascus.*

a. γάρ is supported by ‭א‬[1] B D* F G (reflected in the RSV, NRSV, NASB, NIV). Several early witnesses (𝔓[46] ‭א‬*,[2] A), together with 𝔐, however, read δέ (KJV, NAB, NET). The general scribal tendency to flatten particles in favor of δέ may argue in favor of γάρ, despite the strong evidence for the former (including the fact that the second corrector of Sinaiticus had deliberately altered the work of the first corrector in favor of restoring the blander particle; Silva, *Interpreting Galatians*, 44–50). Paul uses δέ in this disclosure formula in 1 Cor 15:1 (γνωρίζω δὲ ὑμῖν, ἀδελφοί, 1 Cor 15:1; Das, 115), but this usage is due to the lack of any thematic connection between the preceding material and the material introduced by 15:1. Here, the opposite is the case: Paul begins to present evidence for the claims he has made in the opening paragraphs.

b. The words ὁ θεός are omitted in 𝔓[46] B F G, among others (so RSV, ESV, NLT, NET) but are included in ‭א‬ A D 𝔐 (so KJV, NRSV, NASB, NIV). It is easier to believe that early scribes added ὁ θεός to bring greater clarity to the verse than that other scribes omitted the words (with Metzger and Wikgren in Metzger, *Textual Commentary*, 522; Das, 116).

c. The verb ἀνῆλθον is well attested (‭א‬ A K L P Ψ 𝔐) and appropriate for movement toward Jerusalem, which is almost always spoken of as movement "up." Precisely this tendency, however, may argue against this form being original, but rather a correction of the less proper ἀπῆλθον attested in 𝔓[51] B D G or the nondescript ἦλθον in 𝔓[46].

11–12 The first major point that Paul stresses in his narrative is the divine origin of the gospel he had brought to the Galatians. The first and best reason they should resist the leading of the rival teachers is that Paul brought them exactly and fully the message God had for them: "For I want you to know, brothers and sisters, that the message of good news proclaimed[6] by me is not one framed according to human standards. For I didn't receive it from a human being, nor was I taught it by a human being, but I received it by means of a revelation of Jesus Christ." The content of 1:11 grows organically out of 1:10b with its antithesis of human beings, on the one hand, and Christ on the other, whose uncompromised and uncompromising envoy Paul claims to be. The content supports Paul's implicit claim in 1:6–9 that any gospel different from the one that Paul preached to these congregations at the first is not to be received (i.e., because it is set in competition with the message that came from

---

6. The tense of the aorist passive participle εὐαγγελισθέν does not necessarily communicate a temporal component (as in NRSV, "that was proclaimed by me"; see also NIV, CEB), but merely an undefined aspect (hence "proclaimed by me").

God himself) and his explicit claim that those who promote such a different gospel (one that, in the end, is no gospel at all) stand under the anathema (i.e., because they are opposing a divine message and preferring their own contrary message, leading people astray as did the false prophets of old).[7]

Paul addresses his audience here more gently as "brothers and sisters," connecting with them on the ground of their common kinship in Christ under one Father, God (1:1, 3), reassuring them thereby of his goodwill toward them, despite the harsh words of 1:6–9. He asserts that the message that he had brought them was not "according to human thinking" or "humanly devised."[8] It was not a merely human gospel that he had received secondhand from the mouths of other human beings like himself,[9] nor was it the result of Paul's compromising of God's message on the basis of his own human impulses to accommodate people and win them over.

The following verse immediately develops this point in detail, offering further evidence for the claim made in 1:11.[10] Paul makes a claim for his message, his gospel, that closely parallels the claim he made in the opening verse for his commission:

Paul, an apostle not sent from human beings nor through a human being's agency, but through Jesus Christ's agency. (1:1)

I[11] did not receive it from a human being, nor was I taught it, but I received it through a revelation of Jesus Christ. (1:12)

Both the commission and the message have a divine, not a human, origin. The manner in which the truth of the gospel was communicated to Paul proves that his message is not a humanly devised one. He did not "receive" it in the manner of receiving human traditions passed on from teacher to disciple;[12] he was not "taught" it from such human masters.[13] Rather, in

---

7. So also Burton, 35.

8. The prepositional phrase κατὰ ἄνθρωπον reflects a construction that is prevalent in Paul, who uses it with a variety of nouns like "flesh" or "spirit" (κατὰ σάρκα, κατὰ πνεῦμα) to name a particular standard or set of values or impulses in line with which something finds itself.

9. Burton, 37.

10. Paul signals this function with the inferential conjunction γάρ.

11. The explicit nominative pronoun ἐγώ is emphatic. Perhaps we are to hear Paul making an implicit contrast between himself and the rival teachers, who cannot claim such a divine revelation and commissioning.

12. Paul uses the word παρέλαβον, which is a technical term (in tandem with παραδίδωμι) for the handing down and receiving of a tradition (as also in 1 Cor 11:2, 23; 15:1, 3; Phil 4:9; 1 Thess 2:13; 4:1; 2 Thess 3:6). See Schlier, 45; Tolmie, *Persuading*, 49.

13. The agency is omitted but is actually supremely relevant to Paul's point. We should

stark contrast,[14] Paul's message came "through a revelation of Jesus Christ." Paul has omitted the verb from the third member of this verse. We should understand "I received it" or "I was taught it" (the two being essentially synonymous), supplied from one of the first two members.

It is not clear how Paul's hearers would have understood the phrase "a revelation of Jesus Christ." They might have heard it to mean "through what Jesus Christ revealed [to me]" (construing "of Jesus Christ" as a subjective genitive)[15] or as "through an unveiling of who Jesus Christ was" (taking "of Jesus Christ" as an objective genitive).[16] The context of this verse could lend support to either option.[17] The topic of this and the preceding verse is the source or origin of Paul's gospel, which would support the first possibility. The parallel statement shortly to follow in 1:15–16, in which "it pleased God to reveal his Son," retrospectively suggests the latter option. It would be somewhat arbitrary to force a choice, all the more as Paul's main point is not jeopardized on either reading. If Paul is referring to his vision of Christ, naming Christ as the "content" revealed, it is still clear that Paul's commission and message come from a divine rather than a human source (i.e., "through a revelation").

13–14 As proof of the bold claim in 1:11–12,[18] Paul reminds the Galatians of the encounter with the glorified Christ that had turned his own life around (1:15–16), and of the "before" (1:13–14) and the "after" (1:21–23) of his activities that demonstrate, in effect, that something miraculous *must* have happened to bring about such a change. Paul's radical change of allegiance and behavior is the effect that demonstrates the cause, namely, God's direct intervention in his life, which became the source of the gospel he proclaimed.

In what Paul calls his "former life,"[19] he had been more on fire for the To-

---

hear an elided ὑπ' ἀνθρώπου (paralleling παρὰ ἀνθρώπου in the first member of this verse). Paul *was* taught the gospel by God; the point is that he was *not* taught the gospel by a human being mediating God's truth (which was more typically the manner of passing on the gospel; see Acts 18:25–26; 2 Tim 3:14).

14. Paul uses the stronger contrastive conjunction ἀλλά.

15. So Betz, 63; Longenecker, 23–24. This genitive here could also be thought of as a genitive of source ("a revelation that came from Jesus Christ"). This same phrase appears at the outset of Revelation ("A revelation of Jesus Christ," 1:1), where Jesus is clearly intended to be understood as the source of the revelation, as part of the "chain" of revelation that begins with God and passes through John to the rest of the believers addressed. John the Seer's usage is, of course, not determinative for Paul's.

16. So Betz, 63; Burton, 43; Bruce, 89; Fung, 53; Matera, 56; Keener, *Acts: Introduction and 1:1–2:47*, 241. We could also take this genitive as a "genitive of content," a "revelation about Jesus Christ."

17. Silva, *Interpreting Galatians*, 64–68.

18. Paul signals this evidential function by introducing this material with γάρ.

19. Technically, Paul uses an adverbial form here (ποτέ), which is more closely related

rah and the covenant relationship with God that the Torah sustained than his rivals could ever be: "For you heard concerning my conduct when formerly in Judaism, that I used to persecute God's Assembly beyond all bounds[20] and was working to destroy it,[21] and I was making greater progress in Judaism than many of my peers among my race, being more exceedingly an enthusiast for my ancestral traditions" (1:13–14). It is striking that Paul speaks of "Judaism" (*Ioudaismos*, 1:13, 14) here. This was a rare way of speaking about the Jewish way of life, unique here to the New Testament. The term appears to have been coined by Jews in opposition to Hellenism, the Greek way of life that threatened to supplant the native, ancestral customs in Judea during the hellenizing reforms of 175–165 BCE.[22] The first literary occurrence of the term is 2 Macc 8:1, where the word represents the Jewish way of life specifically as something set apart from and distinct from *Hellenismos*, the way of life of the Greeks (which was being foisted and even forced upon Jerusalem and Judea by its hellenizing Jewish elites).[23] Paul's use of the term here to describe the way of life he embraced and zealously defended may signal his awareness of the importance within that way of life of maintaining distinctiveness, maintaining the boundaries that marked Israel off as holy, as well as his awareness of the importance of such boundary issues for his fellow Jews, including the rival teachers. It also suggests Paul's consciousness that the way of life nurtured in Christ is indeed now something other than a variation of Judaism.[24]

Paul's zeal for the Jewish way of life manifested itself in two ways: negatively, as opposition to the early Christian movement (1:13);[25] positively, as wholehearted devotion to studying and bringing his own life into conformity with the Torah as taught by his Pharisaic mentors (1:14). Paul's passionate and even fanatical devotion to the covenant led him to assume the role of

---

to the prepositional phrase that follows than the noun that precedes. A participial form of εἰμί may be considered to be elided, hence "while I was formerly aligned with the Jewish way of life."

20. The expression καθ' ὑπερβολήν is more or less idiomatic for "excessively" (BDAG 1032; Burton, 45).

21. Many translations render ἐπόρθουν as a "conative" imperfect: "I . . . was trying to destroy it" (NRSV; see also NIV, NLT, CEB), which is too weak a rendering (Silva, *Interpreting Galatians*, 70–71). Paul was not merely *trying* to destroy the church; he was on his way to succeeding but was simply stopped in his tracks and thus prevented from completing the action. The verb was often used in military contexts to indicate the destruction or ravaging of cities or physical violence against people (as in 4 Macc 4:23; 11:4; Burton, 45).

22. Dunn, *Theology of Paul*, 347.

23. deSilva, *Introducing the Apocrypha*, 276–78; see also 2 Macc 2:21; 14:38; 4 Macc 4:26.

24. Burton, 44.

25. See also Phil 3:6, where Paul even more closely connects "zeal" with persecution of deviants.

defender of the covenant, striking out against the deviant Jews (i.e., the early Christian movement) taking root in the Jewish communities of Jerusalem and Damascus. The tense of the verbs translated "I was persecuting" and "I was engaged in tearing down" denotes habitual action: attacking the fledgling Christian movement[26] was Paul's regular practice for some period prior to God's intervention—when it became clear to him that this movement was indeed "of God" (1:13), whom he was thereby opposing.[27]

Paul had several important models before him, guiding him to express his zeal in this manner. In Moses's generation, Phinehas son of Aaron manifested zeal for God specifically by killing an Israelite male and his Midianite lover, defending the boundaries of God's people (Num 25:1–13). According to the Scriptures, Phinehas's zeal atoned for Israel's transgression and turned away God's wrath and won for him personally the reward of a "covenant of peace," "a covenant of eternal priesthood" (25:10–13).[28] Elijah's slaughter of the priests of Baal is remembered in the subsequent episode as a display of zeal (1 Kgs 18:40; 19:10).

In history more recent to Paul, Mattathias and his son Judas Maccabaeus, heroes of the Maccabean Revolt (initiated ca. 166 BCE), expressed their zeal in a similar way—and, indeed, Phinehas and Elijah are invoked as precedents for their zeal in the principal history of the revolt (1 Macc 2:26, 54, 58).[29] In his home town of Modein, Mattathias rushed forward to kill a Jew and a Syrian official as the former stepped forward to break faith with the covenant by offering a pagan sacrifice at the latter's invitation. Mattathias and his family then gathered together a guerilla force, inviting "everyone who is zealous for the law and supports the covenant" to join them (2:27). In the initial stages of the revolt, this zeal was directed especially against Jews who were deserting the covenant, enforcing obedience to the Torah or depriving the renegades of life (2:44–47). In this way they, too, "turned away wrath from Israel" (3:8).[30]

---

26. Paul uses the singular ἐκκλησία here to speak of the movement as a whole (against his custom, which is to speak of "congregations" as local bodies), by which he distinguishes the movement from non-Christian Judaism (Ἰουδαϊσμός), of which he was a representative and defender during this period of his life.

27. Mussner, 79.

28. On the legacy of Phinehas, see also Sir 45:23–24; Hengel, *Zealots*, 149–77.

29. During this period, Simeon and Levi—though cursed by Jacob for their anger in Gen 49!—become heroic exemplars of "zeal" for God because, in their abhorrence of the pollution of Israel in the person of their sister Dinah, they slaughtered the males of Shechem (Jdt 9:2–4). The author of Jub. 30.17–20 goes further, saying of their zeal-driven violence that "it was reckoned to them as righteousness and accounted to their credit" (v. 17), with Levi being given the office of the priesthood as a reward for his zeal (v. 18), not unlike Phinehas in the biblical narrative.

30. See further deSilva, *Introducing the Apocrypha*, 257–58, 265; Dunn, *Theology of Paul*, 351–52; Gaventa, *From Darkness to Light*, 26.

Paul thus acted in line with a well-established role as a watchdog for the ancestral ways and for the nation's well-being. Departures from the covenant on the part of Israelites, particularly where their Torah-prescribed distinctiveness that maintained their state of being "holy to the LORD" was at stake, were matters of national security, given the covenant blessings and, especially, the covenant *curses* that ever loomed over Israel (Deut 27:11–30:20). Paul clearly had come to see the Jesus movement as a threat to the nation's fidelity to the covenant, as a movement that might lead to the same sort of large-scale neglect of Torah observance that had provoked God's anger in the past and had led to God's punishing the nation through some foreign power. Rome's presence in Judea made it an ever-present candidate for such divine use.[31] Paul was thus seeking to protect Israel's place in God's favor by punishing those who threatened to violate that covenant bond and incur God's wrath against the whole people.

Nor was Paul alone in this commitment. Even as he writes Galatians, there are non-Christian Jews expressing their zeal for the Torah by putting various kinds of pressures upon Christian Jews. The rival teachers, Paul will claim, promote circumcision and Torah observance among the Christian movement precisely to appease more zealous Jews (Gal 5:11; 6:12–13), who no doubt saw themselves also as defenders of the covenant. Philo (*Special Laws* 2.253) speaks of social reinforcement of obedience to the Torah throughout the diaspora as a pervasive reality: "And these he will never escape; for there are thousands who have their eyes upon him full of zeal for the laws [or 'zealots for the law'], strictest guardians of the ancestral institutions, merciless to those who do anything to subvert them" (LCL). One might also note here the threat to Paul in Acts 21:20–21 from those who are similarly "zealots for the law" *among* the Christ-followers, who have heard reports about Paul inducing fellow Jews to "apostasize from Moses, telling them not to circumcise their children or walk in their customs" (21:21). Paul's purposes in persecuting those who confessed this Jesus to be the crucified but resurrected Messiah were disciplinary, imposing flogging or confinement (the very things to which Paul was later subjected by the Jewish community; see 2 Cor 11:23–24) as means of reclaiming deviants through physical discipline within the bounds of synagogue authority and practice.[32]

---

31. The author of the Psalms of Solomon understood the Roman Pompey's invasion of Jerusalem in 63 BCE, and the havoc he wrought there, as divine chastening for the transgressions and injustice of the later Hasmonean kings and the aristocracy.

32. See Hultgren, "Persecutions," 104, 108–10. Acts 9:1 may engage in hyperbole when describing Paul the persecutor as bent in the first instance on murder, though he is remembered at least as an accessory to murder in the case of Stephen (a mob action without due process; so Hultgren, "Persecutions," 111). On Paul the persecutor, see further Schnelle, *Apostle Paul*, 83–86.

Paul devoted himself to the Pharisaic school within Judaism, being fully dedicated to Torah as interpreted and extended through the "ancestral traditions," which eventually multiplied and became associated with rabbinic Judaism.[33] Paul probably indicates hereby the oral traditions that were accepted by the Pharisaic school as an authoritative complement to the written Torah, referred to in the Synoptic Gospels as "the tradition handed down by the elders" (Matt 15:2 // Mark 7:3–5).[34] He remembers himself as making steady progress in this educational and formational pursuit, distinguishing himself beyond many of his peers—those against whom it is natural to compare oneself and one's progress.[35] He attributes his greater achievement to his "being more abundantly an enthusiast," using the same noun in Greek that gives us the English "zealot."

Paul gives no evidence of having become disillusioned with the Torah-driven life—despite persistent attempts to read Rom 7:14–25 as Paul's confession of his personal inadequacy to keep the Torah.[36] Far from exhibiting any sense of failure to live up to the Torah's standards, Paul claims to have lived in perfect conformity with Torah's demands: "as regards righteousness under the law," Paul was "blameless" (Phil 3:6). This does not imply that Paul thought he never sinned. There was a detailed, Torah-prescribed system of sacrifices that would keep a rightly intentioned Jew "blameless" in regard to accidental sins and slips, at least. The Torah-driven life provided him with all the meaning he required, with a positive self-image, with significant esteem in the eyes of his peers and teachers, and with the assurance that he was walking in the ways of God. Not the deficiency of his religion but an unexpected encounter with the divine explains the radical change.

---

33. Paul appears to have disagreed with his teacher Gamaliel's policy of "live, let live, and leave it to God" (Acts 5:38–39). Paul himself perhaps stood more in line with the stricter school of Shammai within Pharisaism, even though Gamaliel, a disciple of the school of Hillel, was his teacher. See further Wright, *What Saint Paul Really Said*, 26–29.

34. See also Josephus, *Antiquities* 13.297 (LCL): "The Pharisees had passed on to the people certain regulations handed down by former generations and not recorded in the Laws of Moses, for which reason they are rejected by the Sadducean group, who hold that only those regulations should be considered valid which were written down (in Scripture), and that those which had been handed down by former generations need not be observed."

35. The imperfect προέκοπτον ("I was making progress") presents this pursuit as the action-in-progress that God will interrupt, changing the direction of Paul's life in 1:15–16. On the use of προκόπτω in contexts of training or moral formation, see G. Stählin, "προκοπή, προκόπτω," *TDNT* 6:704–7; Luke 2:52; Josephus, *The Life* 2.8.

36. On Rom 7:7–25 as nonautobiographical, see Das, *Solving the Romans Debate*, 204–35. Against psychological explanations for Paul's conversion, see Räisänen, *Paul and the Law*, 229–40; Bornkamm, "Revelation," 92; Dupont, "Conversion," 183; Hengel, *Pre-Christian Paul*, 79; Donaldson, "Zealot and Convert," 661.

Paul's portrait of his former life "in Judaism" allows two relevant inferences. First, no one, including the rival teachers, can pretend to know more about the Torah than Paul. If anyone is in a position to speak authoritatively about that way of life and about its relative value vis-à-vis the Spirit-driven life, it is he. Second, only God's personal intervention in Paul's life could explain his transformation from such a person into a preacher of a Torah-free gospel.[37] It is the second that Paul goes on explicitly to develop.

15–16 When Paul's zeal for Torah was at its most fevered pitch and his opposition to the Jewish Christian movement in its full strength, the inexplicable happened: "But when it pleased the one [or the God] who set me apart from the time I was in my mother's womb and who called me through his generous kindness to make his Son known in me, in order that I should proclaim the good news about him among the nations, it wasn't with flesh-and-blood humans that I went to confer immediately" (Gal 1:15–16). The first thing to notice about these verses is that those subjects that are probably most interesting to us—God's revelation of Christ, Paul's commission to proclaim Christ to the non-Jewish nations—are not Paul's focal concern. Paul's chief point is that, after this life-changing experience, he did not present himself to the Jerusalem apostles as a pupil or ministry candidate, nor did he thus present himself to any other "flesh-and-blood" body of Christians, who could then claim ownership of and authority over him. What he understood to be the significance of the Christ event and the nature of the message he was to proclaim (and that specifically to the gentile nations) took shape independently of the Jerusalem-based Jesus movement.

Is it more accurate to think about the effects of God's dramatic intervention in Paul's life as a conversion or as a prophetic call?[38] One might argue that this experience was not a *conversion*, since Paul was still responding to the same God (the God of Judaism and the God of the church). Paul did not leave behind the faith of Abraham in order to embrace the faith of Christ; he saw himself, rather, as embracing the fulfillment of what God had promised and been driving toward all along. Against this position, however, Paul's own narrative of his life clearly differentiates a "before" ("formerly"), described as living "in Judaism" (Gal 1:13–14), from a radically new "after," to which that description no longer applies.[39] Paul's response to the Christian movement prior to his encounter with Christ demonstrates that Paul regarded it

---

37. The argumentative force of the "before" and "after" was well captured by John Chrysostom (10): "This is a proof that my conversion is sincere, and that the zeal which possesses me is from above. What other inducement could I have to make such a change, and to barter honor for contempt, repose for peril, security for distress? None surely but the love of truth."

38. Stendahl, *Paul among Jews and Gentiles*, 7–23; Hagner, "Paul and Judaism," 93.

39. Beyond Gal 1:13–17, see also Phil 3:5–8. Paul's *rejection* of his past ("sewage," Phil 3:8) is characteristic of converts.

to be "other" than the religion of his ancestors; the postencounter treatment that Paul received from his former associates, who now persecute *him*, bears witness to the same.[40] Most telling in this regard is Paul's changed attitude toward that which centrally defined his preencounter life, namely, the Torah. Paul underwent a paradigm shift of such magnitude as cannot be otherwise described than "conversion."[41] He immediately left off those pursuits that were incompatible with the revelation of Jesus as the Messiah (notably, the persecution of his followers), came to a new understanding of who Jesus was in God's plan for God's people, and radically shifted his allegiance from Torah to Jesus as Messiah and to the Spirit-driven life.

It would be a mistake, however, to think of this conversion in terms of Paul's "personal decision for Christ." It was more an encounter with divine destiny and an acceptance of that destiny. In other words, God had made a "personal decision for Paul," revealed to him the errors in his understanding and direction (hence, converted him), and personally revealed what Paul's task was now to be (hence, commissioned him).[42] The last element suggests that, at the same time and with no contradiction, Paul *also* understood this revelation as a commission to proclaim the good news about Jesus to the gentiles, and from that standpoint, it was a prophetic call.

The language Paul uses in these verses underscores his own sense of continuity with the classical prophets of Israel and his selection of their experience as a framework for understanding his own:

Before I formed you in the womb, I knew you,
and before you were born I consecrated you;
I appointed you a prophet to the nations. (Jer 1:5 NRSV)

---

40. Das, 150.

41. Donaldson, "Zealot and Convert," 681–82; Segal, *Paul the Convert*, 214. The rival teachers might indeed not have converted, regarding "faith in Jesus as the continuation and completion of their system of religious practice. Paul is unique in that he was not only Jewish but a *convert* to Christianity" (Segal, *Paul the Convert*, 214). Admitting that this event effected a "conversion" has significant ideological consequences that are difficult in a post-Holocaust world. If Paul did not *convert*, it becomes easier to affirm that he continued to uphold the validity of the first covenant as the path for Jews to relate to God and connect with God's favor. Paul, however, explicitly affirms the necessity of trusting in Jesus beyond doing "the works of the law," whether the former is added to or fully replaces the latter for Jews like himself (Gal 2:15–16). Paul's rejection of the value of circumcision and the works of the law *for anyone* (Gal 5:6; 6:15) argues against claiming Paul as an ally for parallel paths to justification before God (Segal, *Paul the Convert*, 217).

42. Paul's call was, as he himself recalls it, an imposition against his will; thus it "hardly resembles what we normally call a 'conversion'" (Dupont, "Conversion," 192). But, then, how many people who have experienced a conversion would say that they did *not* feel a compelling supernatural push in that direction, that it was *merely* a voluntary act?

The LORD called me before I was born;
    while I was in my mother's womb[43] he named me. . . .
And now the LORD says,
    who formed me in the womb to be his servant, . . .
"I will give you as a light to the nations." (Isa 49:1, 5–6 NRSV)

In a similar vein, Paul speaks of God "setting him apart"—that is, select-ing him for a special purpose—even before Paul had been born, like Isaiah and Jeremiah. Aside from the subtle support Paul gives to his own claim to be called by God through his use of language from biblical call narratives, Paul also shows here how integral the mission to the gentile nations is to his own sense of God's call. Like Isaiah, Paul is commissioned to bring God's light (i.e., the knowledge of God) to the nations. Like Jeremiah, he is appointed to take God's message to them (though Jeremiah's actual message was notably different, being one of judgment *upon* the nations).

Paul remembers this event as an act of divine grace or favor ("who called me by his grace"). Indeed, Paul becomes a living paradigm of God's gracious action.[44] He had been living as an enemy of God's Messiah, hostile toward that Messiah's followers on account of his own devotion to Torah and the preser-vation of Israel's exclusive covenant, but God turned him into an emissary of that Messiah to proclaim God's acceptance of *all* people on the basis of trust in God's provision in the Messiah. Paul's own experience belied the idea that a person would need to assume a Jewish identity and way of life in order to be accepted by God: he had been the Jew par excellence but found himself opposing God outright when he was himself most committed to doing—and enforcing—the Torah.

Paul writes that God was pleased, in God's timing, "to reveal his Son in me." The precise sense of the prepositional phrase often translated "in me" (as in NIV) or "to me" (as in NRSV, CEB) remains unclear. If Paul had sought to present himself merely as the recipient (the indirect object) of this revelation, a simpler and clearer form of expression was available.[45] The prepositional phrase could suggest a more personal encounter, stressing the internal impact that God's revelation made in Paul's very being (without excluding an exter-nal component along the lines of the account in Acts 9).[46] It is possible that

---

43. Paul recontextualizes verbatim the phrase ἐκ κοιλίας μητρός μου from LXX Isa 49:1.

44. Lyons, *Pauline Autobiography*, 171; Fee, 46.

45. Specifically, the dative pronoun ἐμοί (or μοι).

46. Burton, 50–51; Bruce, 93; Martyn, 158; Matera, 60; Moo, 104. John Chrysostom (11) seems to understand the phrase in this manner: "But why does he say, 'to reveal His Son in me,' and not 'to me'? It is to signify, that he had not only been instructed in the faith by words, but that he was richly endowed with the Spirit;—that the revelation had enlightened his whole soul, and that he had Christ speaking within him."

Paul has already moved beyond thinking about the impact of the experience on himself (God's showing God's Son *to* Paul, to correct Paul's perceptions of who Jesus is) to the impact of God's work in him upon others (God's revelation of the power and reality of God's Son to all who saw the change "in Paul" and heard Paul's preaching).[47] The purpose clause that follows ("that I should proclaim the good news about him among the nations") would then offer a more human angle on how God's revelatory activity worked itself out, namely, in Paul's mission.[48] While this is a point of genuine ambiguity, it makes better sense to understand Paul to speak here of God's action *upon him*, accounting for the change in allegiance and practice, all the more as this narrative is meant to offer evidence that Paul received his understanding of the gospel from God himself (1:12b).

Paul describes the sphere of his commission as "among the nations," but how Paul understood this sphere's coverage is uncertain (see commentary on 2:7–9). On the one hand, he clearly had a particular burden for non-Jewish peoples, extending God's invitation to them to join the "Israel of God" formed as individuals from any ethnic background join themselves to Christ, *the* Seed of Abraham (see below on 3:15–18). On the other hand, he recalls proclaiming the same gospel and extending the same invitation to his fellow Jews (1 Cor 9:20). If the testimony of Acts is to be accepted, it was in fact standard practice for Paul to begin a new mission by frequenting the synagogue in that city.[49] He appears to have understood himself to be called to take the gospel to the non-Jewish lands outside of Israel and to be primarily responsible to extend the invitation to non-Jews, though he would never exclude Jews from his audience or congregation and may even have pursued a deliberate strategy of gathering a core following from among the Jewish and gentile God-fearing adherents of each locality's synagogue.

We come, then, to Paul's first point of emphasis in this narrative, which is reflected in the fact that this is the first independent clause since 1:15 began: "I did not immediately confer with flesh and blood."[50] The adverb "immediately" reflects the fact that Paul would *eventually* "confer with flesh and blood" in limited and carefully selected ways (1:18–20; 2:1–2); the fact that such consultation with the Jerusalem pillars in particular did not occur "immediately" after his divine commission but only in the third year thereafter (1:18) becomes proof of the divine source of his commission and message

---

47. See Gaventa, "Galatians 1 and 2." Das (132) leans in this direction: Christ is revealed "in Paul" by virtue of coming to life "in Paul" (see Gal 2:20), which means that the revelation of Christ is now available to others who encounter Paul. See also Betz, 71, who connects Gal 1:16; 2:20; 2 Cor 4:6 as complementary statements.

48. Wright, *Resurrection*, 380.

49. See Acts 13:14; 14:1; 17:1, 10, 17; 18:4, 19; 19:8.

50. Rightly, Tolmie, *Persuading*, 60.

(thus lending support to the claim Paul made in 1:12a).[51] Referring to human beings as flesh and blood foregrounds the frailty and mortality of such (potential) conversation partners, in stark contrast to the divine conversation partner from whom Paul received his gospel and commission.[52] When Paul goes on to recount his visits with the Jerusalem pillars, his audience will no doubt remember where they fall along this spectrum between God and "flesh and blood."

EXCURSUS: PAUL'S ENCOUNTER WITH THE RESURRECTED JESUS AND PAUL'S PARADIGM SHIFT

Paul claims not only that his commission but also the message of his gospel itself came "through a revelation of Jesus Christ" (1:12), by which he appears to mean the particular revelation of the Son of God that turned him from persecutor to promoter (1:15–16). Allowing that Paul would, of course, learn much about the life and teaching of Jesus and continue to think through his own proclamation and its implications over the course of the decades to follow, we would do well to explore what Paul brought to this encounter and thus how it changed Paul's mind about his most fundamental convictions.[53] Paul knew enough about "the Way" to know that it presented a threat to what he held most dear, namely, Torah and Israel's covenant with God, such that he devoted himself to silencing its preachers and pressuring their followers to renounce their deviant way of life.[54] Paul's distinctive understanding of the gospel and of his own role can, to a surprising extent, be traced to the effects

---

51. Paul uses the verb προσανεθέμην here in the normal sense of "consult" (BDAG 876), not in the technical sense in which it is used in Diodorus Siculus, *Library of History* 17.116.4 (where the term refers to the interpretation of oracles; Dunn, *Jesus, Paul, and the Law*, 109–11). He will use it in an entirely other sense ("to add to") in 2:6.

52. Burton, 54. Paul's stark and uncompromising claims here raise some difficulties vis-à-vis the account of Paul's conversion and postconversion experience in Acts 9:10–20, which speaks of the intervention and, to some extent, instruction of the flesh-and-blood Ananias.

53. See the thoroughgoing attempt to demonstrate the origins of the particulars of Paul's gospel in this encounter in Kim, *Origins of Paul's Gospel*; Kim, *Paul and the New Perspective*. Paul will admit to learning and passing on traditions that he himself had received (e.g., 1 Cor 11:2, 23–26; 15:3–8), which would also include the echoes of dominical sayings found throughout his letters (see Schnelle, *Apostle Paul*, 103–8). This admission does not in itself vitiate Paul's claim in Gal 1:12, however, as he could readily have received such traditions as confirmatory and supplementary to the essential understanding of the Christ event and its significance that came to him "through a revelation of Jesus Christ."

54. Schnelle, *Apostle Paul*, 103. On Paul's encounter with the glorified Christ and its significance, see further Schnelle, *Apostle Paul*, 87–102; Wright, *Resurrection*, 375–98.

of an ecstatic experience of Jesus as risen and exalted upon the knowledge, both in terms of the Jesus movement and in terms of Jewish eschatological expectation, that Paul brought to this experience.

Paul's opposition to the Jesus movement would have begun with his opposition to its leader. Jesus had been recently crucified by the Romans at the instigation of the Sanhedrin, which had condemned Jesus as a blasphemer and a deceiver. To the extent that the Gospels preserve authentic memories of Jesus's teaching, activities, and altercations, the more Paul had heard about this Jesus from his peers and teachers, the less he would have approved of him and the more he would have approved of his leaders' judgment.

Jesus draws criticism for taking a stance regarding work on the Sabbath more liberal than other Jewish groups can affirm. He heals freely on the Sabbath (Mark 1:29–31; 3:1–6) and allows his disciples to gather grain on the Sabbath to satisfy their hunger, making a provocative assertion about his authority being greater than that of the Sabbath (2:23–28). This activity sufficiently alienates the Pharisees to dispose them to seek to eliminate him, no doubt for the good of the nation's covenant relationship with its God. The fact that Jesus deliberately gathers disciples and establishes himself as a teacher raises the stakes concerning his own level of commitment to the Torah, and does so proportionately as his following grows. It is one thing to show modest disregard toward certain pillars of Jewish practice like the Sabbath; it is quite another thing to do so in the role of a teacher, multiplying that disregard exponentially among the people.

Jesus provocatively claims to have authority to forgive people their sins (Mark 2:1–12). He has table fellowship with Jews who exhibit little or no concern with purity regulations, thus jeopardizing his own purity and contributing to the increase of pollution in the land such as might eventually reach the point of no return as far as the holy God in the midst of this land is concerned (2:15–17).[55]

He directly opposes "the traditions of the elders," which the Pharisees revere as an essential part of covenant observance (Mark 7:1–13), of which Paul was an ardent disciple (Gal 1:13–14), and was remembered even to call into question the very idea of pollution being attached to what one ingests (Mark 7:14–23). Whether or not Jesus "thus declared all foods clean" (v. 19), it would have been a radical challenge to the purity maps and boundary lines within and around Judaism.[56] He presumed to correct Moses on the matter

---

55. On the plausible affront presented by Jesus's table fellowship practices to Pharisees' sensibilities, given their understanding of the just requirements of the law regarding purity in the land, see Dunn, *Jesus, Paul, and the Law*, 61–88.

56. On this episode, the differences between the Markan and Matthean versions, and the relationship of both to Paul—namely, the united focus on boundary-making and

of whether or not divorce was permissible (10:1–12), laying down rules that, though stricter than those of the law of Moses, nevertheless were given explicitly to override the law of Moses. Indeed, Jesus's frequent conflicts with the Pharisees over matters of halakah—over how to walk in the way of the law—showed him to be at odds with Torah itself, from the point of view of Paul the Pharisee.

Jesus enters Jerusalem at the peak of his popularity (and apparently just before a major pilgrim festival), acting out a messianic paradigm as if fulfilling prophecy, and is greeted as a messianic figure who will effect deliverance for Israel (Mark 11:1–10; see Zech 9:9). Afterward, he performs a grossly disruptive act in the temple's outer court, the "court open to people of all nations" (4 Macc 4:11), which could be understood as an indictment of the temple and pronouncement of judgment against it and its leadership (Mark 11:15–18). His action also plainly interfered with the procedures that facilitated the offering of sacrifices and the paying of the temple tax, impeding the pious (v. 15).[57] If there had been any doubt about his feelings toward the temple, he teaches his closest followers that the temple will shortly be thrown to the ground (13:1–2).

In sum, Jesus had violated Torah (as Paul and the Pharisaic party would have understood it), stood condemned under Torah, and had been justly executed under the curse it pronounced upon "anyone who does not uphold the words of this law by observing them" (Deut 27:26). Paul might well have mused about the propriety of the particular death Jesus suffered: the one who lived so as to merit Torah's curse and, convicted of a capital crime, died in a manner that singled him out as accursed, "hung on a tree" (21:22–23).[58]

For his followers to proclaim Jesus now as the "Righteous One" (e.g., Acts 3:14; 7:52; cf. Isa 53:11) was an egregious affront to Torah's definition of righteousness and a challenge to the Torah itself and its authorized protectors. Paul saw in the Jesus movement a tendency toward the relaxation of Torah's commands in the name of this crucified one, whom they hailed as the "Prophet like Moses" (Acts 3:22–23; 7:37), who would essentially succeed Moses as the spokesperson of God's covenant requirements, with the

---

boundary-maintaining issues and Jesus's transvaluation of the same—see Dunn, *Jesus, Paul, and the Law*, 37–60; on dietary restrictions, purity maps, and their importance within Judaism, see deSilva, *Honor*, 253–77, and the literature therein cited.

57. Jesus's pronouncement—or threat—against the temple figures prominently in the Gospels and, particularly, in Jesus's trial (Matt 26:61; 27:40; Mark 14:58; 15:29; John 2:19–20).

58. It was not the mere fact of being crucified that would have caused Jesus to fall under this curse in Paul's eyes, as pious Jews (including eight hundred Pharisees under Alexander Jannaeus; see Josephus, *Antiquities* 13.379–83; *War* 1.96–98) had also been thus executed unjustly, but the fact of Jesus's being crucified legitimately. See Donaldson, "Zealot and Convert," 677.

probable result that God would again punish Israel for tolerating such flagrant violations of the covenant in its midst. For his followers to proclaim that the death of this Jesus occurred "for our sins" (1 Cor 15:3) or "for many" (Mark 10:45; 14:24), that is, as an act of atonement, would also have been an intolerable interpretation of a proper execution, not to mention an unacceptable shift in the locus of forgiveness from the temple to the cross of a condemned sinner.[59] The claim that God raised this Jesus from the dead and set him at God's own right hand was a declaration of Jesus's status as the messianic heir to the throne of David—this Jesus, who "in life" showed such disregard for the standards of righteousness laid out in the Torah (and, admittedly, in the traditional accretions to the Torah that were nevertheless embraced *as* Torah by Paul the Pharisee).

Paul could hardly have missed the Christ-followers' claim that covenant-keeping was no longer sufficient prerequisite to experiencing God's deliverance and covenant blessings; rather, alignment with Jesus was now an indispensable requirement.[60] Paul will recall this point as shared knowledge among Jewish Christians in Gal 2:15–16. Such a claim, however, would have been impossible to reconcile with Paul's understanding of the place of the Torah in God's plan for the deliverance of God's people and, indeed, all the nations.[61]

When Paul was confronted, then, with the *resurrected* Jesus, his former interpretation of the world and God's action in that world, which had seemed so secure and certain, was violently and irreparably shaken. This experience was indeed for Paul a "revelation," the making known of the divine perspective on that which was unknown from a human perspective, transforming his prior knowledge and, especially, his prior judgments about Jesus, his followers, and his followers' claims.[62] For Jesus to be alive—and glorified, no less—meant that God himself had vindicated Jesus against the claims of Jesus's enemies (including the authorities whom Paul revered and followed). God had approved Jesus and shown that Jesus was righteous in God's eyes. It is, as it were, that God said afresh to Paul personally: "*This* is my beloved Son. Listen to him!"

---

59. Dupont, "Conversion," 186, 191.

60. Donaldson, "Zealot and Convert," 678–79. It is frequently asserted that Paul took issue primarily with the Hellenist Jewish Christians in Jerusalem on account of their more liberal approach to the Torah. Neither Paul nor the author of Acts, however, makes—or even supports—such a distinction. In Acts, for example, Stephen may be the first victim, but the persecution that erupts upon his lynching is directed toward "the church," and not a particular wing thereof. See Hultgren, "Persecutions," 100.

61. Dupont, "Conversion," 185.

62. Wright (*Resurrection*, 379) eloquently defines the ἀποκάλυψις as "the sudden uncovering of something previously concealed, in particular of something hidden in God's sphere of reality ('heaven'), something which would not normally be visible in the human sphere ('earth'), but which could become so under special circumstances."

Long before Paul's birth, Jews had connected resurrection with God's vindication of the righteous person who had been unjustly killed. Premature death and the loss of covenant blessings could not be the last word on the life of a person who had shown God due obedience. Such an end suited the *ungodly*, not those who loved and honored the covenant. Thus the hope, indeed the expectation, of resurrection rose to prominence as a consequence of the conviction that God was just—so just that, if justice was not done for the righteous in this life, it would be done beyond death.[63] Such resurrection belonged to the end of this age, when God would sort out all things and make all things right at last (see, e.g., Dan 12:1–3).

If Jesus was condemned to death under Torah as a transgressor and blasphemer, but if Jesus was actually so righteous in God's sight that God had *already* raised him from the dead (for Jesus would be the first to enter into the *resurrected* life), then the Torah itself was no longer a reliable guide to what God counted as righteous, nor could it be embraced as something that would reliably make its devotees righteous before God. The problem for Paul was not that Torah *could* not be obeyed, but that Torah was not the final and ultimate revelation of God's righteousness. Jesus was that revelation. A critical effect of his encounter with the risen Lord, then, is that the center of authority and revelation shifts from the Torah to Jesus.[64]

If Jesus was righteous in God's sight, then his followers must be correct in their acclamation of him as Messiah and in their commitment to take their bearings from his teachings above (or as the interpretive key to) Torah. The resurrection and enthronement of Jesus points to him as the heir to David's throne, the one to whom several psalms spoke prophetically: "Sit at my right hand until I make your enemies a footstool for your feet" (Ps 110:1) and "You are my Son; today have I begotten you" (Ps 2:7; cf. 2 Sam 7:14). Here we come to that important role in which Paul finds Jesus specifically in this revelation—he is revealed as "God's Son" (Gal 1:16; see also Rom 1:3–4). As such, Jesus was indeed Israel's Messiah, the one whose rule not only over Israel but over the nations was long anticipated and now inaugurated.[65] The "good news" (*euangelion*) was thus indeed an announcement of accession to rule,

---

63. See especially 2 Macc 6–7, a text known, if not written, in Palestine in the late second-century/early first-century BCE, and Wisdom of Solomon 3:1–9, a diaspora Jewish text written in Greek from the turn of the era. These texts are further discussed in deSilva, *Introducing the Apocrypha*, 142–44, 277.

64. See Beker, *Paul the Apostle*, 182–89. God's resurrection of this crucified Christ signaled that Torah's jurisdiction had come to an end and that God's saving acts were now moving into a new stage.

65. Wright (*Resurrection*, 719–36) provides a masterful discussion of the import of the title "Son of God" within first-century Judaism within the Roman Empire. See also Dunn, "Son of God"; Hengel, *Son of God*; Hurtado, *Lord Jesus Christ*, 102–8.

very much akin to the *euangelia* that announced the accession of Augustus or Vespasian. It was a summons to all the world's inhabitants to acknowledge and give obedience to the new ruler in whose reign God was taking the reins of the kingdoms of the world at last. Encountering Jesus as *resurrected*, furthermore, confirmed for Paul in another way that the last period of this age had begun: the resurrection of the righteous *one* was a harbinger and firstfruits of the general resurrection of the dead expected at the end of this age.

It is at this point that the connection between Paul's encounter with the *resurrected* Messiah Jesus and his commitment to proclaim Jesus as such to the gentiles is forged. Part of the Jewish hope for the messianic age was that the gentiles would come to worship the one God of Israel, bringing their glory to Jerusalem. In Rom 15:9–12 Paul himself cites some of the oracles of God that fed this hope:

> As it is written,
>   "Therefore I will confess you among the gentiles,
>   and sing praises to your name" [Ps 18:49 (LXX 17:50)];
> and again he says,
>   "Rejoice, O gentiles, with his people" [Deut 32:43];
> and again,
>   "Praise the Lord, all you gentiles,
>   and let all the peoples praise him" [Ps 117:1];
> and again Isaiah says,
>   "The root of Jesse shall come,
>   the one who rises to rule the gentiles;
>   in him the gentiles shall hope" [Isa 11:10].

Paul's own nurture in the Old Testament Scriptures would naturally lead him to connect the Messiah's coming with the arrival of the time for the ingathering of the gentiles, who must also bow to the Messiah's rule.[66] What was special to his own calling was that he should take part in this mission to the gentiles as the Messiah's ambassador. The author of Luke-Acts effectively captures the connection of Old Testament hope and the Pauline mission by using Isa 49:6 to illumine the significance of Jesus and the mission of Paul: "I have set you to be a light to the gentiles, to bring salvation to the uttermost

---

66. See Wright, *What Saint Paul Really Said*, 36–37. It is not necessary to reject Paul's own testimony and postulate that Paul and other Antiochene Christians turned to the gentiles out of frustration with Jewish nonacceptance of their message, eliminating the requirement of circumcision to make it easier to have success among the gentiles, and only later developing the theological justifications for this move (Watson, *Paul, Judaism, and the Gentiles,* 34–36). The narratives of Acts could admittedly suggest such an alternative (see Acts 13:46; 28:17–29).

parts of the earth" (Luke 2:32; Acts 13:47; see also Acts 26:18), a text to which Paul himself may already have alluded in Gal 1:15.

The summons to the nations would not be a summons to fall in line with the stipulations of the Torah.[67] First, the final authority of the Torah had come to an end with the resurrection of the One whom Torah had pronounced cursed. Second, Paul, a fully Torah-observant person, found himself in the moment of that encounter as starkly opposed to God as any "gentile sinner," and thus as one who stood in equal need of God's gracious intervention. That which did not bring Paul into line with God's righteousness would not bring the gentiles in line with God's righteousness either.[68] The Torah now takes on a decisively different character. God was calling all nations to acknowledge and heed his rule in the Messiah, to become part of the one, re-created humanity redeemed from their common alienation from God.[69] The Torah, however, essentially functioned to keep Jew and gentile separate, maintaining the "dividing wall of hostility" between them (Eph 2:14–15).

The ingathering of the gentiles was ultimately grounded, for Paul, in the Shema itself, the foundational creed of Israel: "Hear, O Israel: the LORD our God, the LORD is one" (Deut 6:4). The dividing wall of Torah, erected between Jew and gentile, seemed now to belie this essential truth. As Paul would later remark in Romans, "Is God the God of the Jews only? Is God not also God

---

67. There is no solid evidence for a "'Christ-plus-Torah' phase" in Paul's earlier missionary years (Donaldson, "Zealot and Convert," 664). Paul presents his conversion and his decisive break with "Torah-religion" as occurring together in Gal 1:13–16 and Phil 3:5–11 (so Wilckens, *Rechtfertigung als Freiheit*, 13–15). Paul's argument that he received his gospel at his conversion "would have been in serious jeopardy if it was common knowledge that for the first decade of his ministry he had proclaimed the 'other gospel' that he was now opposing with such vehemence" (Donaldson, "Zealot and Convert," 664).

68. As Donaldson ("Zealot and Convert," 656) astutely observed, "The incompatibility of Christ and Torah was the constant element in a syllogism that on one side of the conversion experience led to persecution of the church, and on the other resulted in fierce resistance to the Judaizers," which presupposes Paul's own nonimposition of the Torah upon gentiles turning to God in the Messiah. So also Räisänen, *Jesus, Paul, and Torah*, 47: "The basic Christ *or* Torah antithesis does seem to have been in place from the start—indeed, from Paul's pre-conversion activity."

69. Wright (*Pauline Perspectives*, 201) correctly opposes the view of Sanders (*Paul and Palestinian Judaism*, 443) that Paul reasoned from solution (Jesus as the resurrected Messiah) to plight. The plight was clear enough to Paul from well before his conversion: "the gentile nations' enslavement to idolatry and sin; Israel's enslavement to the gentile empire and her inability to reverse the curse that fell upon the disobedient nation (see Deuteronomy 27–30). The resurrected Messiah Jesus presented Paul with a new, previously unthought-of solution to this well-established problem. It would not be through Torah observance that God would renew the covenant promises, reverse Israel's fortunes, and bring the gentiles to his light. It would be through the way opened up by Christ for all who trust him and his provision."

of the gentiles? Yes, of the gentiles also, since 'God is one'" (Rom 3:29–30). The oneness of God was to be reflected in the oneness of God's people (Gal 3:19–28), as well as in the fact of all people worshiping the one God.[70] Through his encounter with the risen Lord, Paul became convinced that he was the one to bring the promises of God to the gentiles—the promises given long ago to the gentile Abraham—by announcing this new act of God's favor, the arrival of the Messiah and the possibility of deliverance and participation in the Messiah's kingdom through trust in this Mediator of God's favor.[71] In Christ's death and resurrection and in the outpouring of God's Holy Spirit, God has intervened on behalf of both Jew and gentile—and so both Jew and gentile find themselves reconciled to God and brought back in line with God's standards of righteousness in precisely the same way. In such a situation, it no longer made sense to Paul to try to make Jews out of gentiles—all that was important now was to be newly created in the Messiah by the power of God's Spirit.

The essential contours of Paul's gospel and theology can be traced back, therefore, to his encounter with the risen Jesus. While it would remain for him to wrestle with the implications of this revelation for the remainder of his life in the variety of the situations he encounters, his claim that his gospel came through "a revelation of Jesus Christ" (Gal 1:11–12) rather than through human agency or consulting "flesh and blood" (1:16) remains quite credible.[72]

---

17 Paul further affirms: "nor did I go up to Jerusalem to those who were apostles before me, but I went away into Arabia and returned again to Damascus." His purpose here is not to arouse his readers' curiosity about what

---

70. Another important stream of tradition that would feed this expectation concerns the universal dominion of the Messiah, reflected in Pss 2:7–8; 72:8; 89:27 (Wright, *What Saint Paul Really Said*, 55). From this angle, again, Paul would be led to expect one Lord for Jews and gentiles.

71. Again to cite the apposite words of Donaldson ("Zealot and Convert," 668), "Christ has replaced Torah as the center and circumference of the people of God."

72. This same point is also, and perhaps particularly, true in regard to Paul's view of the Torah as expressed in Galatians, as is stressed by Hengel ("Attitude of Paul," 51). Murphy-O'Connor (*Keys to Galatians*, 144–74) argues for a significant development in Pauline thought between Thessalonians and Galatians but does so based entirely on the absence of particular motifs in 1 and 2 Thessalonians, hence offering an argument from silence. Much of what Murphy-O'Connor attributes to the period between the letters could well be placed much earlier, in the immediate aftermath of being confronted by the crucified Messiah, now found out to be indeed the one at God's right hand. The essay is nevertheless full of brilliant insight into the collision of Paul's pre-Christian convictions as a Pharisee, Paul's preconversion knowledge and assessment of Jesus, and Paul's spiritual experience necessitating the paradigm shift that stands at the heart of his mission and message.

he *did* do in Arabia and Damascus,[73] about which he says nothing explicit, but to establish what he did *not* do by remaining in those regions after his conversion. Paul did not present himself to the authorities in the Jerusalem church for their "orders," nor did he present himself to them as their student and disciple. Paul's goal is thus simply to stress his independence from the Jerusalem apostles in regard both to his commission and to his understanding of God's revelation in Jesus Christ. While Paul doubtless would continue to work out the implications of that communication for decades, he insists that the whole gospel was given to him there in seed form.

Paul uses a typical verb for travel toward Jerusalem: to move toward Jerusalem from any compass direction is to "go up," reflecting the slight geographic, but significant ideological, elevation of the city on Mount Zion.[74] Calling the leaders of the Christian movement in Jerusalem "those who were apostles before me" very subtly reinforces Paul's own status as an apostle (see 1:1) alongside them.[75] Rather than consult with them and place himself under their aegis, Paul took off in another direction—Arabia.

What was Paul's purpose in going into Arabia? He himself gives no explicit information regarding either his destination(s) within Arabia or his activities there. Neither does he report on his activities in Damascus following his return from Arabia, nor yet his activities in Syria and Cilicia (1:21). What he does say is that, following all this activity, the churches in Judea were hearing reports that their former persecutor was now proclaiming the faith he once sought to stamp out (1:23). This report would imply at the very least that Paul was actively preaching the good news about Jesus Christ in Syria and Cilicia; it might also suggest that Paul immediately went about his task of proclaiming Jesus to the gentiles in the cities of Arabia and in Damascus following his return.

A great deal of Arabia is essentially barren, unpopulated desert. It is, however, not without major urban centers as well. The Nabatean kingdom, the seat of which was Petra but which included other cities as well (Bozra, Madaba, and, from time to time, certain cities of the Decapolis), sat within this region. A number of factors, not least of which being the hostile interest taken in Paul by the Nabatean king Aretas IV and his representative in Damascus (2 Cor 11:32–33; see Acts 9:22–25), favor locating Paul in the Nabatean kingdom during this early period and favor understanding him to

---

73. That Paul "returned again" (πάλιν ὑπέστρεψα) strongly suggests that Paul had been in Damascus at some prior point as well, perhaps at the time of God's revelation of God's Son to him (1:15–16), thus confirming this facet of the account of Paul's conversion in Acts 9:1–9.

74. Here, a form of ἀνέρχομαι (as in Gal 1:18); forms of ἀναβαίνω are far more common (Matt 20:17–18 // Mark 10:32–33 // Luke 18:31; Luke 2:42; 18:10; 19:28; John 2:13; 5:1; 7:8, 10; 11:55; 12:20; Acts 11:2; 15:2; 18:22; 21:12, 15; 25:1, 9; Gal 2:1, 2).

75. Tolmie, *Persuading*, 62–63.

have begun his objectionable evangelistic activity in the cities there.[76] Paul's commission to preach among the gentiles (Gal 1:16) lends contextual support to such a view as well: in obedience to the divine voice, he set about the task at once.

If the narrative that follows in 1:18–21 is meant to show, among other things, that Paul did not and could not have received the gospel from Peter,[77] the proof would be far stronger if Paul had already been preaching that gospel in Arabia and/or Damascus (1:17; again, see Acts 9:22–25) prior to their meeting (1:18). Indeed, it would almost be necessary.[78] It remains possible, however, that Paul journeyed into Arabia for a time of solitude, prayer, and reflection, perhaps in the wastelands of Arabia. Contextual support for such a supposition is to be found in Paul's claim to have "conferred not with flesh and blood"; by implied contrast, he consulted with God in the desert.[79] Certainty is not possible on the basis of the evidence.

B. PAUL'S FIRST VISIT TO JERUSALEM
AND WORK IN SYRIA AND CILICIA (1:18–24)

18 *Then after three years I went up to Jerusalem to visit with Cephas,*[a] *and I stayed with him for fifteen days.* 19 *But I didn't see any of the other apostles except for James, the Lord's brother.* 20 *Now in regard to the things I am writing to you, look! Before God I swear that I am not lying.* 21 *Then I went into the regions of Syria and Cilicia,* 22 *but I remained unknown by face among the Judean congre-*

---

76. So John Chrysostom, 12; Schlier, 58; Betz, 74; Bruce, 96; Fung, 69; Lührmann, 22; Hengel and Schwemer, *Paul between Damascus and Jerusalem,* 106–20; Witherington, 102; Matera, 61, 64; Murphy-O'Connor, "Paul in Arabia"; Das, 135–37, 153–55. John Chrysostom (12) attributes Paul's silence about his activity in Arabia to his "humility; he speaks not of his successes, nor of whom or of how many he instructed." Another possibility, of course, would be embarrassment at failure (Tolmie, *Persuading,* 62).

77. Dunn, 149.

78. Tolmie (*Persuading,* 62) also recognizes this angle but argues the opposite position: since Paul's earlier preaching would cinch his proof, Paul's failure to mention such evangelistic activity explicitly is either a great blunder or a sign of its nonoccurrence. It is noteworthy, however, that Paul also does not mention such activity in 1:21 (in regard to Syria and Cilicia). It is only the retrospective comment in 1:23 that explicitly mentions *any* evangelistic activity.

79. Burton, 55–57; Hays, *Echoes,* 168–73, 225–26; Longenecker, 34; Fee, 50–51; Tolmie, *Persuading,* 62. Wright ("Paul, Arabia, and Elijah," 685–87) suggests that Paul was acting out the pattern of Elijah, who expressed zeal for God through violent suppression of covenant-breakers (the priests of Baal; see 1 Kgs 19:14), experienced a direction-changing confrontation, sought refuge in the desert of Sinai, and eventually returned to the region of Damascus (see 1 Kgs 19:15).

gations that are in Christ. 23 *They were just hearing, "The one who formerly used to persecute us is now proclaiming as good news the faith that he was formerly trying to destroy,"* 24 *and they were giving God honor in connection with me.*

a. Some manuscripts have replaced the Aramaic name with the more familiar Πέτρον (e.g., א^c D F G 𝔐; so KJV, NKJV), but the Aramaic is undoubtedly original here, supported by the earliest manuscripts (𝔓^{46, 51} א* A B) and widely among early Syriac and Coptic versions (followed by RSV, NRSV, NASB, NEB). Ancient scribes would naturally adapt this wording to reflect the more familiar Greek version of his name (as does the NLT). Similar variation in the manuscript tradition occurs at 2:11 and 2:14.

In this paragraph, Paul does concede that he made an early visit to Jerusalem, but he is also careful to limit this in several ways. It occurred *years* after his encounter with the glorified Christ and possibly after significant activity as a preacher of the gospel in Arabia and Damascus (1:18a). It was undertaken on his own initiative (rather than responding to a summons by superiors), and his goal was to reach out to Peter (Cephas), in particular, and to make his acquaintance (1:18b). It was a collegial visit between two people whom Christ had commissioned and to whom Christ had revealed himself. Paul asserts that he saw only Peter and James on this visit (1:19); there was no meeting with the college of apostles as if with an ordaining or commissioning body. The limited nature of this contact is so important to Paul that he interposes an oath at this point, calling God to witness concerning the truth of Paul's narrative (1:20). Paul also asserts that this meeting did not lead to his working in the other apostles' jurisdiction or under their authority; after the two weeks were over, he went immediately (back?) to his evangelistic work in gentile lands (1:21). At the same time, he implicitly calls the Judean Christians to the stand as witnesses to the divine action behind Paul's transformation from persecutor to promoter of the faith, as they praise God for the change and thus attribute the change to God's direct intervention in Paul's life (1:22–24, returning to the language of 1:13b). In this way, the Judean churches give evidence of the truth of Paul's assertions in 1:1, 11–12 concerning the source of his gospel and apostolic commission.

18–19 Paul must concede to having made contact with the Jerusalem apostles eventually, but he does so in a most carefully limited way, with those limits backed by a formal oath (1:20): "Then after three years I went up to Jerusalem to visit with Cephas, and I stayed with him for fifteen days. But I didn't see any of the other apostles except for James, the Lord's brother." This first postconversion visit to Jerusalem happened at some point within the third year after his encounter with the glorified Christ. The expression "after three years" would not necessitate the passing of three *full* years, as parts of years would tend to be counted as whole years.[80] There is some question concerning

---

80. Matera, 66; Bruce, 97. Schreiner (109) aptly points to the parallel in the reckoning

at what point to begin counting these years—after God's revelation of God's Son to Paul, or after Paul's return to Damascus. The former, as the decisive event underscored in the previous narrative, is the more likely.[81] Paul may thus have been active as an ambassador of the risen Christ for two to three years before he made contact with the Jerusalem apostles. Even then, Paul insists, he met only with "Cephas" (the Aramaic form of Peter's name),[82] and that for only fifteen days, though he admits that he did also see James, Jesus's half-brother (see excursus "James, the Brother of the Lord" on pp. 161–64), during that brief visit. Paul's purpose for this visit was "to make Peter's acquaintance."[83] Paul went up, not as a schoolboy to be taught or corrected, but as a fellow apostle and preacher of the gospel. No doubt Paul learned a great deal from Peter, notably about the earthly life and the teachings of Jesus, whom Paul had not known in the flesh. But Paul presents this visit as a meeting of equals and perhaps also as evidence of Paul's taking the initiative to establish collegial relationships between two major branches of the Christian mission, this relationship becoming the major topic of 2:1–14. Indeed, one might have the sense that this visit is a sign of the esteem in which Paul held Peter and the value that the former placed on making a connection with him.[84]

Paul reinforces this impression by denying that he spent time with any others among the apostles, except James. The Greek of 1:19 admits of two

---

of the timing of Jesus's resurrection vis-à-vis his death, where "after three days" (μετὰ τρεῖς ἡμέρας, Matt 27:63; Mark 8:31; 9:31; 10:34) and "on the third day" (ἐν τρισὶν ἡμέραις, Matt 27:40; Mark 15:29; John 2:19; and τῇ τρίτῃ ἡμέρᾳ, Matt 16:21; 17:23; 20:19; 27:64; Luke 9:22; 18:33; 24:7, 46; Acts 10:40; 1 Cor 15:4) are synonymous. Note particularly that, if Matthew and Luke indeed used Mark as a source, they frequently replaced "after three days" with "on the third day."

81. Schlier, 58; Matera, 66; Das, 137–38; Schreiner, 109.

82. On Peter and Cephas as alternate names for the same person (as were Paul and Saul) rather than two different people, see Allison, "Peter and Cephas"; Das, 138–40. For attempts to argue in favor of two different historical figures, see Lake, "Simon, Cephas, Peter"; Riddle, "Cephas-Peter Problem"; Ehrman, "Cephas and Peter."

83. The verb ἱστορέω is often used to denote making inquiries or observations, but it can bear the sense "to visit" when used with an accusative of the person thus visited (LSJ 842; BDAG 483; see Hofius, "Gal 1:18"; Longenecker, 37–38; Fung, 73–74; Witherington, 119 n91; Das, 138). See the use of this verb in Plutarch, *Theseus* 30.4; *Pompeius* 40.1; *Lucullus* 2.6; Epictetus, *Discourses* 2.14.28; 3.7.1; Polybius, *Histories* 3.48.12.

84. John Chrysostom (13) astutely contrasts Paul's initiative in this scene with the confrontation in Antioch: "He says, 'to visit Peter' (ἱστορῆσαι), . . . a word which those who seek to become acquainted with great and splendid cities apply to themselves. Worthy of such trouble did he consider the very sight of Peter. . . . He premises this, that when he says, 'I resisted Peter,' no one may suppose that these words imply enmity and contention; for he honored and loved his person more than all and took this journey for his sake only, not for any of the others."

possible renderings: (1) "I did not see any others of the apostles, but I did see James (whom I do not enumerate among the apostles)" or (2) "I did not see any others of the apostles except James (whom I thereby enumerate among the apostles)."[85] The second reading is a far more natural construal of the Greek, especially the typical sense of the conjunction rendered "except," and more in keeping with Paul's open acknowledgment elsewhere of James as a witness of the risen Christ and, by implication from his placement within a list of apostles and apostolic groups (1 Cor 15:3–9), an apostle himself—at least, no more and no less than Cephas or Paul in that company (vv. 5–9).[86] Paul tells us nothing at all, however, about the details of his early encounter with James.

EXCURSUS: JAMES, THE BROTHER OF THE LORD

According to the Synoptic tradition, Jesus was part of a large family: "Isn't this the carpenter, the son of Mary and brother of Jacob and Joses and Judas and Simon? Aren't his sisters here with us" (Mark 6:3; Matt 13:55). We learn nothing of Jesus's sisters or two of his brothers (Joses and Simon), but Jacob—whom English readers know better as James[87]—became the leader of the movement formed in their brother's name.[88]

The precise relationship of James (and the other siblings) to Jesus has been a subject of vigorous debate since the patristic period. According to the likeliest view, sponsored by Helvidius, a fourth-century father of the church, James was Jesus's half-brother, sharing a mother but not a father. James would have been a natural child of Joseph and Mary, one of at least six born to the couple after the birth of Jesus (see Mark 6:3). This position understands Matt

---

85. Dunn (76–77) suggests that the Greek here should remain ambiguous, as, he alleges, Paul intends. Dunn suggests further (77) that Paul might have been reluctant to call James an apostle, a man who spent his whole ministry in one city, but this comment overlooks the opportunity James had to reach the world among the constant flood of pilgrims and tourists and assumes that we know everything about James's itineraries (e.g., his movements throughout Judea and the surrounding territories).

86. See also Longenecker, 38; Das, 142–43. Schreiner (110–11) helpfully directs attention to a parallel formula in 1 Cor 1:14: "I baptized none of you, except Crispus and Gaius." Crispus and Gaius are certainly part of the group "of you" (i.e., the Corinthian Christian community).

87. "James" is the Anglicized form of "Jacob"(Ἰάκωβος), the ancestor of the people of Israel.

88. Jude also played some active role in nurturing the new movement, as evidenced by the Letter of Jude. On the authenticity of this letter, see deSilva, *Jewish Teachers*, 45–57.

1:25 to indicate that, while Joseph "did not have sexual relations with her until she bore a son," the couple *did* have sexual relations after Jesus's birth.[89] Paul seems to make this assumption as well, since he refers to James as "the Lord's brother [*adelphos*]," Gal 1:19).[90]

Jesus's siblings do not appear in his earliest circle of disciples.[91] If anything, they are outsiders during the larger portion, if not the entirety, of Jesus's ministry, remembered to have exhibited anything from embarrassed concern (Mark 3:20–21, 31–35) to outright hostility (John 7:1–8).[92] The tradition that nonrelatives saw to the burial of Jesus's body (Mark 15:42–43, 46–47; Matt 27:57–61; Luke 23:50–56; John 19:38–42)—a duty that Jesus's family owed him—is also striking in this regard.[93] Taken together, these episodes preserve at the very least an authentic memory that Jesus's brothers were not among his followers for most of his ministry, and perhaps not until the period after his death, when they begin to appear explicitly in the circle of disciples.[94] The

---

89. See also the Second Apocalypse of James 50.15–22; Meier, "Brothers and Sisters." Epiphanius, Helvidius's contemporary, argued that James, Jude, and the other so-called brothers and sisters of Jesus were actually Joseph's children by a previous wife (*Panarion* 1.29.3–4; 2.66.19; 3.78.7, 9, 13; see also Protevangelium of James). This position is necessitated if one is to maintain, as did Epiphanius, the conviction that Mary remained a virgin throughout her life. Jerome championed yet another theory, namely, that James and Jude were merely cousins to Jesus, but this view requires a great deal of improbable genealogical calculus between the Gospel texts.

90. Though "brother" and "sister" are the terms most commonly used to talk about relationships within the Christian movement, Paul calls no one else "*the Lord's* brother," signaling that this is a special, biological relationship.

91. Tabor sensationally argues that Jesus's half-brothers James, Jude, and Simon are to be identified with the members of the Twelve bearing those names (James the Lesser, Jude "of James," and Simon the Zealot) and even that James was the "Beloved Disciple" of the Fourth Gospel (see *Jesus Dynasty*, 73–81, 162–67, 206–7, 249–54). For a refutation of Tabor's arguments, see deSilva, *Jewish Teachers*, 37–41.

92. In regard to Mark 3:31–35, it is at the very least telling that Jesus's relatives are not *among* those gathered around Jesus, but rather are outside calling for him; see Bauckham, *Relatives of Jesus*, 47; A. Collins, *Mark*, 226. The episode ends with Jesus's brothers remaining outside of the house while Jesus remains within with those whose dedication to Jesus's instruction on how to do God's will make them his more genuine kin. The core saying, if not the whole episode, has a strong claim to authenticity by the traditional criteria of multiple attestation and embarrassment (as a potential insult to revered figures in the early church). If inauthentic, there were witnesses (not least of all James and Jude) available to refute the tradition.

93. Witherington, *What Have They Done?*, 172.

94. Only the Gospel of the Hebrews (frag. 7) places James among the disciples prior to Jesus's passion and death, relating a story about James making a vow not to eat bread from the time he ate the Last Supper with Jesus until Jesus would rise from the dead. The episode itself may have been invented on the basis of 1 Cor 15:7 and Luke 22:18. In Gospel

author of Acts locates them in the company of Jesus's eleven surviving disciples and about one hundred other followers in the period after the ascension (Acts 1:14). A tradition that predates Paul's letters to the Corinthian church speaks of Jesus appearing specially to James after Jesus's resurrection (1 Cor 15:7), perhaps an event more to be compared with Jesus's encounter with Paul than is customarily observed.[95]

James soon emerges as the overseer for the Jerusalem church and its mission (Acts 15:12–21; 21:17–18; Gal 1:19; 2:9, 12). It is not clear how he rose to such prominence. Biological kinship with Jesus appears to have played some role in the selection of leaders in the Jerusalem church. After James, Symeon—a cousin of Jesus, being the son of Clopas, reputedly a brother of Joseph—becomes overseer (Eusebius, *Ecclesiastical History* 3.11; 4.22.42). The grandsons of Jude also exercised some level of oversight in the churches of Palestine during Symeon's long term of leadership (3.32.6).[96] Kinship with Jesus would not have been a sufficient factor, hence the careful preservation of the tradition that James had also seen the risen Lord (1 Cor 15:7).[97]

The New Testament is also far from clear concerning when James's transition to leadership occurred. Acts presents Peter as the de facto leader as the movement begins to organize and expand (1:15–26; 2:14–40; 3:12–26; 4:8–12, 19–20; 5:3–11, 27–32). Paul's persecution of the Jerusalem church provides the occasion for Peter to leave for Samaria and Caesarea. At some point after his return, Peter is imprisoned during a persecution late in the reign of Herod Agrippa I (41–44 CE), by which time James already appears to have risen to prominence (see Acts 12:17). This episode is often seen as the occasion for

---

of Thomas 12, Jesus names "James the Just" as the future leader of the movement, but this comment is ambiguous. It is not clear whether (1) the episode occurs prior to the crucifixion rather than between the resurrection and ascension or whether (2) James is actually a follower at the time of utterance.

95. This is most likely to be James, the brother of Jesus, rather than another early Christian named James, for a number of reasons: (1) An early tradition authenticating James the brother of Jesus alongside Cephas makes good sense in terms of legitimating the actual power structures emerging in the church of the first two decades of the movement; (2) special mention of an appearance to James the brother of John, who was himself one of the Twelve, is redundant *after* the mention of an appearance to "the Twelve" (though it would not have been redundant had Jesus made such an appearance to James alongside Cephas); (3) James the brother of John disappeared from the scene too early (before 44 CE) to become an important leader in the early church and thus to have such an episode enshrined in a tradition making its way throughout the Mediterranean, unlike James the Lord's brother; (4) other early Christian traditions (like the legendary episode in the Gospel of the Hebrews) bear witness to a special appearance to James, the Lord's brother.

96. See Bauckham, *Relatives of Jesus*, 105.

97. This tradition is increasingly embellished, as in the episode from the Gospel of the Hebrews already mentioned.

James's rise to leadership, but it presumes rather that the transition has already taken place.[98] Accepting the plot line in Acts, the transition would have occurred most naturally at Peter's initial departure from Jerusalem. Paul's testimony here in Galatians offers indirect support: when he speaks of meeting with the pillars during his second postconversion visit to Jerusalem, he names James ahead of Peter ("Cephas") and John (Gal 2:6, 9).[99]

James served as the overseer of the Jerusalem church and, with it, exercised some degree of oversight over the whole Christian mission until his martyrdom in 62 CE. During the brief hiatus between the death of the Roman governor Festus and the arrival of his successor, the high priest Ananus the Younger convened the Sanhedrin with a view to acquiring verdicts against several of his enemies in Jerusalem, one of them being James. Ananus's move provoked a substantial backlash among the city's inhabitants, who complained to King Agrippa II about his actions and his procedural missteps (he was not legally allowed to convene the Sanhedrin in the absence of a governor). Agrippa deposed Ananus as a result of his abuse of his power.[100]

---

20 At this point in his narrative, Paul interjects a solemn oath: "Now in regard to the things I am writing to you, look! Before God I swear that I am not lying."[101] He invokes the divine presence "before whom" he is speaking, with the implication that God will judge (and silence) falsehood spoken in God's court, as it were. Swearing such an oath alerts the audience to the seriousness of the matter being discussed: Paul is providing formal testimony concerning his earlier relationship with the Jerusalem apostles to make a point relevant to the case at hand in Galatia. He is not simply reminiscing.[102]

By means of the oath, Paul adds weight to his claims concerning the strict limitations on his interaction with the Jerusalem apostles; the fact that Paul must take an oath to affirm such details also suggests that the nature of this relationship and the contours of this narrative are contested

---

98. Painter, *Just James*, 44, against Dibelius and Greeven, *James*, 13.

99. Eusebius (*Ecclesiastical History* 2.1.3) quotes a tradition from Clement of Alexandria according to which "Peter and James and John" appear for a time to exercise some kind of interim authority together after the ascension that included the authority to name the new overseer.

100. See Josephus, *Antiquities* 20.197–203, on the authenticity of which see Dibelius and Greeven, *James*, 14–15; Witherington, *What Have They Done?*, 211.

101. The words "I swear" do not appear in the Greek but are presupposed by the oath formula of the invocation of God as witness.

102. Sampley, "'Before God, I Do Not Lie,'" 481–82; Burton, 61; Longenecker, 39–40; Fung, 79.

in Galatia.[103] For Paul, there is no room for the suggestion that he was a convert of those apostles, that he was originally taught about the gospel and about its requirements by the apostles, or that he was commissioned by the apostles to preach Christ. Paul acquired all of that from God himself. While this oath could be read as narrowly applying only to the details of this first visit (1:18-19),[104] such a limitation would be artificial indeed. Paul would be most likely heard here to affirm the utter truthfulness—at least from his perspective—of *all* the details in this entire narrative (such that he would also not have omitted all mention of an intervening visit between 1:18-20 and 2:1-10, if such a visit had happened).[105]

21 After this brief encounter, Paul "came into the regions of Syria and Cilicia," by which he means territories within the Roman provincial unit that included the cities of Antioch-on-the-Orontes and his native Tarsus.[106] How broadly Paul ranged throughout this area between his two visits to Jerusalem is unknown; he himself gives no details and, as in the case of Arabia and Damascus, does not even explicitly say that he was engaged in missionary work, leaving this detail to be inferred from his statement of God's purpose (16) and the reports circulating about Paul (23-24). The author of Acts limits Paul to Tarsus (in Cilicia), where Barnabas is able to find him when he wants help for the work in Antioch (in Syria, Acts 11:22-26).[107] By Paul's account, however, he must have been a more active missionary in both provinces—following up perhaps on earlier missionary work in Arabia and Damascus—than Luke cares to report at this point in his own version of the story, since news of Paul's work on behalf of the gospel travels back to the churches in Judea (23-24).

22 Rather than give details of his work in Syria and Cilicia, Paul is more concerned to provide details concerning his *absence* from Jerusalem and, indeed, all of Judea during the period since his conversion, with the single exception of his two-week visit to reach out to Peter: "But I remained unknown[108] by face among the Judean congregations that are in Christ." Paul

---

103. Schreiner, 111; Tolmie, *Persuading*, 66. On the rhetorical weight of oaths, see Anaximenes. *Rhetoric to Alexander* 1432a33.

104. So Schlier, 62.

105. So Burton, 61; Longenecker, 39-40, at least in regard to 1:13-19; Fung, 79.

106. Though the regions had different names, they were administered as a single unit throughout the first century. See Mommsen, *Provinces*, 1:323; 2:120. Judea was technically under the administration of the Roman governor of Syria, but it was also administered semi-autonomously under procurators and, occasionally, client kings of Herod's line. Paul clearly does *not* think of Judea as a subunit of the province of Syria (contrast 1:21 with 1:22-23).

107. On the differences between Paul's and Luke's accounts of Paul's first postconversion visit to Jerusalem (Gal 1:18-19, 22-23; Acts 9:26-30), see the Introduction.

108. The imperfect periphrastic ἤμην . . . ἀγνοούμενος would have a stronger dura-

draws a contrast between the regions where he was active, and thus would be known "by face" (hence "personally"), and Judea, where he was not active— thus neither working under the jurisdiction of the Jerusalem apostles nor poaching in their territory.[109] Paul's commission to preach the gospel "among the gentiles" would have directed him away from Judea and its environs as a whole, which were being effectively evangelized under the direction of the Jerusalem apostles (see also 2:7–10). Paul describes these Judean assemblies as "in Christ," a phrase that will take on increasing importance in this letter (see esp. 3:26–29). It is important to note that, even in the midst of altercations with rival Jewish Christian teachers and the dynamics of competing missions, Paul instinctively thinks of the Judean churches from which they might have originated as "in Christ," in whom is neither Jew nor Greek, along with his Galatian converts.

Paul's claims in these verses raise some questions in light of the accounts of Paul's activity in Acts. Paul was visible as a persecutor in Jerusalem (Acts 7:58–8:3) and as a preacher not only in Jerusalem, however briefly (9:26–30), but according to a later defense speech attributed to Paul, "to those in Jerusalem, throughout the region of Judea, and to the gentiles" (26:19–20). This last statement reflects Luke's interest in displaying the progress of the gospel from Jerusalem, through all Judea, to the ends of the earth (1:8) and is perhaps best not taken as a historical claim about Paul's missionary work.[110] Otherwise, Luke's portrayal remains sufficiently consistent with Paul's firsthand testimony (though the latter is always to be given greater weight in such matters, however true it is that Paul's own account is purposeful rather than dispassionate). Paul is primarily concerned with affirming his (virtual) noninteraction with the Jerusalem leaders during this period. His activity as a persecutor prior to his conversion is immaterial; and if he happened also to engage in public debate with the Hellenists during his visit to become acquainted with Peter,[111] this interaction is only to be expected of the apostle who made the most of every opportunity to advance the gospel.

As for the statement that he was "unknown by face to the Judean assemblies in Christ," it may be pressing Paul's words too far to insist that he

---

tive sense than a simple imperfect indicative (BDF §§352–53; Porter, *Idioms*, 47; Dunn, 80; Tolmie, *Persuading*, 67).

109. By "Judea," Paul may have in mind the whole of the Roman province, which included Galilee and Samaria (see Bruce, 103; Longenecker, 41).

110. See Keener, *Acts 24:1–28:31*, 3529.

111. So also Keener, *Acts 3:1–14:28*, 1690. Witherington (*Acts*, 325) emphasizes Paul's activity among the Jews who were themselves foreigners in Jerusalem here. Even so, Luke leaves the impression of a great deal more evangelistic activity and engagement with the Jerusalem pillars than Paul would allow (rightly Haenchen, *Acts*, 332).

claims that *no one* in all Judea would recognize him if he passed by on the street. To the extent that Acts preserves authentic historical memory, Paul's activity both as persecutor and as preacher were limited to Jerusalem (the latter extremely limited in time as well). This activity is also increasingly removed in time, so that as the movement grows and spreads both in Jerusalem and throughout Judea, the vast majority of Judean Christians would not have known Paul by sight.[112] It is also possible that Paul's claim to be "unrecognized by face" means nothing more than that, throughout this period, he never showed up anywhere in Judea to *be* recognized (apart from his fifteen-day visit). If a mug shot of Paul had been passed around, some Jerusalemites would have recognized him, but no one could have pointed him out on the streets because he simply was not around.

23 Paul was, however, known in Judea by reputation: "They were only hearing,[113] 'the one who formerly used to persecute us is now proclaiming as good news the faith that he was formerly trying to destroy.'" This report significantly reinforces Paul's own presentation of the "before and after" in his life that logically necessitates an intervening cause of the change, namely, God's intervention (1:13–16),[114] which was itself offered as evidence for Paul's claim that his message and his commission came from God rather than from a human source. Indeed, the very words used here explicitly recall 1:13–14:

"I was *engaged in persecuting* the church and *working to destroy* it." (1:13)

"the one who formerly *engaged in persecuting* us . . . the faith he formerly *worked to destroy*." (1:23)[115]

These forms create an inclusio marking 1:13–24 as a discrete segment within the narrative.[116]

There is general agreement that Paul's persecutions of "the Way" happened in and around Damascus; there is less agreement about his starting off in Jerusalem, since the clearly firsthand report circulating in Judea might not

---

112. Das, 144.

113. The imperfect periphrastic ἀκούοντες ἦσαν emphasizes that such rumors were the Judean Christians' only familiarity with Paul for some time. See also on ἤμην ἀγνοούμενος (Gal 1:22) above.

114. Note particularly the juxtaposition of the two temporal adverbs in the clause, ποτε νῦν, "[that] formerly, now [this]."

115. ἐδίωκον . . . ἐπόρθουν (1:13); ὁ διώκων . . . ἐπόρθει (1:23). The use of the present tense participle ὁ διώκων and the imperfect indicative ἐπόρθει again both draw attention to persecution as habitual practice for a season on Paul's part.

116. Gaventa, "Galatians 1 and 2," 316.

have originated from Jerusalem but from Damascus.[117] Nevertheless, these Judean Christians hear reports of Paul's missionary activity in Syria and Cilicia (and perhaps Arabia and Damascus) and bear witness to the activity of God in having turned their former persecutor into a promoter of "the faith" (1:23–24). The report confirms retrospectively that Paul's time in Syria and Cilicia, if not also in Nabatea, was dedicated to preaching the gospel, though he did not previously make this statement explicit in regard to any of these locales. "The faith" here indicates the basic content of the gospel and the way of life it promotes.[118] While Paul himself tends to use the term for the dynamic relationship of trust and faithfulness that exists between Christians and Jesus and God, the use of the term here to refer to a body of convictions and practices also has its roots in the earliest church, whether the usage here reflects Paul's word choice from around 50 CE or an actual report from earliest Judean Christianity circulating around 40 CE.[119]

24 Paul effectively summons the Judean Christians to the stand as witnesses to the divine power at work in his call and apostleship. Observing the transformation in Paul's activity, they attribute the change to God's intervention: "and they were giving God honor in connection with me." The preposition rendered "in connection with" is in most contexts often translated more simply "in." Here, however, it does not denote location ("they were glorifying God-in-me") but rather points to the cause for the Judean churches praising God, with this cause manifested *in* Paul's transformation ("they were glorifying God because of me, because of God's work evident in the change in me").[120]

The Judean Christians' past approbation of the turnaround in Paul does not provide clear evidence that Paul preached a Torah-observant gospel in his earlier years as a missionary. The details of his message might not have been carried along the grapevine as clearly as the more dramatic fact of his

---

117. See Hultgren, "Persecutions," 105–7. Das (144) hears the report as originating in the Jerusalem church. The use of the first person ἡμᾶς here signals that Paul is reporting, as it were, the actual words of the rumor, but it is of no help locating the original "us."

118. Bruce, 105; Fee, 53–54; Schreiner, 113; Das, 146.

119. This early usage of "the faith" is important when assessing the date and provenance of New Testament texts like Jude, which also uses "the faith" (τὴν πίστιν, Jude 3) in the sense of "the message and teachings about Christ handed down to us." Often it is argued that such a petrified use of "faith" is a sign of a later date, after Paul's dynamic understanding of "faith" as "trust in Jesus" has been replaced by "faith" as a body of doctrines to be preserved. In light of the usage of "the faith" in Gal 1:23, however, this particular argument against the authenticity of Jude's letter ought to be abandoned once and for all.

120. Longenecker, 42; Fung, 84; Schreiner, 113; so also NRSV, NIV, CEB, NLT. The strangeness of the wording cannot help but recall the same phrase in 1:16, which raises similar questions.

promotion of "the faith" he had been suppressing.[121] Moreover, even if the details were known, the *implications* of Paul's preaching to gentiles and bringing them into "God's Assembly" without making them Jews were not yet clear for the practice of those who *were* Jews in "God's Assembly," nor were the implications for the role of Torah in the new community. Even in the Acts narrative such opposition to the Torah-free gospel arises late in the story by comparison (Acts 15:1–5). It took the Jewish Christians who would eventually call for the circumcision and full conversion of gentile Christians to the Jewish way of life some time to understand the significance of the trajectory Paul was taking toward "the truth of the gospel"—and to react.

C. PAUL'S SECOND VISIT TO JERUSALEM (2:1–10)

¹ *Then after fourteen years I went up again to Jerusalem with Barnabas, also taking Titus along.* ² *Now, I went up in accordance with a revelation, and I presented to them the message of good news that I proclaim among the nations, privately to the persons of repute, lest somehow I was running or had run for nothing.* ³ *But not even Titus, who was with me, was compelled to be circumcised, even though he was a Greek.* ⁴ *This issue came up on account of the false brothers who were smuggled in, who slipped in to spy out the freedom that we enjoy in Christ Jesus, in order that they might enslave us.* ⁵ *We did not*[a] *give in to them*[b] *in submission even for a moment, in order that the truth of the good news might remain for you.*

⁶ *But from those who had a reputation for being "somebodies"—whatever they were formerly makes no difference to me, since God does not show partiality—for to me those of repute added nothing.* ⁷ *On the contrary, seeing that I was entrusted with the good news for the uncircumcised just as Peter was entrusted with the good news for the circumcised,* ⁸ *since the one who worked through Peter for the purpose of apostleship to the circumcised also worked in me for apostleship to the nations,* ⁹ *and recognizing the generous gift that had been given to me, Jacob and Cephas*[c] *and John—those reputed to be "pillars"—gave the right hand of partnership to me and to Barnabas, in order that we should go to the nations, and they to the circumcision.* ¹⁰ *They added only that we should continue to remember the poor, which very thing I took pains to do.*

a. Several MSS (D* it[d] Marius Victorinus Augustine) omit οὐδέ here, reading "to them we yielded in submission for a moment." The witnesses are, however, neither strong nor widespread (belonging mostly to the Western family), and so the omission is clearly an error, perhaps motivated by a desire to conform the episode concerning Titus to Paul's

---

121. Contra Betz, 80.

accommodationist policy articulated elsewhere (e.g., 1 Cor 9:20–23; Metzger, *Textual Commentary*, 522).

b. Marcion omitted the relative pronoun οἷς, perhaps to emphasize Paul's unwillingness to yield to *any* voice in Jerusalem (Longenecker, 52), but the variant is clearly not original.

c. Some MSS replace Κηφᾶς with the more familiar Πέτρος ($\mathfrak{P}^{46}$ D F G it$^{d,\,g,\,r}$), with most of these (but not $\mathfrak{P}^{46}$ it^r) moving Πέτρος before James and John in keeping with Peter's prominence in early Christian memory. Both variations are clearly secondary (similar variations in the manuscript tradition occur in 1:18 and 2:11).

Paul has shaped the narrative thus far to show that his commission and his message came to him independently of the Jerusalem leadership and in complete dependence on God. As Paul recounts at length this private meeting between James, Peter, and John on the one hand, and Barnabas and himself on the other, Paul moves to the next emphasis, namely, the Jerusalem apostles' validation of his apostleship and message. Paul seeks to strike a delicate balance between (1) affirming the recognition by the pillars of his apostolic mission and message and (2) *not* affirming that they have authority over the same.[122] He lays out the gospel he had been preaching (Gal 1:21–24), bringing along an uncircumcised gentile convert named Titus (2:1, 3). If the Jerusalem apostles felt the need to correct or supplement any aspect of Paul's gospel, *that* would have been the right occasion. Instead, perceiving the hand of God at work in Paul and Barnabas's missionary endeavors just as in their own (2:8), and understanding the success of Paul and Barnabas's work to be an outworking of God's favor (2:9), the Jerusalem apostles affirmed them as partners in mission and "added nothing" to Paul's message (2:6). Why, then, should anyone be calling for circumcision of gentiles now? The Galatians should take this event as evidence that the Jerusalem pillars recognized the validity of Paul's gospel and had all the right reasons for doing so, whatever the rival teachers may have said to the contrary. And if any of the Jerusalem apostles themselves had taken a step back from this along the way (see 2:11–14), they are the ones acting unreliably.

The selectivity of Paul's narrative is especially evident when one considers that he compresses a decade or more of missionary work in Syria and Cilicia into a single verse (1:21) but then gives ten verses to a single episode (2:1–10) followed by at least another four verses to a subsequent episode (2:11–14). This is an additional indication of the specific argumentative purposes behind Paul's autobiographical narrative.

1 Paul moves on to the next significant event in the unfolding chronological narration: "Then after fourteen years I went up again to Jerusalem

---

122. For a fuller investigation of this balancing act, see Dunn, "Relationship between Paul and Jerusalem."

with Barnabas, also taking Titus along." The expression "after fourteen years" could also indicate a span of time at the end of which something occurs.[123] Paul is not clear whether he intends for the episode of 2:1–10 to be understood as happening fourteen years after his encounter with the glorified Christ (1:15–17), as the life-changing event that dominates the narrative, or after his first visit to Jerusalem (1:18–20).[124] The latter seems the more natural reading, given Paul's attention to creating a sequential order of events, but the timing remains another point of uncertainty.

Paul uses the more typical verb for speaking of "going up" to Jerusalem as he begins the narration of his second postconversion visit.[125] Barnabas, who accompanies him, is still clearly Paul's partner at this point in their narrative. Paul presumes that his will be a familiar name to the Galatian Christians, perhaps because Paul and Barnabas founded these congregations together (see Introduction). Titus, who is similarly mentioned without introduction or explanation, and who may therefore already have become a part of Paul's team when he and Barnabas preached in southern Galatia, would become an increasingly important coworker for Paul. His ability to handle delicate relational issues is evident from his role in Paul's dealings with the Corinthian congregations (2 Cor 2:13; 7:6, 13–14; 8:6, 16, 23; see also 2 Tim 4:10; Titus 1:4). The selectivity and incompleteness of Luke's account of the Pauline mission are evident once again from his omission of any mention of this prominent coworker.

Paul gives no indication of his motive in taking Titus along on this visit to Jerusalem. Perhaps it was a natural and naive decision, thinking of Titus simply as a coworker in the mission (and also involved in the collection of the relief funds they were transporting, if Gal 2:1–10 is a parallel account of the visit narrated in Acts 11:28–30). Perhaps it was a strategic move on Paul's part, presenting the Jerusalem apostles with a fine and fully commendable example of the work of the Spirit in and among the gentiles, someone in whom the pillars could see what God was accomplishing through Paul and Barnabas and whose progress in the faith would undermine the suggestions swirling about that circumcision and the like were necessary prerequisites to such progress. What can be affirmed is that the delegation appropriately mirrors the constituency of the Antioch church and, as such, presents a well-rounded picture of its mission.[126]

---

123. BDAG 224; Bruce, 106–7; Longenecker, 45.

124. In favor of the former, see Das, 163; Martyn, 180–82; Longenecker, 45. In favor of the latter, see Betz, 83; Schlier, 64–65; Burton, 68; Matera, 71; Robinson, *Redating*, 37. See the Introduction on the question of Pauline chronology.

125. ἀνέβην (BDAG 58), as opposed to ἀνῆλθον in 1:17, 18. See commentary on 1:17.

126. Dunn, 91.

I went up in accordance with a revelat

2 Paul shares something of his own motivation for the visit, even as he had supplied his motivation for the first visit in 1:18–19: "Now, I went up[127] in accordance with a revelation, and I presented to them the message of good news that I proclaim among the nations, privately to the persons of repute, lest somehow I was running or had run for nothing." Paul offers essential background material in the form of a potentially corrective detail: Paul went up at the instigation of God ("in line with a revelation," 2:2), not in response to being summoned by mortals.

We cannot be certain in what form this revelation came to Paul, whether as a prophetic utterance tested and accepted in the assembly or as a private prompting of the Spirit within Paul. Certainly the phenomenon of a revelation as one of the Spirit's manifestations is well attested in Pauline Christianity (1 Cor 14:6, 26, 30; Acts 13:1–3), one of the many "wonders" worked by God's Spirit in the midst of a congregation (see Gal 3:5).[128] Paul is not concerned to elaborate on this detail, but only to prevent any impression that he and Barnabas went as lackeys of the Jerusalem apostles, either summoned by the apostles to give a report on their preaching and activities or as persons aware of needing to give an account to their superiors.[129] Rather, Paul went because God—the God who gave him his commission—directed him to do so.

Paul's purpose was proactively to present his gospel (and the terms on the basis of which it was offered, as it were, to the gentile hearers) to the Jerusalem apostles. One might infer that he was seeking a ruling from them that would settle the questions being raised about his gentile mission with the hope of walking away in agreement with them, with the doubts raised by other parties silenced and no longer able to undermine his work. Paul adds the qualifying information that it was his goal to do so "privately" in consultation with "those of repute."[130] It does not appear that Paul entirely got his

---

127. On "going up" to Jerusalem, see commentary on 1:17.

128. Fee (*God's Empowering Presence*, 372–73) leans toward a congregationally tested revelation (whether or not the vehicle was Paul), Bornkamm ("Revelation," 95) toward a word spoken to a charismatic in Antioch, and Georgi (*Remembering the Poor*, 24) toward "the outcome of an assembly of the congregation at Antioch, with the final decision understood as a breakthrough of prophetic authority." Georgi (26) affirms that it makes sense for the visit to have been initiated in some sense by the Antiochene Christian community rather than Jerusalem, since they had more at stake as questions began to be raised within the larger movement about the gentile mission and the terms for gentile inclusion.

129. Fung, 87; Longenecker, 47; Dunn, 91.

130. This interjected clause does not give evidence of two meetings—a more plenary session (where Paul presents his gospel to a "them" in general) and an executive session (where Paul meets privately with the pillar apostles), such as we find in Acts 15 (*pace* Dunn, 93). Paul speaks only of a private meeting in Gal 2:1–10. Indeed, the κατ' ἰδίαν δέ functions to correct any possible impression of a kind of general meeting (Das, 166).

way, in light of the fact that some other parties "sneaked in" (see on 2:4). The stress on Paul's intentions for a "private" meeting may serve a strategic end, possibly shutting out the rival teachers and others of their inclination as not in his league or the league of those whom he considers apostolic colleagues.

Paul describes the pillar apostles as "those of repute" or "those thought to be something."[131] The expression does not necessarily convey irony or sarcasm on Paul's part,[132] though Paul may use it to distance himself slightly from the claim. He acknowledges the repute that they enjoy across the broader movement without saying whether he held them in the same esteem. While the expression may not be pejorative, then, it is also noncommittal.[133] The further use of this expression, fleshed out more fully in 2:6 and 2:9, suggests that James, Peter, and John, who are explicitly named as "those reputed to be pillars" in 2:9, are in view throughout.[134]

The last clause of the verse commands attention. In what sense would Paul think his mission so jeopardized by the outcome of this meeting that he faces the danger of having run and continuing to run his course "for nothing"?[135] It is highly unlikely, given Paul's confidence of having been accosted and taught by God himself in his encounter with the glorified Christ, that Paul was experiencing self-doubt, such that lack of affirmation by the Jerusalem apostles would invalidate, for him, his own calling or message. Rather, Paul probably understands that failure to receive the acknowledgment of the Jerusalem apostles would undermine his mission to build, and would mortally impede his vision for, the body of Christ, in which there was "neither Jew nor Greek," since all "are one in Christ Jesus" (Gal 3:28), resulting instead in two separate and divided churches, each with its own mission,[136] and with Paul's

---

131. The use of a substantival participial form of δοκέω to denote "those of repute," as in "the prominent dignitaries," is well-attested in extrabiblical literature: positively in Josephus, *War* 3.453; 4.141, 159; ironically in Plato, *Apology* 21b, c–e; 22a–b; 29a; 36d; 41e. See BDAG 255; also Das, 167.

132. Burton, 71; Bruce, 109.

133. Dunn, 92–93.

134. Matera, 73, suggests that, since Paul does not specify who these "people of repute" are, they might be a larger group of leaders, on whose behalf the pillars will make a final ruling. The persistent use of οἱ δοκοῦντες all the way through 2:9, however, suggests rather a single, consistent group.

135. The marker μή here introduces an undesired outcome ("lest," BDAG 646; BDF §370). τρέχω should be understood as present subjunctive here, coming after μή πως. See Burton, 73–74; Longenecker, 43; Murphy-O'Connor, "To Run in Vain (Gal 2:2)," 384.

136. Burton, 73; Bruce, 111; Dunn, 93–94; Dunn, "Relationship," 468; Fung, 90; Longenecker, 49; Matera, 80; Martyn, 193; Georgi, *Remembering the Poor*, 27–28; Witherington, 134; Wright, *Recent Interpreters*, 340. Murphy-O'Connor ("To Run in Vain," 388) raises the possibility that Paul, rather than expressing a genuine fear, uses the rhetorical device of *concessio*, "in which we seem to allow something damaging, just to show our confidence in

maverick mission being seriously undermined by the lack of support from Jesus's own disciples and family.[137] The unity of the church was at stake in this visit, just as it would continue to be at stake for Paul as he confronted Peter in Antioch, and as he confronts the "other gospel" in Galatia, and as he asks for prayer years later that the collection, the symbol of Paul's faithfulness to his agreement with Peter, James, and John and the symbol of the unity of the Pauline churches with the Jerusalem church, be accepted (Rom 15:30–32).[138]

Paul selects this episode for special focus here in his narrative, furthermore, because he is aware that the Galatians need a standard for discerning the truth of the gospel beyond either himself or the rival teachers. His narration of the agreement between himself and the Jerusalem pillars accomplishes this goal: Paul subjected his message to their scrutiny, and they affirmed that it was indeed in line with their understanding of the gospel, and therefore with the authentic message of Jesus and about Jesus.[139] The rival teachers cannot now claim otherwise, nor can they claim support of the Jerusalem apostles for their position and mission against Paul's. If they urge circumcision upon gentile converts, *they* are the ones who are out of alignment with the Jerusalem apostles in the latter's agreement with Paul, since they persist in foisting their position against the better inclinations of "those reputed to be pillars." Paul thus clearly sees a connection between his current situation (his preaching to the Galatians and the current challenge to his gospel) and this historic meeting with Peter, James, and John. Paul's convictions concerning his divine commissioning and revelation aside, it is important here to note as well that Paul is aware of the need for agreement and acknowledgment of his gospel and commission by those who were apostles before him. The new insights and outreach do not justify divisions within the church; the unity of the movement must be safeguarded if at all possible, and the disintegration of the movement into *movements* would significantly undermine the work of God in the world.

3 Paul's leap to the outcome of the encounter for Titus suggests that this is the matter of greatest significance and relevance: "But not even Titus, although he was a Greek, was compelled to be circumcised!" Paul introduces this outcome with the stronger Greek word for "but," suggesting that 2:3

---

our cause" (Quintilian, *Education* 9.2.51). Paul would be heightening the dramatic tension of the moment by promoting the authority of the Jerusalem leaders and presenting his own work as rising or falling on their judgment, only to heighten the impact of the fact that they did, after all, affirm his calling and his gospel (2:7–9). John Chrysostom (14) regards Paul's visit to have the purpose of demonstrating to his Jewish-Christian detractors that he was not running in vain: this represents *their* supposition, not *Paul's* fear.

137. Schnelle, *Apostle Paul*, 122.
138. Robinson, "Circumcision of Titus," 27.
139. See Bruce, 35–37.

counters the possibility that Paul had been pursuing his mission in vain (2:2). The fact that Titus walked away from a meeting with the Jerusalem apostles uncircumcised should also cast serious doubt upon what the rival teachers are claiming now in regard to the importance, even necessity, of circumcision.[140]

Circumcision was the symbolic mark that distinguished the Jew from the "Greek," or non-Jew more broadly.[141] Its importance as a symbol of Jewish distinctiveness is especially evident from the way in which the practice became a focal point during the Hellenistic reform and the hellenizing crisis of 175–164 BCE. Jews who sought to assimilate to the Greek dominant culture underwent epispasm so that they "might be Greeks even when unclothed."[142] In the prohibition of Jewish practice and forced assimilation that ensued, circumcising one's male children was punished with public execution (1 Macc 1:60–61; 2 Macc 6:8–10). When the revolutionaries began to enact their resistance, forcibly circumcising the Jewish boys left uncircumcised was on the forefront of their agenda (1 Macc 2:46). Later, the Hasmonean rulers would compel the male residents in their conquered territories to be circumcised (presumably in order to meet the requirements of dwelling within the boundaries of the original promised land).[143] The question of whether to compel a person to be circumcised (or to remain uncircumcised) is thus, by the time of Paul, an old and not dispassionate one.

As Paul will suggest in the following verse, some Jewish Christians had called for Titus to be circumcised if he was to be a part of the Jesus movement, or a part of a missionary team representing the Jesus movement. <u>Significantly, the pillars do not get behind this demand.</u> That is all that matters for Paul. It is not clear whether the pillars' actual position was merely negative ("we will not lay upon Titus the demand to be circumcised") or whether it was positive and therefore more broadly applicable ("we recognize that gentiles do not, in fact, need to be circumcised to enjoy all the benefits of Christ's death and resurrection on their behalf"). The former seems more likely, given that Jewish Christians continued to call for the circumcision of gentiles after this ruling in Titus's case, which would suggest some ambiguity in the pillars' position at this point.[144]

---

140. Paul underscored the significance of this outcome for the Galatian situation by using an emphatic negative conjunction ("not even," οὐδέ) and an adverbial participial clause likely to be understood as concessive in this context ("although he was a Greek"; Burton, 76). Ἕλλην could refer to someone who is ethnically Greek but is also used to refer to gentiles more broadly (as in Rom 1:16; 2:9, 10).

141. See Tacitus, *Histories* 5.5.2; Josephus, *Antiquities* 1.192.

142. Josephus, *Antiquities* 12.241; see also 1 Macc 1:15, 48.

143. Josephus, *Antiquities* 13.257–58, 318.

144. Dunn (104–5), however, thinks rather that the pillars did in fact rule decisively in Paul's favor. Robinson ("Circumcision of Titus") suggested that, while Titus was not *com-*

The way Paul has jumped to this outcome at this point in the narrative, ahead even of naming the source of the demand for Titus's circumcision (2:4–5) or the pillars' reception of Paul and his gospel (2:6–10), suggests that he regards it to be highly relevant for the situation he now addresses in Galatia.[145] Indeed, one can trace the issue of compelling gentiles to conform to the practices of the Torah from Jerusalem ("compelled to be circumcised," 2:3) to Antioch ("how can you compel the gentiles to adopt the Jewish way of life," 2:14) to Galatia itself ("those who are compelling you to get yourselves circumcised," 6:12).[146] Paul's second visit produced, for him, the decisive answer: if not Titus, then *no* gentile Christ-followers need to be circumcised.[147]

4–5 The impetus toward circumcision and Torah observance, bringing the gentile converts under the strict tutelage of that outmoded guardian (see 3:23–4:7), is to be traced to a third party: "But on account of the false brothers who were smuggled in, who slipped in to spy out the freedom that we enjoy in Christ Jesus, in order that they might enslave us, to whom we did not yield in submission even for a moment,[148] in order that the truth of the good news might remain for you."[149]

---

pelled to be circumcised, he *agreed* to be circumcised, exercising his Christian freedom in the direction of accommodating for the sake of the work of the gospel among diaspora Jews. He suggests that, as long as it was not regarded as necessary for Titus's place in the people of God, Paul might have approved of asking Titus to be "all things to all people" even as Paul himself was willing to be (1 Cor 9:20–21; Robinson, "Circumcision of Titus," 30–31). This scenario might further explain the possibility of claiming that Paul did preach circumcision elsewhere (see Gal 5:11 and commentary), if not in Galatia (Robinson, "Circumcision of Titus," 37; so also Burkitt, *Christian Beginnings*, 118; Duncan, 41–45). If Titus *had* been circumcised, however, Paul would have needed to explain his motivations far more explicitly in 2:3–5 than he does, rather than simply clouding the issue with a murky denial. Indeed, if Titus had walked away circumcised, it would have constituted the very submission that Paul affirms he resisted for the sake of the persistence of the "truth of the gospel" (Burton, 81; Betz, 89; Longenecker, 50; Dunn, 96; Das, 169).

145. Boers, *Justification of the Gentiles*, 64; Tolmie, *Persuading*, 71.

146. Das, 169.

147. Witherington, 135, 146–47.

148. The expression πρὸς ὥραν emphasizes the fact that Paul and Barnabas did not waver even for the shortest time in this confrontation, an "hour" being the smallest unit of time in common use during the Hellenistic and Roman periods (the ἡμιώριον, "half an hour," excepted; see Rev 8:1). See BDAG 1102; Dunn, 86.

149. Fee (56) suggests that 2:4–5 reveals "the reason for the conference," namely, "the insistence on the necessity of circumcision of gentiles on the part of some Jewish believers." While some people did make this an issue at this meeting, it was not the principal agenda item but more a sidebar that arose outside of, and intruded upon, Paul and Barnabas's meeting with James, Peter, and John. It is tempting to read this phrase in connection with the previous verse ("But even Titus who was with me, although he was a Greek, was not compelled to be circumcised on account of the false brothers who secretly slipped in"), but the presence of

A comment on the style of Paul's writing at this point is in order. Paul starts a sentence in 2:4 that he never actually completes. It remains a sentence fragment by the end of 2:5, at which point Paul starts a fresh sentence (2:6). Neither does Paul seem able to finish this new sentence in the way he started: he introduces the pillars as an object of a preposition at the outset but then starts his sentence over, in effect, by naming these pillars as the subject of the sentence that eventually emerges from the confusion. These false starts and syntactic bumps suggest, first, a rather high level of agitation or emotional investment on Paul's part, particularly as he recalls the intrusion of the "false brothers" into his meeting with the Jerusalem apostles and the conflict over whether or not Titus needed to be circumcised.[150] Part of this flood of agitation may in fact be due to Paul's encounter with similar opposition now in Galatia, when he thought this question had been settled—and that with the full support of the pillars. They also suggest a level of immediacy in Paul's composition of this letter—it is still in rough draft form when he sends it, indicating both his sense of the urgency of the situation and the possibility that Paul did not, in fact, use a secretary in the composition of this particular letter (see commentary on 6:11), who should have caught and smoothed out such rough (even incorrect) syntax.[151]

Paul describes this opposing party in the most unflattering terms. While these people no doubt believed themselves to be Christ-followers, Paul denies them this status. These pretenders pushed their noses in where they did not belong, "weaseling their way in" to the conversation between Paul, Barnabas, and the Jerusalem pillars (2:4).[152] Moreover, they did so with harmful

---

δέ, a conjunction used to introduce a new development in the narrative, precludes such a straightforward solution to the problematic syntax.

150. Fee, 55; Martyn, 194–95. Luther made the apt observation that "the person who is moved by deep emotion when speaking cannot follow grammatical rules at the same time" (WA 40/1:170.10–11, translation mine).

151. The verses have the effect of anacoluthon, a rhetorical ornament involving intentionally disrupted syntax. It could be used by a speaker to give the impression, by his or her broken syntax, that he or she was speaking from the heart (Tolmie, *Persuading*, 82). The syntax could also, however, result simply from the writer actually composing from the heart, betraying genuine agitation (as would certainly be plausible here).

152. The adjective παρείσακτος denotes sneaking in or unauthorized infiltration (BDAG 774). The pretenders were clearly unwelcome as far as Paul was concerned; we cannot tell how the pillars felt about their presence in this meeting (Das, 173). Francis Watson believes that the "false brethren" in 2:3–5 were present in Antioch rather than Jerusalem and that these verses represent a digression rather than belonging to the narrative of the Jerusalem visit (*Paul, Judaism, and the Gentiles*, 50). They weaseled their way into the Antioch congregations, where they spied out the freedom of Jewish and gentile Christians and fomented, by their criticism, a crisis that led to the "revelation" (2:2) that Paul, Barnabas, and Titus should go to the Jerusalem pillars to settle the matter (51, 53; similarly, Georgi,

intent, "to spy out our freedom, which we have in Christ Jesus, in order to thoroughly enslave us" (2:4). Freedom, as the goal of God's provision for human beings in Christ, will become a major theme of the letter, especially in 4:1–5:13. With the prepositional phrase "in Christ Jesus," Paul also anticipates here the discussion of 3:23–4:11 on how the believers' incorporation into, and thus close relationship with, Christ provides a new freedom, zealously to be guarded (5:1).

Paul wants to blame something on these individuals ("But on account of the false brothers"), but he never specifies what it is. In all likelihood, they are the source of the suggestion that Titus needed to be circumcised in order to be fully a member of the new people of God.[153] The "slavery" they sought to impose upon the Pauline mission and its converts, to use Paul's loaded image, was the same kind of practice that Paul's rival teachers are now seeking to promote among the Galatian converts, namely, submission to the yoke of the Torah.[154] The current rivals are also identified with slavery and seeking to enslave (see 4:1–5, 8–11; 5:1), such that the presentation of the "false brothers" in Jerusalem (and the Jerusalem apostles' nonsupport for their agenda) reflects negatively upon the rival teachers here as well, undermining *their* credibility in Galatia.[155]

Paul, however, firmly resisted their pressure and arguments. He emerges from this situation as the champion of the "truth of the gospel," preserving that truth for the benefit of the whole gentile mission (2:5). He presents his actions in Jerusalem, holding his own against the false brothers, as a course ultimately undertaken on behalf of all his converts, specifically including the Galatians ("preserved *for you*," 2:5).[156] The Galatians had not yet been evangelized at the time of this event. Had Paul "yielded in submission" to the false brothers, the "truth of the gospel" would have been compromised before it

---

Remembering the Poor, 24). The action corresponds thus closely with that of Acts 15:1–2. Watson (52) further posits that the false brethren were *sent* by the Jerusalem leaders: "a spy acts on someone else's behalf." Schnelle (*Apostle Paul*, 122) suggests that the false brothers were present in Antioch but also went up to Jerusalem to interfere (from Paul's point of view) with his meeting with the pillars. While these arguments have merit, the narrative of Galatians more naturally and straightforwardly (from outcome in 2:3 to source of the threat in 2:4) suggests pressure brought to bear on Titus in Jerusalem (Longenecker, 49; Das, 170).

153. Longenecker, 47; Schreiner, 124; Dunn, 97.

154. Burton, 82; Schlier, 72; Dunn, 100; Tolmie, *Persuading*, 72.

155. Fee, 62; Tolmie, *Persuading*, 80. The Jewish Christians whom Paul accuses of such an agenda would no doubt have regarded their purposes quite differently, for example, to ensure the proper maintenance of the covenant that God had formed with Israel and that the coming of Jesus did not materially change (Dunn, 99).

156. The prepositional phrase might communicate purpose ("might remain for you" or "on your behalf") or design/destiny ("might remain until [it reaches] you"; BDAG 874).

ever reached the Galatians. The "truth of the gospel" survived rather than perished as a result of his bold resistance. His heroic efforts should arouse due loyalty and gratitude on their part, rather than defection toward those whose message resembles the one that Paul resisted—and the one to which the pillars did not give their support (2:9).

6 However much the "false brothers" might have pressed for circumcision and Torah observance to have been added to Paul's gospel and its requirements, the outcome was quite different: "But from those who had a reputation for being 'somebodies'—whatever they were formerly makes no difference to me, since God does not show partiality[157]—for to *me*[158] those of repute added nothing." Paul had presented the message he proclaimed (2:2) and had no doubt also spoken of the lifestyle changes he required, as well as the signs of God's presence and approval that manifested themselves among his converts, all of which the Jerusalem apostles considered to be adequate (2:6),[159] with one mutually agreeable proviso that Paul will go on to name (2:10).[160]

The principal claim of this verse is presented as a rationale ("for to me . . . ") for some preceding claim, but *what* claim is not immediately apparent. It might be understood to provide support for Paul's refusal to yield to the pressure from the "false brothers" for the sake of the preservation of "the truth of the gospel" (2:5). Paul would be heard to justify his resistance to those lesser figures with the claim that those of repute in the Jerusalem church essentially agreed with Paul's position. It might also be heard as evidence for the implicit claim that the truth of the gospel did in fact remain in play, with the result that the Galatians could benefit from it in due course (2:5), since the pillars added nothing to Paul's gospel but rather affirmed its truth.

Paul continues to refer to the core Jerusalem leaders as "those of repute" (see commentary on 2:2). The verse here admits of two very different readings, both in regard to Paul's extension of this title to "those reputed to be 'somebodies'" and Paul's aside ("whatever they were formerly makes no difference to me, since God does not have regard for a person's appearance").

---

157. Paul employs the idiom πρόσωπον λαμβάνει (lit. "he receives the face"), a Semiticism for "showing partiality" (2 Kgs 3:14; Ps 82:2; Sir 4:22, 27; 35:12–13; 42:1; Mal 2:9; Luke 20:21). We might compare the English idiom "taking at face value." Paul does not explicitly present this truth about God as a rationale for his position, but it does seem to be its argumentative function (hence the addition of "since" in the translation).

158. The dative ἐμοί is emphatic by virtue of its fronted position.

159. Tolmie, *Persuading*, 72.

160. As was the case with 2:4–5, so here Paul begins the sentence in one manner (introducing "those of repute" as the object of a preposition) but continues it in another (reintroducing "those of repute" as the subject of the sentence). We would have expected "But from those reputed to be something . . . I received no additions or corrections."

In regard to the first of these developments, Paul could be referring to the Jerusalem leaders positively as people of genuine account, as opposed to the "false brothers" who were *not* "somebodies" at all but, at best, "busybodies" poking their noses under the tent where Paul and Barnabas met with the pillar apostles. However, Paul might also be maintaining his reserve in regard to the pillars.[161] "Thinking oneself to be something" when one is, in fact, nothing emerges as a serious character flaw in 6:3. The pillars' repute in the eyes of so many Christians does not matter nearly so much as their repute in the eyes of God, who stands behind Paul's mission without question in Paul's mind.

In regard to Paul's aside (which is perhaps responsible for Paul's losing track of how he began this sentence grammatically), much depends on what one decides Paul to mean by "whatever they were *formerly*." What time frame does Paul have in mind? If Paul is speaking favorably of the pillars, the adverb "formerly" could be heard to differentiate "what kind of persons they were" prior to their rising to positions of leadership and oversight in the Christian movement (fishermen and artisans in Galilee, not particularly well schooled in religious matters or regarded as religious authorities) from what they have now become, people "seeming to be something of substance," of *gravitas*, which Paul respects—all the more, no doubt, because they backed him up on that particular occasion. God's choice of former "nobodies" to become principal authorities in the messianic movement is in keeping with the scriptural dictum that "God shows no partiality" (see, e.g., 1 Sam 16:7), choosing whom he will on what basis he will (e.g., the heart over external graces). Paul may have here in mind God's selection of David, the young shepherd in the household, over his taller, finer looking brothers (16:7). This example would also be in keeping with Paul's own philosophy of not reckoning his own life prior to coming to Christ as anything but "sewage" (Phil 3:4b–8).[162]

Reading the aside more negatively, the adverb could refer to the pillars' ecclesial status prior to the meeting that Paul recounts in 2:1–10, or to their closer proximity to Jesus during his earthly ministry and direct commissioning by him, both of which Paul would be dismissing (and alongside which qualifications Paul's own apostleship and calling look quite anomalous).[163] This reading would also suit Paul's theological premise, for *Paul's* calling is also a reflection of God's not showing partiality. Paul could also be heard to express here his lack of regard for the pillars on *this* side of the Antioch

---

161. Lightfoot, 103; Matera, 75; Betz, 92; Dunn, 102.

162. Even this reading could contain a barb: Paul's own religious education and pedigree were actually much stronger than theirs, and he was not some "nobody" in his former life, given the respect he enjoyed among his coreligionists, and all the more if Acts is to be believed on certain points, as, for example, Paul's ability to get a commission from the high priest.

163. So Schlier, 75–76; see also Burton, 87; Schreiner, 126.

incident, in contrast to the esteem in which he formerly held them before their betrayal, and therefore taming, if not undermining, the authority even of the Jerusalem apostles.[164] Paul's sense of having been betrayed at Antioch by Peter and James (through the latter's representatives), and the trouble and frustration to which this incident has given rise both in Antioch and now in Galatia, may suggest that a negative reading would be more in keeping with the dynamics of the situation at this stage in the unfolding drama.

7–9 Paul proceeds to give the positive statement corresponding to the negative "to me those of repute added nothing" (2:6).[165] Galatians 2:6–10 is actually one complex sentence in the Greek, and verses 7–9 in particular need to be taken together: "On the contrary, seeing that I was entrusted with the good news for the uncircumcised just as Peter (was entrusted with the good news) for the circumcised, [8]since the one who worked through Peter for the purpose of apostleship to the circumcised also worked in me (for apostleship) to the nations, [9]and recognizing the gift that had been given to me, Jacob and Cephas and John—those reputed to be "pillars"—gave the right hand of partnership to me and to Barnabas, in order that we (should go) to the nations, and they to the circumcision."[166] The logical flow of this segment of Paul's sentence can be mapped thus:

Reason #1: "seeing that I was entrusted with the good news for the uncircumcised just as Peter was . . . for the circumcised,"

Supporting evidence for reason #1: "since the one who worked through Peter for the purpose of apostleship to the circumcised also worked in me for apostleship to the nations,"

Reason #2: "and recognizing the generous gift that had been given to me,"

Resulting action: "Jacob and Cephas and John . . . gave the right hand of partnership to me and to Barnabas, in order that we should go to the nations, and they to the circumcision."

The Jerusalem pillars' recognition of Paul and Barnabas as divinely called to the work of apostleship came on the basis of the evidence of their

---

164. See, for example, Longenecker, 53–54; Betz, 92; Martyn, 199; Dunn, 102–3.

165. Paul's opening, "on the contrary," refers more precisely to the course the pillars did *not* take, namely, piling on additional conditions to Paul's message and practice among gentile converts.

166. There is a great deal of elision in these verses, with the understood content being supplied in parentheses here.

missionary success.[167] Their account of their message and its fruits would have included testimony concerning the awakening of faith in Jesus among the gentiles, accompanied by the rather visible manifestations of the pouring out of God's Spirit upon those who trusted (see Gal 3:2–5). The similarities between what was happening in their gentile mission and in the Jewish mission spearheaded by Peter[168] constitute sufficient evidence for the pillars that the one God was indeed at work in both missions, extending the deliverance of his Son in both spheres, Jew and gentile (2:8).[169]

Thus the pillars could affirm that God had "entrusted" Paul with "the gospel for the uncircumcised" in the same way that God had entrusted Peter with "the gospel for the circumcised."[170] The fact that the words "circumcised" and "uncircumcised" can function as descriptors of different people groups, as if this is indeed the most fundamental differentiator, indicates the importance of this ritual as a marker of identity and social boundaries.[171] The expressions used are not meant to indicate two different gospels—something that the author of Gal 1:6–9 and 2 Cor 11:4 could hardly applaud—but rather to affirm that the Jerusalem pillars saw the proclamation and enfleshment of the one gospel being appropriately conducted among gentiles by Paul and

---

167. Paul stresses the importance of their acknowledgment, as opposed to their approval or authorization (Tolmie, *Persuading*, 79).

168. The precise function of the dative Πέτρῳ in the phrase "the One working Πέτρῳ," which must be the same as the function of ἐμοὶ in the parallel phrase that follows, is difficult to determine. Burton (94) suggests the category of advantage. It is tempting to treat it rather as location (as in God's sphere of operation, through which God was effective in the spread of the gospel) or even means (with Paul intentionally presenting himself and Peter as only, and as equally, the instruments of God's action).

Paul more customarily refers to his counterpart as Cephas (see Gal 1:18; 2:9, 11, 14; 1 Cor 1:12; 3:22; 9:5; 15:5). The use of "Peter" in 2:7–8 has suggested that Paul may be quoting official language pertinent to the agreement at this point (Betz, 96–98; Dunn, 105; Cullmann, *Peter*, 20). Against this possibility, Das (185) rightly draws attention to the impropriety of referring to the apostle as Peter (his Greek name) in a document written in Jerusalem, with Paul then referring to him as Cephas (his Aramaic name) throughout Galatians, a document written in the diaspora to an audience in Greek Galatia. There appears to be no underlying logic to Paul's choice of "Cephas" or "Peter" in a given instance.

169. Compare the arguments advanced in favor of a mission to the gentiles—specifically one not involving Torah observance—in Acts 11:3, 15–18; 15:12.

170. On the semantics and resonances of τὸ εὐαγγέλιον, see commentary on 1:6.

171. "Circumcision" (περιτομή) is used metonymically, the procedure for the group of people characterized by having undergone the procedure ("the circumcised," hence the Jews). "Uncircumcision" (ἀκροβυστία) is an instance of double metonymy. The word refers literally to the foreskin, thence figuratively for being in such a state as retains the foreskin ("uncircumcision"), thence for the group of people characterized by this state ("gentiles"; John Chrysostom, 17; Burton, 92–93; Matera, 76).

Barnabas and among Jews by Peter.[172] The restatement that follows in 2:8 underscores the emphasis on the audiences that would distinguish the two missions ("apostleship for the circumcision" alongside "[apostleship] to the nations"), reinforcing an understanding of the expression in 2:7 as "[the one] gospel *for* the circumcision" and "for the uncircumcision" (as opposed to "the gospel *of* [i.e., that preaches] circumcision" and "a different gospel *of* [i.e., that preaches] uncircumcision").

The second adverbial participial phrase that supplies a reason for the pillars' affirmation of Paul's ministry ("recognizing the gift given to me," 2:9) is essentially a paraphrase of the first one (2:7). Paul speaks of his commission to this apostolic ministry—his "call"—as an expression of God's favor, a "gift given" to him by God (see also Rom 1:5; 15:15–16; Eph 3:8), a privilege that has fallen to him in God's kindness.[173] The Jerusalem pillars recognize this divine favor operative in Paul's ministry by virtue, again, of the fruitfulness of Paul and E[...]ngle, Paul had spoken of God entrusting hi[...]"I trust, entrust" (*pisteuō*) and its associated [...]auline word "faith, reliability," *pistis*) were frequently invoked in the context of patronage and friendship relations, particularly to speak of one party entrusting another with some task or deposit, or with some request.[174] Here, the superior party (God) has entrusted the inferior party (Paul) with the performance of a service that is a facet of their relationship of reciprocity. But as Paul and his fellow apostles count it, even to be tasked with such a service by the One to whom they already owe everything is a gift, for it is a privilege even to be enabled to serve God in return.

Paul finally, and therefore in mildly climactic manner, names "those of repute" as "Jacob" (James, "the Lord's brother," 1:19), "Cephas" (or "Peter"), and "John." John is here no doubt the son of Zebedee (Mark 1:19–20; Luke 5:10), the brother of the James who was martyred early in the history of the movement upon the order of Herod Agrippa I (Acts 12:2), hence sometime between 41 and 44 CE. Peter and the two brothers, James and John, were remembered as having formed something of an inner circle during Jesus's earthly ministry (Mark 3:16–17; 14:33; Luke 8:51; 9:28). John continues to figure prominently alongside Peter in the opening chapters of Acts (see 3:1–4, 11; 4:13, 19; 8:14) before disappearing from that narrative.

---

172. Dunn, 106; Wright, *Pauline Perspectives*, 89; contra Schnelle, *Apostle Paul*, 128–29.

173. Paul is not speaking here of "grace" as the "forgiveness and redemption" that would be common to all Christ-followers (Longenecker, 56; Das, 189).

174. See BDAG 818. The late-first-century orator Dio Chrysostom devotes two orations to πίστις and ἀπιστία in such contexts (*Discourses* 73, 74). The perfect tense πεπίστευμαι is significant: God's entrusting of this gospel is a past action with ongoing effect, as God continues to entrust Paul with communicating this message and ordering proper responses to it.

Paul refers to these three men as those "who seemed to be" or "were reputed to be pillars." The image of the pillar, a common enough architectural feature in any urban setting in the Eastern Roman Empire, was frequently used of key figures supporting a social body of some kind. Hence, "sons" were the pillars of a household,[175] the patriarchs Abraham, Isaac, and Jacob were the pillars of the congregation of Israel,[176] Rabbi Johanan ben Zakkai was a pillar of the reconstituted Jewish Sanhedrin after the Jewish Revolt.[177] At this point, it is difficult to read 2:9, "those who *seemed to be* pillars," in any way other than with at least a hint of irony.[178] Since Paul will very shortly narrate the failure of one of these three men to walk in line with their agreement, at least in Paul's estimation, it is likely that Paul is expressing some reservation here about people who prove, most obviously in Peter's case (but also implied in the case of James, given the position taken by the "men from James"), "shaky" pillars at best.

The pillars offer Paul and Barnabas "the right hand of partnership,"[179] which indicates the more or less formal sealing of an agreement.[180] But what

---

175. Euripides, *Iphigenia in Tauris* 57.

176. Exod. Rab. 15.7.

177. B. Ber. 28b; 'Abot R. Nat. 25.1. See Burton, 96; Longenecker, 57; Aus, "Three Pillars." There is also the possibility that these three were identified as pillars in an eschatological sense, namely, that they would be "pillars" in the new temple in the new Jerusalem, or of the new community that was the firstfruits of the eschatological people of God (Barrett, "Paul and the 'Pillar' Apostles," 15–19; Dunn, 109).

178. Matera (77) rightly cautions against hearing Paul as being *overtly* sarcastic or ironic here, since the reputation of the pillars also upholds Paul's commission, since they originally gave it their recognition and support.

179. The adjective δεξιάς is used substantivally for "right hand," given "as a sign of friendship and trust" (BDAG 217).

180. Schlier, 79; Georgi, *Remembering the Poor*, 31; see also 1 Macc 6:58; Josephus, *Antiquities* 18.328–29. Francis Watson (*Paul, Judaism, and the Gentiles*, 53) seriously questions the accuracy of Paul's report of the agreement because "the presupposition of Paul's mission to the Gentiles was that the Jewish people as a whole had been hardened by God, so that preaching to them was useless," a presupposition that James, Peter, and John would hardly have accepted, "since they were still carrying on a mission to the Jews." Watson wrongly presupposes that Paul had already by this early date come to the conclusions that he articulates only much later in Rom 11:25. Watson further objects (53) that the pillars would never have "accepted the legitimacy of the principle of freedom from the law," since this "would have fatally undermined their own mission." This conclusion, too, is overdrawn. Paul was asking for the recognition of freedom from performing the Torah in regard to gentile converts and reports the pillars giving recognition only so far. This fact is in itself sufficient to explain the Antioch incident, where emissaries from James insist only that the *Jewish* Christians observe traditional dietary regulations (*kashrut*) more scrupulously. If Paul was holding any cards close to his tunic in his meeting with the pillars, it would be concerning his views on whether or not *Jewish*

exactly was agreed upon at this meeting, if anything beyond the recognition that they are united in a common mission, working for the same Lord and pulling together in the same direction? The emphatic differentiation of the two missions, "*we* unto the nations and *they* to the circumcision,"[181] clearly envisions some kind of division of labor as the focal point of the agreement—but what kind?

The division might have been made along geographic lines, with the province of Judea being the mission field of the pillars, and the territories beyond Judea being Paul's.[182] Alternatively, the division might have had the ethnicity of the people being evangelized in view, with Paul focusing on evangelizing gentiles, while Peter and the other Jewish Christian missionaries focused on taking the gospel to fellow Jews throughout the Mediterranean and Levant. Neither understanding aligns well with the postagreement practice of the parties concerned. Paul does avoid preaching in the territory of Judea, though he does not refrain from preaching the gospel to Jews throughout the diaspora: "To the Jews I became like a Jew, in order that I might win Jews; to those under the law, as someone who was himself under the law (even though I myself was not under the law) in order that I might win those under the law" (1 Cor 9:20). Was the "apostle to the gentiles" dipping into Peter's pond, or did he understand diaspora Jews not to be off limits? Peter is known to have evangelized throughout Greece and Rome, making inroads into Paul's well-established Corinthian mission (1 Cor 1:12; 3:22; 9:5), and James was in touch with Jewish Christians throughout the diaspora (e.g., in his letter). Peter and James clearly did not understand the agreement to limit them geographically, although they might both have concentrated their efforts on Jews in these lands.[183]

Christians needed to observe the Torah and on the direction in which he believed "the truth of the gospel" to be leading for a mixed church of Jews and gentiles. In this regard, Schnelle (*Apostle Paul*, 136–37) is probably mistaken when he asserts that Paul had not yet concluded that the Torah was binding neither on Jew or gentile and "secondary to the promise" at the time of his accord with the Jerusalem leaders, or else the latter could never have accepted Paul's message and mission: rather, Paul may only have remained discretely silent about it.

181. The pronouns ἡμεῖς and αὐτοί are emphatic, and the omission of any verbs makes the point that *is* expressed all the more heavily underscored, namely, the different spheres or targets of the missions. Paul continues to refer to "Jews" by metonymy, naming them by their distinguishing practice of circumcision. While Jews were indeed known throughout the Roman Empire for this practice, Paul may be foregrounding it throughout this section on account of its immediate relevance for the Galatians, who are being confronted with this practice by the rival teachers as if it were an appropriate facet of the "gospel for the nations" or "for the uncircumcision."

182. See Burton, 97–99; Matera, 77.

183. On this evidence, Betz (100), Longenecker (59), and Martyn (213) favor under-

It is possible that the agreement was rather loose, outlining the primary direction of each mission (so as to avoid rivalry in a given locale)[184] or the fundamental sphere of responsibility (or even advocacy) that would define each mission, rather than imposing limitations on either party.[185] It is also, sadly, quite possible that any agreed-upon division of labor dissolved in the wake of the Antioch incident. Paul clearly understood the actions and impact of the "men from James" and of Peter in that episode to constitute a betrayal of their agreement and thus perhaps a nullification of any agreed-upon limitations, such that Paul felt free to evangelize Jews throughout the diaspora and to build thereby his microcosms of the one body of Christ throughout his congregations, in which there would be "neither Jew nor Greek" (Gal 3:26–28). The issues that came to the fore in Antioch might also have given Peter and James fresh pause concerning the idea of two independent missions, particularly since Paul's mission would consistently seek to bring Jew and gentile together and blur the lines.

In theory, a Torah-observant mission to Jews and a Torah-free mission to gentiles could both be affirmed as genuine works of God, and the "right hand of partnership" extended on that basis. It is clear from the events that follow that, at the very least, the implications of this agreement for what should happen when Jews and gentiles came together in the church were not equally clear to all parties. What is especially strange is that the Antioch church was *already* a mixed congregation of Jewish and gentile believers, and this issue appears not to have been addressed in this private meeting, leaving the door open for the conflict that would soon arise.[186]

10 The closing verse in this paragraph, which finally completes the sentence begun in 2:6, connects with the close of 2:6 rather than the immediately preceding verse: "those of repute added nothing to me . . .—only that we should continue to remember the poor, which very thing I took pains to do."[187] "Remembering" here takes on the active sense of "making provision for" the poor, which is an important element of covenant obe-

---

standing the agreement to reflect a more ethnic division of audience. On the authenticity of the Letter of James, see deSilva, *Jewish Teachers*, 45–57.

184. Fung, 100.

185. Georgi, *Remembering the Poor*, 32; Dunn, 110–11.

186. Martyn, 222, who also insightfully observes that the very terms of the agreement—one mission to Jews, another to gentiles—were framed in such a way as to violate Paul's basic insight that, in Christ, there is no Jew or gentile (Gal 3:28).

187. This clause contrasts sharply with Acts 15, where several stipulations, some quite pertinent to the notion of gentile Christians making concessions to Jewish dietary scruples, are reported to have been added (see Acts 15:19–20, 28–29). Among other factors, this contrast weighs against an easy identification of the meeting reported in Gal 2:1–10 with the Jerusalem Conference as narrated in Acts 15. See Introduction.

dience (see esp. Deut 15:11; 24:10–22) and Second Temple period Jewish piety.[188]

Such a request on the part of the pillars, and such a response by Paul, would well suit the context of the visit narrated in Acts 11:28–30 if this private meeting occurred in connection with the delivery of famine relief funds collected in Antioch for the believers in Judea.[189] The pillars would be asking Paul and Barnabas to "keep on doing" what they had been doing,[190] and Paul could rightly assert to the Galatians that he had already demonstrated his eagerness to do this very thing before their request. The willingness of Paul and Barnabas to make care for the needy in the Judean churches a part of their ministry in the mixed congregations of Syrian Antioch and its environs appears already at this meeting to have been a valued sign of the unity of the two missions.[191] It would increasingly become a symbol of the essential unity of the church, as Paul goes on to make the collection of relief funds for Jerusalem a major focus of his evangelizing work after this meeting with the pillars (see Rom 15:25–31; 1 Cor 16:1–4; 2 Cor 8:1–9:15), determined to prove faithful to this agreement and thus to the vision of a single Christian movement.

At this juncture, however, two questions emerge: (1) Who are "the poor" for whom Paul was to continue to make provision through his ministry? (2) What connection exists between the pillars' request and the collection project that dominated Paul's later epistles?

Who, then, are "the poor"? Most likely, the pillars were asking Paul and Barnabas to continue to make provision for the economically challenged members of the Jerusalem church, though this request might have included underprivileged Christians throughout Judea and Galilee, who would have been closely associated with the Jerusalem church as the mother congregation. The portrait of the Jerusalem church in Acts, however stereotypical,

---

188. See Tob 1:3, 7–8; 2:2–3; 4:7–11; 12:8–9, 12–14; 14:2; Sir 4:10; 7:10, 32–35; 29:9–13; also deSilva, *The Apocrypha*, 60–62.

189. Fung, 103; Bruce, 126; Witherington, *Acts*, 371–74.

190. Longenecker (60) correctly observes that the present tense of the subjunctive μνημονεύωμεν ("that we should continue to remember") has the force of calling for an ongoing activity, which could include an activity that Paul and his team had already started. Paul and Barnabas are being asked to make "raising aid for the poor (in the Jerusalem church/ Judean churches)" an ongoing feature of their ministry among the gentiles. It seems doubtful, however, that "remembering the poor" means more than this, for example, that it enjoined caution upon Paul not to do anything in his own mission that would jeopardize the pillars' evangelistic efforts among Torah-observant Jews, as Longenecker (60) suggests further.

191. The verb ἐσπούδασα ("I took pains") is used here in the sense of being "especially conscientious in discharging an obligation" (BDAG 939). The use of the phrase αὐτὸ τοῦτο, which is both unnecessary and unusual with ὅ ("which very thing"), is emphatic.

suggests several ways in which the Jerusalem Christian community was positioned for economic hardship from the outset.

1. First, if the apostles' initial successes were among the great crowds of people who came to Jerusalem at the pilgrim festivals, those who remained with the fledgling movement after their conversion would have been living at some remove from their networks of support in their native countries and would therefore become dependent upon hospitality and charity from their new network of support.
2. Second, the early Christian community is presented not as a community of production that could sustain its own economic needs (unlike the community at Qumran, for example), but a community that continued to fund its focus on mission, study, and fellowship as its members voluntarily liquidated assets. This was not a plan for long-term financial stability.
3. From the start, it no doubt attracted, by its charitable practices, a good number of people who had been unable to support themselves.
4. Their plight was, according to Luke, seriously compounded by the famine of 46–48 CE, the presenting cause for the first collection project associated with the name of Paul (Acts 11:27–30; Gal 2:10).[192]
5. The Jerusalem church was subjected to serious disruption on account of the persecution of non-Christian Jews like Paul himself (if Acts is correct to locate his initial anti-Christian activity in that city) and local kings such as Agrippa I, the economic consequences of which had to be just as weighty as the social and, in some cases, physical consequences.

There is another possible interpretation of the term "poor," however, rooted especially in the prophetic texts of the Hebrew Bible. There, "the poor" could function as a synonym for "the pious," "the just," "the Holy Remnant."[193] The pillars, on this interpretation, used "the poor" as a term for the Jerusalem Christian community as a whole on the basis of their taking their post in the Holy City, refusing to relinquish it to unbelievers. They were committed to remaining as a vanguard awaiting the return of Jesus, the epicenter of which would surely (in their thinking) be Jerusalem, an event that would include the bringing in of the exiles and the nations to the messianic kingdom.[194] Thus "remembering the poor"—in the sense of collecting much-needed material

---

192. So Witherington, 145. Dunn (112), Das (193), Martyn (224–28), and the early church fathers (Longenecker, *Remember the Poor*, 159–76) understand the use of the term "poor" to be strictly economic.

193. See Zeph 3:9, 12; Isa 14:30, 32; Georgi, *Remembering the Poor*, 36–37.

194. Georgi, *Remembering the Poor*, 37.

aid (for all the reasons given above)—would also constitute an acknowledgment of the special eschatological status and identity of the Jewish Christian community in Jerusalem, while also symbolically uniting the universal Christian mission.[195]

As attractive as this alternative is, and while it might indeed reflect the Jerusalem pillars' own (irretrievable) perspective on their community, Paul himself appears to have understood the term only as a designation of material disadvantage. This understanding becomes especially apparent in Romans, when Paul speaks of going to Jerusalem to deliver the contributions made by his Achaian and Macedonian churches "for the poor among the saints who are in Jerusalem" (Rom 15:26). Paul does not identify "the poor" *with* the Jerusalem Christian community, but rather identifies them as a subset of the same.

What connection exists, then, between the pillars' request, made at this early meeting in Jerusalem, and the collection project that dominated Paul's later epistles? It seems most likely that the exchange between Paul and the pillars on this point planted firmly in Paul's mind the importance of producing a tangible sign of the investment of gentile Christians in the well-being of their Judean sisters and brothers. The collection of material aid from Paul's areas of ministry would signal both his own faithfulness to his agreement with the pillars (whether or not the pillars had been able to show faithfulness to match; see on 2:11–14), as well as God's continued empowerment and validation of Paul's apostolic work. If the famine relief brought by Paul and Barnabas was part of the evidence on the basis of which the pillars made this initial judgment about the duo (2:7–9), Paul would continue to bring such evidence before their eyes. Both of these ends served a greater end, namely, the affirmation of the unity of, and genuine partnership/fellowship of, the church made of Jewish and gentile Christians, the church built up by all the apostles, including Paul.[196]

This is not to say, however, that the collection that Paul anticipates delivering to Jerusalem as he writes Rom 15:27–29 is the end result of a single project that he has carried out without interruption since his return to Antioch from Jerusalem around 47 or 48 CE. Paul may have suffered a significant rift with the Antioch congregation in the wake of his confrontation with Peter (2:11–14), essentially necessitating his starting over in the fresh mission fields of Macedonia, Achaia, and Asia Minor.[197] While the churches in Galatia knew of Paul's collection project and had been invited by him to participate even before his writing of 1 Corinthians (see 1 Cor 16:1–4), it is not by any means clear that they chose to do so in the end (the conspicuous mention of

---

195. Georgi, *Remembering the Poor*, 42; less forcefully, Nickle, *Collection*, 60.
196. Nickle, *Collection*, 121–29.
197. Martyn, 222–28.

Macedonia and Achaia contributing in Rom 15:26 makes the silence about other regions conspicuous as well). Nevertheless, Gal 2:7–10 provides the foundation for understanding the importance of this project for Paul and his anxiety that it have its desired effect (Rom 15:30–32).

Leaving Jerusalem after this second visit, then, Paul had the impression that the questions swirling around his gentile mission were settled. He had indeed won a decisive victory over against those who challenged his mission insofar as the pillar apostles recognized Paul and Barnabas as apostolic colleagues and, furthermore, did not support the call for Titus's circumcision. The episode that would follow in Antioch (Gal 2:11–14), however, revealed that many questions remained unanswered—and that these, in turn, called even the most fundamental issues "settled" in Jerusalem into question anew.

The reverence in which Paul is held throughout the church naturally inspires emulation. When it comes to his calling and his relationship with the "apostles before him," however, it is essential also to acknowledge the distance that separates our own experience from his. Most Christians receive the gospel through human teachers in the context of Christian community, and they should acknowledge that source and live from that model, rather than from Paul's model of claiming direct revelation from God (Gal 1:12). God acts, no doubt, to confirm the gospel in the hearts of those who receive it, but they remain thoroughly dependent upon the church throughout the ages for their own reception of that gospel. With two millennia of Christian history behind us, the maverick "apostle" of today is far more likely to be self-pleasing and self-serving than God-pleasing and Christ-serving.

There is therefore all the more need for each Christian, especially each Christian leader, to do as Paul did, continually submitting his or her understanding of the gospel and vision for the church to the scrutiny of other leaders—preferably leaders from other denominations, who see more clearly other facets of the gospel than one's own tradition tends to see. This is not a denial of one's own conviction to have been called by God. It is, however, an acknowledgment in humility that discernment of the truth and of the Spirit belongs to the larger church, not to oneself (or even one's own denomination) alone. In this way, we will best ensure that our message aligns with the faith handed down once for all to the saints (Jude 3). This was the standard beneath which Paul even set his own authority (Gal 1:8–9). Once the apostolic gospel was proclaimed, it became the standard by which *all* Christian preachers were to be weighed and to which *all* preachers were accountable.

Many Christians worldwide face the hostility and pressure of watchdogs for the non-Christian traditions they have left behind. But Paul's example reminds us of the danger of taking on the role of watchdog for *our* tradition, in our case for our own particular brand of Christianity while regarding other brands as hostile competition. Again acknowledging the distance in circumstance and Christian history that separates us from Paul, it seems far more prudent to engage Christians who have come to conclusions about faith and practice different from our own in open, constructive conversation in which both sides hold up their views and practices to scrutiny in the Spirit, realizing that now we all see God's truth reflected as if in a distorted mirror and may see only a partial gospel ourselves (1 Cor 13:12). If Paul could say this about himself and his congregations, how much more should we adopt such a humble attitude in conversation with other Christians. The watchdog (and, in the extreme, the persecutor) stands at the pole opposite from humility.

While Paul's example indeed challenges us to be alert to when we or another Christian preacher or group has lost sight of the core contours on the gospel and begun to preach "another gospel," his encounters with the pillars in Jerusalem and, again, with Peter and their fellow Jewish Christians in Antioch challenge us to look for areas of agreement at the heart of our respective understandings of the gospel, visions for a transformed life, and calls to mission in our local context. Christian groups tracing their theological heritage to the major historic streams of Western Christianity have far more in common with each other than not, and the distinctive elements are less often in areas that one would call core than we tend to admit. United Methodists and Pentecostals have significantly different expectations for how the Spirit will manifest himself among the assembly of believers but would agree that the Spirit *is* at work and that it is essential to nurture and fall in line with that work. Lutherans and Catholics will have different nuances in their expression of doctrines such as justification and sanctification but will agree that God is reconciling us, along with the world, to himself in Christ and that God is at work within us and our churches to make us reflect more and more of his holiness and justice. Anglicans and Anabaptists will practice baptism differently but will agree on the transference of allegiances and the transformation of life from the old person to the new person that baptism represents and will strive after these same ends.

Christians of any one tradition have had a bad habit of stressing the practices and teachings that distinguish them from other Christian traditions or groups at the expense of articulating clearly and honoring appropriately the core beliefs, practices, and hope that they share with their sister churches that fall within the apostolic tradition. Why we do so is quite understandable: the differences, in the end, are what seem to justify our meeting in our own church building in our own denomination (or our "nondenomination") instead of merging our particular group's identity into the larger sea of Christian identity. But the ability of Peter, James, and John, on the one hand, and on the other, Paul and Barnabas to extend and grasp the right hand of fellowship challenges us all to look much more openly and generously at the beliefs, practices, goals, and hopes that are common between us and other Christians—lest we find that we too have run and continue to run in vain. It will enhance the witness of the *whole* church, which suffers as long as Christians of so many stripes give the appearance of an utter lack of unity and agreement as to the heart of the Christian revelation.

The agreement reached in Jerusalem ("they to the Jews, we to the gentiles") may suggest that intentional division of labor and outreach between Christian groups will advance *God's* agenda for the church better than our typical practice. The resources of the church as a whole are often duplicated and thereby wasted as individual churches try to reach out to the same groups of unbelievers and design their ministries to appeal to the same groups of believers. Often, this duplication is driven by a spirit of competition. The gifts and strengths of individual churches, and even individual denominations, are not being maximized for the growth of the body of Christ as one church replicates poorly what another church already does effectively. How much more could the church do to advance God's agenda if each church stopped looking upon other churches as competition and began looking upon them as partners in a common mission instead?

The agreement in Jerusalem also underscores once again what is perhaps one of the most constant themes of Scripture. "Remembering the poor" through acts of real, material support and care is legislated in Deuteronomy, promoted throughout the Prophets (e.g., as the kind of "fast" that God requires, Isa 58:3, 5–7), commended by Jesus as the way in which to lay up treasures in heaven (Luke 12:33; 18:22), and affirmed by his closest disciples as the heart of genuine religion and love for God (Jas 1:27; 2:15–17; 1 John 3:16–18). How a Christian encounters a poor sister or brother is the ultimate test of that Christian's commitment to love the neighbor as oneself. Christ's own example in this regard is stunning: he did not merely empathize with the poor; he *became* poor (2 Cor 8:9). Paul will later urge his converts to "work what is good toward all, and all the more toward the members of the household of faith" (Gal 6:10), challenging us, as we consider the needs of the global church and our own relative prosperity, to enact the biblical vision for the people of God, according to which no one among this people is needy (Acts 4:32–35; Deut 15:4–11).

D. THE CONFRONTATION IN ANTIOCH (2:11–14)

[11] *But when Cephas[a] came into Antioch, I opposed him to his face because he stood condemned. [12] For before certain people came[b] from Jacob, he used to eat with the gentiles. But when they came, he started pulling back and separating himself out of fear of those of the circumcision. [13] And the rest of the Jews were also[c] carried away with him in this charade, with the result that even Barnabas*

was carried away by their display of play-acting. [14] *But when I saw that they were not walking in a straight line toward the truth of the good news, I said to Cephas*[d] *in front of everybody: "If you, though being a Jew, live in the manner of the gentiles and not in the manner of the Jews, how can you pressure the gentiles to take up the Jewish way of life?"*

a. The variant Πέτρος appears frequently, particularly in later witnesses (D F G 𝔐), but this reading is readily explained by the greater familiarity of scribes and their readers with that designation for "the Rock" (see also similar variation in 1:18; 2:9).

b. The variant singular form τινα appears in 𝔓[46] it[d, g, r] and Irenaeus; the singular ἦλθεν replaces ἦλθον here in 𝔓[46] ℵ B D* F G it[d, g] Irenaeus. Thus 𝔓[46] reads "Before a certain person came from James, . . . but when he came. . . ." Uncials ℵ and B support 𝔓[46] in regard, at least, to the singular "when he came" in the second half of the verse. Did one person, or did a group of persons, come to Antioch from James? An original τινα . . . ἦλθεν may have been corrupted to τινας . . . ἦλθον as a harmonization of the situation in Antioch to the situation in Galatia, where the interlopers are almost always described in the plural (5:10 being the singular exception). Alternatively, an original ἦλθον ("they came") may have been corrupted to ἦλθεν ("he came") by assimilation to the sheer number of third singular verbs in its context (συνήσθιεν, ὑπέστελλεν, ἀφώριζεν) and to the opening of the previous verse ("Οτε δὲ ἦλθεν). This early error would have then led a very few scribes to assimilate the indefinite pronoun τινας to the verb they found in the next clause (ἦλθεν, hence τινα; Metzger, *Textual Commentary*, 523). The latter explanation seems the more likely, all the more as we observe no tendency in the manuscript tradition to adapt the singular referent to the intruder into Galatia in 5:10 to the more common references to intruders in the plural throughout the letter, suggesting that we should not explain the scribal corruptions here to result from changing an original singular referent to a visitor to Antioch to a plural out of an alleged desire for conformity. So also Longenecker, 63; against Comfort, *Text and Translation Commentary*, 561–62.

Robinson ("Circumcision of Titus," 40–42) proposed the novel though unconvincing thesis that the variant τινα (for τινας) in 𝔓[46] was the original reading, but that it represented a neuter accusative plural rather than a masculine accusative singular and referred to the apostolic decrees; Peter accepted them after they had been communicated to him in Antioch (why was he not present in Jerusalem when they were formulated?), and Paul regarded Peter's withdrawal (rightly) as Peter compelling the gentiles (knowingly) to accept the decrees.

c. 𝔓[46] and B, along with several other witnesses, omit the adverbial καὶ here; ℵ A C D F G H Ψ include it. The verse reads better with the omission, since it potentially detracts from the emphatic force of the καὶ preceding Barnabas's name and underscoring his defection. Nevertheless, the weight of external evidence is against omission, and, as a stylistic improvement, so is transcriptional probability. See also Longenecker, 63; Fee, 75.

d. Once again the secondary variant Πέτρῳ emerges, particularly in later witnesses (D F G 𝔐), replacing the Aramaic name with the more familiar Greek name (see also on 1:18; 2:9, 11).

Paul's narration has been punctuated by the words "then" (1:18, 21; 2:1) and "but when" (1:15; 2:11). The latter marks a turning point in the narration. The first one was for the better, when Paul encountered the glorified Jesus and was transformed from persecutor to proclaimer. The second one is for the worse, with the accord reached in 2:1–10 jeopardized by subsequent events in Antioch, culminating in Paul's public confrontation of Peter for betraying God's vision for Christian community. The agreement struck in Gal 2:7–10 clearly left room for misunderstanding and conflict. Apparently the question of table fellowship between Jewish Christians and gentile Christians did not come up, to be addressed by all parties face to face, as the sequel in 2:11–14 shows.[198] Each party might have had assumptions about what would be the practice in a mixed congregation, but the incompatibility of these assumptions emerged only later in a tense confrontation.

It is likely that Paul is not the first person to tell the Galatians about this incident, but he is rather put in the position of explaining himself. He would have gained little by being the first person to bring up the fact that James disapproved of a central practice in his congregation, that Peter also withdrew his support and fell in line with James's recommendations, and that his own coworker and most trusted friend had followed suit. It would, however, have served the rival teachers' agenda quite well to point out how the pillars had disapproved of the practice Paul had been nurturing and had set things right in Antioch, even as they were now doing in Galatia.[199] They could have used the episode to demonstrate that the Jerusalem pillars came to understand that gentiles who trusted in Jesus remained, in fact, gentiles nevertheless. If the latter truly wished to become part of the historic people of God and heirs to the promises, and if they had any concern about the unity of the church, they would need to resolve their ambiguous status by adopting the Jewish way of life.

The supposition that his rivals introduced this episode would well explain how Paul has crafted the narrative up to this point. The affirmation and "right hand of partnership" extended by the pillars (2:7–10), together with the pillars' rejection of the demand that Titus, the Greek Christian, be circumcised (2:3), forms the proper backdrop for interpreting what "really" happened in Antioch. According to Paul, James reneged on the agreement, even though he had been convinced by all necessary proofs that God was at work in the mission of Paul and Barnabas; Peter had been cowed into towing the line; even Barnabas betrayed his inner convictions about the place of the gentiles in the one body for the sake of appeasing James (through his repre-

---

198. Robinson, "Circumcision of Titus," 27; Schnelle, *Apostle Paul*, 132–33. There are too many problems with the view that the Antioch incident preceded the conference and agreement of 2:1–10, particularly the question of how Peter could "stand condemned" prior to such an agreement and the lack of any sign of temporal regression in Paul's unfolding sequence (Das, 204; Tolmie, *Persuading*, 83–84; against Lüdemann, *Paul, Apostle to the Gentiles*, 75–77).

199. Dunn, 116; Bligh, 175.

sentatives); and the rest of the Jewish Christians could not help but follow suit. Only Paul had the courage of his convictions, standing strongest for the truth of the gospel because standing most alone. In this way, Paul turns a narrative that demonstrates the Jerusalem pillars' reservations concerning his churches' practice into a narrative that demonstrates Paul's absolute and unshakable reliability where "the truth of the gospel" is concerned.

11–12 The new scene is set quickly, with its denouement announced at the outset: "But when Cephas came into Antioch, I opposed him to his face because he stood condemned. For before certain people came from Jacob, he used to eat with the gentiles.[200] But when they came, he started pulling back and separating himself out of fear of those of the circumcision." Before presenting any details of Peter's visit, Paul affirms that he publically challenged Peter's behavior,[201] because Peter had violated the "truth of the gospel." This wording sounds like an admission of something the Galatians have already heard from other mouths, though Paul will explain what led to this result quite differently. Paul gives no indication of Peter's purposes in visiting, being interested only in Peter's behavior in Antioch before and after the arrival of "some people from James."

When Peter came to Antioch, he found Christians of Jewish and gentile backgrounds worshiping together and expressing their unity by taking their meals together. This picture accords with Luke's account of the mission to Jews and Greeks, which seems to have been distinctive to Syrian Antioch (Acts 11:19–20).[202] Peter appears to have understood that such an arrangement, though in violation of Jewish sensibilities regarding unguarded or overly close association with gentiles, was perfectly in keeping with the purity of the new people God had formed from Jews and gentiles. Indeed, he may have been prepared for this situation himself by his previous experience with the centurion Cornelius and his household in Caesarea (Acts 10:1–11:18), though this history would make his subsequent change in behavior all the more disappointing. Peter therefore joined freely in the practice of the Antiochene church, eating alongside fellow believers in Christ without regard for their ethnicity.[203]

From Paul's point of view, the "truth of the gospel" (Gal 2:14)—the "one body" fashioned by God out of Jew and gentile, slave and free, male and female, all of whom are equally acceptable to God on the basis of Jesus's death

---

200. In the Greek, "with the gentiles" is placed in an emphatic (fronted) position.

201. The idiom ἀνθίστημι κατὰ πρόσωπον carries a sense of confrontation, with the prepositional phrase highlighting the direct manner of the confrontation (cf. "I got in his face"). See LN 83.38; BDAG 888; Tolmie, *Persuading*, 84.

202. Haenchen, *Acts*, 609; Fung, 107.

203. Paul's use of the imperfect tense (συνήσθιεν, "he used to eat together with," 2:12) indicates that Peter adopted this practice for some time.

(2:15–21; 3:26–28)—was being lived out here as Peter, Paul, Barnabas, Jewish Christians, and gentile Christians all shared the common life of the Spirit and had fellowship at table (most especially the Lord's Table, in the celebration of the Lord's Supper, which probably happened in the context of a fellowship meal) as one people, one body. This is the "truth of the gospel" that had been jeopardized by the Jewish Christians (the "false brothers") who wanted to see gentile Christians circumcised and adopt Jewish practices in 2:3–5. This is the "truth of the gospel" that Peter will himself shortly violate as he draws back from this practice to honor, once again, the lines of purity that place gentiles on the outside rather than honoring the new lines of purity drawn by the Holy Spirit poured out on gentile Christian alongside Jewish Christians.[204] Peter thus "stood condemned" even in regard to his own inner convictions (Paul will argue), given his previous welcome of gentile Christians at table.[205]

The catalyst for Peter's change in practice is the arrival of "some people from Jacob (James)" at Antioch. It seems likeliest that these people legitimately represented James, or else Peter would not have been so impressed and Paul would not have admitted a connection between these unwelcome emissaries and the titular head of the Jerusalem church.[206] Paul does not indicate the purpose of their visit, but only the effects, from which we can deduce the position they represented, if not their activity. Paul does not say whether they applied pressure to Peter or confronted him about his practice, or whether their mere presence recalled Peter to a stricter practice where interaction with gentiles was concerned. They clearly stood for the strict observance of boundaries between Jew and non-Jew; they, like James himself, would have regarded the law of Moses in all its particulars as fully binding on Jews, whether or not they were "in Christ."

James and like-minded Jewish Christians were probably content to endorse Paul's mission to the gentiles without the requirement of circumcision. Any converts remained, however, "gentiles" first.[207] Paul remembers his response to Peter on this occasion, and he begins by addressing this very issue: are we "Jews" and "gentiles" first, if we all have come to recognize

---

204. See further deSilva, *Honor*, 280, 283–89.

205. The details that follow are presented as the behavioral evidence (γάρ, 2:12) for Paul's claim in verse 11 that Peter "stood condemned."

206. Matera, 89; Painter, *Just James*, 67–73; Das, 206; Tolmie, *Persuading*, 84–85.

207. Schnelle, *Apostle Paul*, 135. See John Painter, *Just James*, 74–77, on the spectrum of views possibly attested within the early church on the question of circumcision and the interaction of Jewish Christians and gentile Christians. James did not represent the most conservative viewpoint on these questions (against Schnelle, *Apostle Paul*, 123), though he was clearly more conservative than Peter. The rival teachers in Galatia would have fallen to the right of James, alongside those who objected that "it is necessary to circumcise [the gentile believers] and to teach them to observe the law of Moses" (Acts 15:5).

that, without trust in Jesus and what Jesus's death has secured for us, none of us will be brought in line with God's righteousness (2:15–16)? The people from James would have expected to find the Christian Jews maintaining their scrupulous practice of tending the hedge between Jew and gentile in their everyday interactions, which is to say, honoring God's command to the Jew to "be distinct, as I the Lord am distinct."[208] They would not have approved of Peter's practice of eating with gentiles, even if they were gentile *Christians*. The question that Peter's Jewish Christian colleagues asked of him after the Cornelius episode would have been a relevant question in Antioch as well: "Why did you go to uncircumcised people and eat with them?" (Acts 11:3).

Unlike the Peter we find in Acts, however, the Peter Paul knew did not offer a vigorous defense of his practice. Instead, Peter yielded to their pressure, however this was exerted, to return to a more respectable way of life for an "apostle to the circumcision": he drew back from eating with the gentile Christians (see excursus "Eating with Gentiles" on pp. 198–203).[209]

Paul attributes this change in behavior to Peter's "fear," though the verb can also mean "show deep regard for."[210] How one translates this word will determine whether Paul is accusing Peter of outright cowardice (as Paul accuses the rival teachers in 6:12, and denies in his own case in 5:11; 6:17) or people-pleasing (as Paul accuses the rival teachers in 6:13, and denies in his own case in 1:10). The object of Peter's fear (or regard) is "those of the circumcision," Paul once again identifying a group by its distinctive practice of body modification. It is more difficult here to discern whom Paul has in mind. "Those of the circumcision" would logically include these Jewish-Christian colleagues from Jerusalem, as well as the larger group whom they represent (including, most significantly, James himself).[211] Peter might well have been motivated also by how his practice would look in the eyes of his primary mission field, namely, non-Christian Jews throughout the Mediterranean (beginning there in Syrian Antioch), realizing that his looseness of practice in regard to covenant-prescribed boundaries, however well justified from an inner-Christian point of view, might become a stumbling block to his mission.[212] It is also plausible that the people from James had impressed upon

---

208. More traditionally, "Be holy, for I the LORD am holy" (Lev 11:44, 45; 19:2). On the replication and reflection of God's holiness in the activity of God's holy people, see deSilva, *Honor*, 269–74.

209. Jervis, 62–63; Das, 208. The imperfect tense of the verbs ὑπέστελλεν and ἀφώριζεν suggests a gradual move toward what was to become a new pattern of behavior. The latter verb has the sense of "separate to avoid contact" (BDAG 158).

210. See BDAG 1060, 1061.

211. Burton, 107.

212. Martyn, 242; Das, 208; Tolmie, *Persuading*, 86. This scenario would make Paul's

Peter the importance of Jewish Christians showing themselves to be true to the covenant and respectful of the boundaries of the covenant people so that harassment of the Christian movement by non-Christian Jews, zealous for the covenant, would abate rather than grow more acute.[213] Paul will later explicitly name the avoidance of such harassment as a primary motivation behind the rival teachers' activities (6:12), increasing the plausibility of regarding this as a more general consideration behind questions of the Jew-gentile boundary within the Christian movement.

Fear of any human object, however, is not a legitimate motivation in Paul's eyes. From Paul's point of view, fear kept Peter from continuing to walk in line with what Peter himself knew to be true about Jews and gentiles "in Christ," namely, that they were all cleansed by faith in Jesus and by reception of the Holy Spirit. From Peter's point of view, however, he was protecting the Jewish mission and even the unity of the larger Christian movement by yielding to the *visitors'* interpretation of the implications of the earlier Jerusalem agreement for Jewish Christians.[214] What Paul called fear, Peter might have called "not making an issue out of it," not risking alienation from his Jerusalem colleagues and Jewish mission field or the splintering of the movement.

EXCURSUS: EATING WITH GENTILES

Two related questions need to be considered at greater length in regard to the situation in Antioch: What did "eating with gentiles" look like? And why would "people from James" take issue with such practices?

As we read Gal 2:11–14, it might be tempting to imagine the situation unfolding in the setting most familiar to modern Christians in the West—a fellowship hall. Before the people from James arrive, Peter, Barnabas, the Jewish Christians, and the gentile Christians sit at whatever tables they might wish and start to pass the plates of food around. After the people from James arrive, there are two rows of tables, one for Jewish Christians and one for gentile Christians, with Paul ranting in the middle.

All the evidence, however, suggests that Christian groups met in private homes rather than public buildings, and often would have met in a number of different homes in the same city. We might better imagine that, prior to

---

choice of the word "fearing" a highly tendentious way to present Peter's "regard for" his more particular missionary audience.

213. Jewett, *Anthropological Terms*, 340–41; Bruce, 130–31; Witherington, 154–56; Schreiner, 143–44.

214. Longenecker, 74; Fung, 108.

the arrival of the people from James, Peter—a visiting guest of honor—went freely among all the house churches, whether the host was a Jew or a gentile, participating fully in all facets of the community's common life (recitation of and teaching on Scripture, prayer, worship, and fellowship meal, probably with the remembrance of the Lord's Supper), even as all Christians in Antioch felt free to do.[215] After the arrival of the people from James, Peter still goes to the house church meetings in gentile homes, but he excuses himself (together with his guests from Jerusalem) before the meal, whereas he does not leave a Jewish home until the meal is concluded. Other Jewish Christians follow suit, until it becomes painfully obvious that the Jews are once more not eating in the homes of gentiles. The language Paul uses to describe Peter's change of practice suggests that it happened over time, such that it was difficult to notice at first but became increasingly apparent, and all the more as other Jewish Christians in Antioch caught on and followed suit en masse.

Perhaps the situation devolved further. Tired of making excuses or enduring the social awkwardness, Peter (followed by the other Jewish Christians) stops going to the house church meetings in the gentile hosts' homes altogether, holding more frequent meetings in the homes of Jewish Christian householders, with which his Jerusalem guests are more comfortable anyway. If gentile Christians continue to attend such meetings in Jewish homes, the necessary precautions (meaning, mutual reminders of identity and boundaries) are taken.[216] The people from James are satisfied. At some point, Paul still stands up in the middle and rants.[217]

---

215. Dunn (121) identifies as a principal problem Peter's (and perhaps the other Jewish Christians') eating in the homes of gentile Christians without taking appropriate precautions. By being careful to remain *hosts* to gentiles, Jewish Christians could ensure that everything about the meal could be conducted according to Jewish house rules.

216. For example, rabbinic texts instruct Jews to set out personal flagons of wine for themselves and their gentile guests and to set their own flagons on side tables so that, should the gentile pour out a libation to his or her gods, the Jews at the table would not be contaminated by idolatry (Tomson, *Paul and the Jewish Law*, 230–32). The way food and drink was managed would always—and intentionally—remind each party that the other was, indeed, "other." Such rulings provide evidence of table fellowship between Jews and gentiles as an actual practice, though not all Jews approved of the practice, no matter what precautions were taken.

217. Also worthy of consideration is Nanos's hypothesis ("What Was at Stake?," 301–2). What was problematic in Antioch was the way the gentiles at the table were being regarded—not as pagan guests at the table, not as proselytes-in-process, but as full members of the people of God along with the Jews at the table, despite their failure to join the historic people of God by the historic means (i.e., circumcision). Peter and the other Jewish believers withdraw from eating with the gentile believers rather than choosing *either* to continue to eat with them in such a way that reasserted their status as (merely) guests *or* to urge them, contrary to the gospel they had hitherto advocated, to become proselytes by means of cir-

The situation outlined above would not mean that a Jewish Christian would be involved in overt violations of Torah's dietary laws. It is unlikely that eating at the homes of gentile Christian hosts meant that pork and shellfish would have been on the table.[218] Gentiles, especially those who had previously been adherents of the synagogue, knew enough about Jewish sensibilities concerning diet and, in a spirit of friendship and hospitality, would have sought to avoid the obvious forbidden foods.[219] Jewish Christians could educate their gentile hosts about the full lists (e.g., Lev 11; Deut 14), as well as the requirements for the slaughtering and butchering of the animals, or gentile hosts could simply purchase the groceries in Jewish markets, though perhaps one could never be entirely sure that one's gentile sister or brother would observe all the necessary precautions. Within the Christian movement, there would likely not be the danger of the Jewish table partner being contaminated by the gentile's idolatry, since that was one of the first and most necessary things for the gentile to leave behind (1 Thess 1:9–10), though some old habits connected therewith died hard in some settings (see 1 Cor 8:1–13; 10:14–33; Rev 2:14–15, 20), and perhaps one could never be entirely sure what one's gentile sisters and brothers did in secret.

Despite the fact, however, that some Jews who considered themselves entirely Torah-observant enjoyed host-guest relations with gentiles, even those who were themselves idolaters, there were strong currents against table fellowship with gentiles *tout court*.[220] In the book of Jubilees, an expansive paraphrase of Gen 1–Exod 14 written in Judea or its environs by the second century BCE and regarded as authoritative at least within the Qumran community, Isaac instructs Jacob: "Keep yourself separate from the nations, and do not eat with them; and do not imitate their rites, nor associate yourself with them; for their rites are unclean and all their practices polluted, an abomination and unclean. They offer sacrifices to the dead and worship

---

cumcision. Their withdrawal was not meant to be an admission that the gentiles are unclean or unworthy of table fellowship; it was an attempt to avoid the issue until James's emissaries left. Paul objects to withdrawal because what was called for was rather an affirmation of the gentile believers' full status in the people of God. The latter are indeed left "shamed for failing to properly assess who they are—indeed, for having believed what they had been taught by these Jewish Christ-believers about the meaning of the gospel of Christ. . . . Logically, they are thus 'compelled to Judaize' to reduce this dissonance," that is, to restore their place in the people of God (Nanos, "What Was at Stake?," 317).

218. Sanders, *Jewish Law*, 282; Das, 217; Tomson, *Jewish Law*, 228; Nanos, "What Was at Stake?," 301.

219. Das, 218. On gentiles attracted to the synagogue in Syrian Antioch, see Josephus, *War* 7.45. Dunn (121) points out that gentiles seemed willing to adapt at least to some measure in order to enjoy "social intercourse including guest friendship" with Jews.

220. See deSilva, *Apocrypha*, 96–100; Tomson, *Jewish Law*, 233–36.

demons, and they eat among the graves" (22:16–17, APOT). Strict avoidance of table fellowship was to serve both as a symbol of, and as an effective hedge against relaxing, Jewish rejection of gentile practice, as well as protection from contamination from the gentiles' overwhelming pollution (e.g., their ritual uncleanness through corpse defilement).[221]

Jews are known to keep separate in regard to foods and eating, to "sit apart at meals," arousing anti-Jewish prejudices among non-Jews.[222] The Hellenistic Jewish Letter of Aristeas, written perhaps late in the second century BCE in Alexandria,[223] explains the dietary restrictions of the Jewish law as a work of divine social engineering to keep Jews, who have true knowledge of God, from being corrupted by the gentiles' ignorance of God through too close and intimate association.

> All human beings except [the Jews] believe in the existence of many gods, though they themselves are much more powerful than the things that they worship to no purpose. They make statues of stone and wood . . . and worship them, though they have sufficient proof to know that they have no feeling. . . . Therefore our Lawgiver, a wise person and given special endowments by God to understand all things . . . created a fence around us of impregnable barricades and iron walls, so that we might not mingle at all with people of other nations, remaining pure in body and soul, free from all false thinking, worshiping the one Almighty God above the whole creation. (134–35, 139)

Restrictions on social interaction between Jews and gentiles is thus understood to be the goal of a great deal of the Mosaic legislation, a secondary goal that serves, in turn, the primary goal of assisting Israel to maintain its distinctive views of God and practice of worship and a moral life. The images

---

221. In the paragraph that follows, Abraham will also caution Jacob against intermarriage for all the same reasons (Jub. 22.20–23). Klawans (*Impurity and Sin*, 134) argues that the idea of the ritual impurity of gentiles and their territories is a development from the Tannaitic period, but Jub. 22.16–17 shows the idea of the inherent ritual impurity of *gentiles* themselves, if not their lands, to be quite old. And even if gentile Christ-followers ceased to perform idolatrous rites, how strenuously would they avoid pollution from their families, neighbors, and associates who continued to practice such abomination?

222. See 3 Macc 3:3–4; the quotation here is from Tacitus, *Histories* 5. 5.1–2. Diodorus Siculus (*History* 34/35.1.1; 40.3.4) remarks that this practice contributes to the Jews' "unsocial and intolerant way of life."

223. Internal indications of a provenance within the Alexandrian Jewish community include the interest in the origin of the Septuagint in that city and the location of the explicated narrator in Alexandria, even in the court of Ptolemy II Philadelphus. See further Wright, *Aristeas*, 17–20.

of "walls," "palisades," and "hedges," moreover, suggest *radical* limitation of social intercourse as the goal of the Torah. It is noteworthy that, during the seven-day feast that Ptolemy gives for his visiting guests, he sits at his own table and the Jewish scholars at their own tables, so that while they are eating concurrently, they are not eating together.[224] Joseph observes similar boundaries in the romance Joseph and Aseneth: the servants "set a table before him by itself, because Joseph never ate with the Egyptians, for this was an abomination to him."[225] In the Greek retelling of the book of Esther, the heroine professes before God in prayer, "I, your servant, did not dine at Haman's table. Nor did I honor the king's banquet or drink wine that had been offered to the gods" (Add Esth C, 28). Examples could be multiplied.[226]

A major New Testament narrative corroborates the picture of a sizable number of Jews in the ancient world regarding the possibility of table fellowship with gentiles as, simply, off the table. In Acts 10–11, we read of God preparing Peter for an encounter with the gentile Cornelius and his household, the encounter itself, and Peter's defense of the encounter when he returns to Jerusalem. The author presents it as general knowledge "that it is unlawful for a Jew to associate with or to visit a gentile" (Acts 10:28). Peter requires a triple dream-vision on the subject to come to the conclusion that, contrary to this general knowledge (seen from the Jewish perspective), he "should not call anyone profane or unclean" (10:28). The fact that it comes as such a surprise to the Jewish believers who accompany Peter to Cornelius's house that "the gift of the Holy Spirit had been poured out even on the gentiles" points again to their fundamental assessment of the gentile as unclean and thus not a fit receptacle for God's "holy" Spirit. This manifestation of God's acceptance overturns the knowledge with which everyone began the episode, for Cornelius invites Peter to stay in his home for several days and, as the sequel shows, Peter accepts (10:48). When Peter returns to Jerusalem, the circumcised believers[227] challenged his actions: "You went to men having a foreskin and ate with them!" (11:3). Once again, the presupposition is clear: this is not done!

While more open positions on this issue were clearly taken and safeguards developed to allow commensality, the cumulative impression of these texts cannot be ignored. There must have been a significant number of Jews who simply *did not* eat with gentiles. The ultimate warrant for this avoidance

---

224. Esler, 115.

225. Jos. Asen. 7.1 (OTP). This text uses the same verb to speak of habitual (non)eating, συνήσθιε, as is found in Gal 2:12.

226. See, for example, Dan 1:8–16; Tob 1:10–13; Jdt 10:5; 12:1–20.

227. The complaining group is identified as οἱ ἐκ περιτομῆς here, as also in Gal 2:12 (τοὺς ἐκ περιτομῆς).

is to be found in a strict interpretation of Lev 20:22–26: "I am the LORD your God, who set you apart from the peoples [LXX, nations]. . . . You will be holy to me, for I the LORD am holy, and I have set you apart from the other peoples [LXX, nations] to belong to me" (Lev 20:24, 26).

The "people from James" likely shared this conviction. Even the more liberal among them would know that many of their coreligionists held to this conviction. For the sake, at the very least, of the mission to the whole Jewish people, it was necessary for Jewish Christians—and all the more its leaders—to be seen to be strictly concerned with divinely ordained boundaries. There are good reasons to believe that the people from James themselves also regarded those boundaries as divinely ordained and to be observed for the sake of lining up with God's ordering of things.

---

13 Peter's withdrawal from the common table appears to have stung the conscience of the Antiochene Jewish Christians, who then all felt the need to follow Peter's example, giving in to the pressure to eat separately from the gentile converts: "And the rest of the Jews were also carried away with him in this charade, with the result that even Barnabas was carried away by their display of play-acting." Since the celebration of the Lord's Supper involved eating, it is likely that this separation was observed also in connection with this rite.[228] In that context, the reassertion of Jewish distinctiveness would make an especially poignant statement about the nature of the church of Jews and gentiles: "We who are Jews by birth are still distinct from you gentile sinners."

Paul refers to this change of practice among the Antiochene Jewish Christians as "putting on a show," a pragmatic "charade."[229] In their hearts, Paul asserts, none of them really believed that the gentile Christians were still unclean; they were just unwilling to force the issue upon the representatives from the Jerusalem church by making such a forceful statement of their real convictions that "walking in line with the truth of the gospel"—and the affirmation of their gentile sisters and brothers—would have required.[230]

---

228. Fee, 74.

229. Betz, 108; Hays, "Letter to the Galatians," 234; Williams, 58; Witherington, 156; Nanos, *Mystery*, 354.

230. Peter, Barnabas, and the others *may* have actually found the arguments of the people from James convincing (e.g., Jews should still live by the terms of the covenant that God made with the Jewish people; missionaries to Jews should not put such obvious stumbling blocks in the way of the unreached people for whom they are primarily responsible; if anyone is to adapt for the sake of table fellowship, it should be the gentiles, who have a history of being willing to do so in order to enjoy some share in the spiritual heritage of Israel). Paul's

The Greek words used here have given English speakers the loanwords "hypocrite" and "hypocrisy," but the original Greek terms were more at home in the theater.[231] Epictetus, for example, speaks of the gentile who takes on some Jewish practices but does not go all the way as "only acting the part" (*Discourses* 2.9.20). The word group figures prominently in a particular scene in the martyrdom of the aged priest Eleazar, recounted in 2 Macc 6:18–31 and 4 Macc 5:1–6:30. Eleazar is the first to be given the choice by Antiochus IV: eat a mouthful of the meat from a pig offered in sacrifice as a symbol of renouncing Jewish particularism, or be subjected to torture to the point of death. After a protracted beating, Eleazar is given a respite to reconsider his refusal. Some people of long acquaintance come to him and propose to bring him some kosher meat that he can eat, pretending that it is the pork, and thus save his life (2 Macc 6:21). He responds: "Acting out such a role [ὑποκριθῆναι] is not worthy of our old age" (6:24); he will not by such a "charade [ὑπόκρισιν]" (6:25) encourage others toward impiety. Peter in Antioch emerges as a sort of anti-Eleazar here, acting out a role to avoid painful but necessary confrontation. His charade draws others in ("the rest of the Jews") to follow his example, with the result that "even Barnabas"[232] was caught up in their drama.[233]

14 It is from this perspective that Paul confronts Peter and, in his person as their representative and leader, the other Jewish Christians as well: "But when I saw that they were not walking in a straight line toward the truth of the good news, I said to Cephas in front of everybody: 'If you, though being a Jew, live in the manner of the gentiles and not in the manner of the Jews, how can you pressure the gentiles to take up the Jewish way of life?'" In stark contrast to Barnabas, the other Jewish Christians, and Peter himself, Paul responds very differently to the charade and its impetus. He uses a striking fig-

---

perspective is that they are betraying their deeper convictions; we remain ignorant of their motives or understanding as they would give them expression (Dunn, 125–26).

231. BDAG 1038, s.v. ὑπόκρισις.

232. The adverbial καί ("even") emphasizes the following action as particularly noteworthy (in a negative way). Robertson (*Barnabas vs. Paul*, 87) aptly observes that "Paul's words, 'even Barnabas,' are perhaps some of the saddest in all the New Testament" (so also Dunn, 126; Witherington, 157). Paul's friend, mentor, partner, and fellow-champion of the gentile mission "turns his back on the very folk he once welcomed. . . . With those words, 'even Barnabas,' we hear the anguish of a disillusioned friend and mark the beginning of the end of a partnership in ministry." See Acts 9:26–28; 11:25–30; 13:2–14:26. Later references to Barnabas in 1 Cor 9:6 and Col 4:10 give some hope that the breach was not permanent (Dunn, 89).

233. The dative τῇ ὑποκρίσει may express association or instrument here. If the former, Barnabas went along with, and joined in, the others' charade; if the latter, he was led astray by the same (BDAG 965, where the latter is preferred; so also Dunn, 126; Das, 211).

ure to speak of his fellow Jewish Christians' change of course, indicting them for "not walking straight toward the truth of the gospel." Jewish authors are accustomed to speaking of conduct as "walking" (see commentary on 5:16); here Paul speaks of a destination toward which they *ought* always to be walking, but from which they have now turned away—"the truth of the gospel."[234]

The gospel casts a vision toward which Christians-in-community are to be walking and which they are thereby to be realizing. In that vision, Jews and gentiles are being re-created together by the work of the Spirit within them and in their midst. They are coming alive to God as Christ himself comes alive within each one of them, even as each has been submerged into Christ in baptism. They are becoming "a new creation" (6:15; see also 2 Cor 5:17) in which the divisions and dichotomies that belong to the present evil age no longer have value or prescriptive force (Gal 3:26–28). The deity formerly known as "the God of Israel" has shown himself in Christ to be "the God of all people," and the people of God increasingly reflect that unity as the walls of hostility are broken down around the common table and as God, by the indwelling of God's Spirit, comes to be all and in all.

Things veered off sharply from that trajectory in Antioch (even as things threaten to do in Galatia as well). Paul watched the disintegration of the unified Antiochene church into separate tables for Jewish and gentile Christians, the resegregation of the one body of Christ into its former categories of Jew and Greek. The image of the "one new person" in Christ was defaced, and the church reflected once again the divisions that belong to this present evil age and not to the new creation.[235] Paul perceived—while Peter, Barnabas, and the people from James failed to perceive—that treating the gentile Christ-followers as if they are still sinners (and therefore being afraid of being classified as sinners alongside them for mingling with them too freely) made a negative statement about Christ, the value of trusting Christ, and the value of the Spirit and its work. This change in behavior also made a negative statement about the gentile converts themselves, shutting them outside once again and laying upon them, at least implicitly, the challenge of finding their way inside by a means other than trusting Jesus and the Spirit that Jesus had provided.[236]

---

234. The prepositional phrase πρὸς τὴν ἀλήθειαν is often translated "in line with" (NIV; cf. "consistently with," NRSV, CEB). While certainly not impossible, it is more natural to understand πρός as denoting motion "toward," here after a verb expressing movement. See also Dunn, 127; Matera, 86; Nanos, "What Was at Stake?," 284; Tolmie, *Persuading*, 87. BDAG 875, treats πρός in Gal 2:14 under the heading of "in accordance with," though BAGD 710 had treated it as "toward." I understand τοῦ εὐαγγελίου as a genitive of source or origin, "the truth that the gospel generates."

235. Compare Eph 2:11–16, which captures the essence of the Pauline gospel from this angle.

236. As Robertson (*Barnabas vs. Paul*, 89) rightly infers, "Peter's hypocrisy, therefore,

Therefore, Paul publicly confronted the man whose failure of nerve (in Paul's opinion) was directly responsible for this development. Paul openly challenged Peter's honor with this question, trying to bring shame upon him for his action and thereby to affect the behavior of the other Jewish Christians in the situation.[237] Paul makes no mention of trying to confront Peter on this issue privately first, which might have been more in keeping with his own advice (see Gal 6:1).[238] Nevertheless, the public nature of Peter's actions and its impact upon the whole congregation called for these issues to be addressed publicly at *some* point. If Peter, and *even* Barnabas, failed to stand up for the practical consequences of the truth of the gospel—to "make an issue" of free and open association with gentile believers as persons fully acceptable to God and therefore compelling Jews to accept them as such or else have no part of the Christian movement—Paul would do so, and that "in front of everyone." Once again (as in Gal 2:3–5), it is Paul who courageously and uncompromisingly stands up for the truth of the gospel. Whom besides Paul, indeed, can the Galatians trust to tell them the truth?

Paul opens his challenge with a question: "If you, while being a Jew, live in the manner of a gentile and not in the manner of a Jew,[239] how can you pressure the gentiles to take up the Jewish way of life?" This challenge serves as the preface to the fuller discourse that follows in 2:15–21, which becomes an important frame of reference for thinking about what Paul is getting at in this rhetorical question. At the most basic level, Paul is calling attention to Peter's former practice of mingling freely with the gentile Christians and not regulating his interaction with them in accordance with the hedges that Torah and its then-current interpretation placed around the Jewish people, to keep them separate from the nations. Paul is appealing to this practice as

---

was more than a momentary lapse of judgment. His actions were in fact hurting many people, reinforcing that they were not fully acceptable."

237. On the dynamics of honor and shame in this episode, see Esler, 127–29, 132; Witherington, 130.

238. Longenecker, 79; Martyn, 235.

239. The adverbs ἐθνικῶς and Ἰουδαϊκῶς appear only here in the biblical literature, and only rarely outside it. The corresponding adjective ἐθνικός is used four times, always as a substantive to denote "gentiles"; Ἰουδαϊκός is used occasionally to describe something as "Jewish/Judean." There is likely little more to the adverbs than "[doing something] as a gentile would" or "as a Jew would." Dunn (128) suggests that the language of "living like a gentile" was introduced into the situation by the "people from James," who thus upbraided Peter for his practice of eating with gentiles, and that Paul was picking up on the language and using it to advance his own case. This is certainly possible, but the rarity of the adverb in the LXX and NT argues against it. The "people from James" would probably have used some other, more common expression, in which case Paul would not, in fact, be reflecting their language with these terms.

the rule most in line with Peter's own fundamental convictions.[240] It is not that Peter has egregiously violated any stipulation of the Torah in doing so, though he had egregiously accepted gentile Christians as suitable associates at table without preconditions and thereby met them on the common ground of Christian identity rather than observing those practices and regulations that, while they allowed Jew and gentile to eat at the same table, also never let the Jew forget that he or she was not a gentile nor the gentile forget that he or she was not a Jew.[241] Having met his gentile brothers and sisters on that common ground, how could Peter now change course and pressure the gentile brother or sister to meet him on Jewish ground after all? How could he show such regard for the "people from James" that he would show such *dis*regard for his gentile sisters and brothers?

The Greek verb translated "live" has several different connotations in this short letter. While it may refer here simply to Peter's day-to-day manner of conduct, it will shortly, at least, take on significantly expanded senses—the sense of "coming alive to God" (to the life of God's Spirit and God's Son living within and through oneself) and perhaps also entering into life beyond death:

> Through the law I died to the law, so that I might live to God. I was crucified along with Christ. It is no longer "me" living, but Christ lives in me. (2:19–20a)

> It is clear that no one is being justified before God on the basis of the law, because "the just person will live on the basis of faith." (3:11, quoting Hab 2:4)

> If a law had been given that could bring a person to life, then righteousness really would come into being on the basis of the law. (3:21)

> If we have come alive by the Spirit, let us order our steps in line with the Spirit. (5:25)

---

240. Fung, 110; Longenecker, 78. Paul's assumptions about Peter's fundamental convictions are reinforced by the immediately following verse: "*We* who are Jews by birth . . . know" (Gal 2:15). Luke's portrait of Peter's early experience with gentile believers would also lead us to conclude that Peter's personal position would have remained aligned with the heavenly voice that spoke to him within his dream: "What God has cleansed, do not call profane" (Acts 10:15). Indeed, had the "people from James" not come, he would have happily gone on "living in a gentile manner."

241. Dietary regulations were a distinctive mark of Jews throughout the diaspora and, indeed, were geared specifically toward maintaining Jewish social and cultural identity *through* separateness from non-Jews, especially in largely gentile areas. See 3 Macc 3:3–4; deSilva, *Introducing the Apocrypha*, 315–17; deSilva, *Honor*, 260–62, 270–71.

It is worth considering that, since every other occurrence of the verb in Galatians pertains to the higher sense of "coming alive to God" and living the new life of the Spirit, Paul may have this suprapedestrian sense in mind in 2:14 as well.[242] Even if this is not the case, however, Paul's convictions about the proper practice for living together (in the mundane sense) as neither Jews nor gentiles are rooted in his convictions about how God has acted to make both Jews and gentiles come alive to God in Christ, precisely as Paul goes on to express in 2:15–21. Since both "live to God" in the way that has been opened for all, gentile and Jew together—namely, by virtue of trusting in the power of Christ's death on their behalf (2:15–16) and by receiving the promised Holy Spirit that Christ died to provide (3:13–14)—their life together (in the pedestrian sense) should reflect the same nonvalue of their ethnic distinctions that is revealed in their having come alive to God in the common ground of trust and the Spirit.

In light of the same, there is certainly no ground for exerting pressure upon the gentile Christ-followers to value those ethnic distinctions sufficiently to take on the Jewish way of life[243] in order to preserve the unity of the body and to find full acceptance among their Jewish brothers and sisters. Paul's suggestion that Peter's actions apply such pressure upon the gentile Christians to change their practice (and even identity, if they go all the way) might have surprised Peter.[244] It might, indeed, have surprised the "people from James," whose concern was for Jewish Christian believers (and esp. Peter, as the most visible missionary to the Jewish people) to maintain the degrees of separation from gentiles required by the Torah and its then-current application.[245] Neither of these parties likely saw what Paul perceived with

---

242. See the bold and compelling reading given this passage in Nanos, *Mystery*, 355: "To paraphrase this extremely compact argument, Paul was saying to Peter that if he lived (justified) as (an equal, that is, justified in the same manner as) a Gentile (through faith in Christ) and not like (those) Jews (who still relied on the works [status] of the law for their justification), then why would he now withdraw in such a way as to compel the gentiles (also justified by faith in Christ) to believe that they are not equals unless they also live (justified) as Jews (by the works [status] of the law)."

243. The verb Ἰουδαΐζειν, which appears only here in the New Testament, means "to adopt the Jewish way of life," which may further mean "to become a full proselyte by circumcision" (Nanos, "What Was at Stake?," 306–11).

244. Watson, *Paul, Judaism, and the Gentiles*, 54–55, suggests that Peter and the people from James actually were pursuing their course in the full knowledge of its consequences, namely, that they sought quite knowingly and purposefully thus to compel the gentile Christians to accept circumcision and adopt a Torah-observant lifestyle. While certain Jewish-Christian parties advocated for this position, I find it difficult to group James, Peter, and their circles all together as sharing this agenda (see, again, Painter, *Just James*, 74–77, for a more nuanced spectrum of positions).

245. Bruce, *Paul*, 177.

great clarity, namely, that their change of behavior sent a clear message to their gentile brothers and sisters: "You are not really acceptable to God on the basis of your trust in Jesus and your reception of the Spirit after all. If you want to find acceptance before God and enjoy fellowship with God's people, you must make yourselves clean by circumcision and Torah observance."

Paul's objection to such pressuring is rooted in his conviction that the legal code that orders Jews to distinguish themselves from gentiles—the Torah—is no longer in force. For Jewish Christians to *insist* on certain Torah-related practices as a condition for table fellowship was to *force* gentile Christians (for the sake of the unity of the church symbolized at the common table) to put themselves under the pedagogue, the end of whose authority had been signaled by Christ's appearing in the first place. Paul might call upon gentile Christians in other locales (particularly if they were the more dominant group) to exercise their liberty to accommodate their Jewish sisters and brothers, but for leaders like Peter and Barnabas to present a passive-aggressive ultimatum ("table fellowship on Torah's terms, or not at all, because we Jews by nature can't mingle too freely with you sinners from the nations") was a betrayal of the truth of the gospel.

It is likely that Paul left this particular field defeated after his argument with Peter.[246] If it were otherwise, he would have had every reason to add to his narrative that Peter (or Barnabas or the other Jewish Christians, for that matter) was won back to his former practice against the position of the "people from James." The strong possibility remains, however, that this sorry situation was eventually reversed and the fences mended,[247] if the events narrated in Galatians (and, indeed, Galatians itself) preceded the apostolic conference related in Acts 15, which resulted in an admirable compromise—admirable, since no side would be fully happy with the outcome. From that meeting proceeded a clear statement that circumcision was not to be required of gentile converts as a condition of full membership or table fellowship, together with a clear statement of certain regulations that *would* be observed by gentile converts, neatly patterned after the regulations for resident aliens sojourning in the land of Israel with its full citizens in Lev 17–18,[248] such that full social interaction within mixed congregations would be possible on terms that gave some token recognition to the special demands upon Jewish Christians to remain mindful of the historic covenant.[249]

---

246. Dunn, 12, 128; "The Incident at Antioch," 38–39; Martyn, 236.

247. Das, 203.

248. Schnelle, *Apostle Paul*, 124–25. See especially Lev 17:10–14; 18:6–18, 26. The stipulations formulated at the conference answered the question, "Which rules must gentile Christians observe in order to maintain the state of ritual purity required by God?" (Schnelle, *Apostle Paul*, 131).

249. Of course, if the Antioch incident postdated the event known as the Apostolic

The Antioch incident raised an important question beyond the question of whether or not gentiles need to be circumcised to be part of God's covenant people in Christ (the question concerning which Paul and the pillars had come to at least a provisional agreement). If there was to be "one new people" formed in Christ from Jews and gentiles, on whose terms would the new people conduct themselves? Paul's solution—which apparently was Peter's solution for at least a short time—was to practice mutual acceptance at the Lord's Table, valuing the cleansing that came upon both Jew and gentile by faith and the Spirit as sufficiently "kosher" for all parties concerned. The Antioch incident overturned this solution, creating a freshly partitioned church with Jewish Christians placing adherence to Torah in all its particulars ahead of trust in Jesus as sufficient in itself to set the "gentile sinners" apart for God and for free interaction within God's people. Some might well have embraced as the solution to this problem what Paul named only as an even greater problem: pressuring the gentile Christians to take on the yoke of the law. If they were to do so, the Antiochene church could once again come around a common table as one body without the Jewish Christian members first having to relinquish their identity as God's distinctive people. This possibility may, in turn, have given the impetus for some believers there to travel to the daughter churches throughout Galatia to promote the new solution to the problem, namely, calling for circumcision and Torah observance among gentile Christians.[250] They could claim to do so, moreover, with the authority of the pillars behind them, though the central pillar, James, might have been sufficiently happy with Jewish Christian observance of Torah and separate tables for the celebration of the Lord's Supper.

This situation in Antioch provides a close analogy to the Galatian situation (though the rival teachers are not to be identified with the "people from James" and may not, in the end, even have come from the Antioch church).[251] Paul asserts that the rival teachers, like the people from James and like Peter in his vacillation, seek to uphold the old boundaries drawn around the Jewish people by the Torah because they are afraid to tell their fellow Jews (esp. non-Christian Jews) the truth about God's abolition of those boundaries in his new outpouring of favor in Christ.[252] They do not, in other words, "walk straight toward the truth of the gospel." Just as Paul spoke the truth in Antioch—quite possibly to his own

---

Conference, the long-term outcome is more negative. Paul's leaving behind Antioch as a missionary base would be a result not merely of Paul's strategy for reaching lands ever further to the West, but of necessity. Corinth and Ephesus would come to serve as the bases of operations for Paul's mission "for the uncircumcised" (Dunn, 130).

250. Dunn, 14.

251. Witherington, 24.

252. By contrast, Paul, "far from perpetuating old patterns and prejudices, took them on . . . and at great cost" (Robertson, *Barnabas vs. Paul*, 88).

hurt in terms of losing that argument—he will speak the truth in Galatia, without consideration for his own advantage or what is politic (1:10; 4:16).

Paul's response to the Antioch incident challenges us to consider who is not allowed at our tables in our churches and homes, especially where we might say, as did the "men from James" and those who caved in to their pressure, "if you want to have fellowship with us, you need to become like us," but in ways that ultimately no longer matter in God's sight. Difficult as it may be to admit, the communion table is the most blatant place of violation of "the truth of the gospel" as Paul sought to defend it in Antioch. Wherever a church restricts sharing at the communion table to those who belong to its particular stripe or denomination, excluding others who have made the same commitment to follow Jesus and received the same Spirit, Paul would challenge that church that "the truth of the gospel" is at stake in its practice. In recent decades, some of the historic mainline denominations have made important progress toward opening up their tables to Christians of other denominations. Paul would have applauded the conversations that led to the practice of intercommunion between Anglicans, Methodists, and Lutherans, but would urge churches to broaden this conversation more and more.

The question of intercommunion between Catholic, Orthodox, and Reformation churches is far more complex and is inevitably tied up in the history of the irreconcilable differences that led to this plurality of streams. Nevertheless, generations upon generations of Christians have simply been born into each of these streams, and God has blessed *each* stream with the presence and movement of God's Holy Spirit. As a result, it is no longer the case that one stream can say to another with integrity, "You are always welcome to share in communion with us, provided you come back into our fold." Paul would hear such a sentiment as just another echo of the invitation that might have issued forth from the Jewish Christian table in Antioch—the sort of invitation that the rival teachers would extend. Rather, it is now a matter of recognizing the vitality of trust in Jesus and of the indwelling activity of the Holy Spirit in each of these streams, and embracing one another on that basis, honoring what God has done for *all* Christians as the basis for unity rather than insisting that other Christians conform to *our* historic convictions and practice.

But denominational boundaries are not the only considerations that lead us, in our churches, to the practice of separate tables. As we look around our communion table or the tables at our fellowship meals, we need to ask ourselves who is present and who is not. We need to ask whether we are structuring our congregational (and intercongregational) life in such a way as leads, intentionally or not, to the practice of separate tables rather than the celebration of the unity that God has bestowed upon us, all together, as the new humanity God is forming in Christ.

In this same episode (as also in 2:4–5), Paul presents a living example of the courage of the genuine minister of the gospel, in refusing to conform the gospel to the expectations or demands of church or society and in braving confrontation where the truth of the gospel is not being lived out in the church. This is a facet of Paul's leadership that Christian leaders in every generation would do well to imitate. Accommodating the truth of the gospel to the prejudices of our congregations or the values of our constituency would mean preaching a "merely human" gospel, one that has been circumcised and emasculated of its transformative power. Rather, we are called to preserve the challenge that the gospel poses to the world and call our constituencies to conform to the gospel, not vice versa. This is the gospel that has power from God to transform, to justify, to bring us in line with God's own righteousness. It is noteworthy that, in Paul's situation, standing for "the truth of the gospel" meant calling people back to a common table, not finding yet another reason to break out yet another table.

E. THE COHERENCE OF PAUL'S POSITION (2:15–21)

15 *We, Jews by nature and not sinners from among the gentiles,* 16 *[but]*[a] *knowing that a person is not deemed to be aligned with God's righteousness on the basis of the works of the law except by trust in Jesus Christ,*[b] *even we have put our trust in Christ Jesus*[c] *in order that we might be deemed to be aligned with God's righteousness on the basis of trust in Christ and not on the basis of works of the law, since all flesh will not be deemed aligned with God's righteousness on the basis of works of the law.* 17 *But if while seeking to be deemed aligned with God's righteousness in Christ we are also ourselves found to be "sinners," then is Christ a servant of sin? By no means!* 18 *For if I build up again the things I tore down, I prove myself to be a transgressor.* 19 *For I died to the law through the law, in order that I might live to God. I have been crucified along with Christ.* 20 *It's not me living any longer, but Christ is living in me. What I'm now living in the flesh, I live by trusting God's Son,*[d] *who loved me and gave himself up on my behalf.* 21 *I do not set aside God's generous kindness. For if righteousness comes through the law, then Christ died for nothing.*

a. External evidence for the inclusion or exclusion of δέ here is fairly evenly divided. $\mathfrak{P}^{46}$ A D² Ψ 33 1739 1881 𝔐 omit the word; ℵ B C D* F G H include it. Arguments from transcriptional probability can also be made either way. If the connective is original to the text, it *both* suggests that 2:15 should be read as a complete (though verbless) equative sentence *and* marks this clause as a new development in the argument, heard to contrast with the claim made in 2:15, since it would be surprising for "Jews by birth" to come to this conclusion (Matera, 92).

b. A B 33 and some MSS of the Vulgate read "Christ Jesus" (Χριστοῦ Ἰησοῦ), but the external witness for the NA²⁷/UBS⁴ text is too strong to overrule ($\mathfrak{P}^{46}$ ℵ C D F G H 1739 𝔐).

c. The variant Ἰησοῦν Χριστόν appears in 𝔓⁴⁶ B H 33 1739. Interestingly, only 𝔓⁴⁶ A H and 1739 are consistent in the order in which they keep the two components (Ἰησοῦς and Χριστός) in their twin occurrences in this verse. This consistency suggests, however, a harmonizing tendency on the part of these witnesses, lending support to Χριστὸν Ἰησοῦν here, the reverse order of Ἰησοῦ Χριστοῦ just a few words before.

d. Several early and important witnesses (including 𝔓⁴⁶ B D* F G) read "God and Christ" (τοῦ θεοῦ καὶ Χριστοῦ) rather than "God's son" (τοῦ υἱοῦ τοῦ θεοῦ). Paul does not typically write about "God" as the object of "faith" (Metzger, *Textual Commentary*, 524; Longenecker, 82; but see 1 Thess 1:8), though this usage might well have been a central topic of his preaching to gentiles (part of the foundational teaching recalled by Paul's ministry colleague in Heb 6:1). The NA²⁷/UBS⁴ reading τοῦ υἱοῦ τοῦ θεοῦ, which also enjoys early and broad support (א A C D² K L P Ψ 33 𝔐 *pm*), could therefore be explained as an attempt to harmonize this verse with Paul's more normal designation of Christ as the object of faith and τοῦ θεοῦ καὶ Χριστοῦ accepted as the *lectio difficilior*. It would take a creative scribe, however, to change τοῦ θεοῦ καὶ Χριστοῦ to τοῦ υἱοῦ τοῦ θεοῦ rather than just eliminating θεοῦ καὶ and leaving τοῦ Χριστοῦ to stand. It seems more plausible that an early copyist inadvertently omitted τοῦ υἱοῦ before τοῦ θεοῦ by a leap of the eye (not so difficult to imagine when dealing with uncials and nomina sacra). A second copyist, noticing the anomaly of God being described as τοῦ ἀγαπήσαντός με and especially παραδόντος ἑαυτὸν ὑπὲρ ἐμοῦ, correctly reasoned that a reference to Jesus had been omitted somehow and corrected it by adding καὶ Χριστοῦ in the defective manuscript, making this the subject of the following participles.

Though Gal 2:15–21 is often (rightly) recognized as a core statement of Pauline theology, Paul himself contextualizes 2:15–21 in the conflict that erupted in Antioch and presents it as a response specifically to that historical conflict— though in full awareness that this response (like the Antioch incident itself) has direct bearing on what is also happening in the congregations of Galatia.[253] There is no clear point of transition between Paul's reconstruction of his response to Peter and Paul's response to the arguments of the rival teachers within 2:15–21. Rather, the reconstructed response to Peter speaks also and fully to the situation in Galatia.[254]

Verses 15–16 provide argumentation directly in support of verse 14. The fact that Paul, Peter, Barnabas, James, and every other Jewish Christ-follower became a Christ-follower in the first place is evidence that they did not consider aligning themselves with the Torah to be a *sufficient* path to acquittal before God's judgment seat. The fact that they relied on Jesus and what Jesus provided in order to attain that end further suggests, as Paul will seek to demonstrate in the proofs that follow, that aligning oneself with the Torah is also not *prerequisite* to attaining that end. Verse 17 introduces a potential

---

253. So, correctly, Wright, *Recent Interpreters*, 339.

254. See, rightly, Matera, 97–98; Tolmie, *Persuading*, 97. The attempt to find an actual point of transition is a vain pursuit.

objection to Paul's position (and to Peter's former practice in Antioch): if aligning ourselves with the standards of righteousness revealed in Christ as the path to final acquittal leaves us no better than the gentiles whom we have always equated with "sinners," does this not mean that Christ has served *sin's* agenda rather than God's? Paul answers this objection in verses 18–20. The only course of action now that would prove me to be a sinner would be to build up again what God led me to see had been broken down—the "dividing wall of hostility" and the law code that, for a certain span of time that has now come to an end, provided the mortar and bricks for that wall. Trusting in Jesus put an end to all of that for me, made me come alive to God, and allowed Christ himself to come to life within—and, in a very real way, in place of—me: there is no surer path to becoming righteous than that! Paul concludes the paragraph with a strong statement concerning what is at stake in deciding in favor of his position vis-à-vis the rivals' position—receiving well, or ungraciously spurning, God's favor (2:21), a theme to which he returns explicitly in 5:2–4.

Galatians 2:15–21 has been treated as the *propositio* of Galatians, the chief point that would be demonstrated in the course of the speech.[255] Within the narrative framework of the Antioch incident, 2:14 is indeed a *propositio* (in the form of a rhetorical question),[256] while 2:15–21 provides supporting argumentation in favor of that proposition. However, within the framework of the rhetorical situation of the Galatian Christians themselves, 2:11–21, along with the remainder of the letter, is offered rather to *support* the principal point to be demonstrated: "Submitting to circumcision would be a terrible mistake; keep moving in the same direction that Christ set you on when I preached to you and you received the Holy Spirit" (5:1).[257] That Paul's ultimate *propositio* is not explicitly formulated until 5:1 should pose no difficulties for the listeners in Galatia. They will have already inferred this proposition from the content of 1:6–9: "Do *not* listen to the rival teachers! Do *not* do what they are urging!" They will further understand everything that follows that verse to supply the reasons for not doing so.

---

255. See, for example, Betz, 113–14; Hansen, *Abraham*, 69, 100–101. Other proposals regarding the identification of the *propositio* in Galatians have included 1:6–9 (Vos, "Argumentation," 6–7); 1:11–12 (Bullinger, *In omnes apostolicas epistolas*, 346, cited in Vos, "Argumentation," 6); and 3:1 (Melanchthon, cited in Vos, "Argumentation," 6).

256. If we were to restate 2:14 as a proposition rather than as a question, and fill it out in light of the argumentation that follows, we should probably read, "We cannot impose a Jewish identity and way of life upon gentile Christians, since we Jewish Christians have come to understand that, in Christ, the practices that separate Jews as clean from gentiles as unclean have no meaning, since Jews and gentiles are both alike cleansed by faith and the Spirit."

257. See also Hietanen, *Paul's Argumentation*, 181–82.

Even though 2:15–21 is not properly seen as the rhetorical *propositio*,[258] it does introduce many of the key topics and motifs that will occupy Paul throughout the remainder of the discourse, particularly the role of trusting (3:2, 5–9, 11–12, 14, 22–26; 5:5–6, 22; 6:10) and the role of the Torah and its particular prescriptions (3:2, 5, 10–13, 17–19, 21, 23–24; 4:4–5, 21; 5:3–4, 14, 18, 23; 6:2, 13) in bringing about "righteousness" or its acknowledgment by God (3:6, 8, 11, 21, 24; 5:4–5) and bringing about "life" beyond the mere biological sense (3:11, 12; 5:25; 6:8).[259] Paul will develop, in the chapters that follow, (1) why alignment with the prescriptions of the Torah is not, on this side of the coming of the "fullness of time," the path to attaining the righteousness that God will acquit (3:10–14, 19–25; 4:1–11; 5:1–6); (2) why alignment with the prescriptions of the Torah is not the way to join oneself to Abraham and the family of promise (3:6–9, 15–22, 26–29; 4:21–31); and (3) how trusting Jesus has opened up a profoundly more effective means for becoming righteous in God's sight and thus a profoundly more sure means to acquittal (or approval) on the day of judgment (3:1–5; 5:13–6:10).

15 Paul begins his elaboration of his position in a way that plays to Jewish prejudices against gentiles, speaking as if coming alongside Peter and those who had cowed him into changing his practice: "We, Jews by nature and not sinners from among the gentiles."[260] To be a "Jew by birth" (lit. "a Jew by nature," hence "born a Jew") carries with it the great advantage of having been born into God's covenant people and under the Torah, the gracious provision of God for the ongoing covenant relationship between God and this people. All other ethnic groups, lumped together indistinguishably (from the Jewish point of view) as "gentiles," are sinners by definition, since they live outside of God's law and covenant (2:15). Gentiles do not have even the *path* to becoming righteous before God, that is, to becoming anything *but* a sinner.[261] The "we" is emphatic in the Greek, appropriately reflecting the social division between the "us" and the "them" foisted upon the Antioch Christian congregation.

While Paul opens as if embracing this Jewish view of humanity, its divisions, and the ethnic privilege of the Jewish people, which surely reflects the perspective of Peter's critics in Antioch and his own rivals in Galatia,[262] he

---

258. See Fairweather, "Galatians and Classical Rhetoric," 14–15; Kern, *Rhetoric in Galatians*, 105–9; Hietanen, *Paul's Argumentation*, 180.

259. See Das, 238.

260. So also Dunn, 133; Fung, 112–13; Longenecker, 83; Martyn, 248–49.

261. The "sinner" is frequently synonymous with "the non-Jew" or "gentile." See, for example, Ps 9:17; Tob 13:6; Jub. 33.23–24; Pss. Sol. 2.1–2 (Dunn, 132–34; Dunn, "Intra-Jewish Polemic," 462–63; Betz, 115). Reflections of the stereotype of gentiles as de facto sinners also appear in Wis 14:22–31 and Rom 1:18–32.

262. Paul may even echo the language of the "men from James" here as they criticized

will shortly sweep it all away in the following verses (much as he will do in greater detail and with greater finesse later in Rom 1:18–3:20).

16 This verse is perhaps the most dense and most debated in all of Pauline literature. In order to come to a clear understanding of the essence of Paul's position and what is, for him, at stake in the debate in Galatia, we need to grasp what he means in three key phrases, each of which appears multiple times in 2:16 alone: (1) What does Paul mean by "being justified"? (2) What does Paul mean by "works of the law"? (3) What does Paul mean when he speaks of "faith" (or "faithfulness") when this word is qualified by "Jesus Christ"? In this commentary, I argue in favor of the following positions. (1) In Galatians, Paul is concerned with what will bring people into alignment with God's standards of what is "righteous," and thus be declared righteous before God's court on the last day. (2) Aligning oneself with the practices prescribed in the Torah ("works of the law"), which Paul regards as a complete package, though some particular works have come to the fore in the Galatian situation, will not bring people into such alignment. (3) Trust in Christ (the linguistically and contextually more probable solution of the disputed phrase *pistis Christou*) has opened up the path to becoming righteous and thus to receiving God's approbation; but believers must continue to trust in Jesus's mediation and, specifically, in the efficacy and sufficiency of the gift that Jesus's death has secured for those who trust, namely, the Holy Spirit, to lead them into and empower them for the righteous lives that God will affirm.

EXCURSUS: WHAT DOES PAUL MEAN BY "SEEKING TO BE JUSTIFIED" AND "BEING JUSTIFIED"?

The question "What is justification?" is central to Christian theology,[263] and Paul's letters (esp. Galatians and Romans) are foundational texts for any theology of justification. Our inquiry into the specific question of what Paul means, however, in his use of words from the family built upon the root *dikai*—words including "justice/righteousness" (*dikaiosynē*), "just/righteous" (*dikaios*), "acquittal/vindication" (*dikaiōsis*), and "vindicate, acquit, set right"

Peter for his practice of "eating with gentile sinners" and "living like a gentile" (and thus "being no better than a gentile"). See Dunn, 133; Dunn, "The Incident at Antioch," 36.

263. For a representative spectrum of answers, see Beilby and Eddy, eds., *Justification: Five Views*. Some important, recent statements on the topic from different perspectives include Wright, *Justification*; Bird, *Saving Righteousness*; Seifrid, *Christ Our Righteousness*; and Gorman, *Inhabiting the Cruciform God*.

(*dikaioō*)—is more hindered than helped by the many tradition-specific definitions of the theological concept of justification in Christian circles.[264]

As has long been recognized, the courtroom (hence, a "forensic" setting) provides one important mental framework for Paul's use of this language. Specifically, Paul is concerned with *God's* courtroom and the verdict that God will render upon a particular human life. The last judgment occupies a prominent place in Paul's thought (Rom 2:5–13; 3:6; 2 Cor 5:9–10; 2 Thess 1:5–12) and no doubt played a significant role in his preaching, whether as the coming "wrath" of the God who holds all accountable for their ingratitude and disobedience (Rom 1:18; 2:5; 5:9; 1 Thess 1:10; 5:9; Col 3:6) or simply as the day "when God comes to judge the things hidden by people, according to my gospel" (Rom 2:16; 2 Tim 4:1, 8). It is *the* crisis for which people must prepare themselves.[265] Nothing could be more important than settling upon a sound strategy for surviving that encounter, for one's eternal destiny depends upon God's favorable judgment:

> He will pay back to each according to his or her works—eternal life to those who sought glory and honor and immortality on the basis of patiently doing good, anger and fury to those who disobey the truth and follow unrighteousness on the basis of self-serving ambition. Tribulation and distress upon every soul of a person who works what is wicked (upon both the Jew first and the Greek), but glory and honor and peace for everyone working what is good (for both the Jew first and the Greek), for there is no partiality with God. (Rom 2:6–11)

A forensic setting is not made explicit in Galatians, although Paul's reconfiguration of Ps 143:2 ("do not enter into judgment with your slave, for no living being will be acquitted before you") at the end of Gal 2:16 suggests that God's judgment is still very much in the back of his mind. The frequent forensic scene depicted in so many of the Old Testament Scriptures where the verb "to justify" (in the LXX, forms of the verb *dikaioō*) appears—the Scriptures that infuse and inform Paul's thought and the literature of near-contemporary Jewish groups—might also allow us to assume this context in Galatians, though it is not brought into such sharp focus here as in Romans or 2 Corinthians.[266] This verb is also very much at home in courtroom settings in

---

264. Wright, *Justification*, 81.

265. As Stuhlmacher (*Revisiting*, 43) has noted, Paul is intensely concerned with "whether Jews and gentiles will or will not survive before God's throne of judgment." See also Westerholm, *Justification Reconsidered*, 5–6: "With or without an introspective conscience, anyone who takes seriously a warning of imminent divine judgment must deem it an urgent concern to find God merciful."

266. Schrenk, "*Dikē*," 217–18.

the classical world, where it is the duty of the court to "give justice," whether to punish[267] or to acquit, and where the individual may hope "to be given justice" or "to be acquitted" or "vindicated." It is likely, then, that this set of forensic meanings would come into play both for Paul and for his Galatian Christian audience, particularly in the positive sense of "being acquitted."

In Galatians, unlike Romans,[268] Paul *anticipates* justification—being acquitted before God at the judgment—as a result of trusting in Jesus and walking in the new life and the new power of the Spirit that Jesus's death made available to human beings. At no point in Galatians does he speak of "justification" or "acquittal" as an already-accomplished fact.[269] In Gal 2:16 Paul writes about himself and his Jewish Christian colleagues that "we trusted in Christ Jesus in order that we might be acquitted as a result of trusting in Jesus and not as a result of [doing] works of the law" (2:16). While the fact that Paul employed a purpose clause here ("we believed . . . in order to be acquitted"; so also 3:24) is not determinative for this point, it is interesting that he did not instead employ a result clause, which would have unambiguously placed the experience of acquittal in the past ("we trusted in Christ Jesus *with the result that* we *were* acquitted"). Paul speaks unambiguously of nonacquittal in the future tense: "no flesh *will be acquitted* on the basis of works of the Torah" (2:16, echoing Ps 143:2). The explicit contrasts in 2:16 suggest that Paul and his fellow Jewish Christ-followers still *hope* to be acquitted, a hope he denies to those who seek this end by aligning themselves with the Torah.

Most tellingly, Paul considers one possible negative consequence that might occur "while seeking to be justified/acquitted in Christ" (2:17). "Seeking to be justified" here describes a pursuit, a quest still in process *after* an

267. The meaning "execute punishment" is almost unattested in the Septuagint and New Testament. See Schrenk, "*Dikē*," 223; Seifrid, "Paul's Use," 45–50.

268. In Romans, Paul speaks of justification in terms of forgiveness of sins, and therefore of the reconciliation with God *already* enjoyed by the believer (see Rom 4:3–8; 5:10–11); indeed, the range of usage of the same terminology in Romans and Galatians presses upon theologians the problem of the relationship of *initial* justification and *final* justification, all the more as Paul's interest in acquittal at the last judgment is even more explicit in Romans. It is interesting that the word group "save, salvation" (σῴζω, σωτηρία) plays so prominent a role in Romans but *no* role in Galatians, where "being justified" serves as the marker for final deliverance. The introduction of "salvation" alongside "justification" in Romans allows Paul to differentiate between what happens at the outset of the believer's faith journey (justification) and what has yet to happen at the end of the same (salvation; Rom 5:9–10; 13:11), but the shifts in the usage of "justification" have also occasioned no small confusion for theologians, who read Paul's usage of this terminology in Galatians into Romans without differentiation.

269. Moo ("Justification in Galatians," 188, 191), for example, acknowledges that "the timing of justification in other texts in Galatians is surprisingly difficult to pin down," that 2:17, 5:4, and 5:5 may make "reference to future justification," and that, "strikingly, in light of Romans, Paul puts no emphasis on an initial definitive act of justification."

initial response of trusting in Christ.[270] Acquittal ("justification") is the still-future goal driving an entire lifestyle shift, to which lifestyle one commits for the remainder of one's life "in the flesh." Paul reinforces this understanding in the following paragraph, as he speaks about the importance of finishing (and choosing the correct *path* to finishing) the process begun by trust in Jesus (3:3). Paul urges his converts to continue to move forward along the path opened up for them by trusting in Jesus (which brings Paul at last to the indispensable and essential gift of the Holy Spirit), specifically so that they can arrive at the desired goal. "Seeking to be justified" in the sense of "investing oneself in that path that would lead to being acquitted before God's judgment seat by virtue of having fallen in line with God's righteous standards" is also the motivation of the rival teachers and of those who turned to works of the law as the revelation of God's standards, those practices that would shape a life that God would approve and accept. The rival teachers were promoting conforming one's life to the vision for life communicated in the law as a path toward being "set right" in God's sight and therefore "acquitted" before God at the judgment (thus the use of the verb in 5:4). Paul's converts were, at the very least, interested in this as a possible path to advance their own interest in attaining that righteous verdict.

Paul gives particular attention in Galatians also to one of the nouns that belong to this word family, namely, *dikaiosynē*, and the meaning of this word provides a key to understanding Paul's doctrine of how God works to bring those who trust his Son to a place of acquittal, even approbation and vindication, at the judgment. First, it is important to establish what *dikaiosynē* is not: it is not *dikaiōsis*. The latter word speaks of the result of the legal action on behalf of believers and is rightly translated as "acquittal," "justification," "vindication."[271] The former is not, despite the tendency in some English translations to confuse the two.[272] *Dikaiosynē* ("justice, righteousness") was one of the four cardinal virtues of Greco-Roman ethics.[273] It denotes living in line with the ethical norms embraced by one's society and, among Jewish authors particularly, the moral quality and blamelessness of life that finds

---

270. Longenecker (85) rightly opposes Sanders's view (*Paul and Palestinian Judaism*, 544–45) of "righteousness" and its family as "transfer terms" in Paul, since "the issue at both Antioch and Galatia had to do with the lifestyle of those who were already believers in Jesus." Barrett (*Freedom and Obligation*, 65) summarizes: "Justification, then, is a beginning and a process; and it leads to a consummation, at the future judgment, when God's initial gracious verdict on the sinner is—or, it may be, is not—confirmed."

271. BDAG 250; LSJ 429.

272. This error can be observed, for example, in the NRSV of Rom 5:21; 2 Cor 3:9; Gal 2:21.

273. Aristotle, *Nicomachean Ethics*, 5.1–11; Pseudo-Cicero, *Rhetorica ad Herennium*, 3.2.3–3.3.5; reflected in 4 Macc 1:18; 5:24; Wis 8:7; Philo, *Special Laws*, 1.71.

acquittal before the judgment seat of the impartial God. It is an *ethical* term, the quality of living in "uprightness as determined by divine/legal standards."[274] *Dikaiosynē* can provide the *basis* for a legal verdict (*dikaiōsis*) before a human or divine court, but it is *not* a verdict; it is a moral quality embodied in right action. The use of *dikaiosynē* in passages such as Rom 6:12–23 shows clearly that Paul's usage aligns with this more general usage of the word to denote "righteousness."

For Paul, the reason that the Torah is not the path to acquittal is in part that "righteousness" does not come through the law (2:21; 3:21).[275] "Righ-

---

274. BDAG 248. Westerholm (*Justification Reconsidered*, 59) rightly stresses that, in the OT, "the [Hebrew] terms for 'righteous' and 'righteousness' are among the most basic terms in the moral vocabulary: 'righteousness' is what one ought to do (however that is defined), and the one who does it is 'righteous.'" The same can be said for the meaning of the Greek equivalents in classical and Hellenistic Greek literature. Similarly, the δίκαιος is the person who lives in line with what his or her society defines as acceptable norms and practices (BDAG 246; Spicq, *Theological Lexicon*, 1:322–25; Schrenk, "*Dikē*," 182, 185, 189–90, 192, 196). In Hellenistic Jewish writings, the word commonly and quite naturally refers to the person who obeys God's law, the Torah (as in Josephus, *Against Apion* 2.293; *Antiquities* 6.165; 8.208). In the New Testament, which is very much in line with usage in the Greek Old Testament (the Septuagint), the person who is δίκαιος is contrasted with the sinner (Matt 9:13; Mark 2:17; Luke 5:32; 15:7; Rom 5:19), the unjust person (Matt 5:45; Acts 24:15), the disobedient person (Luke 1:17), the ungodly (Rom 5:6–7; 1 Tim 1:9; 1 Pet 4:18), the lawless person (Matt 13:41; 1 Tim 1:9), the wicked person (Matt 13:49), and the play-actor (Matt 23:28; Luke 20:20). Przybylski (*Righteousness in Matthew*, 105) argues that *dikaiosynē* describes "the demand of God upon man to live according to a certain norm, the law," in Matthew and Matthew's Jewish background. Precisely *this* background is also shared with Paul the Pharisee.

Wright (*Justification*, 121) asserts that "*dikaiosunē* really is . . . a *status*, not a moral quality. It means 'membership in God's true family'" (or, later, "membership within the covenant"; 242–43). While he is certainly correct that "the Messiah's death and resurrection *reconstitutes the people of God*, in a way which means that they come out from under the rule of Torah and into the new world which God himself is making," and while it is correct that a major question in both Antioch and Galatia concerns the delineation of God's "true family" (and the role played by Torah observance in that delineation), it does not follow that Wright's emphasis now shapes—indeed, trumps—the well-established meaning of the word δικαιοσύνη, especially as Paul gives the hearer/reader no guidance away from the normal meaning toward the highly specialized and otherwise unattested meaning for which Wright advocates. It would be more correct to say that the rival teachers promote Torah observance (or that Paul promotes the Spirit-driven life) as the way to make oneself a member of God's family/covenant *and* arrive at a place where one will embody the righteousness that God will acquit than it is to conflate membership and righteousness. For a fuller critique of Wright's view of righteousness in Paul as "the status of the covenant member," see Westerholm, *Justification Reconsidered*, 58–73.

275. Nowhere in Galatians does Paul oppose the rival teachers' goal of attaining, and helping the Galatians attain, "righteousness"—only the means by which they are thinking to attain it, urging his converts to make use of the gift of the Holy Spirit as the means to that end.

teousness," that which leads to acquittal before the just Judge of all, who shows no partiality (Rom 2:11),[276] comes by means of the Spirit and on the basis of trusting Jesus and what he has provided (Gal 5:5), a process that involves "being made alive" to God in a way that the Torah could not effect (Gal 2:19–20; 3:21). The Spirit is the agent of God's justifying action in the sense of "setting things right" with human beings,[277] bringing them in line with God's righteous standards and expectations by bringing Jesus, the one in whom God's righteousness was perfectly embodied, to life within them. As Christ comes to life within them more fully, they manifest the loving heart and action for others, as well as the obedience to God's desires, that fulfill God's written and unwritten expectations for God's creatures.[278] "Righteousness," as well as the final "acquittal" rendered on the basis of a life thus lived, remains entirely God's gift to the believer in Christ, as it is brought into being by God's own Spirit.[279] But it is also something for which the believer must "seek"

---

276. Impartiality is essential to the justice of any judge, human or divine. This quality is predicated of God throughout the OT, Second Temple literature, and the NT. See deSilva, *Transformation*, 14–19.

277. The verb can also carry the meaning "to set right" (LSJ 429), which is derived from, but of potentially larger scope than, the courtroom meanings. "To set things right" can mean more than to "give justice" or "vindicate." It can include the reordering of a situation such that injustice is undone, disorder restored to order, and the like. "Since Paul views God's justifying action in close connection with the power of Christ's resurrection, there is sometimes no clear distinction between the justifying action of acquittal and the gift of new life through the Holy Spirit as God's activity in promoting uprightness in believers" (BDAG 249). See also Schrenk, "*Dikē*," 209: "The justifying action of God . . . is always teleological. . . . Thus, without any sense of difficulty or contradiction, the thought of pardoning and forensic righteousness passes over into that of righteousness as the living power which overcomes sin. The righteousness which is given commits the believer to the living power of *dikaiosunē*."

278. In Galatians, contrary to the notion of "imputed righteousness," one finds Paul promoting a view in which God *brings into being* within us the righteousness that Christ exhibited, changing us to become more like him, indeed inviting us to become vessels through which Christ's righteousness continues to express itself in real, impactful ways in the communities and world around us. This righteousness is not what Paul censures as "a righteousness of our own" (see Rom 10:3; Phil 3:9). It is, rather, the "righteousness that comes from God," since it is the product of God's Spirit at work within us, bringing Christ to life within and through us. So also Mark Seifrid, *Christ Our Righteousness*, 149: "Christ—the new person—is present within our faith, performing his works."

279. See also Wright, *Justification*, 251: "The present verdict gives the *assurance that* the future verdict will match it; the Spirit gives the *power through which* that future verdict, when given, will be seen to be in accordance with the life that the believer has thus lived." The life lived by the Christian between coming to trust in Jesus and his or her eventual death certainly matters to Paul (Bird, *Saving Righteousness*, 159; see also Wright, *Justification*, 191; Gathercole, "Law unto Themselves," 48; Moo, "Justification in Galatians," 194–95). This line of thought does not mean that final judgment is ultimately *performance*-based, since, although "God indeed

(2:17) by walking in line with the God-given Spirit (5:16–25), by making sowing to the Spirit his or her habit rather than sowing to the flesh (6:7–10), by crucifying "the flesh with its passions and desires" in union with Christ in his death for them (5:24; cf. 2:19–20). God's gift of the Holy Spirit makes human beings righteous in reality, and not merely "on paper" in God's record book.[280] Paul spends considerable space treating this transformation—*and* affirming it to be prerequisite to entering into life (5:21; 6:7–8; see also Rom 8:13), the consequence of acquittal.

This understanding of justification in Galatians may conjure several unwelcome bugbears of the Reformation and its traditions.[281] If it raises the specter of synergism (the view that people contribute in some way to their deliverance alongside God, who obviously bears the lion's share of contributions), we may be emboldened by the fact that Paul himself frequently speaks of his own investment and effort as he strives "to attain, if possible, the resurrection from the dead" (Phil 3:11–14; see also 1 Cor 9:26–27) and urges Christ-followers to do the same (Phil 2:12–13; 1 Cor 9:24–25; Gal 6:7–10), something he *can* do only because of the freedom that Christ has brought to the Christian.[282] Nevertheless, Paul's robust sense of the Holy Spirit at

---

requires works as the basis for *final* justification," it is nevertheless God himself who "produces in the believer through the Spirit the works he requires" (Wright, *Fresh Perspective*, 148; see also Bird, *Saving Righteousness*, 176). Gathercole ("Law unto Themselves," 48) rightly poses the challenge that, "in the company of statements about the reward of eternal life for obedience in [Rom] 2.7, 10, 26–27, and 29, Rom. 2.13–16 must point to a stronger theology of final vindication on the basis of an obedient life than is evident in most analyses of Pauline theology."

280. Engberg-Pedersen, *Paul and the Stoics*, 173: "What [Paul] means by righteousness is this: God's declaration (possibly in the future, see 5:5) of the positive standing of a human being vis-à-vis God himself in recognition of the fact that the Christ-believer *has now actually become sinless*. He has faith, of course . . . (3:6). But *he also has the inner structure generated* in his response to the Christ event, which means that he never lets himself do any acts of the type listed in the 'vice' list of chapter 5. On the contrary, he constantly acts in accordance with the set of attitudes which constitute the fruit of the spirit. Thus both in relation to God and to other human beings, he is not just 'counted' righteous; he *is* righteous and will therefore also of course be *declared* righteous by God."

281. It does not fail, however, to resonate with important Reformation voices. See, most notably, Philipp Melanchthon, *Apology* 4.72: "And because 'to be justified' means that out of unrighteous people righteous people are made or regenerated, it also means that they are pronounced or regarded as righteous. For Scripture speaks both ways." Jacob Andreae and Johannes Wigand similarly "describe justification as transformation into the likeness of Christ" (Vainio, *Justification and Participation*, 225).

282. Wright (*Justification*, 189) aptly describes this freedom as "a matter of being released from slavery precisely into responsibility, into being able at last to choose, to exercise moral muscle, knowing both that one is doing it oneself and that the Spirit is at work within, that God himself is doing that which I too am doing. . . . The Spirit enables the Christian . . . freely to become that which is pleasing to God."

work within the Christ-follower makes it impossible truly to distinguish a precise division of labor, such that neither foreign, theological categories of synergism nor monergism suffice to capture Paul's understanding.[283] It may also raise the specter of "salvation by [our] works," but this shadow is dissipated, since Paul knows *God* to be the one at work in the Christ-follower by God's Holy Spirit, and thus in and behind all the Christian's "working."[284] It is, however, also not a salvation apart from a changed life, radically brought into alignment with God's values, since God's goal is not merely to get Christ-followers "off the hook" at the last judgment but to make them new creatures who will be at home in his new creation, his kingdom, where "righteousness is at home" (to borrow from 2 Pet 3:13).[285]

In Galatians, then, we find Paul looking forward to acquittal before God's judgment seat and promoting trust in Jesus—in the efficacy of Jesus's death for his sins, in the efficacy of Jesus's death for redeeming him from the curse of the law, in the efficacy of Jesus's death for securing for him the blessing promised to Abraham, namely, the Holy Spirit, and in the efficacy of the Spirit to bring righteousness to life in him, to nurture within him the fruit that pleases God, to form Christ in him and thus transform him into someone who is righteous in God's sight—as the path to acquittal.[286] The death of Christ, as Romans would develop further but as Paul hints at here when he speaks twice about Jesus's death "for our sins" (1:4; 2:20), certainly means acquittal before God now in regard to past misdeeds, on behalf of which Christ offered his own obedience to the point of death as an act of atonement and reconcil-

---

283. See O'Brien, "Was Paul a Covenantal Nomist?," 265. It would be truer to Paul and his context to think rather of grace/gift and natural (but necessary) response to grace (see excursus "A Contextual Understanding of Grace" on pp. 254–62).

284. Wright (*Justification*, 192) describes "the paradox at the heart of the Christian life" that must be integrated into a biblical theology of justification thus: "From *one point of view* the Spirit is at work, producing these fruits (Galatians 5:22–23), and from *another point of view* the person concerned is making the free choices, the increasingly free (because increasingly less constrained by the sinful habits of mind and body) decisions to live a genuinely, fully human life which brings pleasure—of course it does!—to the God in whose image we human beings were made."

285. See Engberg-Pedersen, *Paul and the Stoics*, 142, 173. Scholars who give a similar emphasis on a transformative element within the process of justification include Garlington, *Faith, Obedience, and Perseverance*, 155–61; Jüngel, *Justification*, 208–11; Leithart, "Justification as Verdict"; Gorman, *Inhabiting the Cruciform God*; Garlington, "Even We Have Believed"; Campbell, *Deliverance of God*.

286. Trust in the Holy Spirit is thus an essential component and concomitant of trust in Jesus Christ (Wright, *Justification*, 107; see also 188 and 237: "When, by clear implication, I am charged with encouraging believers to put their trust in someone or something 'other than the crucified and resurrected Savior,' I want to plead guilty . . . that I trust in the Holy Spirit"). The reliability of the Spirit is at the heart of "a Pauline doctrine of assurance."

iation.[287] But Christ's obedient death also opens the way for his followers to be deemed righteous at the *last* judgment on the basis of the transformation God is working within us by means of his Spirit, to whose guidance and empowerment we must yield so that Christ can be formed in us (2:20; 4:19).[288] It is an acquittal, but an acquittal on the basis of God's action in setting things right—of bringing "into order the unruly wills and affections of sinners," to borrow the language of the Book of Common Prayer.

EXCURSUS: WHAT DOES PAUL MEAN BY "WORKS OF THE LAW"?

Paul asserts, echoing the language of Ps 143:2, that all people will fail to be acquitted before God on the basis of "works of the law."[289] The value placed upon "works of the law" is the primary factor that sets Paul apart from the "false brothers" (2:3–5), the "people from James" (2:11–14), and the rival teachers in Galatia. To understand what works Paul has in mind, we must take seriously his own qualification of these works as specifically "works of the law," that is, "works prescribed by the Torah," the law given to the Jewish people.[290] The mutually exclusive alternatives in Galatians are not faith

---

287. Fee (83) defines "justification" thus to mean that "both Jews and gentiles together have received their pardon and right standing with God through the work of Christ."

288. "Being justified" is not here limited to what happens *prior to* sanctification, as happens in many constructions of a "systematic" theology. In Galatians, final acquittal happens *after* sanctification and *as a result* of God's sanctifying work in us. This understanding may indeed suggest a "greater unity between justification and sanctification than has often been supposed" (Hooker, "ΠΙΣΤΙΣ ΧΡΙΣΤΟΥ," 342). See also Spicq, *Theological Lexicon*, 1:336; Longenecker, 84–85; Dunn, "New Perspective," 207–8; Gorman, *Inhabiting*, 55–57, 79.

289. The lack of a definite article before "law" in the phrase ἐξ ἔργων νόμου does not leave the noun indefinite, such that it refers to "legal works" in general (see BDF §258.2; Moule, *Idiom Book*, 113; Moo, "Legalism in Paul," 74–76). The context of 2:11–14 and the extensive discussion of a particular "law" to follow or not to follow in 3:10–25; 4:21–31 make this point abundantly clear.

290. There is a semantic shift as one moves from Hebrew to Greek in the conception of the commandments contained in the Mosaic covenant. It is indeed possible to understand Hebrew תּוֹרָה (*tôrâ*) as "instruction," as well as a body of binding legal stipulation. The choice of νόμος (rather than, for example, διδαχή, "teaching") as the Greek representation of the Hebrew תּוֹרָה, however, reflects Hellenistic Jewish understanding of what the Torah was in their experience and understanding: a body of *law*. This choice is, moreover, a witness to a pre-Pauline Jewish understanding of the nature and function of the Torah. It does not represent Paul's misinterpretation of his own heritage (contra Schechter, *Aspects of Rabbinic Theology*, 117; see also Dunn, *Theology*, 131–32).

over against works: they are "the faith of Christ" (see below) and "works of the law." Paul's polemic against works of the law is not a polemic against good works.[291] On the contrary, Paul expects the Spirit to produce all manner of good works in the life of the disciple (Gal 5:13–25; Rom 2:6–11; 6:12–13; Eph 2:10), and if "neither circumcision nor uncircumcision has any force in Christ," it is striking to read what *does* have force: "faith *working* through love" (Gal 5:6).[292] And according to Paul, one's practice—what one *does*—has eternal consequences, even to the point that one's persistence in *doing* what God hates will mean exclusion from God's kingdom (5:19–21; 6:7–10). The contrast between "works of the law" and "faith of Christ" is not one of achievement versus passive submission.[293]

By "works of the law," Paul has specifically in mind those acts performed with a view to conforming one's practice to the positive and negative stipulations of the Torah, the law of Moses. The hope of those who have thus conformed their practice was that they would be found "righteous" before God, the Judge of all, on that basis and come thereby to enjoy the rewards promised to the righteous.[294] The narrative of the Antioch inci-

---

291. Correctly, Dunn, *Romans 1–8*, lxvii–lxx; Dunn, *Theology*, 354–59, 365; Barclay, *Obeying the Truth*, 82; Sanders, *Jewish People*, 46; Boers, "We Who Are by Inheritance Jews," 275. See also Tyson, "Works of the Law," 430–31; Dunn, "Works of the Law." "The supposed conflict between 'doing' as such and 'faith' as such is simply not present in Galatians" (Sanders, *Jewish People*, 159). While correctly defining "works of the law" as "actions performed in obedience to the law" (Moo, "Law," 92), Douglas Moo (97, 99) goes on to suggest that "Paul appears to criticize 'works of the law' not because they are *nomou* ('of the law') but because they are *erga* ('works')," thus vindicating "the propriety of the application made by the Reformers." I would say, to the contrary, that Paul opposes "works of the law" precisely because they are νόμου ("of the law") and not born from the prompting and empowering Spirit (5:5, 13–14; 6:7–10). Moo ("Justification in Galatians," 180) returns to stronger ground in a more recent essay when he observes that, when Paul abbreviates the phrase "works of the Torah" in Galatians, he uses "Torah" and not "works": "This suggests that Paul's chief concern in Galatians, as we might expect granted the situation being addressed, is with Torah, not with works as such."

292. On the place of works in Paul's view of the Christian life and of the consummation of experiencing salvation, see deSilva, *Transformation*, 19–24, 50–53.

293. Rightly Watson, *Paul, Judaism, and the Gentiles*, 65, who further critiques Bultmann for leaving aside his correct exegetical observations about "works of the law" in Galatians to identify the heart of the problem as legalism, "the problem of good works as the condition for participation in salvation" (*Theology of the New Testament*, 2:111). The "mental leap from circumcision to a wrong understanding of good works is quite illegitimate" (Watson, *Paul, Judaism, and the Gentiles*, 69).

294. Such a conviction is vividly expressed in 4QMMT, "Some Works of the Torah," a document found among the Dead Sea Scrolls that appears to represent a letter from a teacher within the sect (the Teacher of Righteousness himself?) to a priestly counterpart in the Jerusalem temple. The author writes from the perspective of living at "the end of days" (Vermes,

dent provides the immediate context for Paul's exposition of his position in 2:15–21, and thus the immediate point of reference for "works of the law." The arrival of the people from James was the catalyst for Peter and, following in his train, the other Christian Jews in Antioch to fall in line with a particular way of performing works of the law in regard to dietary practice, particularly with a view to honoring the boundaries that Torah drew—and drew quite sharply and explicitly (see Lev 20:22–26)—between Jew and non-Jew as an expression of God's will for the Jew and the special identity and relationship bestowed upon the Jew by God (see Jub. 22.16; Let. Aris. 139, 142; 3 Macc 3:3–4).[295] The pastoral context of Galatians foregrounds circumcision as another "work of the law" that reinforces a clear boundary between Jew and non-Jew, with the invitation having been issued to the gentile Christ-followers to cross that line for the sake of aligning with the Torah and the benefits such alignment would confer (5:1–6; 6:12–15).[296] Paul also mentions other works of the law that his converts have already begun practicing, namely, certain Jewish calendrical observances, at least including observance of the Sabbath (4:10). It can be no accident that Paul, the rival teachers, and the people from James were all foregrounding the works of the law that were also the most visible and widely known marks of Jewish identity, the marks that distinguished Jew from non-Jew, even in the common knowledge of gentiles.[297] The question on the table was very much whether God and his Messiah were still the God and Messiah of *Israel*.[298]

While works of the law such as circumcision, food laws, and Sabbath observance may be foremost on Paul's mind as he remembers Antioch and addresses Galatia, Paul does not limit his understanding of the phrase "works of the law" to these markers of Jewish distinctiveness. Paul considers Torah

---

Complete, 227; see Qimron, Composite Text C14, 247; C16, 248; C30, 251), which calls for a return to faithful and precise observance of the Torah. To this end, he shares some rulings concerning how to perform "some works of the Torah" and commends them to his priestly counterpart: "It will be reckoned for you as righteousness when you perform what is right and good before Him, for your own good and for that of Israel" (Vermes, *Complete*, 228; see Qimron, Composite Text C31–32, 251). See also Dunn ("4QMMT"), who underscores the way in which particular "works of the law" function as a boundary in both 4QMMT and Gal 2:11–21. In the former, it is a boundary between (scrupulously pious) Jews and (covenant-breaking because not as scrupulously pious) Jews. In the latter, it is a boundary between Jews and gentiles (Dunn, "4QMMT," 151).

295. Bruce, 29; Dunn, "New Perspective," 191–94; Barclay, *Obeying the Truth*, 78; Wright, *Justification*, 117.

296. In Rom 4, circumcision functions as *the* representative "work (of the law)."

297. Dunn, 131–50, "New Perspective," and "Yet Once More."

298. A corollary of distinctiveness was ethnic pride in Torah as a sign of God's special favor toward the Jews (hence Paul's castigation of "confidence in the flesh" and of "boasting" in the law; see Rom 2:23; 3:27–30; Phil 3:3–6).

as a *whole* throughout this letter, pointing out its indivisibility (5:3).[299] The Torah as a holistic system of conduct, with its ethical, ritual, and boundary-maintaining regulations, was a temporary measure in God's economy. Its authority was instituted for a particular people (in this regard, Torah was in toto a boundary marker) 430 years after Abraham, and it served a positive function for a prescribed time (see on 3:19–25),[300] but its divinely given mandate came to an end "in the fullness of time" with the coming of faith. With the death and resurrection of Jesus, God was setting in motion his plan to extend the promise and the blessing to all the nations, something that "zeal for the Torah" quite thoroughly inhibited. To reintroduce works of the Torah such as circumcision, dietary regulations, and observance of the Jewish sacred calendar now after the "fullness of time" would be to work against God's purposes for bringing the promise given to Abraham to all people in the new community of Christ, in which the divisions and hierarchies sustained by the labels "Jew," "gentile," "slave," "free," "male," and "female" are transcended (Gal 3:28). Torah as a whole, Paul argues, is simply no longer the means by which people can align themselves with the standards of God's righteousness. This role is now fulfilled by God's own Spirit (3:2–5; 5:13–25), a benefit attained for Jew and gentile alike by Jesus at greatest cost to himself (3:10–14).

In trying to remain *true* to the law, non-Christian Jews and Judaizing Christians were, in Paul's understanding, *betraying* the law, not observing that its goal had been reached in the coming of Christ. Insisting on works of the Torah meant trying to reerect the "dividing wall of hostility" at a time when God had torn it down in Christ and in the outpouring of the Spirit (see Gal 2:18; Eph 2:11–16), thus acting in open defiance of God. Foundational to Paul's position against regulating life in the new community in line with Torah (and its intentional reinforcement of the Jew-gentile distinctions) is the fact that Torah played no role in bringing either the Jew or the gentile to life in this greater sense. Coming alive to God, entering into the life that *is* life, all happened through trusting Jesus and receiving the Holy Spirit, and therefore all happened for the Jew and the gentile in precisely the same way.

---

299. Dunn rightly includes "all or whatever the law requires . . . as a whole" within his understanding of "works of the law" (*Theology of Paul*, 358; "Intra-Jewish Polemic," 466; *New Perspective*, 23–28). He simply emphasizes those identity markers that are also foregrounded by Paul himself (Dunn, 136; so also Yinger, *Paul, Judaism, and Judgment*, 171).

300. Moo ("Law," 97) suggests that "Paul's argument . . . indicates that 'works of the law' have *always* been an improper way to seek God's righteousness." I disagree. Paul viewed conformity with the stipulations of the Torah as quite proper *prior to* the coming of Christ and the path to righteousness opened up by trusting Christ. Obedience to the pedagogue while a child is indeed proper; the matter becomes problematic only with the child's coming of age, the coming of the "time set by the father."

A few clarifications concerning Paul's critique of seeking to be found aligned with God's righteousness by means of doing what the Torah prescribes are in order. First, Paul is not opposed to this pursuit because he views it as an "externalistic" or "legalistic" practice, or as an attempt to earn God's favor, as if one could thereby indebt God.[301] God's giving of the Torah to Moses was itself regarded as an expression of God's incredible favor, God's *grace*, toward Israel, the gift of a covenant with the one God that God did not make with any other nation.[302] Living in line with the Torah was not typically seen as a means of earning God's grace, but rather as the grateful *response* to the God who had graced Israel with the unique privileges of a covenant relationship, and a means by which to remain within that covenant relationship and enjoy its blessings.[303] Doing what Torah prescribed, as the means by which one made a grateful response, was also the means by which to continue to encounter God as benefactor for the future. The opposite, neglecting the Torah and its prescriptions, would display rank ingratitude to the God who called for the obedience and display of loyalty inscribed in the Torah.[304] A gracious and grateful response to a benefactor shows oneself to be the sort of person to whom a benefactor will wish to continue to give (see excursus "A Contextual Understanding of Grace"on pp. 254–62). While Paul now conceived of the decisive manifestation of God's favor and therefore the kind of response that would be appropriate quite differently, he would be no less adamant concerning the importance of a grateful response. Second, Paul does not oppose "works of the law" in the present era because he deems it impossible to live by its prescriptions (see commentary on 3:10). He himself had done so quite well (Phil 3:6). Moreover, God had generously made provisions for failure to observe the covenant in the form of sacrifices, so that forgiveness and reconciliation remained available. Such provisions

---

301. As in Fuller, "Works of the Law" (31), whose goal is to determine whether such legalistic living is inherent in the law of Moses or merely in its abuse, "the legalistic *misin*terpretation of the law advocated by Judaism." See also Burton (120), who defines "works of the law" as "deeds of obedience to formal statutes done in the legalistic spirit, with the expectation of thereby meriting and securing divine approval and award."

302. See Sir 24:1–23; 4 Macc 5:22–26; Dunn, 16–17.

303. Even texts that appear to speak about amassing "a storehouse of works" that results in reward from God (e.g., 4 Ezra 7.77; 8.33) do not abandon this essential framework of regarding acts of obedience toward God's law as a *response* to God's prior acts of generosity (see deSilva, "Grace, the Law, and Justification"). The works that God rewards are those that result from acknowledging and responding to God's just claims on God's creatures and beneficiaries. The only merit that accrues from them is the merit of showing oneself a grateful recipient of God's favors (and thus a suitable recipient of further favor).

304. The rival teachers would also understand themselves to proclaim a gospel of grace, centered on "God's choice of Abraham and his seed from among the nations, to be the recipients of salvation" (Watson, *Paul, Judaism, and the Gentiles*, 65).

show that "flawless performance" was not expected. The principal problem with the Torah was that its term had expired and that what was its strength prior to Christ was now its greatest flaw—the maintenance of the boundary between Jew and gentile on the pretense that the former retained "favored nation" status before God.

EXCURSUS: WHAT DOES PAUL MEAN BY "FAITH" QUALIFIED BY "JESUS CHRIST"?

The Greek phrase *pistis Iēsou* or *pistis Christou* or an equivalent appears at several crucial points in Paul's discussions about how people can pursue justification in God's sight (Gal 2:16 [2x]; 3:22; Rom 3:22, 26; Phil 3:9). There are two significant challenges in the interpretation or translation of this phrase. The first is lexical, since the Greek word *pistis* can have several different meanings. Its principal senses are (1) trust or confidence (in others); (2) faithfulness or that which inspires confidence; and (3) that which is believed, accepted as true.[305] The first two senses are the more likely possibilities evoked in Gal 2:15–16 and 3:22.[306]

The second issue is grammatical and concerns what nuance we should understand to be communicated by the genitive case in which "Jesus" or "Christ" appears. Nouns in the genitive case generally give greater specificity to, and thus limit, another noun by adding a descriptor. In essence, a noun in the genitive case is set in relationship to another noun (say, "love") to supply an answer to a question like Whose love? What kind of love? Love for whom? Love from what source? In the phrase in question, the genitive form "of Christ" tends to be construed either as answering the question "Whose *pistis*?" (a "subjective" genitive, indicating who is showing *pistis*) or answering the question "*pistis* toward whom?" or "*pistis* whither directed?" (an "objective" genitive, indicating the object of the *pistis* of others). A parallel example

---

305. See LSJ 1408; BDAG 818–20. The Louw-Nida lexicon distinguishes between six senses: 31.43 *pistis* [a], "that which is completely believable," "what can be fully believed," hence "proof"; 31.85 *pistis* [b], "faith, trust"; 31.88 *pistis* [c], "trustworthiness, dependability, faithfulness"; 31.102 *pistis* [d], "[Christian] faith"; 31.104 *pistis* [e], "the content of what Christians believe," hence "the faith, beliefs, doctrines"; 33.289 *pistis* [f], "promise, pledge to be faithful."

306. The third sense, as "the faith, beliefs, doctrines," appeared in Gal 1:23. Sprinkle ("πίστις Χριστοῦ as an Eschatological Event") advances an intriguing argument for an alternative that takes πίστις in the expression in question also in this sense ("the faith-message about Christ"), as well as in the equally troublesome expression ἐξ ἀκοῆς πίστεως (3:2), "the message about the faith." On the latter, see commentary on 3:2. This sense has been proposed for the use of the word in 3:23 (see commentary on 3:23).

of the difference between a subjective and objective genitive can be found in the statement "The love of Christ [*agapē Christou*] compels us" (2 Cor 5:14). Is it Paul's team's love *for* Christ (an objective genitive), or Christ's love (a subjective genitive) as experienced by Paul and his team, that compels them to preach the gospel?

These two sets of variables produce four principal possibilities for the interpretation of the phrase *pistis Christou*:

1. Trust directed toward Jesus, reliance on Jesus
2. Faithfulness or loyalty directed toward Jesus
3. Jesus's trust in God, or his reliance on God
4. Jesus's faithfulness toward God (or possibly toward Jesus's followers)

Almost all modern translations resolve the ambiguity of the phrase in favor of the first of these four options, so that the Christian's faith or trust in Jesus is foregrounded (e.g., "faith in Jesus Christ," Gal 2:16 NRSV, NIV, NLT). A growing consensus, however, favors the third or fourth options above (reflected now in the CEB, "the faithfulness of Jesus Christ," Gal 2:16), suggesting that we understand Paul to use this phrase to draw attention to Jesus's own faithfulness toward God as the effective cause by which the possibility of justification has come into the world, a topic certainly brought to the fore in key Pauline texts (e.g., Rom 3:22–26; 5:18–19), even if not in this particular phrase.

The primary arguments in favor of interpreting the phrase as "Jesus's faith" or "Jesus's faithfulness" (hence, taking "of Jesus" as a subjective genitive), then, are as follows. First, it maintains parallelism between the "faith of Jesus" (2:16) and the "faith of Abraham" (3:6–9). No one would suggest that we translate the latter as "believing in Abraham." As a fully human being, Jesus, too, needed to have and to demonstrate trust in and reliance on God, especially as the God who raises the dead.[307] Abraham demonstrated trust in God; Jesus, the "Seed" of Abraham, demonstrated the same faith or faithfulness toward God. Thus the blessing promised to Abraham and to his Seed is secured for all who likewise trust.[308] Second, it avoids the redundancy inherent in the traditional interpretation, which, if followed, means that the disciple's trust is mentioned three times in a single verse (Gal 2:16).[309] Finally,

---

307. Contra Dunn, *Theology*, 382.

308. Hooker, "ΠΙΣΤΙΣ ΧΡΙΣΤΟΥ," 325–31.

309. Hays, *The Faith of Jesus Christ*[1], 158, 171–72; Campbell, *Rhetoric of Righteousness*, 62–63; Hooker, "ΠΙΣΤΙΣ ΧΡΙΣΤΟΥ," 322, 329, though she correctly admits that Paul is no stranger to redundancy. See also the potential redundancy in Gal 3:22: "in order that the promise might be given [*a*] on the basis of trusting Jesus [*b*] to those who continue to trust [Jesus]."

in regard to the occurrences of the phrase in Rom 3:22–26, it is in keeping with Paul's use of unambiguously subjective genitives in connection with *pistis* at Rom 3:3; 4:12, 16.[310]

These arguments, however, are ultimately not strong enough to justify a coup d'état in biblical translation, for several reasons.

1. The example of Abraham points equally well, if not more strongly, in the direction of understanding *pistis Christou* as "trust in Christ," since it is specifically Abraham's "trust in God" that Paul highlights as the response that led to Abraham's justification (Gal 3:6, 9; Gen 15:6). It is not Abraham and Christ, but Abraham and *the believer* who stand in parallel situations where "faith" is concerned (with both Abraham and the believer needing to exhibit trust toward some object), with "those who are characterized by faith," that is, the Christ-followers, becoming Abraham's children by virtue of exhibiting trust as he did.[311] Abraham is *never* explicitly named as a potential object of

---

310. Hays, *Faith of Jesus Christ*[1], 171; Hays, "Pauline Christology," 47; Campbell, *Rhetoric of Righteousness*, 66–67; Stowers, *Rereading of Romans*, 201. Other arguments have been put forward. For example, Rom 3:21–22, which speaks of the manifestation of God's righteousness in the "now" of Paul's era, is often presented as evidence in favor of the subjective genitive reading: is human faith (the sense rendered by an objective genitive reading) the means by which God's righteousness is revealed? Is it not better to understand Jesus's faithfulness as the means to this end? So Hays, *Faith of Jesus Christ*[1], 158–60; Choi, "ΠΙΣΤΙΣ in Galatians 5:5–6," 476; Campbell, "Romans 1:17," 272–76; Campbell, *Deliverance of God*, 379, 610. While establishing the meaning of the phrase in Romans is not essential to establishing its sense in Galatians, a closer look at Rom 3:21–22 suggests that this particular argument is not sound. Its proponents read διὰ πίστεως Ἰησοῦ Χριστοῦ as an *adverbial* prepositional phrase modifying πεφανέρωται and base their claim upon this reading (e.g., Campbell, *Deliverance*, 610: "If the meaning of πίστις is related directly to Christ . . . the exact sense of these Pauline statements [is completed] nicely: 'the δικαιοσύνη θεοῦ [righteousness of God] is disclosed or revealed by means of the πίστις of Jesus Christ'"). Paul, however, gives every signal in his Greek text (particularly by interjecting a second utterance of the noun phrase δικαιοσύνη δὲ[!] θεοῦ) that διὰ πίστεως Ἰησοῦ Χριστοῦ is intended to be heard as an *adjectival* prepositional phrase modifying δικαιοσύνη. If this analysis is correct, then there is no basis at all for the argument. Paul is simply stating that God's long-awaited righteousness has at last been revealed (saying nothing here about the means), and then describing that righteousness as an experience that comes to each believer by virtue of his or her trust in God's agent.

Wright (*Pauline Perspectives*, 201–2) also favors the subjective genitive reading, since, in his view, the primary problem was Israel's unfaithfulness to the covenant: "Israel has been 'faithless' to the commission to be the light of the world (cf. [Rom] 2.17–24). How then is God to reveal his own covenant faithfulness? . . . Through the faithfulness of Jesus the Messiah, the representative Israelite." Those who join themselves to Jesus thus join faithful Israel. See also Wright, *Justification*, 67, 104–5, 198, 203–4.

311. Dunn, 139; Dunn, "Faith, Faithfulness," 418–19; Johnson, "Paradigm of Abraham," 192. Against the objection that Abraham cannot serve as a model of the Christian's faith because he exhibited a purely theocentric faith prior to the coming of Christ and the pos-

faith in Pauline discourse (though reliance on Abraham for acquittal before God is conceivable in the first century; see Matt 3:7–9), but Jesus is so named on numerous occasions (even in this immediate context, Gal 2:16).[312] Abraham's faith in God appropriately parallels the believer's faith in God's Messiah.

2. Redundancy is the hallmark of Gal 2:16, in particular. Apart from the occurrences of "trust in Christ" (*pistis Christou*) and "we trusted in Christ" in this verse, there is a threefold repetition of both (*a*) the verb "to be justified" and (*b*) the prepositional phrase "on the basis of works of the law":

> knowing that a person (*a¹*) *is not justified* (*b¹*) *on the basis of works of the law* . . . in order that (*a²*) *we might be justified* . . . not (*b²*) *on the basis of works of the law*, because (*b³*) *on the basis of works of the law* all flesh (*a³*) *will fail to be justified*.

The presence of such obvious, triple redundancy in regard to the theme of "justification on the basis of works of the law" mitigates the force of any objection regarding redundancy of the theme of trusting in Christ. Indeed, the threefold repetition of "works of law," as well as "to justify," might seem to require a threefold repetition of "trusting in Christ."[313] Closer observa-

---

sibility of "Christian" faith (Campbell, *Deliverance of God*, 1162–63n130; Campbell, "False Presuppositions," 718), Paul claims Abraham's trust in God to be predicated upon Scripture "announcing the gospel to Abraham ahead of time," including the fact "that God would justify the gentiles on the basis of faith" (3:8). The promise given to Abraham in Gen 12:3, which Abraham trusted (and in the Giver of which promise Abraham trusted), is linked by Paul quite explicitly with the gospel that he himself preaches. Abraham's response to that message is thus, for *Paul*, fully a prototype of the Galatian convert's response (rightly, Matlock, "Saving Faith," 82–83).

312. Hooker's attempt to argue in favor of "Jesus's faith" rather than "faith in Jesus" on the basis of the unlikelihood of translating πίστις Ἀβραάμ as "faith in Abraham" is therefore fundamentally flawed. The fact that subjective genitive relationships involving πίστις are more common in Paul than objective genitive relationships is simply to be expected, and not significant (Matlock, "Demons," 304). If the noun accompanying πίστις is not God or Christ, the possibility of an objective genitive does not even arise in Paul.

Some scholars have argued that the use of the genitive to denote the object of trust is contrary to normal Greek usage. Evidence does not support this conclusion. Surveying the usage of πίστις in Plutarch, Matlock ("Demons," 304) found that πίστις is used in the sense of "faith, trust, confidence" about forty times. Half the time the object of trust is not overtly identified. When the object is explicitly named, five times it is indicated by the preposition πρός, once by περί, and thirteen times by the object of trust named as a noun in the genitive case. Matlock does not seek thereby to create prejudice *for* an objective genitive reading in Paul, but to provide counterevidence to the trend in the debate to speak of the objective genitive as less natural (or even improbable). See also Harrisville, "Before πίστις Χριστοῦ"; Porter and Pitts, "πίστις with a Preposition and Genitive Modifier," 49–51.

313. Matlock, "Demons," 307. Hooker ("ΠΙΣΤΙΣ ΧΡΙΣΤΟΥ," 322) attempts to dismiss

tion, moreover, shows that *repetition* here does not amount to *redundancy*: in Gal 2:16, Paul describes first an act of knowing ("a person is not justified . . . except by means of trusting Jesus") and then an act of committing oneself to the path of that knowledge ("even *we* trusted in Jesus, in order that . . .").[314]

3. The fact that Paul uses subjective genitives in connection with *pistis* at Rom 3:3; 4:12, 16 does not tip the balance in favor of reading the genitive constructions involving the same noun at Rom 3:22, 26 as subjective genitives. The context of each fresh occurrence determines which sense of *pistis* will be invoked and what relationship the genitive case will be understood to indicate.[315] The contrast in Rom 3:1-3 between God and the "faithless" or "unreliable" people of God determines the selection of "faithfulness" as the appropriate sense for *pistis* and the selection of a subjective genitival relationship between "God" and "faithfulness" to form an appropriate contrast with Israel's "faithlessness." The context of discussing Abraham (Rom 4:12, 16) as an exemplar of the faith (notably, "faith in God") that leads to justification determines the selection of "faith" or "trust" for *pistis* and the construal of Abraham as the one who is displaying "faith" (hence, a subjective genitive). The question remains, then: what sense of *pistis* and what relationship between the noun *pistis* and the genitive noun *Christou* does the context of Rom 3:22, 26 (or any other such passage) evoke?

To these considerations against the positive arguments in favor of reading *pistis Christou* as "Christ's faith/faithfulness" (a subjective genitive), we may add the following arguments in favor of retaining the reading "trust in Christ" (an objective genitive):

4. Christians closer to Paul in terms of linguistic and cultural context—church fathers like Origen and John Chrysostom—read the relevant passages as speaking about "trust in Christ," not as speaking about "Christ's faith" or "Christ's faithfulness." In several instances the church father does not gloss or comment on the phrase, leaving it ambiguous (for us). But wherever they give an explanation or gloss that resolves the ambiguity of the grammatical construction, it is consistently in the direction of the objective genitive. Indeed, they give no indication that the subjective genitive reading is even a

---

this argument, writing that it "is strange logic! For if the sentence *already* contains an expression of the believer's response to God's actions, do we need another?" Our sensibilities of what is needful, however, hardly constitute a factor in the disambiguation of Paul's writing.

314. Dunn, 139. The same can be said in regard to Gal 3:22. The phrases τοῖς πιστεύουσιν and ἐκ πίστεως Ἰησοῦ Χριστοῦ answer different questions: "to whom" is the promise given and "on what basis or by what means" is the promise conferred. The fact of some overlap in these answers should not result in neglecting the areas' nonoverlap, with the consequent accusation of mere "redundancy."

315. Matlock, "Detheologizing," 16-17.

possible alternative to be weighed.[316] If Eph 2:8–10 and Jas 2:14–16 represent early interpretations of the Pauline antithesis of faith versus works of the law (already truncated to faith versus works), "the 'faith' in question is quite unexceptionally that of believers," and not of Christ.[317]

5. Since "faith toward Christ" and "Christ's faith/faithfulness" are both possible meanings of this phrase, hearers would depend upon the context of the phrase to help clarify which is meant. In the immediate context, the verb *episteusamen* ("we put our trust"), the cognate verb form of *pistis* ("trust/faithfulness"), is used with "Jesus Christ" clearly marked as the object of trust in the middle of two occurrences of the ambiguous genitive phrase "faith of Christ." The clear meaning of the verbal phrase should draw the hearers toward resolving the ambiguity of the noun phrases in favor of the objective genitive,[318] despite the repetitiveness within the verse. If Paul had intended

---

316. Harrisville, "ΠΙΣΤΙΣ ΧΡΙΣΤΟΥ"; see also Silva, *Interpreting Galatians*, 29–31.

317. Matlock, "Detheologizing," 23; see also Matlock, "Demons," 306–7. The qualification "and this not as something coming from yourselves" shows "faith" in Eph 2:8 to be the disciple's faith, which the disciple could, but ought not to, claim as something he or she has generated on his or her own. Foster ("First Contribution") convincingly argues that, when the author of Ephesians writes that "in Christ, we have boldness and confident access through his faithfulness" (διὰ τῆς πίστεως αὐτοῦ, Eph 3:12), he is talking about Christ's display of faithful obedience to God, pointing to essentially the same reality as he did in Eph 2:16 ("through the cross," διὰ τοῦ σταυροῦ) and Eph 2:18 ("through him," δι' αὐτοῦ, notably there affirming that both Jews and gentiles have "access through him"). However, Foster suggests that we must accept one of only two implications of this conclusion for the πίστις Χριστοῦ debate: either (1) the author of Ephesians inadvertently misrepresented Paul's meaning in the latter's use of the phrase πίστις Χριστοῦ or (2) the author of Ephesians purposefully sought to explicate that phrase as a subjective genitive. It seems to me that a third option needs to be considered: (3) the author of Ephesians is using διὰ τῆς πίστεως αὐτοῦ to refer to Jesus's faithful obedience, to which Paul and other members of his team refer using other language (e.g., see Heb 12:2), without any intention thereby of telling the reader of Ephesians how to read the (anarthrous) phrase πίστις Χριστοῦ in Galatians or Romans. (It is the modern exegete, not the Pauline team, that is hung up on this phrase and bent on determining whether it must be subjective or objective, after all.) Foster writes, "It is likely, unless one wants to adopt an imperious attitude concerning the superiority of modern interpreters in comparison to those of the first century, that those who stood so close to the apostle were in fact correctly informed about his meaning" ("First Contribution," 96). While in principle I would agree with him about the need to be humble in the face of early church interpretations of New Testament texts, he seems to me to overplay this particular card: he has *not* shown that the author of Ephesians does intend in any way to make a "first contribution" to this debate rather than simply talk about Christ's faithful obedience, using perfectly natural language for doing so, quite alongside Paul's very natural use of similar language to talk about trusting this Christ.

318. So Hultgren, "*Pistis Christou* Formulation," 255; Schreiner, *Romans*, 185; Silva, "Faith versus Works," 232; Fee, *Pauline Christology*, 224; Matlock, "Saving Faith," 83–86; Tolmie, *Persuading*, 90. Campbell (*Deliverance of God*, 841) engages in a bit of special pleading when he argues that we read ἡμεῖς εἰς Χριστὸν Ἰησοῦν ἐπιστεύσαμεν (Gal 2:16) as "we also

for people to hear *pistis Christou* as "Christ's trust [toward God]" or "Christ's faithfulness [toward either God or us or both]," he would have needed to add something that would bring out this nuance more clearly, since the immediate context is working against hearing this sense.[319]

6. The alternative to *pistis Christou* is "works of the Torah" (*erga nomou*), a succinct phrase signifying "doing what the Torah commands." Since this option clearly falls within the realm of human response to God, context again weighs in favor of hearing *pistis Christou* as "trust in Christ," the alternative human response—the response that Paul wants the Galatians to see as incompatible with "works of the Torah," against the rival teachers' suggestion that these two human responses are fully compatible, even integral. Again, the fact that Paul and his fellow Jewish Christians (the imagined conversation partners in Gal 2:15–16) explicitly choose to respond by "trusting in Christ" ("so even we have put our trust in Jesus Christ," 2:16) reinforces hearing "works of Torah" and "trust in Jesus" as two parallel options for human response.[320]

The traditional translation of *pistis Christou* as "trust in Christ" in Galatians, at least, seems to be the most probable.

The discussion is fraught with theological significance for many of those who have engaged it. Objections have been raised to the traditional translation because it appears to make the human response of faith into the basis for justification in Paul. Does this not make "faith" itself into a "work," resulting in just another kind of "justification by works"?[321] Is it not more in keeping with Paul to locate that basis in the work of Jesus on humanity's behalf, specifically his obedience to God to the point of death (hence a preference for translating the phrase as "Jesus's faithfulness toward God").[322] Such objec-

---

believed concerning Christ Jesus," taking the accusative Χριστὸν Ἰησοῦν as an accusative of respect with εἰς as a redundant case marker (though not one that would normally indicate "reference"), sacrificing a natural and typical reading of ἐπιστεύσαμεν εἰς for the sake of undermining an argument that supports the objective genitive reading (Campbell's main objective).

319. Moule, "Biblical Conception," 157; Dunn, 139; Matlock, "Detheologizing," 13. Dunn (*Theology*, 379–85) observes that we quite naturally and rightly understand πίστιν θεοῦ to mean "faith in God" in Mark 11:22, in large measure because the context clarifies the grammatical ambiguity (see 11:23, where πιστεύῃ refers to the disciple's act of trusting God). He regards the verbal forms in Gal 2:16 (ἡμεῖς εἰς Χριστὸν Ἰησοῦν ἐπιστεύσαμεν) and 3:22 (τοῖς πιστεύουσιν) to provide similar contextual clues in Galatians, leading him to strongly affirm "faith in Christ" as the proper understanding.

320. Dunn, 139; Matlock, "Detheologizing," 12; Hultgren, "*Pistis Christou*," 258–59; Fee, 226; deBoer, 149.

321. Hooker, "ΠΙΣΤΙΣ ΧΡΙΣΤΟΥ," 341. The same objection drives Hays, "ΠΙΣΤΙΣ and Pauline Christology," 45–46.

322. Hooker, "ΠΙΣΤΙΣ ΧΡΙΣΤΟΥ," 337–38. Hooker goes so far as to suggest that "if Paul does not use this idea [namely, of Christ's faithfulness], then he ought to" (324). This is

tions overlook the fact that Paul is not setting "faith in Christ" (or "Christ's faithfulness," for that matter) over against "works" as "human acts," but rather over against "works prescribed by the law," those acts performed out of an attempt to fall in line with God's righteous standards by conforming one's life to the Torah.[323] "Faith in Christ" categorically cannot be a "work" of the kind that actually concerns Paul (esp. a work of the sort that perpetuates the barriers between Jew and gentile and the religious hegemony and privilege of the former).

More important, Paul's antithesis of "trusting Jesus" over against "following the prescriptions of the Torah" does not answer the question "What has saving power, works or faith?"[324] The question is closer to "What path will lead us toward successfully conforming our lives to the standards of a righteous God, in whose eyes we seek to be acquitted?" The answer to the greater question, "What has saving power?" is always, for Paul, the beneficent self-giving of Jesus on our behalf *and* God's gracious provision of the Holy Spirit won for us by the same. This basis, moreover, is explicitly named throughout Galatians quite apart from the resolution of the translation of *pistis Christou* (see, e.g., Gal 1:4; 2:20–21; 3:10–14).[325] "Faith in Christ" is merely our response of recognizing *that* basis as adequate and recognizing Jesus as a trustworthy and reliable mediator of God's favor and agent of reconciliation,[326] such that we receive their gifts and enter into the reciprocal relationship of grace and response to grace into which God in Christ invites us as the means and venue for our justification (our transformation, by God's Spirit's working within us, into people who reflect God's righteousness).

It is probably important to bear in mind that *neither* solution removes the essential content conveyed by the *alternative* solution from Pauline discourse. That is to say, if the proponents of the subjective genitive reading ("Christ's faithfulness") are correct, the place of a human response of trusting and moving forward in trust is not diminished. Paul testifies that he and his fellow Jewish Christians have still "trusted in Christ Jesus" as a prerequisite to being "made right on the basis of Jesus's faithfulness" (Gal 2:16; cf. Rom 3:22).[327] If the proponents of the objective genitive reading ("trusting Jesus")

---

probably the foundational factor in the quest to establish the subjective genitive reading: it is deemed theologically richer.

323. Gordon, "Problem at Galatia," 36; Caneday, "Faithfulness of Jesus Christ," 196–97. Paul has a positive view of and place for "Spirit-driven works." See excursus "What Does Paul Mean by 'Works of the Law'?" on pp. 224–29.

324. Matlock, "Even the Demons Believe," 313.

325. So also, rightly, Martyn, 271; Watson, "By Faith (of Christ)," 163.

326. So rightly van Daalen, "'Faith' according to Paul," 84.

327. Hooker, "ΠΙΣΤΙΣ ΧΡΙΣΤΟΥ," 337. Eisenbaum (*Paul Was Not a Christian*, 189–95, esp. 195), who favors the translation "faithfulness of Jesus Christ," appears to overlook this

are correct, the place of Jesus's own faithfulness and obedience is similarly not diminished. Paul's trust is in the one "who loved me and gave himself for me" (Gal 2:20), whose death redeemed us from the curse of the Torah, the power of the flesh, and the fundamental principles of this world's order (3:10–14; 4:4–5, 8–11; 5:24; 6:14), and won for us adoption into God's family and the gift of God's transforming Spirit.

Reading the phrase as "trusting Jesus" or "faith in Christ," however, what does Paul *mean* by such faith or trust? "Faith" is more than a religious feeling that the disciple manifests or manufactures.[328] It is, rather, an actual and active reliance upon, and the full investment of oneself in, what Jesus, the object of our reliance, has done for us, provides for us, and will yet do within us as we live no longer but as he comes alive within and animates us. Trusting Jesus means relying upon the benefits that Jesus has brought by his death and resurrection (the benefits that faith has allowed the one who trusts to receive), chief among which is the Holy Spirit, and trusting that the latter has power enough to lead the Christ-follower into the righteousness that the God who will judge the living and the dead will approve (5:5–6, 16–25).[329]

In Gal 2:16, Paul continues to relate his (constructed) address to Peter before their fellow Jewish Christians in Antioch. After playing to the general Jewish prejudice, according to which God has given the Jews the special privilege of being taken into the Sinaitic covenant and not being left, as were the gentiles, without law and thus, de facto, "sinners," he takes a further step in which he parts company from *non*-Christian Jews but still speaks in line with what other Jewish Christians would affirm: "Knowing that a person is not deemed

---

point entirely when she claims that, "technically speaking, the Greek equivalent of the phrase 'faith in Christ' never occurs in the undisputed Pauline letters. . . . If Paul did not ever speak of having faith in Christ, that is, having faith in Christ on a par with having faith in God, then Paul's monotheism remained uncompromised." Paul certainly *did* speak about "putting faith in Christ," though this is not to say that he was a polytheist.

328. Hays ("ΠΙΣΤΙΣ and Pauline Christology," 46) claims that reading the phrase as "faith in Christ," that is, as an objective genitive, "verges on blasphemous self-absorption in our own religious subjectivity." Such a claim, however, is based on popular notions of what "faith in Christ" entails rather than a genuinely Pauline notion.

329. See also Gorman, *Inhabiting*, 84, where this trust is described as a "*cruciform* faith, as the response of Spirit-enabled participation in the faithful, loving death of Christ and henceforth in his cruciform resurrection life. This is why Paul can affirm that justification is by faith alone [*sic*: Paul himself never qualifies "faith" with "alone"] and also affirm, with utmost seriousness, that God judges and justifies on the basis of doing the law (Rom 2:13). This is the law of love manifested in the obedience/faith/death of Christ, the law or 'narrative pattern' of the Messiah, the fulfillment of which is made possible by the indwelling, living Christ."

to be aligned with God's righteousness on the basis of the works of the law except by trusting Jesus Christ, *even we* have put our trust in Christ Jesus in order that we might be acquitted as people aligned with God's righteousness on the basis of trusting Christ and not on the basis of the works prescribed by the law, since all flesh will not be deemed aligned with God's righteousness on the basis of law-prescribed works."

The core of this very involved sentence is the emphatic declaration that "even we" Jews by birth have turned to Jesus in trust in order to attain the desired outcome—acquittal on the day of judgment as people who have lined themselves up with God's standards for righteousness.[330] Second, Paul may have used the literary device of chiasm to underscore this phrase as the focus point:

> A   that [*hoti*] a person is not justified
> > B   on the basis of Torah-prescribed works
> > > C   except through trusting Jesus
> > > > D   even we trusted in Christ Jesus
> > > C'   in order that we might be justified on the basis of trusting Christ
> > B'   and not on the basis of Torah-prescribed works
> A'   because [*hoti*] all flesh will fail to be justified on the basis of Torah-prescribed works[331]

Even the privileged Jews have taken the step of trusting Jesus, which has implications shortly to be drawn out for the "privilege" that has *hitherto* set the Jew apart from the gentile "sinner."

Paul and his fellow Jewish Christ-followers have taken this step because they came to know that "a person is not deemed to be aligned with God's righteousness on the basis of the works of Torah except by trusting Jesus Christ."[332] Throughout this verse, Paul uses a preposition to introduce "works

---

330. Paul underscores this core in two ways. First, he uses an adverbial καί ("even") in conjunction with a redundant, and therefore emphatic, nominative pronoun (ἡμεῖς, "we").

331. The chiasm is arranged slightly differently (and perhaps more precisely) in Tolmie, *Persuading*, 98–99, and the fact that chiasms can often be construed in multiple ways should make us hold them but lightly as rhetorical devices. Even here, the third appearance of "Torah-prescribed works" is arbitrarily sidelined. The microchiasm is, however, a well-attested ancient practice, unlike the macrochiastic outline of major sections of texts or even entire texts. On the problems with the latter, see deSilva, "X Marks the Spot?"

332. The adverbial participial phrase introduced by εἰδότες is construed here as causal. The repetition of "trusting Jesus" in 2:16 is not merely redundancy. Paul first describes an act of knowing ("justification comes by means of trusting Jesus") and then, as a consequence, an act of committing oneself to the path of that knowledge ("even we trusted in Jesus, in order that . . ."). So, rightly, Dunn, 139.

of the Torah" and "reliance on Jesus" that is most commonly used in a spatial sense, denoting movement out of or from some space. Here, however, it is being used in one of its derivative senses, most likely "basis" or "means."[333] A paraphrase of the verse intending to capture the nuance that this preposition brings to the relationship between "works of the Torah" and "being acquitted" or "being set right" might read: "Conforming one's life to the requirements of the Torah, unless this is joined with trusting in Jesus, does not result in (or does not lead to) acquittal before God."[334]

Because Paul is still speaking alongside and from the perspective of his fellow Jewish Christians, he allows for a moment that "trusting Jesus" is a necessary *supplement* to "conforming one's life to the requirements of Torah." This is not a concession, but a strategy.[335] Paul does not endorse the view that Jewish Christians must observe works of the law *plus* trust in Jesus in order to fall in line with God. Rather, Paul first states a position with which even the rival teachers (like the "people from James" in Antioch) would agree so as to

---

333. See BDAG 295–97 (s.v. ἐκ). The single use of διά here is probably the result of "paradigmatic variation" and bears the same essential sense as ἐκ (which replaces διά the next time the expression "trusting Jesus" appears in this verse). See Campbell, "Meaning of πίστις," 95, 98–99; also Dunn, *Romans 1–8*, 189, 193.

334. Some have suggested that the prepositional phrase be understood as adjectival, describing "a person" and therefore qualifying "what kind of person is not justified" (Seifrid, *Christ Our Righteousness*, 106; Caneday, "Faithfulness of Jesus Christ," 193–94). While this interpretation creates a good parallel with the use of the prepositional phrase ἐξ ἐθνῶν in 2:15 (ἀμαρτωλοὶ ἐξ ἐθνῶν, 2:15 // ἄνθρωπος ἐξ ἔργων νόμου, 2:16) and while adjectival uses of similar prepositional phrases introduced by ἐκ are well documented elsewhere in Galatians (e.g., τοὺς ἐκ περιτομῆς, 2:12; Ὅσοι ἐξ ἔργων νόμου, 3:10; οἱ ἐκ πίστεως, 3:7, 9), reading it thus at the outset of 2:16 would necessitate being able to sustain this reading throughout its recurrences in the verse, which becomes impossible. One can, however, readily construe all the prepositional phrases as adverbial (so also Das, 242–43).

335. The ἐὰν μή is almost certainly exceptive ("unless," "except") here, as has been well demonstrated by Das, "Another Look." ἐὰν μή has an exceptive meaning everywhere else that Paul uses the expression (Rom 10:15; 11:23; 1 Cor 8:8; 9:16; 13:1; 14:6, 7, 9, 11, 28; 15:36; thus Das, "Another Look," 530–31; see also Burton, 121; BDAG 267–68). Some scholars defend an adversative reading ("but rather"; Zerwick, 158 §470; Schreiner, 162–63; BDAG 378), claiming that Paul uses a similar—but significantly not identical!—expression (εἰ μή) in an adversative sense in Gal 1:7, 19. Walker ("Translation," 516) affirms an exceptive translation but relates it to "a person is not justified" rather than "by Torah-prescribed works." He suggests an ellipsis of this phrase, rewriting Paul thus: "Knowing that a person is not justified by works of law ([a person is not justified] except through faith in Christ), we also have come to faith in Christ Jesus" (517). For this reading to be plausible, Paul would have to be seen to rely on his hearers (1) to understand the ἐὰν μή clause as parenthetic and (2) to understand that they must supply "a person is not justified" again. Given that almost all readers prior to Walker have not made these two leaps, it seems likely that most of Paul's audience in Galatia would not have done so either.

lead the Galatians (the principal audience of this passage) to see the absurdity of the rivals' position that "works of Torah" are essential for gentiles when they were not even sufficient for Jews.[336] The very fact of Jewish *Christians* is an admission by all parties that "trusting Jesus" is essential and indispensable for justification. If Torah was going to carry people through to God's ends for them, what was the point of Jesus dying on a cross (Gal 2:21; 3:21)?

Paul's next step is to present what he regards as the only logical inference:[337] If the Torah-prescribed works are an insufficient basis for justification, they constitute *no* basis for justification ("and not on the basis of works of Torah").[338] Paul will argue the case for this inference in greater detail in 3:10–14, 19–22. At this point, he offers a significantly rewritten version of an authoritative Scripture (Ps 143:2 [LXX 142:3]) as a rationale for this inference. The psalmist prays to God, "Do not enter into judgment with your slave, because no living being will be acquitted before you." In the Hebrew text, the psalmist acknowledges his own imperfection in God's sight, asking nevertheless that God would indeed enter into judgment against, and destroy, the psalmist's enemies.

Paul alters this in two important ways. Paul reads "all flesh" rather than "every living being." He looks at humanity here specifically in its frailty, its vulnerability to the powers that lead it away from fulfilling God's standards of righteousness toward all manner of harmful self-indulgence (see Gal 5:13–25). He may also be thinking about humanity as a collective whole, "all flesh" including Jew and gentile, and stating the obvious: the law, whose self-avowed function is to keep Jew and gentile separate (Lev 20:22–26), is not going to be the means by which "all flesh" shall come to be held righteous before God at the judgment and thus be acquitted. And if the law has an expiration date,

---

336. See, similarly, Dunn, 137–40; Das, "Another Look," 534.

337. Paul's rivals would not, of course, regard this as a *necessary* inference. They might have regarded it as thoroughly logically consistent to have put their trust in Jesus as Israel's Messiah and in his death as an act of obedience that erases past sins—even the sins of willful neglect and intentional disobedience, for which there were no prescribed sacrifices—under the covenant for those who believe, setting them right with God and giving them a clean slate for renewed obedience to the historic covenant.

338. Because Paul moves so swiftly to this inference and defends it so thoroughly, there is little if any possibility that Paul would "confuse the Galatians" (contra Schreiner, 162) if he intended ἐὰν μή to be heard as exceptive—which is, after all, how they would most likely hear the phrase, no matter *what* he intended, given that this is its overwhelmingly typical sense. This logic may incidentally illustrate Paul's allergic reaction to adding Torah-prescribed works to the way of life opened up by trusting Jesus. If the rival teachers were saying (or were to say), "We know that a person is not justified by trusting Jesus except through doing what Torah prescribes," Paul would follow this thought to the (for him) logical conclusion, "Therefore we are really dispensing with trusting Jesus, since this proves insufficient for justification in itself" (as he does in 5:2–4).

as Paul had come to believe (see 3:15–25; 4:1–7), it will indeed not supply the means by which "*any* flesh" shall come to be held righteous before God at the judgment and thus be acquitted. Second, Paul adds (and indeed foregrounds by stating ahead of the verb it qualifies) the phrase "on the basis of Torah-prescribed works," which makes his claim quite different from that of the psalmist. Paul may be justified in so doing, however, since the psalmist could safely be presumed to have made his declaration that "no one will be justified" in God's sight in the context of the covenant community, and thus in the context of living by "Torah-prescribed works." The addition limits the scope of the psalmist's declaration of the impossibility of acquittal before God to acquittal that is pursued by one particular avenue ("by works of the law"), leaving open the possibility of another successful avenue to the desired end (namely, trusting Jesus).

Paul's presumption in Galatians is *not* that it would be impossible for a person to live by the Torah. He considered himself "blameless" in his performance of the Torah (Phil 3:6). His near-contemporaries, the Jewish authors of 4 Maccabees and 4 Ezra, presumed that it was possible to live by Torah, even though it was difficult and demanding. Paul's presumption is that, now that the fullness of time has come, falling in line with Torah is not the way to fall in line with God, as Paul's own experience had most dramatically proven. God had now moved salvation history into a whole new stage with the death and resurrection of Christ and the formation of one body out of divided humanity. Torah was simply never the means by which God purposed to bring "all flesh"—Jews and gentiles together—to acquittal. Torah's role was more limited in God's plan for the justification of *all* flesh. Indeed, its role was limited to one particular people for the duration of its term, with the "works of the law" functioning to keep that people separate from the gentiles. That term being ended with the coming of "the fullness of time," God's provision for setting "all flesh" right again in his sight is now available: the provision of the Holy Spirit for all, Jews and gentiles alike, who, by trust in Jesus, join themselves to Jesus as the particular Seed of Abraham to whom the promise was given. Paul will provide an elaboration of this point in 3:15–4:7, supporting his claim that "no flesh will be acquitted on the basis of works of the law."

Within these terse phrases—"relying on Jesus" and "conforming one's life to the Torah's regulations"—are encapsulated two processes of transformation. The latter process happens as one becomes an embodiment, on a day-to-day basis, of the stipulations in the Mosaic law; the former happens as one relies on the power and guidance of the Holy Spirit that God has given to make the individual an embodiment of Christ's own spirit. Paul parts company with many of his fellow Jewish Christians in that Paul believes that all Jewish Christians who *are* Christians ought now to seek to be acquitted by relying wholly on Jesus and on what Jesus, in his death and resurrection, has brought to light, and not relying any longer on conforming their lives to the Torah for this purpose, and certainly not conforming their lives to the Torah where this reintroduces the divisions between those Jews who are in Christ and those gentiles who are also in Christ, as happened in Antioch. Even though the "people from James" and the rival teachers in Galatia would not accept Paul's inference concerning the "works of the Torah," Paul's act of speaking alongside them in this verse has the advantage of showing to the Galatians, at least, how the rival teachers' practice and position is fundamentally inconsistent with their own identity as people who have trusted Jesus and as a departure from shared Christian knowledge.[339]

17 Paul is well aware of the objection that non-Christian Jews and Jewish Christ-followers could raise, and perhaps have raised, against his position (and even, perhaps, against Peter's former practice in Antioch): "But[340] if while seeking to be deemed aligned with God's righteousness in Christ we ourselves also turn out[341] to be 'sinners,' is Christ then[342] a servant of sin?" If Jews, who have been historically obliged to show their loyalty to their covenant God by observing Torah, now begin to set aside its regulations as they pursue realignment with God on the basis of trusting Jesus and living the Spirit-led life, that makes Christ into an agent of sin as sin is defined by Torah. If Jewish Christians start neglecting the behaviors that keep them set apart from gentile "sinners"—becoming in this way "sinners" themselves and no different from gentiles (2:15), contrary to God's express command to and purpose for Israel (Lev 20:22–26)—then Jesus has become the excuse for violating the historic covenant and disobeying God through neglect of the Torah.

The most immediate referent for understanding this implied accusation is the practice of Jewish Christians in Antioch prior to the correction introduced by the people from James.[343] In the eyes of the latter, joining the Christian movement has become an excuse for mingling more freely with non-Jews ("sinners from the gentiles," 2:15) and not attending to the divinely sanctioned boundaries of Israel. The laxity of those who claim to follow Jesus

---

339. Tolmie, *Persuading*, 96.

340. The δέ here introduces a new development in the argument; because the new development involves posing an *objection*, the connective is generally translated "but."

341. The meaning of εὑρέθημεν is not so much "be found out" by someone as "turn out to be" (Burton, 125).

342. There is some discussion concerning whether αρα here should be read as ἆρα (an interrogative particle introducing a question; BDAG 127) or as ἄρα (an inferential particle introducing a logical consequence). Since the latter is far more frequent in Paul (indeed, there are no *clear* uses of the former at all), it seems preferable to translate it here as "then" (Bruce, 141; Lambrecht, "Line of Thought," 489–90; Tolmie, *Persuading*, 91). This word still occurs, however, in the context of a question.

343. Fung, 120; Shauf, "Galatians 2.20," 91, 94.

will have the effect of portraying Jesus as an enemy of the covenant, "one who advances sin's agenda"[344] rather than God's agenda for God's people.

Paul is speaking as if he were coming alongside Peter in 2:17 and showing him how to deflect the rebuke of the "men from James" and how to reject the perspective that gave rise thereto. He accepts that following Jesus has led him and his fellow Jewish Christians to be no different from "sinners," namely, the gentiles who are following Jesus.[345] They might indeed be sinners according to Torah's norms, but, Paul claims, that does not make Christ a servant of sin, since Torah, taken as a whole, no longer defines sin. Eating with redeemed and sanctified gentiles (sanctified, that is, by virtue of and as evidenced in their reception of the Holy Spirit) does *not* show that Christ is advancing sin's agenda, but that the old lines that defined "sinner" and "not sinner" have been redrawn. The "wall of hostility" (Eph 2:11) has been broken down by God, and Jewish Christians are following *God's* lead by observing these *new* lines. Galatians 3:26–28 is a climactic expression in this regard. Walking in line with the Torah's stipulations, which were intended (and were clearly *understood*) to keep Jews separate from gentiles, means, for Paul, rebelling against God's new act in Christ, God's new drawing of the lines.

It is important that Paul speaks about the life of the Christ-follower even after the initial act of trusting as a life of "seeking to be acquitted" or, to flesh this out more fully, "seeking to be aligned with God's righteous standards so as to be acquitted at the judgment."[346] This expression signals that, when Paul speaks of being acquitted "on the basis of trusting Christ," he understands that basis to involve not just an initial act of belief but the process of being transformed into a righteous person that Christ opens up for the one who

---

344. Understanding ἁμαρτίας as an objective genitive, modifying διάκονος. As "sin's servant," Christ would be "serving sin," advancing sin's interests and its agenda.

345. Williams, 72; Shauf, "Galatians 2.20," 89–90; Tolmie, *Persuading*, 91. Das (259) suggests that the Jewish Christ-followers are found rather to be "likewise guilty of sin before being justified by Christ," for which Gal 3:22 could offer support. However, this understanding would occasion no surprise for anyone in the context of Antioch. From the earliest Jewish Christian tradition, Jesus's death was a death "for sin," bringing forgiveness to "sinners." The way in which Paul presents the outcome as unexpected—that "even we ourselves" (καὶ αὐτοί) are found to be "sinners"—suggests that Paul is speaking here of Jews now being ranged alongside "gentile sinners" in their *Christian* practice.

346. The present participle ζητοῦντες denotes a pursuit, a quest still in process after an initial response of trusting in Jesus (see also 3:3). The goal, δικαιωθῆναι, still therefore lies in the future, at the end of this "seeking" (Martyn, 254; Seifrid, *Christ Our Righteousness*, 82). Das (258) objects that "the apostle certainly does not consider justification as a prize to be sought or achieved," but this objection stems from his theological commitments regarding "justification." Paul himself has no difficulty speaking of his own striving after the prize of "gaining Christ" and thus "attaining to the resurrection from the dead," which is certainly a consequence, at least, of justification (qua acquittal at the last day) in Phil 3:8–14.

trusts. Paul will go on to spell out this implication more fully in 2:19–21, in 3:3 (where he speaks of finishing, by means of the Spirit, the process begun with the Spirit), and in much greater detail in 5:13–6:10. Indeed, Paul here chooses to associate a different expression with "attaining acquittal," namely, the enigmatic phrase "in Christ." While this phrase lies beyond absolute definition,[347] Paul does give us several frames by which to think about its significance. First, believers are submerged "into Christ" and have "put on Christ" as a kind of overgarment in consequence of their baptism (3:27) and therefore can be said to live a new existence "in Christ" thereafter (3:26, 28). Second, Christ himself is coming alive within the believer, who thereby has come alive to God in a new and qualitatively different way, and who therefore can be said to live a new existence "in [association with] Christ" thereafter (2:19–20).[348] It is the person who lives this new existence "in Christ" that God, the just Judge, will acquit, and not merely the person who believes and then experiences as little change in his or her life as the demons, who likewise believe (Jas 2:19).

18 Having flatly denied the possibility of drawing the conclusion that Christ is becoming "sin's servant" in Paul's churches, Paul offers an alternative perspective on the question:[349] "For if I build up again the things I tore down, I prove myself to be a transgressor." If we allow the scenario described in Gal 2:11–14 to continue to guide us, then it becomes clear that Paul is speaking here about first tearing down and then reinstating the dividing lines between Jews and gentiles erected and enforced by Torah (in Antioch, in particular, through its regulations about maintaining some level of separation from gentiles in regard to foods).[350] After eating freely with gentile Christians, Peter turns himself into a transgressor only when he acknowledges anew the lines that, according to the Torah, should be drawn between Jews and gentiles— the very lines that he had previously crossed in obedience to the leading of the Spirit (and, quite possibly, the dream vision of Acts 10)—and begins to withdraw from unregulated table fellowship with gentile Christians.

If Paul were, hypothetically, to act as did Peter, he would establish himself to be a transgressor in two important respects. First, his return to Torah-reinforced separateness would amount to an admission that his previous conduct was a transgression (and thus, being again "under law," he would confirm his status as a temporary transgressor of that law). Second, and far more crucially, his return to Torah-reinforced separateness would amount

---

347. "The phrase ἐν Χριστῷ (κυρίῳ), which is copiously appended by Paul to the most varied concepts, utterly defies definite interpretation" (BDF §219.4).

348. Schreiner, 168.

349. Barclay, *Obeying the Truth*, 79–80; Longenecker, 90; Martyn, 255; Matera, 95.

350. Wilckens, "Entwicklung," 170; Longenecker, 90; Martyn, 256; Barclay, *Obeying the Truth*, 80; Das, 265.

to disobedience to, and denial of, what God is doing *now* in the Spirit-led community of Jews and gentiles in Christ (as in 3:23–28).[351] It is in rebelling against what God has done in Christ, reversing one's path and turning away from "the truth of the gospel," that one demonstrates oneself to be a *genuine* "transgressor." In 2:19–21 Paul will present a confirmation of the rationale offered in 2:18. Paul believes that returning to alignment with the Torah would nullify what God has accomplished in Paul's life by means of Jesus's death on Paul's behalf and be a rejection of God's purposes for all the nations in Christ. It would be an ungracious repudiation of Jesus's supreme generosity—his love—manifested in his giving over of himself for Paul, and ultimately a repudiation of God's grace manifested in the Christ event.[352] Transgressing the grace relationship that God has renewed with human beings in Christ is far less "just" and far more worthy of "just judgment" than sharing a table with those for whom Christ also died.

Being found to be on an equal footing with "gentile sinners" does not pose a danger to eschatological deliverance; being found to be a "transgressor" of God's purposes for Jews and gentiles on this side of the death and resurrection of Jesus, however, poses great threat. With heavy irony, Paul applies the name "transgressor" (typically, one who violates a stipulation of the Torah) to the person who tries to *reinstate* the Torah (particularly as it relates to the boundaries around the Jewish people and their "favored nation status" before God on this side of the Christ event).[353]

19–20 Paul offers a personal statement as a further elaboration of the rationale for why that which was torn down (2:17–18) should not be erected afresh.[354] To do so would be to undo all that is spoken of in 2:19–21. He gives us thereby one of the most beautiful expressions of the essence of the Christian life: "For I died to the law through the law, in order that I might live to God. I have been crucified along with Christ. It's not me living any longer,

---

351. Paul will return to this topic more fully in 3:23–4:11 under a different metaphor—that of trying to turn back the clock, as it were, on the fullness of time.

352. Lambrecht, "Transgressor," 235. Gombis ("Transgressor," 88) rejects Lambrecht's view that the transgression in 2:18 is not against the Torah but against "the new command to live for God" in 2:19, asserting that there is "no basis for viewing God's new initiative in Christ as an implied command." Admittedly, the term "transgressor" normally refers to one who runs afoul of a particular prescription in the Torah (Dunn, 142–43; Betz, 120), but there is *indeed* an implied command in the obligation to show gratitude where grace is extended and received. See excursus "A Contextual Understanding of Grace" on pp. 254–62.

353. John Chrysostom, 21; Hays, "Letter to the Galatians," 242, based on Martyn, 256; also Hansen, 72–73; Das, 266. "Sinner" has become a more neutral term here, while "transgressor" names the willful violator of God's revelation (Dunn, 143).

354. Note again the presence of the inferential conjunction γάρ ("for") at the outset of 2:19. Longenecker, 91; Martyn, 256.

but Christ is living in me. What I'm now living in the flesh, I live by trusting God's Son, who loved me and gave himself up on my behalf." Paul describes a paradigmatic "dying" that opens up the possibility of a new kind of "living," all the result of Jesus's own dying for the sake of, out of love for, and in order to benefit Paul—and it is significant that, while Christ did this for "all" (see 2 Cor 5:14–15), he also did it for "each," and thus for "me" (2:20). In this way, a general benefaction ("for all") remains also a very personal benefaction ("for me"), calling for a very personal response and creating a very personal bond.[355] It is this bond that Paul takes every pain not to violate, this response of gratitude to which Paul yields all that he is, such that "it is not me living any longer." Returning to the Torah-driven life would mean, for Paul, setting aside the favor, the generous love, that Christ has shown at ultimate cost to himself, which is something he will neither do himself nor suffer others to do without being held accountable (2:21).[356]

Paul claims that his movement away from seeking to align himself with God's purposes and standards through continuing to align his life with the Torah, accompanied by his movement toward aligning himself with God's purposes and standards through trusting Jesus and allowing Jesus to come alive within him, was itself a journey undertaken "*through* the Torah." Paul will explain further below (3:11–14, 19–25; 4:4–5) how "dying to the Torah" is in fact in accordance with God's ultimate purposes for, and revealed in, the Torah. That Torah should pronounce Jesus accursed while God pronounces Jesus righteous by means of resurrection represents Torah's own claim of incompatibility with Jesus. Indeed, by contributing to bringing about Jesus's death, the Torah helped to effect Paul's liberation from its own authority and power.[357] Torah has a positive function, but only as a temporary measure set

---

355. John Chrysostom (23), perhaps not surprisingly, given his location in a cultural milieu much closer to that of Paul than to our own, captures this sense most vividly: "This language teaches that each individual justly owes a great debt of gratitude to Christ, as if He had come for his sake alone, for He would not have grudged this His condescension though but for one, so that the measure of His love to each is as great as to the whole world." Joubert (*Paul as Benefactor*, 51) rightly observes that "for a service to qualify as a benefit it must have been undertaken because of a specific individual, and not just bestowed on him as one of the crowd." Compare Seneca's comments on this distinction (*On Benefits* 6.18.2; 6.19.2–5).

356. Räisänen ("Galatians 2.16," 544) is probably correct that, in light of "Paul's critique of the law" and statements of "dying" to the law, "we should not shrink from speaking of his 'break' with Judaism," as his own language suggests in 1:13–14.

357. Tannehill, *Dying and Rising*, 58–59. See also Schlier, 101; Bruce, 142; Eckstein, *Verheissung und Gesetz*, 62; Martyn, 257–58n142; Barclay, *Obeying the Truth*, 81n14; Witherington, 189; Schreiner, 171; Das, 268. Dunn (143) suggests that Paul refers here to his former zeal for the law, which led him to act against Christ and eventually to be accosted by Christ. While this view is certainly not impossible, Paul takes pains to provide more explanation than this in support of his implicit claim that embracing Christ's gift means a death to the Torah.

in place to provide protective discipline for the particular people out of which the Seed (see 3:15-18) would arise. It had to give way to the more powerful means by which God would bring *all* people, and not just Jews, into alignment with God's righteousness—namely, identification with Christ in his death and rising to new life, and the gift of the Spirit to direct and empower righteousness from the heart.

Paul's identification with Christ in his death, because he is now in Christ (who had been crucified and rose to a new life) and Christ is now in him, frees him from obligation to the law, which "has authority over a person while he or she is alive" (Rom 7:1).[358] It is a death to living under the authority of the Torah, constrained by its regulations and practices, but it is also, as Paul recognizes here, a death to "the jurisdiction of one's own ego,"[359] or as he will express it later, a death to the power of the "old person," the "flesh" with its cravings and urges (Gal 5:24), so that one can follow the Spirit's leading in all things, manifesting the righteous character and practices that fulfill the Torah's vision for righteousness—becoming the sort of person that Torah would affirm as reflecting God's holiness, even though the Christian arrives at that point by a completely different path (5:22-23; see also Rom 6:1-14; Col 3:1-17).

This dying in union with Christ allows Paul to enter into a new kind of living—not merely existence as a biological organism, but a coming alive to God in a wholly new way, a life before God characterized by the freedom of God's mature children (3:23-25; 4:1-7), who have the capacity to do what pleases God because God's Spirit, living within them and empowering them to live this life, guides them (5:13-25).[360] Gratitude, the full-bodied response to grace shown, is the path into, and driving force of, this new life.[361] Paul remains ever mindful of the generous kindness of Jesus, "the Son of God

---

358. This view is corroborated in rabbinic literature: "As soon as a person is dead, he or she is free from obligation to the commandments" (R. Johanan in b. Šab. 30a). See Tannehill, *Dying and Rising*, 58-59. Paul's choice of the perfect tense form συνεσταύρωμαι is significant, as he himself will emphasize not only the past action but its ongoing effects, namely, his ongoing state of being dead not only to his past life (so Das, 236) but also, in a sense, in the midst of his new life, where it is Christ living now in Paul.

359. Longenecker, 92. See also Dunn, 145, who notes that the "old Paul" of Gal 1:13-14 is gone.

360. There is also an eschatological dimension to the phrase "living to God." While indeed enjoying a new quality of life now before God, Paul ultimately embraces the death and life of Christ in his mortal body as the path to sharing in Christ's resurrection, "living to God" for eternity (see Gal 6:8b-9). On "living to God" as a way of speaking about resurrection or postmortem life, see 4 Macc 7:19; 16:25.

361. The triple occurrence of δέ punctuating 2:20 gives the sense that Paul is coming to a series of climactic steps in the development of his position.

who loved me and handed himself over on my behalf" (2:20b; see 1:4). Jesus displayed the highest form of generosity that any benefactor could, giving not his resources but his very life to bring benefit to others. Such commitment ought to awaken an equal commitment to respond with a proportionate degree of gratitude. Paul describes this response as nothing less than a life for a life. In a very real sense, Paul has given over to Jesus the remainder of his life in the body ("flesh" here does not yet carry the negative hues with which it will be colored in Gal 3–6 but speaks only of "this mortal body," as in 1:16).[362] Paul has put himself out of the way so that "the one who loved [him] and gave himself over for [him]" could have the remainder of Paul's life as a fair return. As a gift in return, it may not be of equal *value*, but it shows equal commitment to the grace relationship. Christ's self-giving becomes the focal act, the stimulus, that defines all of Paul's responses—all of life is thenceforth lived first and foremost with a view to giving oneself to Christ, to his interests, his agenda, his pleasure.[363]

An essential component of this response to costly favor is to move forward with unflagging trust in such a benefactor, and Paul expresses his own commitment to continue in this response: "What I now live in the flesh, I live by trusting in the Son of God" (2:20). The "faith in Christ" that is the means to acquittal ("justification") includes this new life of "living by faith in God's Son," a new life in which the "I" no longer drives what is lived in the body, but Christ does by the power and means of his indwelling Spirit.[364] Much of the central argumentative section of Galatians can be read as Paul's attempt to encourage the believers to show more complete confidence in Jesus's ability to bring them into God's household and in the sufficiency of the gifts that Jesus's death has secured for them. Central here is trust in the sufficiency of the Holy Spirit, the blessing once promised to Abraham and now available to all who trust Jesus (3:14), to lead them to life and righteousness before God (3:21; 5:13–6:10) by causing Christ to take shape within, and to live in and through,

---

362. See also 2 Cor 10:3; Phil 1:22, 24; Fee, 92; Das, 271.

363. Engberg-Pedersen (*Paul and the Stoics*, 145) eloquently captures the place of this grace-response exchange in the transformation and setting right of the individual: "Christ had the very specific role in the Christ event of *enabling* human beings to *respond* to the event *in the way they were meant to by God*. When Christ, the mediator, bent down in love and gave *himself* up 'for *my* sake' (2:20), that is, by *his* suffering (vicariously) in order to bring '*me*' help in a situation which was negative for '*me*' (cf. 1:4 and 3:13), then "I" *responded in kind* and through that response came to live for God and so 'live'" (emphases original).

364. See Gorman, *Inhabiting*, 64; Ziesler, *Meaning of Righteousness*, 165. The new life described here is something that the Spirit works. See Rom 8:9–10 ("Christ by his Spirit lives in me"); Fee, *God's Empowering Presence*, 374; Ridderbos, 106; Bruce, 144; Dunn, *Baptism*, 144; Campbell, *Quest for Paul's Gospel*, 93. On the connection between this work of the Spirit within the believer and justification, see Williams, "Justification and the Spirit," 98.

them (2:20; 4:19).[365] This is the "new creation" (6:15; cf. 2 Cor 5:16–18) that renders all concern over circumcision or uncircumcision misplaced.

Paul offers his own experience as a paradigm of response to Christ's love manifested in his self-giving death. Paul emphasizes how deeply personal this statement is by his repeated use of the nominative pronoun *egō*, explaining why he himself cannot think as did the "people from James," could not do as Peter did, and cannot abide what the rival teachers are now seeking to do. The experience of "dying to the Torah" is, moreover, a particularly Jewish one and not one with which the gentile converts among his audience can immediately identify.[366] Nevertheless, Paul's response in 2:19–20 is paradigmatic insofar as gentile Christians must also experience a death, a cocrucifixion with Christ, to "the flesh with its passions and desires" (5:24) and to "the world" (6:14) with *its* fundamental rules and ordering principles (4:3, 8–11) in favor of Christ coming to life within them and making them "new creation" in whom "righteousness" comes to be embodied (5:5–6; 6:15).[367] Paul is in labor for his converts until "Christ is formed" in them (4:19), even as Christ has taken shape in Paul (2:20). He will speak more fully in 5:13–6:10 of the process by which this formation becomes reality.[368]

The narrative of Jesus's giving of himself for Paul out of love for him becomes the act that defines Paul's response, namely, dying with Christ in return and, in some sense, *for* Christ in return so that Christ may now live in Paul. This narrative must, in turn, be allowed to awaken the same response in every person who trusts in Christ's death: "One person died on behalf of all; therefore all died. And he died on behalf of all in order that those who continued living might live no longer for themselves, but rather for him who died and was raised on their behalf" (2 Cor 5:14b–15).[369] This response frees the human being from the condition of being "curved in on itself"[370] and restores to it the God-centeredness and other-centeredness that is at the heart of righteousness under the old covenant and under the new.

Taken as a whole, Gal 2:15–21 demonstrates the fallacy of choosing *either* "justification by faith" *or* "participation in Christ" as *the* center of Paul's theology. The two represent facets of a single center. Indeed, if we under-

---

365. Christ indwelling the believer (Gal 2:20; Rom 8:10; 2 Cor 13:5; Col 1:27; Eph 3:17) is less common in Paul than either the believer living "in Christ" or the Spirit [of Christ] indwelling the believer, but all name the same experience (so Dunn, 145).

366. McKnight, "Ego and 'I,'" 279.

367. Shauf, "Galatians 2.20," 98; Wright, *Recent Interpreters*, 344.

368. Fee, *God's Empowering Presence*, 374.

369. Tellingly, this process leads to becoming "new creation" in both 2 Cor 5:17 and Gal 6:15.

370. Schnelle, *Apostle Paul*, 285, using Luther's famous diagnosis of the fundamental human problem.

stand "justification" in its fullest sense—God intervening to bring back in line what was out of alignment in human beings and their relationship with the divine—then "participating in Christ" or, perhaps better, "Christ's participation in us" is an essential mechanism of that justification. Paul speaks of Christ's participation in us as the Spirit's activity within and among us (4:6–7; 5:16–25), of "Christ being formed" among the believers (4:19), and of Christ "living" in Paul (2:20). Christ participating in us, changing us to the point that we are not "ourselves" any more, with Christ, rather, taking on new flesh in us—this is the means by which the righteousness that God seeks in God's people (6:7–10), for which the Christian hopes (5:5), is formed within us (a righteousness that the Torah could not effectively nurture, 2:21). Paul's interest in God's justifying ("rectifying") initiative includes a highly "formational" or "transformational" element.[371]

21 The description of Jesus as the self-giving and committed benefactor provides the grounds for Paul's trusting Jesus *and* for Paul's unwillingness to carelessly cast aside a gift that cost the giver so much to make available: "I do not set aside God's generous kindness. For if righteousness (comes) through the law, then Christ died for nothing." The favor of God lavished upon human beings in Christ and the significance of Christ's death are ultimately what is at stake for Paul in Galatia.[372] The second half of the verse explains why:[373] if observing the Torah would bring "all flesh" in line with God's righteousness and righteous purposes for humanity, thus leading to acquittal on the last day, what was the purpose—and what is the value—of Christ's self-giving death?[374]

---

371. Shauf ("Galatians 2.20," 87) rightly understands 2:20 to describe "how Christians are justified by faith and not by works of the law." See also deBoer, "Paul's Use," 214–15. Schreiner (*Faith Alone*, 264) writes: "But my confidence on the last day will not rest on my transformation. I have too far to go to put any confidence in what I have accomplished. Instead, I rest on Jesus Christ. He is my righteousness." Schreiner is indeed correct that the Christian's confidence will not be in the degree to which he or she has been transformed; he is incorrect to view that degree of transformation, whatever it is, as "what I have accomplished," and perhaps therein lies a major stumbling block to joining together once again what Reformed theologians long have separated. Our confidence is in Jesus *and* in the power of Jesus's Spirit—and this not only on the last day, but *every* day as we strive merely to let Christ's self-giving love provoke the gratitude in us that it merits, and then let gratitude have its way as the Spirit directs and empowers.

372. By "grace," Paul does not mean here specifically (or "obviously," *pace* Dunn, 147) the grace/gift of God manifested in his commissioning. It is the grace of God manifested in Christ's death and resurrection on behalf of each and every person, not a peculiar gift given to Paul.

373. Paul signals this argumentative function by presenting the material with the inferential conjunction γάρ, "for."

374. The rival teachers, of course, might have had an answer to this question: Christ's death was an offering *within* the covenant on behalf of the many transgressions of the many

It would seem that, if Torah observance could achieve these results, this costly gift was, in the end, superfluous.[375]

It is possible that the rival teachers had first charged *Paul* with nullifying God's grace (i.e., by setting aside the special grace given to Israel),[376] since the Torah was indeed regarded as a manifestation of divine favor to be embraced and treasured as such. The statement is thoroughly intelligible, however, as originating with Paul himself. In stating that *he* does not set aside God's grace, Paul is also indirectly charging his *rivals,* who would restore the walls of Torah and reject what God has graciously accomplished (at great cost!), with acting ungraciously.[377] "Setting aside God's gift" or "favor" is precisely what Paul sees happening when one follows the course of action that Paul has rejected, namely, returning to the Torah-prescribed practices that maintain the "dividing wall of hostility" as if that is the path to falling in line with God's purposes for humanity (2:18; see also 5:2–4).[378] The way Paul has phrased this sentence poses an implicit challenge to the Galatian converts as well: *they* must take the greatest care in their present situation not to "set aside God's gift (or generosity)." It is important, perhaps not incidentally, to note that *Christ's* self-giving love is understood by Paul completely as an act of *God's* generosity. Christ does not mediate between alienated sinners and an angry God; Christ's self-giving love *is* the manifestation of God's own initiating and outreaching favor.

But why should Paul consider Torah and trust in Christ so fundamentally at odds? The answer seems to lie in Paul's understanding of the universal scope of God's new outpouring of favor. God was at last bringing together Jew and gentile into one, united people (Gal 3:28)—the oneness of the God who is God both of Jew and gentile (Gal 3:20; Rom 3:29) being reflected not only in the new people being formed in the name of Jesus, but also in the single basis on which both Jew and gentile were brought into that united people (Gal 2:15–16), namely, God's generosity toward all as expressed in Jesus's death on behalf of humanity. God thus fulfills at last the promise made to Abraham, making him the spiritual ancestor of many nations. After Jesus's death, a *return* to works of Torah as if these could *add* to what Jesus had done

---

transgressors; his death spares the larger people of God (the Jews), and all the gentiles who would join themselves to God's people, from God's anger against transgression and gives them all a fresh opportunity to renew their obedience to the covenant. For Paul, however, such an answer would be insufficient.

375. Das (274) and Hays ("Letter to the Galatians," 245) underline the implicit pun as Paul speaks about a costly gift (see δωρεά, "gift," Rom 5:15) as "gratuitous" (δωρεάν).

376. Burton, 140–42; Schlier, 104; Fung, 125; Longenecker, 94–95.

377. With Shauf, "Galatians 2.20," 95–96; Matera, 96–97; Tolmie, *Persuading,* 94.

378. The verb ἀθετῶ does not mean "render ineffective, inoperable" in this context (as in Dunn, 147), but "reject," with the result that the grace relationship is broken off.

would amount to a repudiation of Jesus's ability to connect us to God and an insultingly low evaluation of the potential of the Spirit, the promised gift won for us at such cost, to transform our lives (5:13–6:10).

The appearance in this verse of the word "righteousness" (*dikaiosynē*), an ethical term, rather than the forensic term "justification" (*dikaiōsis*),[379] is significant for at least two reasons. First, it reminds us that Paul's polemic throughout Galatians is not against "doing good works" but against doing "works of the Torah" out of a conviction that the Torah still regulates the life of the people of God. Paul expects the Spirit to produce all manner of "good works" in the life of the disciple (Gal 5:13–25; see also Rom 2:6–11; 6:12–13; Eph 2:10). He understands the Christian hope to entail, in part at least, attaining "righteousness" through the Spirit's transforming work in disciples' lives (Gal 5:5). And when Paul has swept aside both circumcision and uncircumcision as meaningless characteristics before God, the only thing left holding value in God's sight is not mere "faith" but "faith *working* through love" (Gal 5:6). Second, it reminds us that Paul's concern is not simply with "justification" in the sense of "acquittal" or forgiveness of sins, being made initially right with God,[380] but with "justification" in the sense of being brought fully in line with God's standards of "righteousness" (*dikaiosynē*),[381] which happens as Christ comes more and more alive within and through the believer.[382]

Will the Galatians appreciate and accept what God has done for humanity in the cross of Christ? Will they trust the efficacy of that single act of costly obedience to join them to the family of Abraham and the family of God, without trying to turn the clock back to a time before Jesus's death by aligning themselves with the Torah's prescriptions? Will they place sufficient value upon the resource God has provided in the Spirit—ever so much more

---

379. Tyson ("Works," 429), like the NRSV, mistranslates Gal 2:21: "If justification were possible through the law."

380. BDAG 250.

381. BDAG 248.

382. I disagree with Fung (123–24) and Moo ("Justification in Galatians," 165), who argue that the meaning of δικαιοσύνη ("righteousness") is controlled by the forensic/declarative character of the verb δικαιόω ("I justify, acquit") that appears in 2:16. Since Paul *knows* the noun that is truly the cognate of this verb (i.e., δικαίωσις, see Rom 4:25; 5:18), his choice of δικαιοσύνη ("righteousness") represents an intentional decision to expand the scope of the discussion of God's purposes in Christ for the believer. The continuity of Paul's argument is not compromised by understanding δικαιοσύνη as "righteousness"—an ethical quality recognized on the basis of a life lived in line with God's standards, a life that is, in turn, justly acquitted at the last judgment. Righteousness is still God's gift to human beings (as Schreiner, 157, affirms), but God's gift of the Holy Spirit gives human beings righteousness "in reality," and not merely "on paper" in God's record book (Engberg-Pedersen, *Paul and the Stoics*, 173). Paul spends considerable space treating this transformation (*and* affirming it to be prerequisite to entering into life; see 5:21; 6:7–8).

effective and empowering a guide to God's heart than the Torah—to lead them into righteousness? All of these questions are wrapped up in the catch-words "grace" and "trust" that so dominate this letter.

Paul's summary statement of his position assists us in discerning the genuine gospel from "other gospels" that are *no* gospels. What should we expect from God as a result of our turning in trust toward his Son? Some voices speaking in and around the church suggest that we should expect God to pour out material blessings on us in abundance, or to open doors to advancement in the structures and systems of our corrupt world, or to spare us from the experience of pain or sorrow. These voices set their hearers up not only for disappointment but even for apostasy, for when prosperity fails to come, or prayers to be spared anything unpleasant do not prevent the experience of grief, the individual becomes embittered against God, revokes his or her trust, and turns away.

Paul preaches a different set of expectations: we should expect God to be at work in our lives to form Christ in us, that is, to deepen our capacities for love and other-centered service, to change our hearts from a focus on ourselves and our interests toward a focus on the needs and good of another person, to break us out of our self-centeredness and our immersion in the values of this world so that we will be free to serve and love God as our Cre-ator merits. Paul lost his prestige, his social power, and his personal safety and comfort (Phil 3:5–8; 2 Cor 11:21b–33). What he found as a result of his conversion and call was that the power of Christ was coming to life in him, transforming him into a person who pleased God—indeed, refashioning him into the likeness of *the* person who pleased God: "It's no longer me living, but Christ is living in me" (2:20). This transformation was the most important thing he could seek for himself, the thing he wanted most from God, for which he counted the loss of everything else to be just so much trash (Phil 3:7–11).

Paul reminds us that God is not out to make us rich. He is not out to make our lives easy or pain-free. He is, rather, out to make us more like Jesus, able to use everything that comes our way to strip away the old person and form us a bit more into the new person. If the Son learned obedience through the things he suffered and experienced (Heb 5:7–10), how much more should the many sons and daughters prepare themselves to endure rigorous training in this life (Heb 12:5–11), rather than expect ease and prosperity, so as to be fully formed in the image of the Son? Western images of "Christian" life are of-ten very misleading in this regard, reflecting the difficulty Western Christians have divorcing the pursuit of the kingdom of God from the pursuit of "the American Dream," and reflecting as well the very real danger that, in holding on to the latter, we will miss the former. If God brings enough resources our way for us and our families to live on, it is enough. If God brings more material wealth our way than our needs require, it is so that others and their families will have enough to live on by virtue of our sharing with them as conduits of God's gracious provision.

EXCURSUS: A CONTEXTUAL UNDERSTANDING OF GRACE

Paul developed his theology of grace and preached about the generous favor of God in Christ in a socioeconomic environment very different from the emerging mercantile economy of the Reformation period or the modern economies that have arisen since. As a result, theologians are much more prone to speak of God's grace in terms of one-way, commercial transactions rather than in terms of relationships of reciprocity, the native socioeconomic context of Paul, his converts, and his writings. Such theologians speak about God's grace in terms of some transfer of a commodity (salvation, justification) to a human recipient, and there an end, understanding God's action of "freely giving" to mean "given with no cost laid upon the recipient." Paul and his hearers would understand God's "freely giving" to mean "without any external force coercing the *giving*," without the recipient having done something to leverage the gift. And while they would understand that a gift, to be a gift, *comes* "at no cost," they would understand that it cannot be *received* and *retained* "at no cost," for receiving something of great value meant accepting the obligation to return something of great value. The failure to do so would mean fracturing the relationship—and the relationship is the very thing that an act of grace seeks to create, solidify, celebrate, or deepen.

Understanding the real-life settings of "grace" language in the New Testament is therefore of great importance if we are to understand the unity of gift and response, grace and discipleship, theology and ethics in Paul and in early Christian texts more generally.[383] Better-placed individuals helped less

---

383. For a more detailed overview of the nature and kinds of relationships of reciprocity in the Greco-Roman world, the ethos embodied in these relationships, and the relevance of this background for understanding the New Testament, see deSilva, *Honor*, 95–156. Seminal works on the Greco-Roman context of patronage and reciprocity include Saller, *Personal Patronage*; Wallace-Hadrill, ed., *Patronage in Ancient Society*; Gill, Postlethwaite, and Seaford, eds., *Reciprocity in Ancient Greece*; Griffin, "*De Beneficiis* and Roman Society." Studies exploring the relevance of this context for interpreting the New Testament include Danker, *Benefactor*; Moxnes, "Patron-Client Relations"; deSilva, "Exchanging Favor for Wrath"; "Grace, the Law, and Justification"; *Letter to the Hebrews*, 95–138; *Perseverance in Gratitude*, 59–64, 215–48, 474–77; "We Are Debtors"; Joubert, *Paul as Benefactor*; "Religious Reciprocity in 2 Corinthians 9:6–15"; Harrison, *Paul's Language of Grace*; Engberg-Pedersen, "Gift-Giving and Friendship"; Briones, "Thankless Thanks"; Blanton, "Benefactor's Account-

strategically placed individuals get access to what they needed or desired, and received honor, loyalty, and support in their own endeavors in return. Social equals helped one another in the same way. Rich citizens lavished benefactions on their own or other cities and were granted perpetual honors for their generosity. Poor villagers extended grace to one another in the normal course of living lives. Seneca observed that the giving and receiving of such mutual assistance was "the practice that constitutes the chief bond of human society" (*On Benefits* 1.4.2). Relationships of reciprocity formed the fundamental weave of the social fabric of the Greco-Roman world (including its Jewish inhabitants).

It was in these relationships, and not in the specialized vocabulary of Christian theologians, that the word "grace" (Greek *charis*, Latin *gratia*) was primarily at home. The Greek *charis* conveys a range of meanings, most of which are at home in relationships of reciprocity. It is used to refer to (1) the disposition to show "favor";[384] (2) the "gift" or "assistance" given;[385] (3) the response to favor received, hence "gratitude" or "thanks."[386] The three basic senses of the word already hint at what Greco-Roman poets and moralists made explicit: an act of grace goes hand in hand with a response of gratitude.

One of the cultural icons of the ancient world—attested not only in Italy, but also Greece, Asia Minor, and Cyrenaica—was the image of the Three Graces, three goddesses dancing hand-in-hand or arm-over-shoulder in a circle. The image exemplified the ethos of grace relationships. As Seneca relates,

> There is one for bestowing a benefit, another for receiving it, and a third for returning it. . . . Why do the sisters hand in hand dance in a ring which returns upon itself? For the reason that a benefit passing in its course from hand to hand returns nevertheless to the giver; the beauty of the whole is destroyed if the course is anywhere broken, and it has most beauty if it is continuous and maintains an uninterrupted succession. . . . They are young because the memory of benefits ought not to grow old. . . . the maidens wear flowing robes, and these, too, are transparent because benefits desire to be seen. (*On Benefits* 1.3.3–5)

Book"; Mathew, *Women in the Greetings*; Oropeza, "Expectation of Grace"; and, now, Barclay, *Paul and the Gift*.

384. As in Aristotle, *Rhetoric* 2.7.1 (1385a16–20); LXX Gen 6:8; 18:3; LXX Exod 33:13; LXX Prov 3:34; 22:1; Luke 1:30; Rom 5:15, 17; Heb 4:16; Jas 4:6.

385. LXX Esth 6:3; Sir 3:31; Wis 3:14; 8:21; 4 Macc 5:9; 11:12; Rom 12:3, 6; Heb 12:15; 1 Pet 1:10, 13; 3:7; 4:10; 5:10.

386. Evident in Demosthenes, *On the Crown* 131; 2 Macc 3:33; 3 Macc 1:9; Luke 17:9; Rom 6:17; 7:25; 1 Cor 10:30; 2 Cor 8:16; 9:15; 1 Tim 1:12; 2 Tim 1:3; Heb 12:28. On the polyvalence of χάρις, see Harrison, *Paul's Language of Grace*, 51, 179–83; BDAG 1079–81.

This line of ethical commentary on the Three Graces extends at least as far back as Aristotle, who spoke of the public shrines dedicated to the Graces as reminders to all to return kindnesses (*Nicomachean Ethics* 5.5.7).

Initiating the circle dance with a gift was a matter of choice on the part of the giver. For the gift to *be* a gift, it had to be offered primarily in the interest of the recipient and not with a view to gaining some specific gift in return. The noble giver could expect gratitude,[387] but he or she could not expect to be able to leverage a particular return.[388] The hand that extended a gift at the same time extended an invitation to this dance. Accepting the gift, which is also a matter of choice, meant accepting the relationship with—and the obligation to—the giver. If one decides to dance, one must dance gracefully and in step with one's partner.[389]

A grace-act was a social act, both naturally evoking goodwill from the one to whom grace is shown and laying the person who accepts a gift or assistance under an obligation.[390] Thus Sophocles could say that "favor [*charis*] gives birth to favor [*charin*]" (*Ajax* 522) in a natural and uncoerced cycle; at the same time, Euripides could affirm that "favor [*charis*] is due for favor [*anti charitos*]" (*Helen* 1234). Offering a gift and accepting that gift did more than effect the transfer of a commodity: it created (or continued) a relationship, a bond, that would be further sustained by the return of favor by the one who accepts and by future acts of favor and returns of favor. Graceful receiving and returning involved expressing thanks personally and giving testimony publically to the giver's generosity and virtue, thus augmenting his or her honor.[391] It involved showing loyalty ("faith," Greek *pistis*, Latin *fides*) toward the giver, even when such action would prove costly.[392] Giving and receiving created and was symptomatic of *relationship*, and it is to this relationship that one must prove loyal. It also involved looking for the opportunity to render timely gifts or services in return.[393] This response does not "pay back" the giver or "settle" a debt; it is itself an act motivated by the desire to be gracious in response.[394] It does not bring an exchange to an end, but rather allows a grace relationship of ongoing exchange to continue.[395]

---

387. Isocrates, *To Demonicus* 29; Seneca, *On Benefits* 4.10.4; Sir 12:1.

388. Aristotle, *Rhetoric* 1385a35–b3; Seneca, *On Benefits* 3.15.4.

389. Seneca, *On Benefits* 1.4.3; 2.22.1; 2.25.3; Cicero, *On Duties* 1.47; Aristotle, *Nicomachean Ethics* 8.14.3 (1163b12–15); Isocrates, *To Demonicus* 26; Sir 35:2.

390. Seneca, *On Benefits* 5.11.5.

391. Aristotle, *Nicomachean Ethics* 8.14.2 (1163b1–5); Seneca, *On Benefits* 2.22.1; 2.23.1; 2.24.4; Ps 116:12; Tob 12:6–7.

392. Seneca, *Epistles* 81.27; *On Benefits* 4.20.2; 4.24.2.

393. Seneca, *On Benefits* 2.33.3; 2.35.1; 6.41.1–2.

394. Seneca, *Moral Epistles* 81.9–10.

395. See Seneca, *On Benefits* 2.18.5. Engberg-Pedersen ("Gift-Giving and Friendship," 20) well captures this dynamic: "The mutual emotional attitude and relationship between

For a person in the first-century Roman Empire—more particularly, for a first-century *recipient* of grace—to regard an act of grace as a one-way transaction would therefore be unthinkable. If such a person were to regard it as such and leave it at that, it would be beyond reprehensible. Rather, an act of grace was a snapshot within an ongoing and ever-flowing relationship—one beautiful step in an ongoing *dance*. And there was no stepping on one's partner's toes. Failure to show gratitude was regarded as supremely dis*grace*ful, the cardinal social and ethical sin in the Greco-Roman world.[396] It could turn a person's desire to benefit into a desire for satisfaction against insult and publically mark the ingrate as a person on whom not to waste favor.[397]

The ethos of reciprocity (though not all of its forms) permeated all levels of society, from the city-state to the household, from senators to agrarian peasant villagers.[398] It is therefore not surprising to find this ethos reflected in Paul's letters to his congregations, all the more as Paul himself would have been located in the mid-to-upper hues of this spectrum, and the members of his congregation would reflect a broad palette of the same.[399] It is particularly evident in his letters to Philemon (from whom he seeks to gain a favor on behalf of Onesimus) and the Philippians (whom he considers to be his friends in a sense inclusive of mutual beneficence), though it also emerges in his promotion of the collection as an act of reciprocity (e.g., Rom 15:25–27).[400] It is also not surprising to find Paul sharing in the broader conception of the Divine as the benefactor(s) par excellence, a conception shared by the Greco-Roman and Jewish cultures, and of human duties toward the Divine as essentially motivated, shaped, and necessitated by gratitude.[401]

---

giver and receiver . . . defined the gift element in those acts. By giving, accepting, and returning benefits between one another, giver and receiver establish, support, and give expression to a personal involvement with one another that generates a space of sharing and community within which they may live."

396. Seneca, *On Benefits* 1.4.4; 3.1.1; Dio Chrysostom, *Discourses* 31.37.

397. Aristotle, *Rhetoric* 2.2.8; Seneca, *On Benefits* 4.18.1; conversely, Sir 3:31; Seneca, *On Benefits* 1.10.5; Isocrates, *To Demonicus* 24, 29; Dio Chrysostom, *Discourses* 31.7.

398. Harrison, *Paul's Language of Grace*, 64–95; Peter Garnsey and Greg Woolf, "Patronage of the Rural Poor in the Roman World," 153–70 in *Patronage in Ancient Society*, ed. Wallace-Hadrill; deSilva, *Honor*, 99–100; Hesiod, *Works and Days* 342–51; 401–4.

399. On the diversity in social level within a Pauline congregation, see Theissen, *Social Setting*, 69–119; Meeks, *First Urban Christians*, 51–73; Holmberg, *Sociology and the New Testament*, 21–76.

400. See deSilva, *Honor*, 123–26; "We Are Debtors," 161–65.

401. It is commonly asserted that, when applied to the relationship of human beings with the gods, the ethos of reciprocity functioned on the principle of *do ut des*, "I give in order that you might give." It is important to note that both Jewish and Greco-Roman worshipers bear frequent testimony to the principle of *do quia dedisti*, "I give because you have given." See Aristotle, *Nicomachean Ethics* 8.14.4 (1163b16–18); Seneca, *On Benefits* 1.1.9; 2.30.1–2;

The fundamental problem in the human condition is ingratitude toward God. God has graced all who *are* with the gift of life and made provision to sustain them, but human beings did not return the honor, loyalty, and obedience that were God's due, giving these instead to their idols, to their own created things rather than the Creator, despite all the evidence that ought to have directed them to God (Rom 1:18–21, 25; see also Wis 13:1, 5–9). As a result, God's wrath—the anger of the slighted benefactor—hovers over the heads of humanity.[402] An important goal of Paul's mission is the reversal of the general population's ungrateful and highly insulting behavior in denying their Creator his due acknowledgment, in favor of awakening them to God's gifts and their reciprocal obligations (1 Thess 1:9).

What is surprising about God and God's grace is the degree of God's desire to benefit and of God's generosity as God extends a fresh invitation to receive and respond to God's gift of life appropriately. Rather than act swiftly and decisively to avenge his slighted honor, as would have been fully justified, God invests himself in restoring the relationship that the ingrates had broken. Rather than wait for the ingrates to come to their senses, God takes the initiative; rather than merely extend a further gift, God extends the most lavish display of love and self-giving possible. In this regard, God's grace is still "amazing"—but in degree, not in kind. Other slighted benefactors have occasionally extended further acts of grace to quicken gratitude even in the soil of the ingrate's heart,[403] but God has embodied the most extreme *degree* of generosity and desire to benefit.

Paul expects, and suggests rather plainly that *God* expects, this second act of grace to produce rather different results from the first acts of grace manifested in creation and the preservation of life. God's gift of the life of his Son on behalf of human beings is intended to lead these human beings into changed lives such that they no longer use their created bodies to multiply sin (affronts against the Creator) but to do what is righteous (in line with the values and purposes of the Creator; Rom 6:1–23). The response of the redeemed to his or her Redeemer will bring him or her *also* in line with the just response of the created to the Creator, "one whose daily experience is shaped by the recognition that he [or she] stands in debt to God."[404] Ac-

---

4.26.1; 4.28.1; Ps 116:12–19. For other Jewish expressions of the divine-human relationship in terms of benefaction and gratitude, see Exod 20:2–3; Deut 5:6–7; Num 18:9; Philo, *On Planting* 126–31; *Embassy* 118; *On the Creation of the World* 169.

402. See also 4 Ezra 7.20–25, 37; 8.59–60; 9.18–20; deSilva, "Grace, the Law, and Justification," 27–33.

403. See Seneca, *On Benefits* 7.31.1–7.32.1. Seneca also knows that the gods give their gifts of sun and rain to the worthy and unworthy alike (4.26.1, 4.28.1), providing an example of nobility to human benefactors (7.32).

404. Dunn, *Romans 1–8*, 59; see also Engberg-Pedersen, "Gift-Giving and Friendship," 41; Oropeza, "Expectation of Grace," 220.

cording to Paul, we are indeed "debtors"—just not debtors "to the flesh" (Rom 8:12).[405]

It is in this framework that we rightly hear passages such as 2 Cor 5:15: "He died on behalf of all in order that those who continue living might no longer live for themselves, but for the one who died on their behalf and was raised" (see also Rom 6:4–5; Gal 2:19–20). God's act of grace invites a response that shows an appropriate assessment of the value of his gift—in this case, a life for a life. Only a life given back shows the giver that we have properly valued his gift to us—his death on our behalf.[406] But this very giving *back* to God effects the transformation of the believer's life that allows him or her to live in a manner that is actually righteous in God's sight, thus in a manner leading to his or her justification in the fullest sense—that is, justification as "acquittal" as a result of having been "brought in line with God's righteousness."

Human sin (the failure to live out a response of obedient gratitude to the Creator) was followed by the further generous acts of God, extending the means of reconciliation and restoration to a grace relationship. At this point, however, continuing to live for one's own ends is not an option: "Are we to persist in sin in order that favor may be multiplied further? Certainly not!" (Rom 6:1); "Shall we keep on sinning because we are not under law but under favor? Certainly not!" (Rom 6:15). Being "under grace" and having experienced Christ's deliverance from slavery to sin mean investing ourselves fully in a reciprocal God-ward act: "Don't offer your life-in-the-body to sin as a vehicle for unjust action, but offer yourself to God as people now living from among the dead and offer your life-in-the-body to God as a vehicle for just action" (Rom 6:13). The person who has previously failed to respond to God's creative gift is now, by virtue of encountering and receiving God's love in

---

405. Jewett, *Romans*, 493. See also Furnish, *Theology and Ethics*, 226: "God's *claim* is regarded by the apostle as a constitutive part of God's *gift*. The Pauline concept of grace is *inclusive* of the Pauline concept of obedience." Barclay (*Obeying the Truth*, 214) similarly affirms that the gift of the Spirit "involves both gift and obligation." The full clause in Rom 8:12 is frequently mistranslated, particularly in markedly conservative translations, as "We are not indebted to the flesh" (HCSB, GW, TLB, NLT). It is, however, translated more accurately (note the position of the negating adverb: ὀφειλέται ἐσμὲν οὐ τῇ σαρκὶ), "we are indebted, not to the flesh" (as in the KJV, RSV, NRSV, ESV, GNT). The NIV is particularly strong: "we have an obligation—but it is not to the flesh, to live according to it" (similarly, CEB).

406. So, rightly, Barrett, *Second Epistle*, 169; Furnish, *Second Corinthians*, 328. Paul is not afraid to put his converts' obligation to God even less delicately when they are behaving less than graciously: "You were purchased with a price, so bring honor to God with your body" (1 Cor. 6:20). Redemption was an act of generous kindness—of grace—but being ransomed carries obligations toward the ransomer, if we appreciate the freedom that was purchased for us.

Christ, awakened to gratitude and its obligations and is thereby positioned to give God his due—to act justly rather than unjustly.[407] "Eternal life" remains God's gift (Rom 6:23)—but given to those whose lives reflect their reception and response to his beneficent creating and redeeming interventions, who have put their lives at his disposal rather than at the disposal of their own sinful, self-centered, self-gratifying impulses (Rom 6:20–22).[408]

Paul also expresses an awareness, however, that failure to respond in a manner that appropriately values Christ's selfless investment in the believer and the efficacy of the Spirit as an inner guide and power against sin and the flesh jeopardizes one's place in God's favor. A return to or embracing of the Torah becomes an affront to the honor and generous investment of the One who secured the Holy Spirit for his client-followers (Gal 2:21; 5:1–6). Failure to allow God's gift to have its full, transformative effect in the life and practice of the believer and believing community jeopardizes one's enjoyment of the eschatological favors of life and welcome into the kingdom of God (Gal 5:13–14, 19–21; 6:7–9; Rom 8:13–14).[409]

Critics of attempts to read Paul's discussions about God's grace against the background of reciprocity in the Greco-Roman world sometimes seek to distinguish the social practice from God's giving by pointing out that God's favor is so immense that it *cannot* be repaid, almost drawing the corollary that it is pointless for the recipients of God's favor to regard it as their absolute duty to *try*. Ancient moralists, however, were well acquainted with the case of the gift that cannot be repaid. Aristotle appears to have viewed this as a *typical* situation.[410] Seneca advises concerning it that, even though the recipient may never offer anything of the same value, he or she may offer what will give the superior benefactor equal pleasure through his or her expressions of joy and appreciation, commitment to bring honor to the giver, devotion to the relationship, and watchfulness for seizing any opportunities to offer the superior a pleasing and beautiful gift.[411] The giver's act of unmatchable favor irrevocably binds the recipient to himself or herself and, indeed, binds the two parties together, which is an underlying purpose in the giving and the returning of favor. The obligation of gratitude is not a burdensome debt to be discharged, but a delight to be ongoingly remembered and acted upon as a constant renewal of the relationship of favor. Returning to the specific case

---

407. Jewett, *Romans*, 412; see also the analysis of Paul's metaphor of the Christians as obligated beneficiaries in Rom 6:12–23 in Harrison, *Paul's Language of Grace*, 234–42.

408. Donfried, "Justification and Last Judgment," 97, 99.

409. Donfried, "Justification and Last Judgment," 99: "One negative role which the last judgment will play is the withholding of the final gift of salvation from those baptized Christians who have been disobedient."

410. Aristotle, *Nicomachean Ethics* 8.14.2 (1163b1–5).

411. Seneca, *On Benefits* 2.24.4; 2.30.2; 5.3.3; 5.4.1; 7.14.4, 6.

of God's matchless favor, it is because God's gift *cannot* be repaid that it is transformative. We are moved to give our *all* in return, to let the grace shown us become the initiating act that calls forth our grateful responses ever afresh in each new situation, in every moment, with no time or energy free to be given to the "flesh" or to the "world."

Any expectation that human beings must *do* anything also raises objections that salvation is no longer "by grace alone" (a phrase that, like "faith alone," Paul never actually uses) or that it reintroduces "earning salvation" or that it yields a theology of merit *as opposed to* grace. The theologian's distinction between "free grace" and "cooperant grace" makes a categorical distinction where Paul would have seen *no* distinction. Grace, in his world, is always both *free*, since giving is uncoerced, and *cooperant*, since grace *must* be met with grace (gratitude, return). As long as theologians cling to such categories, they will continue to parse grace in a way that is foreign to the New Testament authors on whose writings they typically seek to ground their theologies.

That the understanding of grace articulated here leads to the notion of "earning salvation" is also a misperception. Paul is clear that no human being, by the very fact of being a *creature*, can indebt God with a view to leveraging future favors: "Who has anticipated God in giving a gift, so that it will be repaid to him or her?" (Rom 11:35). The rationale is telling: "Because all things are from him and through his agency and directed unto him" (11:36), an obvious formula about creation, and thus positing indebtedness to God— specifically, indebtedness to give *back* to God—as the starting point for every created being. Nevertheless, Paul *does* advocate very strongly a mentality of "I give because you have given" (*do quia dedisti*), which is entirely in keeping with Greco-Roman convictions about the absolute *necessity* of meeting favor with favor, of recipients of favors responding to their benefactors and friends with equal commitment and investment. Thus, even as one insists on the necessity of responding to grace well and fully if we are to remain in a relationship of grace, one does not suggest *earning* God's grace.

Finally, opposing "merit" to "grace" in another categorical distinction is also highly problematic.[412] Paul understands a grateful response to have merit, and to contribute to the ongoing nurturing of the grace relationship, just as ingratitude contributes to the dissolution of the relationship (as in Gal 5:2–4), but God's grace is still the initiating force, and the human recipient always remains in the position of the one indebted to God. "Merit," in other words, exists in Paul's framework, but does not earn by indebting God. Rather than regarding this model as a return to "salvation by works," I would propose that it be regarded as "letting God's grace have its full effect" in and upon the recipients of God's favor, where that effect includes the response of reoriented

---

412. Westerholm, *Justification Reconsidered*, 29–30.

lives that God's favor naturally and necessarily provokes where it is received well. God's initiating acts of grace provoke the response and determine the structure of the response that sets one on the path to responding justly to God (and thus to being acquitted as just). Moreover, as Paul himself will never allow us to forget, it is God himself working in us, through the *gift* of God's Holy Spirit, to make possible this very response that transforms our lives from unjust to just in our relationship with our Creator-Redeemer.[413]

I would also propose that the model finally allows disciples to hear statements like Gal 2:19-20; 1 Cor 6:19-20; 2 Cor 5:14-15; Rom 6:15-23 and to give them their full weight rather than mute their force in favor of traditional positions emerging from the Reformation period and thereafter. For, finally, where transactional understandings of God's grace (an isolated act that transfers something irrevocably to me on the basis of "belief") trump dynamic, relational understandings of grace, theologians are wrenching Paul and his message out of the social, ethical, and *lived* contexts in which Paul was shaped and his gospel formulated, preached, and heard.

---

413. See Gal 3:2-5; 5:16-25; Phil 2:12-13; Rom 8:4, 9-11. As Käsemann ("Righteousness of God," 170) formulated it so well, "Paul knows no gift of God which does not convey both the obligation and the capacity to serve."

IV. ARGUMENTS AGAINST ADOPTING
TORAH OBSERVANCE (3:1-4:11)

Paul sets forth the argumentative underpinnings of his implicit claim that righteousness does not come through aligning one's life with the stipulations of the Torah, the obvious conclusion to be drawn from his contrary-to-fact statement in 2:21 (since no party in this altercation would be willing to admit that "Christ died for nothing," v. 21c). Paul's anchoring arguments are grounded upon the Galatians' firsthand experience of having received the Holy Spirit and continuing to experience this Spirit at work in their lives and in their midst (3:1-6; 4:4-11). This experience, Paul asserts, ought to have been sufficient to cause the Galatian converts to realize that their trust in God had already attained for them all that was needful for "righteousness" (5:5-6) and that they were already sons and daughters in God's household and thus heirs of God's promises. Any further attempt to reinforce these gains through Torah observance would, on the contrary, undermine these gains (4:8-11; see also 5:2-4).

The premise behind this argument, which Paul will develop in 3:7-14 (climactically in 3:14b), is that the reception of the Spirit signals the fulfillment of God's promise to Abraham and to Abraham's "Seed," whom Paul identifies as the singular offspring, Jesus (3:15-16). This premise calls for an acknowledgment that the experience of the Holy Spirit, as well as the consequent action of the Holy Spirit in the believer and believing community, is of much greater importance for Paul than is captured in the Nicene and Apostles' Creeds, or in any systematic theology wherein "pneumatology" is an afterthought to, rather than an integral part of, "soteriology." The *further* premise behind this premise, which Paul will develop in 3:15-25, is that the promise to Abraham and his Seed, and *not* the giving of the law, is the fulcrum point of God's plan to bring human beings back into line with God's righteousness. This position requires, in turn, that Paul address God's reason for the giving of the law in the first place (3:19-22), if it was not for the reasons that the rival teachers allege, and that Paul establish the precise relationship of Christ's death to the Torah and its term limits (3:10-14, 23-25; 4:1-7).

Evident throughout this section is the importance of establishing what makes a person a son or daughter or Abraham and thus an heir of "the promise":

> You all know, then, that those who exhibit trust, *these* are the ones who are Abraham's sons and daughters. (3:7)

> Christ redeemed us from the curse of the law . . . in order that the blessing of Abraham might come to the nations in Christ Jesus, so that we might receive the promise of the Spirit through trust. (3:13-14)

If you are of Christ, then you are Abraham's seed, heirs in accordance with promise. (3:29)

You are no longer a slave, but a son (or daughter)—and if a son (or daughter), then also an heir through God. (4:7)

Paul devotes so much attention to this point, which is largely ancillary to his own argumentation, that it seems likely that the rival teachers had been making much of circumcision and Torah observance as the means by which to become part of the family of Abraham and thereby heirs of God's promises. Were others *not* making this case, it would have been enough for Paul to draw upon the Galatians' experience of the Spirit and perhaps to argue for the temporary role of the Torah in God's economy.

This larger argumentative block can be outlined as follows:

3:1–6: Proof from the experience of the Spirit

3:7–9: Proof of the sufficiency of trust from Abraham's precedent

3:10–14: Deductive proof from the Scriptures that trust, and not Torah observance, is the way to righteousness and life

3:15–18: Proof from an analogy with testamentary law

3:19–22: An explanation of the Torah's limited role

3:23–29: Proof from an analogy with coming of age in a household, with inferences to be drawn up to this point

4:1–7: A resumption of the analogy, returning to the reception of the Spirit

4:8–11: Further conclusions to be drawn from the analogy, in the form of a rebuke.

A. PROOF FROM EXPERIENCE:
THE GALATIANS' RECEPTION OF THE SPIRIT (3:1-6)

¹ O unthinking Galatians! Who has put a spell on you,ᵃ before whose eyes Jesus Christ was vividly portrayedᵇ as crucified?! ² This one thing only do I want to learn from you: Was it on the basis of works of Torah that you received the Spirit, or on the basis of the message that aroused trust? ³ Are you all so thoughtless [that], after beginning with the Spirit, you are now going to finish by means of flesh?! ⁴ Have you experienced such great things for nothing—if indeed it was for nothing?! ⁵ The one, then, who keeps on supplying the Spirit to you and working miraculous signs among you, does he do this on the basis of works of Torah or on the basis of the message that aroused trust, ⁶ just as Abraham trusted God, and it was accounted to him as righteousness?

a. A number of later MSS (C D^2 K L P Ψ 33^c 𝔐, hence its appearance in the KJV) add "in order that you should not obey the truth" (τῇ ἀληθείᾳ μὴ πείθεσθαι), a secondary borrowing and insertion of the same phrase from Gal 5:7.

b. A number of Western and Majority MSS add ἐν ὑμῖν (D E F G K L 𝔐, hence the KJV), "vividly portrayed *among you*," a clearly secondary attempt at clarification and improvement.

With this paragraph, Paul begins to make his case for the truth of his position (2:14–21) on the basis of the addressees' experience of God's Spirit and God's working in their midst, on the basis of arguments from Scripture, and on the basis of the understanding of salvation history that Paul's reading of Scripture nurtures. All of this argumentation contributes directly to his primary proposition: the Galatians should keep moving forward in the direction in which Paul started them off rather than adopt the rival teachers' proposed "course correction" (5:1). Paul will continue to give attention to argumentative proofs through 4:11, with 3:1–5 and 4:8–11 forming a kind of *inclusio* marking the opening and closing of this segment. Both 3:1–5 and 4:8–11 involve a series of pointed rhetorical questions, using the technique of interrogation to lead the audience to a particular conclusion. Both passages also contain direct statements to the audience that are at home in letters of rebuke ("You unthinking Galatians," 3:1; "I am afraid for you," 4:11).[1] The moral philosophers in the marketplace often called into question the intelligence of passers-by who were not yet taking the "larger view" on life that philosophers promoted, such that Paul's challenge to the soundness of his converts' reasoning, while abrupt and attention-getting, was not out of line with rhetorical practice. Paul will continue to offer arguments in support of his advice beyond 4:11, but these arguments become more fully intertwined with exhortations to (and warnings about) action and allegiances.

Galatians 3:1 marks a clear start of a new discursive step. After a lengthy narration, Paul opens with a commanding direct address and poses a direct question to his audience, focusing them afresh on their immediate situation. While there is continuity of topic (i.e., the antithesis between pursuing justification by the path opened up by trusting Jesus and the path of conforming to the Torah's stipulations), Paul also introduces fresh subject matter, namely, the topics of the Holy Spirit and of Abraham. Galatians 3:1–14 forms a coherent unit of argumentation in three discernible steps. In the first step, Paul calls attention to the Galatians' reception and experience of the Holy Spirit on the basis of responding with trust to the gospel message as evidence that the path of trust is, indeed, the sufficient path by which to reach the end of the journey on which they have set out (3:1–5). Galatians 3:6, which

---

1. Longenecker, 97.

introduces the figure of Abraham as a historical example of faithful response leading to righteousness, is sometimes taken as part of 3:1–6,[2] sometimes as the beginning of a new paragraph.[3] The former position is almost certainly to be preferred, however, since the coordinating conjunction translated "just as" functions more naturally as a direct continuation of the question posed in 3:5. Abraham is thus introduced as a precedent whose case should lead the hearers to a particular answer: we received God's gifts, know God's power, and will arrive at God's goal for us by pursuing the path that trusting the word about Christ opened up.

Galatians 3:7–9, then, posits that "faith" is the point of family resemblance that defines Abraham's sons and daughters, those to whom the blessing promised to Abraham would come. Galatians 3:10–14 returns to the topic of "works of the Torah" by way of contrast, establishing the Torah-driven life as a life lived "under a curse" rather than a life of confident expectation of the blessing, which comes from moving forward in trust. Paul rounds out this period of argumentation in 3:13–14 by bringing together the topics of Christ crucified, the Spirit, blessing, curse, law, and faith: Christ fell under the law's curse to redeem, by exchange, those who labored under the threat or experience of the law's curse so that the blessing promised to Abraham, even the Holy Spirit, might come to all nations on the basis of faith.

1 Paul signals a shift in the flow of discourse with an arresting, direct address: "O unthinking Galatians! Who has put a spell on you, before whose eyes Jesus Christ was vividly portrayed as crucified?!" Calling the addressees "Galatians" here is an effective way to refocus their attention on their immediate local situation, completing the bridging of the Antioch incident (2:11–14) and Paul's theological response thereto (2:15–21) with the challenge of the rival gospel in Galatia.[4] Calling them "unthinking" is an effective way of challenging their openness to the message and advice of the rival teachers. While it is tempting to translate the Greek here as "stupid," Paul is not making a statement about the Galatian believers' intellects per se, but about their refusal or failure to apply them in their current situation.[5] Had they done so, they would not have been led so easily to give the rivals' advice serious consideration.

Paul opens his interrogation by asking, "Who has put a spell on you?" using a verb that often refers specifically to casting a spell by giving someone

---

2. UBS[4]; NEB; ESV; NIV; Bruce, 152; Matera, 113; Silva, *Interpreting*, 219–20 (though not insistently).

3. NA[27, 28]; NRSV; NLT; Burton, 153; Longenecker, 112; Tolmie, *Persuading*, 100–101.

4. Tolmie, *Persuading*, 103. On the relevance of the term "Galatians" for discerning the location and composition of the audience, see the Introduction.

5. Burton, 143; Matera, 111; LN 32.50.

the "evil eye."[6] The evil eye, an expression of evil intent often motivated by envy incurred by the good fortune of its object, was regarded as a potent and pervasive force. A second-century mosaic in the Archaeological Museum in Antakya, Turkey, bears witness to the interest in warding off the evil eye in Roman-period Anatolia. The mosaic features an eyeball surrounded by various talismans against the evil eye, including a trident and a sword with their points touching the eyeball, a bird pecking at the eyeball, as well as a centipede, scorpion, snake (with a knot in its body), dog, and leopard all poised as if to strike this eyeball. The magic is completed by a goblin-like figure walking away from the eyeball and holding skewers, while its erect phallus is (impossibly) turned backward to ward off the power of the eye, ranged alongside the other talismans keeping the evil eye at bay. The mosaic contains the two Greek words for "you also," pronouncing an "and also with you" upon whoever would enter the house, whether that visitor brings blessing or curse.[7] One popular antidote against the evil eye was apparently spitting three times into one's breast.[8]

This is a rhetorically charged characterization of the strategies employed by, and fundamental motivation of, the opponents. It is unlikely that they used magic against the Galatian converts, but it is strategic for Paul to cast their influence over the Galatians in as negative and sinister light as possible. The Galatians are not merely being "persuaded" otherwise than Paul has taught them; they are being subjected to dark forces to seduce them to the rivals' position.[9] Their response should be now to ward off their spell as quickly as possible. Paul also shifts the blame for the Galatians being duped to the rival teachers, such that the latter's malevolence is ultimately responsible for the Galatians' present lack of clarity (thus also lessening any resentment toward Paul for pointing this out so brusquely).[10] He suggests that the rival teachers' influence specifically clouds their vision of what was of central importance to the gospel message: Christ crucified.[11]

The evil eye was associated particularly with envy, and Paul may be

---

6. BDAG 171.

7. The image can be found in Cimok, *Journeys of Paul*, 104.

8. In Theocritus, *Idyll* 6.39, in response to fear of the evil eye, Polyphemus, having aroused Galatea to jealousy, responds thus: "Lest I be cursed, I spat three times into my breast." See discussion in Clayton Zimmerman, *The Pastoral Narcissus: A Study of the First Idyll of Theocritus* (London: Rowman & Littlefield, 1994), 45–46; also Pliny, *Natural History* 28.7 §§36, 39; BDAG 309.

9. Longenecker, 100; Witherington, 201–4; see Betz, 131 for examples of the figurative sense of the word in classical literature.

10. Tolmie, *Persuading*, 104.

11. Paul may be making something of a word play as he conjoins the evil eye with what the Galatians themselves have essentially seen with their own eyes (Fee, 104).

hinting that this plays a part in motivating the rival teachers. He had already suggested that another group opposed to Paul's gospel looked begrudgingly upon the "freedom" of his converts and took steps to draw them back into slavery, though Paul successfully thwarted their attempts (2:4–5). He will go on to accuse the rival teachers specifically of courting his converts, pretending to seek their good but in actuality trying to deprive them of their standing in Christ, all to improve the teachers' *own* standing (4:17), turning the Galatian Christians into trophies (6:12–13).

Paul clearly expresses his expectation that the Galatians should have been more critically reflective in their assessment of the truth of the rival teachers' message, and that, if they had exercised their brains more, they would not have come under the spell of these outsiders so easily. Had they reflected more on the message about "Christ crucified" that Paul had clearly laid out before them during his first visit to their cities—and on their own experience of having been loved and accepted by God (i.e., their experience of the Holy Spirit soon to be foregrounded in 3:2–5)—they would have seen through the rival teachers' false reasoning. The verb Paul uses here can mean either "display prominently" or "announce beforehand," the latter typically in writing. The first sense fits the context better, as Paul recalls how, in his initial proclamation of the gospel to those who would become his converts and his early instruction of the same, Paul set the crucified Messiah right in front of their eyes.[12]

"Christ crucified" is Paul's shorthand expression for the larger proclamation of the gospel, holding up the most distinctive image and facet of that message (see also 1 Cor 1:23; 2:2). It is also the image that captures most graphically the costliness of this gift or favor of God that some Galatian Christians are, in Paul's view, in danger of setting aside (2:21).[13] The emphasis on Paul's proclamation of the crucified Messiah in 3:1 grows organically out of Paul's emphasis on the death of Christ in 2:21 and his conviction that the very

---

12. So Fung, 129; Longenecker, 100–101; Matera, 112. Burton (144) offers "placarding" as an equivalent. Vivid presentation, making something to appear before the mental eyes of an audience, was an oft-articulated goal of persuasive speaking, in which "things are set before the eyes by words that signify actuality" (Aristotle, *Rhetoric* 3.11.2). Quintilian (*Education* 6.2.29–32) similarly speaks of the creation of mental images by means of words, such that "absent things are presented to the mind in such a way that we seem actually to see them without eyes and have them physically present to us," with the result that the speakers "seem not so much to be talking about something as exhibiting it" (both texts are cited in Murphy-O'Connor, "The Unwritten Law," 229). Bryant (*Risen Crucified Christ*, 171) correctly observes that, while Paul usually downplays his rhetorical ability, here he appears to celebrate it. Davis ("Meaning of προεγράφη") goes too far in suggesting that Paul used his own bodily scars (6:17) as a crude visual aid in this proclamation.

13. Shauf, "Galatians 2.20," 96.

value of Christ's death is now at stake. We might paraphrase Paul's underlying challenge thus: "We emphasized the redemptive and eschatological significance of Jesus's costly death on the cross while we were among you; how could you now, then, be so unreflective as to begin to entertain the idea that you will fall in line with God's righteous standards by following the Torah?"

2 Having brought home the significance of his statement of his position (2:14–21) for the Galatians in their current deliberations (3:1), Paul demands an answer from them in regard to one question: "This *one thing only* do I want to learn from you" (3:2a). The placement of "this one thing only" (the direct object of the infinitive "to learn" that follows) at the beginning of the sentence is emphatic, adding force to the question and creating audience anticipation concerning "*this* one thing" yet to be named. While Paul actually follows this up with four questions (possibly five, if 3a is treated separately from 3b) in relentless succession, these are all foundationally related to a single issue: "Was it on the basis of works of the law that you received the Spirit, or on the basis of the message that aroused trust?" (3:2b). The answer to this question, which can only be "by trust," drives the deductive process of the paragraph, leading the Galatians to an inevitable conclusion regarding their present situation.

Rhetorical theorists advised that a strong argument, if not the most compelling, should be placed up front in the proof section of one's address. In this way, the speaker would convince the audience early on, with all following proofs serving to confirm the hearers in their decision. Paul exhibits such a strategy in Galatians. If he can gain the Galatians' assent concerning "this one thing only," he believes that it will provide the decisive evidence that settles for them the issue of whether Torah observance is indeed the next step forward in their journey toward acquittal.[14]

This passage in particular (as, in greater detail, 5:13–6:10) points to the significance of the reception of the Holy Spirit in the Pauline mission and in Paul's understanding of how God was at work among his converts, bringing them to the end God promised for them. The Spirit itself is, for Paul, an essential component of the promise that is now coming to fulfillment in the Christian assembly (3:14). In Ezekiel, for example, God promises to send a new spirit into God's people, empowering obedience to God's statutes (Ezek 11:19–20; 36:26–27). Ezekiel might have expected the fulfillment of this promise to result in the perfect and internally driven observance of the Torah, but Paul understands the Spirit to empower obedience to God's universal norm for humankind, not to the specifically Jewish law code (see 5:13–25).

---

14. Thus, for example, Burton, 147; Betz, 130; Dunn, 151; Matera, 112; Tolmie, *Persuading*, 101, 104. Authors who regard 3:1–5 as a digression or interlude (e.g., see Drane, *Paul, Libertine or Legalist?*, 24) miss the importance of this passage, as well as the decisive importance of the reception of the Holy Spirit for Paul's theology.

Whether the Galatian Christians received the Spirit is not in question. Paul knows that they did, and knows that *they* know they did. Paul's description of the Galatians' initial encounter with the gospel as a combination of hearing the proclamation and experiencing the conviction brought by the Spirit and power of God is a common feature throughout the Pauline mission. Paul reminds the converts in Corinth of a similar experience (1 Cor 2:1–5), and the member of the Pauline team who wrote Hebrews reminds his addressees of their experience of God's power and distributions of the Spirit that confirmed the proclaimed word (Heb 2:3–4). The nature of the experiences left little doubt that something supernatural was happening in the converts' midst (see also 1 Cor 12:1–14:40, esp. 14:24–25). The unmistakable experience of the pouring out of God's Spirit upon his gentile converts becomes a foundational premise in Paul's own thinking about what God is doing in and through his mission.[15] It becomes empirical proof of the Galatian Christians' status before God and thus proof against the rival teachers' assertions.[16]

Paul makes his converts recall this facet of their experience and asks on what basis or from what source they received the Spirit, offering them two possible answers from which to choose: on the basis of "works of the Torah" (*ex ergōn nomou*) or on the basis of "the message that awakened faith" (*ex akoēs pisteōs*). The first phrase appeared already in 2:15–16 (three times!), and its meaning is by now familiar. The second phrase is a new and highly imprecise expression, open to a number of potentially legitimate interpretations. The Galatians themselves might have found Paul's precise meaning elusive here, as they would have faced the same ambiguities therein as does the modern interpreter (though with the benefits of having more extensive exposure to Paul's thought and expression, as well as an insiders' grasp of the nuances of the language).

As with the phrase *pistis Christou*, to which this expression is related (since it now replaces that expression in this new antithesis with "works of the Torah" and features *pistis* once again), the ambiguities reside both in the meaning of the head noun *akoē* and in the relationship between *akoē* and *pistis* communicated by the genitive case of the latter.[17] The noun *akoē* could

---

15. "At the heart and at the start of the Christian life of the Galatians is the existential experience of the Spirit" (rightly, Rabens, "Indicative and Imperative," 300).

16. See Lemmer, "Mnemonic Reference"; Fee, *Empowering Presence*, 378, 381–89.

17. Although ἐξ ἀκοῆς πίστεως and ἐξ ἔργων νόμου are parallel expressions, it would be a fallacy to suggest on that basis that the grammatical and syntactic components making up the two prepositional phrases need to be understood in parallel fashion (rightly Hays, *Faith of Jesus Christ*[1], 147). Two radically different senses of the genitival relationship can exist within the same sentence, as Matlock ("Detheologizing," 16) has shown in regard to Acts 9:31. For a fuller discussion of the options, see Hays, *Faith of Jesus Christ*[1], 143–49.

signify either (1) the faculty or the act of hearing[18] or (2) the thing heard, hence "report" or "message."[19] The second noun (*pistis*) would probably be heard to denote "trust" or "faith" (rather than "faithfulness" or "the faith," i.e., the essence of the Christian gospel, as in 1:23), particularly in retrospect, since Abraham's believing response to God is presented as a precedent and analogous situation (although 2:16–21 also predisposes the hearer toward this understanding). Hearing and believing is what one finds both in Abraham (3:6) and in those who become his sons and daughters (3:7–9; in response to Paul's preaching, 3:1–2). Faith in both cases signifies "trusting acceptance of God's word and obedient compliance with the divine purposes it expresses."[20]

The genitive case of *pistis* may suggest that "faith" is a quality of the "hearing" in some sense, hence "faithful hearing" or "hearing characterized by trusting." This reading—"hearing (and trusting what has been heard)"—offers a better parallel and foil to the contrasting action, namely, the implied performance of the "works of the Torah." It also conforms closely to the forthcoming example of Abraham (3:6), to whom God announced the promise, and who heard the promise and trusted it.[21] The preceding verse, which recalls Paul's presentation of a specific message ("Jesus Christ crucified"), also naturally gives way to a focus on the response of listening and trusting.

The genitive could also be taken to describe *akoē* in terms of naming the direction or purpose of this noun,[22] yielding "a message (or, possibly, the act of hearing) that awakens faith." In favor of this reading is a statement Paul would later make in Rom 10:16–17 about the proclamation of the gospel and the awakening of faith or trust. There Paul takes Isa 53:1 as a starting point for arguing that Christ's word is disseminated through the message of apostles like Paul, resulting in the arousal of a response of trust or faith.[23] While interpreting an earlier document by a later one is not without methodological problems, the fact that both Gal 3:2 and Rom 10:16–17 are written by the same author, appearing in documents that clearly have a close relationship with one another, invoking a similar constellation of topics, may be sufficient to allay these reservations. This understanding also takes its bearings from Paul's ex-

---

18. As it does, for example, in LXX Isa 6:9; Matt 13:14; Mark 7:35; Luke 7:1; Acts 17:20; 1 Cor 12:17; 2 Tim 4:3–4; Heb 5:11; 2 Pet 2:8.

19. As in LXX Isa 52:7; 53:1; LXX Jer 6:4; 30:8; Matt 4:24; 14:1; 24:6; John 12:38; Acts 28:26; Rom 10:16–17; 1 Thess 2:13; Heb 4:2 (John 12:38; Acts 28:26; Rom 10:16 are all citations of LXX Isa 53:1).

20. Williams, "Hearing of Faith," 87.

21. Fung, 132; Bruce, 149; Schreiner, 182–83; Williams, "The Hearing of Faith," 86–87. Longenecker (103) may also be aiming in the same direction when he glosses the phrase as "believing what you heard."

22. BDF §166.

23. Martyn, 288–89.

plicit, contextual reminder of the gospel *message* that Paul proclaimed ("Jesus Christ . . . crucified," 3:1), which the Galatians trusted.[24]

Either option renders the antithesis in 3:2 consonant with the earlier antithesis involving "works of the Torah" and "trust in Jesus Christ" in 2:16, since both readings continue to foreground the response of trust directed toward Christ as a result of hearing Paul's initial preaching, as opposed to another human response, that of conforming one's practices and person to the stipulations of Torah.[25]

It seems, in the end, impossible to determine precisely how the audience in Galatia would have construed this phrase, and what variety of interpretations might have existed among them as they listened to the letter being read to them. Nevertheless, this much is unambiguous: God had already poured out God's Holy Spirit upon the Galatian Christians because they responded with trust to the message Paul preached regarding the significance of Jesus's death for their connection with God, long before they were considering submitting to circumcision and adopting any part of a Torah-observant lifestyle. Moreover, whether the Galatians would have understood *akoē* as their act of listening or as the message to which they listened, it was Paul who spoke in their hearing and Paul's message that awakened their faith, with the result that they received God's Holy Spirit. This, too, should have obvious implications for them in regard to choosing now between trusting Paul and trusting the rival teachers. They will, perhaps most important, understand quite clearly that "doing what the Torah prescribes" was *not* the means by which they have received and continue to experience the Spirit.

If the Galatian Christians can attest from their own religious experience that they had received God's Holy Spirit and experienced God's presence in their midst as a result of trusting in Jesus and in what his death secured for human beings, they will come to see that (1) they have received the blessing that was promised to Abraham concerning "all the nations" (3:14), (2) they have enjoyed God's complete acceptance and are already sons and daughters of the living God and thereby also heirs of God's promise (4:6–7),[26] and (3) they have received from God all that they need to live beyond the power of the flesh and to conform

---

24. Sprinkle, "Eschatological Event," 177. See also 1 Thess 2:13: "the word of the report [ἀκοή] . . . of God."

25. Williams, "Hearing of Faith," 86. Other possibilities arise if one understands the genitive πίστεως to name the "content" of the head noun, hence (3) "hearing about faith," less likely (4) "hearing about (Christ's) faithfulness" (taking πίστις in its other principal sense) or (5) the "report" (Paul's preaching) about "faith." The last is essentially the meaning espoused by Betz, 133; Matera, 112. Again, however, the example of Abraham exhibiting trust in response to God's promise heightens the probability that πίστις will be understood as "trust" here, if only in retrospect.

26. A similar point is made by the extensive episode of Cornelius and its interpretation in Acts 10:1–11:15.

to God's righteous standards, thus enjoying God's approval at the end (5:13-25; 6:7-10), all on the basis of having trusted in Jesus and relying upon the favor God is showing to the world through Jesus. They are poised to deduce that they could not gain anything more by turning to performing the works of the Torah. Their trust in Jesus was enough to render them holy to the Lord, hence allowing the Holy Spirit to rest upon them and dwell among them. There was no need to perform the traditional rites by which Jews had kept themselves holy to the Lord, with holiness being defined in terms of maintaining their ethnic distinctiveness from the gentile nations. Indeed, turning to the Torah as a means of making their possession of these blessings more secure would express a "vote of no confidence" in Jesus, whom they had hitherto trusted solely (cf. 2:21; 5:2-4).

3 Paul presses his interrogation forward with a second, related question: "Are you all so thoughtless that, after beginning with the Spirit, you are now going to arrive at the end by the flesh?!" (3:3). He creates a genuine chiasm of two contrasting pairs in the second half of this verse to highlight the absurdity of exchanging "spirit" for something pertaining to "flesh," as though the latter could improve upon or contribute to the former:

> A after beginning
>   B with the Spirit,
>   B' with the flesh now
> A' are you making an end?[27]

The Galatian believers had begun their journey of transformation (Christ being formed in them, 4:19; becoming righteous before God, 2:16) by their reception of the Holy Spirit. The question before them concerns how they will best bring this journey to a successful completion. The rival teachers are promoting close observance of the Torah, the commitment to which would be inscribed into the flesh of the male Galatian converts' foreskin, as the securest way to reach the goal. The connection of the covenant, circumcision, and "flesh" is strongly forged in the scriptural and parabiblical texts that promote circumcision as the sign of belonging to Abraham's family and to the covenant God made with him and his offspring:

> You shall circumcise the flesh of your foreskins, and it shall be a sign of the covenant between me and you. . . . So shall my covenant be in your flesh an everlasting covenant. (Gen 17:11, 13 NRSV)

---

27. Tolmie (*Persuading*, 106) quite plausibly regards νῦν ("now") to be an independent element (a "C") at the central focal point of the chiasm, calling the hearers to think about the moment at which they find themselves between start and finish: (A) ἐναρξάμενοι (B) πνεύματι (C) νῦν (B') σαρκὶ (A') ἐπιτελεῖσθε.

[Abraham] certified the covenant in his flesh, and when he was tested he proved faithful. (Sir 44:20 NRSV)

The opponents themselves might well have viewed an act performed "in the flesh" as having great ethical significance and thus holding value for making progress toward the end of the journey begun with trusting Jesus. Philo of Alexandria, for example, praises circumcision as an act that in itself limits lustful passions by diminishing the pleasure of intercourse. It becomes thus a potent symbol of a whole life dedicated to the taming and mastery of the desires in favor of living a life of virtue (*Migration* 89–94).

Paul accepts this connection between circumcision and flesh but portrays it quite differently. He assumes that the congregations will share his evaluation of the Spirit as far more positive and valuable a force than the flesh, a safe assumption, given the widespread devaluation of flesh (as "physical body") below spirit (as a person's "nonphysical essence," like a "soul," or as divine spirit indwelling and leading a person) in Greco-Roman philosophical writings and, no doubt therefore, in speeches in the marketplace of every city. Paul himself does not share in this general devaluation of the body, since he clings to the hope of the resurrection of the physical body in some sense, insisting on some connection between one's future, eternal body and the physical body of our mortal life (see 1 Cor 15:35–58; 2 Cor 5:1–4). He does, however, capitalize on it from the outset of his argument: flesh (as "body," "physical existence") is certainly less powerful than Spirit (which is, throughout Galatians, not the human spirit or soul but God's Holy Spirit) when it comes to pursuing the life of righteousness that God seeks in God's people.

In Gal 5:13–6:10 Paul will go on to develop the concept of flesh as a collection of destructive drives within the individual human being and even in the midst of human community—that is, not limiting flesh to the physical aspects of being human but extending it to embrace also the realms of our interior life and our social existence. Hence the "works of the flesh" include the ways in which we rebel against God's righteous standards with our bodies (lust, gluttony, drunkenness, and the like), but also with our minds and in our relationships (enmities, factions, anger, envying, and the like). Paul will make it clear, however, that flesh as a power in our midst that turns us away from God's righteousness and Christ's example of self-giving love is not the same as the flesh that serves as the soft tissue covering our bones.

At this point, Paul is content to play on the generally accepted evaluation of flesh as that which participates in our mortal weakness. When Paul denies that he conferred with "flesh and blood" (meaning the apostles who had accompanied Jesus, 1:16–17) after his divine commission, he expects his hearers to understand that "flesh and blood," being of a lower order and possessing a weaker insight than God, could add nothing of value to what he had already received from God in his experience of the glorified Christ. He uses the term again when he speaks of the impossibility of "all flesh" (meaning "all humanity") being justified, or brought in line with God's righteous standards, by means of the Torah (2:16). He uses the term more neutrally in 2:20 when he speaks of the life he now lives "while in the flesh," but this is neutral rather than pejorative because Paul lives within the relationship of trust or faith with Jesus, such that Jesus is coming to life within Paul, living through him, giving him a new life that is beyond the limitations of flesh on its own or even flesh aided by the guidance and guardianship of Torah.

Here in 3:3 Paul consigns Torah itself to the realm of flesh and thus the realm of that which is impotent to help bring human beings to where God wants them to be. Paul's argument works by reducing his rivals' position to absurdity: if the Galatian converts already have experienced the Holy Spirit of God working in their midst collectively and in their lives individually, what could they possibly think that cutting around the flesh of their foreskin would add? If they had begun their journey in the power of the Spirit, how could they possibly think they could make greater forward progress now by turning to the "flesh" (both as attention to the physical alteration of the penis and as a collection of commandments that were concerned about such things as circumcision, what foods a person ate, and what one did to rinse pollution off the body)?[28] They have already made a good beginning in the Spirit and can make progress now only by heeding the Spirit (hence the attention to this topic in 5:13–6:10, esp. 5:16–25), which will prove to be the sufficient source of guidance and empowerment for the whole journey.[29]

4 Paul's next question suggests that, were the Galatians to turn now to circumcision and other works of Torah as a means of making progress in their life before God, they would betray everything with which God had graced them up to that point: "Have you experienced such great things for nothing—if indeed it was for nothing?!" The opening verb is properly translated here

---

28. Paul connects "works of the law" in the plural with the "flesh" in this paragraph; "flesh" therefore does not refer only to the act of circumcision (against Burton, 148; Betz, 133–34; with Bruce, 149; Schlier, 123; Barclay, *Obeying the Truth*, 85–86), though it clearly plays upon such resonances. The unflattering linking of Torah with flesh continues in 4:21–31, as Paul connects Ishmael, the child born of the "flesh" (4:23a, 29) as opposed to the child born of "promise" (4:23b) or of "Spirit" (4:29), with those people who remain under the covenant of Sinai, that is, the Torah (4:24–25).

29. Moo ("Justification in Galatians," 166) mistakenly identifies "hearing characterized by faith" as "the means by which they will sustain their Christian experience (see 3:3)" here; it is not *faith* per se, but rather the *Spirit* that Paul foregrounds as the means by which they will move from the beginning to the end of the journey on which God set them when they first "heard with faith."

"you experienced," and not "you suffered."[30] While the verb is often used to speak of painful or otherwise negative experiences, it is the context that determines whether the things experienced are negative or positive. Paul refers here to the Galatians' experience of the Spirit and of God's power working in their midst (2–3, 5)—clearly positive experiences—asking if it was all for nothing. Paul had already hinted that turning now to the Torah would amount to repudiating God's generous kindness (2:21), and he will again raise this alarm in 5:2–4 as part of his climactic appeal on this topic. Their religious experience from conversion to the present moment is on the line. Paul adds the final phrase, "if indeed it was for nothing," as a way of calling this possible outcome into doubt. He expresses the hope that his converts will indeed draw the correct conclusions about the matter at hand on the basis of their past experience.[31]

5–6 It is so important to Paul that the Galatians reflect on their own, firsthand experience of God's favor and acceptance on the basis of their having responded to the gospel with trust (rather than by adopting a Torah-observant lifestyle) that he essentially repeats the question first posed in 3:2: "The one, then, who keeps on supplying the Spirit to you and working miraculous signs among you—does he do this on the basis of works of Torah or on the basis of the report that awakens trust, just as Abraham trusted God, and it was accounted to him as righteousness?" The perspective shifts here subtly from what the Galatians had experienced ("you received," 3:2) to what God has continued to work in their midst and on what basis God has done it.[32] Paul refers here to their ongoing experience of the Holy Spirit and of miracles or wonders divinely wrought.[33]

With his question and, especially, the conjunction "then," Paul presses his converts to draw the logical inference from their own experience. The

---

30. BDAG 785; LSJ 1347; Burton, 149; Schlier, 124; Fung, 133; Longenecker, 104; Fee, *Presence*, 387; Matera, 113; with the NRSV, NIV, CEB, NLT, against the KJV, GW. "Have you suffered" was a fine translation of Gal 3:4 in 1611, when "to suffer" meant "to passively experience" something, and not just "experience painful things," as it does in contemporary English.

31. So, rightly, Tolmie, *Persuading*, 108, who considers the phrase "if indeed it was in vain" to be an example of self-correction, softening the previous statement; see also Hietanen, *Paul's Argumentation*, 86.

32. This is the import of the continuative aspect of the participles ἐπιχορηγῶν ("supplying") and ἐνεργῶν ("working").

33. This is the sense of δυνάμεις here, rather than the power behind such manifestations (BDAG 263). Despite the absence of experiences of God's Spirit supernaturally at work in many Western contexts, we should not doubt that Paul's churches were accustomed to seeing in their midst what could be attributed only to the wonder-working power of God. See Keener, *Miracles*.

Galatians have known God's power to be at work in their midst. On what basis, then, has God been thus active among them up to this point? Once again, on the basis of their response of trusting what Paul had proclaimed concerning the death and resurrection of Jesus and the benefit to them of the same.

Also new in this iteration of the question (as compared with 3:2) is Paul's introduction of the historical example of Abraham in 3:6 as analogous to, and thus a precedent for, the experience of the addressees and their position vis-à-vis God.[34] Although often treated as the beginning of a new paragraph, this verse is better construed syntactically as a continuation of the preceding material, guiding the resolution of the rhetorical question of which it forms a part. Abraham's example adds the weight of historical precedent to the addressees' experience of being made righteous by God on the basis of trusting God and God's provision—here, prominently, the Spirit.

Paul recites LXX Gen 15:6 almost verbatim.[35] In context, the promise that Abraham trusts concerns a multitude of descendants (15:5). Paul does not neglect this facet of the promise; on the contrary, it remains central to his argument throughout Galatians, beginning in the next verse (see, e.g., 3:7–9, 26–29; 4:21–31). Paul, however, understands the giving of the Holy Spirit as a fulfillment of the promise as well, and he will make the connection between "the blessing of Abraham" and receiving the Spirit explicit in 3:14, at the close of this first cycle of argumentation. Here, then, he cites Gen 15:6 as a scriptural precedent for the Galatians' reception of the Spirit by faith after the pattern of Abraham, though Gen 15:6 says nothing explicitly about the Spirit.[36]

It does, however, speak explicitly about righteousness: Abraham's response of trusting God's promise "was credited to him in the 'righteousness' column" (the language is that of accounting).[37] This text gives Paul a warrant for claiming that trusting God's word of promise is in itself something that God considers a righteous response to God's initiative. We also see here something of the connection for Paul between the Spirit, received by faith, and the goal of being accounted righteous, a connection that will be made explicit in 5:5–6 and explained in 5:16–25.

---

34. καθώς introduces Abraham as an analogous historical situation to the one being considered in 3:2–5; it does not merely function as an introduction of the scriptural quotation that follows (with Lightfoot, 136; Martyn, 296; Witherington, 217; Tolmie, *Persuading*, 112; contra Betz, 40; Dunn, 160).

35. In Genesis, the episode precedes Abraham's change of name, hence it reads Αβραμ rather than Αβρααμ; the name also comes after, rather than before, the verb ἐπίστευσεν.

36. Silva, *Interpreting*, 220.

37. See BDAG 597. The latter clause also appears in LXX Ps 105:31 in regard to Phinehas's act of zeal (see Num 25:1–13), in whose steps Paul had once walked but had come to reject.

Paul's introduction of Abraham as a prototype of trust leading to being accounted righteous effects a smooth transition to the next step in his argument, where he begins to consider how God was bringing about the fulfillment of his promise to multiply Abraham's descendants (3:7–9).

Paul's argument stands or falls depending on his converts' awareness of the Holy Spirit present among them and working within them. In our endeavors to *know* the truth and make it *known*, Paul reminds us not to neglect the surpassing importance of *experiencing* the Holy One. This is the bedrock of Paul's proof, and it is often the bedrock of our personal perseverance in faith as Paul expected it would be for the Galatian Christians. In the face of the challenges posed to faith throughout the course of a life, faith must be more than doing the right rituals and knowing the right doctrines; it must be grounded in a living, ongoing relationship with God through the Spirit.

Paul's reliance upon the converts' awareness of this Spirit urges us to value the living experience of God in our times of worship and to help our fellow disciples cultivate an awareness of God's presence and of God's hand at work in their lives. Pastor and parishioner, counselor and counselee, teacher and student alike must be able to find the irrefutable signs of God's love, acceptance, and favor in their lives, and our life together as a Christian community should be directed, at least in part, toward positioning people for transforming encounters with the living God. Without the active presence of God's Spirit in our lives, we lack, in Paul's view, the very inheritance promised in Christ (3:14) and the key to our transformation into the likeness of Christ (5:5–6, 13–25).

B. PROOF FROM ABRAHAM'S PRECEDENT (3:7–9)

7 You all know, then, that those who exhibit trust, these are the ones who are Abraham's sons and daughters. 8 Now the Scripture, perceiving in advance that God would bring the gentiles in line with his righteousness on the basis of trust, announced the message of good news ahead of time to Abraham that "All the nations will be blessed in you." 9 So then, those who exhibit trust are blessed along with Abraham, who exhibited trust.

A major question to which Paul returns throughout Gal 3:6–4:31 concerns the identity of the children of Abraham.[38] Answers to this question, affirming the Galatian Christians, in particular, to be among this number, punctuate this central section:

---

38. Wright, *Justification*, 122; Fee, *Empowering Presence*, 379.

Those who exhibit trust, *these* are the ones who are Abraham's sons and daughters. (3:7)

So then, those who exhibit trust are blessed along with Abraham, who exhibited trust. (3:9)

If you belong to Christ, then you are Abraham's seed, heirs in accordance with promise. (3:29)

Abraham had two sons, one from the slave woman and one from the free woman. . . . And you, brothers and sisters, are—in line with Isaac—children of promise. (4:22, 28)

Therefore, brothers and sisters, we are not children of the slave woman but rather of the free woman. (4:31)

It is clearly important to the Galatians to know that they belong to Abraham's family, and important to Paul to demonstrate that they *already* do.

The sudden introduction of the topic of the identity of Abraham's children in 3:7, and that by way of forceful affirmation that a *particular* group (those characterized by trusting) constitute his children, strongly suggests that Paul has to discuss Abraham here in Galatians because the rival teachers had already promoted their own answer to the question, "Who is the heir of the divine promises?" on the basis of their reconstruction of Abraham's story.[39]

Abraham was regarded as the ancestor of the Jewish people, the people of God. To be a child of Abraham, then, was to be part of God's people and an heir of the divine promises given to Abraham. Abraham was, moreover, the exemplary convert. He began life as a gentile and a worshiper of idols in the house of his father, Terah, but he left these idols behind in his quest for the living God, who created heavens and earth.[40] God chose him, therefore, to be the vehicle of blessing for all nations, and to make of him a great nation. As a seal upon this agreement, Abraham accepted the sign of circumcision upon himself and upon every male in his household in perpetuity (Gen 17:9–14). The rival teachers had, in Abraham, a strong argument

---

39. Burton, 153; Tolmie, *Persuading*, 109; Das, 302. For a creative attempt to reconstruct the kind of sermon the rival teachers might have preached on Abraham, see Martyn, 302–6.

40. Stories of Abraham's preconversion involvement in idolatry, questioning of the validity of idolatrous worship, and prayer that the real God would reveal himself were popular in the intertestamental period. See Jub. 11–12; *Apocalypse of Abraham*; Josephus, *Antiquities* 1.154–57. These texts and topics are discussed in deSilva, "Why Did God Choose Abraham?"

in favor of circumcision, insofar as Scripture explicitly prescribed it as prerequisite to being part of Abraham's family and thus an heir of the promise.

Moreover, although Genesis does not make the anachronistic suggestion that Abraham observed the Torah, by the second century BC this suggestion had become a firm tradition. The Jerusalem sage Ben Sira writes:

> Abraham was the great father of a multitude of nations, and no one has been found like him in glory. *He kept the law of the Most High*, and entered into a covenant with him; he certified the covenant in his flesh, and when he was tested he proved faithful. Therefore the Lord assured him with an oath that the nations would be blessed through his offspring; that he would make him as numerous as the dust of the earth, and exalt his offspring like the stars, and give them an inheritance from sea to sea and from the Euphrates to the ends of the earth. (Sir 44:19–21 NRSV, emphasis mine)[41]

In Ben Sira's configuration of Abraham's story, the patriarch's observance of the law was, like the ritual of circumcision and his obedience when tested (the near-sacrifice of Isaac is no doubt foremost in mind), prerequisite to his reception of God's promise. If the rival teachers held to this tradition as well, the example of Abraham would serve their desire to promote the whole of Torah alongside the initiatory rite of circumcision.

For Paul, however, it was Abraham's response of trust when he encountered God's promise and neither his circumcised flesh nor his alleged observance of the law of Moses in some pre-Mosaic form that secured his hold on God's promise and resulted in his being accounted righteous in God's sight.[42] In this way, Abraham could indeed become the ancestor of many nations, the vehicle for God's blessing "all the nations" (Gal 3:8). Circumcision marked one as a Jew; trust marked one as an heir of Abraham, whether Jew or gentile.

Galatians 3:7–9 establishes that "trust" or "faith" toward God's promises is what defines Abraham's family and marks out those destined for the blessing; the section that follows will demonstrate how devotion to the "works of the law," by contrast, defines those who labor under a curse (3:10–12) and how Christ redeemed people from that condition so as to experience the

---

41. See also Jub. 24.11 on Abraham's flawless observance of God's "commandments and my laws and my ordinances and my covenant"; m. Qidd. 4.14: "And we find that Abraham our father had performed the whole Law before it was given" (trans. H. Danby).

42. Paul's view of the limited duration of Torah—something that came late upon the scene and has since passed from the scene—is aptly captured by John Chrysostom (25): "What loss was it to [Abraham], not being under the Law? None, for his faith sufficed unto righteousness. The Law did not then exist [when Abraham was accounted righteous], he says, neither does it now exist, any more than then."

blessing granted them in Abraham, particularly the reception of the Holy Spirit (3:13–14). In this way, 3:7–14 continues to develop the antithesis of trust in Christ and works of the law that dominated 3:1–6 (picked up, in turn, from 2:15–21).

7 Paul would develop his interpretation of Gen 15:6, cited in Gal 3:6, in two ways when he later turned to write Romans. In Rom 4:3–8, being "accounted righteous" is presented in terms of God's forgiveness of sin in line with the psalmist's words, "Blessed is the person whose sin the Lord does not hold in his account" (Ps 32:1). In Rom 4:9–11, Abraham's being "accounted righteous" (Gen 15:6) prior to receiving the sign of circumcision (Gen 17:9–14) signifies God's acceptance of Abraham while uncircumcised, presaging God's acceptance of the gentiles who would become Abraham's children alongside the Jews and would similarly hold a place in the family on the basis of trust.

Here, however, Paul exploits neither of these possibilities. Rather, he goes on immediately to define who constitutes Abraham's descendants, the children of promise: "You all know,[43] then, that *these* people[44]—the ones who exhibit trust—are Abraham's sons and daughters." The essential point of family resemblance is not the condition of the foreskin, but rather the exhibition of trust in (and, consequently, steadfastness toward) God's announcement of his promise.

Living as a Jew (walking within the prescriptions of the Torah) as opposed to living as a gentile is an issue that was brought to the fore in 2:14 and frames all that follows. As the "father of many nations," however, Abraham cannot be the spiritual ancestor only of those who live as Jews; indeed, to insist upon conformity with the Jewish way of life, as the rival teachers are doing, is to deny this basic fact of Abraham's paternity. Since the Galatians already share the essential "gene" of Abrahamic lineage, namely, trust in God's

---

43. The form Γινώσκετε could have been heard either as an indicative ("you know, then") or a command ("know, then!"). The sustained argumentation throughout this section does not assist in making a determination, as a passionate speaker such as Paul could easily drive an argument forward with imperatives, impressing the conclusions upon the hearers by way of command. An indicative here would have a similar force, as the hearers probably had not thought this issue through prior to hearing the letter (thus Paul is not assuming this indeed to be a premise already known to and accepted by his auditors, but speaks as if they are drawing this inference alongside him). The force of the statement is: "The conclusion from this that you ought to be drawing is that the ones characterized by faith, *these* are Abraham's children."

44. The word for "these people" (οὗτοι) is emphatic by virtue of its position in its clause; see also Schlier, 128; Tolmie, *Persuading*, 113. If the more difficult reading found in $\mathfrak{P}^{46}$ ℵ* B is correct, "sons" is also emphatic by virtue of being fronted ahead of the verb and away from its modifier (υἱοί εἰσιν Ἀβραάμ).

promise, there is nothing to be gained from circumcision or taking up the yoke of the law—indeed, only something to be lost.[45]

The step from Gal 3:6 to 3:7 is supported implicitly by the context of Gen 15:6. The promise that Abraham believed, with the result that he was accounted righteous, was that God would give Abraham descendants as countless as the stars of the sky, with God assuring Abraham that he would have heirs from his own "seed" (Gen 15:5). Paul uses "sons and daughters" here rather than "seed" or "offspring" (*sperma*), the word used in Gen 15:5, as Paul will take the interpretation of that particular term in a very different direction in Gal 3:15–18. Nevertheless, it is clear in Gen 15:5 that numerous descendants (and not one particular descendant, one particular "seed") are the substance of the promise at that point. Paul presents the good news of Christ and the response of trusting this message (and moving forward in line with this trust) as the means by which God's promise to multiply Abraham's descendants is being fulfilled in their time.[46]

8 Paul takes another step forward in his argument as he cites a particular word of promise spoken by God to Abraham as, somewhat surprisingly, the result of "Scripture" announcing the gospel ahead of time to Abraham: "Now the Scripture, perceiving in advance that God would bring the gentiles in line with his righteousness on the basis of trust, announced the message of good news ahead of time to Abraham that 'All the nations will be blessed in you.'"

In this citation, Paul blends together God's initial word of promise to Abraham ("all the tribes of the earth will be blessed in you," Gen 12:3) with a second utterance spoken by God about Abraham ("all the nations will be blessed in him," Gen 18:18). Paul retains the direct address of the first, but uses the phrase "all the nations" from the second, as it better underscores God's purposes for the gentile nations as well as the Jewish nations within the scope of God's promise. The promise to Abraham focused on land, descendants,

---

45. Thielman, *Paul and the Law*, 131.

46. The expression οἱ ἐκ πίστεως is generally intelligible as "the ones who are characterized by trusting" (understanding the preposition to indicate the larger group or people to which one belongs; BDAG 296). However, the expression is a bit unusual. οἱ τῆς πίστεως would have communicated this idea far more clearly and naturally. The use of the prepositional phrase ἐκ πίστεως here to define one group, as also the use in 3:10 of the prepositional phrase ἐξ ἔργων νόμου ("as many as are characterized by works of the law") to define a contrasting group, recalls and may even be guided by the appearance of these same prepositional phrases, used adverbially moments before (2:16). If the Galatians make this connection, they will hear 3:7 identifying Abraham's children more along the lines of "those who are (lining themselves up for acquittal) on the basis of trusting (Jesus)." Similarly, the group in 3:10 would be understood as "as many as (are lining themselves up for acquittal) on the basis of works of Torah."

and the blessing of the nations through him or through his seed. It is the third element of the promise that most captures Paul's attention—and that most defined his own understanding of his call as apostle to the nations (1:16; 2:9). It is foregrounded in the first utterance of the promise in Gen 12:3, perhaps accounting for Paul's choice of this text here, in combination with Gen 18:18.[47]

Paul presents the word of Gen 12:3/18:18 as a proleptic announcement of the gospel to Abraham. "All the nations will be blessed in you" (3:8b) thus becomes the equivalent of "God will make the nations righteous on the basis of faith" (3:8a)—the plan of God as ordained from before Abraham and thus preannounced to Abraham. This was therefore God's plan for all the nations from the beginning (with Torah playing a decidedly different and more limited role; see Gal 3:19–25). Paul's view of God's plan renders Abraham's faith even more similar to the Galatian converts' faith: in both instances, it is trust in the *gospel*! Paul's move here is not without precedent. His claim that Scripture "proclaimed the gospel to Abraham in advance" mirrors the similar claims of earlier Jewish authors that God had revealed the Torah to Abraham (and the other patriarchs) "in advance," with the result that Abraham, Isaac, and Jacob all lived Torah-observant lives prior to the revelation of the Torah on Sinai.[48] Paul will develop the continuity between the promise to Abraham and the good news of Christ in 3:15–22, 29.

It is "Scripture" that both foresees and, on that basis, fore-evangelizes.[49] Although it is tempting to understand "Scripture" merely as a metonymy for God (the product for the producer, or the writing for the writer),[50] such a move may not do justice to Paul's sense of Scripture as indeed something that "speaks," a medium of divine revelation and almost an independent witness to the plans and promises of God—something "living and active" in itself, to borrow the language of Paul's ministry colleague (Heb 4:12), and not mere ink on parchment.

The expression "*all* the nations" (3:8b) implicitly includes the Jewish nation alongside non-Jewish nations (the latter being referred to simply as "the nations" in Jewish literature; also in 3:8a). Paul underscores the fact that Abraham is the vehicle for God's blessing of *all* nations, and that the non-Jewish nations, in particular, are made righteous by God on the basis of their

---

47. Wisdom, *Blessing for the Nations*, 42, 221–22. The blessing of "all nations" is a consistent and prominent feature of God's articulation of his promise to Abraham in Genesis (12:3, 7; 13:15–16; 15:5, 18; 17:7–8, 19; 18:18; 22:17–18; 26:4; 28:14). Paul addresses the promise of descendants in Gal 3:9, 26–29; 4:21–31; the promise of "land" may be reflected in language about inheriting the "kingdom of God," as in Gal 5:21.

48. See, once again, Jub. 24.11; Sir 44:20.

49. The adverbial participle προϊδοῦσα ("foreseeing") may indeed best be taken as causal here, that which motivates the fore-evangelizing (so, rightly, Das, 278).

50. Bruce, 155–56; Dunn, 164; Tolmie, *Persuading*, 114.

trust, in imitation of their spiritual progenitor.[51] Perhaps not accidentally, the element "in you" in 3:8b most closely corresponds to the element "on the basis of trust"—the trust that Abraham also showed and that therefore characterizes those who are "in him" as his family, his body of heirs—in 3:8a. Genesis 12:3/18:18, understood as God's communication of the essence of the *gospel* to Abraham, establishes "trust" as the basis upon which (or means by which) the blessing of "righteousness" is bequeathed upon "all the nations," insofar as their members (Jew or gentile) exhibit the same trust and reliance upon God's provision that Abraham himself exhibited, becoming thereby his spiritual descendants and proper heirs (see 3:7, 9). This is also the context for Paul's critique of and complaint against the Torah, which serves to keep Jews and gentile nations separate from one another, preventing the formation of the one family God promised to Abraham.[52] In presenting the promise to Abraham (Gal 3:8b) as a proleptic announcement of the justification of the nations (Gal 3:8a), Paul is giving specific content to the general "blessing" that is promised to the nations through Abraham (Gen 12:3/18:18): the blessing is to be "made righteous" by God, even as Abraham's own trust led to righteousness for him (Gen 15:6/Gal 3:6).

9 Paul draws the logical conclusion or result of the foregoing information about Abraham: "So then, those who exhibit trust are blessed along with Abraham, who exhibited trust."[53] Abraham remains a prototype, but not just for gentile proselytes. Rather, he is the prototype showing how all people—Jew or gentile—will fall in line with God's righteousness and find acquittal together at the judgment. The rhetorical force of the repetitions of "blessing" ("will be blessed," 3:8; "are blessed," 3:9) in close association with the response of "trusting" God ("Abraham trusted," 3:6; "those who display trust," 3:7, 9; "on the basis of trusting," 3:8) will not be fully felt until Paul arrives at 3:10, where he introduces the major alternative course, "works of the law" ("as many as occupy themselves with the works of the Torah," 3:10), in close association with "curse" ("under a curse," "cursed," 3:10). This double contrast between "blessing" and "curse," associating the former with "trust" and the latter with "works of the Torah," continues to sever as incompatible the pairs that the rival teachers are promoting as complementary and mutually completing ("works of the law" and "blessing"; "works of the law" and "faith"). "Blessing" here encompasses the Spirit (3:14) and righteousness (3:6), a pair that Paul sees working in tandem (5:5–6).

---

51. Thus Hays (*Echoes*, 105) rightly concludes: "Scripture already proclaims and authorizes a Law-free community of God's people, that is, a church in which Jews and gentiles stand on common ground."

52. Wright, *Pauline Perspectives*, 212; *Climax of the Covenant*, chap. 8.

53. More woodenly, "with trusting Abraham" (τῷ πιστῷ Ἀβραάμ).

C. DEDUCTIVE PROOF FROM THE SCRIPTURES (3:10–14)

10 *For as many people as are [seeking to be declared righteous on the basis]*[a] *of the works of the Torah are under a curse, for it is written: "Cursed is everyone who does not remain in all the things that stand written in the book of the Torah, to do them."* 11 *And it is clear that no one is being lined up for the verdict of righteousness in God's estimation by means of Torah, because "the one who is righteous will live on the basis of trust."* 12 *Now, the Torah does not involve operating on the basis of trust; on the contrary, "the one doing them will live by means of them."*[b] 13 *Christ redeemed us from the curse of the Torah by becoming a curse on our behalf—because it is written: "Cursed is everyone who is left hanging upon a tree"—* 14 *in order that the blessing of Abraham might come to the nations in Christ Jesus,*[c] *so that we might receive the promise*[d] *of the Spirit through trust.*

a. I here supply the context of the first (threefold) utterance of the prepositional phrase ἐξ ἔργων νόμου from 2:16, as the issue of how to arrive at "righteousness" is thematic from 2:16 through 3:14 (acquittal/justification as a goal continues to appear in 3:8, 11). Modern translations often move in this same direction (hence, NRSV: "all who *rely on* the works of the law"; see also NIV, CEB). See also commentary on ἐκ πίστεως in 3:7. Silva (*Interpreting*, 228) rightly encourages interpreters to look for the "verbal idea implicit in the construction" (since "prepositions are most frequently ruled by verbs").

b. The antecedents of the neuter pronouns αὐτά ("them") and αὐτοῖς ("by them") here are, in the context of LXX Lev 18:5, προστάγματα ("commands") and κρίματα ("judicial decisions"; Das, 279).

c. Codices ℵ and B (among a few others) read Ἰησοῦ Χριστῷ, although the external evidence favors the NA[27]/UBS[4] reading Χριστῷ Ἰησοῦ.

d. A number of MSS (𝔓[46] D*, c F G) read τὴν εὐλογίαν for τὴν ἐπαγγελίαν here, but this wording is readily explained as a carryover from the appearance of the noun εὐλογία, visually quite similar to ἐπαγγελία, in the previous—and parallel—clause (so Metzger, *Textual Commentary*, 525). The early scribe of 𝔓[46] simply misread the text at this point and was followed by a few other scribes in the history of transmission.

Paul advances his argument by creating a matrix of contrasting, irreconcilable pairs. The first of these focuses on the "blessing" versus the "curse" (3:6–14). The blessing is the result of trust and moving forward in the path opened up thereby; the curse is the threat that looms over and often falls upon those who tread the path of "doing what Torah prescribes." Paul here drives a wedge between trust and works of the Torah, demonstrating from Scripture the incompatibility of the two paths that the rival teachers urge his converts to combine. He gives initial expression to the idea that the period of living "under law" belongs to the past, as Christ has redeemed people from the curse that the Torah pronounces; the present time is now for walking in the Spirit, the blessing surprisingly identified with the promise. The former topic will continue to be developed in 3:15–25; 4:1–7; the latter topic in 5:5–6, 13–25.

10 Paul introduces an argument from the contrary as a rationale in support of the immediately preceding claim that trusting, as Abraham trusted, leads to the experience of blessing (3:7–9).[54] Having described those people who *are* Abraham's children and heirs ("the ones who are of faith," 3:7), Paul turns to those who, by implication, are neither:[55] "For as many people as are [seeking to be declared righteous on the basis] of the works of the Torah are under a curse, for it is written: 'Cursed is everyone who does not remain in all the things that stand written in the book of the Torah, to do them.'" Trusting leads to blessing because the alternative—submitting oneself to the Torah-driven life—means submitting oneself to live under the threat of curse. The Scripture quotation from Deut 27:26 is offered, in turn, as a confirmation of this rationale,[56] the warrant for connecting "works of the law" and "curse."

In its original context, Deut 27:26 is the climactic curse of twelve curses to be pronounced by the Levites after the twelve tribes had crossed over the Jordan (Deut 27:11–26). While the first eleven reinforce specific commandments (regarding setting up an idol, failing to honor parents, moving a boundary marker, misleading a blind person, failing to give justice to orphans, widows, and aliens, various kinds of incest and bestiality, murder, and taking a bribe), the twelfth is comprehensive, reinforcing "all the words of this law." After each statement of curse, the people are to respond "Amen," affirming their agreement to and acceptance of the consequences of the covenant and any breach thereof. The phrase "the words of this law" may have been intended, in the first instance, to refer to the encapsulation of the ethical commands in Deut 27:11–26. Paul has given Deut 27:26 its broadest application, however, by replacing "all the words of this law" with "all the words written in the book of the law," weaving language from related statements in Deut 28:58 and 30:10 into this quotation.[57] The verb "remains" is used metaphorically to describe

---

54. Paul underscores this argumentative function by introducing this material with the conjunction γάρ.

55. Silva, *Interpreting*, 230. While Paul may be thinking primarily of the rival teachers as the individuals who occupy this category (Wisdom, *Blessing*, 223), with an implicit warning to the Galatians, should they join themselves to the rivals by accepting their (per)version of the gospel, Paul would view all Jews who are not Christ-followers (and, moreover, who do not place the unity of the body ahead of the stipulations of Torah, as he himself does) as populating this group together.

56. Paul continues to give guidance in regard to the argumentative flow with another use here of the conjunction γάρ.

57. Other minor differences between Paul's recitation and known LXX representations of Deut 27:26 include the following: the omission of ἄνθρωπος ("the person") as the antecedent to ὅς ("who"); the omission of the (redundant) ἐν prior to πᾶσιν ("in all"); the change of the final αὐτούς (masculine "them") to αὐτά (neuter "them") to agree with the new antecedent (τοῖς γεγραμμένοις "the things written"). None of these differences carry exegetical significance.

conduct: the person who acts outside of the bounds (i.e., does not *remain* inside the bounds) of what is prescribed by the Torah falls under its curse (see Deut 27:11–26; 28:15–68). The infinitive phrase "to do them" or "to put them into practice" explains what it means to "remain" in the things written in the book of the Torah.[58] Paul makes the unobjectionable point here that those who, like Israel, place themselves under this covenant place themselves also under the threat of its curse.

The text from Deuteronomy, however, would more naturally be heard to *promote* Torah-obedience, threatening the curse upon those who neglect its decrees. Indeed, it *may* have been introduced into the debate by the rival teachers, and not by Paul, to serve that very purpose.[59] Paul uses it, however, to assert Torah's essential *character* as "curse" rather than "blessing," since the blessing in any case belongs to the promise and to trust. It is important to observe that Paul does *not* say that those who live under the Torah are automatically accursed, but rather that they live under the constant *threat* of curse if they step to the left or the right of the Torah's prescriptions.[60] Paul depicts living "under law" as a slavish existence, living in thrall to its regimentation of all life (without the Torah providing access to the life that matters), held in bondage by its power to curse, even while it imparts no power to the individual to walk in line with its demands.[61] His claim functions, at least in part, as a warning to his audience about the nature of life "under law" and the consequences of failure to do all that the law requires.[62] This is a sufficient point for him to make, however, since his converts would regard living under a curse to be far less desirable and advantageous than continuing to live out a

---

58. On the basis of the presence of the verb "to do" here and in 3:12, Moo ("Justification in Galatians," 167, 180) reaffirms the traditional Reformation antithesis of trusting and doing, but Paul *himself* is not actually opposed to "doing" (5:5–6, 13–15). Paul finds fault specifically with doing "the works prescribed by Torah" because it involves lining oneself up with the wrong standard on this side of Christ's coming. One should still "work" what is good for all without growing weary in "*doing* good" (6:9–10).

59. Watson, *Paul, Judaism, and the Gentiles*, 71.

60. "The curse, like the blessing, is *conditional.* . . . The Israelites are not cursed *because* they are a people whose charter is the law of Moses. Rather, they are *subject* to the curse of God's punishment *if* they disobey that Law" (Williams, 89). So, similarly, Mussner, 224; Stanley, "Galatians," 500; Longenecker, 117; Witherington, 233; against Silva, *Interpreting*, 221, 227. We should recognize that Paul is trying to attach certain associations to Torah and to trusting Jesus that will prejudice his hearers against the former in favor of the latter. According to Deuteronomy, it is also the case that everyone living under the Torah lived under the constant promise of blessing for obedience (Deut 28:1–14; 30:15–20). Those living in trust toward Jesus, however, *may* find themselves in danger of breaking faith with Jesus, thus ceasing to enjoy the greater blessings won by his beneficent self-sacrifice (Gal 5:2–4).

61. Bruce, "The Curse of the Law," 27.

62. Tolmie, *Persuading*, 119.

confident response to divine favor, even divine love, as shown forth in Christ's self-giving death (2:20), enjoying the empowerment of God's Holy Spirit to walk in the way that pleases God.

Does Paul assume that those who rely on works of the law are "under a curse" because it is categorically *impossible* for anyone to do all the commandments without misstep, with the result that all such people inevitably end up accursed? It is frequently asserted that this is the implicit premise that completes the logic of Paul's syllogism here.[63] Paul would no doubt have admitted that a vast number of Israelites have failed to keep the law,[64] but there are strong reasons to doubt that his objection to Torah as the path to justification was predicated on his belief that it was an *impossible* path.

First, Paul would well know that Deuteronomy itself asserts the feasibility of keeping the covenant sufficiently: "Surely this commandment that I am commanding you today is not too hard for you, nor is it too far away" (i.e., "out of reach," Deut 30:11 NRSV).[65] The authors of both 4 Maccabees and 4 Ezra believed that it was indeed feasible to live in line with Torah. Indeed, for the former, the giving of the commandment is in itself proof that the prescribed behavior can be performed (4 Macc 2:5-6). The author's assumption is that God does not play games with his creatures by making rules that cannot be kept; rather, God shows his love for his creatures by giving rules that allow the human being to fulfill God's best vision for his or her existence (4 Macc 2:21-23; 5:25-26). The author of 4 Ezra admits that keeping the law is indeed a difficult struggle in the face of the power of the "evil inclination," but it remains a struggle that can be won (2 Esd 7:127-29). Indeed, so powerful is the "evil inclination" that the majority of humankind will fail to attain the life of the age to come, but it remains *possible* for the person who applies

---

63. See Kim, *Paul and the New Perspective*, 128-64, esp. 141-43; Burton, 164-65; Longenecker, 118; Fung, 142; Thielman, *Paul and the Law*, 124; Andrew Das, *Paul, the Law*, 145-70, esp. 145-46; Das, *Paul and the Jews*, 36-42.

64. Many individual Jews fell into the curse by their willful acts of disobedience; the nation as a whole suffered the curse because of the apostasy of its leaders and rampant disregard for the covenant's stipulations at several points in its history. Several texts suggest that Jews understood themselves to be experiencing the result of the curse by virtue of their having been scattered and having fallen repeatedly under foreign domination, most recently in the Roman period (e.g., Bar 4:5-16; T. Lev. 15.1-2; 16.5; T. Jud. 23.3; T. Zeb. 9.6, 9; T. Dan 5.8; T. Naph. 5.8; 4 Ezra 3.20-27; 14.29-34). This understanding is reflected also in the hope for regathering in the eschaton as the reversal of curse (as in Sir 36:13-17; Tob 13:3-6; 14:4-7; Bar 4:21-23, 28-29, 36-37; 5:5-6; T. Jud. 23.5; T. Zeb. 9.7; T. Dan 5.9, 13; Pss. Sol. 17.26-28, 31; 4 Ezra 13.12-13, 39-50), though there are also contrary positions that regard dispersal positively as a kind of colonization (notably in Philo, *Embassy* 36, 281-83).

65. The law "was given to be obeyed," not to be broken because of the impossibility of its demands (Dunn, *Theology*, 135).

himself or herself to this contest to keep the commandments and enter into life (7:45–60, 70–73, 127–31).[66]

Paul also believes that the law could be kept (Rom 7:7–24 notwithstanding).[67] As he looks back upon his life "while in Judaism" (Gal 1:13), he sees a person making confident progress toward conforming his life fully to the Torah's prescriptions (1:14). He can say of his performance that he was, "with regard to the righteousness that is defined in the Torah, blameless" (Phil 3:6).[68] The Torah made provision for blunders, though not for deliberate transgressions that flouted God's honor. Jews did not understand the Torah as a collection of laws that they had to fulfill perfectly or else fail to attain God's favor.[69] Rather, the commandments of the Torah constituted the way of life they were to embody in response to God's favor, and the sacrificial system was God's provision for imperfect people trying to live out this pattern of life. The "curse" of the law did not fall on those who failed to do everything perfectly, but on those who sinned willfully, committed idolatry, or otherwise turned away from the covenant God.

Where Paul differs from the authors of 4 Maccabees and 4 Ezra, then, is not in a conviction about the feasibility of doing the Torah, but (1) in his conviction that Christ has secured for his dependents something far better able to align human beings with God's righteousness in the gift of the Holy Spirit and (2) in his conviction that the Torah was instituted for a limited term

---

66. Thielman (*Paul and the Law*, 130) thus rightly observes that the most obvious remedy to "violation of the Mosaic law" is not "to dispense with the law," but rather "to devote oneself all the more strictly to observing the law."

67. Thus the implied premise must be different than what is commonly assumed (so Schlier, 133), perhaps simply "if they abandon any of the stipulations of the covenant" (so also Young, "Who's Cursed?," 87).

68. The Greek reads γενόμενος ἄμεμπτος, but the participle γενόμενος is rarely translated. As an aorist participle, it is not communicating "progress toward blamelessness," as would a present participle at this point, but rather "arrival at the state of blamelessness." On Paul's successful alignment with the demands of the Torah, see O'Brien, *Philippians*, 378–81. Paul is the "chief of sinners" only in his persecution of Christ's followers (1 Tim 1:13–15; Gal 1:13), not in regard to his alignment with the stipulations of the Jewish law. Indeed, this dissonance is probably of great importance for his emerging view of the Torah on this side of the Christ event.

69. So Nock, *St. Paul*, 30; Cranford, "Possibility of Perfect Obedience," 244–45, 248; Wisdom, *Blessing*, 61; Young, "Who's Cursed?," 82–83. Some rabbis may indeed have thought that failing to keep one commandment would result in the curse or in death. Rabbi Gamaliel was said to have wept at the implications of "he that does them shall live," that one must do *all* the commandments in order to live, and not just one (b. Sanh. 81a). But Rabbi Akiba would later retort that, in doing each one, individually, is life. Even if Gamaliel's response to hearing Lev 18:5 is to be interpreted as his recognition of how difficult it is to attain life through obedience, this position is contradicted within the rabbinic tradition itself.

to play a very limited role in God's larger economy of making people righteous (3:15–25). The law does not give life, because that is the role of the promise and of the faith that receives what was promised, and the law was a temporary arrangement with a fixed endpoint, whose term expired with the coming of the Christ and the completion of his work on behalf of Jew and gentile. This point is underscored for Paul in his experience of seeing gentiles accepted by God on the basis of their response of trust in Jesus, an acceptance that he deduces from their reception of God's Holy Spirit. The ongoing value of the boundary-maintaining function of the Torah as pedagogue over Israel[70] was now sharply called into question by the Christ event and the pouring out of the Holy Spirit upon Jew and gentile alike.

Paul held to the conviction that the Torah essentially bore witness to its own demise as a valid force in the plan of God. In his broadening of the application of Deut 27:26 to "all the things that stand written in the book of the law," Paul may be thinking beyond the performance of individual commandments and considering the observance of the entirety of the Torah. This broad view would include heeding the prophet whom God would "raise up" after Moses (Deut 18:18, understood in early Christian discourse to refer to Christ, as in Acts 3:22–23), as well as the model of Abraham, whose trust in God the readers of the Torah are taught to imitate. Through their zeal for the Torah and their resistance to what God was doing in Christ in the new phase of salvation history, Israel had made itself an enemy of God (Rom 10:2–4; 11:28, 31), refusing to submit in obedience to God.[71]

Paul's assessment of his own standing before God prior to his conversion—zealous for the Torah, yet the enemy of God's Messiah—would plausibly have led him along such a train of thought. As such, Israel's "doing" of the Torah, and his own in particular, was only partial and misguided, so that they did not in fact "observe and obey all the things written in the book of the law" (Deut 27:26; 28:58, as rendered in Gal 3:10). In trying to keep the Sinai covenant alive after Christ in the way that was appropriate before Christ, they actually used the law in a manner contrary to the purposes of the God who gave it, the purpose revealed in that very law itself (qua Scripture), as Paul would go on to demonstrate.[72] Such a path would lead to inheriting curse rather than blessing. We should also bear in mind that Paul understands life

---

70. See Gal 3:23–25 and cf. Lev 20:22–26; Let. Aris. 139–42.

71. Bruce, 160.

72. Gal 4:21–31 is again instructive, particularly v. 21: It is possible to "do" the law without "hearing" what the law has been saying. Paul will return to this point (perhaps more clearly) in Rom 3:21: the Law and the Prophets bear witness to the epochal, game-changing event of Christ. Thus, at this stage in God's dealing with humanity, "Jewish restriction of the covenant in narrowly national and ethnic terms is to be designated *un*faithfulness (rather than as covenant loyalty)" (Dunn, "What Was the Issue?," 311).

in the Spirit to be qualitatively different from, and superior to, life under the Torah, as freedom is superior to slavery. He has discovered, by virtue of encountering Christ and receiving the Spirit, the life that the Torah was intrinsically unable to provide (Gal 3:21).[73]

11–12 Trust is associated with blessing and with righteousness (3:7–9), Torah with curse and failure to fall into alignment with God's righteousness (3:10). Paul takes another step forward in his argument, suggesting that the way of Torah, the mode of existence under the threat of the curse, is not the way forward into the righteousness that God will acquit: "And it is clear that no one is being lined up for the verdict of righteousness in God's estimation by means of Torah, because 'the one who is righteous will live on the basis of trust.'[74] Now, the Torah does not involve operating on the basis of trust; on the contrary, 'the one doing these things will live by means of them.'"

In 3:11b Paul introduces a modified citation of Hab 2:4 as evidence in support of his claims that Torah observance is not the way to acquittal before God as righteous persons.[75] In so doing, he brings together in short compass the only two texts from the Jewish Scriptures that combine a focus on "trust" and "righteousness" (Gen 15:6 in Gal 3:6; Hab 2:4 in Gal 3:11).[76] If one hopes to be a "righteous person," then one is compelled to look to the path opened up by trust in Jesus and by the gift of the Spirit. This path aligns with Abraham's experience and Paul's interpretation of the promise given to Abraham that all nations would be blessed (i.e., made righteous) insofar as they walked in his example of trust (Gal 3:6–9). Since doing the Torah is based on something other than this trust, it cannot lead to becoming righteous.

But why, then, does the response of trust exclude the response of conforming oneself to the stipulations of the Torah? Paul anticipates the question

---

73. Bruce, "The Curse of the Law," 34; Martyn, 310.

74. Thielman (*Paul and the Law*, 127–28) argues that the first ὅτι in 3:11 is causal, with δῆλον serving as the predicate adjective for the second ὅτι-clause in this verse ("And because no one will be justified before God, it is clear that 'the just person will live on the basis of trust'"). This reading is unlikely from the point of view of the logical progress of Paul's argument. Thielman's reading assumes that Paul has in fact established that "no one achieves alignment with God's righteousness through following the Torah" (3:11a) and that he can move from there to the establishing of further points (3:11b). In fact, however, 3:11a is a highly controverted point in Paul's situation, one that requires demonstration, which is precisely what he provides in 3:11b–12. The more traditional construal also preserves the rhythm of claim followed by supporting scriptural evidence, which otherwise runs throughout 3:10–13. See Aristotle, *Metaphysics* 982a1–2 for a classical example of the ὅτι clause preceding the δῆλον.

75. Habakkuk 2:4 in the Hebrew Bible differs from the version in the Greek Septuagint in regard to whether or not a person would live by "his (or her) faith" (Hebrew) or by "my [i.e., God's] faith" (LXX). Paul, however, omits *any* personal pronoun, putting the entire focus on "trust" or "faith" *tout court*.

76. See Sanders, *Palestinian Judaism*, 483–84.

and supplies both the answer ("Now the Torah does not involve operating on the basis of trust,"[77] 3:12a) and the Scripture that supports the same ("on the contrary, 'the one doing these things will live by means of them'"). Following the Jewish exegetical principle of *gezera shawa*, whereby the meaning of one verse is drawn out by means of interpreting it in light of another scriptural text containing the same key word or words—here, the key word "he or she will live" (in Greek, the single word *zēsetai*)—Paul brings Lev 18:5 into the conversation alongside Hab 2:4. The structural parallels that would recommend these two texts as related and mutually interpreting go far beyond the occurrence of this shared word:

Hab 2:4	Lev 18:5
the one who is righteous	the one who does these things
will live	will live
on the basis of trust[78]	through them

In this juxtaposition, being "righteous" is linked only with the first path, the path of trust. The problem with the law is not that doing what the law commands is impossible. Paul could not be unaware of Israel's failure to "live by" God's commandments, with the result that they did not enjoy the life that God had held out before them.[79] But Paul's point here is even more basic: the law was not given as the way forward for all people to receive the promise and thereby arrive at acquittal and life.[80] That way is the way of "trust," or "faith,"

---

77. It is possible that the phrase ἐκ πίστεως should be heard here as a deliberate echo of the focal phrase in Hab 2:4: "Now the Torah is not 'on the basis of trust' [ἐκ πίστεως], as in the text I just cited." Either way, Paul asserts that the Torah fails to align with that which *does* lead to righteousness, acquittal, and life.

78. This parallelism strongly suggests that the prepositional phrase "on the basis of trust" (ἐκ πίστεως) modifies the verb ("will live," ζήσεται; thus Schlier, 131; Betz, 145) rather than the substantive ("the righteous," ὁ δίκαιος, specifying the manner in which the person became such; thus Watson, "By Faith [of Christ]," 162; Tolmie, *Persuading*, 120). Contra Fung (146), the two Scriptures do not answer the question "*Who* shall enter into life?" but "*How* will one enter into life?" This is clearly the thrust of the Leviticus text (which includes the element "by means of them [i.e., the commandments performed]"), and the Habakkuk text should be read in a parallel fashion, given Paul's careful antithetical framing of these two texts.

79. The language of Lev 18:5 reappears even in Ezek 20:11, 13, 21 and Neh 9:29 in the context of explaining Israel's failure (Das, 324; Sprinkle, *Law and Life*, 34–51; Willitts, "Context Matters," 112–14): "I gave them my statutes and showed them my ordinances, *by whose observance everyone shall live*. . . . But the house of Israel rebelled against me in the wilderness; they did not observe my statutes but rejected my ordinances, *by whose observance everyone shall live*; and my sabbaths they greatly profaned. Then I thought I would pour out my wrath upon them in the wilderness, to make an end of them" (Ezek 20:11, 13 NRSV).

80. On this point, Paul stood diametrically opposed to his coreligionists as articulated,

which is simply not the way of "law," as "law" involves something other than trust, namely, the performance of its specific, boundary-maintaining regulations. It is, again, not the *doing* that Paul opposes, but the doing of the *Torah* in the age of the Spirit and the fulfillment of God's purposes for *all* nations.[81]

As in Gal 2:19, the verb "to live" carries again the more special sense of "to gain life before God," a quality of life resulting from God's blessing upon the person. This is certainly how the Palestinian targumim (early Aramaic paraphrases of the Pentateuch) interpreted Lev 18:5: the life of which it spoke was "everlasting life" or "the life of eternity" (Tg. Onq. and Tg. Ps-J. Lev 18:5).[82] For Paul, trusting God in Christ brings a person into the life of the "new creation," which is ultimately "eternal life" (2:19–20; 6:10).[83]

13–14 Relying on works of the Torah as the path to righteousness and life, or putting oneself under the yoke of Torah on this side of the Christ event, is ultimately contrary to God's purposes in Christ—purposes achieved only at the greatest and grisliest cost to Jesus himself: "Christ redeemed us from the curse of the Torah by becoming a curse on our behalf (because it is written: 'Cursed is everyone left hanging[84] upon a tree') in order that the blessing of Abraham might come to the nations in Christ Jesus, so that we might receive the promise of the Spirit through trust." Paul speaks here about the purposes of Christ's death and thereby the benefits that Christ's death have brought—benefits that are jeopardized where "grace" is set aside (2:21). To prefer slavery to liberation won at great cost alienates the liberator (5:2–4).

Paul quotes an excerpt from Deut 21:22–23, a regulation originally limiting the amount of time an executed criminal's body should be displayed on a tree or a pole to further degrade that criminal and serve as a warning to others.[85] The regulation stipulated that the body of the deceased criminal was to be buried before nightfall, so as not to defile the land of Israel, "because anyone hung on a tree is under God's curse" (Deut 21:23 NRSV). Curiously, we do not find Jewish authors connecting the victims of crucifixion with this verse, deducing therefrom that they die accursed. Philo and Josephus refer frequently to crucifixion—Philo, five times (*Flaccus* 72, 83); Josephus,

---

for example, in Pirke Aboth 6.7: "Great is Torah, for it gives to them that practice it life in this world and in the world to come" (Charles).

81. See also Watson, *Paul, Judaism, and the Gentiles*, 67.

82. Longenecker, 120. The targumim, notably, were affirming that the doing of Torah was, in fact, the way to attain this life. See also Rom 8:11.

83. So also Martyn, 315; Schreiner, 209. See also 2:14, 19 on the use of this verb.

84. The imperfective aspect of the participle κρεμάμενος might suggest "cursed is everyone left hanging."

85. The word ξύλον means "wood" (as material) or "tree" (as living source of material) in the first instance, but it can also refer to any one of several objects constructed out of wood (e.g., a pole, stocks, gallows, or a cross or stake used for execution; BDAG 685).

seventeen times (*Antiquities* 13.380–81; *War* 5.449–51), never speaking of the victims as cursed. Blame falls instead upon the perpetrators of these executions: upon Flaccus, Alexander Jannaeus, and the soldiers who crucified refugees fleeing Jerusalem during the siege. Even in the *Testimonium Flavianum*, the somewhat doctored reference to Jesus in Josephus, there is no mention of curse. Pesher Nahum (4QpNahum fragments 3–4, col. 1, lines 7–8) also recalls the acts of Alexander Jannaeus, who crucified 800 of his enemies (presumably Pharisees, as that party opposed him most virulently), but this text envisions God vindicating the victims against Alexander Jannaeus's heirs. The Testament of Moses (6.9; 8.1) also speaks sympathetically of faithful Jews who are the victims of crucifixion, clearly not cursed by God for standing by the covenant and being "hung on a tree" as a result.[86] The Temple Scroll, by contrast, does apply Deut 21:22–23 to crucifixion, reversing the order of the killing and the hanging, such that the hanging now becomes the mode of execution (11QTemple 64.6–13). This is perhaps the only text that understands both the "hanging" (on a cross) to indicate the mode of death and God's curse to fall upon the victim as a result.[87] Crucified Jews were otherwise not widely viewed as automatically cursed apart from the justice of their sentence and execution—hence, the fact that they had indeed been transgressors of such a kind as merited capital punishment and postmortem degradation.[88]

There is therefore almost no evidence that Deut 21:22–23 figured prominently in Jewish criticism of Christians and their Messiah.[89] It may have been sufficiently problematic that the one proclaimed by Christians as Messiah had been subjected to suffering, degradation, and death, without critics also feeling the need to bring up (or perhaps not perceiving the possibility of applying) Deut 21:22–23. These verses, however, do rise to the fore in Christian texts, which focused in some instances not on the fact of the curse but on the command to bury the crucified victim the same day (as in John 19:31). The passage is also referred to obliquely in Acts 5:30; 10:39; 13:29, texts that focus on Jesus's innocence. In the resurrection of Jesus, God had personally intervened to vindicate Jesus as righteous (hence not guilty of the capital crime

---

86. For these three citations, see O'Brien, "Curse," 64, 68–69.

87. See Fitzmyer, "Crucifixion in Ancient Palestine"; O'Brien, "Curse," 64, 66. The evidence of Justin Martyr (*Dialogue with Trypho* 10.3; 32.1; 38.1; 89.2; 90.1), who portrays Trypho, his Jewish conversation partner, voicing "doubt whether the Christ should be so shamefully crucified, for the law declares that 'he who is crucified is to be accursed,'" is compromised by Justin's obvious knowledge of Paul and by questions about the extent to which the arguments he *places* on Trypho's lips represent actual second-century Jewish discourse or Justin's crafting of a straw man (rightly, O'Brien, "Curse," 60–61).

88. Fredriksen, "Judaism, the Circumcision of Gentiles," 551–52.

89. O'Brien, "Curse," 71; against Hengel, *Crucifixion*, 84–85, whose evidence for the linkage of crucifixion and curse comes exclusively from the rabbinic period.

for which he was executed) and not as accursed, overturning the verdict of the Jewish authorities, the Roman enforcers, and (in Christian discourse) the Torah itself.[90]

Paul may introduce the quotation here not because of popular anti-Christian application calling for rebuttal, but because it affords him an opportunity to demonstrate how Jesus's death announces an end to the rule of the law and its power to curse. The principle of *gezera shawa* is again operative in the selection and juxtaposition of Deut 21:23 and Deut 27:26:

Cursed is everyone who . . . (Deut 27:26).

Cursed is everyone who . . . (Deut 21:23).

Christ suffered crucifixion—was hung upon a tree—so as to die accursed[91] under the Torah, specifically in order to redeem all those who had been born under the threat of Torah's curse (or who, because of their actual disobedience during their lives, suffered the curse itself). The word translated "redeem" probably carries the sense of "secure the rights to someone by paying a price," as in the purchase or sacral manumission of a slave.[92] The use of this verb anticipates Paul's depiction of life under Torah as a form of slavery (3:23–25; 4:1–4; 4:21–5:1). Christ made himself an "exchange curse" for all who lived under the threat of curse and brought the authority of Torah to an end by buying out all who lived under its jurisdiction.[93] With the term of Torah—that which separated Jew from gentile—ended, God would now deliver the blessing, promised through Abraham, to "all the nations," Jewish and gentile alike (3:14).

When Paul speaks of Christ as cursed by virtue of hanging upon a cross, it is unclear whom he regards to be doing the cursing. He has omitted the phrase "by God" in his citation of Deut 21:23, which may be an indication of his desire to suggest that not God, but Torah, pronounces Jesus ac-

---

90. Wilcox, "Upon a Tree," 92–93.

91. Paul uses metonymy here, using "a curse" to speak of "one accursed." The adverbial participle γενόμενος ("by becoming") expresses the mode in which the main action was achieved (Das, 279).

92. BDAG 14.

93. Longenecker, 121. The exchange theme occurs frequently throughout the New Testament, as for example in the following texts: "He made him who did not know sin to become sin on our behalf, in order that we might become God's righteousness through him" (2 Cor 5:21); "You know the generous kindness of our Lord Jesus Christ, that, though he was rich, he became poor on account of you, in order that you might become rich through his poverty" (2 Cor 8:9); "Christ suffered for sins once for all, a just person for the unjust, in order to lead us back to God" (1 Pet 3:18).

cursed.[94] As a result, Torah itself would appear to have been ranged against God and God's Messiah by virtue of pronouncing the latter "cursed" when, in fact, he was the first human being to experience the ultimate blessing of resurrection from the dead (the sign of God's vindication of the righteous person). It is also possible, however, that Paul assumes—and knows that his readers would assume—the curse pronounced *in* Torah to be pronounced *by* God.[95] In this case, Paul would regard Jesus as willingly enduring *God's* curse in order to redeem those laboring under the curse of the law, with God, however, nevertheless also affirming Jesus to have been righteous and to have died to advance God's own salvific purposes for all peoples.[96] In either understanding, returning to the Torah-observant way of life as a means to acquittal before God entails placing oneself back under the slavish existence from which Christ redeemed that individual by dying accursed on the cross—and thus also entails a "setting aside of God's favor" (2:21), a repudiation of this death on the person's behalf by repudiating its beneficial consequences.

EXCURSUS: PRONOUNS, PEOPLE GROUPS, AND THE PLAN OF GOD IN GALATIANS 3-4

The interpretation of several passages within Galatians hinges on the reader's understanding of the likely referents of the various pronouns found therein, with "likely" being perhaps more helpfully assessed both in terms of the point of view of Paul as he writes and that of his audience as they hear. This issue is especially acute in regard to passages speaking about the redemption of an "us" from the Torah, hence to Gal 3:13-14, 3:23-26, and 4:3-7, and has particular significance for the reader's understanding of Paul's view of the various stages of God's salvific plan and the relationship between the redemption of the Jewish people and the redemption of the nations.

> Christ redeemed *us* from the curse of the Torah by becoming a curse on
> *our* behalf—because it is written: "Cursed is everyone who is left hanging

---

94. Burton, 164; Martyn, 320-21.

95. Tolmie, *Persuading*, 122.

96. Caneday ("Redeemed from the Curse") presents an interesting analysis of Deut 21:22-23 as apotropaic ritual in this context. The criminal is hung up to be exposed to God's curse such that it falls upon the guilty individual rather than the nation as a whole, among whom the crime occurred. In fulfillment of this "obscure and repugnant regulation" that itself foreshadowed redemption, Jesus, the righteous victim hung on the cross, bears God's curse on behalf of unfaithful Israel (Caneday, "Faithfulness," 200).

upon a tree"—in order that the blessing of Abraham might come to *the nations* in Christ Jesus, so that *we* might receive the promise of the Spirit through trust. (3:13–14)

Before the faith came, *we* were being guarded under Torah, hemmed in together until/unto the faith that was about to be revealed, with the result that the Torah has been *our* pedagogue until/unto Christ, in order that *we* might be lined up for acquittal on the basis of trust. But with faith having come, *we* are no longer under a pedagogue. For *you* are all sons and daughters of God in Christ Jesus through faith. (3:23–26)

We also, when *we* were minors, were enslaved under the fundamental principles of the cosmos: But when the fullness of time came, God sent his son, coming into being from a woman, coming into being under Torah, in order that he might redeem *those under Torah*, in order that *we* might receive adoption as children. And because *you* are sons and daughters, God sent the Spirit of his son into *our* hearts, crying out "Abba, Father!" The result is that *you* are no longer a slave, but a son or daughter—and if a son or daughter, then also an heir through God. (4:3–7)

The following salvation-historical schema emerges rather clearly from each of these passages:

a. the mention of a group and its plight (3:10, 13; 3:23–24; 4:3, 5)
b. Christ's identification with the group in its plight (3:13; 3:23, 24, 25; 4:4)
c. Christ's redemption of the group (3:13; 3:25; 4:5)
d. the enjoyment of the promised blessings by *all* believers (3:14; 3:26–29; 4:5b–7).[97]

The question that remains concerns whether Paul focuses *within this schema* on (*a*) the plight specifically of Israel, the former experience of Jewish Christians, with which (*b*) Christ specifically identifies and (*c*) from which Christ has specifically redeemed *them* as a precursor, if not prerequisite, for (*d*) all Christians, Jewish and gentile, to receive the promised blessings.

If we were to read some number of the occurrences of the pronouns "we," "our," and "us"[98] to refer specifically to Jewish Christians as those who

---

97. Donaldson, "Curse," 95; Hays, *Faith of Jesus Christ*, 86–121.

98. It would be a mistake to insist that *all* occurrences of a "we" pronoun have the same referent. Pronominal referents change constantly, depending on the context of each utterance; there are instances in these passages where Paul *must* include his Galatian converts, both Jewish and gentile, in a given "we" or "us," as in 3:14b ("so that *we* might receive the

are, in fact, born "under Torah" and thereby labor under its threat of curse (esp. those pronouns in 3:13, 23–25; 4:4–5), we would answer this question affirmatively: Paul *does* regard the eschatological redemption of the people of Israel from the Torah as a prelude and prerequisite to all nations enjoying the promised blessing.[99]

While I do not embrace this reading, there are several factors that lead others to do so. Paul's use of "we" language in 2:15–16 certainly calls for ongoing, careful attention to the question of whether or not a "we" refers specifically to Jewish Christians elsewhere in the letter. Paul speaks of gentiles elsewhere as being "without law" or "not having law" (Rom 2:12a, 14; 1 Cor 9:21), placing them in a category distinct from those who are "under law" (Rom 2:12b; 1 Cor 9:20). It is reasonable to think that he would, at some level, hold to such a distinction also as he wrote Galatians, with the result that those "under law" (3:23), or needing redemption from "the curse of the law" (3:13), would be the Jewish people and, in some passages, specifically the Jewish Christians who have embraced this redemption. The emphatic placement of the word "us" in 3:13 and of the phrase "to the gentiles" in 3:14 may suggest a pointed contrast between two people groups, two *different* objects of God's salvific activity, hence may reinforce the identification of the "us" as the nongentiles within the Christian movement.[100] A number of Second Temple Jewish texts present the eschatological restoration of Israel as a precursor to the inclusion of the gentiles (e.g., Tob 14:5–7).[101] While Paul would give this topic a decidedly different accent (in other Jewish texts, the gentiles come under the aegis and, in some cases, the domination of the restored Israel), it would stand to reason that his own soteriology would be informed by this broader hope.[102]

Paul would certainly affirm that the path from Abraham to the blessing of the nations does not *bypass* Israel or make an "end run" around the

---

promise of the Spirit through trust"), given Paul's emphasis on the *gentile Galatians'* reception of the Spirit in 3:2, 5. So also Martyn, 334–36; Williams, 94; Tolmie, *Persuading*, 122–23.

99. See Donaldson, "Curse," 94, 100; Betz, 148; Hays, *Faith of Jesus Christ*, 86–92, 116–21; Belleville, "Under Law"; Lagrange, 71–73; Burton, 169; Matera, 120; Witherington, 236–38; against the view that the "we" is inclusive of Jewish and gentile Christians taken by Schlier, 136–37; Fung, 148–49; Sanders, *Jewish People*, 68–69, 72, 81; Bruce, 166–67; Howard, *Crisis in Galatia*, 58–60; Tolmie, *Persuading*, 121. Admittedly, Paul does appear to come to such a position and state it more explicitly by the time he writes Rom 1:16–17; 2:9–10.

100. Lagrange, 71; Donaldson, "Curse," 97. In both verses, the word or phrase in question appears in the second position and ahead of the verb, which is atypical and therefore emphatic (Χριστὸς ἡμᾶς ἐξηγόρασεν . . . ἵνα εἰς τὰ ἔθνη ἡ εὐλογία τοῦ Ἀβραὰμ γένηται).

101. Donaldson, "Curse," 99.

102. See Isa 2:2–3; 25:6–10; 56;6–8; Mic 4:1–2; Zech 8:20–23; Tob 13:11; 1 En. 90.30, 33; Sib. Or. 3.710–23, 772–76; cited in Donaldson, "Curse," 110.

law.[103] Yet, it would be theologically difficult, if not impossible, to go so far as to affirm that Paul promotes a view in which the redemption of Israel *precedes*, in some manner, the redemption of the gentile nations, as there is but *one* act of redemption—the once-for-all crucifixion of Jesus on behalf of all (2 Cor 5:15). Nevertheless, there is an undeniable "priority" in another, nonchronological sense, to the Messiah's engagement with the historic people of God. It was indeed essential for the Messiah to be born "under law." God's giving of the law had the positive effect of *maintaining* (by preserving its distinctive identity) a people that would carry with them the awareness of the one God and the righteousness that God required, bearing witness to both (Gal 3:19–25). The law confined the people, but it also made them a distinct group by means of this confinement. It threatened with the curse any who dared to neglect those group boundaries maintained by the doing of the law in all its particulars. It was God's good pleasure that the Seed should come through the people that knew the one God—with what other people group could the Seed possibly have identified, and within what other people group could he have possibly *been* identified as acting on behalf of the one God to accomplish that God's purpose, the fulfillment of that God's ancient promise? This people did not escape the law's curse, and now they are redeemed alongside the rest of humanity. But the death of Christ is a single event: in 29 or 30 (and one must, in this salvation-historical context, use "AD"), both Jews and gentiles were redeemed at a single time, together, from their imprisonment under sin (though formerly held under different wardens and in different wings). Without the act that redeemed Israel, the blessing would indeed not come to the gentiles (or to Israel, for that matter); but the same act accomplished the redemption of both and the unleashing of blessing upon all at the same time.[104]

There is another set of lenses, however, by means of which we might approach the question of Paul's pronouns and their referents, which is to consider Paul's persuasive goals and how his use of pronouns in particular contexts might advance those goals. These statements might not have rigorous theological or salvation-historical precision, but they might, for all that, better accomplish the task of persuading his audience. Interpreters tend to focus first and foremost on the interpretation that lends itself to abstract precision, losing sight of the fact that Paul's primary interests are pastoral and persuasive.

First person plural pronouns ("we, us, our") tend to be associative unless context suggests otherwise. While the "we" of Gal 2:15–16 is indeed not

---

103. Donaldson, "Curse," 102.

104. In the end, Donaldson ("Curse," 102) might not disagree on this point: "The way forward for both Jew and Gentile required the redemption of Israel from its plight ὑπὸ νόμον."

inclusive of the Galatian audience, there are also explicit contextual clues that would lead the Galatians (whether themselves Jewish or gentile)[105] to understand that they are not part of this "we." Paul clearly identifies Peter as the primary audience of his speech in those verses and identifies a "them" that constitutes the Antiochene audience to the historic exchange. The Galatians will understand, given this framework, that the "we" of 2:15–16 is primarily "Paul in association with Peter," as representative Jewish Christians (given the actual content of 2:15). But what would lead the gentile Christians among the Galatian congregations to exclude themselves from the "we" or the "us" in 3:13–14, 23–25; 4:3–7?

The clear definition of the "we" of 2:15 does not determine the constituency of the "we" in 3:13. In the intervening space, the Galatians have encountered Paul's "I" (2:19–21) and been themselves addressed as a "you (pl.)" (3:1–5), which could also come together to form a "we" as the discourse moves forward (and as Paul intentionally and strategically joins himself with the Galatians as a single party).[106] Paul will provide no contextual clues here, as he did so thoroughly in 2:14, to lead any of the Galatians to dissociate themselves from the first plural pronoun in 3:13. Paul would indeed have good reason, from a pastoral point of view, to *invite* particularly the gentile Christians among the Galatian churches to insert themselves into the "we" in this passage, drawing them in to identify with the state of having been confined under the law and having the law as a guardian, so as to identify also with having been enabled to cast off the oversight of that guardian (3:23–25). Paul needs to teach the gentile Galatian Christians, now that they have inherited the Scriptures of Israel containing Israel's law, how they are to relate to this law as they engage these Scriptures *as their own* sacred story. The rival teachers are doing nothing other and no less in their dialogue with the Galatians, affirming that the Galatian Christians, both Jewish and gentile, *belong* under law.

Despite the possible lack of historical precision involved, Paul invites both the Jewish and gentile Galatian converts to regard themselves as among those who have been redeemed from the curse of the law by Jesus's death on their behalf. If they did so, it would better position them to reject the rival teachers' summons to take on the yoke of Torah and to place themselves (back) under its threat of curse (5:1), as this step would be to relinquish a great benefit that Jesus won for *them* at significant cost (2:21; 5:2–4).[107] They

---

105. I have argued (see Introduction) in favor of the view that this letter addresses Christian assemblies in the cities of South Galatia, assemblies that, according to Acts, include both Jewish and gentile adherents (see Acts 13:42–43, 48; 14:1).

106. On this phenomenon, see Tolmie, *Persuading*, 249; he incidentally regards 3:14, 23–25 and 4:3–6 as examples of such strategic association—though not 3:13.

107. It has, however, also been suggested that gentiles *require* redemption from the curse of the law every bit as much as the Jewish people; since its curse falls upon nonob-

will be less likely to choose, in response to the rival teachers' challenge, to identify themselves among "those who seek status before God through Torah observance" (the topic of 3:10–12),[108] if they understand themselves as having been redeemed from the law's claim on them, whether or not they lived in line with that claim (or perceived themselves to be liable to such a claim) in the past. While, if pressed on the point, Paul might admit that what he says in 3:13 applies *historically* only to the Jewish people or the Jewish Christians, *rhetorically* he has much to gain by inviting the Galatian Christians to hear the statement to apply to them in association with himself and others of like mind.

The same holds true, then, for Gal 3:23–25. The gentile Galatian Christian hearers are given no clear contextual indicators that they should exclude themselves from the "we" of Paul's narrative. Paul's language invites them to take a narrative that might more narrowly and properly belong to the Jewish Christian (from a historical or biographical point of view) and to make it their own from the point of view of their ideologically constructed "faith narrative." Again, this rhetoric is highly strategic, as it locates the law in *their* past as well, putting them in a clear relationship with this prominent entity in the scriptural heritage, but in a relationship that excludes its playing a role in their present and future (at least, the role that the rival teachers are recommending). The transition from the "we" of 3:25 to the "you" of 3:26 is significantly eased by such a reading. The latter verse is presented as a rationale in support of the claim made in 3:25 and makes far better sense as such if the personal referents do not radically change between the verses: "We (all of you Christians in Galatia, both gentile and Jewish converts, and I) are no longer under a pedagogue because you *all* (and this would be true for me, Paul, as well, but I want to focus on the implications here for you all in particular, given what other people are telling you about your status) are sons and daughters of God."[109] Paul writes a common story throughout 3:23–29 for the Jew and

---

servance of the Torah, it must fall de facto upon all gentiles (Martyn, 317; Das, 331). From another perspective, gentiles were redeemed from the curse of the law in that, apart from Christ, they would have had to place themselves under the law in order to be a part of God's people (Williams, "Justification and the Spirit," 91–92).

108. As Donaldson ("Curse," 97) renders the phrase.

109. If we were to read these two verses as saying "We *Jews* are no longer a guardian because you *gentile converts* are all, in Christ Jesus, sons and daughters of God through faith," the logic *might* work if one considers Paul to emphasize the protective role of the pedagogue (the Torah) for the Jewish people. The pedagogue's restraints can now be safely removed, and the Jews may now begin safely to rub shoulders more closely with gentiles, because the latter have now become God's sons and daughters in Christ and are thereby now more fit for free social intercourse. We would, however, create several problems. First, the redemption of the Jewish people from the law would now become dependent upon, and theoretically subsequent to, the gentiles' conversion to trust in Christ. Second, we would have to overlook

the gentile in Christ, affirming the gentile Christian's liberation from the pedagogue, along with that of the Jewish Christian, as a means of reinforcing the gentile Christian's determination not to return to the pedagogue.[110]

In Gal 4:3–7 the Galatian converts will likely associate themselves with every occurrence of a first person plural pronoun. Paul has named the Galatians "heirs" in 3:29; when he speaks, then, about the representative "heir" in 4:1, the Galatians are likely to continue to identify with this heir as representative of any one of them. When Paul moves then from the hypothetical representative heir living under the domination of "guardians and custodians" (4:2) to the condition of some "we" group, the Galatians have every reason to continue to identify themselves as members of this "we" who formerly lived under the domination of "the elementary principles of the world" (4:3). Paul's exclamation of surprise that they might wish to return to such slavery in 4:9 would confirm them retrospectively in this reading.

In this context, however, Paul *may* speak more explicitly of Christ's identification not only with the universal plight of humanity ("come into being from a woman," 4:4) but with the particular plight of the Jewish people ("come into being under law," 4:4)[111] with the aim of redeeming "those under law" (presented now as a third person party, 4:5), with the result that all believers together ("we") receive the blessings of adoption and the Holy Spirit, who demonstrates and/or actualizes this adoption by God (again, with special emphasis on the enjoyment of this benefit, given what competing voices are saying to them, by the Galatian converts, sporadically addressed directly in the second person as a subgroup of this "we").[112]

Two purpose clauses close this segment of Paul's argument:[113] Christ redeemed us from the curse of the Torah "in order that the blessing of Abra-

---

the fact that Jews become "sons and daughters of God" also through trusting in Christ and receiving the Holy Spirit, such that it is not the gentile Christians' adoption into the family that renders them "clean" for Jews to mingle with apart from the "pedagogue," but their adoption *together* into the family of God that renders the separation thenceforth inappropriate.

110. The gentile convert is not, of course, *returning* to this particular pedagogue—but it is rhetorically strategic to tell his or her story in this way. See commentary on 4:3, 8–11 on Paul's placement of the Torah among a larger group of enslaving "elementary principles of this world."

111. Donaldson, "Curse," 106.

112. Even though Paul does not mention it explicitly, the redemption also of gentiles from their plight of slavery (4:3) must also be assumed here.

113. This verse closes the loop opened in 3:2: compare "did you receive the Spirit . . . on the basis of hearing characterized by faith?" with "in order that we might receive the promise of the Spirit through faith" (Hays, *Echoes*, 110).

ham[114] might come to the nations in Christ Jesus, in order that we might receive the promise of the Spirit through trust." The careful parallelism of the components of these two clauses underscores their mutually interpreting quality: they give expression to the same spiritual reality, the second giving more specific definition to the first.[115] The Holy Spirit *is* the content of the blessing of Abraham that was promised to the nations, the promised gift (Gal 3:14).[116]

On what basis could Paul make this identification, when the Holy Spirit is not mentioned in the promises given to Abraham in Genesis?[117] First, Paul, along with other early Christian leaders, witnessed the Spirit coming upon all who trusted in Jesus, whether Jews or gentiles. It was as universal in scope as had been the promise to Abraham: "in you all the nations will be blessed" (Gen 12:3; Gal 3:8). Second, the giving of the Spirit signified the believers' adoption by God as sons and daughters; the phenomenon of being filled with the Spirit led the early Christians, who thenceforth called upon God as "Abba, Father" (Gal 4:6–7), to understand this experience as a spiritual begetting by God's own self, making them spiritual children of Abraham (Gal 3:26–29; 4:21–28), just as Isaac was the spiritual child of Abraham, having been born on the basis of God's promise rather than on the basis of what was possible for the flesh. Paul could readily deduce that, through the giving of the Spirit, God was making Abraham the father of innumerable descendants—of all those who, through baptism, were being incorporated into Christ, the Seed of Abraham (see on 3:15–18; also 3:29; 4:21–31).[118]

---

114. The genitive τοῦ Ἀβραάμ is probably to be understood as an objective genitive ("the blessing originally granted to Abraham"). Abraham had been introduced as the object/recipient of blessing in 3:8–9.

115. Burton, 177; Bruce, 167–68; Martyn, 323; Schreiner, 219; Fee, *Empowering Presence*, 394–95. Wright (*Justification*, 124–25, 171) takes the two clauses in Gal 3:14 in two separate senses, with the "we" indicating "presumably Jews who believe in Jesus" (124) as recipients of the promised Spirit. Such a limitation is highly problematic in light of Paul's emphasis on the Galatian addressees receiving the Spirit *as gentiles* in 3:2–5 and 4:6–7. Surely the Galatians, given the preparation in 3:2–5, would understand Paul to be referring to a group that includes them in 3:14b.

116. I read the genitive τοῦ πνεύματος as explanatory (i.e., epexegetical; with Williams, "Promise in Galatians," 711–12; Tolmie, *Persuading*, 123). Since "the blessing of Abraham" might easily be understood as the prerogative of the Jewish people, Abraham's physical descendants, Paul explicitly states in the first subordinate clause (3:14a) that it is "the *gentiles*" (in Christ) who receive the Abrahamic blessing.

117. See also Martyn, 323; Thielman, *Paul and the Law*, 135. The giving of the Spirit figures prominently, however, in other passages bespeaking eschatological promise such as Ezek 11:19; 18:31; 36:26–27; 37:1–14.

118. Das (334) insightfully notices the connection between the pouring out of the Spirit and the blessing of "seed" and "descendants" in Isa 44:3, a text that Paul might have heard

The Holy Spirit is the God-given resource for our transformation into people who are indeed righteous before God, people in whom Christ himself comes to life and through whom he lives. It is by the action of the Spirit that those who have trusted in Jesus, whether Jew or gentile, are "set right," or "brought in line with God's righteous standards." Sending the Spirit into the hearts and lives of believers was the way in which God would "justify the nations" (3:8), making it possible for them to find acquittal on the day of judgment. Paul will say more about *how* the Spirit intervenes to empower the fulfillment of God's righteous requirements in 5:16–6:10, proving his claim that the Spirit—the gift bestowed on the basis of trust in Jesus—is indeed sufficient not only for starting the disciples on this journey but for bringing them to the completion of their transformation (3:3) without the disciples relying on "works of the Torah." At this stage, it is sufficient for Paul that he has demonstrated to his converts that they had already received the blessing promised to and through Abraham, and thus their response of trust toward God[119] was sufficient to join them to Abraham without any need for circumcision or other "works of the law."

"In Christ Jesus" may recall, in abbreviated fashion, the previously mentioned cause of extending the blessing to the nations (hence a fuller statement would be "by means of Christ Jesus becoming a curse on our behalf, thus releasing the blessing"). Alternatively, the phrase could be heard to define the sphere of the blessing, as Paul will go on to name Jesus as the particular and sole Seed to whom the blessing was promised (3:15–18) and to define the people who experience the blessing as those who have incorporated themselves into Christ Jesus, the one Seed (i.e., through baptism, 3:26–29).

Paul's description of life under the Torah as an existence "under a curse"—an existence from which Jesus went to and through great pains to redeem people—challenges us to exercise care lest we create an ethos of "living under a curse" within the Christian community rather than helping fellow Christians experience life in Christ as freedom and blessing (i.e., blessing in terms of the enjoyment of the Spirit's guidance and empowerment and in terms of knowing God as our Father).

Wherever a church's culture is characterized by a "do this and be damned, do that and be damned" mentality, the power of the curse is revived and the gospel emasculated. Yes, there are genuine ethical dangers that jeopardize our forward progress in "Christ being formed in us," which are therefore to be avoided (Gal 5:19–21), but churches and their leaders cannot

---

spoken spiritually to Abraham: "For I will pour out water on the thirsty land, and flowing streams on the dry ground; I will pour out my *Spirit* upon your seed [LXX: σπέρμα] and my *blessing* on your descendants."

119. The phrase διὰ τῆς πίστεως here echoes 2:16, where the phrase first appeared.

create new bodies of regulations (now not even given by angels, but just formulated by mere human beings) in order to confine their congregations under the protective custody of human-made regulations, hedging them in and imposing authoritarian rule over them.

Wide-open spaces are scary for people who ultimately trust in walls. The freedom that God's sons and daughters are meant to enjoy requires responsible use of that freedom, as Paul will develop at great length (5:13–6:10), but ultimately Spirit-directed freedom is God's will for God's people in Christ. New Torahs, while having the appearance of nurturing obedience, in fact constitute *dis*obedience to God's purposes for us and a repudiation of Christ's death to bring us that freedom.

D. PROOF FROM ANALOGY: TESTAMENTARY LAW (3:15-18)

15 *Brothers and sisters, I am speaking at a human level here. All the same, no one sets aside or adds to a person's testament once it has been ratified.* 16 *The promises were spoken to Abraham and to his "seed." It does not say "to seeds," as concerning many, but as concerning one, "and to your seed," which is Christ.* 17 *This I say now: The Torah, coming into existence 430 years later, does not nullify a testament previously ratified by God,*[a] *so as to make the promise void.* 18 *For if the inheritance comes on the basis of Torah, it is no longer on the basis of a promise—but God graced Abraham with a promise.*

a. A number of later MSS (D F G I 𝔐) add εἰς Χριστόν here (hence the KJV, "the covenant, that was confirmed before of God in Christ"), which is best understood as a secondary gloss introduced to give Christ a place in the economy explicated in the verse as the one with a view to whom God had ratified his "testament" to Abraham—but this understanding is already sufficiently clear from the context. The earliest manuscripts are unanimous in their witness that these two words are a later addition.

Paul has given attention to the promise God made to Abraham and the response of trusting God's promises that constitutes the family resemblance between Abraham and those who are his genuine sons and daughters (3:6–9), connecting this promise specifically with the Galatian converts' reception of the Spirit on the basis of their trusting God through Jesus Christ (3:1–5). He has given attention, by way of contrast, to the life of conforming one's practice to the regulations of the Torah under the threat of the curse that is pronounced therein upon the disobedient (3:10–12), doing so specifically in connection with Christ's redemption of human beings from Torah's curse and, once again, their consequent reception together (whether Jew or gentile) of the promised Spirit (3:13–14). Now he takes a step forward to discuss the relationship between the promise and the giving of the Torah, demonstrating why the latter cannot be understood as an alteration of the former and presenting a distinctive construction of the story of God's salutary interventions on behalf of humankind ("salvation history").

God's new act of favor shifts the center of gravity of God's beneficence away from the Torah to the self-giving of Jesus and the consequent reception of the Spirit (Gal. 3:10–14), understood by Paul as the fulfillment of the promise made to Abraham concerning the blessing of "all nations."[120] As a result, the promise given to Abraham, together with its fulfillment, emerges as the focal point in God's plan for redeeming humankind "in the fullness of time" (4:4), with the Torah, now more of a parenthetical element, being assigned a much more limited (and limiting) function within God's plan.

In this new section, signaled by a fresh address of the hearers as "brothers and sisters," Paul seeks to advance his case by creating a quasi-legal argument concerning the promise to Abraham as "bequest" and focusing on the specific terms of that bequest, which names Abraham and his singular Seed—namely, Christ—as the beneficiaries. He relies on general knowledge about last wills and testaments to demonstrate that a later, independently made agreement (i.e., the Torah as covenant with the Jewish people) does not change the terms of a previously ratified agreement. This argument will lead Paul in the paragraphs that follow to explore what positive purposes and functions can be assigned to the Torah as a temporary measure in God's purposes for Israel in the working out of God's purposes for all nations (Gal. 3:19–25),[121] as well as to demonstrate how the promise of "many descendants" is finally fulfilled, namely, through the incorporation of people from all nations into the one Seed, Christ, through baptism and adoption by the Holy Spirit (Gal. 3:15–18, 26–28; 4:4–5).

15 Paul advances his version of the story of God's provision for making human beings righteous before him by introducing an argument from analogy, in which he asks them to take a general principle from the realm of testamentary law in human legal practice: "Brothers and sisters, I am speaking at a human level here. All the same, no one sets aside or adds to a person's testament once it has been ratified." Paul takes, and allows his hearers to take, a breath as he begins to address them afresh as "brothers and sisters," which also allows him to normalize the tone of the letter after the harsh address of 3:1 and the rigorous cross-examination of 3:2–5 and arguments of 3:6–14.[122]

The prepositional phrase translated above as "at a human level" could also be understood as "in line with human affairs." Taken in the latter sense, it would signal to the hearers the shift in Paul's argumentation from a deduc-

---

120. See Gen 12:3, 7; 13:15–16; 15:5, 18; 17:7–8, 19; 18:18; 22:17–18; 26:4; 28:14.
121. For a fuller treatment of this topic, see Dunn, *Theology of Paul*, 143–50.
122. Lightfoot, 139; Tolmie, *Persuading*, 125.

tive mode based on logical inferences from authoritative Scripture (3:6–14) to a looser form of inductive argument based on the comparison of the unclear (God's "covenants" and their relationship) with the well-known (human testamentary law).[123] Taken in the former sense, the phrase allows Paul to distance himself from the difficulties inherent in the argument he is about to make, as Paul acknowledges in advance his own lack of complete satisfaction with the analogy because he knows that it inevitably breaks down at certain points.[124] This sense might be reinforced for the hearers by the following word, which is often translated "nevertheless, notwithstanding, for all that,"[125] or the like, as if also indicating at the outset Paul's awareness of the imperfections of his analogy—not that the analogy is lame, but there are obvious difficulties involved in using a "last will and testament" as an analogy for an act of the immortal God, and a critical audience could quickly press Paul's analogy beyond its capacity to fit the dealings of an immortal deity and human beings.[126]

The Greek word here translated "testament" can refer to a variety of legally binding agreements. In addition to a covenant struck between two parties by mutual agreement (such as the covenant made at Sinai), it is very commonly associated with the practice of drawing up a document granting one's property to designated heirs upon one's death, hence the "testament" or "will." The latter sense is rather clearly in view in this paragraph, given both the strictly promissory, one-sided nature of the particular agreement to which Paul refers (the promise to Abraham), as well as the mention of "inheritance"

---

123. John Chrysostom, 27; Tolmie, *Persuading*, 126. Most commentators are content to consider this an "argument from analogy" (e.g., Bruce, 169; Betz, 154; Witherington, 240), though Schlier (144) and Tolmie (*Persuading*, 124–25) have suggested that it is more properly considered an argument "from the lesser to the greater," with the inviolable force of human testaments supplying the "lesser case" that demonstrates the ultimately inviolable nature of God's bequests. These are not mutually exclusive categories, since the argument from lesser to greater applies only in analogous cases.

124. Dunn, 181. John Chrysostom (28) seems to intuit both senses himself as he adds that Paul says that he is "speaking of human affairs" so as to warn the hearers not to deduce anything from the imperfect analogy "derogatory to the majesty of God," for example, that God, who gave the law, was trying to break his promise to Abraham thereby. See also Cosgrove, "Arguing like a Mere Human Being," 537, 549. Paul uses this phrase in Rom 3:5 principally to distance himself from the content expressed there.

125. So LSJ 1230.

126. The author of Hebrews will try to solve this problem in his own way by speaking of the death of Jesus as the necessary death upon which the provisions of a will take effect (Heb 9:15–17), though this interpretation introduces problems of its own, as now it is the mediator of the will/covenant, and not the benefactor making the will, who dies. Both Paul and the author of Hebrews clearly assume that their hearers will grant them some degree of looseness in using this particular analogy.

in 3:18 as the practical consequence of this agreement.[127] The hearers would also have been more familiar with last wills and testaments as a feature of their everyday legal world and thus might be predisposed to understand the word in this sense (rather than confuse it with a "covenant") after Paul's announcement that he is drawing an analogy from human practice.[128]

The facet of testamentary law upon which Paul wants his hearers to focus is the fact that, once a person's will is made and ratified, that person's property has to be distributed (and other stipulations executed) as specified therein. Its provisions cannot simply be ignored, altered, or encumbered by additional stipulations later on (by other parties).[129] A person may typically change his or her will prior to dying, such that wills tend to be revocable in the ancient world, though Paul and his hearers would also have known of a kind of irrevocable will whereby a person actually passes on possession to other parties while he or she is still living, with the provision that he or she will continue to enjoy the use thereof until death.[130] The force of the analogy does not depend on the hearers' deciding what kind of will Paul has in mind or settling upon a specific legal background (e.g., Roman versus Greek versus indigenous Phrygian), but on a general acceptance of the premise that ratified wills tend to have binding, legal force, even if they may sometimes be altered by a person prior to, or even contested after, his or her death.[131]

16 Paul takes a step forward in his argument as he applies the elements of the analogy of testamentary law to the specifics of God's promise and the outworking of salvation history: "The promises were spoken to Abraham and to his 'seed.' It does not say 'to seeds,' as concerning many, but as concerning one, 'and to your seed,' which is Christ." Abraham's "seed" figures prominently in a large number of passages in Genesis in which God articulates his

---

127. The sense preferred here by John Chrysostom, 28; Matera, 126; Witherington, 240–41.

128. Bruce, 169.

129. Bruce, 171; Fung, 154. The verb ἐπιδιατάσσω is not found elsewhere in extant Greek literature, though its meaning can readily be deduced from its component parts (see Burton, 180; Longenecker, 128; BDAG 370). Paul may assume, and may expect his hearers to assume, that the "no one" represents "no one else"; no one can come along later and change or add provisions to a(nother) person's will. The interjection of other parties besides God into the giving of the law (a "mediator," no doubt Moses and angels) may further serve to combat any reading of the giving of the law as God's own revision of his bequest "to Abraham and to his seed."

130. Longenecker, 129–30.

131. Hietanen (*Paul's Argumentation*, 122) rightly suggests that Paul's case would have been more sound had he written: "A human testament is normally meant not to be annulled or added to. In the heavenly realm, where such intentions are always realized, testaments are not annulled, nor added to."

promises (his bequests of land, innumerable descendants, and the blessing of the nations).[132] Abraham and his seed are specifically named as *joint* beneficiaries of the promise in Gen 13:15 ("all the land that you see I will give to you *and to your seed* forever"); 17:8 ("I will give to you *and to your seed* after you"); and 24:7 ("To you I will give this land, *and to your seed*"). Paul might have the larger body of promissory texts in mind, though the four words cited at the end of Gal 3:16 correspond exactly to the wording in these last three passages—and Paul presents his argument as one founded on the precise verbiage of the "testament" to Abraham.

The singular noun "seed" (Greek *sperma*) is typically understood as a collective noun, much as the English word "offspring" can refer to a single child or to all of one's natural descendants (even through the generations).[133] Gen 15:13 assumes a collective understanding, using the pronoun "them" to refer back to the seed; Gen 13:16; 15:5; and 22:17 promise that Abraham's "seed" will be "like the dust of the earth" or innumerable even as the stars in the sky or the sand beside the sea cannot be counted, again assuming a collective reading: "Thus shall your 'seed' be" (Gen 15:5). The Aramaic paraphrases of the Hebrew Bible (the targumim) also tend to explain the singular, collective "seed" as "sons and daughters" or some other plural noun.[134]

Here Paul offers a stunning interpretation, presenting his conclusion as the result of a close examination of the literal wording of the Genesis text as a lawyer might examine the precise terms of a will. He notices that the word "seed" (*sperma*) is in the singular, and not in the plural (*spermata*, "seeds"), deducing that God had in mind a particular descendant of Abraham as the recipient of the promises and as the agent of the blessing of the nations ("by your 'seed' shall all the nations of the earth be blessed," Gen 22:18), rather than all the natural descendants of Abraham.

The history of the Jewish people could easily have led Paul to reject the collective understanding of "seed" (*sperma*), since the promise of God's blessing all the nations had not come to pass through the nation of Israel at any point. Now, however, it was coming to fulfillment where the gospel was proclaimed and the Holy Spirit poured out upon people from any and every nation who trusted God's promises in Jesus. Nor is this an entirely idiosyncratic reading, as other Jewish authors are known to have applied the promises to Abraham and David concerning their "seed" to the single figure of the Messiah.[135]

---

132. See Gen 12:7; 13:15; 15:5, 18; 16:10; 17:8; 22:17–18; 24:7; see, in regard to Isaac's "seed," 17:19; 26:3, 4; in regard to Jacob's seed, 28:4, 13; 35:12; 48:4.

133. BDAG 937.

134. See Wilcox, "Promise of the 'Seed.'"

135. See Wilcox, "Promise of the 'Seed,'" 16.

Paul does not, moreover, ignore the fact that the focal point of the promise concerned God's multiplying Abraham's seed and granting divine favors to this large collectivity (Gen 13:16; 15:5; 16:10; 22:17–18). However, the means by which God would multiply the heirs of the promises was quite unlike anything foreseen by other Jewish interpreters of those passages. The promise comes to pass as people join themselves not to Abraham's collective "seed" in the form of the Jewish people (defined by Torah observance), but to Abraham's singular "Seed" in the form of Jesus the Messiah, clothing themselves with Christ in their baptism. Paul sees God's promise resulting in far more numerous descendants than a few million physical descendants (the Jewish people). Rather, countless millions would become Abraham's seed by means of joining themselves to *the* Seed that is Christ (Gal 3:26–29).[136] For this reason, Paul also regards the prophecy of Isa 54:1 to be fulfilled as Sarah's spiritual progeny (those born "in trust" and "on the basis of God's promise") are multiplied through the proclamation and reception of the gospel across the Mediterranean (see Gal 4:26–28 and commentary). All who are in Christ, therefore, are incorporated into the promise quite apart from Torah's stipulations.

17 Paul marks this verse as introducing a new step in the argument by drawing attention to his immediately forthcoming words: "This I say now: The Torah, coming into existence 430 years later, does not nullify a testament previously ratified by God, so as to make the promise void." We arrive here at the relevant point that Paul had in mind when he asked his hearers to consider the common practice among human beings of making "wills," legal dispositions of goods to which no one else could add any further provisions or make any alterations after the will had been ratified, as Paul applies the analogy from testamentary legal practice to salvation history.

The figure of "430 years" comes from Exodus 12:40, where it is given as the length of time "that the Israelites had lived in Egypt."[137] The time between Abraham's reception of the promise and the migration of Jacob and his family to Egypt would have added substantially to that tally, but Paul is simply using a well-known biblical number associated with the exodus rather than trying to provide a precise calculation of the time elapsed between the promise being given to Abraham and the Torah being given to and through Moses. Paul's description of the law as something given 430 years after the promise to Abraham is one further indication that, by "law," he specifically means the

---

136. Das, 352. See also Barrett (*Freedom and Obligation*, 38), who rightly asserts that Paul "break[s] down the old collectivity of race in order to establish the new collectivity which is coming into being, in an inconceivable unity, with and in Christ."

137. Compare Gen 15:13, where the time of Israel's bondage in Egypt is given as 400 years.

Mosaic law as communicated on Mount Sinai and laid out in Exodus through Deuteronomy, which will be the referent of occurrences of "law" throughout this section.[138]

Paul stands starkly against the contemporary Jewish tradition of the eternity of the Torah here. The second-century BCE book of Jubilees, for example, retells the stories of the patriarchs in a way that depicts them following and teaching their descendants the precise stipulations of the Torah during their lifetimes, long before Torah was revealed to Moses on Mount Sinai. This is one means by which Jews gave expression to their conviction that the Torah had always regulated, and would always regulate, God's people's practice and relationship with God.[139] The rival teachers would agree with Paul that the law does not "set aside" or "annul" the promises given to Abraham (3:17), but they would rather stress that the law, assumed to be in some sense contemporary with (and even to predate) the promises to Abraham, is the means of their fulfillment.[140]

In Paul's configuration of the story of God, the death and resurrection of Jesus—and the consequent outpouring of the Spirit—represent the decisive advance of God's agenda for bringing blessing to all the nations (inclusive of Israel) in fulfillment of God's bequest "to Abraham and to his 'seed.'"[141] The Torah postdates the latter by a considerable span and cannot be understood to

---

138. Dunn (*Theology*, 132–33) rightly cautions that no hard and fast significance can be attached to the presence or absence of the article with νόμος ("law"), and that context must guide the hearers in determining when a particular law (e.g., the Torah as legal code) is in view and when the word may mean "principle" or "law" in a more general sense (as in certain phrases in Rom 3:27; 7:21, 23; 8:2).

139. On the eternity of the Torah, see also Bar 4:1; 4 Ezra 9.37; Gen. Rab. 1:4; b. Pesaḥ. 54a.

140. Silva, *Interpreting*, 190–91.

141. Wright's major thesis regarding salvation history is that "God had a single plan all along through which he intended to rescue the world and the human race, and that this single plan was centered upon the call of Israel, a call which Paul saw coming to fruition in Israel's representative, the Messiah" (*Justification*, 35). This call is further refined in terms of God's covenant with Israel, with Paul agreeing in this regard with "second-temple Jewish literature": "*God's way of putting the world right is precisely through his covenant with Israel. . . . God's single plan to put the world to rights is his plan to do so through Israel*" (Wright, *Justification*, 65, emphasis original). I find such a view, however, to give too much weight and centrality to the "covenant *with Israel*," which would typically indicate the Mosaic covenant, as opposed to the promise *to Abraham and his seed*, which is an agreement concerning all nations, to be a fair representation of *Paul's* view of God's plan. Wright later defines the plan as "*God's single plan, through Abraham and his family, to bless the whole world*. That is what I have meant by the word *covenant* when I have used it as shorthand for writing about Paul," specifically, "*the covenant made with Abraham in Genesis 15*" (Wright, *Justification*, 67). This is a far better statement, but it is now a very different understanding of "covenant" than we find in most "second-temple Jewish literature," the frame of reference with which he began.

represent the addition of fresh terms thereto. For anyone (like the rival teachers in Galatia) now to represent fulfillment of the stipulations of the Torah as prerequisite actions to qualify one for "the inheritance" would be to assault the legal validity of God's promise "to Abraham and to his seed" and to make of the law an illegal codicil altering the terms of the promise and interfering with God's gracious and duly ratified bequest to Abraham and his seed. The parallelism in sentence structure between 3:15 and 3:17 helps the hearer to map the former onto the latter as an interpretive frame:

> a person's ratified will/covenant [direct object] no one sets aside or adds to. . . . (3:15)

> the previously ratified will/covenant [direct object] the law coming into being 430 years later does not nullify. . . . (3:17)

According to Paul, the Scriptures are unambiguous: the inheritance was promised to Christ (the singular Seed) and becomes available to those who then receive it from, in, and through Christ. The Torah cannot add stipulations either regulating Christ's reception of the same or limiting Christ's passing along of the same, nor can it offer the inheritance to other people apart from Christ.[142] It belongs to him and those to whom he chooses, in turn, to give it.

18 Paul adds an argument from the contrary in support of the claim that he has made in the preceding verse: "For if the inheritance comes on the basis of Torah, it is no longer on the basis of a promise—but[143] God graced Abraham with a promise." Another important antithesis emerges in Galatians at this point: Law versus Promise. Does the inheritance come about "on the basis of law" or "on the basis of promise"? The word "inheritance" here includes "righteousness and life" (see 3:21) and, indeed, all the benefits (some presently enjoyed, some yet to come) of which Paul has spoken from the beginning: justification, the Spirit, and redemption.[144] Paul's statement here is perhaps best understood in tandem with a similar statement he will make in the subsequent paragraph: "Is the law, then, against God's promises? By no means, for if a law that had the ability to give life had been given, then righteousness would indeed have been on the basis of law" (3:21). Paul is getting at a similar point in both of these verses, namely, the

---

142. Cosgrove, "Arguing," 547–48. The concept of inheritance will remain prevalent throughout the letter (Gal 3:29; 4:1, 7, 30; 5:21), continually reminding the hearers of the priority of God's promise to Abraham and the Seed (Christ) over the Torah.

143. The connective δέ is often (correctly) translated in an adversative sense here, since the clause is refutative.

144. See Silva, *Interpreting*, 189; Esler, 194; Tolmie, *Persuading*, 130.

fact that the Torah is not and was never, in fact, an alternative means to attaining righteousness, "life," or the inheritance. If aligning one's practice with the stipulations of the Torah *were* a viable path to the goal of justification for all people, then the law would indeed be opposed to the promises by virtue of providing a competitive alternative, one that particularly interfered with God's blessing "all nations." Based on his conviction that God's intent to bless "all nations" means God's dealing with all nations on the same terms (see 2:15–16), Paul assumes that the inheritance cannot be "by promise" and "by law" at the same time, or "by promise" for some and "by law" for others.

Here, the fact of God's having graced Abraham with the promise (3:18b) is taken as historical evidence that the inheritance *cannot* come from doing the law (3:18a), or, perhaps better, that the doing of the law cannot now be imposed upon people as a necessary condition of receiving the inheritance, for it was given on other terms (the argumentative point of 3:15–17). This historical evidence shows the conditional clause that opens the verse to be a contrary-to-fact condition, despite the lack of grammatical indicators to that effect. The verb "graced" is cognate to the noun "grace" that plays such a crucial role in the argument of Galatians (as in Pauline thought generally; see excursus "A Contextual Understanding of Grace" on pp. 254–62). The promise to Abraham, the promise of the gift of the Holy Spirit, was the fruit of God's disposition to be generous (to "show grace"), hence properly to be met with trust (trust that God would give, that the gift would be good and sufficient, and the like). The perfect tense is significant: Paul calls attention to the lingering effects of God's act of kindness toward Abraham and thus the lingering summons to trust as the perpetually appropriate response to this act of favor.

It is not God who is in jeopardy of acting "illegally" (i.e., as regards his prior bequest "to Abraham and to his 'seed'") in giving the law in 3:17–18, for God's purposes for the law were different from those proclaimed by the rival teachers.[145] God never *meant* for observance of the Torah in all its particulars to be the means by which a given individual could enter into the inheritance of Abraham, but God had a very different purpose in mind—to which Paul will give expression in 3:19–4:7.

E. WHY, THEN, THE TORAH? (3:19–22)

19 *Why, then, the law?*[a] *It was added for the sake of transgressions, until the seed/descendant to whom the promise was made should come. It was es-*

---

145. With the phrase "if the inheritance comes on the basis of the law," Paul addresses what he believes to be a basic premise of the rival gospel (rightly Silva, *Interpreting*, 192).

tablished through angels by the hand of a mediator. 20 *The mediator is not a representative only of one, but God is one.* 21 *Is the law, then, against God's*[b] *promises? By no means, for if a law that had the ability to give life had been given, then righteousness would indeed have been on the basis of law.* 22 *But the Scripture has consigned all things under sin, in order that the promise might be given on the basis of trusting Jesus Christ to those who continue to exhibit trust.*

a. 𝔓[46] adds τῶν πράξεων, "the law *of deeds*," perhaps under the influence of Paul's tendency to qualify "law" in various ways with nouns in the genitive in Romans ("the law of sin," Rom 7:23; "the law of works" or "of faith," Rom 3:27 etc.).

b. The important early witnesses 𝔓[46] and B omit τοῦ θεοῦ, though the inclusion of this phrase is supported by ℵ A C D 𝔐. It is more likely that these two words were added by scribes wishing to make clear what promises were meant by Paul (hence, a scribal "improvement" of the text) than that two very early witnesses omitted the words, for which there would be no motive (or easy explanation of an accidental oversight). The addition could also be motivated by the tendency to harmonize texts, here in the direction of Rom 4:20 and 2 Cor 1:20. The existence of an alternative reading in MS 104 (τοῦ Χριστοῦ) adds weight to the argument that τοῦ θεοῦ represents an expansion as well (if τοῦ θεοῦ were original, there would be no reason to change it to τοῦ Χριστοῦ). The scribal addition "of God" nevertheless captures Paul's meaning correctly.

Having raised the problematic nature of Torah's "intrusion" into God's plan in 3:15–18, Paul must now explain what role the God-given Torah in fact served, if not—as the rival teachers are arguing—as the God-given means of aligning oneself with God's righteousness.[146] Even though Paul appears to be about to focus on explaining the positive function of the law, the bulk of the material in this and the following paragraph is actually given to speaking of the law in ways that further demonstrate its inferiority to God's promise and to the way of relating to God based on faith. The law was a mediated arrangement, hence inferior (3:19–20); the law was an arrangement that could never "make alive" (3:21; see Rom 8:11); the law was an arrangement that further consigned all things "under sin," hence placed humans in need of redemption (3:22); the law was an arrangement the quality of which was akin to the child's life under a pedagogue (3:23–25). A recurring topic is the *temporary* quality of these arrangements: "it was added," 3:19; "until," 3:19; "before faith came," 3:23; "no longer," 3:25. The paragraph contributes more to further establishing the *limits* of the law's value and validity than to offering a balanced answer to the question with which Paul opened it ("Why, then, the law?").[147]

---

146. So, rightly, Thielman, *Paul and the Law*, 124.
147. Tolmie, *Persuading*, 131–32.

Paul's answer in Romans will show considerably greater nuance and development than here in Galatians. Comparing the two is inevitable, but it is probably a misstep to assume that Romans explicates Galatians. Paul's reflection on this topic may well have undergone considerable change in the intervening period (possibly as long as seven or eight years).[148]

19 The conjunction translated here "then" typically introduces a logical inference drawn from preceding material. Here it invites further discussion of a topic made problematic by the preceding material, namely, the reason for which God gave the law after having already established a perfectly valid and sufficient arrangement with Abraham.[149] Paul's answer, unfortunately, is quite cryptic: "Why, then, the law? It was added for the sake of transgressions, until the Seed to whom the promise was made should come. It was established through angels by the hand of a mediator." What *is* clear from Paul's answer is that the Torah was introduced as a temporary measure, to serve some function for the limited time between God's making promises to Abraham and the "fullness of time" (4:4)—which was by the time of Paul's writing already in the past—in which the promised blessings would be delivered in the singular Seed (3:16), namely, Christ.[150] Paul connects this new step in his discourse with the previous one as he continues to speak of the Torah as "added," as a subsequent arrangement that does not alter the promise to Abraham but serves some intermediate and temporary purpose inferior to the purpose of the promise that is the controlling arrangement.[151]

What is not clear, however, is the meaning of the law being added "for the sake of transgressions."[152] The ambiguities in this terse phrase lead to significantly different understandings of the role of Torah in God's economy:

---

148. The Mosaic law (νόμος) is a major topic only in Romans and Galatians (Dunn [*Theology of Paul*, 131] counts 72 occurrences of the noun in Romans and 32 in Galatians—104 out of a total of 119 occurrences of the word in Paul's undisputed letters).

149. BDAG 736. The unspecified agent of the passive verb προσετέθη ("it was added") is God, the ultimate source of the Torah (Matera, 128; Schreiner, 239; contra Hübner, *Law*, 26–27, 82–83), even as God is the agent of the next passive verb (ἐπήγγελται, "it was promised") in the same verse (Wallace, "Galatians 3.19–20," 235). Paul cannot ultimately deny that *God* added the law; he can only explain why and for how long.

150. Betz, 168; Bruce, 176; Lull, "Pedagogue," 483; Wallace, "Galatians 3.19–20," 239–40; Witherington, 255.

151. Schlier, 153; Longenecker, 138. The verb that Paul uses to speak of the angels' activity (διαταγείς, "established") is related to the verb he used to name the action of "adding" (ἐπιδιατάσσεται) to a person's ratified will in 3:15, which may provide further verbal reinforcement of this connection between 3:15–18 and 3:19.

152. The Greek is τῶν παραβάσεων χάριν. The accusative form χάριν is used here as a preposition to indicate cause or goal/purpose (BDAG 1078–79; Burton, 188), but its precise meaning here is unclear, and Paul does not clarify.

1. Torah exercises a limiting or restraining force against transgressions.[153]
2. Torah provides a means of dealing with transgressions (e.g., punishing offenders against God's righteousness and making amends by means of the sacrificial system), though not eliminating transgression.[154]
3. Torah provokes transgressions.[155]
4. Torah brings an awareness of transgressions by identifying them as such and, thus, of the distance between human behavior and God's righteousness.[156]

The latter two options are most in line with Paul's later statements about the Torah in Romans. There, law brings "knowledge of sin," the recognition of certain patterns of behavior as being contrary to God's standards of righteousness and holiness (Rom 3:20), but it also gives an opportunity for Sin, as a suprapersonal power wreaking havoc in the lives of human beings, to provoke people's impulsive desires to move in directions contrary to God's law (Rom 5:20).[157] The very command "do not covet" gives Sin an opportunity to provoke covetousness in all directions in the human heart, taking advantage of the commandment (Rom 7: 7–8). The commandment thus provokes transgressions, although indirectly. The way the question is framed in Gal 3:19, however, predisposes the hearer to expect a *positive* function of *some* kind,[158] which would lead us away from either of these options.

It is possible that Paul is not seeking so much to offer a precise answer about the law's function as to forge a connection between Torah and *transgression*, countering the link between Torah and *righteousness* that the rival teachers promote and that Paul opposes (see, in the immediate context, 3:21).[159]

---

153. Engberg-Pedersen, *Paul and the Stoics*, 171; Lull, "Law Was Our Pedagogue"; Belleville, "Under Law"; Brawley, "Contextuality," 106–8.

154. Dunn, 188–90. Paul could grant the law a limited effectiveness in this regard while still reserving decisive efficacy for the death of Jesus in regard to sins, both unintentional and even willful transgressions, as God offers a fresh start to all who have alienated themselves from him.

155. Betz, 165–66; BDAG 1079. Martyn (354–55) favors this sense, on the ground that, since transgression is technically a violation of a law, the law must be given and known before there can be any transgressions.

156. Longenecker, 138; Matera, 128; Witherington, 256.

157. "Sin" may name the same inner-personal reality or dynamic that Paul speaks of under the label "flesh" in Gal 5:13–6:10.

158. Tolmie, *Persuading*, 133. Similarly Dunn (*Theology*, 139), specifically against the later idea that the law was given to *multiply* transgressions (Rom 5:20): "Without knowledge of the later Romans text it must be judged doubtful whether any Galatian believer would have heard Gal. 3.19 as a criticism of the law." See also Sanders, *Law*, 66; Keck, *Paul*, 74; contra Betz, 165.

159. Longenecker, 139; Tolmie, *Persuading*, 133.

Nevertheless, if one were to choose among these options, the best appears to be the first. Paul might well be attributing to the Torah a certain power to limit the multiplication of sin, to exercise some level of restraint upon human behavior. While he would credit the Spirit with the power to effectively restrain and even overcome "the flesh," with the result that a person is freed to live in line with God's righteousness (see on Gal 5:13–25), the analogy that Paul is about to introduce in 3:23–25, in which the Torah's role is compared with that of the "pedagogue" (essentially the disciplinarian over young children), would most favor the idea that the Torah helped to keep sin under control in the interim period between promise and fulfillment, at least for the particular people to whom the Torah was given and in whose consciousness it was front and center, the people from whom the Messiah would be born for the sake of all nations.[160] The contribution of the Holy Spirit is still far superior in this regard, so admitting that the "disciplinarian" does *some* good for a limited—and now past—period of time is not damaging to Paul's case. This notion of the purpose of the giving of *any* body of law would be in line with Stoic thought. Seneca (*Moral Epistles* 90.5–14), for example, writes that, "after the end of the Golden Age, laws had to be introduced as a check on the degenerating culture."[161] The major difference concerned the timing of this "Golden Age," which, for Paul, had begun only recently with the pouring out of the Spirit and the possibilities for life (living "to God," living a qualitatively different, righteous life, but also living beyond death) that it brought. The second option merits consideration alongside the first, perhaps more as a complementary sense, as punishment for wrongdoing and instructing the children on how to make amends were also functions of the pedagogue.[162]

Paul goes on to say that the Torah "was established through angels by the hand of a mediator." Moses's role as a mediator of the law—the agent through whom God revealed, recorded, and instituted the Torah and the covenant based thereon—was well established in the Pentateuch (as early as Exod 20:18–22a). The giving of the law "in the hand of Moses" is a frequent

---

160. Thus John Chrysostom: the law was given to the Jewish people "as a bridle, guiding, regulating, and checking them from transgressing, if not all, at least some of the commandments" (28), lest "all would have been wrecked upon wickedness, and there would have been no Jews to listen to Christ" (29).

161. Schnelle, *Apostle Paul*, 288.

162. Callan ("Pauline Midrash," 561–64) emphasizes the punitive function of the law on the basis of midrashic traditions concerning the aftermath of the golden calf incident that suggest that "the law . . . worsens the human situation by explicitly proscribing the sins of human beings, thus making them liable to punishment, namely, death" (563), with Moses breaking the stone tables so as to free the Hebrews from liability. But just as prominent within the Torah itself is the propitiatory and restorative function of its prescriptions for transgressions committed.

expression throughout the Pentateuch.[163] While Moses is not called a "mediator" in the Pentateuch, he is called by this term in first-century Jewish texts.[164] The role of angels in the giving of the law is not nearly so apparent from the beginning. Recollections of the appearance of God at Sinai, however, increasingly depict God coming with his angelic retinue (as in Ps 68:17), with the result that angels were commonly associated with the giving of the law—indeed, providing a distinct link in the chain of the giving of the law—by the first century CE.[165]

20 Paul takes a step forward in his argument to explain the significance of the mediation involved in the "adding" of the Torah, which becomes another indication of its inferiority, perhaps even of its failure to align with the most central creed of Judaism: "The mediator is not [a representative only] of one, but 'God is one.'" Paul hints suggestively at the inferiority of the Torah to the promise with which "God graced Abraham" in two ways, based on its being a mediated arrangement. First, the chain of mediation begun in the preceding verse paints a picture in which God is operating at a greater distance in giving the Torah than previously in giving the promises to Abraham, with the result that the latter is the more reliable.[166] Paul does not deny the divine origin of the law, but he paints a picture of the giving of the law in which angels act on behalf of God, who is not immediately present in the picture. This portrayal would be in line with the reimaging of the same scene in Jub. 1.29–2.1, where the angel of the presence appears to Moses to *relate* "the word of the Lord." Jewish authors before Paul gave voice to the view that mediated revelation is inferior to God speaking directly. Philo, for example, wrote that "wise men take God for their guide and teacher; but the less perfect take the wise man; and therefore the Children of Israel say [to Moses] 'Talk thou to us, and let not God talk to us lest we die' (Ex. 20:19)" (*Who Is the Heir?*, 5.19; LCL).[167] Indirect evidence for this negative evaluation of mediated revelation comes from later rabbinic texts that explicitly deny the increasingly popular tendency to view the law as given "through angels."[168]

---

163. See, for example, Exod 34:29; Lev 26:46; Num 4:37, 41, 45, 49.

164. See T. Mos. 1.14; Philo, *On the Life of Moses* 2.166; Callan, "Pauline Midrash," 555.

165. See Jub. 1.27–29; Heb 2:2; Acts 7:38, 53; Philo, *On Dreams* 1.140–44; Josephus, *Antiquities* 15.136; Callan, "Midrash," 550–54; Longenecker, 140. The verse is not a *denial* of God as the ultimate originator of the Torah, though Paul is conspicuously silent in regard to *affirming* God as such (see Schnelle, *Apostle Paul*, 289–90). It is still given "through angels" and not "by angels," as if originating with them—and certainly not "by evil angels" (a tradition dating back to Barn. 9.4, but not to Paul, contra Hübner, *Law*, 26, 29–31).

166. Burton, 190–92; Betz, 171–73; Callan, "Pauline Midrash," 555–67.

167. Das, 365; other texts are presented in Callan, "Pauline Midrash," 555–59.

168. See Sipre Deut. 42 [on 11:14]; 325 [on 32:35]; 'Abot R. Nat. B 2; discussed in Goldin, "Not by Means of an Angel"; Longenecker, 136–37.

Second, a mediator, by definition, does not represent or stand associated alongside only one party, but multiple parties. Torah is a mediated treaty, whereas the promise is the absolute declaration of the one God, dependent on one party alone, guaranteed to the Seed (Christ) and all those who join themselves to the Seed by trust. The second part of this verse quotes the opening of the Shema, the fundamental credal statement of early Judaism recited twice daily by pious Jews: "Hear, O Israel: the LORD our God, the LORD is one" (Deut 6:4). By setting the involvement of multiple parties (hence requiring a mediator) in the giving of the Torah over against the essential oneness of God, Paul suggestively distances God from the giving of the Torah, hence calling into question the absoluteness of Torah as the revelation of God's will and God's covenant.

There is also a more subtle problem inherent in the Torah—whose effect was to set Jews apart from gentiles—in regard to the one God who is God both of Jews and gentiles, whose oneness is to be reflected in the oneness of the people of God, as would eventually come to pass in Christ Jesus. The logic is murky here when compared to the much clearer statement in Rom 3:27–28, where Paul, there also reciting the Shema as foundational evidence for his case, more explicitly opposes the ultimacy of the Torah as God's arrangement through which to bless humankind on the basis of Torah's historic function of dividing humanity into two groups (Jew and not Jew), which does not reflect the oneness of God: "Is God only the God of Jews? Not also of gentiles? Yes, also of gentiles, since God (who will make the circumcision righteous on the basis of faith and the uncircumcision through faith) is one" (Rom 3:29–30). It would be risky to interpret Gal 3:20 on the basis of the later letter, but some internal evidence within Galatians also points in this direction. Where there is Torah, there are Jews and gentiles; where people have joined themselves to the Seed on the basis of trust, "there is not 'Jew' or 'gentile,' there is not 'slave' or 'free,' there is not 'male and female,' for you are all one in Christ Jesus" (Gal 3:28), the people of God reflecting at last the oneness of God (Gal 3:20).[169]

21 Paul draws out a possible logical consequence of the foregoing statements, which he then takes care to reject with a careful explanation:[170] "Is the law, then, against God's promises? By no means, for if a law that had the ability to give life had been given, then righteousness would indeed have been on the basis of law." It is not that the (admittedly) God-given Torah

---

169. Paul reads the Shema in terms of philosophical monotheism rather than in line with ethnic particularism (where God's care for all is predicated upon his particular care for Israel). See Dahl, "The God of Jews and Gentiles," 178–91.

170. Mussner, 251; Silva, *Interpreting*, 85; contra Lambrecht, "Tracing," 495; Tolmie, *Persuading*, 137, who regards the γάρ as introducing "a new idea" rather than "explaining why he states that the law is not against the promises of God."

was opposed to the (certainly) God-given promises.[171] The Torah was simply not part of God's plan to deliver the promised blessings: it had no power to "give life," since it had no power to make righteousness take root among the people, righteousness being the prerequisite to finding "life" before God. Paul presents an argument from the contrary as evidence in support of his denial that "the law is against the promises": if the Torah *had been* a viable path to life and righteousness, then the Torah *would* have been opposed to God's promises, because it would have offered an alternative means to the same end (or even annulled the earlier promises).[172] This is a more specific statement of the similar argument from the contrary (and its refutation) found in 3:18.[173] The law is not against the promise, as long as the law is allowed to become a datum of history rather than retained as the modus vivendi for Jews and gentiles—human categories that no longer have prescriptive value or force anyway (Gal 3:28)—in the new epoch. The rival teachers, in contrast, threaten to make the Torah an enemy of the promise by imposing it, now that "faith" has come (3:23–25), upon those who have trusted in Christ for the reception of the promise.

The verb "to make alive" speaks of a quality of life beyond mere biological existence, since Paul addresses (as the Torah addressed) people who already breathe and move and conduct their affairs.[174] Torah cannot "make alive" in the sense of opening its adherents up to living a new kind of existence in the here and now, which happens through the work of the Spirit, who has already come to indwell the believers (2:20; 3:2, 5; 5:25). Life and righteousness are bound together in this verse;[175] if righteousness does not come by way of the law, since the law cannot "make alive," it must come by means of that which *does* "make alive," namely, the Spirit (see 5:5).[176] "Making alive" also pertains to conferring the power to live an eternal life beyond death, beyond God's judgment, beyond the consequences of our first parents' disobedience, which brought death into the world (see Rom

---

171. Understanding τοῦ θεοῦ as a subjective genitive ("the promises God made") or a genitive of source ("the promises received from God").

172. John Chrysostom, 28; also Belleville, "Under Law," 69; Silva, *Interpreting*, 188.

173. Silva, *Interpreting*, 190.

174. The law did, in one sense, promise "life" to those who obeyed it, namely, ongoing enjoyment of life in this world, particularly in the land of Israel, for generations (Deut 30:15–20). Paul is concerned throughout Galatians with a qualitatively better life than the secure possession and prolonged enjoyment of some Mediterranean real estate (see commentary on Gal 2:19–20).

175. Moo ("Justification in Galatians," 169) suggests that the meaning of these terms is virtually identical; Fung (163), that righteousness is the path to (and thus the prerequisite for) life.

176. Williams, "Justification and the Spirit," 97.

5:12–21).[177] Making alive was, according to Paul, simply never the Torah's purpose. It is, however, the purpose of the giving of the Spirit, who opens people up to the life of Christ taking on flesh within them (Gal 2:19–20; 4:19) and, ultimately, to eternal life (6:7–8).

Paul's claim that Torah is not the path to life in every meaningful sense runs directly against contemporary Jewish views concerning the Torah; witness, for example, m. 'Abot 6.7: "Great is the Torah, for to those who practice it, it gives life both in this world and in the world to come." Paul's experience, however, of the surpassing power of the Spirit to "make alive" and to enable people to do what is right in God's sight (see commentary on 2:19–20) would have been sufficient cause for him to disagree. Despite his own success in regard to fulfilling the stipulations of the Torah, from the new vantage point he could discern how Torah, though it promised life, fell far short of empowering people to find life by means of keeping its commands, lacking the power to overcome the forces drawing individuals away from righteousness (whether conceived of as Sin, as in Romans, or Flesh, as more prominently in Gal 5:13–6:10).[178] Israel's collective experience down to the time of Paul (and all the more in the decades after!) could have served to confirm him in his new understanding of the Sinaitic covenant essentially ensuring a fairly consistent state of "curse" for Israel because of its collective failure to keep the covenant, which resulted, in turn, in the Assyrian invasion and deportation of the Northern Kingdom; in the Babylonian invasion, deportation of Judean elites, and destruction of the first temple; in Persian, then Greek, then Egyptian (Ptolemaic), then Syrian (Seleucid) domination; in the desecration of the temple and desolation of Jerusalem under the Seleucid monarch Antiochus IV; and, finally, after temporary independence under the Hasmonean family, in the establishment of Roman domination by Pompey the Great in 63 BCE. How much, really, did Israel ever see the *blessings* of the Sinaitic covenant in its collective life? "Righteousness" thus did not come through the Torah (3:21), and the people therefore did not experience the blessings of the Torah ("life"), but only its curse.

22 If the preceding verse represents the incorrect conclusion to draw in regard to the relationship between the law and the promises, Paul now introduces what he considers to be the actual state of affairs. The law that was given was not able to give life or to bestow righteousness before God;

---

177. On the fuller sense of "life" here, see also Fung, 162–63; Seifrid, *Christ Our Righteousness*, 82; Engberg-Pedersen, *Paul and the Stoics*, 170. See also 1 Cor 15:22, 45, where the verb forms ζῳοποιηθήσονται ("they will be made alive") and ζῳοποιοῦν ("to bring to life") appear in the context of discussing the consequences of Christ's achievement as it pertains to the resurrection from the dead.

178. Schnelle, *Apostle Paul*, 282, 296.

on the contrary, "the Scripture has consigned all things under sin, in order that the promise might be given on the basis of trusting Jesus Christ to those who continue to exhibit trust" (3:22). "Scripture" again appears somewhat strangely as the subject of a sentence (see 3:8), not as though it were itself an independent force, but as the revelation of the purposes of God, whose movements and actions Scripture reveals. God has consigned all things under sin; Scripture simply makes this fact known.

Paul does not specify here how Scripture accomplishes this action or where Scripture communicates such a revelation. He may have some particular scriptural text in mind here (e.g., Deut 27:26, which had placed all those who seek to live on the basis of works of the law "under a curse");[179] he may equally think here of the general witness of Scripture to the failure of all human beings, Jew and gentile, to live in line with God's righteousness and thus falling into the power and consequences of sin, needing liberation together therefrom.[180] The verb here translated "consigned" essentially means "to confine" but can be used in contexts where that confinement means "imprisonment." Paul intuits some connection between confinement under the power of Sin (so here) and confinement under the guardianship of the law (3:23), the repetition of forms of this same verb linking the two parallel agents.[181]

This verse describes the end result of life under the law. The promise of righteousness and of life would be given not through Torah, as history has demonstrated, but on the basis of God's promise to Abraham and to Abraham's Seed, and thus received as one joins oneself to that Seed in trust. There are two significant points of grammatical ambiguity in the second half of this verse. The first concerns whether the prepositional phrase "on the basis of faith" describes "the promise" (thus, "the promise [made] *on the basis of faith* ... will be given to those who keep trusting"; so NRSV, ESV, CEB) or "will be given" (thus, "the promise will be given *on the basis of faith* ... to those who keep trusting"; so NIV). Two factors would incline the hearer to the latter possibility. First, Paul omits the second definite article, which would clearly signal to the hearer that the prepositional phrase ought to be taken adjectivally. New Testament authors are admittedly far from consistent in supplying such markers, so this point is hardly determinative, but the hearer would have to work against the syntactic clues in the text as it stands to understand the promise, rather than the giving, to be "on the basis of faith." Second, the contrast between 3:21b and 3:22b would dispose the hearer to

---

179. Burton, 195–96; Longenecker, 144.

180. See, for example, the string of quotations from Scripture that Paul later brings together in Rom 3:10–18 to establish the point that "all—both Jews and Greeks—are under sin" (Rom 3:9); Schlier, 164; Fung, 164.

181. συνέκλεισεν, 3:22; συγκλειόμενοι, 3:23.

understand the phrase "on the basis of trust" in the latter to correspond anti-thetically to "on the basis of law" in the former. Paul fronts the prepositional phrase "on the basis of law" in 3:21b—meaning that he places the adverbial prepositional phrase ahead of the verb it qualifies, which would make the prepositional phrase the emphatic element in that sentence: "then, truly, *by law* would righteousness come." The hearer, already well familiar with the contrast between these two particular prepositional phrases, would now be positioned to process 3:22b in a parallel fashion, hearing "on the basis of trust" as a fronted adverbial prepositional phrase as well, and thus better taken in relation to the verb that follows.

The second point of ambiguity, embedded in the first, concerns the relationship of the genitive "of Jesus Christ" to the governing noun "trust"—and, thus, to the by-now familiar options.[182] The promise will be given:

(*a*) on the basis of trust in Jesus Christ or
(*a'*) on the basis of Jesus Christ's faithfulness
(*b*) to those who continue to display trust.

The role of a trusting response to God's promise on the part of the recipient is unambiguously affirmed in the second element (*b*).[183] The question concerns, as in Gal 2:16, the first element. If contextual indicators are any guide, we would once again have to resolve this ambiguity (with the verbal expression in the second element guiding the resolution of the nominal expression in the first) in the direction of "trust in Jesus Christ" (the "objective genitive," wherein "Jesus Christ" is the object of trust), despite the *apparent* redundancy.[184] Taking the larger context of Paul's argument into consideration, it also seems unlikely that such a key phrase would be used one way so prominently in 2:16 and then in essentially the opposite way in 3:22.

I call the redundancy "apparent" because, even on an objective genitive reading, the two elements above answer different questions: (1) "on what basis or by what means" is the promise conferred, and (2) "to whom" is the promise given. The fact of some overlap in these answers should not lead us to ignore the significant points of nonoverlap, such as happens where this reading is accused of leading to mere redundancy. The tense of the participle

---

182. See excursus "What Does Paul Mean by 'Faith' Qualified by 'Jesus Christ'?" on pp. 229–37.

183. Williams, "Hearing of Faith," 89.

184. Once again, nothing is lost hereby theologically: Jesus Christ's faithfulness toward those he came to redeem remains an essential, if not *the* essential, element in the narrative of redemption, captured in such verses as Gal 1:4; 2:20; 3:13, even if not also expressed in this controverted phrase. Jesus's faithfulness to God is also amply attested elsewhere in Paul, as, for example, in Phil 2:5–8.

underscores that the promise is given to those who "*continue* in trust," which no longer *merely* answers the question "to whom," but also "under what conditions"—conditions that, according to Paul, are very much in doubt, since ongoing reliance on Jesus and his gifts, to the exclusion of turning to other means of aligning with God, is at issue in Galatia.[185]

F. PROOF FROM ANALOGY: COMING OF AGE IN THE HOUSEHOLD, PART 1 (3:23–29)

23 *Before faith came, we were being guarded under Torah, hemmed in together unto/until the faith that was about to be revealed,* 24 *with the result that the Torah has become our pedagogue unto/until Christ, in order that we might be lined up for acquittal on the basis of trust.*[a] 25 *But with faith having come, we are no longer under a pedagogue,* 26 *for you are all sons and daughters of God in Christ Jesus through faith:* 27 *for as many of you as were baptized into Christ clothed yourselves with Christ.* 28 *There is no "Jew" or "Greek"; there is no "slave" or "free"; there is no "male and female"—for you are all one in Christ Jesus.*[b] 29 *And if you are of Christ, then you are Abraham's seed, heirs in accordance with promise.*

a. On the meaning of "being lined up for acquittal" ("being justified") and "on the basis of trust," see commentary on 2:16.

b. Two important MSS ($\mathfrak{P}^{46}$ A) read "for you are all of Christ" (ἐστε Χριστοῦ) at this point. This wording effects a smoother transition to the following claim ("and if you are Christ's," 3:29) and may therefore result from an early attempt to improve Paul's expression.

Paul continues to advance the view of salvation history articulated in 3:15–22, with the period of Torah's authority yielding to the period of the Spirit's guidance in Christ, by formulating an argument from analogy based on the common experience of children growing up in households of more-than-moderate means, that is, households that could afford to own several slaves (3:23–25). Such children moved through several stages of care—first nannies or wet nurses, then pedagogues, then (while still being ushered about by the pedagogue) teachers—before reaching maturity, the age at which they become adult sons and daughters within the household and participants in the life of the city. Paul likens the period of the Torah's authority over human action and interaction to the period of the pedagogue's authority over the minor children in a household, and the coming of faith to the chil-

185. Paul uses the present tense (continuative aspect) participle πιστεύουσιν, with the article (τοῖς), to describe this group here.

dren's coming of age in the household, at which time they pass into a new status and a very new set of conditions and circumstances. The stereotype of the pedagogue as a despot-disciplinarian would reinforce Paul's earlier descriptions of life "under law" as life "under a curse" (3:10–14), as well as the *intrinsically* temporary nature of such conditions in God's larger plan for humankind (3:15–22).

Paul then turns in 3:26–29 to the rite of baptism and its significance (probably as spelled out, in part at least, in early Christian baptismal liturgies) to explain why Torah's continued authority would be incompatible with their new status. Within the body of God's sons and daughters, among whom Christ is all and in all, the old categories of Jew and gentile no longer hold any value: the Torah, which was principally concerned with the maintenance of these categories, would only work against what God has accomplished among them in Christ (3:26–28). Paul also returns to the legal argument of 3:15–18, drawing out the implications for his Christian converts: if they have been immersed into Christ, they have joined themselves to the Seed and have thereby become valid heirs of the promise (3:29).

Paul will continue to develop this analogy in 4:1–11, where the implications for the Galatians' current situation are drawn out. Just as the child who has come of age cannot (and should not want to!) turn back the clock to return to the time that he or she was under the discipline of the pedagogue, so those who have come to know Jesus and his gifts cannot now turn back the clock to the period before Christ's coming, so as to return to live under the Torah or any of the other enslaving powers that dominated people before "the fullness of time" (4:8–11).

23–25 Paul has been arguing that the Torah's authority extended only until the coming of Christ and the possibility thereby opened up to all people of joining oneself to Abraham's Seed in trust, imitating Abraham's own response to God's promise (3:15–19, 22). Now, he speaks of the arrival of this turning point, considering both the before and the after: "Before faith came, we were being guarded under Torah, hemmed in together unto/until the faith that was about to be revealed, with the result that the Torah has been our pedagogue unto/until Christ, in order that we might be lined up for acquittal on the basis of trust. But with faith having come, we are no longer under a pedagogue."

Referring here to the turning point as the coming of "faith" or "the faith" (3:23, 25) is unexpected. In light of 3:15–18, we might have expected Paul to have written "before Christ (or the Seed) came" (3:23) and "with Christ having come" (3:25), but instead he speaks of "faith" or "the faith" coming at these points. The coming *of* faith is conceived of here as an objective, historic event comparable to the coming of the Seed (i.e., the coming of Christ), not as the individual, personal, subjective experience of coming *to* faith, by which both Jew and gentile continue to appropriate the benefits of this event for themselves wherever the gospel is proclaimed.[186]

There would have been several ways in which the first-century Galatian Christian could have understood Paul's meaning here, given the contextual clues Paul provides. The most likely would seem to be to understand "faith" in contrast to "law" and the conditions of and parameters for living "under law" (3:23). "The faith" names a way of being and living before God that became a possibility only at a certain point in time, namely, in the coming of Christ (4:4–5 etc.), the Seed (3:15–18), just as "the law" was a mode of living in response to God that came at a specific time (i.e., shortly after the exodus event). Like law, the coming of faith set in motion an all-encompassing way of responding to God for those who identified with it—a new kind of "economy" (in the ancient sense of ordering a household) in God's dealings with humanity in general and in forming a people in particular. Specifically, the possibility came of exhibiting Abraham-like trust toward God in regard to what God was making available through Jesus Christ, and living in line with this trust.[187]

This economy is clearly also the direct result of the Christ event, the faithful death of the Messiah and the consequences of the same for humanity: the availability of the Spirit and thereby the hope of righteousness for all who respond in line with the values of the new economy, namely, trust.[188] Paul has firmly established the temporal scheme of Promise—(Torah)—Coming of the Seed/Christ by this point (3:15–17, 19). The Galatians will hear the "coming of faith" as parallel to the arrival of Christ, the Seed whose "coming" signaled the end of Torah's term of authority (3:19).[189] "Before faith came," then, could be heard as shorthand for "Before the period of Torah's authority came to an end because the Seed to whom God's promises were given had arrived" or, equally, "Before the necessary events took place (i.e., Christ's coming, death, and resurrection) that would allow us to be aligned with God's righteousness on the basis of trusting the effects of Jesus's death and the power of the Holy Spirit that would be shed abroad in our hearts."

In the end, these resonances may not represent such very different usages of "the faith" from the usage Paul attributed to the early Judean Christians in 1:23, namely, the message about the newly instituted relationship of trust established by God in Jesus and the life-changing and life-shaping re-

---

186. See Burton, 202; Betz, 176; Wallis, *Faith of Jesus Christ*, 87–88, 113; Choi, "ΠΙΣΤΙΣ in Galatians 5:5–6," 475; Campbell, *Deliverance of God*, 869–74, esp. 869.

187. Das similarly understands "faith" here as "an alternative religious system to that of the Mosaic Law" (376).

188. Compare Wright, *Justification*, 128. It would be too limited, however, to understand "faith" here as "the pattern of faithfulness revealed in Jesus," as does Hays (*Faith of Jesus Christ*, 231–32).

189. Martyn, 361–62.

sponse to that message.[190] There is no reason to truncate "the faith" in Gal 1:23 to mean merely a body of doctrine or tradition encapsulated in a message; what Paul opposed and then promoted as "the faith" was far more than that.[191] The shift from focusing on the coming of the Seed (3:15–16) to the coming of faith (3:23–25) is, moreover, rhetorically astute, as it is also foregrounds, by association with the usage of "faith" (*pistis*) throughout Gal 2:15–3:14, the appropriate response to God that is at issue now in Galatia, whether to continue to live "in trust" regarding God's provision in Jesus (and walking forward and growing in what God has provided) or to place oneself "under law" as a necessary component of attaining God's good ends.

Paul likens life under law to that experienced by minor children under the pedagogue in households of some means.[192] He arrives at this image or model by way of describing the experience of those under law as "being guarded" over a period of time and "being hemmed in together."[193] Paul continues to have the Mosaic law, the Torah, in view throughout the letter,[194] and

---

190. See Sprinkle, "πίστις Χριστοῦ," 177–78.

191. Similarly, the expression "I have kept the faith" in 2 Tim 4:7—whether Pauline or Paulinist—does not merely mean "I kept the message intact," but rather "I have lived out my life to the end within the parameters of and in line with the new economy of God revealed in Christ to those who trust; I have lived in line with the gospel message."

192. Wilson ("Under Law") argues that "under law" is a rhetorical shorthand for "under the curse of the law," though he falls short of demonstration. He assumes the expression needs to be "decoded" (365), even though the expression, taken essentially at face value ("under the law's authority"), is meaningful and well suited to its contexts of use. It is problematic that Wilson speaks of the phrase "under the curse of the law," even re-creating it in Greek and citing 3:10, 13 as references (365–66), when the phrase itself *never* appears in Galatians. Although he acknowledges this fact in a footnote, the realization does not adequately impact his own argument in favor of "under law" as a shorthand for a longer phrase that simply does not exist in Paul. Paul would no doubt be pleased if his hearers continued to think about life "under law" as life lived under the perpetual threat of a curse ("under curse"), and therefore a condition undesirable in itself, but this interpretation is to stop well short of claiming that "under law" means, quite consciously for Paul and his attentive hearers, "under the curse of the law." Galatians 1:8–9 is, incidentally, not relevant for "the curse of the law" (contra Wilson, "Under Law," 367), as Paul is there imposing his *own* curse at this point upon those who are perverting holy things.

193. The imperfect tense of the verb ἐφρουρούμεθα ("we were being guarded") and the present tense (continuative aspect) of the participle συγκλειόμενοι ("being hemmed in together") both underscore a state or condition that persisted over time—indeed, the whole length of time between the promise and its fulfillment. "Imprisoned" (as in NRSV and ESV) is a possible sense (BDAG 1066–67) but may be *too* negative a translation choice, given Paul's conviction that the Torah served *some* positive purpose in God's plan.

194. The fact that Paul writes "law" and not "*the* law" at this point does not mean, as Fung (167) asserts, that Paul has now switched his focus to "the general principle of law." Paul reverts immediately in 3:24 to speaking of "*the* law," signaling that his focus has not left the *Jewish* law, the Torah.

its effects upon those following its stipulations could well be described as "hemming them in" and "closing them off" on every side.

Other Jewish authors would also speak about the regulations of Torah effecting the purposeful confinement of a particular people from other groups—cordoning them off from bad influences. Thus in the Letter of Aristeas, the high priest Eleazar explains to his Greco-Egyptian visitors that:

> Our Lawgiver, being a wise man and specially endowed by God to understand all things, took a comprehensive view of each particular detail, and fenced us round with impregnable ramparts and walls of iron, that we might not mingle at all with any of the other nations, but remain pure in body and soul, free from all vain imaginations, worshipping the one Almighty God above the whole creation. . . . Lest we should be corrupted by any abomination, or our lives be perverted by evil communications, he hedged us round on all sides by rules of purity, affecting alike what we eat, or drink, or touch, or hear, or see. (139, 142; APOT)

This cordoning off is viewed as entirely positive and beneficial in this text; it protects the Jewish people from the influence of gentiles and their "vain imaginations" by preventing too intimate a social intercourse and thus maintains the virtue and purity of their conduct. The author is well aware of the social-engineering function of the purity laws of the Torah: attention to what one can or cannot eat, or to how food has been properly or improperly prepared, for example, creates and maintains social boundaries. The connection between Torah's distinctive practices and the maintenance of Israel's distinctive identity is reflected quite clearly even in as early a text as Lev 20:22–26: by making its careful distinctions between "clean and unclean," Israel both mimics God's own making distinctions between Israel as "clean" for God's self and the nations as "unclean" (and, therefore, not God's own) and, at the same time, actualizes that call to be separate from the nations, fencing itself off, as it were, by its practices. It is also reflected in 3 Macc 3:4, where observing the dietary laws of Torah causes the Jews to keep clear lines of separation from people of other races.[195] For these authors, Torah's "guarding and hemming in together" of the Jewish people was a state of affairs that was not set to come to an end, at least not before the gentiles came to the light of God and walked in the ways of God's righteousness themselves. Particularly the Letter of Aristeas reflects Paul's estimation of the Torah taken as a whole as a boundary marker—the whole way of life that it prescribed, and not just some of its more obvious "works" (circumcision, Sabbath-keeping, dietary restrictions).

---

195. See further deSilva, *Honor*, 260–62, 269–74.

The confining, guarding, strict supervisory function of the Torah suggested to Paul that the pedagogue set over young children in a household was an apt metaphor. Though no doubt his charges often chafed against his guardianship, and though popularly lampooned as a despotic disciplinarian over the same, the pedagogue nevertheless serves a positive purpose in the lives of underage children in the household—though, notably, *only* up to a certain point in the child's life. Paul's identification of the Torah as pedagogue (as opposed to taskmaster, slave driver, or warden) suggests that 3:23–25 offers, among other things, a positive continuation of the answer to the question raised in 3:19: "Why, then, the law?"[196]

In English, "pedagogue" and "pedagogy" are words associated with the education of children. The latter, in fact, concerns the methods used in the classroom to teach children, youths, and even older learners (though "andragogy" is increasingly popular for the last). In the ancient (more or less elite) household, however, the pedagogue was a slave entrusted with the care and discipline of minor children.[197] He was clearly distinguished from the tutors or teachers that educate the child.[198] In practice, the pedagogue performed a necessary and positive role at a certain stage in a child's early development (generally from the ages of six to seventeen), serving to keep the child safe, to teach good manners, to correct bad behavior and discipline the misbehaving, and generally to supervise.[199] It is not an entirely positive image: whatever the benefits, existence under the pedagogue and thus, by extension, "under law" is slavish (3:23; 4:1–2), a descriptor that Paul will persist in applying to life under the Torah (4:7, 8–9, 21–31; 5:1).[200] The pedagogue does not educate

---

196. Paul's moderation in presenting the Torah as a disciplinarian is all the more striking, given the availability of popular philosophical critiques of living under particular, national laws as slavery under a despot in comparison with living by the natural or universal law (see discussion in Betz, 166–67).

197. On the person and role of the pedagogue in the Greco-Roman world, see the still-unsurpassed survey of ancient sources in Young, "*Paidagogos*," 151–69. See also Bonner, *Education in Ancient Rome*, 38–46; Longenecker, 146–47; Longenecker, "Pedagogical Nature," 53–56; Belleville, "Under Law," 59–61. Classical texts that provide windows into the pedagogue's functions and quality include Plutarch, *Moralia* 4A–B; 439F; Epictetus, *Discourses* 2.22.26; 3.19.5–6; Xenophon, *Constitution of the Lacedaemonians* 3.1; Philo, *Sacrifices* 4.15; *On the Change of Names* 39.217; Plato, *Lysis* 208c; *Laws* 7.808d–809b.

198. Thus, rightly, Engberg-Pedersen (*Paul and the Stoics*, 349): "It is important not to read into Paul's picture of the pedagogue the idea that he serves in the institution of 'education toward virtue.'"

199. Dunn, *Theology*, 142; Tolmie, *Persuading*, 140; Das, 374.

200. "Under law" (3:23; 4:4, 5) is also ranged alongside living "under sin" (3:22), "under guardians and custodians" (4:2), "under the elementary principles of the world" (4:3), and "under a curse" (3:10), each of which names an undesirable existence, and all of which together name that condition from which Christ has liberated Paul's converts.

so much as keep the unruly in line, protecting them with a tyrant's authority from bad influences (in the case of Israel under its pedagogue, from mingling with gentiles) *and* from themselves, so as to bring them safely to the time of their maturity.[201] Torah served this function, moreover, not in order to provide the means by which to be aligned with God's righteousness—that role belongs to trust and to the promised gift that is bestowed upon those who trust (3:24b)—but merely to preserve Israel during the intervening period between the promise to Abraham and the coming of the Seed, keeping intact the seedbed into which Christ would be born.[202]

Paul's view of the Torah is markedly different from that of Jewish authors nearly contemporary with him.[203] The author of 4 Maccabees, for example, very much viewed the Torah as the instructor (5:34) and not merely the pedagogue. The aged priest Eleazar praises the education that Torah offers: "It teaches us self-control, so that we master all pleasures and desires, and it also trains us in courage, so that we endure any suffering willingly; it instructs us in justice, so that in all our dealings we act impartially, and it teaches us piety, so that with proper reverence we worship the only real God" (5:23-24, ESV). The language throughout this passage links Torah with Greek *paideia*, the formative education that made children into virtuous and competent adults. It is quite possible that the rival teachers tapped into this kind of tradition, promoting Torah as God's trainer for virtue and for rising above the power of the passions of the flesh, such that Paul responds by demoting Torah to the function of the pedagogue and asserts that the Spirit is alone sufficient to tame the passions and desires of the flesh and to bring forth the fruit of virtue in a person's life and relationships (5:16-6:10).[204]

From a strictly historical point of view, of course, it was the Jewish people as a whole who lived a segregated life as a result of Torah's close regulation

---

201. I think of this role, now assigned chiefly to parents, as saving underage children from natural selection. Dunn (*Theology*, 142) and Longenecker (146-48) provide a well-balanced view of the positive contributions and negative conditions of life under the pedagogue/Torah; Schlier (168-70) and Betz (177-78) regard the image as wholly negative and therefore denigrating to the Torah. Of course, life under the Torah would be entirely negative if chosen on this side of the "coming of faith" (see Sanders, *Jewish People*, 66-67, and Engberg-Pedersen, *Paul and the Stoics*, 349).

202. As John Chrysostom (29) observed: "Had the Law not been given, all would have been wrecked upon wickedness, and there would have been no Jews to listen to Christ."

203. Josephus (*Against Apion* 2.174-75), however, similarly—though without any of the negative overtones that we find in Paul—speaks of Torah's oversight as like that of "a father and a master" from a person's infancy onward, regulating everything from diet to social intercourse to patterns and ethos of work and rest, and the like.

204. Certainly, Paul would not have advocated for Torah as an effective check on the passions and desires of the flesh (contra Lull, "Law Was Our Pedagogue," 495).

of their conduct and practice; rhetorically, however, it is strategic for Paul not to give the same clear contextual clues here as he did in 2:14 (where he guided the gentile converts in Galatia to exclude themselves from the "we" in 2:15 and to place themselves in the scene merely as spectators to the exchange). Paul may indeed be *inviting* the Galatian converts here to identify the Torah (and the regulation of their lives in line with Torah) as something belonging in their past as well, so as to help eliminate it as an option for their present or future. Paul would certainly find it desirable if they could affirm with him that, "with faith having come, we are no longer under a pedagogue," and thus recognize that Torah observance is not a viable option for the present and for moving forward.[205]

I have deferred discussion of a particular grammatical point that appears both in 3:23 and 3:24, namely, the sense of the preposition *eis* ("until/unto") in Paul's statements:

> We were . . . hemmed in together *until/unto* the faith that was about to be revealed.[206] (3:23)

> The law was our pedagogue *until/unto* Christ. (3:24)

The preposition *eis* here could have a directional or a temporal sense, thus "unto Christ" or "until Christ."[207] The former sense is far more common in terms of the overall usage of the preposition, but context is always more important for determining the meaning of any particular use. Context certainly supports hearing *eis* in a temporal sense.[208] These two statements occur within the context of Paul's sharp division of periods of time—one in which the Torah (the "pedagogue") had authoritative force, and a subsequent one, commencing with the advent of Christ, in which it no longer had that force.

Is there any cause, though, to affirm that Paul would allow the preposition *also* to exercise a directional/spatial sense here? One indication favoring an affirmative answer would be Paul's choice of the image of the pedagogue, whose supervision is *purposeful*. The pedagogue admittedly exercises authority for a period of time "until" something happens to signal the end of that

---

205. Hartman, "Galatians 3:15–4:11," 141–42; Tolmie, *Persuading*, 141. See excursus "Pronouns, People Groups, and the Plan of God in Galatians 3–4" on pp. 296–302.

206. The participle μέλλουσαν points to an imminent action in regard to (ending) the past state of being kept under guard; it is already past, of course, by the time Paul writes.

207. The potential for ambiguity is much clearer in the Greek than in most English representations; Paul has, moreover, *not* chosen a word that would unambiguously or, at least, more typically communicate temporal limitation (e.g., ἕως or μέχρι[ς]).

208. See Longenecker, 148–49; Dunn, 199; Das, 375; strictly so, Betz, 178. NRSV, ESV, NIV, NLT, and CEB all give the preposition this sense.

time, but he also exercises authority over his charges to bring them "unto" a particular goal. A second indication would be the fact that, if the Torah hemmed the Jewish people in, corralling them like cattle into one large pen separate from all the other herds of animals (to alter the metaphor somewhat), when "faith" came, rather than the fences all falling down, a single gate was opened for them.[209] Paul would affirm that the Torah positioned the Jewish people to respond to their Messiah; the retrospective use of the Torah in early Christian apologetics and evangelism demonstrates this to have been a foundational conviction of the early church prior to and contemporaneous with Paul.[210] When Christ did come, there was a core of Jewish people who saw what God was doing, saw how texts throughout their Scriptures were pointing in this direction, and thus trusted in Jesus as the Jewish Messiah (see Gal 2:15–16). To be sure, most Jews in Paul's time never left the corral of the Torah to enter into the fields of freedom in Christ, a fact most grievous to him (see Rom 9–11). Paul is admittedly not introducing here the full-blown notion of "preparation for the gospel" (*preparatio evangelica*) that would dominate patristic readings of the law and interpretations of the history of the Jewish people,[211] but he may leave some room for the Torah to point the Jewish people in the right direction—"unto faith" and "unto Christ"—and not merely exercise a restraining force "until" the same.

In 3:25 Paul returns to the claim he had already made in 3:19, namely, that the Torah had a temporary role in God's plan, one that came to an end with the coming of Christ and the means Christ opened up for *all* people to be aligned with God's righteousness through trust and all that trust receives.[212] This claim is true not only for Jewish Christians, who historically had spent their lives prior to *their* coming to faith living under the authority of the law, even as the Jewish people had for centuries prior to *the* coming of "faith"; it is also true for the gentiles among the Galatian converts, who are also "no longer under a pedagogue," whether the "elementary principles" that dominated their pagan past (4:2–3) or the Torah, the regulatory system that dominated the Jews before faith came, to which some Jewish Christians wish to remain in

---

209. I take here the opposite view of the one that sees Paul presenting the law as "a hard taskmaster, driving us to despair of ever accomplishing its demands, so that we would be forced to flee to Christ and find an easier way, namely, faith" (Wright, *Justification*, 129, who also opposes this view). The movement from Torah to Christ happens as a result not of the human being's flight but of the Torah's directional pressure.

210. As Wright (*Justification*, 123) has suggested, "God always intended that this single-plan-through-Israel-for-the-world would be fulfilled, as announced to Abraham, on the basis of faith, and the Torah, by sealing off every other route, has made sure that will indeed be the outcome."

211. So, rightly, Belleville, "Under Law," 60; a bit too trenchantly, Betz, 178.

212. Burton, 201; Matera, 137.

submission, and to which the rival teachers are inviting the Galatian converts as a body to submit.

The analogy of children who pass on from being under the authority of the pedagogue to young adults who are "no longer under a pedagogue" (who thenceforth enjoy greater liberty and answer to the internal norms of virtue) makes Paul's salvation-historical claim seem more natural, more in keeping with "the way things operate," and thus more persuasive. It also reinforces the propriety of applying the schema of a decisive transition point in a person's (or in a *people's*) life, calling for leaving behind one stage (the stage of being "under law" as "under a pedagogue") and entering a new stage (being "in Christ," enjoying a new freedom while being accountable to the Spirit).[213] Jesus's death and resurrection mark a kind of rite of passage, a collective "coming of age," from which there is no turning back. Wherever the gospel is preached and received in faith, and wherever the Holy Spirit is poured out by God, individual people enter into this "coming of age," as it were. Paul's declaration also prepares for Paul's castigation of his converts in 4:8–11: the law served a good purpose in its time, but to continue to live under it as though the pedagogue still exercised rightful authority, a practical denial that the "fullness of time" has come, would constitute an act of defiance against God's own ordering of the times.

Theologians from the Alexandrian school of the second and third centuries through the Protestant Reformation and Catholic Counter-Reformation of the sixteenth century have divided the Torah into the "moral law" and the "ritual law" (John Calvin further differentiated the "civil law," the regulations that applied to the polity of ancient Israel), teaching that the "ritual law" is fulfilled in the sacrificial death and ongoing mediation of Christ, but that the "moral law" remains binding on Christian disciples. Paul himself appears to have advocated a more radical position in Galatians.[214] While the Torah as "the first five books of Scripture" would continue to have educative value for the believer, as Paul amply demonstrates in Galatians and throughout his letters (see, notably, Gal 4:21; 1 Cor 10:11), the Torah as legal code and guardian of behavior has no prescriptive value for the believer's life. Its term has expired, and to make it continue to function in its previous role is tantamount to idolatry (see discussion of 4:11).

26 We arrive at this point at one of Paul's most marvelous declarations of the change that has come about (and that cries out to be fully actualized)

---

213. This freedom would include the freedom of Jews to continue to live a Jewish lifestyle (as in Rom 14:1–15:7), as long as it did not violate the greater principle of the unity of all baptized Christ-followers, as it was being violated in Antioch (Gal 2:11–14).

214. John Chrysostom, 29; Longenecker, li; Westerholm, *Justification Reconsidered*, 77–80.

in the common life of human beings because of Christ and wherever people join themselves to Christ and, in Christ, to one another:

> For you *all* are sons and daughters of God in Christ Jesus through faith: for as many of you as have been baptized into Christ have put on Christ as one would put on one's clothes. There is no "Jew" or "Greek"; there is no "slave" or "free"; there is no "male and female"—for you are all one in Christ Jesus. (3:26–28)

By joining themselves to God's Son in trust, the many have also become God's sons and daughters, sharing in the status of the Son, Christ, who is taking shape himself within them, changing them from the inside out to become righteous in God's sight (2:20; 4:19), so that all are moving toward reflecting the family resemblance of the righteousness of God shown in Jesus. Inclusivity is the essence of this passage. The word "all" is emphatic by virtue of its position at the beginning of the Greek sentence, speaking in the first instance to the whole company of the Galatian Christians, whatever the ethnic derivation of any particular individual within the assemblies.[215] The title "sons of God" or "children of God" was applied restrictively to ethnic Israel in both the Jewish Scriptures and extrabiblical Jewish texts.[216] Here it is purposefully applied to Jewish and gentile Christians together, since the distinction is no longer observable once both have "put on Christ" (3:27–28), with trust in Christ as the decisive criterion of adoption. "Sons and daughters" renders a Greek word that can be translated simply "sons," but it is to be understood as inclusive not only on the axis of ethnicity ("neither 'Jew' nor 'Greek'") but also on the axis of gender, given the similar claim about "not 'male and female'" that follows (3:28).

Paul presents Gal 3:26 (and thus all of 3:26–29) explicitly as a rationale for the preceding declaration "we are no longer under a pedagogue." Living under the Torah is no longer appropriate or possible because of the decisively new condition in which those who are "in Christ Jesus" find themselves, namely, the condition of having been adopted together into God's family, becoming a new social entity in which the old lines of division and differentiation no longer have normative value. The analogy that Paul had been

---

215. The move from first person plural in 3:23–25 to second person plural address in 3:26 ("*you* are all . . .") brings the implications home for the addressees specifically; it does not necessarily signal a switch from a "we" that does not also include them (so Tolmie, *Persuading*, 143; against Betz, 185). This understanding is all the more accurate if we read Galatians as addressing the Christian assemblies in South Galatia, which, at least to some extent, according to Acts (13:43; 14:1), were ethnically mixed congregations.

216. See, for example, Exod 4:22–23; Deut 14:1–2; Hos 11:1; 3 Macc 6:28; Pss. Sol. 17.27; Jub. 1.22–25. A seminal study of this phenomenon is Byrne, *Sons of God*, 11–63.

developing in 3:23–25 (and to which he will return in 4:1–11) here admittedly shows its imperfections, since adoption into God's household as sons and daughters actually takes place through faith and thus after the coming of faith and at the *end* of the period of living under the authority of the pedagogue (or, in 4:1–7, under the authority of the larger body of "guardians and custodians"). If the analogy were perfect, one would have begun as a son or daughter in the household and have come, in due course, under the authority of the pedagogue (or the multiple guardians), and thence into adulthood within the family. Adoption as God's sons and daughters happened for the Jew as well as the Greek with the coming of faith; Paul makes no distinction between the Jews, as if they were the "minor children" already in the household, and the gentiles, as if they alone were "slaves" in the household awaiting adoption. *Both* receive adoption as sons and daughters as a result of baptism into Christ (3:26–28) and reception of the Holy Spirit (4:5–6).[217]

In this new social entity, there is no place for the continued separation of Jewish Christians from Christians of other ethnicities: the former are no longer in danger of learning "vain imaginings" from the latter, or being led astray by their idolatrous or immoral practices. No danger exists there from which a pedagogue (the Torah) must fence them off. To continue to live under the regulatory principles of the Torah would be, in fact, to divide again into two what God has joined into one, to deny the consequences of Jew and gentile having been immersed together into Jesus Christ (3:27–28) or having jointly received the gift of the Holy Spirit, the spirit of adoption (4:4–7).[218] And if it is inappropriate for the Jewish Christians, who had been placed by God under the pedagogue for a period of time, to continue to allow that pedagogue to determine their every step and social interaction, how much less appropriate is it for the rival teachers to attempt to extend the authority of the pedagogue over the gentile Christians, who were never "under Torah," never under *this* particular pedagogue before, presumably so that the gentile converts could become true sons and daughters of Abraham, heirs of the covenant blessings, and "clean" partners for Jewish Christians in the common life of Christian assembly.[219]

---

217. Contra Donaldson, "Curse," 104. Paul will reinforce such a view in his innovative interpretation of the "lineage" of Sarah and Hagar in 4:21–31. See Alan Segal's discussion of the shift in boundary markers around the people of God from those set by the Torah to those created around a shared conversion to Christ-faith and an experience of the transformation that resulted from conversion (*Paul the Convert*, 205–7).

218. Dunn (*Theology*, 145) suitably emphasizes the role of the Holy Spirit in redefining the people of God, observing that Paul challenges "Israel's continued assumption that it enjoyed a favoured nation status before God," since "the promised Spirit was rendering all such evaluations outdated, in Rome ([Rom.] 2.28–29) as in Galatia (Gal. 3.1–5, 14)."

219. Young ("Social Setting," 173) aptly summarizes: "In Christ this separation of Jew

English translations that render 3:26 as "you are all sons and daughters of God through faith in Christ Jesus" (e.g., CEB, NLT) obscure the possibility that Paul intends the two prepositional phrases—"through trust" and "in Christ Jesus"—to be understood separately, making two distinct affirmations in parallel fashion: "you are God's sons and daughters *by means of trust*" and "you are God's sons and daughters *in Christ Jesus*," that is, as believers enter "into" Christ and wrap Christ around them in the rite of baptism (3:27).[220] The focus of the following verses specifically on the element "in Christ Jesus" might incline the hearer toward thinking of the prepositional phrases in 3:26 as parallel elements (thus with the NRSV and NIV, against the CEB and NLT).

27-28 Paul introduces these verses as a further rationale in support of the claim he made in 3:26, technically therefore as a "confirmation of the rationale" that was offered in support of 3:25. Here he explains how the believers have become God's "sons and daughters" by virtue of being joined to the Son in baptism and how this new status affects personal identity and social relationships within the Christian assembly: "For as many of you as have been baptized into Christ have put on Christ as one would put on one's clothes. There is no 'Jew' or 'Greek'; there is no 'slave' or 'free'; there is no 'male and female.'"

Paul draws on the powerful image of the ritual of baptism, and quite plausibly on the ritual language already in use among the Christian assemblies in connection with baptism.[221] Similar formulas appear elsewhere in Paul's letters:

> For indeed we were all baptized into one body in one spirit, whether Jews or Greeks, whether slaves or free persons, and we all drank in one spirit. (1 Cor 12:13)

> Putting off the old self with its practices and putting on the new one, which is being renewed in knowledge in line with the image of the one

---

and Gentile which the law demanded was abolished (3:28)." See also Howard, *Crisis in Galatia*, 60–62.

220. The NRSV and NIV separate the two prepositional phrases so as to convey this reading clearly. Had Paul meant for ἐν Χριστῷ Ἰησοῦ to be understood as a subordinate descriptor of πίστεως, he might have more properly written διὰ τῆς πίστεως τῆς ἐν Χριστῷ Ἰησοῦ (as he did, essentially, in 2:20, though the rule about including the second article to indicate adjectival use is not rigorously observed in Koine Greek); alternatively, he might have used the (for him) more typical expression διὰ πίστεως Ἰησοῦ Χριστοῦ (so Fung, 171–72; see 2:16; 3:22). The scribe of 𝔓[46] came close to this wording with the variant διὰ πίστεως τοῦ Ἰησοῦ Χριστοῦ, though this is readily explained as a harmonization in the direction of Paul's language in 2:16 and elsewhere.

221. See the discussions in Betz, 181–85; Longenecker, 154–55.

who created it, where there is not "Greek" and "Jew," circumcision and foreskin, a barbarian, a Scythian, a slave, a free person, but Christ is all things and in all things. (Col 3:9–11)

Notable parallels emerge among these three passages: (1) attention to the "all" who have become "one" in Christ and through the action of the Spirit; (2) attention to specific pairs of categories that create socioethnic differentiations; (3) declarations that these categories that differentiate (and thereby divide the "all") are overcome in the new unity of the people joined together in Christ and no longer have any prescriptive or evaluative force. Common to 1 Cor 12:13 and Gal 3:27–28 is the connection of the rite of baptism with the decisive change. Common to Col 3:9–10 and Gal 3:27 is the language of putting on the garment of the new person. The similarities may best be explained as the result of dependence on a common source, the baptismal liturgies of the earliest Christian congregations. Internal parallelism and rhythmic cadence in Gal 3:26–28 itself also reflect more the loftier prose of liturgy than the quotidian prose of argumentation.[222]

Paul explicitly reminds the Galatians about what happened to them, in some sense objectively, as they underwent the Christian rite of initiation.[223] The symbolism of baptism by immersion, as it was no doubt most commonly practiced in the early church, is powerful indeed. Paul could liken it to burial, such that one dies with Christ in baptism to one's former life and its connections, and rises to a new life as one emerges from the water (Rom 6:1–14). In Galatians, Paul uses the image to underscore the submerging of each individual convert *into* Christ,[224] with Christ engulfing, covering, enveloping the convert like a garment.

While the imagery of garments and changing garments is used powerfully in Col 3:5–17 to capture the thorough transformation that God is seeking to effect within and among us,[225] here Paul focuses on the social rather than the ethical implications of this "putting on." Once "covered" by Christ, former distinctions ceased to hold any value or significance. What they (ought to) see now when they look at each other is Christ in them, over them, surrounding

---

222. Betz (181) draws attention to the parallelism of both the outermost phrases (Πάντες . . . ἐστε . . . ἐν Χριστῷ Ἰησοῦ, 3:26, 28) and the internal phrases (οὐκ ἔνι . . . οὐδέ . . . , 3:28a, b).

223. Schlier, 174–75; Betz, 185.

224. The preposition εἰς here, as typically, denotes movement into some space, physical or figurative. This image provides an interesting counterpart to other expressions of the intimate connection and communion that the believer enjoys with Christ (2:20; 4:19), though this image looks at the transformation "externally" (i.e., as Christ envelops the believer) rather than from the inside (i.e., as Christ is formed and comes to live through the believer).

225. See deSilva, *Transformation*, 53–58.

them. As a result of being submerged into Christ, they form an essential unity. What they share as "new creation" is exponentially more important than what had distinguished—and thereby divided—them while they belonged to the old creation. Those learned lines that divide humanity and that protect systems of inequality no longer have force in the Christian assemblies, where all are "one in Christ Jesus": thus, "there is no 'Jew' or 'Greek'; there is no 'slave' or 'free'; there is no 'male and female.'"

The elimination of the social value of the first pair—"neither Jew nor gentile"—is of obvious relevance to the situation in Galatia. For the Galatian Christians to adopt a Torah-observant lifestyle would mean reintroducing the value of the distinctions that baptism obliterated over and above the value of shared identity in Christ. While Paul affirms the elimination of the social value of the second pair (especially bold under the system of Roman imperialism, the economy of which depended entirely upon slavery), he does not deal with the relationships between slaves and free persons in Christ in any focused way in the letter (though he will foreground the imagery of slavery and freedom). The third pair, however, may be of secondary relevance alongside "neither Jew nor gentile." While circumcision is most often discussed in terms of distinguishing the Jew from the gentile, it does so only in regard to Jewish *males*, thereby also serving as a perpetual reminder (at least, whenever the subject arises or the rite is performed in the case of male infants) of the distinction between male and female.[226] Two factors suggest that Paul has interjected this particular dyad here, expanding the traditional baptismal formula. The first is the difference in form. The "there is not . . . or" pattern in the first two pairs is broken in the "there is not . . . and" of the third because of Paul drawing here from the exact wording of Gen 1:27—where God made humanity "male and female," the prototypical dyad of the old creation transcended in the new creation[227]—rather than from existing liturgy, which, as a genre, is more disposed to value parallelism over exact reproduction of a source text. The second is the absence of any reference to this dyad in the otherwise very similar passages in 1 Cor 12:13 and Col 3:11, which are also taken to reflect early Christian liturgy.

These pairs represent not merely alternative states of being but power relations and evaluations. They are categories not merely of self-identification but also of other-identification, from which the former is inseparable as long as one knows oneself in terms of the categories operative within and sustain-

---

226. For a fuller exploration of gender issues in Galatians, see the provocative study by Kahl, "No Longer Male."

227. "Male and female" is also one of Aristotle's pairs of στοιχεῖα (which he calls συστοιχεῖα), the foundational pairs that order the cosmos. See excursus "What Are the Elementary Principles (*Stoicheia*)?" on pp. 348–53.

ing the structures of "this present, evil age." Each of these three pairs reflects the racism and chauvinism that pervaded the ancient world (though, from the Greek perspective, the first pair would be given as "Greek and barbarian," with Jews included with all other non-Greeks in the pejorative second term of that pair).[228] For example, Diogenes Laertius attributes to Socrates and Thales the words of this thanksgiving: "first, that I was born a human being and not a brute animal; next, that I was born a man and not a woman; thirdly, a Greek and not a barbarian" (*Lives of Eminent Philosophers* 1.33; LCL). Similarly, Rabbi Judah prescribed for the Jewish male three blessings to be recited every day: "Praised are you, O Lord, who has not made me a gentile," "Praised are you, O Lord, who did not make me a boor," and "Praised are you, O Lord, who did not make me a woman" (b. Menaḥ. 43b; t. Ber. 6.18a; trans. J. Neusner). In the new unity of Christ, these manifestations of the divisive categories of "this present, evil age" are no longer appropriate or welcome; indeed, their persistence is a betrayal of what faith and baptism are meant to accomplish within the new social entity of the church.[229]

The final part of 3:28 ("for all of you are one in Christ Jesus") is presented explicitly as a rationale in support of the claim made in the first half of the verse. Since each individual now has put on Christ in baptism and wrapped Christ about himself or herself like a garment, each individual now wears, as it were, the same uniform; the differentiating marks that belong to the prebaptismal self no longer appear or have value. Where all are "one," dyadic differentiators no longer have place. The declaration that "you are all one in Christ Jesus" ultimately reflects the central affirmation that "God is one" (Gal 3:20, reciting Deut 6:4) and answers the objection to the mediated arrangement of the Torah as somehow violating the very oneness of God that it announced. The oneness of God, the God of Jew and gentile, would at last be reflected in the new humanity coming together in Christ, in freedom from the Torah and the other "elementary principles of the world" that created lines of differentiation to serve as barriers to and boundaries on human interaction and potential.[230]

---

228. See Longenecker, 157.

229. Gaventa, *Our Mother*, 72, 74. Engberg-Pedersen (*Paul and the Stoics*, 146–48) explores the connections between the change in self-identification Paul exemplifies (leaving behind self-identification in terms of the more limited categories of particular ethnic groups and social structures for the sake of affirming a new identity that comes from belonging to "something . . . outside [his own] more immediate, individual self") with Stoic ethics, particularly the Stoic theory of οἰκείωσις, whereby awareness of being indwelt by (and thus defined by) the divine creates a new identity and corresponding social body. Galatians 2:19–20, 3:26–29, and 4:20 reflect this model quite strongly.

230. Paul's meaning is well captured in Eph 2:14–16, regardless of the authorship of that text: "[Christ] himself is our peace, he who made the two one and destroyed the en-

29 Paul now comes full circle, unfolding the logical consequences of the preceding discussion for the question under debate in Galatia, namely, Who are the heirs of the divine promises? Answer: "And if you are of Christ, then you are Abraham's seed, heirs in accordance with promise."[231] English translations typically understand "if you are of Christ" to mean "if you belong to Christ" (taking "of Christ" as a genitive of possession, so NRSV, NIV, CEB; see also NLT, ESV). The preceding material, however, might more readily dispose the hearer to understand the meaning as "if you are a part of the larger whole that is Christ" (a "wholative" genitive, also called a partitive genitive). Paul has been speaking of the many, both Jews and gentiles, being incorporated together into Christ, even being "plunged into Christ" through baptism.

Paul has been addressing this question from the outset of chapter 3, first calling the Galatian converts to remember their actual experience of receiving the Spirit and of God's working in their midst (3:1–5)—in other words, to remember that they had already received *what* was promised (3:14). He went on to demonstrate from Scripture that "those who exhibit trust," following Abraham's example, are Abraham's genuine sons and daughters (3:7) and receive the blessing along with Abraham (3:9). He demonstrated from a close reading of the promises themselves that God bequeathed this blessing upon Abraham and upon a *particular* offspring of Abraham, and not Abraham's descendants generally, such that those who joined themselves to that particular Seed (Christ) joined themselves to the heir, to share the inheritance (3:15–18). He returns to this argument, claiming that he has now demonstrated what he had set out to prove, much as a mathematician signs "Q.E.D." at the conclusion of a mathematical proof. In baptism, the Galatian converts joined themselves to Christ, the Seed of Abraham, thereby becoming *collectively* that Seed of Abraham to whom God gave the promise, the true heirs of God's promise of the Spirit and of righteousness and, thereby, the life that the Spirit was given to nurture and bring to completion (3:29).[232] There is nothing more that Torah observance or circumcision could do for the Galatian Christians, save *un*do the work of the Spirit in their midst.

A major goal for Paul in Galatians is to demonstrate that the social lines of division created by the distinctions made between Jew and gentile and

---

mity—the wall that divided them—in his flesh, having set aside the law consisting of commandments in decrees. He did this in order that he might create out of the two one new humanity in himself, making peace and reconciling the two to God in one body through the cross, killing enmity upon it."

231. Wright (*Justification*, 35–36) correctly observes this to be the climactic point in the argument.

232. This verse consists of a first-class condition of the "equivalency" type: "If A is B (and B is C), then A is C." Paul holds the protasis to state a truth about his converts, leading several translators to render the "if" as "since."

enforced by the regulations of Torah for keeping the two groups separate are transcended in the new community formed in Christ, with the result that the regulatory principles of the "old creation" (even those once given by God!) no longer have authority over relationships in the community of the "new creation" (Gal 6:15).[233] Paul's vision continues to challenge the global Christian community wherever Christians allow longstanding ethnic and racial divisions, prejudices, and hostilities to guide their interactions with one another ahead of our unity in Christ. To name just the largest of a herd of elephants in the room for American Christianity, Christians of European descent and Christians of African descent often find the history of race relations in America regulating and restricting their relationships to a far greater extent than their mutual experience of being submerged into Christ and adopted into God's one family. Paul's vision challenges us all to work very diligently, and in the Spirit's power, to love one another as sisters and brothers—and address the very real issues that continue to plague race relations in America from that mutual love and commitment—rather than continue to live out the scripts that the broken domination systems of America have written for us over the centuries. "New creation" is indeed waiting to be birthed in this regard.

One could rewrite the preceding paragraph, changing what is required, again and again in country after country. In Sri Lanka, it is the challenge to live and love as brothers and sisters in Christ first, rather than as Sinhalese and Tamils in line with the scripts written for these ethnic groups over decades of alienating practices and civil war. Whatever its particular local manifestation, Paul's vision calls Christians to take the necessary steps to come to a place where Christ's actions on behalf of Christians from both groups (or from multiple groups) are valued more highly and regulate interaction more completely than the history of those groups as written in and by "this present, evil age."[234]

Paul goes on to include two other pairs reflective of social divisions and vast inequalities. He denies any prescriptive relational value to the labels "slave" and "free person" in the Christian community. While Paul in the context of the Roman Empire could not abolish slavery per se any more than he could abolish the valuing of ethnic distinctions in the world at large, he *could* urge members of the new community in Christ to reject those distinctions and the regulatory weight they exercised on the lives of individuals and on their interrelationships. Such urging is seen most clearly in his letter to Philemon. Tragically read in ways that supported the institution of slavery

---

233. Schüssler-Fiorenza, *In Memory*, 210.

234. It is perhaps always necessary to remind ourselves that the elimination of the *normative value* of these distinctions is not accomplished by the elimination of distinctiveness. Paul's statement in Gal 3:28 concerns "communal Christian self-definition rather than . . . the baptized individual" (Schüssler-Fiorenza, *In Memory*, 236).

in the antebellum American South, this letter actually challenged Philemon forcefully to make his *own* Christian identity real by honoring the new identity of the newly converted Onesimus as a brother above—and even in place of—their former relationship of master and slave.[235] Christians are challenged by Paul's vision not to allow the socioeconomic or caste divisions in their societies to limit, constrain, or regulate the life of and relationships within the community of the new creation.[236] This community is called to order its common life in ways that demonstrate the lack of stratification (and the affinities and avoidances such stratification nurtures) among those whom God has made sisters and brothers in the one family of God.

Finally, while the physical differences between, and hence the division of humanity into, "male and female" are inherent in nature (see Aristotle, *Politics* 1.2 [1252a25–32]) and perhaps even in God's design for creation itself (Gen 1:27), the expectations that relegate females to supporting roles are not. These are, instead, inherent in the fall and the curse (see Gen 3:16c). A Christian husband and wife are first and foremost fellow heirs of the gift of life and are called to bestow *mutual* honor (1 Pet 3:7), and on that basis to extend *mutual* submission (Eph 5:21).[237] This mutuality extends, of course, into the larger life of the Christian community, which is to become a place where one's immersion into Christ and one's responsiveness to the Holy Spirit—and not one's gender—guide how one will contribute, and be valued as a contributor, to the life of the church.[238] We can look to certain scriptural texts for support in resisting this vision, but when we do so, we should also bear in mind that the rival teachers could and did do so as well.[239]

In the one family that God has created in Christ, the dividing walls of ethnicity are torn down, social prejudices are neutralized, and gender inequalities and male chauvinism are negated. Paul challenges us to continue to examine

235. See further deSilva, *Introduction to the New Testament*, 668–83.

236. On the caste system in India and the ongoing challenge the churches face in regard to enacting Paul's vision in place of this persistent system of divisions and its regulation of relationships, see Jayakumar, "Caste."

237. A Bible that introduces a section heading separating Eph 5:21 from Eph 5:22 was edited by people seeking to underscore the wife's submission above the mutual submission that frames everything said of wives and husbands. Ephesians 5:22 is a verbless dependent clause leaning upon the main clause of 5:21.

238. Schüssler-Fiorenza, *In Memory*, 212–13.

239. Two factors are rarely appreciated in regard to texts maintaining the normative value of gender roles and female subordination: (1) the desire on the part of the author to foster acceptance of the vulnerable Christian minority among the broader society and, perhaps, to facilitate mission; (2) the subtle challenges being lodged against the rationales for and practices of domination in the household, even within, for example, New Testament "household codes."

our hearts and our practice along these lines, asking continually, what would life in our congregation (and all its components) look like if we approached all such issues from the position articulated in Gal 3:26–28 and committed ourselves to live out fully this facet of the baptismal life, the new creation? Does our practice perpetuate these divisions and the social inequalities they inscribe, or does our practice challenge them, witnessing to the "new humanity" being formed in Christ in their communities, where Christ is all and in all?

G. PROOF FROM ANALOGY:
COMING OF AGE IN THE HOUSEHOLD, PART 2 (4:1–7)

1 *And I say, for the extent of time that the heir is a minor, he or she differs in no way from a slave, even though he or she is master of all,* 2 *but he or she is under guardians and stewards until the time set by the father.* 3 *In this way, we also, when we were "minors," were enslaved under the elementary principles of the world:* 4 *But when the fullness of time came, God sent his son, coming into being from a woman, coming into being under Torah,* 5 *in order that he might redeem those under Torah, in order that we might receive adoption.* 6 *And because you are sons and daughters, God sent the Spirit of his Son*[a] *into our*[b] *hearts, crying out "Abba, Father!"* 7 *The result is that you are no longer a slave, but a son or daughter—and if a son or daughter, then also an heir through God.*[c]

a. 𝔓[46] omits "of the Son" (τοῦ υἱοῦ) here, perhaps because this designation of the Holy Spirit is unusual, whereas "his [i.e., God's] Spirit" is common.

b. Many later MSS (D[c] E K L Ψ 𝔐) read ὑμῶν, which can be explained either as an intentional correction (to regularize the use of the pronouns in this verse, converting an apparently aberrant first person plural into another second person plural form) or an error in hearing ("your" and "our" differ in Greek only in the opening vowel, and these opening vowels came increasingly to be pronounced alike in the Byzantine period), in either case motivated by the second plural address of the verse established by ἐστε near its beginning. The earliest manuscripts unanimously favor "*our* hearts."

c. There are a number of variant readings representing attempts to "correct" the odd idea of being heirs "through God" rather than heirs "of God" (Comfort, *New Testament Text*, 568), none of which can claim to be more likely original than the well-attested διὰ θεοῦ (𝔓[46] ℵ* A B C* 33 1739*[vid]). F G 1881 read διὰ θεόν ("on account of God," cause rather than agency); 81 630 1739[c] attribute agency to "Christ" or "Jesus Christ" in place of "God." ℵ[2] C[3] D 𝔐 (hence the KJV) fill out the theological proposition as "an heir of God through Christ" (κληρονόμος θεοῦ διὰ Χριστοῦ). Most of these variant readings represent attempts to clarify and emphasize Christ's role in our becoming heirs at this climactic point in Paul's argument.

Paul returns to develop further the analogy he had introduced in 3:23–25, comparing the experience of both Jews and gentiles in the unfolding plan of God to the experience of coming of age in a household. As he revisits the topic, Paul moves away from the image of the children living under the strict guardianship of the pedagogue (3:23–25) to the image of the underage heir living under the authority of legal guardians and custodians, prior to the time he or she comes of age to exercise legal control over self and property (4:1–2). As before, there is a decisive moment that changes the situation: as the coming of "faith" marked the end of the pedagogue's legitimate authority (3:24–25), so God's sending of his Son marks the end of the authority of the "elementary principles of the world" over human beings (4:4–5). In a sudden shift within the analogy, slaves become sons and daughters by adoption because of God's sending of the Son, a change of status demonstrated by the reception of the Holy Spirit, whose indwelling leads each disciple to call upon God as "Abba, Father" as the result of having entered into a new and intimate relationship with God (4:5–7; see 2:19–20). This paragraph cannot help but recall Paul's earlier invocation of the Galatian Christians' experience of the Spirit (3:1–5), the argumentative step with which Paul began his demonstration of the reliability of his position (2:15–21).

The analogy of coming of age—a process that can move in only one direction—provides a strategic frame for the appeals that will follow, beginning pointedly in 4:8–11 (see also 5:1–6). Just as the heir cannot turn back the clock to return under the guardians of his or her minority, and just as the adult cannot turn back the clock to place himself or herself under the discipline and authority of the pedagogue once again (and would be utterly senseless to do so!), so the Galatian Christians must take adequate stock of what it means that "faith has come" and that "the fullness of the time" has already come and gone. They cannot now jeopardize the gains Christ has won for them by choosing a course of action that would effectively repudiate what God accomplished when "he sent his Son" (4:4).

1–2 As Paul resumes his argument from analogy, he portrays the plight of the underage heirs in the household in even bleaker terms than he had in 3:23–25: "For the extent of time that the heir is a minor, he or she differs in no way[240] from a slave, even though he or she is master of all, but he or she is under guardians and stewards until the time set by the father." Paul has left behind his exclusive focus on the pedagogue and, with it, the Torah in its regulatory function (3:24–25), positing now a multiplicity of "guardians and stewards" in anticipation of introducing the "elementary principles of the world" (the *stoicheia tou kosmou*), which these figures represent in Paul's analogy and which, he will claim, enslaved all people prior to the coming of Christ (4:3–5).[241]

The scenario that Paul imagines is likely that of the surviving minor child after the father's death; the terms of the inheritance, the selection of

---

240. Understanding οὐδέν as an adverbial accusative indicating manner or extent.

241. Schlier, 189; Martyn, 388; Tolmie, *Persuading*, 146–47; Das, 434.

the guardians, and the timing of the heir's coming of age are all spelled out in the father's last will and testament. The word here translated "guardian" can refer to the manager or steward of a household, estate, or similar unit, but it can also refer to the person granted legal care of and authority over some charge, the more likely sense here.[242] The term rendered "steward" refers to the person entrusted with care or custodianship of the property. The two terms would not necessarily designate different persons, but only different functions, potentially of the same person, who might be guardian of both the minor's person and his or her property.[243]

The minor heir lives out his or her life under the authority of these masters "until the time set by the father"[244] for the minor child to enter into his or her inheritance and the accompanying authority over his or her own person and property. The specific legal practice serving as a background to Paul's analogy remains uncertain, despite extensive investigation.[245] In favor of local Galatian practice is the fact that local law allowed the father some flexibility in terms of the setting of the age of coming to majority, whereas this age tended to be fixed by Roman and Greek law (though with some degree of flexibility, in the provinces, even here).[246] As with the analogy drawn from testamentary law in 3:15–18, however, Paul's analogy remains at a general level and works based on his hearers' consent to his representation of the *general* situation of the oversight of underage children, the change of legal status and authority over self and goods at a certain age, and (awkwardly juxtaposed to the situation of *heirs*) the dynamics of adoption. The force of his analogy does not depend upon him conforming his analogy to a *particular* legal background (nor his hearers' identification of the same). Indeed, Paul may just as easily be adapting actual legal practice somewhat to better parallel his understanding of salvation history and the coming of the "fullness of time" in the Father's own good time.[247]

Prior to his or her coming of age, the minor child has no right to dispose of the property that he or she will inherit; the child likewise does not have authority over his or her own person or actions. Living "under guardians and stewards" (4:2), like the experience of living under a pedagogue (3:25), is portrayed as a restrictive and oppressive (rather than a beneficially forma-

---

242. BDAG 385. ἐπίτροπος even enters Hebrew as a loan word from the Greek in this sense (Taubenschlag, *Law of Greco-Roman Egypt*, 123–24).

243. Burton, 214.

244. The genitive τοῦ πατρός is here understood as a subjective genitive.

245. Ramsay, 391–93; Burton, 212–15; Betz, 202; Schlier, 189; Longenecker, 162–63. Das (427–38) provides a thorough review of possible Jewish, Roman, and Hellenistic legal backgrounds.

246. Longenecker, 163; Das, 434–36 and literature therein cited.

247. Fung, 180; Tolmie, *Persuading*, 146.

tive) existence.[248] Indeed, being governed by others in respect of person, property, and action, the minor child's life (Paul suggests) resembles more the life of a slave than the life of a free person, even though he or she simultaneously possesses the title to the entire estate.[249] Paul introduces the language of slavery (here as hyperbole) that he will use to great effect throughout the remainder of the letter: the state of slavery versus the event of adoption that makes people sons and daughters in the household of God (4:3, 5); slavery to the rules and powers of this age versus the freedom for which Christ liberated people (4:3, 8–9a), a freedom people are to defend against every enticement to fall back into bondage to this world's rules and ruts (4:10–11; 5:1b), but a freedom also not to be misused to cater to one's self-centered drives and desires (5:13–25).

3 In 4:3–7 Paul applies this domestic analogy to his own and his Galatian converts' location in the timeline of salvation history: "In this way, we also, when we were 'minors,' were enslaved under the elementary principles of the world [*stoicheia tou kosmou*]." Two questions need to be considered in regard to this and the following verses: Who is included among the "we"? and What are the "elementary principles of the world"?

As already explored above (see excursus "Pronouns, People Groups, and the Plan of God" on pp. 296–302), Paul gives his hearers no reason to exclude themselves from the group labeled "we" in this passage. Particularly in the wake of 3:26–29, in which Paul declared the solidarity of all Christians, Jew and gentile, and named them "heirs," together with the last word of 3:29, each Christian in Galatia would have strong cause to identify himself or herself with the "we" group that emerges as Paul continues to consider the backstory of these heirs.[250] That is, Paul invites the Jewish Christian converts among the Galatians (alongside himself) to think of their pre-Christian

---

248. DeBoer, "τὰ στοιχεῖα τοῦ κόσμου," 212.

249. Belleville, "Under Law," 63; Martyn, 388. A similar comparison of the pedagogue to a prison warden, and of the children placed under the care of such a guardian as no better off than slaves, appears as early as the writings of Plato (see *Laws* 7.808d–e). Paul presents this as an everyday situation in the life of many a household, not as a specific reference to Israel in Egypt (contra Wilson, "Wilderness Apostasy," 560; Byron, *Slavery Metaphors*, 185–90; Wright, *Justification*, 136). Exodus has left its imprint at the most general level of the Christian framing of the redemption story, but that influence does not mean that an author refers to the former every time he or she speaks of the latter.

250. With Burton, 215; Betz, 204; Tolmie, *Perusuading*, 150; Martyn, 391 (more particularly in reference to 4:6); contra Longenecker, 164; Belleville, "Under Law," 68; Witherington, 284. DeBoer ("Meaning," 209–10) believes Paul to be purposefully blurring the distinctions between Jews and gentiles among his audience through his rather inconsistent use of pronouns, a suggestion that has merit, given Paul's core convictions about the lack of value of these distinctions "in Christ" (3:26–28).

lives as lived "under the elementary principles of the world," even as he invited the gentile Christian converts to think of their conversion as also their own release from the authority of the Torah (the pedagogue, 3:23–25). The group of those who lived "under the *stoicheia tou kosmou*" (4:3) is inclusive of those who were "under law" (hence, Jewish Christ-followers, 4:5), as well as those who formerly served things that were *not* gods in their ignorance of and alienation from the one God (hence, gentile Christ-followers, 4:8–9). If there were any doubt on this point after hearing 4:3–5, it would be retrospectively removed after hearing 4:8–11, where Paul explicitly connects the observance of the *Jewish* calendar of sacred days and seasons with a *return* to the *stoicheia* on the part of the Galatian Christians.[251] This is a stunning thing for a Jew to consider, let alone say.

We turn, then, to the second question: What are the *stoicheia tou kosmou*, these enslaving powers from which Christ redeemed the Galatians? They represent the fundamental building blocks of the world, but not in the sense of the physical elements from which the physical world is constituted, though this meaning does provide a close analogy. In Paul's usage here, they are the basic, fundamental principles upon which social reality (the "world" of human systems, interaction, and activity) is constructed and by which it is governed. They are, especially, the categories (like those listed but swept aside in Gal 3:28) that divide, order, and create hierarchy within social reality, as well as the rationales that undergird the same. They are the rules and values that each child, born into and confronted with the society that had long since taken shape on the basis of such rules and values, must inevitably internalize, accept, and live by. They are the individual parts of "the way the world works," to which each child must adapt himself or herself, by which each child must be willingly constrained as his or her mind, practices, and life trajectory are shaped thereby. The *stoicheia* are happiest (if the conceit be allowed that impersonal forces can be happy) when this child arrives at his or her grave without having questioned them. This is the slavery into which every person is born, and which most never recognize as such.

---

251. Thus, rightly, Donaldson, "Curse," 97: to be "under law" is one particular way of being "under the elements of the world." So also Bruce, 30; Longenecker, 181; Martyn, 393. Barclay (*Obeying the Truth*, 210–11) suggests that the polemic situation in which Paul finds himself, and within which he is hammering out his theology of Torah's limited role in the overall plan of God, leads him to make more extreme statements here. His view becomes more balanced, and more positively inclined toward Torah, by the time he writes Romans (i.e., when the heat of controversy on this topic is passed).

EXCURSUS: WHAT ARE THE "ELEMENTARY PRINCIPLES" (*STOICHEIA*), AND IN WHAT SENSE ARE THEY "OF THE WORLD" (*TOU KOSMOU*)?[252]

In and prior to the first century, *stoicheia*—and especially *stoicheia* in relation to the word *kosmos*—most widely denotes the elements out of which the natural world was believed to have been made, namely, earth, water, air, and fire.[253] These elements were often divinized, either in themselves or in connection with a particular deity associated with each element, a fact to which Jewish authors drew attention. The first-century Alexandrian Jewish author Philo, for example, observed that gentiles "call fire Hephaestus . . . air Hera . . . water Poseidon . . . and earth Demeter" (*On the Contemplative Life*, 3–4; see also *On the Decalogue*, 53–54, and *On the Eternity of the World*, 109). Similarly, the author of Wisdom of Solomon, a Hellenistic Jewish work from around the turn of the era, wrote that gentiles "were unable from the good things that are seen to know the one who exists, nor did they recognize the artisan while paying heed to his works; but they supposed that either fire or wind or swift air, or the circle of the stars, or turbulent water, or the luminaries of heaven were the gods that rule the world" (Wis 13:1–2).[254] In this reading, slavery to the "elements" would communicate much of what Paul and other Hellenistic Jews communicate elsewhere as they speak of gentiles worshiping facets of the created order rather than the Creator himself.[255]

An identification of the *stoicheia* as "the natural elements," however, does not well suit the context of the usage of the phrase in Gal 4:3, 9. The

---

252. As deBoer ("Meaning," 204) helpfully breaks up the question.

253. For lexical data, see Blinzler, "Lexicalisches," 439–41; Rusam, "Neue Belege"; Schweizer, "Slaves of the Elements"; Wink, *Naming the Powers*, 67–77. Martyn (395) additionally cites Philo, *Who Is the Heir?*, 134; Wis 7:17; 19:18; 4 Macc 12:13; 2 Pet 3:10, 12 in support of a connection of the term with the physical elements of the world. It is, however, essential to remember that the particular context determines the sense of a word or phrase, not the preponderance of overall lexical usage in *other* contexts. The exact phrase στοιχεῖα τοῦ κόσμου, moreover, appears only in Paul (Gal 4:3; Col 2:20); it is not a technical term for the natural elements from which the cosmos is made (Burton, 516).

254. See also Homer, *Iliad* 20.67; Empedocles, *Fragment* 6; DK 1.311 (found in Freeman, *Ancilla*, 52; Kirk and Raven, *Presocratic*, 323).

255. See also Guthrie, *History of Greek Philosophy*, 2:144–46. The word *stoicheia* comes to be used to speak of actual gods, demons, and other spirit beings, but not until the third or fourth century CE (as in Pseudo-Callisthenes, *Alexander Romance* 1.1). See Bruce, 193–94; Martyn, 395; Moore-Crispin, "Galatians 4:1–9," 211. On the population of Paul's invisible cosmos and the language Paul uses (concrete, abstract, or purely metaphorical) to represent them, especially those powers hostile to humankind, and the relationship of Paul's powers to those found in Jewish apocalyptic and Greek philosophical (including Hellenistic Jewish) writings, see Forbes, "Paul's Principalities and Powers"; "Pauline Demonology."

term could also be applied in antiquity to the heavenly bodies, such as the sun, moon, and other stars and planets—what the author of Wisdom of Solomon would call the "luminaries of heaven" (13:2). These celestial "elements" exercised influence over people and were of obvious importance for establishing any group's calendar of religious observances. Their domination over human life is further reflected in popular gentile obsession with horoscopes and astrology. Paul's specific reference to the Galatians' observance of a ritual calendar as a sign of their renewed bondage to the *stoicheia* (4:9–10) could be seen to lend support for the view that *ta stoicheia* refers to the celestial bodies and, by association, the religious practices associated with the elements, particularly the annual cycles of holy days and festivals that dominated both Jewish and non-Jewish practice throughout the ancient Mediterranean.[256] In the mind of the ancients, these heavenly bodies were themselves connected with spiritual beings or powers, often hostile toward humans and thus needing to be heeded and placated. External evidence for such usage of the term *stoicheia*, however, is lacking until the second-century Christian author Justin Martyr (*Apology* 2.5.2; *Dialogue* 23.3), with the result that it would be surprising to find Paul using it in this sense so early. It would also be artificial to limit the *stoicheia* in Galatians to calendrical observances, in light of other available "regulatory principles" in the context, like circumcision as a regulation based on the distinction between "Jew and Greek" as a fundamental conviction about the world order.[257]

In the particular context of Gal 3:23–4:2, in which discipline and child-minding have been prominent images and in which Paul specifically connects the *stoicheia* to the term during which we were children, the word (which can refer to a series of things lined up in a row—even the letters of the alphabet) could be heard to signify the "ABCs," or fundamental tenets, of some body

---

256. Betz, 205; Bruce, 204; Martyn, 395; Blinzler, "Lexicalisches," 439; deBoer, "Meaning," 206, 223.

257. Comparison with Colossians, another Pauline text that speaks of the authority of the "elementary principles of the world" and the Christ-followers' changed relationship to the same, would support this counterclaim. While the author (whom I take to be Paul; see deSilva, *Introduction to the New Testament*, 696–701) refers to disputes over "a festival or a new moon or Sabbaths" (Col 2:16) in connection with having been liberated "from the elements of the world" by dying with Christ (2:20), he also speaks in the even more immediate context of dietary restrictions and taboos against touching or handling certain things (2:21), faulted because they are in line merely with "the precepts and teachings of human beings" (2:22). It is interesting that in Colossians, as in Gal 5:13–6:10, we find a desire on the part of the Christian addressees to discover that which has power to "put the flesh in check" (Col 2:23): rival teachers in Colossae may also have been promoting Torah-based practices as means to this end (in an admittedly different constellation of practices from what we find in Galatia).

of teaching,[258] in this case the fundamental principles belonging *to this world* (the *kosmos*, which is also this "present, evil age," 1:4).[259] This understanding could be extended to signify the ABCs of human and institutional logic as it has taken shape in our rebellion against God.[260]

Paul would not be using the term to speak positively about some elementary teaching serving as a preparation for the gospel, but rather to denote a set of rules, ideas, values, prejudices, and divisive categories (like "slave versus free," "male versus female," "Greek versus barbarian," "Jew versus Greek") that imprison and constrain those who grow up knowing nothing else and nothing better, limiting and regulating human action and interaction.[261] In this sense, Paul would be speaking about slavery to "the way the world works," however the society in which a person is born and bred defines the rules and sets the parameters on life.[262] Seneca, a Roman philosopher contemporary with Paul, had a clear sense of the ways in which the individual would encounter such sociocultural logic as something outside of and greater than himself or herself, and would therefore tend to conform himself or herself to the same *and* stand in need of deliverance from the control it exerted. He writes: "We do not know how to weigh matters; we should take counsel regarding them, not with their reputation but with their nature. . . . For they are not praised because they ought to be desired, but they are desired because they have been praised; and when the error of individuals has once created error on the part of the public, then the public error goes on creating error on the part of individuals" (*Moral Epistles*, 81.29; LCL). For Seneca, Stoic reflection on the nature of things is a means to liberation from this deeply ingrained—and socially or systemically reinforced—error.

As *literal* children, Paul and his Galatian converts were exposed to precisely this kind of socialization into the rules and regulations imposed upon them as they were enculturated into systems of "foundational principles," from whose stranglehold Christ freed them in principle and the Spirit works to free them in actuality. Paul may indeed offer the opposing pairs of Jew/Greek, free/

---

258. See Aristotle, *Politics* 1309b16; Plato, *Laws* 7.790c; Xenophon, *Memorabilia* 2.1.1; Col 2:8, 20; Heb 5:12.

259. Burton, 512, 517–18; Longenecker, 165; Matera, 150. Burton and Matera limit the principles to *religious* principles of this age, but that qualification seems unnecessarily limiting, especially if Gal 3:28 names sample στοιχεῖα.

260. Burton, 510–18; Belleville, "Under Law," 67–68; Young, "Paidagogos," 172.

261. Martyn (404) helpfully underscores this connection: "The formula of Gal 3:28— with its announcement of liberation from enslaving pairs of element opposites—constitutes a key part of the context in which, in 4:3–5, Paul explicitly speaks of liberation from the enslaving elements of the cosmos."

262. Martyn (389) insists on this negative evaluation of the *stoicheia* and their impact on a person's experience of life, community, religion, and so forth.

slave, male/female as examples of *stoicheia*, "universal polarities that the Greeks and others thought to be the basis of the cosmos."[263] In his *Metaphysics* (1.986a 22–27), Aristotle identified twenty foundational *stoicheia*, articulated as ten pairs of corresponding opposites: (1) Limit and the Unlimited, (2) Odd and Even, (3) Unity and Plurality, (4) Right and Left, (5) Male and Female, (6) Rest and Motion, (7) Straight and Crooked, (8) Light and Darkness, (9) Good and Evil, (10) Square and Oblong. These became principal categories by means of which reality could be described, sorted, and otherwise ordered.[264]

Each pair often also includes an implicit hierarchy of value: the un-limited is better than that which has limits; unity is better than a plurality; right is better than left; good is better than evil. Aristotle could overlay the pairs of natural elements (fire, air, earth, water) upon the above categories to derive hierarchies and provide rationales for the same: he named fire and air the dominant elements and related them to the "Male" (both were elevated, active agents, and more rarified, hence came out "on top"), while naming water and earth the inferior elements and relating them to the "Female" (both were lower, passive, less rarified, hence coming out "on the bottom").[265] Paul might very well be heard to have laid out sample *stoicheia* in Gal 3:28—some of which have been named in philosophical discourse before ("male and female") and some of which perhaps had not, but could be recognized as appropriate candidates for related pairs of *stoicheia* by analogy. With these opposing pairs still in their ears, the Galatians would be further disposed to push beyond hearing *stoicheia tou kosmou* as a reference to "the four natural elements" (even if this was their preliminary understanding) toward the "el-ementary categories that regulate human existence."[266]

Such an understanding of the *stoicheia tou kosmou* well suits the fact that Paul considers the Torah itself to be a representative of this group. To-

---

263. Kahl, "No Longer Male," 44, drawing upon Martyn, 393–406.

264. In an interesting correlation, the natural elements (*stoicheia*) were also orga-nized in terms of opposites (air vs. earth, fire vs. water); both the physical and the social universes were ordered "in binary oppositional pairs" (Kahl, "No Longer Male," 44). See also Sir 33:15: "Consider all the works of the Most High—two by two, one opposite another." Aristotle could, in the same discourse, also speak of the *stoicheia* as the material elements (*Metaphysics* 1.985a32–33).

265. Kahl, "No Longer Male," 44, citing Aristotle, *Metaphysics* 1.986a.

266. The adjectives "weak" and "beggarly" (4:9) are also less appropriately applied to the elements of the physical universe (though such application is not impossible) than to the principles on which the world's logic, shown to be foolishness by God (see 1 Cor 1:18–20; 3:19), is based (so Burton, 517). Belleville ("Under Law," 68) foregrounds their governing and constraining function in the translation "regulatory principles of the world," which is quite on target, passed over here primarily for the sake of preserving the double entendre in *stoicheia* as "elements" and "elementary" instruction.

rah quite obviously has a dimension of "fundamental instruction" regarding the way the world worked, investing this instruction with an aura of divine legitimacy. Its regulation was built upon binary oppositions that resemble (and in some cases include) other well-known pairs of *stoicheia*—Jew and Greek, male and female, even slave and free. It, too, had a cosmic dimension, instructing those under it to observe particular signs in the sky and regulate their lives accordingly (i.e., by observing sacred days and seasons, and setting them apart from ordinary days, on which to attend to other business), thus giving celestial bodies like sun and moon authority over the human sphere.

Understanding the *stoicheia tou kosmou* here to represent the "world [*kosmos*]-defined regulatory principles [*stoicheia*]"—which, though impersonal, confront the individual as a suprasocial being with a life and power of its own[267]—also aligns well with the further uses of these two morphemes (*stoich-* and *kosmos*) in Galatians. Paul will direct those liberated from these "regulatory principles" to "regulate themselves by" (better, "walk in step with," *stoichōmen*) the Spirit (5:25). He will also declare himself dead to the world (*kosmos*)—by which he means not the world as God's creation but the world as "present, evil age," a collection of systems ruling not on behalf of God but in place of God—and the world to him on account of Christ's cross, pronouncing the "new creation" (which stands in stark contrast to the *order* that has taken hold over the first creation) to be the only thing that now has value (6:14–15).[268] Those who are in agreement with him on this point—who "regulate themselves by" (again, better, "walk in line with," *stoichēsousin*) this rule (6:16) and reject the paired *stoicheia* of "circumcision" and "uncircumcision" (6:15)—are those upon whom he wishes grace and mercy at the end of his discourse and whom he names "*God's* Israel" (6:16).[269]

The *stoicheia*, then, are the guiding powers and principles of this age, the building blocks (metaphorically speaking) from which the *kosmos* as "present, evil age" (1:4) is composed—which have contributed to perverting and

---

267. Caird (*Principalities and Powers*, 51) links these *stoicheia* with the "principalities and powers" (see Col 1:16). Paul says both that the Galatians were serving beings that were not by nature gods and that the Galatians were formerly enslaved to τὰ στοιχεῖα τοῦ κόσμου, which does not imply that the latter are personal beings: "The same fact may be, and often is expressed both in personal and impersonal terms" (Burton, 517).

268. On "the world" (κόσμος) in Paul, see Wink, *Engaging the Powers*, 51–59.

269. Kahl ("No Longer Male," 44–45) makes a brilliant observation in this regard: "The oneness of the new creation attacks the old age by constantly undermining the hierarchical structuring of difference either as repressive sameness (= the other made similar to the one, e.g., all males to be circumcised) or as imperial oneness (= the one, e.g., Jew, superior to the other)." Being "one" in Christ means no identification of "the other" to subject or to objectify.

corrupting the present age. These "elementary principles" divide the world and all that constitutes it, creating the categories, hierarchies, and evaluations that guide, limit, and constrain human beings in their thoughts, behaviors, and interactions, keeping them in a form of ideological and systemic bondage. They include, especially, all that contributed to the internal and external divisions among human beings, the power differentials across those divisions, and the ideologies that sustained those divisions and power structures. Living "under the elementary principles of the world" (4:3) is on the same level and of the same kind as living "under a curse" (3:10), "under law" (4:4, 5); "under a pedagogue" (3:25), "under guardians and custodians" (4:2), and, finally, "under sin" (3:22). From his present vantage point in experiencing God's dealings with humanity, Paul sees that this existence was a prolonged state of being enslaved.[270]

4–5 Paul returns to the moment that effected a decisive change in the human condition, ending the repressive rule of the "elementary principles of the world": "But when the fullness of time came, God sent his son, coming into being from a woman, coming into being under Torah, in order that he might redeem those under Torah, in order that we might receive adoption." The "time set by the father" for his minor children's accession to authority over their own persons and property (4:2) corresponds to the "time set by the Father" in heaven for the removal of the spiritual and social pedagogues, guardians, and custodians. It marks the ending of the period of Torah's legitimate authority to constrain the Jewish people and maintain their separation from "all the nations"; it similarly marks the end of the authority of those worse "guardians and stewards" regulating the minds and lives of the other nations. It makes it possible for all people, Jews and gentiles, to come into the possession of the inheritance promised to them.

Paul has already spoken of this inheritance as the reception of the Holy Spirit (3:14), which would lead Jew and gentile alike to become righteous and obedient from the heart (5:5, 16), and which would bring to life within them the very life of Christ, the "Righteous One" (2:20; 4:19). The Spirit would succeed where the Torah had failed, empowering victory over the impulses of the flesh and bringing righteousness to fruition in the lives of Christians individually and corporately (5:13–6:10). Paul will shortly turn once again to the topic of God's sending of the Spirit as the sign and proof of his converts' adoption into God's family (4:6–7).

---

270. The pluperfect periphrastic tense ἤμεθα δεδουλωμένοι appropriately signifies a past action that had long-term consequences for the subjects.

The idea of "the fullness of time" and the view of the positive progression of history from plight to deliverance and new existence that it assumes might be seen to stand at odds with the more apocalyptic—and therefore *pessimistic*—view of history that Paul adopts when he speaks of "the present evil age" (1:4), from which people required rescue, as well as the "new creation" (6:15), which takes shape within but stands starkly opposed to the first creation (which has become the "present evil age").[271] It is not, however, as if Paul speaks of a "new epoch" that is universally experienced: what came "in the fullness of time" was nothing other than "rescue from the present, evil age" (1:4), a rescue experienced only by those who join themselves to Christ in faith. For all others, "the present evil age" continues as they remain under the power of the same, ignorant of or willfully rejecting the way out from its stranglehold that Christ has effected. Only in the future will this age come to a decisive end for *all* people.

This invasive act of deliverance involved God's sending his Son to redeem the slaves and make them sons and daughters. Paul departs in a significant way here from the analogy with which he opened this round of argumentation (3:23–25; 4:1–2). He began with the image of a natural-born child living the *life* of a slave under guardians and then coming of age and coming into his or her own. Now he shifts to the image of adoption, whereby those who were not part of the family (and, indeed, were slaves to second-rate masters) are made part of the family and, thus, heirs in the family, by the action of the paterfamilias (here, the action of God). The former analogy was insufficient to capture the real plight of humankind or the significance of God's intervention. The coming of Christ, the unique Seed of Abraham (3:16, 26–29) and unique Son (1:16; 4:4), redeemed *slaves* so that God could give them—Jews as well as gentiles—the gift of adoption into God's family. The Roman practice of adopting even adult children, most famously the adoption of Octavian by Julius Caesar as a means of designating Octavian as Julius's personal and political heir (a practice that would continue throughout the Principate), would be well known to the addressees. The radical transformation from slave to son or daughter is a witness to the experience of Jewish Christians like Paul, who discovered for themselves a new quality of relationship with God, described in the intimate terms of becoming God's child and knowing God as Parent.[272]

The expression "God sent his Son" may suggest implicitly here what Paul and members of the Pauline circle will elsewhere affirm explicitly, namely, the preincarnate existence of the Son (see 1 Cor 8:6b; 10:4; Phil 2:5–8; Col 1:15–17; Heb 1:1–4), a conviction that itself might have arisen from the early

---

271. Barclay, *Obeying the Truth*, 99.
272. Longenecker, 172.

Christian identification of the Son with the figure of Wisdom.[273] The action parallels God's sending (the same Greek form is used) the Spirit of his Son in 4:6, a Spirit that would be presumed to exist and be active prior to its appearance on the human scene. The Son "came into being[274] from a woman," thus sharing our humanity; furthermore, he "came into being under the Torah," sharing in the particular experience of the Jewish people, to redeem them, allowing the blessing promised to Abraham thence to flow forth to the gentile nations.

The affirmation here in 4:4–5 repeats from another angle the argument of 3:13–14, with which it shares several structural similarities: an act by a divine being (Christ, 3:13; God, 4:4); two parallel purpose clauses outlining the beneficent aims (and, in retrospect, effects) of that act.[275] In both passages, Paul gives particular attention to Christ's redemption of those who live under the particular bundle of *stoicheia* undergirding (and undergirded in turn by) the Torah, which means, in practical terms, God's historic people Israel. Paul elsewhere speaks of gentiles as being "without Torah" or "outside the Torah" (Rom 2:14; 1 Cor 9:20b–21), their lives constrained and limited by other *stoicheia*. Here he nods to this historical fact by speaking of "those under law" in the third person, though he also invites both Jewish *and* gentile Christians in Galatia to understand themselves to have been redeemed from the law's curse by Christ's death and to regard the law as something that belongs only to the *past* of their story, not their present or future (in contrast to the preaching of the rival teachers). Nevertheless, Paul acknowledges in both passages that the parenthesis opened by God in the giving of the Torah ("430 years later" than the promise) to a particular people needed also to be purposefully closed, which Christ's coming (and dying accursed) achieved.

God's sending of the Son makes the gift of the Spirit (the focus of 4:6–7) and the adoption into God's family that the Spirit effects (4:5b) available to *all* people. Paul makes no distinction between minor sons and daughters in the household (denoting Jews) and slaves (denoting gentiles) such that the former are merely "redeemed" while the latter are "adopted" into a family within which the former already belonged.[276] *All* are adopted into God's fam-

---

273. Longenecker, 167; deSilva, *Introducing the Apocrypha*, 149–52. Dunn, *Christology in the Making*, 39–40, however, sees in this verse merely a reflection of Jesus's own tendency to speak of himself as "son" and as "sent by God" (as in Mark 9:37; 12:6)

274. The Greek γενόμενον is often translated "born," which is a fair contextual rendering of "coming into being" here. It is less likely that this meaning is the result of confusion between γενόμενον and γεννώμενον (from γεννάω, "I bear, beget") than that the verb γίνομαι simply carried the connotations of "coming into being through birth" in certain contexts (contra Bligh, *Galatians*, 160; Das, 398).

275. This repetition has also been noted by Williams, "Justification and the Spirit," 98.

276. Contra Donaldson, "Curse," 104.

ily together as they are submerged into Christ (3:26–29), an adoption that became real through the sending of the Holy Spirit into the heart of the Jew, just as into the heart of the gentile (3:14; 4:6–7). All were slaves to various *stoicheia* before Christ without distinction, and now, in Christ, all can receive adoption into God's family without distinction.[277]

6–7 The importance of the early Christians' experience of the Holy Spirit comes to the fore once again (see 3:1–5), an experience of a spirit being, an "other" from outside the person, coming to encounter and indwell the human person: "And because you are sons and daughters, God sent the Spirit of his Son into our hearts, crying out 'Abba, Father!' The result is that you are no longer a slave, but a son or daughter—and if a son or daughter, then also an heir through God." Paul marks this verse as a further step in his argument,[278] as he identifies their *experience* of the Holy Spirit (4:6–7) as evidence for the *conviction* that God has adopted them into God's own family (4:5).[279]

Paul points the Galatians to their own experience of entering into a new relationship with the one God, whose Holy Spirit within them has enabled them—and continues to enable them[280]—to call upon this God as "Abba, Father," even as the Son addressed God as "Abba" during his lifetime (Mark 14:36).[281] The appearance of the Aramaic term *Abba* here is striking (as again in Rom 8:15). To be a meaningful part of Paul's argument, it must reflect the actual use of this foreign term among Greek-speaking, gentile congregations,

---

277. John Byron (*Slavery Metaphors*, 193) speaks of the Galatians as being in danger of "rejecting their new status and position as God's slaves" as they contemplate returning "to their previous form of enslavement" (see also 202). This seems to be a strange way of putting the case, when Paul himself adamantly affirms that the Galatians have moved from the status of "slaves" to that of "sons and daughters of God" ("you are all sons and daughters of God," 3:26; "adoption as sons and daughters," 4:5; "because you are sons and daughters," 4:6; "no longer a slave, but a son or daughter," 4:7), rejecting slave language where God is concerned (though not, indeed, the *stoicheia*). Byron's admission that Paul "does not, of course, press the imagery and call the Galatians δοῦλοι θεοῦ here" (192) is not sufficient; after reading Gal 4:1–7, no Galatian would think of himself or herself as occupying the "status and position as God's slaves."

278. Paul signals this progression with the particle δέ.

279. The logical flow between these verses requires that the change in pronouns here (from the "we" of 4:5b who receive "adoption as sons and daughters" to the "you" of 4:6 who "are sons and daughters") not indicate a radical shift of reference. In 4:5 the fact of a "we" group's adoption into God's family is asserted; in 4:6 the consequence of this adoption is posited, with its relevance for a subgroup of the "we" (the "you" [pl.]) especially highlighted (so also Burton, 224; Tolmie, *Persuading*, 150; Das, 408).

280. The present tense (continuative aspect) of the participle κράζον suggests that this Spirit-empowered activity is ongoing or habitual.

281. See Joachim Jeremias, *The Prayers of Jesus* (London: SCM Press, 1967), 11–65; Meier, *Marginal Jew*, 2:294, 358–59; Fee, *Empowering Presence*, 410–12.

even as the phrase *maran atha* (Aramaic for "Our Lord, come!") came into us-age in Greek-speaking congregations (as presumed in 1 Cor 16:22; Did. 10.6).[282] Paul writes to the Christians in Rome in strikingly similar terms, assuming that the practice of calling upon God as "Abba" is familiar there as well.[283] This suggests that Paul was aware of the practice in congregations beyond his own sphere of influence (as he had personally played no part in the formation of the Roman churches before that point). Whether this practice was introduced into diaspora Christian congregations by Jewish Christian evangelists like Paul in imitation of the Lord, or whether it resulted from a manifestation of the Spirit moving Jewish and gentile converts to address God using a foreign term (corresponding, supernaturally, to the actual practice of Jesus and Ju-dean Christians), cannot be known.

Paul's argumentative use of the practice of calling upon God with a word that would have been foreign to the Greek-speaking Galatians suggests the implicit meaningfulness of the practice itself. It was not enough for them to identify God as "Father" (using their native Greek *patēr*); they sought to iden-tify with Jesus's own experience of God as "Abba," claiming for themselves the quality of that intimate relationship and that confident self-knowledge as being not merely God's creature, but God's child, seeking to know and experience God precisely as Jesus knew God and made God known.[284] The foreign word *Abba* was capable of encoding and invoking this more precise experience of the fatherhood of God. The linguistic anomaly is similar to, though much more specific than, the much more prevalent use of the Hebrew loan-words "Hallelujah" and "Amen" in Christian churches throughout the ages, the self-conscious awareness of standing in and living from a tradition of worship that is native to a particular source (in these instances, the worship life of Israel and Judah).

---

282. The Didache, the short title for the "Teaching of the Twelve Apostles," is an early church manual on ethics, baptism, the Eucharist (or communion), discerning the true prophet from the false, and other such topics. It may date from the late first or early second century and derives from Jewish-Christian circles in Syria or Palestine.

283. Bruce, 199. The argumentative use to which Paul puts the phenomenon is also essentially the same as in Galatians: "For as many as are led by God's Spirit, *these* people are God's sons and daughters. For you did not receive a spirit of slavery leading again into fear, but you received a spirit that conferred adoption, by means of which we cry out 'Abba, Father.' This spirit bears witness along with our spirit that we are God's children—and if children, then heirs, heirs of God and fellow heirs with Christ, if indeed we suffer with him in order that we may be glorified with him" (Rom 8:14-17).

284. Heeding the critique in Barr ("'Abba' Isn't Daddy," a critique accepted by Jere-mias, *New Testament Theology*, 67), I do not wish, in speaking of an "intimate" relationship between a father and a child, to lend credence to the idea that "Abba" means "Daddy" or belongs on the lips of immature children as opposed to adult children of a father. See also George, 308; Das, 417; deBoer, 266; Jewett, *Romans*, 499–500; Witherington, 291.

Paul's own point here is that the cry "Abba, Father" is not mere wishful thinking or role-playing on the part of the gentile Galatian Christians. It is, rather, a Spirit-driven and Spirit-enabled utterance that reflects the reality of the relationship that God has created with those people, whether Jew or gentile, who have joined themselves to the life of his Son Jesus Christ by water and the Spirit. God has sent the same spirit that is in Jesus (the Son) to dwell within believers (the adopted sons and daughters), making them to share in the spiritual identity of the "Seed" and bringing Christ to life within them (hence the claims found in 2:19; 4:19). This experiential knowledge of God (see also 4:8–9) should give them all the evidence of their acceptance by God and their place in God's family as God's sons and daughters that they might require.[285] For Paul, such assurance comes to the believers from their experience of the Holy Spirit and the inward testimony of the same; it is notably not manufactured on the basis of attaining certainty in regard to claims about what happened "the hour I first believed."

Paul is primarily interested in engendering this assurance for the sake of stabilizing the Galatian converts in the path on which Paul had set them and defusing the anxiety that the rival teachers have provoked so as to motivate the Galatians to adopt the path *they* promote. For this reason, I would not read 4:6 as an absolute affirmation concerning the order in which two things happen for the Christ-follower, namely, adoption *followed by* reception of the Spirit.[286] Here it suits Paul's purposes to present these acts in this order, since the unquestionable experience of the latter can provide the basis for assurance concerning the former. However, Paul can elsewhere express the relationship differently. In Romans, Paul can assert that one is not a son or daughter of God *before* and *apart from* God's bestowal of the Holy Spirit (Rom 8:14). Without the Spirit, we are not Christ's own (Rom 8:9). The Spirit itself *is* the "spirit of adoption" (Rom 8:15–16), whose indwelling actualizes God's intention to adopt people into God's own family. Receiving the Spirit and being a son or daughter of God are so intimately connected that the chronological priority of one or the other aspect is impossible to establish.[287] All of this suggests that Paul does not actually view a chronological progression here in Gal 4:6, but rather a logical interdependence.[288]

Receiving Christ's Spirit made the Galatian Christians to be numbered among Abraham's seed by virtue of being united with the one Seed, which

---

285. Once more, the word υἱοί is no doubt inclusive of Christians of both genders, the distinctions between which no longer have value (3:28), hence "sons and daughters."

286. As does Fung (184), for whom "sonship logically precedes the gift and operation of the Spirit, which in turn attests the reality of sonship," with "sonship" being "not the result of the operation of the Spirit, but [something] attained through faith (3:26)."

287. Longenecker, 173.

288. Rightly Longenecker, 173; Das, 414.

is Christ. This makes each one of them—Paul repeats for the Galatians' benefit—"an heir through God" already on the basis of trusting Jesus and apart from taking on the yoke of the law (see 3:29). The shift to the second person singular in 4:7 is especially striking and personalizing here, as Paul invites each member of his congregations to identify himself or herself personally with this conclusion, even as Paul identified Christ's death not merely to be "for all" in general, but "for me" in particular at the same time (2:19–20).

Galatians 4:1–7 reinforces for all Christ-followers the importance of the experience of the Holy Spirit and, by means of the Spirit, the awareness of living as people personally adopted by God into his family as we have been joined by baptism with the unique Son, Jesus Christ. In his first letter to the Christians in Corinth, Paul would address the problems that arise when one unduly emphasizes certain experiences of the Spirit's working in the midst of the congregation and, worse, uses these experiences to establish a kind of inner-church hierarchy of more and less spiritually empowered members. In Galatians, Paul reminds us that, abuses aside, the experience of the Holy Spirit is foundational to discipleship, confirming for us who we are, *whose* we are, and how we are to live together as "new creation" (see commentary and reflections on 3:1–5; 5:13–26).

This passage also provides foundational insight into our lives in the "old creation" (the cosmos that God created "good" [Gen 1:4, 10, etc.] but that has been malformed into "this present, evil age" [Gal 1:4]) and the challenges that we face as we seek to live into the new creation as Paul describes it—a community in which the multiple identifications of "us and them" cannot continue to guide the valuation of, regulate relationships between, or constrain the contributions of any person "in Christ" (3:28), a community in which the fruit of the Spirit rather than the works of the flesh are to be the natural outcomes of our common life in the Spirit (5:16–6:10).

Paul describes life prior to Christ as life lived in slavery to the "elementary principles of the world-as-present-evil-age," which confront human beings as powerful, constraining forces. They exercise authority over the entire human race, some in universal, most in more-or-less local ways. They represent the power of the basic principles of the way things are done in our particular societies, a way of doing things that existed prior to our being born and into which we have ourselves been socialized from birth so that we would, in our turn, preserve the institutions of our society and the values and practices they embody and engender and participate in passing them on, in turn, to the generation that would survive us.[289] They represent the ideologies of nation, of militarism, of economics (whether capitalism, socialism, or

---

289. For a classic primer on such "socialization," see Berger, *Sacred Canopy*, 3–52; *Invitation to Sociology*, 66–121.

communism), even of religion and how far the sphere of religion is permitted to extend. They determine how these ideologies take shape in our society and control and constrain us. What encounters us from outside as we are growing up in this world finds its way inside us as we internalize the logic, the values, the practices, and the boundaries that we are taught and observe, guiding and limiting the options we are even able to imagine for our responses, our relationships, our ambitions, and, ultimately, our discipleship.

Paul challenges us to discern how these *stoicheia*, which we could think of somewhat glibly as the "isms" that exist within our particular sociopolitical context, have been operative in our lives *and* in the life of the church, so that we may become ever more free to respond to one another and to the world on the basis of the ideals, values, and practices taught by God. The importance of the Spirit here cannot be overestimated: only by hearing and following the Spirit, in conjunction with studying the Scriptures and listening to our Christian sisters and brothers across the globe, can we begin to discern the invisible walls of the prisons our particular societies construct around us from birth.

Consider, for one example, militarism and its guiding beliefs that violence can produce peace, that the power to destroy any threat is the foundation of national security, that the successful suppression of resistance means that concerns regarding justice and peace have been addressed. This is a bundle of *stoicheia* that has carved deep ruts in the human consciousness, having exercised its logic and indoctrinated generation after generation into its creed since prehistory. Of course, it is bound up with other *stoicheia*, notably nationalism and imperialism—the development of a systemic "us" that is separate from a systemic "them" and the idea that "we" should be poised to take more of what is "theirs" for ourselves or make "them" more like "us," by force if necessary. These systemic arrangements and individuals' ongoing subscription to their underlying convictions do, in fact, make strong militaries essential on all sides. One nation cannot simply dismantle its military so as to pour those immense resources and personnel into more creative pursuits for the good of its own people or the world population (like healing broken lives, educating and fostering sustainability for at-risk people groups, researching the cures for cancer, AIDS, and other global ravagers of lives) because of what would happen to them at the hands of the other nations out there. And so we are *compelled* to sustain and even to keep upgrading our military capacity. Therein our slavery to the *stoicheia* of militarism comes out into the open. What the nation *cannot* do, however, Christians have been freed to do, and we begin by dismantling for ourselves throughout the global church those fundamental convictions and replacing them with the fundamental convictions in line with which God would have us live together as a global faith community.

Capitalism is a driving ideological force that has taken on embodied form throughout Western societies like no other. A friend, half-joking, once shared with me that he did his part to ensure the survival of capitalism across the generations by teaching his two-year-old niece the words "mine" and "more." His grasp of the fundamental *stoicheia* undergirding a now-global machine was profound. Capitalism represents a way of life that many Christians are committed to living and to zealously defending. As far as national economies go, it is no more beset with evils than socialism or communism and, historically, it appears to be far *less* beset with evils than either. But ought Christians to allow it to define *our* way of life? In the way of life that Christ would engender among his followers, the final argument is not profit, such that we ought to privilege the well-being of something that has no God-given life, like a corporation, over the well-being of the people who constitute the real life of the institution. The purpose of wealth is neither to make more wealth nor to secure my own well-being in the distant future of retirement (itself an assumed good), but to relieve the presently pressing need of our neighbors. The driving force and the sought-after end of our actions is not "more" (and especially not "more for me and 'my own'") but God and what service I can render to advance God's pleasure.[290]

All facets of our learned existence need to be reexamined and, in many instances, unlearned if we are to experience the freedom of the sons and daughters of God. The way our society draws the lines that become the grid for our existence—its paired *stoicheia* of "private and public," "kin and nonkin," "male and female," "black and white,"[291] "native and immigrant," and so forth—cannot, in the end, be allowed to encumber our living into God's vision for human community as it is becoming new in Christ. An essential component of the "good news" of the gospel is that we have been liberated from continuing to live out our lives in servitude to these ideologies and structures. A new Spirit has been poured into our hearts, driving out the spirits of this age, so that we can apply ourselves to building our lives around the teachings and example of Christ, the guidance of the apostles, the counsel of fellow Christians—trying to discover together what authentic life free from the domination of these *stoicheia* will look like.[292] If our liberation is to be-

---

290. To be fair, it is also not government-enforced redistribution of wealth either to make everyone more equally equipped to succeed in a capitalist economy or to be sustained without discovering their own capacity to contribute, so as to realize their dignity as producers of good for their neighbors.

291. The ideology of ethnicity—the formation of personal identity grounded in belonging to a particular ethnic category, the regulation of relationships on the basis of remaining associated with people of one's own ethnic group, the belief that members of one's own ethnic group are superior in some way, or have superior claims in some regards, than members of another ethnic group—is another of the most powerful and abiding *stoicheia*, indefatigable in its regulation of the lives of Christians.

292. There are many books that help us think about the "powers and principalities" that

come real, we need to attend to the long process of discovery of those areas in which we (as individual disciples and church bodies) continue to act upon what we have internalized from these *stoicheia*, discarding these practices, and inquiring into what Christ-formed practices could take their place if we rebuild our lives together as faith communities and as the worldwide kingdom ruled by God *from the ground up* on the basis of the "elementary principles" that Christ, in concert with the prophets and apostles, taught.

H. REBUKE BASED ON ARGUMENT FROM ANALOGY (4:8-11)

8 *But formerly, not knowing God, you were enslaved to things that were not gods by nature.* 9 *And now, knowing God—and, what is more, being known by God—how can you turn back again to the weak and impoverished elementary principles, to which you desire to submit yourselves to live as slaves*[a] *all over again?* 10 *You are observing days and months and seasons and years!*[b] 11 *I am afraid where you're concerned, lest somehow I have labored*[c] *over you for nothing.*

a. א and B read an aorist infinitive in place of the present infinitive δουλεύειν, which is, however, very strongly attested otherwise. The imperfective aspect of δουλεύειν suggests the more durative "live as slaves" rather than simply "enslave yourselves."

b. 𝔓⁴⁶ extends the question of 4:9 through 4:10 by the change of the indicative παρατηρεῖσθε to the participle παρατηροῦντες: ". . . to which you again wish to be enslaved by observing . . . ?"

c. 𝔓⁴⁶ reads the corresponding aorist form at this point.

In Gal 3:23-29 and 4:1-7, Paul has established the framework of the "before" and the "after" created by God's action in the moment that separated the two—the moment "when faith came" (3:25). Paul now personalizes this framework for the Galatian Christians, particularly for the gentiles among the congregations, since they are also the principal focus of the rival teachers' interest. He contrasts the "before" of their lives prior to their trusting encounter with Christ (4:8) with the "after" of their lives since receiving God's Spirit and entering into a new and intimate relationship with the one God, all with the aim of laying bare the absurdity of the change in course they are contemplating (4:9) and, to some extent, beginning to undertake (4:10).

The paragraph recalls the earlier rebuke of Gal 3:1-5, not merely in the directness of Paul's language, but in the subject matter. In both passages,

---

constrain human society, the foundational logic of the world-gone-astray from God. I have found the following most helpful: White, *Making a Just Peace*; Wink, *Naming the Powers*; *Unmasking the Powers*; and *Engaging the Powers*; Ramachandra, *Subverting Global Myths*.

Paul's recollection of the Galatian Christians' experience of the Holy Spirit (3:2, 5; 4:6–7) is materially connected to Paul's frustration with their inability to draw the correct (and, to him, obvious) conclusion about the illegitimacy of the rival teachers' position (3:3; 4:9b–10). In both passages, Paul expresses this frustration in terms of questioning whether all his investment (and, indeed, God's investment) in them has been "for nothing" (3:4; 4:11). At the same time, it anticipates a further exhortation to the Galatians not to trade their costly freedom for a return to slavery (5:1), an exhortation that Paul would support by laying out the consequences of their repudiation of the freedom Christ won for them (5:2–4).

The heightened and heated tone of the rebuke affords Paul a natural segue into the appeal that follows, based largely on the relational connection that Paul and his converts had enjoyed (4:12–20), in the course of which he is able even to make good use, by way of explanation, of the stronger outbursts such as we find here in 4:11.

8–9 Paul has been speaking in terms of a "before" and an "after" in regard to God's intervention in human affairs, sending his Son to effect a decisive change. He now applies this more directly to the Galatian Christians: "But formerly, not knowing God, you were enslaved to things that were not gods by nature. And now, knowing God—and, what is more, being known by God—how can you turn back again to the weak and impoverished elementary principles, to which you desire to submit yourselves to live as slaves all over again?!"

Paul focuses particularly on the gentiles among his congregations, as they are most targeted by the rival teachers and, therefore, most at risk of making a terrible mistake under their influence. In stark contrast to the Galatians' present state of knowing the one God intimately as God's own sons and daughters (4:9), they formerly lived ignorant of and alienated from this one God (4:8).[293] Paul stands alongside other Hellenistic Jewish authors on this point: "All people who were ignorant of God were foolish by nature; they were unable, on the basis of the good things that are seen, to know the One who is" (Wis 13:1). Gentiles failed to move from contemplation of the created order to the discovery of the Creator, falling instead into serving "things that are not divine by their very nature" (Gal 4:8):[294] "Those who call 'gods' the

---

293. The strong temporal contrast in these verses is heightened in Greek through the use of the correlatives μέν and δέ.

294. Hardin (*Galatians and the Imperial Cult*, 126), pointing to Betz, 214–15, suggests that Paul's description of "things that are not gods by nature" recalls the distinction between gods who are divine "by nature" and those who are gods "by official recognition," for example, the emperors. Winter (*Seeking the Welfare of the City*, 132) had similarly read the "so-called gods" of 1 Cor 8:5 as inclusive of the emperors who were worshiped as gods. But Paul would hardly accord to *any* of the Greco-Roman gods (divinized humans, demigods,

products of human hands—gold and silver items carefully sculpted, images of animals, a useless stone worked by someone's hand long ago—are pitiful, setting their hopes on dead things" (Wis 13:10). The Galatians might hear Paul naming their past failure to know God as in fact the cause of their previous enslavement to the *stoicheia*.[295] Paul would include idolatrous religion as a facet of the *stoicheia* that dominated and regulated gentile life in society (as in 1 Thess 1:9), but he was looking beyond merely the practice of idolatry to the larger ways in which gentiles, like Jews, were slaves to the ideological and social structures around them.[296]

That state of benighted alienation came to an end when they encountered the gospel, responded with trust, and received God's Holy Spirit. Their coming to a place of knowing God—or, rather, being known by God (here Paul uses the rhetorical device of self-correction to highlight *God's* taking the initiative in reversing their condition of alienation-through-ignorance)[297]—ought to have positioned them to recognize and reject any attempt to persuade them from their position. They ought to have valued the testimony of the Spirit in their inner person more than the testimony of the rival teachers. Thus Paul makes no attempt to hide his exasperation with them: "How can you turn back again to the weak and impoverished elementary principles, to which you desire to submit yourselves to live as slaves all over again?!"[298] (4:9b).

Just as the adult cannot again be a child, the person who drinks deeply of God's Spirit cannot again look backward to any of the *stoicheia*, Torah or

---

or full-fledged Olympians) the status of being gods *at all*. Thus it is difficult to agree that *Paul* would be making the kinds of distinctions that Hardin and Winter suggest. *None* of the gentiles' gods are gods "by nature"; *all* of the gentiles' gods fall into the category of "so-called gods." None of this, therefore, can be taken as evidence in favor of regarding the imperial cult as particularly foregrounded in Paul's thinking or the addressees' situations (see excursus "Galatians and the Imperial Cult," on pp. 368–75).

295. This would be one possible way to construe the adverbial participial phrase οὐκ εἰδότες θεόν ("not knowing God").

296. Bruce (30) comments on the essential difference between Torah as a *stoicheion* and the *stoicheia* to which gentiles were enslaved: "According to Paul, pagan worship was always culpable because it involved idolatry and the vices which followed from idolatry; Jewish worship in the pre-Christian stage of God's dealings with humanity was far from being culpable—it was divinely instituted—but it had the character of infancy and immaturity as compared with the coming of age into which human beings were introduced by faith in Christ."

297. Das, 420. See also John Chrysostom (31): "How great and bitter will be the chastisement ye draw upon you, if, after such a treatment, ye relapse into the same disease. It was not by your own pains that ye found out God, but while ye continued in error, He drew you to Himself."

298. The two adverbs πάλιν ἄνωθεν are mutually reinforcing (with both individually meaning "again"), hence, colloquially, "all over again."

otherwise, for the way forward. More insidiously, turning back to the *stoicheia* would mean repudiating the freedom, the new and glorious status of "heir" and "son or daughter," that Christ won for the believer at such great cost through his death "under the Torah" (Gal 4:4–5). Paul's rhetorical question suggests that he finds it incomprehensible—as indeed his Galatian converts *ought* to have found it unthinkable—that they would seriously contemplate taking on the yoke of Torah, that passé pedagogue, after all that God had done and Christ had opened up for them.[299] The language of slavery here connects this paragraph with the preceding analogies in 3:23–25 and 4:1–7, depicting the Galatians' contemplated course of action as all the more unnatural and unnecessary a return to a most disadvantageous condition.[300]

In Paul's view, the Torah, which regulated the life of Jews apart from Christ, is on a par with the (other) *stoicheia tou kosmou* that had regulated the life of the gentiles apart from Christ. Both equally enslaved human beings, and the binding power of both was equally broken by the coming of Christ.[301] For this reason, Paul can speak of the (gentile) Galatians' move toward taking on some of the works of the Torah (which they had *not* practiced before converting to Christ) as essentially a *return* to slavery to the *stoicheia tou kosmou* (others of which they had served, as idolaters and products of their upbringing in Greco-Roman society, before converting to Christ). Paul continues to

299. Paul's assertion that they want to be slaves again (4:9) directly parallels the assertion that they want to be under law (4:21; deBoer, "Meaning," 215).

300. Wilson ("Wilderness Apostasy") suggests that Paul is drawing heavily upon the story of God's redemption of the Hebrews and their subsequent apostasy as a frame for the Galatians' situation in 4:8–9 (and elsewhere). In support, he points to correlations between Galatians and the exodus narrative in regard to the experience of deliverance and redemption from slavery, in particular the appearance of deliverance language (forms of ἐξαίρειν) in Gal 1:4; Exod 3:7–8; 18:4, 8, 9, 10, etc.; and redemption language (forms of ἐξαγοράζειν) in Gal 3:13; 4:4–5. He also notes correspondences in regard to adoption into God's household as sons and daughters (see Exod 4:22; Hos 11:1) and moving forward toward entry into the promised kingdom (Gal 5:21). More to the point, paired references to the converts' rescue and contemplated apostasy occur throughout Galatians (1:1–4/1:6–7; 4:3–7/4:8–9; 4:21–5:1a/5:1b; Wilson, "Wilderness Apostasy," 552). He is on firmest ground (561–63) in regard to Paul's comment concerning turning back to other gods and to slavery in 4:8–11, which resonates strongly with the folly of the Hebrews in the wilderness.

It may rather be sufficient to say that the story of the exodus is so fundamental and foundational a story line for the Jewish people that it shapes, to some extent, all future stories, even at a subconscious level. I would not agree that Paul is "making references" so much as being shaped, in regard to his thinking, at a structural level quite apart from his conscious choice (see Deut 6:20–22 for a hint that this story essentially precedes all other stories in the experience of the Jewish child of Jewish parents, at least for children of those parents who followed Deuteronomy's regulations).

301. Vielhauer, "Gesetzesdienst," 553; Bruce, 30, 202; Longenecker, 181; Martyn, 393.

drive a wedge of incompatibility between two facets of practice that the rival teachers promote as completely, even necessarily, complementary (namely, faith toward Jesus and observance of the requirements of Torah).

10–11 The Galatians, of course, had not been looking at their choices in terms of returning to their preconversion slavery: this spin is part of Paul's rhetorical strategy. Indeed, it is quite possible that the rival teachers had themselves discussed the *stoicheia* in their preaching, contrasting the gentile Galatians' slavish worship of the elements (in the form of their idolatries and worshiping of the created things instead of the Creator, as well as in their own calendrical observances based on their observation of the stars) with the possibility they now have, by adopting the Torah-prescribed way of life, of worshiping the one and only God aright and observing the calendar that God himself enjoins upon people, having given the heavenly bodies as indicators of that calendar (and not objects of veneration in their own right). Convinced at least in a preliminary way by these teachers, the Galatian Christ-followers had begun to conform their practice to their recommendations: "You are observing days and months and seasons and years! I am afraid where you're concerned,[302] lest somehow I have labored over you for nothing!"

Paul's words here indicate that some of the Galatian Christians, at least, had begun to observe a particular calendar of religious festivals, most likely the sacred days of the Jewish religious calendar as an initial step toward conforming their lives to Torah's regulations, as the rival teachers were urging.[303] The language of this verse specifically recalls the old Greek translation of Gen 1:14, where the stars and other astronomical bodies are created to serve "for signs and for seasons and for days and annual festivals." These are precisely the same terms as found in Gal 4:10 (with the substitution of "months" or "new moon" festivals for "signs").[304] The Galatians were beginning to observe the Sabbath days (Exod 20:8–11; 31:16–17; Deut 5:12–15), quite possibly the new moon festivals (Num 10:10; 28:11–15), and could be expected, then, to observe the seasonal feasts (feasts lasting more than a day, like Passover, Tabernacles, and Booths)[305] and annual commemorations, like the New

---

302. The pronoun ὑμᾶς is understood here as an accusative of respect. Paul is not afraid *of* the Galatians themselves, but *for* them.

303. This verse also provides clear evidence that the rival teachers were promoting more than merely circumcision, as John Chrysostom (31) recognized: "Hence is plain that their teachers were preaching to them not only circumcision, but also the feast-days and new-moons."

304. Fung, 192–93; Bruce, 205–6. The use of "and" to separate each constituent in this list also reflects the syntax of Gen 1:14, though Tolmie (*Persuading*, 154–55) suggests that this may have the effect of emphasizing the tediousness of the endless observances to which the Galatians are about to commit themselves.

305. See Exod 13:10; 23:14–17; 34:23–24; Lev 23:4–8, 15–22, 33–36, 39–41; Num 9:2–3.

Year.[306] The observance of the Sabbath, together with circumcision and the distinctive dietary practices, were the most obvious and most universally well-known "works of the law" that set Jews apart from gentiles.

The rival teachers would have had material at their disposal to continue to use Abraham as a model here of the ideal proselyte who moves from idolatry to correct observance of the one God's liturgical calendar. While the Genesis account does not suggest that Abraham observed the Sabbath and other such religious days, Jews began to retell the story of Abraham and the other patriarchs with a view to showing how even they, long before Moses, observed the Torah before it was given in written form. For example, the book of Jubilees, written in Judea sometime prior to 150 BCE, recounts how Abraham, in response to the visit of the three angels who confirmed to him God's promise of an heir (as in Gen 18:1–15), offered animal sacrifices to God daily for seven days while living in booths (Jub. 16.20–27). "Because he celebrated the festival at its appointed time," God "blessed him forever, and all his descendants after him for all the generations of the earth" (v. 28); moreover, on the basis of Abraham's precedent (!), it becomes an ordinance that Israel must continue to observe "the Feast of Tabernacles for seven days with joy" (v. 29).[307]

In submitting themselves to the Jewish ritual calendar, the Galatian Christians were submitting themselves to the authority of the stars and other heavenly bodies that determined the timing of the holidays and thus regulated the lives of Jews "under law" (see Jub. 2.8–10 and 1 En. 82.9). Giving sun, moon, and stars such authority over one's life and practice amounted, for Paul, to a return to idolatrous service to things that were not in themselves divine. They were also submitting themselves to the authority of the custodian who had kept Jews and gentiles corralled in separate pens, drawing back from the work of Christ creating the one, new humanity out of the two. If they are all now part of one family (3:26–29; 4:5–7), and that on the basis of the action of the Holy Spirit within them, there is no value in continuing to adhere to (or take up) practices that were in force while they were not

---

306. Burton, 233–34; Dunn, "Intra-Jewish Polemic," 470–73; Longenecker, 182. One need not suppose that enough time had passed for the Galatians to observe everything in the calendar; it was enough that they had begun to observe the cycle. Genesis 1:14, not the list of actual festivals already observed by his converts, accounts for the scope of Paul's language. Hardin (*Imperial Cult*, 121) claims that it would have been impossible for the Galatians to have actually observed the annual festivals by the time Paul writes, as they were not yet circumcised (note Exod 12:43–51, which explicitly excludes the uncircumcised from celebrating the Passover along with Jews). He deduces from this restriction that Paul *cannot* be referring to the Jewish calendar of observances, but this deduction depends on not allowing Paul any room for exaggeration.

307. Martyn, 397–400.

kin—either to God or to each other. Whether they reverted to their pagan past religious calendars driven by the imperial cult and the rhythms of indigenous observances,[308] or reverted to Paul's own pre-Christian practice (the close observance of Torah), as was immediately the case, it was all the same to Paul: they were throwing away the freedom that Christ had died to give them and moving against the Holy Spirit of God that was at work sanctifying one people together for God. The seriousness of the situation in Paul's eyes is underscored by his exclamation of fear that his work among them might turn out to have been all for nothing (4:11, also 3:4).

EXCURSUS: GALATIANS AND THE IMPERIAL CULT

The cult of the goddess Roma and the emperors was a major ideological, architectural, and liturgical feature of the life of most cities in the Roman East, including the cities of southern Galatia, as exemplified by Pisidian Antioch. The gospel Paul preached in Galatia interacted with the claims of Roman imperial ideology at many points, and his Galatian converts (and Galatian non-converts!) would likely have made many of these connections. The changes in

---

308. Witherington, 298–99. Martin ("Apostasy to Paganism"; "Pagan and Judeo-Christian Time-Keeping Schemes") has argued that the Galatian Christians were actually returning to participation in pagan religious rituals, and that this is Paul's primary concern throughout the letter and the specific target of Paul's rebuke in 4:8–11. According to Martin, the Galatian converts were indeed persuaded by the rival teachers but, being loath to undergo circumcision, abandoned the Christian project altogether and returned to their pre-Christian religious practices. Paul's goal was to show that the rival teachers' gospel was no gospel and not a true and necessary supplement to the gospel, so that the Galatians could return to embrace their Christian identity, beliefs, and practice ("Time-Keeping Schemes," 116). I have several difficulties with his position. (1) Paul's use of language directly reminiscent of Gen 1:14 at Gal 4:10 strongly suggests that a *Jewish* calendar of observances is in view. (2) If Gal 4:21–5:6 is an address not to the Galatian converts but to the rival teachers, as Martin suggests, Paul gives no signal of such a shift in his intended audience. On the contrary, he gives every indication that he is addressing Galatian Christians on the fence: (2a) The rival teachers cannot be addressed as "those wanting [θέλοντες] to be under Torah" (4:21), for they are already under Torah; (2b) Paul would not name the rival teachers "children of promise, in the manner of Isaac" (4:28) alongside himself (4:31); (2c) Only the Galatian Christians can decide to "stand firm and not submit to a yoke of slavery" (5:1) by stepping back from being found among the circumcised at this point (5:2–3). (3) Even apart from 4:21–5:6, Paul speaks to the converts as those who are inclined to hold onto Christ while adding Torah-prescribed observances rather than as those who have abandoned Christ out of revulsion for the requirement of circumcision (3:3) and as those who are turning from one version of the gospel *to* another (1:6–7), not turning away from the gospel *tout court* because of the "gospel" presented by the rival teachers. See Hardin, *Imperial Cult*, 128–29, for an alternative critique.

practice that Paul demanded of his converts (e.g., leaving behind all idolatrous practice; see 1 Thess 1:9–10) would have changed his converts' relationship with the imperial cult, alongside the many other Greco-Roman religious cults with which they had been familiar and in which they had participated. It is well worth considering, therefore, both the phenomenon of imperial cult in Galatia and the implications of Paul's gospel for the gospel of empire and its cult. At the same time, it is important not to make more of this background than Paul himself makes. The surge of interest in the imperial cult and Roman imperial ideology in recent decades has led to a swell in attempts to locate concern with this cult at the center of the issue in Galatia to which Paul must respond as he writes this letter. For reasons that will be laid out in the second half of this excursus, these currents threaten to throw off course our understanding of the situation in Galatia and the program of the rival teachers.

Even during the era of the Roman Republic, Rome was an *empire* insofar as it exercised domination over lands around the Mediterranean. Long before Rome had emperors, cities (such as Smyrna in 195 BC) erected temples to the goddess Roma, the divinized personification of Rome, in acknowledgment of Rome's power, in expression of the locals' loyalty, and in hope of beneficent relations. From the earliest years of the rule of Octavian (Augustus), cults of Rome's rulers, deceased and living, exploded throughout the cities of Italy, Greece, Anatolia, Syria, and the territories in between and beyond.[309] Two authors—Nicolaus of Damascus (a personal friend of Herod the Great) and Philo of Alexandria—give eloquent testimony to this phenomenon and its motivation:

> People gave him this name [Augustus] in view of his claim to honor; and, scattered over islands and continents, through city and tribe, they revere him by building temples and by sacrificing to him, thus requiting him for his great virtue and acts of kindness toward themselves. (Nicolaus of Damascus, *Life of Augustus*, 1; trans. Clayton Hall)

> If ever there was a man to whom it was proper that new and unprecedented honors should be voted, it was certainly fitting that such should be decreed to . . . Augustus, not [only] because he was the first, and greatest, and universal benefactor . . . but also because the whole of the rest of the

---

309. Seminal studies on the imperial cult in the Roman world include Mellor, *ΘΕΑ ΡΩΜΗ*; Price, *Rituals and Power*; Scott, *Imperial Cult under the Flavians*; Taylor, *Divinity of the Roman Emperor*; Zanker, *Power of Images*, 297–333. Information on the imperial cult in particular cities and helpful summaries of the data can be found in Friesen, *Twice Neokoros*; *Imperial Cults and the Apocalypse of John*, 1–131; deSilva, *Seeing Things John's Way*, 37–48; *Unholy Allegiances*, 11–34; Crossan, "Roman Imperial Theology." On the "Roman peace" in particular, see Wengst, *Pax Romana*, 7–54.

habitable world had decreed him honors equal to those of the Olympian gods. And we have evidence of this in the temples, and porticoes, and sacred precincts, and groves, and colonnades which have been erected, so that all the cities put together, ancient and modern, which exhibit magnificent works, are surpassed, by the beauty and magnitude of the buildings erected in honor of Caesar, and especially by those raised in our city of Alexandria. (Philo, *On the Embassy to Gaius*, 149–50; trans. H. D. Yonge)

Not merely the phenomenon of the worship of the emperors and Roma, but the ideology of the beneficent and divinely instituted ordering of the *orbis terrarum*, the circle of the inhabited lands about the Mediterranan, through their rule is a foundational and loudly trumpeted component of the public discourse of the entire region and therefore an important backdrop for thinking about the significance of the Christian gospel, the challenges faced—and also posed—by the early Christian movement, and the ways in which the imperial cult factors into the situations addressed by the New Testament writings themselves.[310]

The cities addressed by Paul's letter to the Galatians were no exception to this enthusiasm for the Roman emperors and the cultic expression thereof. Here we focus on Pisidian Antioch, the leading city of South Galatia, though much of what is said below could also be affirmed, with slight modifications, in regard to Ancyra, the leading city of North Galatia. The Antioch that Paul knew was a revitalized Roman colony dominated architecturally and spatially by edifices related to imperial cult and the honoring of the imperial family more generally. Phrygia and Galatia came under direct Roman rule in 25 BC, united in the new Roman province of Galatia. Augustus, the then-ruling emperor, injected new life into the city by settling upwards of three thousand veterans and their families there as citizens of the newly refounded Colonia Caesarea Antiochia.

By far the most impressive structure on the modern archaeological site, as no doubt in Paul's lifetime as well, is the Augusteum, a monumental temple built to honor Augustus as a god. It was likely to have been completed by the turn of the era. The central feature was a temple with a footprint of about 85 by 50 feet. The original height of the temple has been estimated at between 45 and 55 feet. Within the temple would have sat or stood a colossal cult im-

---

310. The greatest energy and attention has been devoted to the relevance of the imperial cult for the interpretation of Revelation; see especially Friesen, *Imperial Cults and the Apocalypse of John*, 132–217; Kraybill, *Imperial Cult and Commerce*; Biguzzi, "Ephesus"; deSilva, *Seeing Things John's Way*, 93–116, 193–215, 257–84; *Unholy Allegiances*, 35–76; Frey, "Relevance of the Roman Imperial Cult." Studies covering the whole of the New Testament include Cuss, *Imperial Cult and Honorary Terms*; Winter, *Divine Honours*, with varying success in regard to particular texts.

age of Augustus. The sacred space was rendered far more impressive by the construction of a two-story semicircular portico behind the temple. Porticoes extended from the tips of the semicircle past the temple, creating an open courtyard of about 300 by 300 feet surrounding the temple. The whole was graced with ornate carvings on every horizontal face, for example, garlands and bulls reminiscent of the sacrifices performed here to honor Augustus on the twenty-third of every month, in celebration of his birthday on September 23, to express loyalty and gratitude to the emperor for his divine gifts and as the particular benefactor of this colony, and to petition the other gods, like Jupiter Best and Greatest, for the emperor's continued well-being during his lifetime. The worship of Augustus continued long after his death and his official recognition by the Senate as a god, after which it was customary to refer to him as "the Divine Augustus" in all public inscriptions.

The residents of Antioch further aggrandized this monument by constructing a massive gateway, called a Propylaeum, to the sacred area. Although almost nothing remains of this building today except for its footprint, this was originally a tall structure decorated with statues of members of the imperial family. One of these showed a male figure, perhaps Augustus himself, with a barbarian kneeling before him as a captive. Such "art" also communicated a clear message to the indigenous inhabitants around Antioch: one way or another, they would submit to Roman rule.

Civic improvements continued in this area under the reign of Tiberius, Augustus's successor. A rich citizen named Titus Baebius Asiaticus paved a large open area in front of the Propylaeum, dedicating it to Tiberius. This area functioned as a place for recreation and commerce, to judge from the shops, bars, and restaurants found surrounding the square and in close proximity. Some of the few remaining paving stones still bear game boards that had been scratched into them in antiquity. Citizens were invited to enjoy some of the benefits of the imperial peace here in the shadow of the great Augusteum complex.

One of the most important inscriptions from the Augustan period is "Res Gestae Divi Augusti" ("the things accomplished by the divine Augustus").[311] The emperor composed this text himself in the months prior to his death, intending it to be the epitaph on his life's achievement. The inscription documents his deliverance of the Roman world from civil war, his successful neutralizing of threats to the borders, his lavish benefactions upon the Roman people, the staggering number of public buildings erected at his expense (i.e., from his share in the spoils of war), his diligence in rewarding veterans, and the many public honors awarded to him on account of his virtue. Augustus

---

311. The full text in English can be found in Danker, *Benefactor*, 256–80; the Latin and an older translation can be found in F. W. Shipley, trans., *Velleius Paterculus; Res Gestae Divi Augusti*, LCL 152 (Cambridge, MA: Harvard University Press, 1924).

ordered that this lengthy document be engraved on bronze plates and placed in front of his mausoleum in Rome. A copy in both Latin and Greek was found inscribed on the ancient temples of Rome and Augustus in Ancyra (modern Ankara) and in Apollonia in Pisidia (modern Uluborlu); it was also engraved in full on the Propylaeum in front of the Augusteum in Pisidian Antioch (about a hundred pieces of this inscription were found in the area of "Tiberius Square").

Two sentences from the Res Gestae are particularly appropriate as we consider Antioch. Augustus recalls how "citizens everywhere, privately as individuals and collectively as municipalities, sacrificed unremittingly at all the shrines on behalf of my health," which included the Augusteum in Antioch and its surrounding shrines. In another place, Augustus recalls how "in Africa, Sicily, Macedonia, the two Spanish provinces, Achaia, Asia, Syria, Narbonian Gaul, and Pisidia, I settled colonies of soldiers." Pisidian Antioch was one such colony.

The prominence of the imperial cult and of the ideology of the emperors that the cult represented suggests that Paul's audience would have heard significantly political overtones in his proclamation of a son of a god who came as a savior to bring deliverance to the whole world, whose coming was "good news" ("gospel") for all people. The term "gospel" (*euangelion*) appears in imperial as well as Christian contexts. An inscription from Priene, near Ephesus in Asia Minor, looks back upon the birth of Augustus as "the beginning of good news" for the whole world.[312] Josephus uses the term to refer to the accession of Vespasian to the imperial power (*War* 4.656). It appears also in an inscription from Pergamum by a gymnasiarch honoring Augustus.[313] Augustus was lauded as *divi filius* ("son of the deified [Julius]") on coins, inscriptions, and the like, as were his own successors in relationship to him after his death and formal divinization by the Senate. He was also hailed as "Savior," as, for example, in the inscription on the Temple of Augustus and Roma on the Acropolis in Athens. What Paul calls "this present *evil* age" is celebrated as the *Golden* Age of the Augustan Peace in all manner of public discourse. Paul's message was a challenge to imperial ideology on all fronts, as would be the witness of Christians increasingly during the first three centuries of the church.

It is not surprising, therefore, to find inquiries made into the degree to which the phenomenon of imperial cult might have played a part in the

---

312. For the full text, translation, and discussion, see Danker, *Benefactor*, 215–18.

313. *IGR* 4:317; see Taylor, *Divinity of the Roman Emperor*, 275. These three known instances, however, hardly justify claiming that the word "was *often* used in contexts dealing with imperial good news (e.g., the birthdays, victories, and health of the emperors)" (Hardin, *Imperial Cult*, 139; emphasis mine).

situation addressed by Galatians. To what extent did local pressures to participate in the imperial cult's calendar of festivals weigh on the gentile Christians
in Galatia? Was circumcision an attractive possibility because it would clarify their status in the community as full proselytes to Judaism and therefore
exempt them from participation in the worship of the emperors and other
iconic rites in which gentiles typically engaged? Jews were allowed to demonstrate their loyalty to the emperor in ways appropriate to their historic commitment to henotheism.[314] In Jerusalem, sacrifices were offered in the temple
on behalf of the emperor, rather than *to* the emperor in his own temple. Only
Caligula challenged the practice, but he was—in all respects—an aberration.
Diaspora Jews enjoyed the covering, as it were, provided by the rites in their
central temple, though they also honored the emperors in their synagogues
with inscriptions and other aniconic honors, as well as, no doubt, prayers on
behalf of the rulers.[315] Were the rival teachers in fact motivated to promote
circumcision among the gentile converts to the Christian movement out of a
desire to preserve a uniformly Jewish face to the movement and thus simplify
the movement's relationship to this ubiquitous cult?

The early Christian movement was fairly adamant in regard to promoting nonparticipation in the cults of the traditional gods and, indeed, any other
gods besides the God of Israel. Gentile converts to the movement would have
realigned their practice in ways that would have provoked a considerable
amount of peer pressure from their non-Christian neighbors to return to their
former *pious* practice. Nevertheless, it seems highly unlikely that they have
returned to observing any of the rites on the pagan religious calendars at the
time of Paul's writing, including imperial cult festivals.[316] The rival teachers,

---

314. Although Hardin's discussion (*Imperial Cult*, 102–14) of the forms of honor shown
the emperor by the Jewish people in various locales is generally quite solid, it blurs the
distinctions too much to say that "Jews did not have special exemption from observing the
imperial cult, but in fact were active participants *along with Gentiles*" (110, emphasis mine).
No Torah-observant Jew would have been an active participant *along with* a gentile, for the
gentiles participated in some form of idolatrous rite as part of their observance of the imperial cult. Jews were "active participants" in their own, carefully qualified and restricted ways
and also off on their own rather than alongside their neighbors in the latter's rites. It is also
appropriate to ask whether the Jews' displays of loyalty and gratitude constitute imperial
cult rather than political honors that could in no way be understood by the participants or
observers as *worship*.

315. See the fine discussion of Jewish displays of loyalty both in Israel and throughout
the diaspora, as well as imperial responses to the same, in Winter, *Divine Honours*, 94–114.

316. Hardin (*Imperial Cult*, 120) claims that "Paul does not actually employ any Jewish terms" when speaking of the religious calendar of festivals to which the Galatians have
begun to return. However, the unmistakable resonance with Gen 1:14 in Gal 4:10, which
Hardin discusses only briefly in a footnote, seems far more significant here than he allows.
Paul directly recalls God's own purposes in setting sun and moon in the heavens, namely, to

being committed to the Torah in all its particulars, would have opposed such practice as adamantly as Paul.

It has been argued that concerns over the imperial cult nevertheless motivated the rival teachers to urge, even constrain (to the extent possible), the gentile converts in these cities to accept circumcision. If all the males among the Christian groups were circumcised, the groups would enjoy the same toleration as the synagogue, since they would also clearly identify themselves as *Jewish* groups. According to this view, the persecution that the rival teachers seek to avoid (6:12b) comes from local Roman authorities.[317] The boast that Paul imagines the rival teachers making in Gal 6:13, however, could be made only before a Jewish court of reputation; no other group would give honor to Jews who talked gentiles into undergoing what was, in their eyes, a disgusting body modification procedure. It is before their fellow Jews that Paul accuses the rival teachers of wanting to "look good" (6:12a) by their actions among gentiles in the (renegade Jewish) Christian movement (6:12).[318] Jewish Christians who meet together are not legally endangered by the presence of uncircumcised gentiles in their midst; such gentiles are to be found, in admit-

---

provide guidance for the observance of particular rites. Paul *must* have Jewish rites in mind, as he would never attribute pagan ritual calendars to God's intentions. And while Paul is not hostile to the Jewish calendar in other contexts (Hardin, *Imperial Cult*, 120–21), this is no evidence against reading Gal 4:10 as Paul taking the Galatian converts to task for adopting these observances *as part of the package* of aligning oneself with the Torah as the means of attaining righteousness and entering into "life" before God. Hardin (141) is correct that, "far from being a Christian ghetto with no pressures from society, the Galatian Jesus-believers were forced to negotiate their obligations in society vis-à-vis the imperial cult." This fact does not, however, provide any evidence that they are succumbing to *those* particular pressures at this time.

317. Winter (*Divine Honours*, 243–49; *Seeking the Welfare*, 137–40) asserts that the rival teachers' "wanting to show a good face in the flesh" (6:12) means "wanting to secure a good *legal* face or standing." Such an interpretation, however, essentially requires mapping one set of meanings of the Greek word "face" (πρόσωπον), which apparently does carry legal connotations in the idiom "have face" (πρόσωπον ἔχειν), over the meanings of words belonging to the εὐπρόσωπος word group, which tends to denote a pleasing appearance and, by extension, a specious concern with outward appearances (LSJ 728). This basic lexical fallacy is to be avoided. The interpretation also leaves aside the important qualifier "in the flesh."

318. One reason that Winter (*Divine Honours*, 244) rejects the typical meaning of εὐπροσωπῆσαι ("to make a fair showing") here is that he finds it "difficult to see how the outcome of circumcision could ever have been construed as a 'fair show' in the flesh with the male genital organ bereft of its adorning foreskin." The difficulty remains only because he never questions his decision about the panel of judges that would be making this determination, namely, Greeks or Romans; he also subtly shifts the subject of what is going to "look good" from the rival teachers (those who actually hope to improve their reputation) to the penis, which is a bit of rhetorical sleight of hand as he does not retain this shift in his own interpretation—merely using it to discredit the traditional view.

tedly smaller numbers, in the synagogues as well. Indeed, the full proselytization of gentiles tended, throughout the first century and beyond, to *invite* rather than *alleviate* negative attention from Roman authorities, resulting in expulsion from Rome on at least one occasion.[319] The practice of circumcising gentiles would come to be subjected to severe, restrictive legislation in the period after Hadrian.[320] It still makes better sense, therefore, to regard the persecution that the rival teachers seek to avoid also to come from a Jewish quarter. The agitators seek to turn a cause for persecution into a boast before the same court of opinion: non-Christian Jews.[321]

Paul's gospel challenged Roman imperial ideology by clearly rejecting the dominant culture's claims on behalf of Augustus's achievement and by telling an alternative story of universal rescue by a different Son of God and Savior. Gentile Christian practice challenged Roman imperial ideology by withdrawing from former cultic displays of loyalty and gratitude toward *all* the Greco-Roman gods, including the divinized emperors. Gentile Christians would face increasing pressure from their neighbors and, eventually, local and imperial authorities because of this withdrawal. In the early second century, Pliny the Younger, governor of Bithynia and Pontus in northern Turkey, would require of Christians that they offer wine and incense to the statues of the emperor Trajan and the traditional gods or else suffer execution (or detention for further trial in Rome). Nevertheless, in their burgeoning awareness of this background, interpreters run the risk of seeing the imperial cult and the ideology of Rome and her emperors as the focal issue behind *every* text on the slimmest of evidence.

---

319. See Tacitus, *Annals* 2.85; Josephus, *Antiquities* 18.65, 81–85; Suetonius, *Tiberius* 36, all of which treat the expulsion of Jews under Tiberius in connection with the purging of Rome of religious practices deemed infectious superstition.

320. Winter, *Divine Honours*, 231–32.

321. Das (636) decisively and rightly concludes: "Paul, for his part, does not mention the emperor cult as a factor in the rivals' or the Galatians' motivations. He never alludes to any pressure on the gentiles from the governing authorities. He never mentions other gentiles at Galatia who might be pressuring the Christ-believers. Throughout Galatians, persecution always derives from Jewish groups or communities, and never from pagan communities or the government (see 1:13, 23 [Paul himself!]; 4:29; 5:11; cf. 2 Cor 11:24–25)."

V. A RELATIONAL APPEAL (4:12-20)

12 *I beg you, brothers and sisters, become like me, because I myself became like you. You injured me in no way.* 13 *And you know that I originally proclaimed the message of good news to you on account of a sickness of the flesh,* 14 *and you neither scorned nor spat*[a] *in response to the trial you*[b] *endured in my flesh, but rather you received me as an angel from God, even as Christ Jesus.* 15 *What happened, then, to your earlier pronouncement that I was a person specially favored by God? For I bear you witness that, if it were possible, you would have dug out your eyes and given them to me.* 16 *So then, have I become your enemy by being truthful with you?* 17 *They are not courting you with noble intent, but they desire to shut you out in order that you might begin courting them.* 18 *It is always a noble thing to be courted with noble intentions, and not only while I am present with you.* 19 *My children, with whom I am again in labor pains until Christ takes shape in you:* 20 *I have been wishing that I could be present with you even now and change my tone, because I am at a loss where you're concerned!*

a. 𝔓⁴⁶ omits οὐδὲ ἐξεπτύσατε, "nor did you spit," probably as an oversight.

b. A number of MSS read τὸν πειρασμόν μου ("the trial *I* endured," 𝔓⁴⁶; μου τὸν πειρασμόν, C*vid D¹ Ψ 𝔐 *pm*) in place of τὸν πειρασμὸν ὑμῶν, probably from the difficulty of making sense of how the Galatians could experience "trial" in *Paul's* flesh (Comfort, *New Testament Text*, 568). ὑμῶν is well supported by early and reliable manuscripts (ℵ* A B C² D* F G 33) and best explains the other variants. Paul is calling attention to the burden his physical condition made him to the Galatians ("*your* trial in my flesh"). On either reading, Paul acknowledges that his physical condition could have made the Galatians reject and despise him.

Having shared his deeply personal fear that his work among them may prove to be all for nothing (4:11), Paul continues to write in a more personal vein throughout this next paragraph, returning to the task of supporting his cause with appeals to ethos and pathos (specifically invoking feelings of friendship, shame, and indignation). He purposefully recalls his former connection with the Galatians, forged during his earlier time with them, and adds the weight of this connection to the force of his reasoning in 2:14–4:11. Remembering the "good old days" in their relationship before the rival teachers came along, nosing their way in to break up the relationship to their own advantage, also allows him to rouse hostile feelings toward, and undermine the credibility of, those who have broken in with self-serving intent.

After much argument, Paul here begins to turn to explicit exhortation: what should the Galatians *do* in light of all that Paul has said in 2:14–4:11? In this paragraph, the answer emerges first in relational terms: the Galatians should continue to remain steadfast in their relationship with Paul and move forward along the path on which he set them (rather than allow themselves to be talked into a detour—or, perhaps more accurately, waylaid—by others).

The material here will be reinforced by further assaults on the rival teachers' credibility, affirmations of Paul's own reliability, and attempts to arouse strategic emotions in 5:7–12 and 6:11–18. Paul's lack of concern for following formal rhetorical structures too closely is incidentally revealed in the fact that he will return to logical argumentation in the form of the interpretation of authoritative Scripture once again in 4:21–31 before continuing his appeal to the Galatian converts to take decisive action in regard to their situation.

12 Paul makes his first direct appeal to the Galatian Christians at this point: "I beg you, brothers and sisters, become like me, because I myself became like you," adding that "you injured me in no way." After an expression of exasperation (4:10–11), Paul does indeed "change his tone" (4:20), addressing them afresh as "brothers and sisters," using a term of connection and kinship strategically once again to foster the same. His appeal here is both cryptic and terse. In the Greek, one readily sees that Paul has elided several words that he would expect his hearers to supply ("Become as I, because I also as you").[1] The effect of the elision, however, is to foreground the reciprocal exchange for which Paul calls.[2]

Paul occasionally sets himself forward as a positive example of discipleship to be imitated, particularly insofar as he successfully imitates Jesus (1 Cor 11:1; Phil 3:17). Here Paul has emphasized not his own imitation of Jesus but his correct understanding and application of two facts: (1) the significance of Jesus's death and the gift of the Spirit for his relationship to the Torah, which formerly kept Jews separate from the gentiles, whom God was now also calling to be God's people (Gal 2:14–18); (2) the genuinely transforming gift of God received by trusting (2:19–21). The imperative "become" commends Paul's stance to his converts as one that is to become habitual and persistent among them as well.[3]

Paul's becoming like the Galatians is the result of what he himself became: a person who understood that the term of Torah's authority had come to an end and that God was now reaching back in fulfillment of his promise to Abraham to bring people from all nations together into his family as they joined themselves to the Seed, the Messiah, by faith. Ethnicity was a line to be crossed for the sake of serving this vision, not a boundary to be maintained. What Paul means here is perhaps best illumined by his later statement in 1 Cor 9:20b–21: "To those under Torah I became as one under Torah, though not

---

1. The initial ἐγώ governs an unstated εἰμί; κἀγώ is the nominative subject of an implied γέγονα or ἐγενόμην; and ὑμεῖς the nominative subject of an implied ἐστε: "Become as I [am], because I [became] as you [are]."

2. "Y'all [-εσθε] as I [ἐγώ] because I too [κἀγώ] as y'all [ὑμεῖς]."

3. Paul employs the present tense imperative Γίνεσθε; its continuative aspect communicates not merely "become" (as would an aorist imperaitve) but "engage in the process of becoming" or perhaps "become and continue to be."

being myself under Torah, in order that I might win those under Torah. To those without Torah, I became as one without the Torah—not being without God's Torah but rather keeping within Christ's law—in order that I might win those without Torah."[4]

Paul went to the gentiles on their turf and on their terms, interacting and eating freely with them, all to share Christ and to demonstrate what it now meant that God was bringing Jews and gentiles alike into God's new people in Christ. His example was the polar opposite of the practice of the "men from James" who had gone to Antioch, whose behavior proclaimed to the gentile Christians there: "become as we are, if unity is important to you, because we're certainly not going to become as you are" (see commentary on 2:14).[5] Paul was willing to behave like someone who was dead to the Torah (2:19)—to count himself as a "former Jew," in effect—for the sake of connecting the gentile Galatians with their inheritance in Christ. He calls here for some reciprocity from his converts (explicitly in the "because"). They too should consider themselves dead to the Torah, as well as to any and all *stoicheia tou kosmou* for the sake of holding onto that inheritance, and for the sake of remaining true to their good friend who had so well and so genuinely served their interests during his earlier times with them.

The focus has already moved to how Paul approached the Galatians when he first came to them ("becoming as they were"); he now begins to move more fully in that direction, beginning by affirming that they did him no injury.[6] Paul may be making this claim with more limited reference to

---

4. Each instance of "Torah" here is represented in the Greek by the word νόμος, which simply means "law." Paul clearly has a particular legal code in mind here, however—namely, the Mosaic law, the Torah, which created the distinct identities of these two groups in the first place.

5. The Galatians might hear an echo of this verse in 4:17, where Paul will accuse the rival teachers of courting (another connotation would be "being emulous of") the Galatians in order that the Galatians might, in the end, court ("be emulous of") the rival teachers. The direction in which one's emulation is focused is crucial: the Galatians should direct theirs toward Paul and continue to be "as he is" insofar as that focus leads to becoming as Christ is, and not toward the rival teachers, who are zealous for the Galatians to the latter's harm.

6. Reading οὐδέν as an accusative of respect or extent ("you injured me in no respect" or "in no way"). Das (451) offers a novel reading of this verse based on repunctuating: "Become as I [am], because I—inasmuch as you [are] brothers (and sisters)—am not requesting anything of you. You wronged me." Against the first part of his rereading, ὡς ἐγώ and ὡς ὑμεῖς are clearly meant to be heard as parallel elements, a parallelism Das destroys. For Paul allegedly not to request anything of the Galatians, moreover, hardly provides a motive for them to become as he is. His good observation that the Galatians had, in fact, done Paul wrong might suggest that we consider taking the traditional "you did me no wrong" rather as a question: "did you not wrong me?" But then the aorist tense seems less natural than a present tense, "are you not wronging me?" The old is indeed better here, with Paul deliber-

that earlier period in which they received him graciously and responded to him warmly, as he will go on to relate (4:13–14). It might also be heard as a blanket dismissal on Paul's part of any injury, even though the Galatians are clearly doing him wrong at the moment by giving greater credence to the rival teachers and departing from his teaching. Paul would be offering amnesty, as it were, with a view to facilitating reconciliation by showing them that he bears them no ill will and that nothing stands in the way of their resuming their devoted friendship in the gospel.

13–14 Paul takes a step forward by introducing further background material:[7] "And you know that I originally proclaimed the message of good news to you on account of a sickness of the flesh, and you neither scorned nor spat in response to the trial you endured in my flesh, but rather you received me as an angel from God, even as Christ Jesus." As we have explored already in the Introduction, Paul recalls his first visit to the Galatians quite differently from any accounts of Paul's activity in Galatia (whether South or North) in Acts.[8] But Paul's is a firsthand remembrance of that evangelistic visit, the details of which are therefore likely to be far more reliable than those reconstructed by Luke several decades later (all the more as Paul expects his audience's memory to corroborate his recollections).

Paul suggests that it was not his plan to spend time in the region of Galatia at all. Perhaps it had been his original intent to go directly to the major centers of Asia (e.g., Ephesus) and Greece, from which he expected the word to spread in all directions, including back into less-developed Galatia. Paul's body, however, did not cooperate. The word translated "sickness" (another possibility would be "weakness") suggests an illness or other physical condition that halted Paul's westward progress.[9] There is no way of knowing the nature of Paul's illness or infirmity, though there has been no shortage of theories. We only know that it slowed him down considerably. Paul, however, turned an annoying setback into an opportunity for proclaiming the gospel.[10] Finding the people in Galatia receptive, he changed

---

ately denying any wrongdoing—more to the point, showing that he holds nothing against them—so as to facilitate reconciliation.

7. Paul signals this intention with the particle δέ.

8. Paul refers to this evangelistic visit as τὸ πρότερον, meaning either "the first" (i.e., original) visit or "the former" visit of two or more such visits. Reading τὸ πρότερον in the second sense contributes nothing to resolving the "North versus South Galatia" debate, as paired visits are envisioned in both Acts 13:13–14:28 and Acts 16:6; 18:23 (though the latter is by no means clearly a journey through *North* Galatia). Moulton and Milligan (*Vocabulary*, 554) have also established, based on their study of Roman-period papyri, that τὸ πρότερον could simply carry the looser meaning "originally" or "previously."

9. Hafemann, "Role of Suffering," 168–70; Schreiner, 286; Matera, 159.

10. Mussner, 307; compare Paul's attitude about his imprisonment in Phil 1:12–14.

his plans so as to spend more significant time in the southern cities of that province.

Paul's physical condition was such that he might have expected the Galatians to turn away from him in contempt and reject anything he might have had to say. Bodily ailment or disability could be interpreted as a sign of divine displeasure or as shameful defect, and therefore "despised."[11] How could a person who was so obviously *not* enjoying the favor and protection of the gods (indeed, appearing more as one who endured their disfavor) claim to be speaking on behalf of one of them? What kind of spiritual power could he have, or could this Christ give, if Paul, Christ's ambassador, could not gain the upper hand over his own sickness or infirmity? Or perhaps he had himself been overcome by the evil spirits by means of which he worked his magic?[12] The Galatians might have "spat" at the sight of Paul (pretending to speak on behalf of some deity), whether as the result of pure contempt[13] or as an attempt to ward off the ill effects of the spell, bad luck, or other magical contagion Paul was clearly carrying.[14]

While the Galatians would have had several culturally conditioned reasons for despising Paul, they did not let his condition—or the evident inconveniences it caused them ("the testing you endured in my flesh")[15]—stand in their way of hearing the gospel and warmly embracing its messenger. So enthusiastic, indeed, was their response, as Paul recalls it, that he likens it to the kind of response they might have shown had an angel from God[16] or even Christ Jesus himself appeared in their midst to announce the good news of God's acceptance. At that time at least, they indeed did not wrong him in any regard (4:12b).

Paul was aware throughout his ministry of the need to allow his hearers to encounter not just a persuasive speaker but the very power of God. He did not want anyone's faith to rest on the strengths of the human messenger, but on the experience of the living God and God's Spirit:

---

11. See Savage, *Power through Weakness*, 19–53; also Fung, 198.

12. Martyn, 421.

13. The two verbs ("despising" and "spitting") are also used synonymously in Joseph and Aseneth 2.1: "Now Aseneth despised [ἐξουθενοῦσα] all men and regarded them with contempt [καταπτύουσα]" (OTP).

14. See BDAG 309; Hafemann, "Role of Suffering," 173; Schreiner, 287. Theocritus (*Idyll* 6.39) has his character Polyphemus, having aroused Galatea to jealousy, spit three times into his breast to ward off the ill effects of the evil eye (discussed in Zimmerman, *Pastoral Narcissus*, 45–46). See also Pliny, *Natural History* 28.7 §§36, 39).

15. Reading ὑμῶν as an objective genitive ("your test" = "the testing of you," "the testing you endured").

16. Reading θεοῦ as a genitive of source. A superhuman emissary (an "angel") is probably intended (cf. 1:8), not merely a messenger.

> When I came to you, brothers and sisters, I announced God's mystery to you not with flowery speech or rhetoric, for I decided to know nothing among you except Jesus Christ—and him crucified. I was among you in weakness and apprehension and great fear, and my speech and my proclamation was not executed with well-crafted and strategic words, but with a demonstration of Spirit and power in order that your trust might not be grounded in the cleverness of human beings but in God's power. (1 Cor 2:1–5)

> We do not announce ourselves, but we announce Jesus Christ as Lord and ourselves as your slaves on Jesus's account. The God who said "let light shine out of darkness" shone his light into our hearts to shed abroad the light of the knowledge of God's glory in the face of Christ. But we have this treasure in clay pots, in order that the abundance of power might be God's and not our own. (2 Cor 4:5–7)

God showing up to work wonders and to send his Spirit into the hearts of those in Galatia who heard the weak and ailing Paul (Gal 3:1–5; 4:6–7) was very much in line with what would become Paul's conscious philosophy of evangelism and ministry.[17]

15 The experience of the Holy Spirit showed the Galatians that, appearances notwithstanding, Paul's God was powerful indeed and that Paul was a divinely favored messenger. Paul now holds before them the gulf between the way they received and embraced him formerly and the way they are now allowing themselves to come under the spell of teachers who are taking them in a different direction from the course he originally set out for them: "What happened, then, to your earlier pronouncement that I was a person specially favored by God? For I bear you witness that, if it were possible, you would have dug out your eyes and given them to me."

In the context of this question, the word "then" calls the Galatians to account for the logic behind an apparently illogical step. What could possibly account for the Galatians' inexplicable change of stance toward the apostle they had so recently and so fully favored? Aristotle defines the kind of pronouncement alleged by Paul to have been made by the Galatians as one that acknowledges a person or group to be "divinely favored," "privileged," "honored."[18] This kind of pronouncement is common throughout Scripture, seen throughout the Psalms, the Prophets, and New Testament, wherever

---

17. See deSilva, *Introduction to the New Testament*, 586–89; Martyn, 421.

18. Aristotle, *Rhetoric* 1.9.34, on the μακαρισμός. See further deSilva, *Seeing Things John's Way*, 274–76; so also Fung, 198 ("an act of declaring or counting as blessed or happy"); BDAG 611.

someone or some group of people are pronounced "blessed." The Galatians formerly pronounced Paul to be "divinely blessed" and therefore worthy of their attention and embrace.[19] It is an expression of the high esteem in which they once held Paul.

Paul offers solemn testimony ("I bear witness") as evidence for the Galatians' former stance toward him, and thus *against* the logic of their current aloofness from him. Their former regard for and attachment to him was so great that, were it possible,[20] they would have been willing to pluck out their own eyes for him. The eyes were often spoken of as the most precious part of the body, and so Paul's graphic image here is a reminder to them of how much they cared for and esteemed Paul (rather than a clue that his own eyes were the source of his troubles).[21] Paul is referring to a proverbial saying along the lines of such modern expressions as "he'd give his right arm for me."[22] This reminder might indeed serve to make the Galatians feel ashamed of how they have proven less than reliable in their relationship with Paul, once wholly devoted and now entertaining second thoughts about him and his reliability as God's messenger.

16 What, he asks, had he done to change their opinion of him? Paul's rhetorical question is in fact a strident claim that he has given them *no* cause: "So then,[23] have I become your enemy by being truthful[24] with you?" The "truth of the gospel" has been a prominent topic in Galatians, and Paul has

---

19. See Fung, 198. Since Paul had just been speaking about the Galatians' regard for him and the awestruck reception they gave him, and since he will continue in the following verse to focus on their perception of him (now as enemy rather than friend?), understanding ὁ μακαρισμὸς ὑμῶν as "your act of pronouncing [me] favored" (taking ὑμῶν as a subjective genitive; so also Das, 465) seems far more likely than reading it as a reference to the Galatians' own former state of "being blessed," a state that has now come to an end (Longenecker, 192; ESV) or the view that the Galatians pronounced *themselves* privileged or favored (BDAG 611; Burton, 243; Bruce, 210)

20. The parenthetical remark εἰ δυνατόν acknowledges the hyperbolic nature of what Paul is here about to express.

21. John Chrysostom (32) essentially understands the saying in this manner ("counting me more precious than your own eyes"). See also Fung, 199; Longenecker, 193; Martyn, 421; Bruce, 210; contra Witherington, 309–10.

22. Das, 466; Betz, 228; Longenecker, 193. Lucian in the second century AD narrates a story that reflects the cultural assumptions behind Paul's figurative expression (*Toxaris* §§40–41). In it, Dandamis managed to negotiate the release of his friend Amizoces from captivity by sacrificing his own eyes. Amizoces was so moved by the gesture that he had his own eyes removed as well.

23. The conjunction ὥστε typically introduces a result clause, here in a question with the force of "So, then?"

24. Taking the adverbial participle ἀληθεύων as communicating the (ironic) means by which Paul has alienated the Galatian Christians.

maintained that he has consistently spoken and acted in line with this truth (2:5, 14). He defended it in the course of the developing Christian mission so as to preserve it for the Galatians, and he brought this truth to the Galatians, but the rival teachers appear to have called Paul's message and motives into question, perhaps suggesting that he was not such a good friend to the Galatians after all, withholding the critical information about the ongoing authority of Torah and circumcision as the seal of the covenant.[25]

Paul has by this point spent several chapters demonstrating that he did indeed proclaim the true message of God's actions in Christ, recalling twice the Galatian converts' own experience of acceptance by God in their receiving God's Holy Spirit as the divine witness to the genuineness of his message (3:1–5; 4:6–7). On this basis he asks indignantly how he can be considered now to be their enemy,[26] as if he did not have their best interests at heart and did not deal truthfully with them about God's plan for their inclusion in God's family. If anyone should be treated like an enemy in this situation, it is not Paul but the rival teachers, as Paul goes on immediately to assert in the following verse.

The frank speech of the letter itself is also an indirect witness to Paul's commitment to speak the truth, as is proper for friends to do, seeking always that which will benefit one's friends (however difficult) rather than taking the easier path of withholding difficult truths or even flattering them to their harm.[27] Even as Paul upbraids the Galatian Christians (3:1–5; 4:8–11), he is speaking sincerely as a friend.

17 Paul accuses the rival teachers of showing interest in the Galatian Christians out of selfish motives: "they are not courting you with noble intent, but they desire to shut you outside in order that you might begin courting them." The Greek verb translated here "courting" belongs to a word group whose forms frequently named the feeling of emulation, admiring someone with a view to imitating them and acquiring thereby the good reputation or success that they had also enjoyed.[28] Here, however, the verb carries more the sense of "making a big deal of someone," "showing earnest interest in someone," hence "courting."[29] It is used to speak both of the behavior of men

---

25. Martyn, 420.

26. The verse could also be read as an indignant exclamation: "So, then, I have become your enemy by telling you the truth!" (Burton, 245; Longenecker, 193).

27. See the discussion in Plutarch, "How to Tell a Flatterer from a Friend" 1–2, 5 (*Moralia* 48E–49B, 50B, 51C–D).

28. See Aristotle's discussion of the emotion of ζῆλος (the noun form of the verb ζηλόω, used here) in *Rhetoric* 2.11.1–7.

29. LSJ 755; Martyn, 422. Paul uses the verb also in this sense in 2 Cor 11:2, where he presents himself as courting the Corinthian Christians on behalf of Christ, wishing to present them to Christ as a pure bride.

and women amorously pursuing one another and, by figurative extension, of the relationship of teachers and students (both of the teachers' quest for followers and of followers' attachment to their teachers).[30] Paul alleges that the rival teachers are showing a great deal of interest in the Galatians, but not to the latter's advantage. Instead, the rival teachers' goal is to "exclude" the Galatians—to shut them back outside of the people of promise (i.e., by convincing them that, as gentiles, they have no place in the people of God) so that the Galatians will be put in the position of trying to reenter the people of promise by courting the rival teachers and becoming their followers.[31] The rival teachers' actions represent the antithesis of Paul's own, a contrast implicitly supported by the parallelism between 12 and 17.[32]

18 Paul takes a step forward in his argument by quoting what appears to be a proverbial saying: "It is always a noble thing to be courted with noble intentions, and not only while I am present with you."[33] The prepositional phrase translated "with noble intentions" could indicate the manner of the courting, hence "in a noble way,"[34] in contrast to the courting in which the rival teachers are engaged ("*not* nobly," 4:17). It could also indicate the direction of the courting, hence "toward a noble end," "for the good."[35] "With

---

30. Bruce, 212; BDAG 427; Longenecker, 193–94; Plutarch, *Moral Virtue* (*Moralia* 448E).

31. The focus of the rival teachers' (alleged) goal of "shutting the Galatians out" is not on alienating the Galatian Christians from Paul (contra Longenecker, 193–94; Tolmie, *Persuading*, 161; NIV, NLT), but on alienating them from the people of promise (rightly, Burton, 246; Martyn, 423; NRSV, ESV, CEB).

32. Compare "Become as I, because I also [became] as you" (Γίνεσθε ὡς ἐγώ, ὅτι κἀγὼ ὡς ὑμεῖς) with "They are courting you . . . in order that you might court them" (ζηλοῦσιν ὑμᾶς . . . ἵνα αὐτοὺς ζηλοῦτε).

33. Burton, 247; Betz, 230; Witherington, 313. Longenecker (194; also Lappenga, *Paul's Language*, 124) translates this maxim as "good is always to be courted in a good way," taking καλόν as the subject of the infinitive ζηλοῦσθαι. While this translation is not impossible, the opening καλόν is far more likely to have been heard as part of an impersonal verbless clause ("it is good" or "it is a noble thing"), with καλόν and αἰσχρόν being very common openings for maxims or other statements coordinating some attitude or behavior with the "noble" and the "shameful," the primary axis of value in the Hellenistic-Roman world (for examples with αἰσχρόν, see, 4 Macc 6:20; 16:17; 1 Cor 14:35; with καλόν, LXX Prov 17:26; 18:5; 24:23; Matt 18:8–9; 26:24; Luke 9:33; 1 Cor 7:1, 8, 26). Additionally, if Paul had meant for καλόν to be heard as the subject of the infinitive, he would likely have introduced it with the article, τὸ καλόν, as in 6:9 (against Lappenga, *Paul's Language*, 124, I regard the presence of the article in 6:9 as a mark of *differentiation* on Paul's part, not an indication that he uses καλόν with or without the article indiscriminately).

34. BDAG 330; Lappenga, *Paul's Language*, 124.

35. See BDAG 327; Schreiner, 283. One would typically expect the prepositions εἰς or πρός rather than ἐν, but the last can indicate movement toward a goal that is understood to lie *within* a particular space or condition.

noble intentions" seeks to preserve the ambiguity (and perhaps a double meaning).

Paul indirectly affirms that such "courting" happened for the Galatian converts while Paul was present with them, wooing them to the genuine gospel, intending to facilitate the full formation of Christ within them (4:19),[36] making himself available, in turn, as a model for emulation that would lead them in the right direction (unlike the rival teachers' courting, the goal of which is to lead the Galatian Christians in an ignoble direction vis-à-vis the grace God has shown them in Christ). It would be a good thing, Paul affirms here more directly, for them also to have been "nobly courted" in his absence. Paul would not have objected had the other teachers who followed him worked for the Galatians' good, advancing God's interests (cf. 1 Cor 3:4–15; Phil 1:15–18).[37] His annoyance at the rival teachers does not spring merely from jealousy or an awareness that his "turf" has been violated. In Paul's absence, the rival teachers courted his converts with a self-interested agenda (and a false gospel). Paul's indirect affirmation may also suggest, however, that in his absence he is *still* courting the Galatians with noble intentions, unlike the rival teachers who are now present among them. Paul is here already heading in the direction of Gal 4:20, where he will express the wish to be present with them again,[38] since they seem to be having difficulty maintaining their direction in his absence.[39]

19 Paul's noble intentions for courting the Galatians are clearly stated in 4:19: he has sought from the outset that Christ take shape in them, that they be transformed fully into the image of Christ, God's righteous one: "My children, with whom I am again in labor pains until Christ takes shape in you!" Syntactically, this verse could be taken either as a continuation of the preceding verse[40] or as an introduction to the verse that follows.

Paul expresses clearly here the essential formational element of justification, namely, God's desire to restore his image within us by conforming

---

36. Fung, 202.

37. Martyn, 423; Matera, 161.

38. Note the repetition of the infinitive παρεῖναι, "to be present," in both 4:18 and 4:20.

39. An alternative reading that merits consideration is that Paul is here drawing a contrast not between the rival teachers' courting of the Galatians and his own, but the Galatians' emulation of the rival teachers ("in order that you might be zealous for them," 4:17) and their former emulation of Paul, such as their initial welcome and honoring of Paul presaged (4:14–15). See Lappenga, *Paul's Language*, 118–40 for a discussion of the history of the two views and a case in favor of the latter, though in my view the former leads naturally to the latter (as 4:12 and 4:17b suggest in this context).

40. "It is a fine thing always to be courted to a noble end, and not only while I am present with you, my children, with whom I am again in labor pains until Christ takes shape in you!"

us to the likeness of Jesus, his Son, the perfect human bearer of that image. In this process of transformation, we *become* righteous (hence, are justified, brought into alignment with God's standards and heart) as we *become* more like God's Son, who comes to life within the believer by the action of the Holy Spirit. Whether Paul speaks of Christ taking shape in and among the believers (4:19) or of Christ living in the believer (2:20) or of believers being shaped into Christ's likeness (as in Phil 3:8–11; 2 Cor 3:18), such transformation is the passionate heart of Paul's gospel and theology.[41]

Paul's passion for seeing this transformation continue unimpeded in his converts' individual and collective lives comes through clearly in the images he chooses in order to communicate the pitch of his emotional and personal investment in the process. Calling the hearers his children, Paul claims to be "again in labor pains until Christ takes shape in you" (4:19). Although he usually addresses his converts as brothers and sisters, Paul occasionally addresses them as his children when he wants to draw attention to the fact that he has been the active agent—their "spiritual father"—in bringing them to the new birth of the faith (e.g., see 1 Cor 4:15; Phlm 10). Here, however, the role of the father simply does not suffice. Such is his personal investment in, and his anguish over, the successful "birth" of the Galatians into the new life of Christ that he identifies more with mothers in labor, "who because of their labor pains have a deeper sympathy toward their offspring than do fathers" (4 Macc 15:1).[42] Paul's metaphor is somewhat more complex, however, since ultimately it is Christ who is the one being born ("taking shape") in the midst of the Galatian community, and so Paul is casting the Galatian Christian community itself as a kind of womb, in whom—individually and collectively—Christ, like the fetus, is taking shape.[43] The image of Paul's "birthing" the Galatian church, whose members are thereby his children, is meant to evoke strong reciprocal emotions in the hearers, even as it reveals Paul's deep feelings for and investment in them. The work of the rival teachers has put this process of formation in jeopardy, and Paul is in anguish to get his converts back on track.

The formation of Christ in the believer is not to be reduced to a sharing, on the part of the believer, in the faith of Christ and the concomitant abandonment of relying on works of the law.[44] The Christian, in Paul's view, does

---

41. See also Martyn, 425, 430–31; deSilva, *Transformation*, 10–14, 44–66.

42. The idea of being in labor pains a second time to "give birth to children for immortality" appears in 4 Macc 16:13, where a mother endures watching her seven sons tortured to death—even spurring them on to continue to resist the tyrant, despite the heart-wrenching grief it causes her—as a second round of labor pains to give them "rebirth for immortality." On Paul as a mother figure, see Gaventa, "Our Mother St. Paul"; Gaventa, "Maternity of Paul."

43. Longenecker, 195; Schlier, 214.

44. Contra Hooker, "ΠΙΣΤΙΣ ΧΡΙΣΤΟΥ," 342.

not reject the works of the Torah simply to rely on "faith alone" (whether Christ's or his or her own). Rather, the Christian relies on that which faith has allowed him or her to receive—the Holy Spirit, which is truly that which stands in contrast with Torah in Galatians, and not "faith." "Faith in Jesus Christ" is an abbreviated expression for "relying on that which trusting Jesus has brought to the one who trusts," namely, the actual benefits of Christ's passion, death, and resurrection. In Galatians, the most fully foregrounded of these benefits is the Holy Spirit, that divine, indwelling gift who empowers the recipient for, and guides the recipient into, a life of righteousness, that is, conformity with the righteous demands of the God who will judge the living and the dead. Paul expresses this end result more eloquently as "Christ living in me" (2:20) or "Christ [being] fully formed in you" (4:19).

20 This anguish, Paul confesses, has led to the severity of his tone throughout the letter from the outset (e.g., 1:6; 3:1–5; 4:11): "I have been wishing that I could be present with you even now and change my tone, because I am at a loss where you're concerned!" The tense of the verb "I have been wishing" suggests ongoing action in some past time;[45] Paul indicates at this point in his letter that he has been wishing to be able to deal differently with his dear friends in Galatia for some time prior to getting to this point in his harsh letter. This tone—and the developments in the situation that have led to his taking this tone in the first place—is not what Paul would have chosen. He has, however, just communicated quite clearly in the preceding verse where his annoyance, angst, and anger come from: he believes that the formation of Christ within them and in their midst is in jeopardy of being stalled, even stillborn, and he is in anguish over that possibility. Paul's perplexity concerning the Galatians is also the cause of his desire to be present with them (and thus to learn the facts more clearly and intervene more directly), with the implied hope that such direct intervention would lessen his anxiety about them, prove the matter not to be so dire, hasten correction, and thus allow him indeed to adopt a kinder, gentler tone.

The potential rhetorical gains of this verse are significant.[46] Paul is able to challenge and to express his exasperation at the Galatian Christians' responses and, at the same time, distance himself from any alienating effects that such expressions might cause by wishing *himself* distanced from those very expressions. He affirms, quite directly, his goodwill toward his audi-

---

45. Paul employs the imperfect ἤθελον.

46. John Chrysostom (33) similarly recognized the rhetorical force of this passage: "This weeping is not only a reproof but a blandishment; it does not exasperate like reproof, nor relax like indulgent treatment, but is a mixed remedy, and of great efficacy in the way of exhortation. Having thus softened and powerfully engaged their hearts by his tears, he again advances to the contest."

ence, essential to securing a receptive hearing; if his wishes could become reality, the causes of his distress over them would evaporate, his tone would be modulated, and the current breach in their relationship would be quickly repaired. He also prepares for the challenges that he will pose afresh as soon as the following verse, having established that the source of his speech is his deeply felt affection for his converts and his desire to bring them to an eternally good end.

Paul's reflections upon his ministry in Galatia, together with his criticisms of his rivals' mission, invite examination of our own motives and practice in ministry against the examples we find in this paragraph. Paul was ever attentive to how to advance God's work (or how God's work was advancing), investing himself in this cause even in the midst of apparent setbacks (the illness that held him in Galatia and kept him from moving on to his intended destination; imprisonment in the location from which he wrote Philippians). Are we similarly committed to advance God's cause in both circumstances of our choosing and circumstances against our choosing? He prioritized living with the people to whom he offered Christ rather than living as a Jew, not that he engaged in the gentiles' activities that were displeasing to God, but that he engaged the gentiles fully on their own ground. Are we similarly committed to live with the people among whom we are serving rather than to continue to live in the manner to which we have been accustomed? From another angle, Paul's comments on how the Galatians *might* have received Paul, given their cultural prejudices and convictions, hold up a mirror to us as well. What prejudices do we harbor concerning who might or might not have anything to say to us as messengers of God?

Paul poses another challenge as we consider his approach to mission vis-à-vis the approach taken by the rival teachers. The Judaizers are one example of a Christian mission coming into foreign territory with an agenda to impose upon the people in that territory. The Galatians, perhaps out of their own lack of confidence in their discipleship or in their own discernment in the Spirit, seem all too willing to accept whatever program the Judaizers have to offer them. Paul had approached the Galatians in a very different manner. Paul, the Jew from Cilicia, can urge the Galatian converts to become like him, because he first became like them, stripping himself of the culturally bound practices of his own ethnic and religious background. He sees far better than the rival mission what is at the core of the transformation God wants to work in the lives of human beings, and therefore he is focused on helping the gentiles among the Galatians to discover how to be Spirit-led Christ-followers *as gentile Galatians* rather than seeking to make them Jewish Christians. He does have a message to preach, and he does have boundaries to mark out around genuinely Christian practice and belief, but he does not import a program of imposing one form of the contextualization of the gospel (how Christianity takes shape in a Palestinian Jewish context) on another group in another context. While Christian missions has become far more careful in this regard than it has been in generations and centuries past, there is still an insidiously pervasive tendency to export Christian practice and ecclesiastical strategies rather than to build truly indigenous Christian communities.

Paul's passionate outcry in 4:19 reminds us of the fundamental driving goal of his ministry: Christ taking shape in and among his converts. Paul's ministry is ultimately *formational*. Bringing people to the point where they trust in what Christ's death has achieved for them is merely a beginning. Paul regards it as essential that they continue in the *trajectory* of "faith," following what was received by trust (the Spirit) all the way to the endpoint whither it leads ("Christ formed in/among you"). We cannot look for less, or work for less, in ourselves or in those among whom we exercise pastoral responsibility. Whether using the language of formation (see Rom 8:29; 12:2; 2 Cor 3:18; Phil 3:10, 21) or related images, like the putting away of whatever belongs to the old self and the nurturing of the life of the new self (Col 3:1–17), or dying and rising to new life with Christ as slaves of righteousness (Rom 6:1–14), Paul puts the transformation of the inner person and the outward practice of the disciple front and center in God's interest and purposes for us. This transformation is ultimately, for him, what the gospel is all about, and therefore his example recommends that we become most passionate about this as well.

VI. A SCRIPTURAL COUP DE GRÂCE (4:21–31)

21 *Tell me, you who wish to be under the law, do you not listen to the law?*
22 *For it is written that Abraham had two sons, one from the slave woman and*
one from the free woman. 23 *But the one from the slave woman has been born*
in accordance with the flesh, while the one from the free woman has been born
through a promise.[a] 24 *These things are communicating something else: for these*
women are two covenants, the one from Mount Sinai, bringing people to birth
unto slavery—this is Hagar. 25 *And Hagar is Sinai,*[b] *a mountain in Arabia. She*
corresponds to the present Jerusalem, for she is enslaved along with her children.
26 *But the Jerusalem above, who is our mother,*[c] *is free,* 27 *for it is written: "Re-*
joice, barren woman who is not giving birth; writhe and cry out, you who are
not in labor, because many more are the children of the desolate woman than of
the woman who has a husband." 28 *And you,*[d] *brothers and sisters, are children*
of promise in the manner of Isaac. 29 *But just as at that time the one born in line*
with the flesh was persecuting the one born in line with the Spirit, so also now.
30 *But what does the Scripture say? "Cast out the slave woman and her son, for*
the son of the slave woman will by no means inherit along with the son of the
free woman." 31 *Therefore,*[e] *brothers and sisters, we are not children of the slave*
woman, but of the free woman.

a. Some MSS (B D G) and 𝔐 read *"the* promise," since a particular promise has indeed been previously specified.

b. There is some discrepancy among manuscripts, even among the earliest ones, as to (1) whether one should read δέ or γάρ here and (2) whether Hagar is actually named in this verse ("And Hagar is Sinai, a mountain in Arabia") or not ("And Sinai is a mountain in Arabia"). 𝔓⁴⁶ reads simply τὸ δὲ Σινᾶ; ℵ C F G 1739 concur in the absence of Hagar's name but differ in regard to the conjunction, reading τὸ γὰρ Σινᾶ. Ψ 33 1881 𝔐 read τὸ γὰρ Ἀγὰρ Σινᾶ; A B D support τὸ δὲ Ἀγὰρ Σινᾶ (favored by Martyn, 438). The weight of external evidence on its own favors the originality of the particle δέ over γάρ. Transcriptional probabilities, however, suggest to Metzger that an original γάρ led to the accidental omission of Ἀγάρ by homoioteleuton (*Textual Commentary*, 527), though Comfort (*New Testament Text*, 569) comes to the opposite conclusion: Ἀγάρ is *introduced* into the verse by dittography and under the influence of the proximity of the conclusion of 4:24 (ἥτις ἐστὶν Ἀγάρ). The decision does not affect the interpretation of the allegory, since Hagar is already firmly linked to Sinai in 4:24.

c. Many witnesses add πάντων after μήτηρ ἡμῶν ("the mother of us all," ℵ² A C³ 𝔐, hence the KJV); the shorter reading ("our mother") has the stronger external support (𝔓⁴⁶ ℵ* B C* D F G Ψ 1739). The longer reading can be explained as an attempt to broaden the application of Paul's statement to include wider circles of readers (perhaps under the influence of Rom 4:16, which describes Abraham as "the father of us all"; Zuntz, *Text of the Epistles*, 223; Metzger, *Textual Commentary*, 528).

d. The earliest manuscripts are split between reading "and *you*, brothers and sisters, *are* children of promise" (ὑμεῖς ... ἐστέ, 𝔓⁴⁶ B D* F G 33) and "and *we*, brothers and sisters, *are* children of promise" (ἡμεῖς ... ἐσμέν, ℵ A C D² Ψ 𝔐). This is a common kind of variant in New Testament manuscripts, since the pronouns differ only in the initial vowel (vowels that came, moreover, to be pronounced increasingly alike). Here it is more likely that scribes were influenced to replace an original "you" with "we," conforming this verse to the "we" statements that surround it in its paragraph (4:26, 31; Metzger, *Textual Commentary*, 528). The second plural forms are both well attested and also the more difficult reading.

e. There is considerable disagreement concerning the inferential particle that opens 4:31. διό is supported by ℵ B D*; ἄρα appears in its stead in 𝔓⁴⁶ Dᶜ; ἄρα οὖν in F G; merely δέ after the pronoun in A C. All variants, however, point to hearing 4:31 as a logical inference of the preceding material (even δέ, understood in a continuative sense).

Paul launches one more argument from Scripture in support of his position, specifically his affirmation that "those who are characterized by trust" are the heirs of the promise, a topic that has dominated the letter since 3:7. Here he does so by offering an allegorical reading of a number of episodes from Abraham's story, particularly those concerned with his attempts to secure an heir by means of what lay within his and his partner's natural powers (i.e., "the flesh") and by means of the path designated by God (i.e., "the promise" or "the Spirit").

It is somewhat surprising to find Paul returning to an argumentative mode after making such an earnest and personal appeal in 4:12–20. Paul is not concerned, however, to make a clear-cut distinction between an argumentative section and an exhortative section; rather, he is concerned to move the Galatians back on course by whatever path seems to him the most salutary.[1] We find, then, that Paul uses an interlocking structure whereby 4:12–20 indeed begins to exhort in earnest, leading into 5:1–6:10 (which nevertheless also contains significant supporting argumentation), but where 4:21–31 closes off the arguments based on Scripture, offering a virtuoso interpretation in support of both preceding and subsequent exhortations.

Paul focuses in this passage on the antithesis of slavery and freedom. Having used the former advantageously to characterize the converts' past life, whether lived under Torah or under any of the other configurations of "elementary principles of the world" (4:3, 9), thus rendering a return to either highly unattractive, he cements the identification of the Sinaitic covenant with slavery and the life into which Paul had already led his converts with freedom, hence a good to be preserved at any cost. Paul's reading of the Hagar and Sarah episodes thereby positions the Galatians perfectly for hearing and embracing Paul's proposition—"Christ liberated us to live in freedom: stand

---

1. It is therefore a mistake to hold Paul too closely to the structure of a standard oration, arguing, for example, that, since Paul's exhortation began in 4:12, 4:21–31 "should be seen not as part of Paul's argumentative *probatio* but as part of his appeals and exhortation" (Longenecker, 199). The theoretical structure Paul is presumed to follow should not trump what Paul actually writes.

firm, therefore, and don't bow down to take on a yoke of slavery again" (5:1)—along with its further supporting argumentation (5:2–6).[2]

21 Paul opens this new paragraph with a direct challenge: "Tell me, you who wish to be under law,[3] do you not listen to the law?" Paul has not, in fact, been able to significantly alter his tone (4:20), though he has prepared his hearers to understand what is behind the vehemence of his arguments and rebukes (4:19). Here he speaks particularly to those among his audience who will self-identify with the description "you who want to be under law." The clear implication of the question is that, were they actually to pay attention to what is spoken in the Torah, they would not thus self-identify! In this way, he prepares them for an interpretation of an episode from the Torah that should convince them that Torah itself—rightly understood—would counsel them not to heed the rival teachers' advice, but to continue in the way that Paul had taught them.[4] Paul gives another indirect indication here that the gentile Christians among the Galatian congregations have not yet taken the decisive step of receiving circumcision and initiation into a Torah-observant lifestyle, as he describes them as not yet "under law," but "wanting to be under law."[5]

This verse bears witness to the ambiguity of "Torah," or "the law," for Paul in the era after Christ's death. In the first instance, "the law" refers to the enslaving power of the Mosaic Torah, Israel's pedagogue and custodian, from whose authority Christ liberated those who would respond in trust. In the second, however, the term refers to the text of Scripture, which functions as an ongoing witness to God's purposes, as a collection of oracles to which Christians should pay attention and that they should heed (see also 1 Cor 10:1–11).[6] A similar ambiguity appears, also in stark juxtaposition, in Rom 3:21, where Paul speaks of a "righteousness of God manifested apart from law, attested by the Law and the Prophets." "Law" continues to have authority as divine witness, but not as prescriptive legislation.

22–23 Paul presents the material in 4:22 as a rationale explaining the implicit claim made in 4:21, namely, "if you listened to the law [i.e., the Scriptures], you would know that it was not a desirable thing to be 'under law'":

---

2. Hietanen (*Paul's Argumentation*, 159) rightly observes that 5:1–6 advances further—and stronger—argumentation than 4:21–31, such that the allegory is not the climactic argument per se.

3. The prepositional phrase ὑπὸ νόμον is made emphatic by virtue of its position in the sentence, though it is difficult to capture this nuance in English.

4. "Rightly heard, the Law itself contains (*a*) a witness to the birth of the Galatian churches into freedom, and (*b*) a command that they evict the Teachers from their midst, thus sealing the freedom given them by Christ" (Martyn, 26).

5. Longenecker, 206–7.

6. Martyn, 433.

"For it is written that Abraham had two sons, one from the slave woman and one from the free woman. But the one from the slave woman has been born in accordance with the flesh, while the one from the free woman (has been born) through a promise." The formula "It is written" characteristically precedes the recitation of a particular text; here, however, Paul uses it to introduce a summary statement of the contents of several passages (Gen 15:1–6; 16:1–16; 21:1–14). This usage might seem less anomalous if we bear in mind that "summary" was a form of recitation practiced in the elementary rhetorical exercises known as the progymnasmata, with which the well-educated Paul might have had some familiarity.[7]

The way Paul introduces the story suggests that he expects the audience to be quite familiar with it. He mentions no proper names, expecting his hearers to know whom he means by "the handmaid," "the free woman," and their respective sons, as well as the general contours of the story (at least those elements found in Gen 15:1–6; 16:1–16; 21:1–14). It is quite possible, though by no means necessary, that the rival teachers had used this very story to advance their own interpretation of how one becomes an heir of Abraham. The fact that Paul uses words and expressions both in this passage (Jerusalem as "mother," "Sinai") and elsewhere in Galatians ("seed of Abraham") that appear in no others of his letters shows these topics to be specific to the situation in Galatia and possibly first introduced into the situation by another party, such that Paul had to take up these topics to give them a different interpretation or application.[8]

If the rival teachers had spoken of this story in their preaching, they could have advanced their cause by means of a quite literal reading. Abraham fathered Ishmael with his wife's female slave, Hagar. Thirteen years later, he fathered Isaac by his own wife, Sarah. Only the descendants of Isaac would, however, be counted as Abraham's heirs and the people of the promise and, indeed, only the descendants of Isaac's younger son Jacob (renamed "Israel") would be counted as heirs as well. The "law" demonstrates thereby that only the Jews—and those who join themselves to the Jewish people by submitting to circumcision and adopting the distinctively Jewish way of life spelled out in Torah—are Abraham's heirs. The blessing that comes to the nations is the invitation issued through God's Messiah to join the historic people of God, and thus share in the inheritance of God's promises.

---

7. See, for example, Theon, *Progymnasmata* 15, particularly paraphrase "by subtraction" (Kennedy, *Progymnasmata*, 70); also relevant are the exercises involving the expansion and abbreviation of *chreiai* (Theon, *Progymnasmata* 3; in Kennedy, *Progymnasmata*, 19).

8. Barrett, "Allegory of Abraham, Sarah, and Hagar," 9; Longenecker, 207–8; Barclay, *Obeying*, 91; Martyn, 437; Das, 484–85. Di Mattei ("Allegory," 119) is correct, however, that the passage also serves Paul's own argument so well, once one understands it to "speak allegorically," that he might plausibly have introduced it into the situation himself.

Paul will draw radically new lines through this story, wreaking havoc with the ethnic lines drawn in connection with the emphasis on physical descent from Sarah through Isaac and Jacob when it comes to defining the "children of promise." He accepts the well-known contrast between the two children in the story in terms of their lineage (4:22), but he adds a critical element, namely, his summary of the basis on which or means by which each child was born, which becomes *the* distinctive characteristic not only for the historical children but for the spiritual extension of their lineage (4:23). The story demonstrates God's rejection of those who are born into the family "in line with the flesh"—pertinent to Ishmael, "in line with fleshly powers and the normal ways of procreation," but also pertinent to people who seek to establish their place in the family by means of Torah observance—and God's establishing of those who are born into the family "through promise."[9]

24 Paul claims that the story of Hagar and Sarah reveals something beyond (and *other than*) what can be learned by taking it at face value: "These things are communicating something else: for these women are two covenants, the one from Mount Sinai, bringing people to birth unto slavery—this is Hagar." Paul's language clearly indicates that he is about to engage in an allegorical reading, in keeping with a well-established tradition of reading texts, especially "sacred" or "canonical" texts in the ancient world, whereby an element "signifying one thing literally" is taken to mean something else.[10] Ancient allegorical readings followed a "this-signifies-that" mode of interpretation that suits 4:21–31 perfectly ("these woman are two covenants").[11]

---

9. Das (494) calls attention to the practice of Jewish authors both of Old Testament and later Jewish texts to use the phrase "son of your slave woman" (more poetically, "son of your handmaid," υἱὸς τῆς παιδίσκης σου) as a self-designation: "Save me, the son of your handmaid" (Ps 86:16 [LXX 85:16]); "I am your slave and the son of your handmaid; save me" (Ps 116:16 [LXX 115:7]; also Wis 9:4–5; 1QS XI.16 [4]: בן־אמתך; 4Q381 frag. 15; 4Q381 frag. 33; see also Di Mattei, "Paul's Allegory," 114n43, 121–22). Perhaps such usage performed some role in Paul's thinking, as he came to invert the natural sense of the story of Abraham's two sons and their begetting, taking a phrase associated with Jewish privilege in his liturgical tradition and turning it into a designation of bondage under the law.

10. The Greek reads ἅτινά ἐστιν ἀλληγορούμενα, directing the hearers toward a specific practice of reading and interpretation ("allegory") familiar from ethical philosophers' interpretations of the (ethically problematic) stories from Homer's epics or the Greek myths. See Tryphon, *De tropis* 1.1 (late first-century CE): "*Allegoria* is an enunciation which while signifying one thing literally, brings forth the thought of something else"; Heraclitus, *Homeric Allegories* 5.2 (late first- or early second-century CE): "The trope that says one thing but signifies something other than what is said is called by the name *allegoria*." These are quoted and discussed in Di Mattei, "Paul's Allegory," 105–6.

11. Di Mattei," Paul's Allegory," 109. Di Mattei demonstrates quite convincingly that, by first-century definitions, Paul truly engages in allegorical interpretation (as opposed to the position that his use of the Sarah-Hagar story is typological *rather than* allegorical).

Paul's allegory works at several levels, something of which he is aware as he speaks of the various correspondences "lining up"[12] on one side or another of the fundamental contrast between the "slave girl" and the "free woman."

lexical term	"slave girl"	"free woman"
signification A (historical)	Hagar	Sarah
signification B (transferred)	Covenant A	Covenant B
signification C (transferred)	the present Jerusalem	the Jerusalem above

It is not immediately clear whether Paul himself understands the story to be "allegorically spoken" (thus, originally written with the *intent* of communicating something more) or that the story is to be "interpreted allegorically." In 1 Cor 9:9–10 Paul attributes allegorical *intent* to the author of the particular law prohibiting the muzzling of an ox while it treads out the grain, claiming that the lawgiver was not himself concerned about oxen but revealed a principle applicable to human workers' access to the fruit of their own labors and right to sustenance for their labors.[13] The usage of the same verb and specific construction in Philo, Plutarch, and other ancient sources strongly favors the view that Paul himself understands the story to have been communicated with allegorical intent.[14]

Philo of Alexandria, an older contemporary of Paul, presents a very different allegorical interpretation of the same story. In Philo's reading, Sarah represents moral virtue, and Hagar the preliminary studies—that is, the course of formal education, whether formally or informally pursued. "We are not yet capable as yet of receiving the impregnation of virtue unless we have first mated with the handmaiden, and the handmaiden of wisdom is the culture gained by the primary learning of the school course," or "the lower branches of school lore" (*On the Preliminary Studies* 9–10, 14). In Philo's hands, the story really does "communicate something else," something quite divorced from the historical dynamics of the narrative.

Paul's allegorical reading is more reserved, insofar as he is not seeking to eliminate the historical specificity of the story in favor of some timeless philosophical principle.[15] Rather, he has discovered a principle at work specifically *within* the world of the story of Sarah and Hagar (expressed indirectly in 4:23), which he then applies to the larger story of God's fulfillment of the promises

---

12. This is the sense of the verb συστοιχεῖ, which Paul will use in 4:25.

13. Longenecker, 209.

14. Di Mattei, "Paul's Allegory," 106–9, on ἐστιν ἀλληγορούμενα; contra ESV, NIV; Longenecker, 208; Dunn, 247; Hays, *Echoes*, 113. Other translations resolve the problem by offering a paraphrase of the Greek: "Now this is an allegory" (NRSV; see, similarly, CEB, NLT).

15. Hanson, *Allegory and Event*, 82–83.

given to Abraham. That principle concerns the way in which God's promises come to fulfillment. They do not come about on the basis of "flesh," that is, what human beings can manage for themselves on their own strength and with their own resources (corresponding to Ishmael's birth as a result of Abraham and Hagar's natural procreative power). Rather, they come about "through promise" (4:23), namely, through what the Spirit works among and within human beings, empowering them beyond their own capacity (corresponding to Isaac's birth as a result of God's empowering Abraham and Sarah to attain what their natural powers could not). Paul's substitution of "according to the Spirit" (4:29) for "through promise" (4:23) in a later contrast with "flesh" is in keeping with Paul's identification of the Spirit as the promised inheritance (3:13–14) and looks ahead to his discussion of the Spirit's empowerment of the human being to rise above the power of the flesh and live a righteous life before God (5:13–6:10). The application of this principle (and thus of the allegorical reading) to the situation in Galatia becomes immediately apparent: circumcision of the physical flesh and the adoption of a Torah-observant lifestyle are all things that human beings can manage on their own in an attempt to align themselves with God's righteousness, but God has decreed that the promise of righteousness will be attained on the basis of trusting Jesus and trusting the Spirit's guidance and empowerment (3:11).

The principal shift in Paul's allegorical interpretation involves moving away from reading the narrative as a story about two women to reading the narrative as a statement of principles concerning two covenants. One is depicted thereby as an arrangement based on the flesh and perpetuating slavery;[16] the other covenant is presented as an arrangement based on promise and the Spirit, leading to freedom. Even before Paul's identification of the former with Sinai, Paul's hearers could have plotted where Paul was heading, for he has already connected living under the Torah (the Sinaitic covenant) with living in a state of slavery (4:3–5) and the action of the Spirit with becoming an heir of God's promises (4:6–7). It is important to realize from the outset that the two covenants are not conceived of here as "the old covenant" and "the new covenant" (though Paul can use this language elsewhere, as in 1 Cor 11:25; 2 Cor 3:6), but as the "old covenant" (Sinai) and "the *even older* covenant" (the promises to Abraham, about which Paul has made so much, as in 3:8, 15–21).[17] The chronological priority of the covenant (*diathēkē*, 3:15, 17) with Abraham has been an important piece of evidence for its legal priority in God's economy.

---

16. The present aspect of the participle γεννῶσα is appropriate to Paul's presentation of the Sinai covenant as ongoingly "begetting" people into slavery (so also Witherington, 330). Paul is assuming the Roman legal ruling that, if a person's slave bears children, those children also become that person's slaves (so Burton, 258).

17. Rightly, Hays, *Echoes*, 114.

25 Hagar was a young and fertile woman, with whom Abraham could have children on the strength of their mutual reproductive capabilities alone (i.e., "in line with flesh"). Paul therefore connects the path promoted by the rival teachers—the path of submitting to circumcision and doing the works of Torah—with Hagar, since it promotes practices that belong to the realm of what lies within the power of human beings to perform, and not what the provision of God alone empowers.[18] The Sinaitic covenant (the Torah) is thus connected not with Sarah, the free woman, but with Hagar, the slave woman. This connection is now supported by the geographic reference to Mount Sinai being in the territory of Arabia, with which Hagar was also associated: "And 'Hagar'[19] is Sinai, a mountain[20] in Arabia. She corresponds to the present Jerusalem, for she is enslaved along with her children."

Though originally from Egypt, Hagar ended up settling somewhere in Arabia (traditionally in the area of Petra) after her expulsion from Abraham's camp.[21] There is a mountain in Arabia named Hagra, which is connected with Hagar in the tradition of the Aramaic paraphrases of the Torah (the targumim).[22] This Hagra facilitates the connection between Hagar and a(nother) mountain in Arabia and, thus, with the covenant associated with that mountain.

Paul takes a second step in his allegory as he not only aligns Hagar, "the slave woman," with the Sinaitic covenant, but asserts further that "she lines up with the present Jerusalem, for she is in slavery along with her children" (4:25). The verb Paul employs here was originally used to speak of soldiers

---

18. Martyn, 436.

19. The τό in the opening phrase τὸ δὲ Ἁγάρ signals, in effect, quotation marks around "Hagar," as if to communicate: "The lexical entry 'Hagar' in this story represents . . ." (Di Mattei, "Paul's Allegory," 111; Turner, *Syntax*, 182).

20. In the NT and LXX, ὄρος almost always occurs before Σινᾶ when it signifies part of the title "Mount Sinai." Here, following Σινᾶ, ὄρος is probably to be understood in apposition.

21. McNamara, "*To de (Hagar) Sina*," 36.

22. See Tg. Onq. and Tg. Ps.-J. on Gen 16:7, discussed in Di Mattei, "Allegory," 112; more extensively in Gese, "τὸ δὲ Ἁγάρ." Elliott ("Choose Your Mother") points to the "mother mountain" Mount Dindymus overlooking the temple state of Pessinus and the self-castrated *galli* serving as priests of the mother goddess Cybele as an informative, native background for Gal 4:21–31. While it is indeed likely that readers in *Pessinus* would make such connections, for *Paul* to have done so would require (1) a North Galatian ministry and destination, (2) a special interest in Pessinus among North Galatian sites or a presumption that converts in Ancyra (for example) will have some general knowledge of the tradition sufficiently foregrounded in their minds to make these connections, and (3) a desire to draw on local religious tradition as a supplement to exegesis of the Old Testament, masked by a marked avoidance of making any specific references to this local tradition as such.

lining up in columns or rows.[23] Paul draws attention to the way in which he is creating, in effect, two rows of columns and asking the Galatians to find themselves lined up with the second column rather than the first (see the table in the commentary on 4:24).[24] Paul presents the alleged slavery of his contemporary Jerusalem—the conceptual center and focal "place" for all who relate to God by way of the Sinaitic covenant—as a rationale for his identification of Jerusalem with Hagar. This allegation depends upon prior acceptance of his connection between the Torah and the condition of slavery (as compared to the condition experienced by those who approach God by trust and through the Spirit).[25] It would have no probative value for the rival teachers, but Paul hopes it will win the assent of his converts by this point in his discourse.

In the other column, Paul is lining up "Sarah," the "promise/Spirit," the "Jerusalem above" (and all who look to that city as their mother), and "freedom" and being born into freedom. In so doing, he makes the radical suggestion that the *physical* genealogy of the Jewish people (who trace their lineage naturally from Isaac, not Ishmael) is not in line with their *spiritual* genealogy. Paul contends that the narrative's lesson is that those who are born into the new life of "living to God" on the basis of God's promise and the Spirit are the ones who inherit the blessing of Abraham (Gal 4:30–31); in the immediate situation, this group would include the Galatian Christians (whether Jew or gentile), but *not* the rival teachers, who still labor in slavery and seek to enslave the converts as well.[26]

"The present Jerusalem" and "the Jerusalem above" enter the discourse as the "mothers" of two people groups at the allegorical level. The former "is in slavery together with her children"; of the latter, Paul will say "she is *our* mother" (4:26). Paul has moved away from any interest in descent from Hagar or Sarah.[27] Paul now builds upon a long tradition of faithful Jews looking to Jerusalem as mother, a testimony to the ideological importance of the space of the Holy City on the conceptual map of Judaism.[28]

Whom does Paul have in mind as he writes about "the present Jerusa-

---

23. Burton, 261–62.

24. Martyn, 438, 449–50.

25. As Hays (*Echoes*, 115) rightly observes, Paul's judgment on life under the law as "slavish" is "grounded upon a new communal experience of freedom in the power of the Holy Spirit, as he affirms in 4:4–7."

26. Eastman, "Cast Out the Slave Woman," 315.

27. Di Mattei ("Allegory," 113) rightly affirms that the point of the allegory is misrepresented in statements such as "those under the Sinaitic covenant are actually sons of Hagar," which would be to conflate the literal and figurative levels of meaning inappropriately.

28. For notable examples, see Isa 49:19–22, 25; 50:1; 51:17–20; 54:1–17; Bar 4:8–37; 5:5–6; 4 Ezra 10.6–10.

lem" that is "in slavery along with her children"? It has been suggested that Paul limits his allegory to the two Jewish Christian missions directed toward gentiles—one promoting Torah observance as a condition of conversion and membership, and one proceeding free of the Torah (i.e., Paul and his team, and other Jewish Christian missionaries sharing his position).[29] It does indeed seem likely that foremost in his mind as he writes Gal 4:21–31 is the kind of mission—indeed, the *very* mission—represented by the rival teachers. It is essential to his success that the Galatian Christians come to identify them with those who are excluded from the promise, with the same fate looming over any who yield to their persuasion. Paul, however, gives no indication that he *limits* "the present Jerusalem" to the Torah-observant Jewish Christian mission. On the contrary, all the clues he does give point to his inclusion of all non-Christian Jews among those "born into slavery" and thus among the children of "the present Jerusalem" in his allegory. Paul ranks *all* who are "under Torah" as slaves (4:3–5).[30] Given Paul's assessment of his own former life, and even the essentially non-Christian character of the rival mission as he perceives them (if they lead people to be cut off from Christ, Paul could not affirm them to be "in Christ" themselves), Paul could only affirm all non-Christian Jews to be "in slavery" along with, and as part of, "the present Jerusalem."[31]

26 Paul points his hearers—the children of promise, born by the working of the Holy Spirit (4:28–29)—to a different ideological space as their mother city: "But the Jerusalem above, who is our mother, is free" (or, "the free woman").[32] We might have expected "the present Jerusalem" to be contrasted with "the future Jerusalem," but instead Paul speaks of "the above Jerusalem," suggesting that the mother city exists not merely in future hope but as a heavenly reality now, even if its manifestation within the realm of human experience lies in the future.[33] By speaking of this heavenly city as "our" mother, Paul again makes strategic use of associative language, distinguishing Paul and his converts together from those who are born into slavery to the law (a group that includes the rival teachers).[34]

---

29. Martyn, 457–66; Martyn, *Theological Issues*, 191–208.

30. So, for example, Fung, 209.

31. Martyn (38) admits that Galatians "does contain an *implication* with regard to Judaism: Paul's zealous observance of the law failed to liberate him from enslavement to the elements of the old cosmos. That liberation came through God's apocalypse of Jesus Christ, not through any religion, including that of Judaism."

32. Di Mattei ("Allegory," 115) notices this possible double entendre. The lack of an article with ἐλευθέρα is to be explained by its occupying the position of the predicate nominative (cf., famously, θεός at the end of John 1:1).

33. Rightly Hays, *Echoes*, 118.

34. Tolmie, *Persuading*, 173.

Claiming a city as a mother is a declaration of citizenship, as Paul expresses more explicitly in Philippians: "Our citizenship is in heaven" (Phil 3:20). This is the land that the spiritual descendants of Abraham will inherit (cf. Gal 5:21) in line with God's promise that he would provide them with territory. Paul is thus in tune with other early Christian voices who declare that the Christian hope is no longer bound up with the future of an earthly city, even one with so distinguished a pedigree in the history of God's acts as Jerusalem. Rather, Christ-followers look for "a better, that is, a heavenly homeland" (see Heb 11:11–16; 13:13–14) or await "the holy city, New Jerusalem" that does not belong to this creation (Rev 21:1–22:5); they do not set their sights on any disputed stretch of land in the Middle East. For the author of Hebrews, John the seer, and the author of 2 Peter, earthly Jerusalem is merely a part of the visible, manufactured cosmos whose elements will be consumed with fervent heat (2 Pet 3:5–6, 10) or shaken and removed so as to reveal the way into our heavenly homeland (Heb 12:26–28).

This verse affords a rare glimpse into Paul's eschatology. While the earthly Jerusalem is bound up with the history of a particular ethnic people (the Jewish people), Paul looks to a heavenly city as an appropriate future dwelling place for the multinational, multi-ethnic people of God formed in Christ. Paul might find himself perplexed at the interest of twenty-first-century Christians (especially the more evangelical Christians) in the affairs and their investment in the promotion of the interests of earthly Jerusalem and the modern State of Israel. Galatians is decidedly *not* a Zionist text. The "present Jerusalem" is not the focal point of the promise; the God of Jew and gentile is interested in peace with justice for all peoples, not the one-sided privileging of any people at the expense of another. In light of Paul's redefinition of who constitute Abraham's seed, Christians might consider whether their first allegiance ought to be, not to the State of Israel (or to the Palestinian Authority), but to Israeli and Palestinian *Christians*, with their agenda being to actively promote the mutual good of these brothers and sisters in Christ.

27 Paul now recites Isa 54:1–2 as an authoritative text that provides confirmation (*gar*) of his reading of the Hagar and Sarah story, particularly that the "barren woman" aligns with "the Jerusalem above," introducing this quotation with the customary formula: "For it is written, 'Rejoice, barren woman who is not giving birth; writhe and cry out, you who are not in labor, because many more are the children of the barren woman than of the woman who has a husband'" (Gal 4:27).[35] While, by the standards of the modern study of the Old Testament, Paul may be faulted for failing to read Isa 54:1 first as a word to the

---

35. It is occasionally suggested that Isa 54 was read alongside Gen 16–17 as the haftarah that accompanied that specific reading from Torah in the synagogue cycle, though there is but slender evidence for such practice prior to 70 CE (Di Mattei, "Allegory," 114).

returning exiles from Babylon, by first-century standards, Paul handles this text as a responsible and well-trained exegete with a high level of sophistication.

First, Paul connects Isa 54:1, which addresses the "barren woman," with the story of Sarah, who is also called "barren" in Scripture.[36] Paul follows a practice of biblical interpretation known as *gezera shawa*, whereby two texts sharing a common term or phrase are brought together to interpret one another. Moreover, Sarah did "shout for joy" giving birth to Isaac (Gen 21:6–7), as the "barren woman" in Isaiah is exhorted to do.[37] Paul applies this promise from Isaiah, then, to the (Torah-free) gentile mission, which was in fact making many more spiritual descendants for Abraham (born through promise by means of the Holy Spirit) than proselytism to either Judaism or Torah-observant Christianity (born into the family on the basis of the flesh, that is, through circumcision of the flesh).[38] This result is in keeping with Isaiah's own anticipation of gentiles being included in God's people, expressed frequently in the context of this quoted verse.[39] Paul also has latched onto a passage that addresses "Jerusalem," the "barren woman" of Isa 54:1, for a while rendered desolate but yet again to be the object of God's compassion.

Paul may be reading Isaiah even more closely that this, however. The verse that he recites (Isa 54:1) follows immediately after the famous fourth Servant Song (Isa 52:13–53:12), in which the righteous one bears the sins of many, ransoms many, makes many righteous, and sees his offspring despite being cut off from the land of the living. Indeed, he engenders offspring precisely in being offered up for sin:

> When you make his life an offering for sin,
>> he shall see his offspring, and shall prolong his days;
> through him the will of the LORD shall prosper.
>> Out of his anguish he shall see light;
> he shall find satisfaction through his knowledge.
>> The righteous one, my servant, shall make many righteous,
>> and he shall bear their iniquities. (Isa 53:10–11 NRSV)

---

36. Sarah is described as στεῖρα in LXX Gen 11:30, as here in Gal 4:27 (using the language of Isa 54:1).

37. Isaiah 51:1–3 may also inform Paul's linkage of 54:1 to the story of Sarah (Hays, *Echoes*, 119–20).

38. Fung, 211. John Chrysostom (34) had made this observation long ago: "Who is this who before was 'barren,' and 'desolate'? Clearly it is the Church of the gentiles, that was before deprived of the knowledge of God. Who, 'she which hath the husband?' plainly the Synagogue. Yet the barren woman surpassed her in the number of her children, for the other embraces one nation, but the children of the Church have filled the country of the Greeks and of the Barbarians, the earth and sea, the whole habitable world."

39. See Isa 51:4–5; 52:10; 54:2–3; 55:5; also 2:4; 42:1, 6; 49:6.

Jesus, the messianic servant who brings blessings to many who are then accounted his offspring, makes the "barren one" (heavenly Jerusalem) to enjoy an abundance of offspring, multiplying endlessly the children and heirs of Abraham through the Torah-free gentile mission.

Prior to the birth of Isaac, Abraham and Sarah both regard Ishmael (born through Hagar) as the fulfillment of God's promise to Abraham. But Hagar—the Sinaitic covenant—represents only the temporary solution to the barrenness of Sarah, the period during which the promise to Abraham did not bear fruit, such that "the Jerusalem above" remained desolate.[40] It is indeed temporary, even in the Genesis narrative taken at the historical level, which Abraham understands only after Gen 17:19–21.[41] The story, read allegorically, well supports Paul's earlier presentation of the Torah as the temporary, interim "fix" (3:19–25), as well as his view of salvation history as a whole.

28 Paul affirms in regard to his converts: "And you, brothers and sisters, are children of promise[42] in the manner of Isaac." In line with his description of the "Jerusalem above" as "our mother," Paul continues to emphasize the affective ties of kinship that unite him with the Galatian Christians, his "brothers and sisters," who resemble Isaac in the most important respect: they, like Isaac, were born into the family of Abraham in line with God's promise, specifically through their reception of the promised Holy Spirit (28), rather than by flesh-based means, like Ishmael.[43] Paul does not specify the second of the two covenants, the one represented by Sarah (24), as he does so explicitly in regard to the first (24b–25). Given the prevalence of the language of promise and the focus on Abraham, he can only be thinking of the promise given by God to Abraham (3:15–18), which was also given in terms of a covenant (3:15, 17).

29 Again looking to the story of Sarah and Hagar for a historical precedent to the situation of the Torah-free gentile mission, Paul claims that "just as at that time the one born in line with the flesh was persecuting the one born in line with the Spirit, so also now." There is very little in the Genesis narrative to suggest that Ishmael harbored hostile intent toward Isaac. In the Hebrew text, we read that Sarah observed Ishmael "playing" or "laughing." While in certain contexts with certain additional markers, this verb *could* bear the darker sense of "mocking" or "toying with," those markers are simply absent, as is Isaac (at least, there is nothing to suggest that Ishmael was playing with his infant half-brother).[44] Sarah, after simply observing Ishmael

---

40. Di Mattei, "Allegory," 18.

41. Di Mattei, "Allegory," 119. Indeed, even the covenant that "the angel of the Lord" makes with Hagar in Gen 16:9–10 does not alter God's determination to fulfill his promises to Abraham through Isaac as the promised Seed (Di Mattei, "Allegory," 119).

42. I understand ἐπαγγελίας as a genitive of source ("children born of promise").

43. Matera, 171.

44. It is therefore interesting to note that many English versions persist in translating

playing during the party for Isaac's weaning, tells Abraham to send Hagar and Ishmael away so that the latter will not inherit alongside her own child (Gen 21:9–10; Gal 4:30). Later retellings of the story seek to justify Sarah's rather cold-hearted command, which would have resulted in the deaths of both Hagar and her son had God not intervened (Gen 21:14–21), by suggesting that Isaac was in some danger from Ishmael.[45] Paul appears to have been familiar with these developments of the original story and to have valued them insofar as they helped to cement his point that what happened long ago was paradigmatic for what was happening in the immediate situation of his mission to the gentiles.

Whom would Paul have considered to have been persecuting the children born of the Spirit in his own setting? Paul might refer to the activity of the rival teachers themselves, their dogging Paul's steps and putting new pressure on Paul's converts, as persecution.[46] Indeed, Paul regards certain Jewish-Christian parties as particularly hostile to himself (Gal 2:3–5) and might even have begun to regard their activity as persecution. However, the other four explicit references to persecution in Galatians point more directly toward non-Christian Jewish opposition to the Christian movement. Paul twice refers to his own former activity as persecuting the church while still "in bondage" himself (Gal 1:13, 23). He also refers to the persecution that he alleges the rival teachers to be avoiding by promoting circumcision (Gal 6:12), which Paul could have hoped to avoid were he to do likewise, but does not (Gal 5:11). Such persecution is more likely to be coming from the moderately empowered non-Christian Jewish community, which had a certain authority over its own and used this authority to restrain deviance (see Acts 9:1–2; 2 Cor 11:24; 1 Thess 2:13–16). This persecution targets most directly the Jewish Christians who appear to go beyond the pale of Torah or speak against the

---

this verb in a manner that might provide at least some justification for Sarah's cruelty. The KJV and NIV, for example, read "the son [Ishmael] . . . was mocking," rightly adding no direct object (e.g., "Isaac"), as there is no direct object in the Hebrew. Without an object, however, the verb should be taken in an intransive sense, "playing" or "laughing." The NLT introduces such an object into its translation to make the sense of "mocking" more natural ("making fun of her son, Isaac"), but without warrant in the Hebrew text. The LXX does add an object in the form of a prepositional phrase, but the choice of the preposition unmistakingly leads to the translation "playing *with* her son Isaac" (LXX uses μετά, whereas πρός or an accusative direct object would have been required to yield the sense "make sport of [someone]"; so LSJ 1288). The NRSV follows the LXX well at this point ("playing with her son Isaac"), though, again, the Hebrew text gives us no indication that Isaac is anywhere on the scene.

45. See, for example, Gen. Rab. 53:11; Tg. Ps.-J. Gen 21:10; Tg. Onq. Gen 21:9; Josephus, *Antiquities* 1.215; Callaway, "Mistress and the Maid."

46. Martyn, 445; Longenecker, 217; Fee, *Empowering Presence*, 413, 415; Tolmie, *Persuading*, 169, 174. Fung (213) allows for this possibility.

central pillars of the Mosaic covenant,[47] but makes itself felt among gentile Christians as well—the rival teachers are, according to Paul, troubling the Galatian churches on account of a desire to avoid persecution themselves by persuading gentile converts to Christianity to become circumcised, thus making the whole Christian movement essentially an effort of Jewish proselytism.[48]

Ishmael's (alleged) persecution of Isaac, mapped onto the persecution occurring in Paul's context, signals the true identity of each party. The ones who are doing the persecuting are enacting the role of Ishmael, "the one born in accordance with the flesh"; the Jewish Christians involved in the Pauline mission (and others of similar mind)—together with those who align themselves with *this* mission—are cast in the role of "the one born in accordance with the Spirit," hence children of promise.

30 To bring this point home, Paul follows the story of Ishmael to its end in the Genesis narrative. While Ishmael was raised in Abraham's tents for thirteen years, he was destined to be disinherited: "But what does the Scripture say? 'Cast out the slave woman and her son, for the son of the slave woman will by no means[49] inherit along with the son of the free woman.'" Paul recites the words of Sarah to Abraham, urging the eviction of Hagar and Ishmael. He has changed the quotation in one particularly significant way: where Sarah had hoped to prevent Ishmael from inheriting along "with my son Isaac" (Gen 21:10), Paul changes this to "with the son of the freewoman" so as to make the quotation more immediately applicable to the Galatians, who are tellingly *not* descended through Isaac but only *in the manner of* Isaac. Paul also refers to this command as spoken not by "Sarah" but by "Scripture." At a certain level, this claim is true by virtue of the latter's subsuming all the recorded speech of the former. Paul's change may also reflect an awareness that, though initially spoken by Sarah, God confirms the course of action for which Sarah called (Gen 21:12). It was only after God's confirmation that Abraham consented to Sarah's demand. The words of Sarah to Abraham have, in any event, become for Paul the very words of Scripture, passing sentence on those who seek to attain God's promises by trusting in physical descent, circumcision, and joining the covenant of Moses.[50]

The Galatians might have heard, in the recitation of Gen 21:10, a summons (with scriptural authority) to definitively set aside any thoughts of taking on the yoke of the Torah ("the slave girl" having been explicitly identified

---

47. See, for example, the circumstances surrounding Stephen's murder in Acts 7–8, Paul's former activity as a persecutor, and the hostility he reported in 1 Thess 2:13–16.

48. Schlier, 227. Fung (213) prefers this scenario.

49. Paul uses οὐ μή followed by a subjunctive for emphasis: this is an outcome that *will not* eventuate.

50. So also Hays, *Echoes*, 116.

as a cipher for "the Sinaitic covenant").[51] They may also have heard a summons to break off relations with the rival teachers and send them on their way, which would no doubt have pleased Paul.[52] Paul himself, however, seems to be more interested in the second half of the quotation, in which "Scripture" declares the rival teachers and all those who remain "under Torah" with them to be outside of the inheritance, and declares only those who have been born in the freedom of the promise and the Spirit to be God's heirs. This is the part of the quotation on which he actually comments in 4:31. The recitation perhaps most importantly communicates a warning to the Galatians of their own potential loss of inheritance should they follow the rival teachers back into slavery, since only the children of the "free woman" will inherit.[53] The response to God being promoted by the rival teachers is not, for Paul, simply an alternative route to justification, not even an inferior route to justification. It is, simply, *no* route to justification at all. God's promise cannot be attained in a fleshly manner, but only by the power of the Spirit.

31 Once again addressing his converts in associative, familial terms, Paul presents this verse as a logical conclusion derived from preceding material: "Therefore, brothers and sisters, we are not children of the slave woman, but of the free woman." Paul has returned a final time to the topic that has run throughout his letter since 3:7, namely, who the sons and daughters of Abraham are, specifically those who constitute the heirs of the divine promises

---

51. Di Mattei, "Allegory," 121; Stanley, *Paul and the Language of Scripture*, 250.

52. Matera, 173. Eastman (*Recovering*, 132–33; "Cast Out the Slave Woman," 320–24) has argued against hearing this as a summons to the Galatians to evict the rival teachers. Whenever Paul enjoins an action upon the Galatians, he consistently employs second person plural imperatives (4:12, 21; 5:1, 13, 15, 16; 6:1, 2), third person singular imperatives (6:4, 6, 17), or the hortatory subjunctive first person plural (6:9–10). Despite the variety of verb forms, Paul consistently avoids any use of a second person singular imperative (like ἔκβαλε in Gal 4:30) for directives to his congregations. Indeed, when Paul issues an imperative to one of his congregations in the language of the Scriptures in 1 Cor 5:13, he alters the Septuagint's *singular* form (the imperative future ἐξαρεῖς, "you [sg.] shall purge out," in, e.g., LXX Deut 17:7; 19:19; 21:21; 24:7) to his own customary *plural* imperative form, ἐξάρατε, "(you [pl.]) purge out." The imperative in this verse is therefore not issued as a command, which will come rather in 5:1.

While this argument exhibits good reasoning, the immediate context points in a different direction here. The preceding sentence has set up a correspondence between the ancient story and the contemporary situation: "as at that time, so also now." This wording sets up the expectation for a correlation between the solution to the problem "at that time" and the solution to the present (corresponding) problem. Indeed, Paul's introduction—"what does Scripture say?"—could readily be heard as an announcement of that solution, that is, urging the hearers to take the same steps "now" that Sarah and Abraham took to safeguard the promise "at that time."

53. Schreiner, 306; Tolmie, *Persuading*, 175.

(see 4:30, which has explicitly raised again the latter issue). The conclusion here is logically possible because Paul has already proven that the Galatians *have* inherited what was promised through Abraham, namely, the Holy Spirit (3:1–5, 13–14; 4:6–7). While not Sarah's physical descendants, and while not joining themselves to the community of Sarah's physical descendants (i.e., the Jewish people), the Galatian Christians nevertheless legitimately belong to that which "Sarah" represents at the allegorical level—they are the heirs of the promise given to Abraham, the "older" covenant recently activated with the coming of Christ, the Seed, and those to whom "the Jerusalem above" will be given as an inheritance. With this, Paul is prepared to present his proposition, the advice that he has been preparing his converts to embrace and act upon.

VII. PAUL'S PRINCIPAL ADVICE (5:1–12)

We have been reading Galatians essentially as a specimen of deliberative rhetoric,[1] a communication aimed at having an impact on what course of action the audience will take in a particular situation. In Gal 5:1 Paul forcefully states his advice in the form of his recommendation regarding the course of action the Galatian Christians should pursue (and not pursue), toward which all the preceding argumentation has been leading and for which it has been building support.[2]

The structural parallels between 5:1 and 5:13 strongly suggest that Gal 5:1–12 is a discrete unit, with 5:13 opening a new but closely related unit. Both 5:1 and 5:13 begin from the same premise, stated in similar terms ("Christ freed us for freedom," 5:1; "you were called to freedom," 5:13), which provides the launching-off point for the exhortation to follow in the second half of each verse.[3] Paul's clearly constructed parallelism here weighs against the view that 5:1 *concludes* the preceding section (4:21–31) with 5:2 starting a new section.[4] The first of these parallel sections (5:1–12) establishes that the gift of freedom must be preserved; the second (5:13–26) establishes that it must not be misused against the Giver's purposes for it, but rather used fully in line with the same.

Galatians 5:1–12 clearly divides into two subsections (vv. 1–6 and 7–12), both focused on the task of dissuasion and thus supporting the proposal made in 5:1. Galatians 5:2–6 outlines the negative consequences of failing to heed this exhortation (5:2–4) and reaffirms the positive consequences of walking in line with trust in Christ and with the Spirit (5:5–6). Galatians 5:7–12 adds support from another angle, namely, by raising further questions about the credibility of those who have been urging the Galatians to change their course

---

1. "Deliberative rhetoric," not a "deliberative oration" per se.

2. Rightly Dunn, 260; essentially, Hietanen, *Paul's Argumentation*, 164, 181–82, although Hietanen focuses on 5:2.

3. Longenecker, 224. Galatians 5:13–26 is the "positive, protreptic part" that follows upon the conclusion to the "apotreptic" portion of the letter, in which "Paul does his utmost to dissuade the recipients from submission to the law and circumcision" (Dahl, "Paul's Letter," 137, who speaks of Galatians as containing elements that fulfill the dual goals of "the symbouleutic [i.e., 'deliberative'] genre of speech").

4. Commentators and translations that treat 5:1 as the conclusion of what precedes include Bruce, 226; Fung, 216–17; Martyn, 432; Witherington, 321, 340; Tolmie, *Persuading*, 175; NRSV, CEB, NLT. This verse is treated as initiating a new step in the discourse in Burton, 269; Lagrange, 134; Schlier, 228 (the verse begins with "a powerful, new approach"); Betz, 255; Dunn, 261; Moo, 319; NIV, ESV, NJB. Hietanen (*Paul's Argumentation*, 165) treats 5:1 as transitional, with 5:1a providing the conclusion to the Sarah and Hagar allegory and 5:1b beginning a new paragraph with its "therefore." The parallelism between 5:1a and 5:13a, however, argues strongly against this analysis.

midstream by adopting circumcision and Torah observance. Paul will begin a supplementary, and more constructive, exhortation in 5:13 to answer the remaining question: if the Galatians do keep themselves from Torah's yoke, how will they attain mastery of the passions without the discipline of law? This positive exhortation extends through 6:10, after which the formal conclusion (which closely resembles the *peroratio* of a spoken address) begins.

A. PAUL'S RECOMMENDED COURSE OF ACTION (5:1–6)

¹ *Christ freed us for a life of freedom: Maintain your stance, then, and do not again bear a yoke of slavery.*[a] ² *Look: I, Paul, am saying to you that, if you get yourselves circumcised, Christ will not benefit you at all.* ³ *I am testifying again to every man who is getting himself circumcised that he is a debtor to perform the entire Torah.* ⁴ *You were cut off from Christ, you who are bringing yourselves in line with the Torah; you fell from favor.* ⁵ *For we are awaiting the hope of righteousness by the Spirit on the basis of trust.* ⁶ *For in Christ Jesus neither circumcision nor uncircumcision has any force, but rather faith working through love is what has force.*

a. A number of Western scribes had difficulty with Paul's expression here. Some (F G) change the article τῇ into its corresponding relative pronoun, making the first part of the verse an internally headed relative clause (ᾗ ἐλευθερίᾳ ἡμᾶς Χριστὸς ἠλευθέρωσεν, στήκετε οὖν) dependent upon 4:31 ("for which freedom Christ freed us, stand firm therefore . . ."). 𝔐 incorporates the first half of the verse syntactically into the command in the second half, transposing οὖν and also introducing a relative pronoun: τῇ ἐλευθερίᾳ οὖν ᾗ Χριστὸς ἡμᾶς ἠλευθέρωσεν· στήκετε (hence the KJV, "Stand fast therefore in the liberty wherewith Christ hath made us free"). The sense of the verse remains consistent in these various readings, though the unanimous witness of ℵ, A, and B argues strongly in favor of the reading given in the main text above.

Earlier rhetorical analyses of Galatians tended to identify 2:15–21 as the "proposition" of the speech, the overall point or position to be established.[5] In large measure, this determination was born of the assumption that the parts of a classical deliberative (or judicial) oration would all be found in Galatians, and would all be found in the "proper," textbook order. Thus, having passed through an exordium (1:1–10) and a narration (1:11–2:14), and facing what was clearly a series of proofs (3:1–4:7, at minimum), the intervening verses (2:15–21) *must* represent the intervening section of a speech: the proposition. While 2:15–21 certainly lays out a number of Paul's core convictions, this material is *not* what he seeks to support with the argumentation and precursory

5. Betz, 113–27, esp. 113–14; Witherington, 169–94, esp. 169–71.

appeals of 3:1–4:21. Rather, if there is anything in Galatians that functions as a *propositio*, it is 5:1, Paul's proposal of the course of action that the audience is to adopt, and the contrary course of action that they are to avoid.

This proposal is followed immediately by a series of terse arguments that are themselves summary statements of, or inferences finally drawn from, the arguments that have preceded this paragraph.

- Christ has brought us into freedom (5:1): 3:23–25; 4:1–7, 21–31.
- To put oneself "under law" is to commit to doing "the whole law" (5:3): 3:10–14.
- The paths of trusting and of Torah observance are not compatible (5:2, 4): 2:15–21; 3:10–14, 15–25; 4:21–31.
- Being "in Christ Jesus" nullifies the value of being (or not being) circumcised (5:6): 3:26–29; 4:26–28.
- Returning to live "under law" means nullifying (and repudiating) Christ's death on behalf of the disciple (5:2, 4): 2:19–21; 3:21; 4:8–11.

At the same time, several of these statements in support of the proposal look ahead to further, detailed argumentation that will confirm these statements:

- The Spirit brings righteousness into being among those who trust in Christ's provision and commit themselves thereunto (5:5): 3:2–5; 5:16–25; 6:7–10.
- Walking in love fulfills God's demand for righteousness, even as Torah itself bore witness (5:6): 5:13–15.

As the nexus of the argumentative web of the whole of Galatians and the locus of its primary exhortation, this paragraph far more resembles the "proposition" of the discourse as a whole.

It is a mistake to think of Paul's antithesis in 5:2–6 as one of "faith versus works."[6] This sort of language perpetuates a major error in representing Paul's message, for Paul no more makes "works" in general the target of his polemic than he makes "faith" in general the subject of his approbation. Just as it is only "faith in Christ" that he promotes as the path to justification, so it is only "works of the Torah" that he opposes here as a dead-end path to the same. In the context of 3:1–6:10, moreover, we should bear in mind that "faith in Christ" is closely related to the "Spirit" for Paul, since the Spirit is what "faith in Christ" receives (3:2–5, 13–14), and the Spirit drives the disciple *to* works—the works of love by means of which faith becomes effective.

---

6. As in the section heading in Fung, 221.

1 Paul's urgent goal for this communication is stated most clearly here as Paul directly appeals to his converts to choose *against* the course of action that the rival teachers promote: "Christ freed us to live in a state of freedom; maintain your stance,[7] therefore, and do not again place your neck under a yoke of slavery." This is not *just* a transitional verse,[8] though it *also* effects an admirable transition by displaying the connection between the "indicative" of what God has done for the Galatians (the subject matter of 3:1–4:7, 4:21–31) and the "imperative" that the Galatians must now live out in light of God's favor and gifts (preserving their "freedom" as children of God and heirs of the promised Spirit, and as people who have been redeemed from slavery to the principles and powers of this age). More important, the verse articulates the principal exhortation toward which all of the preceding argumentation has been leading.[9] Its importance is highlighted by its syntactic isolation from what precedes and follows: "No particle or conjunction binds it to what precedes, and no conjunction or particle in 5:2 connects verse 1 to what follows."[10] The most pressing need, according to Paul, is for the Galatians to decide in favor of holding onto their freedom rather than putting their necks under Torah's yoke or the yoke of any other worldly system of rules and values ever again.

Representing the Greek text more woodenly in English, we would read "for *freedom* Christ freed us." The prepositional phrase is fronted for emphasis.[11] "Freedom" is the destination or purpose behind Christ's liberating action.[12] Adolf Deissmann found this expression used in documents recording

---

7. The present tense στήκετε appropriately conveys a durative or habitual sense ("maintain a firm stance"). Schlier (230) thinks of "standing tall" as opposed to stooping down once more to allow a yoke to be placed upon one's shoulders.

8. Against Burton, 270; Fung, 216. The absence of transitional phrases or particles (Betz, 255) helps to establish that this verse has more than a transitional function.

9. Thus deBoer, 327; Dahl, "Paul's Letter," 142; Engberg-Pedersen, *Paul and the Stoics*, 329. The return to this topic in 6:12–16 further indicates that "to be, or not to be, circumcised" is the main and immediate point at issue (Witherington, 364).

10. Williams, 132; so also Dunn, 261.

11. This emphasis is nicely captured by the NIV: "It is for freedom that Christ has set us free." See also Tolmie, *Persuading*, 176.

12. So NRSV, NIV, CEB, representing the dative case noun phrase τῇ ἐλευθερίᾳ. The category "dative of destination" is rare (cf. Acts 22:25; Burton, 271; see "dative of place whither" in Smyth, *Greek Grammar*, §1531) but well suits the context. Schreiner (307) treats this as a dative of purpose (see also Betz, 255–56; Longenecker, 224; Matera, 180; Barrett, *Freedom and Obligation*, 55), a well-established category in Latin but disputed in Greek. Nevertheless, this sense would be essentially the equivalent of the dative of destination here, since the destination is a new state of being rather than a physical place. Betz (255) helpfully observes that the dative here and the prepositional phrase ἐπ᾽ ἐλευθερίᾳ in 5:13 are parallel expressions, reinforcing the understanding of this dative as indicating purpose, goal, or

"sacral manumission," a procedure for freeing a slave in which a slave was liberated from his or her human master, with "ownership" passing to a particular god.[13] Hence, Paul is saying that Christ freed us from bondage to the demonic *stoicheia* in order to allow us to live as free persons ("for freedom"), though still in service to the God and Father of Jesus (as Paul will go on to develop in 5:13–6:10). Freedom speaks here of the new quality of relationship with God and the new level of personal responsibility that comes from being sons and daughters who have come of age (4:1–7).

Indicative and imperative play an important role here in Paul's argumentation (see excursus "Indicative and Imperative in Paul" on pp. 473–76). The word "therefore" in 5:1b signals that this verse as a whole presents itself as an enthymeme, an abbreviated form of syllogistic argument (often simply a statement supported by a single explicated rationale). The action being urged in the imperative clause is presented as the logical conclusion (5:1b) derived from the premise that opens the verse (5:1a). Audiences would be trusted to supply, often intuitively, the missing premise or premises that completed the syllogism (see Aristotle, *Rhetoric* 2.21.2).[14] Paul has given significant attention in the preceding chapters to establishing the premise "for freedom Christ set us free." While the language of freedom and slavery was most prominent in the immediately preceding allegory of the Sarah and Hagar story (4:21–31), freedom, slavery, and release from enslavement (or confinement) have been focal topics in 2:4–5; 3:23–25; and 4:1–11. In the first passage, Paul simply describes his and his converts' state as freedom enjoyed "in Christ"; in the latter two he speaks of God's purposes and the specific results of Christ's death as ending a period of slavery (whether under Torah or under other regulatory principles) and bringing liberation to those who have trusted in Jesus.

What would the audience need to supply in order for the argument to work, that is, in order to effect the all-important transfer of assent to the premise ("Christ freed us to live in a state of freedom") to assent to the conclusion ("Keep standing firm and do not again take up a yoke of slavery")?[15] The audience would readily recognize "freedom" as a good and "enslavement" as

---

destiny/destination. A similar parallelism of expression has been noted in Paul's letter to the Romans (ἐφ᾽ ἐλπίδι, Rom 8:20; τῇ . . . ἐλπίδι, Rom 8:24; see Longenecker, 224).

13. Deissmann, *Light from the Ancient East*, 326–28.

14. See Quintilian, *Education* 5.10.1–3 for several other kinds of enthymeme, and discussion in Aune, "Use and Abuse." It is important to observe that, while the goal of dialectic is logical *necessity*, the goal of rhetoric is merely logical *probability*.

15. See Perelman, *Realm of Rhetoric*, 21. One of the rhetorical benefits of enthymemes as opposed to syllogisms is that they thus invite the audience to "think with" the one who addresses them, to arrive at the speaker's conclusions on their own and thus "own" those conclusions the more securely and personally.

an evil, potentially supplying "freedom is better than slavery" as the premise that completes the syllogism, or the even more general premise that "good things are to be preserved wherever possible."[16] The implicit argument would thus utilize the deliberative topic of expediency.[17]

Paul has also set up the audience, however, to think in terms of costly acts of beneficence and the obligations of beneficiaries. The supporting arguments that will immediately follow (5:2-4) move explicitly in this direction. By stating "Christ freed us" (5:1) rather than "you are free," Paul invites the audience to remember that this condition of freedom was conferred on the believers at significant personal cost to Christ, who "gave himself on account of our sins" (1:4), who "loved me and gave himself for me" (2:20),[18] who "became a curse on our behalf" by being left hanging on a cross (3:13). The addressees would thus also be poised to complete the syllogism by drawing on their awareness of what is appropriate in response to costly gifts and exceptional benevolence (e.g., "that which cost the giver so dearly must be dearly preserved").[19] The audience would infer its obligation to protect and preserve this state of freedom that was conferred on them at such personal cost to Christ. This implicit premise would utilize the deliberative topic of what is just, which includes "repaying one's benefactors" appropriately (Anaximenes, *Rhetoric to Alexander* 1421b38-40; see also Pseudo-Cicero, *Rhetoric for Herennius* 3.3.4).

Paul has facilitated his audience's assent to his proposal by strategically labeling the course of action he wishes for them to reject as submission to a "yoke of slavery." This is a striking way for a Jew to describe the Torah-observant way of life promoted by the rival teachers, but it is potentially effective in nurturing aversion to that way of life. Jewish authors used the image of the yoke to speak about their submission to the Torah (m. Ber. 2:2),

---

16. This logic aligns with Betz's analysis (256): "Given the opportunity of freedom, . . . the task is then . . . the *preservation* of freedom."

17. Anaximenes (*Rhetoric to Alexander* 1421b23-30) finds speakers urging an audience to pursue a certain course of action by showing that course to be "just, lawful, expedient, honorable, pleasant and easily practicable" or, at least, "feasible and unavoidable," and urging an audience to desist from a particular course of action by showing it to be the opposite of these. The "expedient" is further defined as "the preservation of existing good things, or the acquisition of goods that we do not possess, or the rejection of existing evils, or prevention of harmful things expected to occur" (1422a5-7).

18. Paul has already thus articulated his own understanding of his obligation to live the life for which Christ redeemed him as the logical consequence of having experienced this costly redemption (Gal 2:19-21), thus perhaps modeling it for his converts to emulate.

19. John Chrysostom (36) reveals an insider's sensitivity to this implicit dimension of Paul's argument when he writes that the audience "would be convicted of neglect and ingratitude to their Benefactor, in despising Him who had delivered, and loving him who had enslaved them."

but this is a yoke that brings freedom from more oppressive burdens. Rabbi Nehunya ben Haqqaneh, a slightly later contemporary of Paul, is reputed to have said: "From whoever accepts upon himself the yoke of Torah do they remove the yoke of the state and the yoke of hard labor" (m. 'Abot 3.5; Neusner). Wisdom teachers like Ben Sira and Jesus used the image of taking on a yoke as they invited people to learn wisdom from them (Sir 51:26; Matt 11:29). In Ben Sira's case at least, "wisdom's yoke" is the equivalent of Torah's yoke.[20] In all such instances, the "yoke," while signaling submission, is nevertheless beneficial. Paul assures that his hearers will understand the image negatively by describing it as a "yoke of slavery."[21] This yoke is a burden that brings no benefit and, more specifically, is a burden that God does not wish for people to continue to bear—to such an extent that he even sent his Son to die to redeem people from every "yoke of slavery."

So Paul exhorts the Galatians not to "bear[22] *again* a yoke of slavery," signaling once more his equation of the Torah that dominated Jews alongside the *stoicheia* that dominate gentiles (4:8–11). The gentile Christians among the Galatians formerly bore the enslaving yoke of the latter; for them to turn to the Torah is to return "again" to an enslaving yoke.[23] While Paul's characterization of the Torah contrasts sharply with his contemporary Jews' assessment of the same, his position on the ethnic law code of the Jewish people as enslaving would resonate with popular Stoic philosophy. The philosopher and statesman Dio Chrysostom, who was born about the time Galatians was written, defined freedom as "the knowledge of what is allowable and what is forbidden, and slavery as ignorance of what is allowed and what is not" (*Discourses* 14.18). Freedom is not autonomy, nor is it absolute license to do what one wishes in every situation (14.3–6), but rather an opportunity to conform to the absolute law of God. Slavery, in contrast, consists in being unclear on the laws God has laid down for humankind, and in being bound instead by ever-multiplying human-made laws (80.5–7). For Dio, following local, ethnic, national laws while remaining ignorant of "the ordinance of Zeus" is "the grievous and unlawful slavery under whose yoke you have placed your souls"

---

20. See Sir 24:1–23, where the author identifies Wisdom with "the book of the covenant of the Most High God."

21. δουλείας can be understood as an attributive or descriptive genitive.

22. The present tense imperative ἐνέχεσθε is appropriate to the whole lifestyle change to which Paul envisions circumcision obligating the proselyte, namely, keeping the whole of the Torah (5:3). Alternatively, it may more simply suggest that "the action hangs in the balance" (BDF §336.1). The NIV appropriately reads this verb as a passive, introducing a permissive sense ("do not *let* yourselves be burdened") that is well within the semantic range of passive commands.

23. Lagrange, 135; Schlier, 231; Betz, 258; Longenecker, 225; deBoer, 309; Moo, 320–21; Dunn, 262.

(80.7). Paul now classes the Torah with such second-rate law codes, calling it also a "yoke of slavery," relegating it to the period of humanity's ignorance of the law of God written on the heart by the Spirit.[24]

2 The argumentation that follows in 5:2–4 shows clearly that, for Paul, this gift of freedom and this obligation to preserve freedom go hand in hand: "Look: I, Paul, am saying to you that, if you get yourselves circumcised, Christ will not benefit you at all." Paul begins most emphatically, both with the attention-getting command ("Look!") and the underscoring of Paul's personally addressing the Galatians ("I, Paul, myself am saying to you"; see also 2 Cor 10:1).[25] He wants to have their full attention and to bring the full weight of his personal experience and authority (at least his expertise) to bear on the pronouncement he is about to make. Paul, who formerly outstripped his peers in zeal for the Torah (1:13–14), who was formerly a true believer in the value of the Torah-driven life, can speak even more authoritatively than the rival teachers concerning the very course of action *they* are recommending![26]

Paul lays out what is at stake in the decision they have been contemplating: "If you get yourselves circumcised,[27] Christ will not benefit you in any way" (5:2). This is the first time that Paul explicitly speaks of circumcision as an option on the table in Galatia, though it will be prominent hereafter (5:3, 6, 11; 6:12, 13, 15). In this and the following two verses, Paul is drawing a sharp line dividing "grace" from "law." One must choose whether to rely on Torah

---

24. Thielman (*Paul and the Law*, 137–38) argues too strongly for a new exodus background to the language of slavery in Galatians to the exclusion of other immediate backgrounds, especially the use of slavery and freedom as moral categories in terms of ethnic laws (versus God's universal law) and in terms of one's relationship to one's own passions (see below on Gal 5:13–25). These uses pervade Hellenistic Jewish literature (Philo's *Good Person* being an especially concentrated example) and their exclusion in favor of Old Testament resonances is artificial.

25. The explicit subject pronoun ἐγώ is emphatic. The NIV and NRSV appropriately supply idiomatic English equivalents ("Mark my words" and "Listen!" respectively) for the Greek Ἴδε, traditionally rendered "Behold!" ("Look," CEB).

26. Schlier (231) observes that Paul's authority, in part, comes from the fact that he is not a Jew of some liberal or hellenizing disposition but was once a champion of observing the covenant obligations as Israel's way of aligning itself with God's righteousness.

27. Longenecker, 225; Witherington, 365. Whether this form is understood as middle or passive in voice, it can still yield a permissive sense (e.g., "allow yourselves to be circumcised"). See BDF §§314, 317; so NRSV, NIV; CEB gives the verb a causative nuance ("if you have yourselves circumcised"), as here. The third-class condition suggests that the majority, at least, of the gentile Galatian Christians have not yet taken the step of submitting to circumcision. DeBoer (311) suggests that we read this sentence more in terms of ongoing community practice: "If you all were to take up the practice of circumcision." His grammatical arguments, however, do not make it less likely that Paul is indeed very much concerned with what individual Galatian Christians are about to do right then and there.

for aligning oneself with God's righteousness *or* on the favor that God has shown in the Messiah's ransoming death and in the gift of the Holy Spirit, and thus also on the sufficiency of the Spirit to bring righteousness to life within and among the Christian disciples.

The consequence of accepting circumcision on the rival teachers' terms is that "Christ will not benefit you at all" (5:2).[28] The verb here speaks of the action of a person who offers help or assistance to another person and thus is well suited to the benefactor-beneficiary relationship that is presupposed (and presupposed as *endangered*) in these verses.[29] Christ will cease to act as the personal patron of the converts, and all the gifts bestowed because of his generous favor will cease to be operative.[30] He "gave himself to ransom them from this present, evil age" (1:4), but this act would do them no good if they put themselves back under the power of this present, evil age.

An argument from the consequences is, according to Quintilian (*Education* 5.10.1–3), another kind of enthymeme. What would help the audience agree that the proposed consequence would indeed follow from the action named in the protasis (i.e., accepting circumcision at this point in the journey and the Torah-observant lifestyle it presupposes)? Paul has been preparing them to fill in the necessary logical steps throughout the preceding arguments. Paul had previously asserted, in speaking of his own case, that returning to lining up one's life with the Torah would have meant setting aside God's favor shown in Christ—thus, in refusing to do the former, he was able to claim: "I do not void out God's favor" (2:21). He further asserted that, had Torah been the divinely appointed means for all people to fall into line with God's righteousness, then Jesus would have died for nothing. The implication

---

28. The case of οὐδέν can be understood as an accusative of respect ("in regard to nothing"), accusative of extent ("not . . . at all," as here and in the NIV), or adverbial accusative ("in no way").

29. BDAG 1107; LSJ 2042; see also 1 Cor 14:6. The NIV ("Christ will be of no value") uses a gloss for the verb ὠφελήσει that is more suited to an inanimate subject than a person (BDAG 1107; thus in Rom 2:25) and so represents Christ more as a commodity than a party who will or will not continue to accept a particular role in a particular relationship. The CEB misses the mark further by representing the subject not as "Christ," but as "having Christ" ("having Christ won't help you"), representing Christ as an object possessed by the audience rather than as the subject who will decide whether to continue in a grace relationship with the audience.

30. While some scholars associate the future tense of ὠφελήσει only or primarily with Christ's assistance at the last judgment (Schlier, 231; Betz, 259; Witherington, 367; Tolmie, *Persuading*, 179), it is more correct to hear it as an affirmation that Christ will no longer help the converts at *any* point after they undergo circumcision (Longenecker, 226; deBoer, 312). The absolute pronouncement of being severed from favor "already" (in effect) in 5:4 supports this reading. One enjoys Christ's benefits only by continued connection with him: "God's grace does not yet endow the individual with irreversible benefit" (Das, 529).

is that one cannot both adopt a Torah-observant lifestyle and properly value Christ's giving of himself over to death. Paul followed this argument immediately by reminding the hearers that they received a precious and powerful gift from God—the Holy Spirit—solely on the basis of trusting Jesus to provide them with God's means for justification (3:1–5). According to him, turning now to circumcision and Torah observance to secure alignment with God's righteousness is the product of a lack of confidence—a lack of "faith"—in the adequacy of the ability of the Spirit, the divine gift secured for the converts by Jesus's self-giving death, to effect that end.[31] Such a turn would effectively repudiate the effects of Jesus's death in the economy of God (3:23–25; 4:1–11), showing contempt for the same rather than due gratitude, and thus breaking the relationship of favor.[32]

3 Paul follows this pronouncement of a negative consequence with a second, which he begins with equal solemnity, continuing his expert witness ("I testify again").[33] The word "again" does not imply that Paul has taught the Galatians about the unified nature of Torah observance on a previous visit. Rather, it signals that this statement of testimony reinforces what Paul has just asserted in 5:2, though now from another angle.[34] Galatians 5:2 states the loss,

---

31. Paul is, of course, not talking about Jewish Christians, whose circumcision was decided for them on their eighth day of life, or about Jewish Christians who continue to circumcise their infants for cultural reasons, but about those currently on the verge of undergoing the procedure because they have been convinced that trusting Christ and receiving the Spirit are not enough (Lagrange, 136; Schlier, 232; Fung, 222). "If you let yourselves be circumcised" (5:2) addresses adult gentile Christians about to make a decision based on an assessment of the sufficiency or insufficiency of the Holy Spirit. Similarly, Paul's words "to every person undergoing circumcision" (5:3) speak about those now in the process of making that decision, not those for whom that decision had been made in infancy.

32. See deSilva, *Honor*, 110–12, 115–16, 145; also Wright, *Justification*, 138. Commenting on this passage as a whole, John Chrysostom (36) drew similarly upon the social logic of reciprocity: "He that is circumcised is circumcised for fear of the Law, and he who fears the Law, distrusts the power of grace, and he who distrusts can receive no benefit from that which is distrusted."

33. Greek, μαρτύρομαι δὲ πάλιν. The particle δέ introduces a new development in the argument, here as Paul supplies a second argument from the consequences (the first was presented in 5:2) in support of the course of action recommended in 5:1. The middle voice μαρτύρομαι carries a greater degree of solemnity than its active form (Lagrange, 136; Burton, 274).

34. Lagrange, 136; Matera, 181, who draws attention to 1:8–9 as a similar instance; Longenecker, 226; deBoer, 313; Moo, 322. Such "redundancy . . . indicates emphasis and importance" (Witherington, 368). Paul has, however, also already hinted at this "all or nothing" requirement of Torah previously in Galatians itself, at 3:10, where he adaptively quotes the words of Deut 27:26 ("Cursed is everyone who fails to live by *all* the things written in the book of the law, to do them"), and so Paul might well have this in mind as a previous statement concerning the burden of the law (so Tolmie, *Persuading*, 180). See also Rom 2:25–29; Jas 2:10; m. 'Abot 2.1; 4.2; 4 Macc 5:20–21; Sir 7:8 (cited in Witherington, 368).

and 5:3 the "gain," which is a fearsome obligation indeed—"Good lost, and Evil got" (*Paradise Lost* 9.1072): "I am testifying again to every man who is getting himself circumcised that he is a debtor to perform the *entire* Torah."[35]

Paul wants to emphasize that the Torah is a complete package deal, even as Christ's death and provision of the Spirit constitute a complete package. Circumcision is a ritual initiation into a covenant that regulates every facet of one's life and of one's dealings with God. Christ and his gifts, on the one hand, and on the other, Torah and its stipulations are not all laid out buffet style for the consumer to select so many items from this cart and so many items from that cart. Paul subtly reinforces the incompatibility of enjoying Jesus's favor and choosing to align oneself with Torah as the means of securing acquittal before God with a clever word play: Christ will not "benefit" or "oblige" (*ōphelēsei*, 5:2) those who, by accepting circumcision, make themselves "debtors," or "people obligated to" (*opheiletēs*), the whole law (5:3).[36]

The rival teachers would, of course, have also stressed to the hearers that circumcision was an induction into a Torah-driven lifestyle. Indeed, it was typically the climactic move in a non-Jewish male's process of bringing his life into alignment with God's law, and not a first step. But Paul speaks as if his rivals have not told the *whole* story concerning their future dependence upon Torah. What does he think he is revealing to the audience here that they have not already heard from his rivals? The rival teachers would have looked to Jesus's death as the locus of saving benefits and encouraged the hearers that they would continue to enjoy these benefits, even as they now began to look to the Torah for other saving benefits. Paul, however, has been preparing the hearers to recognize the incompatibility of the two. "I do not set God's gift aside, for if righteousness is through the Torah, then Christ died for nothing" (2:21). Entering into the Torah-observant lifestyle as the means of bringing oneself in line with God means repudiating the benefits of Jesus's death on their behalf. If Christ died to "rescue us from this present, evil age" (1:4), then putting oneself back under the powers of this age means repudiating the benefits of Jesus's death.

When Paul wrote this letter, the sacrificial cult prescribed by Torah and conducted in the Jerusalem temple was bustling with the activity of people bringing sin/guilt offerings, purification offerings, and well-being offerings, not to mention the twice-daily offering (the *tāmîd*) that was Israel's sign of

---

35. The phrase ὅλον τὸν νόμον is underscored by virtue of being fronted before ποιῆσαι (rightly, Fung, 222). A gender-specific rendering of the Greek ἄνθρωπος (so also NRSV, NIV, CEB) is appropriate, given the context, though not inherent in the word itself. DeBoer (313) suggests, however, that Paul has used ἄνθρωπος specifically to stress that the issues are relevant for Galatian Christians of both genders, even though the particular rite of circumcision applies only to one gender.

36. Dunn, 265.

perpetual loyalty to their covenant God (Exod 29:38–42; Num 28:1–8). Trusting in Torah means going back to trusting in—and having to perform—those sacrifices as the means of mediation between God and the community of God, the means of sustaining and repairing the relationship between God and the person. One cannot hold to Christ's death as the fulfillment of a portion of Torah (the cultic aspects of its ritual law) while clinging to the validity of other portions.[37] Once the Galatians express distrust for Jesus, they also renounce the Christ who "died for our sins" (1:4). Thus, if the Galatian Christians submit to circumcision,[38] Christ's death also "will not benefit" them. They commit themselves to the whole ritual-cultic system of dealing with God—something even the rival teachers have not figured out for themselves in their selective attention to the Torah (6:13).

4 Paul restates the consequence he posited in 5:2: "You were cut off from Christ, you who are bringing yourselves in line with the Torah; you fell from favor." While this verse does not significantly advance the logical argument (though it certainly reinforces the point), it contributes to the appeal at other levels. Paul maintains that those who are thinking to bring themselves in line with God's standards by performing circumcision and observing other "works of Torah"[39] have grossly underestimated what Christ's death has ac-

---

37. I do not believe that "the only way 5:3 can function as a technique of *dissuasion* is if obeying the whole law is difficult or impossible" (Das, 325; see also Gundry, "Grace, Works, and Staying Saved," 23–27; Schnelle, *Apostle Paul*, 293) or if Paul is asserting that "the law is an absolute demand which must be perfectly fulfilled" (Watson, *Paul, Judaism, and the Gentiles*, 71). The Torah did not require perfect obedience, as it made provisions for atonement for unwitting transgressions. See commentary on 3:10–11; also Cranford, "Possibility of Perfect Obedience"; Dunn, 266–67. Paul claims rather that, even though obeying the whole law is feasible, those who turn to the Torah will be parting company with Jesus entirely. And it was that encounter with the living Jesus through the Spirit, after all, that made these Galatians leave their former way of life and religious practice—and all the social systems that sustained and were nurtured by the same—out of a desire for a closer walk with this Jesus. That is a huge chip to put on the table, asking, "Are you really sure you want to let *this* ride?"

38. Whether one construes περιτεμνομένῳ as a middle or a passive voice form, a permissive sense remains possible (i.e., "allow yourselves to be circumcised"; BDF §§314, 317). Paul uses the present tense here in part because he could not have used an aorist or perfect without impugning Jewish Christians, who are already circumcised.

39. The person who is δίκαιος ("righteous") is righteous in regard to a particular standard. The present tense of the verb δικαιόω is being translated accordingly here as "lining [something] up with a standard so as to render it 'just' in regard to that standard." Many English translations render δικαιοῦσθε with a modal verb ("You who *want* to be justified," NRSV, cf. ESV; "You who *are trying* to be justified," NIV, cf. CEB; emphasis mine). Though allowed by standard grammars (see BDF §319; Smyth §1878; Wallace, *Greek Grammar*, 535), Fee (*Empowering Presence*, 416n170) rightly objects that introducing a modal verb here is superfluous, reading the phrase instead as "you who are achieving righteousness by law." The NRSV and ESV may have introduced modal verbs out of a desire, conscious or otherwise, to

complished, undervalued God's gift of the Spirit, and not preserved Christ's gift of freedom. These affronts to the Giver stand behind Paul's dramatic language of the breaking off of the "grace" relationship between the believer and Christ: "you were cut off from Christ . . . you fell from favor" (5:4).[40]

"Grace" ("favor") is probably *not* best thought of "as a sphere or 'domain' in which one stands,"[41] unless we are very clear that we are speaking about a *relational* space. Grace must never be depersonalized, never seen as something separate from or even having any existence apart from the One who is graciously disposed, which disposition itself constitutes this "grace in which we stand" (Rom 5:2).[42] And Paul has hitherto painted a winsome picture of what it means to "stand" in favor: reception of God's Holy Spirit (3:2–5), which assures the disciples also of adoption into God's own family as people joined together with the Seed par excellence (3:15–18, 26, 29; 4:6–7); the promise of deliverance from the present, evil age ultimately (1:4), enjoyed proleptically in being freed from the domination of the *stoicheia* of this age (4:1–5, 8–9a) with the lines they have drawn through human community, severing and perverting the same (3:26–28); the enjoyment of a new quality of relationship with God, unattainable in previous arrangements, that can be described only as "coming alive" to God (2:19–20; 3:21). All of this is now in jeopardy, as Paul's converts flirt with the alternative in what he has laid out as a pair of incompatible options.[43]

The use of the aorist tense in this verse ("you were cut off," "you fell") is striking, but not terribly problematic. Paul does not mean that these actions

---

ensure that Paul is not seen to admit the possibility of justification by means of law. Translating the verb δικαιοῦσθε with less theologically laden language ("lining yourselves up with the law's standards for 'righteousness'") accomplishes the same end without overloading the present indicative. The form used in Gal 5:4 could be taken as a passive voice ("you who are being aligned") or a middle voice ("you who are aligning yourselves"). Both the historical and the literary context—where the hearers are taking steps to bring themselves in line with what the rival teachers say God requires—suggest that we understand the middle voice here. The prepositional phrase ἐν νόμῳ can be understood as essentially a dative of reference or instrument. Burton (276) suggests that it is functionally equivalent to the phrase ἐξ ἔργων νόμου in 2:16.

40. NIV "alienated" and CEB "estranged" capture well the sense of the verb κατηργήθητε in the context of the breaking off of a relationship and with it, as in Rom 7:1–6, any ongoing mutual obligations (see BDAG 526; so also Matera, 182; Williams, 137).

41. Against the position of Fung, 223.

42. To the extent that (particularly) Protestant theologians conceptualize grace as the isolated transference of a commodity (like "salvation" or "righteous status" or whatever) as opposed to the initiation of an ongoing relationship of gift and response, they are out of touch with Paul's native conception of grace and disposed, as a result, to underestimate the consequences of the recipient's actions or failures to act for his or her eschatological destiny (see deSilva, "We Are Debtors").

43. Schlier, 228.

have indeed already befallen his addressees.[44] The aorist tense is chosen, not to be temporally precise, but rhetorically effective. Paul makes the consequences more vivid and thereby potentially heightens a response of fear that will motivate an immediate volte-face—"you stepped off the cliff, so turn around and grab on to what you once had as fast as you can!"[45] He points back to the place where they began to look to Torah observance as the effective means of their transformation into people who would be righteous in God's sight and says, "There—right there's where you alienated Christ, right there's where you broke off this grace relationship." Aristotle observed that speakers could induce fear by portraying seriously unwelcome consequences as imminent, and conversely that consequences perceived as more remote do not arouse sufficient fear to provoke a response on an emotional basis (*Rhetoric* 2.5.1). Paul's statements in 5:2–4 cumulatively place the hearers in a very unwelcome situation, with 5:4 stating the danger most starkly (with the absolute loss of that which initially attracted them to the Christian movement to begin with). Paul nurtures a connection between the course of action the Galatians are considering and a gut-level response of fear that will stimulate aversion from that course.

5 Paul gives clear signals in 5:5–6 that he is advancing the rational argumentation behind his appeal. Each of these two verses is introduced with the conjunction "for," which signals that the material is being presented as a supporting rationale for what precedes: "For we are awaiting the hope of righteousness by the Spirit on the basis of trust. For in Christ Jesus neither circumcision nor uncircumcision has any force, but rather faith working through love is what has force." But for *what* preceding claim are these statements offering argumentative support?

The most natural, because sequential, reading would be to understand the claim of 5:5 as a rationale, specifically an argument from the contrary, supportive of the material in 5:4.[46] The two verses are certainly connected in Paul's argument. Paul creates a contrast between two groups in 5:4–5, under-

---

44. Burton (276) reads this as a factual statement about some Galatians who have gone ahead with the procedure, though it remains possible, even probable, that Paul would not regard this as an irreversible loss for those who came back around to his way of thinking (Jervis, 132–33; Das, 525). Most translations render the aorist as an English perfect ("*have been* cut off," "*have* fallen") rather than simple past to make the juxtaposition of an action in progress with a past consequence of said action still in progress (!) stylistically more palatable (so NRSV, NIV, CEB).

45. See Turner, *Syntax*, 74; Zerwick, *Biblical Greek*, 84 (§257); Witherington, 368–69. The NLT weakens the rhetorical force of the verse significantly by turning it into a conditional clause.

46. Burton, 278; Fung, 224: specifically "against the validity of reliance on works of the law for justification."

scored by careful parallelism in phrasing and wording, between a hypothetical "you" who "are lining yourselves up with 'righteousness' by means of Torah" (5:4) and an emphatic "*we*" who are awaiting "the hope of righteousness by the Spirit on the basis of faith" (5:5).[47] After the dire consequences predicted—and even announced as fulfilled—for the "you" who are on the path to circumcision (5:2–4), the hearers have additional motivation to identify themselves with the "we" of 5:5, for whom beneficial consequences are anticipated.[48] Galatians 5:5 might be heard to provide a rationale in support of an unexpressed inference to be drawn from 5:4,[49] namely, that those who seek to embody the righteousness that God will approve at the last judgment by the path of aligning themselves with the stipulations of Torah will *fail* to attain that righteousness (something expressed explicitly in 2:15–16; 3:10–14). Such righteousness comes through an entirely other path now that "faith has come" (3:23).

One might also consider 5:5 to offer evidence—at least indirectly—in support of the primary exhortation of 5:1, providing a positive incentive after the negative disincentives of 5:2–4. The Galatians can "maintain their stance" (5:1) knowing that the course on which they have been heading leads to "righteousness," the result of which is acquittal on the last day. Galatians 5:5 is itself a terse summary of Paul's position, articulated and established in 2:14–4:31.[50] Trusting and the consequent walking in the Spirit, who was given as an inheritance to those who trust (3:14; 5:5; 5:16–6:10), is the basis for attaining and the means to attain righteousness (alignment with God's standards), in contrast with aligning oneself with the Torah (5:4).[51] This po-

---

47. The nominative pronoun ἡμεῖς is emphatic, highlighting the contrast. The contrast between 5:4 and 5:5 is underscored by Paul in the repetition of words formed on the δικαι-root and by the by-now familiar contrast between "law" and "faith" (ἐν νόμῳ δικαιοῦσθε, 5:4; ἐκ πίστεως . . . δικαιοσύνης, 5:5).

48. While some commentators argue that the "we" still refers here to Paul and Jewish Christians, as in 2:15–16 (Longenecker, 229; Witherington, 369), the contextual indicators that would be necessary to signal to the hearers that they ought to exclude themselves (indicators that were present in 2:14–16) are lacking here. This "we" more likely distinguishes Paul and, he hopes (see 5:10), his Galatian converts from the rival teachers and those who succumb to their teaching, "effectively inviting the Galatians to see the matter as he does, and so to stand fast (5:1)" (deBoer, 315–16; so also Das, 527; Tolmie, *Persuading*, 181).

49. On this phenomenon, see BDAG 189.

50. Betz, 262; Longenecker, 228.

51. The prepositional phrase ἐκ πίστεως may be understood as indicating basis or means. The latter is favored by Burton (278), who regards trust as the "subjective condition" that complements the Spirit as "objective power," both of which contribute to the end result. By this point in the epistle, Paul may assume that his audience will hear this phrase as an abbreviated expression for ἐκ πίστεως Χριστοῦ, trust directed toward Christ (Betz, 263; Choi, "ΠΙΣΤΙΣ in Galatians 5:5–6," 467). See the extended note on this much-debated phrase and the functionally equivalent διὰ πίστεως at the commentary on 2:16. DeBoer (316–17),

sition has been thematic throughout the preceding argumentation. Paul has sought throughout 2:14–4:31 to win assent to the premise articulated in 5:5, which, if accepted, lends further support for accepting the conclusion of 5:1.

Galatians 5:5–6 contributes to developing a larger picture of justification as transformative process rather than a forensic, declarative act. Paul is not talking about the goal as merely being *declared* righteous while not actually *being* righteous in God's sight. The Christian hope as he expresses it is nothing less than transformation into Spirit-led and Spirit-empowered people who do and are what pleases God, as Paul will develop in 5:13–6:10. "Righteousness," an ethical quality that the Spirit is nurturing within the believer (see 2:21 and comment), remains God's goal for the believer (Gal 5:5).[52] Paul's objection is that *lining oneself up with Torah* (5:4) does not make one righteous before God, in large measure because doing so *both* continues to maintain the lines that God has obliterated in Christ *and* fails to respect the limited term that God had prescribed for Torah's operation. Instead, God "justifies" ("rectifies") people—God makes people righteous, bringing them in line with his standards—through the Spirit.[53] Indeed, Paul will go on to explore at length, in 5:13–6:10, how this process of "walking in line with the Spirit" (5:25) leads to genuine righteousness.[54] God sends the Spirit into Jew and gentile alike to bring all who believe into conformity with God's character

---

who favors understanding the expression in 2:16 as "Jesus's faith or faithfulness" (hence as a subjective genitive), understands "faith" here as an abbreviated reference to "Christ's faithful death," though that interpretation asks far more of the reader in terms of what must be supplied than the more common reading. For the arguments in favor of reading the prepositional phrase adverbially (describing the action of "eagerly expecting") rather than adjectivally (describing the Spirit), see Das, 528.

52. With Burton, 278; Ziesler, *Meaning of Righteousness*, 179; Dunn, 269–70; Gorman, *Inhabiting*, 72 ("The phrase 'hope of righteousness' in Gal 5:5 implies a full, future transformation, not merely acquittal"); contra, for example, Schreiner, 316; Moo, 327. Moo believes that a "purely forensic sense" is "in keeping with δικ- language throughout the letter," but an ethical sense is no less in keeping with Paul's interest in the ethical transformation of the person who has trusted Christ and received the Spirit *precisely* for this purpose (5:13–6:10). See 2:16 and the extended note on justification language in Galatians. Though generally supportive of final justification on the basis of a transformed life, Wright (*Justification*, 144) similarly reduces "the hope of *dikaiosunē*" ("righteousness") to "the verdict that is still eagerly awaited." Again, other Greek words were readily available had Paul intended to denote "verdict" rather than "a moral quality manifested in a particular set of commitments and practices" (the widest and most natural sense of δικαιοσύνη in Greco-Roman and Jewish discourse) that will, incidentally, be recognized as such at the last judgment.

53. The "Spirit" (πνεύματι) is the means by which, or perhaps the sphere in which, God's righteousness takes shape in the disciple.

54. This is an important indication that the remaining material in Gal 5–6 is an integral part of Paul's strategy for intervening in his converts' immediate situation.

and purpose, transforming them into the image of the Righteous One, Jesus himself (Gal 4:19; 2:20), and causing the people of God to reflect the unity of the one God (3:20, 28). Righteousness is something that Paul and his faithful converts look forward to in hope as the outcome of this transformative process (5:5).[55] Because this transformation depends entirely upon the action and empowerment of God's Spirit, it remains fully justification on the basis of faith and on the basis of that which faith has received from God, namely, the promised Spirit.[56]

6 Paul adds a confirmation of the rationale articulated in 5:5, specifically offering evidence that faith has the necessary efficacy, and indeed is the only thing that has such efficacy, to bring one in line with God's righteous standards: "For in Christ Jesus neither circumcision nor uncircumcision has any force, but rather faith working through love is what has force." This verse also provides an effective summary of Paul's preceding argument and a précis of the contribution that the following section (5:13–6:10) will yet make to his argument. The first half of the verse ("neither circumcision nor [having] a foreskin has any impact") is a concluding summary, essentially, of Paul's refutation of the rival teachers' position in favor of undergoing circumcision.[57] Most specifically, it recalls the climactic remark in Gal 3:28 (it-

---

55. The genitive noun δικαιοσύνης should be understood either as an objective genitive ("the righteousness for which we hope," as in NIV; Schrenk, "Dikē," 207–8; Dunn, 270) or genitive of apposition ("what we hope for, namely, righteousness," here understanding ἐλπίδα metonymically, the "hope" in place of "the thing hoped for"; see Burton, 279; Lagrange, 137); so also Silva, *Interpreting*, 182; Tolmie, *Persuading*, 181. One may profitably compare the Pauline phrases "the hope of glory" (Rom 5:2; Col 1:27) and "hope of deliverance" (1 Thess 5:8). "Righteousness" has also been named as a prominent goal in 2:21; 3:21, making it therefore a suitable object of hope here in 5:5.

In an awkward attempt to avoid the ethical focus of Paul's language in 5:5-6, Fung (226) tries to construe "righteousness" as a subjective genitive. He argues that 5:5 should be understood as "we look for that which righteousness (= the righteous) hopes for" or "the hope to which the justification of believers points them forward." In either case, the reader is having to import a great deal more semantic material to arrive at this understanding. Lagrange (137) also favors this understanding but is more forthright about the theological presuppositions that *demand* that the verse be read this way: "Righteousness *cannot* be the thing hoped for by the Christian, *since* justification, in Paul's teaching, is the entrance into the Christian life. . . . δικαιοσύνης *must* therefore be a subjective genitive" (my translation and emphases).

56. On this point, Bultmann ("Das Problem der Ethik," 140) was quite correct.

57. Longenecker, 228. The usefulness of this formulation in the Galatian situation is shown by its repetition, with some modification, in 6:15: "For neither is circumcision nor a foreskin anything of significance, but rather a new creation!" The coordinating conjunctions οὔτε . . . οὔτε link περιτομή and ἀκροβυστία as equal subjects of ἰσχύει and thus equally without positive significance or effect in the economy of God. The indefinite pronoun τι is to be understood either as an accusative of reference ("in regard to anything") or perhaps as

self supported by the argumentation of 2:14–3:27) that "there is neither Jew nor Greek," circumcision and lack of circumcision being defining physical marks of the distinction between Jew and Greek and ciphers for the *value* in God's sight of that distinction.[58] The dividing lines drawn by Torah no longer have any value or force in God's economy. The claim also rests upon the arguments in 3:15–4:7 that proposed that Torah, with circumcision as the mark of being "under Torah," had a defined term limit that was now expired. It rests upon Paul's sense that a decisively "new creation" (see the parallel statement in 6:15) is taking shape "in Christ"—that is, among the global community of people who have put on Christ in baptism (3:27) and within whom Christ is being formed (2:20; 4:19). In this way, 5:6 supports Paul's claim that "the hope of becoming righteous" (5:5) belongs to those who rely on the Spirit rather than those who align themselves with the stipulations of the expired Torah, since the latter offers *no* means to that end at all.[59]

The second half of this antithesis, "but a faith that keeps on making itself effective through love is what has force,"[60] names the path that effectively leads to righteousness by the working of the Spirit. This important qualification of "faith" anticipates the final major section of the epistle (5:13–6:10), wherein Paul will describe how trust and the provision of the Spirit are, in fact, sufficient to bring a person into conformity with God's righteousness, and thus to lead to acquittal at the judgment (see esp. 5:21; 6:7–8).

It is theologically significant that Paul does *not* write that "the only thing that counts is faith." Rather, he carefully qualifies what kind of faith counts before God,[61] namely, "faith that continues to invest itself in loving

---

the accusative direct object of an unexpressed complementary infinitive ("has force/power *to accomplish* anything").

58. The phrase ἐν . . . Χριστῷ Ἰησοῦ in 5:6, naming the sphere within which the claim is true, closely recalls the language of 3:26–27 (ἐν Χριστῷ, εἰς Χριστόν).

59. Paul's antithetical formulation also effects a strategic reduction of the scope and significance of the opposing party's concern (to the condition of the foreskin, whether or not an individual has undergone a ritual peculiar to one ethnic group), contrasting something now trivial and superficial with a concern tied to moral value and other-centered behavior ("faith working through love").

60. Technically, the words "is what has force" are supplied and do not stand in the Greek. πίστις is the nominative subject of an elided ἰσχύει, which is clearly to be inferred as the verb for the second half of the statement, even as it functioned thus in the first half, completing the antithesis.

61. Fung, 229; see also Bird, *Saving Righteousness*, 178: "Works as christologically conceived, pneumatically empowered, and divinely endowed are necessary for salvation in so far as they reveal the character of authentic faith expressed in the form of obedience, love, faithfulness, righteousness and holiness." Fung (230), however, is compelled to affirm that this does *not* mean that love such as we show plays any real role in justification, as this would

action."[62] This is the formula for righteousness under the new covenant and under the Spirit's guidance and empowerment. This is the kind of "faith" that leads disciples toward the realization of their hope to attain righteousness in the Spirit and through faith (5:5).[63] "Thus 'faith' is not some form of 'easy believism'; neither does the elimination of Torah observance thereby eliminate righteousness. Rather, faith 'works'—expresses itself—in the ultimate form of the Christian ethic, love."[64] Such love is possible, of course, only because of God's gift of the Holy Spirit, who brings the Spirit's fruit to maturity within us and in our lives (as Paul will go on to develop in 5:13–25). Love (in Greek, the familiar *agapē*) will become a keyword in Paul's positive discussion of the life that is aligned with God's Spirit, as love for neighbor represents the core command of the Torah (such that the person who loves the neighbor essentially *fulfills* the Torah without *doing* Torah; 5:13–14) and is the primary fruit of the Spirit (5:22).[65]

---

suggest some kind of synergy of God's action and ours. It is sufficient for me to note that faith that *fails* to express itself in works of love is not the kind of faith that brings one in line with God's righteousness, and hence does not lead to justification before God.

62. "Investing itself in . . . action" and "making itself effective" are attempts to capture the significance of the middle voice of the participle ἐνεργουμένη. The form could technically also be construed as passive, but the absence of any agent responsible for the action tips the scales against this interpretation (see Mussner, 353–54; Lagrange, 138). The verb appears in the middle also in Rom 7:5; 2 Cor 1:6; 4:12; Eph 1:11; 2:2; 3:20; 1 Thess 2:13; 2 Thess 2:7; Col 1:29, and never as a passive in the Pauline or para-Pauline corpus. Paul uses a present tense (i.e., a participle with an imperfective aspect) participle to portray "working through love" as a process or a habit of the "faith" that has such value in God's sight. The prepositional phrase δι' ἀγάπης specifies the means by which faith invests itself or makes itself effective.

63. Schlier (235; my translation) rightly observes, "Of course this is to be understood as 'trust in the Son of God', but here it is not a matter of its . . . object, but a matter of the manner of its manifestation." The connection between faith and obedient response to God is forged even more closely by Watson (*Paul, Judaism, and the Gentiles*, 64): "For Paul, faith is inconceivable without, for example, the abandonment of participation in idolatry (1 Thes. 1:9) or the practice of 'love', i.e. commitment to the new community of the church (Gal. 5:6). It is not simply that these things inevitably *follow* from faith, so that one could theoretically distinguish them from faith; on the contrary, faith *is* the abandonment of old norms and beliefs and the adoption of new ones."

64. Fee, *Empowering*, 420; see also Barclay, *Obeying*, 94: "Although the true Abrahamic family are free from the yoke of the law, they are not free from the obligation to *work*—to turn their faith into loving behavior. Once again it is clear that Paul is not at all concerned in this letter to attack 'works' as such, only works of *the law*."

65. DeBoer (318) reads Gal 5:6 completely in light of Gal 2:20 and also in light of a subjective-genitive reading of "faith of Jesus Christ," with the result that 5:6 is taken as an extremely abbreviated phrase for "Christ's faith(fulness) becoming effective through his self-giving love for us." This reading, however, seems to conflict with deBoer's own (correct) understanding that Gal 5:5–6 looks ahead to 5:13–6:10, "where the unifying theme is the love

A watchword of Galatians is "freedom," brought home most forcefully in the climactic command of 5:1. The passage summons disciples in every age to take care what they bind to themselves and upon those in their charge. Traditions are valuable, decorum in worship is valuable, guardrails on behavior are valuable, but Spirit-led freedom is more valuable than any of these. There is a great deal of wisdom in the Christian tradition about Christian practice, but "wisdom" is not "law." *Devotion* to tradition or to our sense of decorum or our own valued guardrails can easily slide into *slavery* to the same—and not just our own enslavement, but we quickly find ourselves expecting other Christian disciples to shoulder the same yoke or else we judge them to be the less for it. Paul would also be quick to remind us, as he reminded the Galatians, that this freedom is at the same time freedom *for* the pursuit of righteousness by the Spirit on the basis of trusting Jesus. It is not freedom from having to do something, but freedom in the way in which one moves forward into the righteousness that pleases God, because this righteousness is being fashioned within us by God.

Circumcision as a rite of entry into the people of God is no longer a significant issue among Christian churches. Nevertheless, Paul's stern warning about the incompatibility of trying to align ourselves with God's righteousness by means of following the Spirit in faith and by means of following external regulations, whether based in the Torah or created within Christian culture, remains an important reason to examine our practice and the practice of our churches in this regard.

The historic Torah as external code to be followed still plays an important role in several Christian denominations. It does so, moreover, in ways that serve as boundary markers between those who are "in" and those who are "out," just as it did in Paul's situation. One example would be the role of the Sabbath among Seventh-day Adventists or the Worldwide Church of God, where it becomes a distinctive mark of genuine obedience, even of one's identity as a "true Christian."[66] Where Christians practice Sabbath obser-

---

produced by the Spirit" (315), thus the ethical response manifested in the way Christians practice love toward one another and toward non-Christians. Choi ("ΠΙΣΤΙΣ in Galatians 5:5–6," 482–89) argues for a similarly forced interpretation of "faith" as Jesus's faithfulness here, against reading πίστις δι᾿ ἀγάπης ἐνεργουμένη as "an ethical principle of Christian behavior" (470).

66. "The fourth commandment of *God's unchangeable law requires* the observance of this seventh-day Sabbath as the day of rest, worship, and ministry in harmony with the teaching and practice of Jesus, the Lord of the Sabbath" (www.adventist.org/en/beliefs/living/the-sabbath, emphasis mine); "The seventh day of the week is the Sabbath of the Lord our God, and on this day humans are commanded to rest from their labors and worship Him. Established and blessed by God at creation, the seventh day of the week begins at sunset on Friday and continues until sunset on Saturday. The Sabbath is an identifying sign

vance as an expression of their own commitment to honor God (the God who created the heavens and the earth and rested on the seventh day, the God of the exodus, who gave rest to oppressed slaves), Paul would affirm their practice. Where Christians practice the observance of the "Lord's Day" (the first day of the week, hence Sunday) as an expression of their own commitment to honor God (the God who vindicated Jesus as the Christ on the first day of the week, the God who gives life to the dead), Paul would affirm *their* practice. Where Sabbath-observant Christians tell other Christians that they are breaking God's law and outside of God's will because they worship on Sunday, or harbor in their hearts the notion that they are themselves more acceptable to God because they observe Saturday rather than Sunday as their day of worship and rest, Paul would take serious issue. (Indeed, he *does* take serious issue with this specifically in Rom 14:1–12.) The question of observing one day or another reflects a persistent use of Torah to create divisions again between the "true people of God" and "second-rate Christians" or even "false Christians." An extreme example of the latter would be the interpretation of Sunday-worship as the mark of the beast.[67] One could go on to examine the use of other Torah-based practices as litmus tests of one's true standing in the people of God, such as the practice of tithing (with the strict accounting of the 10 percent).[68]

If alignment with Torah's stipulations is not a viable path to attain the hope of righteousness, how much less is alignment with the many human-made regulations that are frequently imposed upon Christians in an attempt to replace Christian freedom in the Spirit with hard-and-fast rules. Many denominations insist upon total abstinence from alcohol, condemning even the moderate use of alcohol and those "looser" Christians from other denominations who permit such practice. We should pay attention here to the fact that Paul condemns drunkenness as a work of the flesh, not drinking wine in and of itself (which, indeed, is promoted on one occasion as a treatment for Timothy's stomach problems). Some churches forbid social dancing as if the practice is in and of itself always contrary to Christian holiness. If the cardinal difference between works of the flesh and the Spirit's fruit has to do with self-centered versus other-centered behavior, we should bear in mind that good dancing is one of the most other-centered activities in which we might engage. Moreover, if one's goal in going out to dance is to give one's

---

and a perpetual covenant between God and His people. *True Christians follow the example of Jesus Christ, the apostles and the New Testament Church in observing the seventh-day Sabbath*" (http://cogwa.org/about/fundamental-beliefs, emphasis mine).

67. Kenneth Holland, ed., "The Amazing Prophecies of Daniel and Revelation," *These Times* 88.4 (1979): 55.

68. Given Jesus's teachings on our obligation to those in need (i.e., to love our neighbor as ourselves), it seems likely that the Spirit would lead us to do far more than tithe.

husband or wife an enjoyable evening and thus to promote marital health, this would more surely fall in the column of Spirit-inspired behavior rather than indulgence of the flesh.

Attempts to legislate the behavior of our fellow Christians in such matters is a repudiation of the freedom for which Christ freed us. Outside of Galatians, Paul returns to this point again most clearly in Colossians: "Let no one, then, judge you in regard to food or drink or a festival or new moon celebration or Sabbath day. . . . If you died with Christ to the elementary principles of this world's order, why do you put yourselves, as though living within this world's order, under rules and regulations—'Don't participate in this; don't eat that; don't touch this' (all with reference to things that don't outlast the using of them)—in line with human rules and teachings" (Col 2:16, 20–22). We cannot legislate the Christian life. We *can* and *should*, however, invoke the presence of God's Spirit and invite our fellow Christians to examine whether or not their practice is fully consonant with walking in the Spirit rather than gratifying the flesh, but we also have to be ready to accept different answers in indifferent matters.

Galatians 5:1–6, like many passages in Paul's writings, also raises questions about the adequacy of the prominent Reformation-era expressions "justification by faith alone" and "justification by grace alone" as soteriological formulas. At the very least, it challenges us to reexamine our understanding of the *import* of these formulations, which have taken deep root as absolutes in Reformed theology. While they were appropriate within the context of an ideological campaign against a distinctive theology of merit and a near-commodification of the same,[69] they have often conduced, among the descendants of the Reformation, to a reductionistic soteriology that is distinctly un-Pauline, where "faith alone" is taken to mean that faith-in-isolation-from-everything-else is sufficient unto salvation.

Significantly, neither expression—"faith alone" or "grace alone"—*ever* appears in the Pauline corpus (whether the disputed or undisputed letters). The addition of the qualifier "alone" radicalizes and thereby distorts Paul's thought, especially in light of the fact that Paul himself qualifies "faith" here in Gal 5:6 not as "faith alone" but as "faith working through love." Furthermore, Paul does not treat even *such* faith in isolation, but connects it closely with the Holy Spirit, which God gives to those who are "of faith" (Gal 3:2, 5).[70] The

---

69. A complicating factor here is one's understanding of justification, whether it is understood merely as "forgiveness of sins" or as "transformation in alignment with God's standards for righteousness."

70. This inseparability was a point also stressed by the Reformers themselves. John Calvin writes, for example, that "it is not our doctrine that justifying faith stands by itself. We maintain that it is always joined with good works. What we say is that faith alone is sufficient for justification, *but true faith cannot be separated from the Spirit of regeneration*" (Commen-

slogans "faith alone" and "grace alone" have made it all too easy to overlook the Spirit's importance in Paul's understanding of the disciple's journey to righteousness (5:5) and, as Paul will state explicitly three times despite later Protestant discomfort with the idea, the importance of our *cooperation* with the Spirit by "conducting ourselves by the Spirit" (5:16), "walking in line with the Spirit" (5:25), and "sowing to the Spirit" (6:8). A faith that acts in line with the Spirit to produce the fruits of love-in-action—*this* faith, and this faith *alone*, attains the hope of righteousness and, with it, approval before the judgment seat of Christ "when, through Jesus Christ, God will judge the secrets of human beings, according to my gospel" (Rom 2:16).[71]

In Paul's economy, faith in Christ is important because this faith has led to the Galatians' reception of the Spirit (3:2–5, 13–14). The Spirit, in turn, nurtures righteousness in the believer, particularly moving us to walk in love toward our neighbor; the end result is justification—being brought in line with God's norms, with the result that one is acquitted at the judgment (for God would not condemn his righteous Son, who has come to life in and through the believer).[72] The slogan "justification by faith *alone*" draws a sharp line between "faith" and the very thing that faith was awakened to obtain, namely, the Spirit. Moreover, the absolute insistence that "justification" happens entirely upon the initial exercise of faith draws an even sharper line between faith, that which faith was quickened to receive, and that which the Spirit was sent to work in the life of the one who trusts God's gift of the Spirit, namely, the righteousness that the just God may justly approve.[73]

---

tary on Galatians, in Bray, *Galatians, Ephesians*, 176; emphasis mine). But if true faith cannot be separated from the Spirit, why must we still speak of "faith alone" in the same breath?

71. Engberg-Pedersen (*Paul and the Stoics*, 176) is exemplary in his fuller understanding of what the "faith" that matters (5:6) entails for Paul: "God will justify (in the future) on the basis of faith *with all that this implies* (now). There is no faith which is *merely* a relationship with God. . . . Nor, consequently, is there any justification on the basis of faith which does not presuppose the whole range of attitude and behaviour . . . which we have seen to be built into Paul's notion of faith" (emphasis original). See also Schlier, 235.

72. Das (531) is therefore correct to stress that "faith's working in love is really the work of God. . . . It is no longer we who live, but Christ who lives in and is being formed in believers (2:20; 4:19)."

73. Moo (329) recognizes that "a deep-seated confidence in the Spirit's power to transform believers lies at the heart of Paul's teaching about Christian obedience," further suggesting that "that confidence in the Spirit should be a hallmark of any faithful teaching about the nature of the Christian life." Paul sought to call the Galatians, and thus modern disciples as well, to share his confidence—his *faith*—in the Spirit when it comes to final justification as well and, in our case, to include this confidence in our understanding of "faith." Erasmus Sarcerius violates both "faith" and "hope" when he writes: "If faith justified us through love or by the addition of love, our righteousness would be uncertain because nobody would know at what point he had loved enough to obtain righteousness"

"Justification by grace *alone*" has also tended to result in a stunted understanding of Paul's robust (and contextually informed) theology of how grace works among human beings to bring about final deliverance to those for whom only condemnation was otherwise possible. Here the problem may lie less in the emphasis on "alone" than in the typical understanding of what "grace" means. Yes, "grace" includes here God's initiating act of reconciling an alienated and ungrateful humanity through the death of Jesus on their behalf, but not in isolation either from the gift of the Holy Spirit (toward the giving of which Jesus's death was, in part at least, a *means* to an *end*, Gal 3:13–14) or from the response of grateful trust on the part of the beneficiaries, which is all but assumed in a grace-act.[74] This response of gratitude includes, at the very least, "walking in the Spirit," valuing the gift and allowing it to fulfill the Giver's intentions for it. All of this is still moved "by grace," but not "by divine favor in isolation from what is given and from how the recipients are moved and changed thereby."

If Paul believed and had taught the Galatians that "justification by grace" was indeed a fait accompli the hour they first believed, he could not expect the threat of "Christ not benefitting you" or "falling from grace" to carry any force. His warning presupposes that people well into the journey of Christian discipleship still need grace, still need Christ's beneficence, still need to act

---

("Annotations on Galatians," in Bray, *Galatians, Ephesians*, 176). The assumption here is that our subjective experience of assurance in regard to righteousness is a determinative factor in sorting out the question of justification in Paul. Paul states, quite to the contrary, that righteousness is yet the object of our hope and that a facet of faith is trust in the Spirit's competence to produce the fruit of righteousness in us.

74. Moo (326–27) opposes "pursuing the law" as "wrong . . . because the pursuit of the law as a means of justification involves an attempt to find security with God by means of human effort, a 'doing' of the law (cf. v. 2) that, with whatever attitude it is pursued, introduces into the divine-human relationship a nexus of obligation that is incompatible with the nature of our gracious God." I would say, first, that it would be more precise to say that, for Paul at least, pursuing the law is wrong because it says "the Spirit isn't sufficiently powerful or reliable to get this job done; God's best gift, which Christ died in order to secure for us, is not good enough." Second, Paul positively proclaimed "a nexus of obligation" where human response to God is concerned and that such obligation on our part toward God is certainly compatible with God's gracious nature. Indeed, it is a consistent feature of God's gracious dealings with humankind from Adam to Abraham to Sinai to Christ. Of course, Paul was also outspoken against the idea that human beings could obligate *God* (Rom 11:35 particularly comes to mind). If doing the law were seen as an attempt to obligate God, then, indeed, such an effort is incompatible with the nature of God (as the One who is, by definition as Creator, the initiator of every grace relationship, the One to whom *all* start out obliged by virtue of *being* at all). But God may *certainly* obligate us and impose consequences, positive and negative, upon our fulfillment of those obligations, especially in a "grace relationship."

so as to maintain rather than break off that grace relationship, if they are to arrive at the goal, here described as righteousness (5:5) such as inherits the kingdom of God (see the statement from the contrary at 5:19–21) and leads to "reaping" eternal life (6:7–10).

We are not reading Galatians *with Paul* when we are thinking that he is most concerned with establishing "faith" or "grace" as "the valid 'external' soteriological basis of justification."[75] He is most concerned with moving Christ-followers forward in the process of transformation that Jesus has opened up for us by God's fresh supply of God's Holy Spirit, and not allowing us to be turned back from the direction in which Jesus has invited us (and that at the cost of his own life), because Paul is convinced that persistence in this trajectory is our only "hope of righteousness," of standing approved before God at the last day. Attempts to isolate the point of justification in a particular transactional moment with the analytic precision of Aristotelian logic (something for which the Reformers, ironically, sharply criticized medieval Scholasticism and its consequences for the practice of the sixteenth-century Catholic Church) threaten to obscure Paul's deeply dynamic and relational understanding of how God was at work setting things right in God's creation, and thus his understanding of both "grace" and "faith" (see excursus "A Contextual Understanding of Grace" on pp. 254–62).

B. A STRATEGIC RESUMPTION OF APPEALS TO ETHOS (5:7–12)

7 You were running well. Who cut in on your lane in order that you should no longer obey the truth? 8 This persuasion is not from the one who is calling you. 9 A little yeast leavens[a] the whole lump. 10 I myself am confident concerning you all in the Lord that you will think nothing else, but the one who is disturbing you will bear the judgment, whoever he is. 11 But as for me, brothers and sisters, if I am still[b] proclaiming circumcision, why am I still being persecuted? In this case, the offense that the cross presents would be made void. 12 I wish that those upsetting you would cut something off themselves!

a. In place of ζυμοῖ, D* reads δολοῖ ("a little leaven *adulterates* the whole lump") both here and in 1 Cor 5:6. The variant has no claim to be original, given its meager attestation. It may have arisen in an environment in which the maxim itself was well-known in a different form. Nevertheless, the variant accurately captures the fact that "leavening" is here regarded as a corrupting, souring process.

b. A few witnesses (D* F G it Ephraem) omit ἔτι here, clearly a scribal "improvement" of the text to remove the difficulty of deciding when it was that Paul did, in fact, preach circumcision.

---

75. Choi, "ΠΙΣΤΙΣ in Galatians 5:5–6," 487.

With this paragraph, Paul moves away from giving attention primarily to *logos* (sustained, reasoned argument in support of his position and against the position of the rival teachers) to giving more direct attention to *ethos* (creating positive connections with the hearers and breaking connections between the hearers and the rival teachers) and *pathos* (arousing strategic emotions in the hearers, particularly negative ones toward the rival teachers, so as to better win the Galatians' assent to his own proposal). In both language and rhetorical focus, 5:7–12 resonates strongly with 1:6–9, forming something of an *inclusio* around the main body of the letter in support of the primary appeal (5:1).[76] Though the sentences that compose this paragraph are indeed abrupt, they are not without logical progression, as Paul drives a wedge further between his converts and those who are leading them along a dangerous path.

7 Paul commends his converts for the progress that they had made prior to the rival teachers' intrusion into their community: "You were running well. Who cut in on your lane in order that you should no longer obey the truth?" He uses the image of running a race as a metaphor for pursuing a particular course of life, as he had done when referring to his own missionary activity in 2:2.[77] The image allows him to cast the rivals' intrusion in a particularly negative light. Like people cheating in a footrace, they crossed over into the Galatians' lane, trying to trip them up and break their stride.[78] The use of a simple infinitive more typically indicates purpose than result, and Paul quite plausibly seeks to attribute bad motives to his rivals rather than merely point out the negative consequences of their work.[79] Paul is concerned that he and his fellow Jewish Christian missionaries "walk straight in line toward the truth of the gospel" (2:14); his converts in Galatia were making good strides in that same direction, living into the new creation that the gospel announced and called into being. The rival teachers are now trying to trip them up, just as the "men from James" had made Peter and Barnabas miss a step in Antioch.

---

76. With Gal 5:8, "from the one who called you" (ἐκ τοῦ καλοῦντος ὑμᾶς), compare 1:6, "the one who called you" (ἀπὸ τοῦ καλέσαντος ὑμᾶς); with 5:10, "the one troubling you" (ὁ δὲ ταράσσων ὑμᾶς), compare 1:7, "those who are troubling you" (οἱ ταράσσοντες ὑμᾶς); with 5:10, "he will bear the judgment," compare 1:8–9, "let him be accursed." Dunn (273) colorfully likens this paragraph to "snorts of indignation."

77. See also 1 Cor 9:24–26a; 2 Tim 4:7.

78. See Gardiner, *Greek Athletic Sports*, 146, 278–79; Lagrange, 139; Matera, 183. The NIV makes the imagery more explicit: "You were running *a good race*" (emphasis mine; see also NJB, NLT).

79. Lagrange (139) explains the sense of μή in μὴ πείθεσθαι as falling appropriately "after a verb of hindering as after a verb of intending, because the person who hinders intends that the thing not come to pass."

Even as Paul nurtures his connection with his converts by praising their former progress, fostering good will by expressing esteem,[80] he also seeks to arouse feelings of enmity toward the rival teachers by suggesting that they have done the Galatians wrong, getting in the way of their steady, continued obedience toward the truth of the gospel.[81] The rival teachers' interference has put the Galatians' progress toward alignment with God (and hence their attainment of righteousness, 5:5) in serious jeopardy. Paul frames this allegation in the form of a question ("Who has cut in on you?"), much as he did as he began his argument ("Who has bewitched you?" 3:1), even though Paul knows full well *who* is responsible.[82] With these open questions, Paul invites the hearers to be the ones to identify the rival teachers as the "problem people" in their own minds.

8 Paul continues to call his rivals' credibility into question by asserting that their influence is leading his converts away from God's direction for them: "This persuasion is not from the one who is calling you."[83] The last phrase would recall Paul's opening allegation against the Galatian Christians ("I am astonished that you are so quickly deserting the one who called you," 1:6). The rivals' "persuasive influence"[84] does not come from a divine source

---

80. The author of *Rhetorica ad Herennium* expects that the hearers' goodwill toward the speaker will be aroused "if we reveal what esteem they enjoy and with what interest their decision is awaited" (1.5.8). Similarly, the speaker's credibility is augmented as the credibility of rival speakers is diminished: "From the discussion of the person of our adversaries we shall secure goodwill by bringing them into hatred, unpopularity, or contempt" (1.5.8), something Paul seeks to do throughout 5:7–12 (as also in 1:6–9; 6:12–13, as is particularly appropriate for the opening and closing of an address).

81. Paul uses a present infinitive (πείθεσθαι; the subject is an implied ὑμᾶς) to denote the action of "obeying" (BDAG 792). The context here, in which Paul has noted the Galatians' prior obedience ("running well"), suggests that it would be appropriate to translate this clause "so as *no longer* to obey the truth" rather than merely "so as not to obey the truth."

82. John Chrysostom (37) had observed this similarity. On the basis of comparison with a single verse ("Satan got in my way," ἐνέκοψεν ἡμᾶς ὁ σατανᾶς, 1 Thess 2:18), Betz (264) thinks that Paul intends for his audience to understand the one who "got in your way" (ὑμᾶς ἐνέκοψεν) here to be Satan as well. There is, however, no demonic connection in the other two verses Betz references (Rom 15:22; 1 Cor 9:12, which uses the related noun ἐγκοπήν), so it is far from clear why there should be such an overtone here. The persistent references through the end of this passage to human beings who are getting in the way of the Galatians' progress toward the truth proclaimed in the gospel (5:10, 12, as indeed throughout the letter) weigh heavily against Betz's suggestion.

83. The present participle τοῦ καλοῦντος here suggests an ongoing summons in the direction of the goal.

84. The Greek word πεισμονή appears here for the first time in Greek literature (Longenecker, 230), making determination of its precise significance more difficult. It is a noun formed from the verb "I persuade" (πείθω, πείσομαι), and could be taken in either an active or a passive sense, hence the rival teachers' "persuasion/persuasive influence" (favored by

and should therefore be rejected. Paul has sought to establish the truth of this assertion in his lengthy argument against their position, showing it to be contrary to God's purposes on the basis of Paul's interpretation of the divine oracles. By contrast, Paul suggests implicitly here (as he has already stated explicitly in 1:6) that his persuasive influence was exercised on behalf of God.[85] He relies in no small part on the addressees' own sense of having experienced the divine as an outcome of Paul's proclamation and ministry among them (3:2–5; 4:6–7), and thus their equation of Paul's message with a genuine invitation from God into this new relationship they have experienced in some way.

9 Paul applies a bit of proverbial wisdom to demonstrate that the rival teachers and their influence represent a danger to the entire Christian enterprise in which the Galatians are engaged: "a little yeast leavens the whole lump" (5:9).[86] The proverb is effective, since everyone would be familiar, given the ubiquitous practice of baking bread, with how a small amount of leaven (the ancient equivalent of a sourdough starter) gets worked into the whole lump of flour and makes the whole lump puff up equally (transferring the sour smell of fermentation also equally throughout the lump).[87] Paul no doubt wants the connotations of corruption and souring to be transferred and applied to the rival teachers' influence; if he was effective in demonstrating the divergences between God's plan and the teachers' advice, he will be successful here as well.

---

most commentators; see Lagrange, 139) or the Galatian Christians' "conviction." The same ambiguity exists in the English equivalent "this persuasion," with no lack of clarity, however, concerning the essential meaning: the influence of the rival teachers is not a godly one. The article identifies a specific persuasion—the one leading the hearers away from "the truth" spoken of in the preceding verse (cf. Burton, 282). Later Christian authors (Epiphanius, *Refutation of All Heresies* 30.21.2; John Chrysostom, *Homilies on 1 Thessalonians* 1.2) use the term in the sense of "sophistry" or "flattery," but (contra Longenecker, 231) it seems unadvisable to read this richer, more specific, and *later* connotation (which is probably influenced by Paul's own reflections on the distinctions between his own and others' rhetoric, as found for example in 1 Cor 1–4) back into Paul's early—and perhaps original—use of the term.

85. Witherington, 371.

86. A number of translations, including NRSV, NIV, and CEB, add "of dough" to make the image even more explicit.

87. Although leavened bread was a welcome and fundamental staple across the Mediterranean world, "leaven" itself often had negative connotations in both Jewish and Greco-Roman contexts. See Philo, *Special Laws* 1.293; 2.184–85; Matt 16:6 // Luke 12:1; Plutarch, *Roman Questions* 289F; cited in Betz, *Galatians*, 266. Positive applications of the image are also attested (as in Luke 13:21 // Matt 13:33). Burton (283) suggests that the present tense verb ζυμοῖ be heard as action in progress ("a little leaven is leavening the whole lump"), referring more directly to the growing influence of the rival teachers, but this nuance seems to run counter to the proverbial nature of the maxim.

Paul uses this same proverb in 1 Cor 5:6 to talk about the corrosive effects of one shameless sinner on the moral fabric of the entire community.[88] A little shamelessness in regard to sin in one small pocket of the community has the power to erode the entire community's sensitivity to sin and to God's ethical standards. So here, being persuaded by the rival teachers on a small point (e.g., the necessity just of circumcision, let alone obeying the whole Torah) or allowing their influence to take hold in a small pocket of the church would lead to the reintroduction of slavery to the whole.

10 Paul then offers an even stronger statement of confidence in the Galatians, showing that he still bears them good will and holds them in high esteem, expecting the best for them and from them (5:10a). He reflects here a common strategy for rendering an audience well-disposed toward the speaker by showing himself or herself well-disposed toward them.[89] The explicit subject pronoun (*egō*) in the opening declaration ("I myself am confident") is emphatic.[90] The emphasis may suggest contrast with the preceding statement, setting Paul's confidence in the Galatians over against the intruders' souring influence. Paul identifies the "Lord," by which he probably means Jesus, rather than God the Father,[91] as the basis or cause of his confidence. The expression is not as precise as we might wish, whether the sense is "I know that the Lord will work this all out among you" or "I have assurance from the Lord about where your hearts really are." It is also not exactly clear what conclusion Paul confidently expects the hearers to reach (they will "think nothing other"—*than what?*). Perhaps the Galatians will think nothing other than what Paul has essentially said in 5:8–9, identifying the influence of the rival teachers as corrupting leaven working its way through the congregation and counter to the influence God would wish to

---

88. Hardin (*Imperial Cult*, 92–94) asserts that the agitators come from within the congregation, in part on the basis of the use of the maxim in 5:9, which is used also in 1 Cor 5:6–8 to refer to the influence of people *within* the congregation. This argument, however, is weak, for the maxim is inherently flexible. That it applies to insiders in one instance in no way prejudices its use in another instance.

89. See again Pseudo-Cicero, *Rhetoric for Herennius* 1.5.8 and, more generally, Aristotle, *Rhetoric* 1.8.6; 2.1.3, 5. Betz (266–67) observes that this tactic is also an epistolary commonplace. See also Olson, "Pauline Expressions," 289. The NIV opts not to translate the prepositional phrase εἰς ὑμᾶς in this clause, perhaps considering it to be redundant, but this omission blunts what is potentially a principal goal of Paul's in this verse: to express confidence "where you are concerned" and thus to keep fostering restored connection.

90. So also Tolmie, *Persuading*, 184. On translating πέποιθα with an English present tense (as the present result of a past action), see Wallace, *Greek Grammar*, 574–76; Moule, *Idiom Book*, 13. Words based on the root πεισ-/πειθ- create thematic coherence in 5:7–10 and, quite probably, an intentional word play (πείθεσθαι, 5:7; ἡ πεισμονή, 5:8; πέποιθα, 5:10).

91. Burton, 284–85; Longenecker, 231.

have.[92] Perhaps they will think "nothing other *than Paul thinks*" in regard to the issues on the table in general. The main point is clear, however: Paul expresses the conviction that the Galatians will arrive at a point of agreement with him against the rival teachers. In making this pronouncement, he may be subtly challenging them (as a parent might; see 4:19) to live up to his confidence in them by doing the right thing.[93]

Paul's confidence in their good decision is matched by his confidence that the "one troubling" them will have to answer to God for what he or she has done in their midst (5:10b).[94] There is rhetorical weight in Paul's identifying any given rival teacher as "the one troubling you"—as an agitator, a troublemaker, a person who is disturbing the peace of the community (see 1:7, where Paul describes the rivals using the same expression, though in the plural, and also 5:12).[95] The rivals are creating turmoil and division, not acting with a view to the health and harmony of the Christian community. They are enemies of the peace and, according to Paul, are answerable to God for the damage they are causing among God's churches. Such claims may help the hearers disassociate themselves from the rival teachers, both by arousing feelings of hostility against them and by suggesting the disadvantage of being allied with those who stand under God's judgment.[96] Once again, Paul avoids giving any hint that he knows—or even cares—about the rivals' identity ("whoever he or she is").[97] Orators in the Greco-Roman world frequently speak about their rivals or enemies in this manner, not even giving them the honor of being named.[98]

---

92. Burton, 284; Lagrange, 141; Longenecker, 231; Moo, 335. This seems to be the sense in NIV and CEB.

93. Moo, 335; essentially also Dunn, 277.

94. The particle δέ introduces a new step in the argument. This connective is often (correctly) interpreted in an adversative sense ("but") here, since the new step involves a contrast between Paul and a(ny) representative of the rival teachers.

95. Paul's use of the singular here in 5:10 ("the one troubling you") appears to be a "generic singular" (Bruce, 235; Longenecker, 232; essentially also Dunn, 278) representing any and each member of the group of teachers who have come into the Galatians' midst, to whom Paul more regularly refers in the plural ("the ones troubling you," 1:7; "those who are upsetting you," 5:12; "those who want to make a good show in the flesh," 6:12).

96. Judgment by God is certainly in view in 1:8-9. In light of the connections Paul weaves between 1:6-9 and 5:7-12, and the absence of any additional information that would suggest a change in reference from 1:6-9, Paul warns here also of divine judgment hanging over the intruders.

97. This nuance is strengthened by the fairly rare use of ὅστις (rather than ὅς) with ἐάν, which introduces a heightened sense of generality and lack of specificity to the clause ("whoever he might be").

98. A convention noted by John Chrysostom (38): "Observe that [Paul] never mentions the name of these plotters, that they might not become more shameless."

11 The next verse introduces a new topic rather abruptly: "But *I*, brothers and sisters—if *I* were still promoting circumcision, why am I still being persecuted?" (5:11).[99] As such, it implies a contrast between Paul and "the one currently troubling you," the general representative of the group that *is* openly, aggressively, and unquestionably "preaching circumcision." At this point Paul's thought jumps to what appears to have been a claim made about Paul by the rival teachers: "Paul still promotes circumcision, elsewhere at least, if not among you." The charge must have been made (or at least Paul must *believe* the charge to have been made) in Galatia for 5:11 to make sense as it stands. Paul does not explain the charge, believing that his hearers know all about it. He raises it only to refute it, to remove a particular blot upon his own credibility that he believes someone else to have introduced.[100]

Where would the rival teachers get the idea that Paul promoted circumcision? Paul's use of the adverb "still" in the first clause most naturally suggests that he would himself admit that there *was* indeed a time when he stood behind circumcision (and all that it represents) as a necessary requirement for aligning oneself with God and God's people.[101] Such an admission, however, would not imply that Paul formerly preached a Judaizing *gospel* like that of the rival teachers.[102] Paul himself grounds his learning of the Torah-free gospel—*his* gospel—in his encounter with the risen Christ (Gal 1:11–17). From the beginning of his Christian preaching, he would have preached a

---

99. The explicit nominative pronoun ἐγώ is emphatic; fronted as it is (the pronoun properly belongs within the "if" clause as the subject of κηρύσσω; it stands, however, before the εἰ as the first element in the sentence), it is doubly emphatic. This heightened emphasis is not represented in the NIV or CEB, although it does come through well in ESV, NJB, and KJV.

100. If this were in fact an appeal to pathos in the sense of Paul's attempt to arouse pity toward himself (Witherington, 363), we should expect Paul to be more *piteous*: "If I were still preaching circumcision, why am I driven out from city to city among you like a thing hated and unclean, why am I stoned and left for dead, why is my name treated as a curse word among all the people of my own race?" Paul merely mentions the fact of his ongoing experience of opposition; if he were seeking pity, he would dwell upon its particulars, its cost to himself, and its unmerited character.

101. The presence of this qualifier argues against the view (advanced in Das, 539–40) that Paul is raising a purely hypothetical issue rather than explaining a claim actually made about him.

102. For an attempt to advance precisely this position, see Campbell, "Galatians 5.11." My own principal reservation concerning Campbell's proposal stems from the likelihood, in my reading of Paul, that he regarded the Torah-driven path to approval before God to be antithetical to following Jesus, such that, at the very least, a *radical* relativizing of the value of Torah-prescribed works would have been a direct and immediate consequence of his conversion, leaving no room for him to spend years preaching a Torah-observant version of the gospel to gentiles.

Torah-free gospel. If he ever truly "preached circumcision," it was in his pre-Christian zeal for promoting Torah observance among Jews (not all of whom consistently sealed their sons with the sign of the covenant) and perhaps even among gentiles prior to his conversion and commissioning by the glorified Christ.[103] The rumor that Paul here opposes might alternatively, but less plausibly, have arisen from a misunderstanding of his policy of allowing circumcision among Jewish believers and their families—*letting* Jews remain Jews and continue to make their offspring Jews, but also still letting gentiles remain gentiles (see 1 Cor 9:20–21; Acts 16:1–3).[104] The rival teachers may have argued that Paul, who supported circumcision elsewhere, must believe in his heart that undergoing circumcision is the right thing to do. They may have suggested that he was reluctant to share this conviction with the Galatians, perhaps because he thought he would have better success among them if he left that part out. Pointing out Paul's inconsistencies and omissions would have served their interests in establishing their greater credibility, just as Paul's pointing out of their inconsistencies and mixed motives serves his interests (e.g., in 6:12–13).[105] It should also be pointed out that their report

---

103. Lightfoot, 207; Burton, 286; Fung, 238–39; Longenecker, 232–33; Dunn, 278; Witherington, 373; Matera, 184; Moo, 337; Donaldson, *Paul and the Gentiles*, 270–71, 277–83. This promoting of Torah observance need not imply active, far-ranging proselytizing on Paul's part. Borgen (*Philo, John, and Paul*, 236–54; also "Paul Preaches Circumcision," 37–41) has advanced a distinctive theory. Paul's ethical teaching concerning the cultivation of virtue and the taming of the passions of the flesh overlap considerably with Hellenistic Jewish teachings concerning the value and fruits of circumcision. His rivals recognized that Paul was promoting "the ethical meaning of circumcision," which should now be "followed by bodily circumcision and a life in accordance with the Law of Moses. In this way they had grounds for claiming that Paul still preached circumcision" (*Philo, John, and Paul*, 236). Borgen's argument has not won wide assent. First, Paul's use of the word "still" implies an admission on his part that, at some point, he was an advocate for the *bodily* circumcision that his rivals currently advocate *and* implies that this was a position that he no longer supports. Second, although the ethical interpretation of particular commandments is widespread in Hellenistic Judaism, the ethical interpretation of circumcision as a cutting away of excess passion is novel and (so far) found only in Philo (see Barclay, *Obeying*, 50–51).

Francis Watson explains this verse as an indication that Paul did "preach circumcision," in a manner of speaking, at the Jerusalem Conference. He cites Rom 3:1–2 and 15:8 as examples of the kind of thing Paul *could* have said at that meeting to give the "appearance of regarding circumcision and Jewish privilege very highly" so as to facilitate the attainment of his goals: acceptance by the Jerusalem leaders and their willingness to recall their agents, in effect, who are creating trouble for him in Antioch (*Paul, Judaism, and the Gentiles*, 55).

104. Dunn, 279.

105. It is not certain that this was the rival teachers' intent here: they might have had the goal of establishing that their own message was not really so different from Paul's own elsewhere, asking for the opportunity to complete his work (see Lagrange, 141).

may not have been entirely factual but, rather, highly prejudicial.[106] We need not attribute to them a higher standard of accuracy when it comes to attacking a rival teacher's credibility than we find in Paul (see, again, 6:12–13).

Paul, however, can readily refute this charge and thus reaffirm his absolute consistency (a major point in Gal 2:1–14): if he still promoted circumcision as part of his mission, he would not continue to be persecuted by his fellow Jews (see Acts 13:50; 14:2, 19–20; 2 Cor 11:24) because his gospel would no longer be a threat to the Mosaic covenant and to the loyal obedience of all Jews (whether or not they claimed Jesus as Messiah) to that covenant.[107] If Paul promoted circumcision, he would remove "the stumbling block of the cross," the "offense that the proclamation of a crucified Messiah offers."[108] There was already significant offense in the claim that, by virtue of his formal condemnation and execution, God's Messiah died accursed under God's law (see also 1 Cor 1:23). But there was even greater offense in the conclusion that finally impressed itself upon Paul after his encounter with the vindicated Jesus—that the Torah itself was thus discovered to be out of line with God's

---

106. This factor of veracity is one that Campbell does not take into account. He writes, for example, "Understood as a reference to pre-call activity, on the one hand, Paul's critics would seem to gain little if anything by introducing it into discussion. And neither would Paul. On the other hand, Paul would not really need to refute it, and certainly not in these terms. So in all respects the argumentative function of the pre-call view is problematic" ("Galatians 5.11," 337). The points Campbell goes on to raise about how Paul *could* have defended himself if the charge concerned is preconversion activity are excellent, *assuming* that the rival teachers are presenting an accurate charge by saying that Paul preached a gospel involving circumcision *and* that the Galatians would give credence to Paul if he simply denied the charge. Neither can be taken for granted, and so he presents a refutative sign, namely, the ongoing opposition he endures from pious Jews. At the same time, Paul knows that he was once an ardent supporter of circumcision. along with wholehearted devotion to the Torah, hence the "still."

107. Fung, 238. Longenecker (233) thinks that Paul is pointing here to persecution at the hands of people like the rival teachers, but this interpretation is unlikely. The rival teachers are themselves (allegedly) promoting circumcision in an attempt to avoid persecution; Paul has suffered physical punishments—apparently *legally*—as a result of his obedience to Christ (6:12, 17). These factors point to persecution by the non-Christian Jewish community, whose leaders enjoyed the authority to administer limited discipline among their own. The force of the second ἔτι in this verse may be to denote logical opposition ("yet, nevertheless"; so Burton, 287) rather than persistence of an action ("still"), as it does in the first use in this verse.

108. The genitive phrase "of the cross" (τοῦ σταυροῦ) can be understood as a genitive of definition, supplying the specific content of the "stumbling block" (Fung, 240; cf. genitive of apposition, in Moo, 337), or a genitive of source, naming that which causes non-Christian Jews to take offense (here, particularly because of Paul's understanding of the implications of the cross for the authority of Torah in the present time). "Cross" is probably to be understood as an abbreviated expression for "the crucified Messiah."

purposes in the Messiah, and therefore the Torah's authority was shown to have come to an end.[109] This conclusion would certainly be a stumbling block to Paul's fellow Jews and sufficient cause to arouse violence against him. Preaching circumcision would not alleviate the first stumbling block, but it would certainly remove the second one. Paul will claim in 6:12 that the rival teachers are unwilling to pay the price in their own flesh of living into the new creation that God has set into motion "in Christ," as he himself has done (5:11; 6:17).

12 Paul concludes this series of "snorts of indignation" with a snide comment about castration, expressing the wish that the rival teachers who are so eager to circumcise the Galatian gentile Christians would "go all the way" with themselves instead.[110] It is striking that Paul, himself a Jew and well aware of the scriptural discourse concerning circumcision, nevertheless now locates circumcision (the sign of the covenant) along the same spectrum as castration: both are now mutilations, differing only in degree.[111] A similar statement is found in Phil 3:2, where Paul makes a crass pun to refer to Judaizers as "the mutilation party" instead of "the circumcision party."[112] By so doing, Paul appears to be playing on Greek and Roman sensibilities in regard to the Jewish rite of circumcision, which was regarded as an incomprehensible bodily mutilation.[113] Some translations make the reference to castration or emasculation explicit (NRSV, NIV, CEB, ESV) while others leave it muted (e.g., as "mutilate," NJB, NLT). The verb used here ("cut [something] off") recalls the ruling in LXX Deut 23:2 that excludes the man whose male member "has been cut off" from entering the assembly of the Lord. Paul *may* have this commandment in mind, wishing that the rival teachers would render themselves unfit for the congregation of Israel, even

---

109. Similarly, but less radically, Dunn, 281: "the cross as marking the end of a clear dividing line between covenant Jew and outlaw Gentile."

110. Whether this formula (ὄφελον followed by the future indicative) is understood as an essentially *unobtainable* wish (Moule, *Idiom Book*, 137) or an *attainable* wish (BDF §384) is not germane; Paul's wish will clearly not be fulfilled by his rivals but serves only a rhetorical purpose. The middle voice of ἀποκόψονται is significant: Paul hopes for the rival teachers to turn their attention to performing their surgeries on themselves.

111. Some scholars have suggested that Paul's wish be heard against the background of the self-emasculation performed by the priests of Cybele, a goddess with a wide following in central Anatolia, but known more widely throughout the region as well (Lightfoot, 206; Burton, 289; LaGrange, 143; Betz, 270; Dunn, 283; Elliott, *Cutting Too Close*, 258–86). This much would be in keeping with Paul's relegation of circumcision, in this context at least, to a meaningless, superstitious, masochistic, pagan blood rite.

112. The play on words is evident in Greek: τὴν κατατομήν ("the mutilation," Phil 3:2) for τὴν περιτομήν ("the circumcision").

113. See Dio Cassius 79.11; Diodorus Siculus, *History* 3.31.

as their desire to circumcise his converts threatens *the gentile Galatians'* place in the assembly of Christ.[114]

Paul's emotional words also reveal the depth of Paul's concern for his converts.[115] This concern may, in turn, arouse reciprocal feelings in the audience in response to Paul's evident passion for them and in response to the seriousness of the action they are contemplating (as a complete betrayal of Paul, who is set so strongly against the rival teachers). If there are yet feelings of attachment toward Paul, in other words, this outcry may serve to reawaken sympathy for him and a corresponding inclination to take his position seriously. Paul continues here to characterize the opponents as disturbers of the peace, employing a phrase used in normal political discourse to describe agitators or rabble-rousers, with the goal of caricaturizing and discrediting the rival teachers (see also 1:7; 5:10).[116]

The situation in Galatia, and in particular the introduction of a new teaching into the congregations, underscores the importance of exercising discernment. This must be exercised in two directions—discerning when we are being led away from obeying the truth, but also when we are *not* being shaken from the ways in which we do *not* obey the truth. The latter is inherently the more difficult, as one faces the paradox of being tasked with seeing what neither oneself nor one's teachers are seeing.

The surest way to recognize a counterfeit, however, remains extensive familiarity with the genuine. What is the "truth"—the reality, the quality of human relationships, the new ordering of human community, the realignment of the individual person's drives and desires—that the good news of God in Christ proclaims and seeks to summon into being? Intentional and ongoing examination of the scriptural witness and identification of those places and moments in which the "truth of the gospel" has been lived out give us the familiarity with the genuine that will allow us both to discern the detours and to discover those areas in which we have been walking far from the path ourselves.

Another angle from which to approach this issue is to ask where we blunt the offense of the cross (and, with it, the power of the cross to liberate and usher in a new creation) for the sake of our own comfort, quiet enjoyment of this life's goods, and well-being (whether as preachers or as communities of disciples), so as to come less under fire. The particular form that this issue took in Galatia is now quite remote from us, but there are plenty of corollaries to be drawn on the basis of Galatians alone, plenty of other facets of the

---

114. Fung, 242; Dunn, 283.

115. Witherington, 375.

116. Betz, 270. The imperfective aspect of the participle οἱ ἀναστατοῦντες again suggests that these agitators are in the thick of their activity.

"offense of the cross" before which we may be tempted to retreat rather than plunge courageously toward the truth of the gospel.

If in Christ there is neither Jew nor gentile, then there is also no room "in Christ" (i.e., in Christ's body, the church) for any of the many other lines drawn between ethnic groups with the concomitant devaluing of the group on the other side of the line. Somewhere in small-town Florida is a preacher who does not challenge the deep-rooted prejudice against African Americans and Hispanic Americans rampant in his or her congregation and town. The offense of the cross is thereby removed. If in Christ there is neither slave nor free, there is also no room for other dividing lines between people of different social and economic status and the tendencies of both to withdraw from meaningful fellowship with the other even as the Jewish Christians at Antioch withdrew from their gentile sisters and brothers. Somewhere in a wealthy church in Atlanta is a pastor who does not challenge his or her congregation not merely to engage in charity toward the poor and homeless but to engage in relationship with them. The offense of the cross is blunted here as well. And of course many churches are more intent on preserving the gender-based lines and limitations imposed for millennia by the *stoicheia* of the patriarchal ordering of domestic and social life than discovering the full freedom of what the Spirit would do through its gifting of people in Christ of either gender.

The cross is an offense in many more ways to the domination of the *stoicheia* (the fundamental values and principles that order life under the powers of this age; see commentary on 4:3) and thus to social groups whose sense of a secure existence in a well-ordered universe is based upon the tutelage of those *stoicheia*. Christ's command to love one's neighbor as oneself is an offense to worldly wisdom regarding finance and to a culture that values self-gratification. Christ's example of other-centered, selfless service is an offense to a rights culture that promotes self-actualization. The extent to which we remove that offense as preachers and teachers of the Word, however, is the extent to which we limit the ability of the "truth of the gospel" to become manifest in our own communities of faith and across the global community of faith.

VIII. SPIRIT-EMPOWERED RIGHTEOUSNESS (5:13–6:10)

Galatians 5:13–6:10 is the strategic *continuation* and, in a sense, the *climax* of the case Paul has been making in the first four and a half chapters of this letter against taking on the yoke of the Torah as the way forward in discipleship.[1] Paul is, moreover, not addressing these words about the flesh and the Spirit to people who wish to indulge their passions, but to people seeking help in overcoming the passions and who therefore might "wish to be under the law" (4:21).[2] They are receptive to the rival teachers and to embracing the Torah-driven life because they want all the help they can find in overcoming the cravings and impulses of their "old selves" so as to live more closely in line with the ethical ideals taught by Paul (see 5:21, "as I warned you beforehand"). Part of their attraction to the Torah was that it provided them with a concrete and regimented guide to ordering their new lives and identifying clearly what God expected from them, so as to make orderly progress in their moral transformation—to move on to "perfection" (3:3). Paul therefore has to do more than argue *against* turning to Torah and circumcision. He must also show how the Spirit, which the Galatians have already received from God in Christ on the basis of their trust, provides sufficient guidance and support for them to rise above the power of the flesh and to live virtuously in God's sight.[3]

A. THE SPIRIT'S SUFFICIENCY TO NURTURE RIGHTEOUSNESS (5:13–26)

[13] *For you were called to freedom, brothers and sisters—only not freedom as an opportunity for the flesh.*[a] *Rather, through love*[b] *keep serving one another*

---

1. Betz, 8–9, 273–74; Betz, "Spirit, Freedom, and Law"; Engberg-Pedersen, *Paul and the Stoics*, 131; Matera, "Culmination," 80–82; Fee, *Empowering Presence*, 423–24. This understanding of Gal 5:13–6:10 is elegantly refined and developed in Barclay, *Obeying*, 68–72, 106–77. The role of 5:13–6:10 within the larger letter has been much debated. The most radical position views it as a later interpolation of Pauline ethical instructions into Galatians, having no particular connection to the problem Paul addresses in Galatia (thus O'Neill, *Recovery of Paul's Letter*, 65–71). A slightly less radical approach affirms this passage to be integral to the letter, but still without any particular relevance to the question on the table before the Galatians or Paul's answer to the same (so Dibelius, *From Tradition to Gospel*, 239). Others have regarded it both integral to Galatians *and* related to the situation in the churches there, but to a wholly different aspect of that situation from the one addressed in Gal 1:1–5:12. According to this view, Paul begins at 5:13 to address a second problem, namely, libertinism—a tendency toward self-indulgence born of the conviction that traditional morality does not apply (most starkly, Lütgert, *Gesetz und Geist*, and Ropes, *Singular Problem*).

2. So, rightly, Barclay, *Obeying*, 20.

3. Lagrange, 144; Dunn, 284–85; Matera, "Culmination of Paul's Argument," 85.

as slaves. 14 *For the whole Torah has been fulfilled in one statement: "You will love your neighbor as yourself."* 15 *But if you bite and eat one another up, stay on the lookout lest you be consumed by one another!*

16 *But I say, make it a habit to walk by the Spirit and you will certainly not fulfill what the flesh desires.* 17 *For the flesh yearns against what the Spirit desires, and the Spirit against what the flesh desires, for these stand opposed to one another in order that you may not do whatever you want.* 18 *But if you are being led by Spirit, you are not under Torah.* 19 *And the works born of the flesh are clearly evident: sexual immorality,*^c *impurity, shameless debauchery,* 20 *idolatry, drug-induced spells, displays of enmity, strife,*^d *fanaticism, angry outbursts, self-promoting acts, dissensions, factions,* 21 *acts born of envy,*^e *drunken bouts, gluttonous parties, and other things like these.*^f *Concerning these things I tell you in advance, just as*^g *I warned you before: Those who keep on practicing such things will not inherit the kingdom of God.*

22 *But the fruit produced by the Spirit is love, joy, peace, patience, kindness, goodness, faithfulness,* 23 *forbearance, self-control.*^h *Against such things there is no law.* 24 *And those who are Christ's*ⁱ *crucified the flesh along with its passions and desires.* 25 *If we live by the Spirit, let us also keep falling in step with the Spirit.* 26 *Let us not become conceited, challenging one another, envying one another.*

a. The negative μή is used here in an abrupt expression without a verb (BDAG 646). An imperative of some kind is probably to be inferred (e.g., "only *do* not *use* this freedom as" or "*do* not *turn* this freedom into an opportunity to privilege the flesh"; see Burton, 292; Longenecker, 239; Das, 544). The presence of an explicit imperative in the following clause (δουλεύετε) balancing the present clause strengthens this view. The article τήν before ἐλευθερίαν looks back to the occurrence of the noun in the first half of the verse.

b. A few Western MSS (D F G) read τῇ ἀγάπῃ τοῦ πνεύματος in place of διὰ τῆς ἀγάπης. In the variant, "love" becomes the means, and the Spirit is identified as the source of this love ("the love that the Spirit provides"). This is an obvious expansion, interpreting 5:13 in light of 5:22 (treating love as a fruit of the Spirit).

c. Scribes tended to expand this list to include vices that were present in other New Testament vice lists, making Paul's catalog of "works of the flesh" more comprehensive. Many MSS (א² D [F G] Ψ 1739^mg 𝔐 syr^h Ambrosiaster) add μοιχεία ("adultery") before πορνεία ("sexual immorality"), harmonizing Paul's list with Jesus's list in Mark 7:21–22; the latter passage may also have exercised some influence on MSS including φόνοι after φθόνοι in 5:21). External evidence also favors the exclusion of μοιχεία from this particular list (it is not found, for example, in the very early and important MSS א*, A, or B), hence its absence from modern translations of this list.

d. Many MSS (C D^{2,3} F G K L N P 𝔐) read the plural ἔρεις. The singular is well attested by both early Alexandrian and Western MSS (א A B D* 1739) and is probably original. The change could be due to harmonization with Paul's tendency to list these vices, beginning with the preceding ἔχθραι, in the plural (with the exception of ζῆλος in B D* P 33; even this noun is given in the plural in א C D^1), or to the fact that the singular and plural would have increasingly been pronounced the same way.

e. A preponderance of MSS (A C D G K P Ψ 88 1739 𝔐 *pm*) add φόνοι after φθόνοι. It is possible that φόνοι was originally included in this list but was omitted by error because of homoioteleuton; the emotional-ethical journey from "envying" to "murder" is well attested in other Jewish ethical texts (see T. Sim. 3.2–3; 4.7–8; T. Benj. 7.1–2; Jas 4:1–5). This same point (that it would be an expected partner to envy) could, however, also support the position that φόνοι was added to the list as a glaring omission. The addition also may reflect the harmonizing influence of Rom 1:29, where the two vices appear in succession. Metzger (*Textual Commentary*, 529) thinks the latter more likely. The external support for the shorter reading is also very strong and early (𝔓[46] ℵ B 33 81). Jesus's list of vices in Mark 7:21–22 also includes φόνοι, as it had also included μοιχεία (see earlier note), possibly contributing to scribes' tendency to include both in this list as well.

f. The NIV divided the works of the flesh into four subgroups by introducing semicolons and inserting an "and" before the last member of each subgroup ("sexual immorality, impurity and debauchery; [20] idolatry and witchcraft; hatred, discord, jealousy, fits of rage, selfish ambition, dissensions, factions [21] and envy; drunkenness, orgies, and the like"). However helpful this may be, Paul himself indicated no such subdivisions.

g. A few manuscripts (ℵ[2] A C D Byz) read καθὼς καί rather than simply καθώς (𝔓[46] ℵ* B F G). The longer reading would simply add greater emphasis ("just as I *indeed* warned you before").

h. Following this noun, several MSS show an expansion of Paul's list of virtues, none of which can claim to be original. The addition of ἁγνεία ("chastity") in D* F G is particularly interesting, perhaps because of assimilation to 1 Tim 4:12, or perhaps because of the increasing emphasis on that ideal in the postapostolic church.

i. οἱ δὲ τοῦ Χριστοῦ Ἰησοῦ ("those who belong to Christ Jesus") is perhaps better attested in the manuscript tradition (ℵ A B C P Ψ 33 1739 *pm*) than οἱ δὲ τοῦ Χριστοῦ ("those who belong to Christ," hence "those who are Christ's"), but the shorter reading has the support of 𝔓[46] D F G 𝔐 *pm*, and the strong tendency to expand occurrences of "Christ" or "Jesus" to "Christ Jesus" or "Jesus Christ" throughout the epistolary literature weighs equally heavily against the longer reading.

In this important section, Paul affirms that the Christians have already received all that is necessary (and effective!) for living transformed lives of righteousness, that is, for living in line with God's standards (5:5–6). If the freedom for which Christ liberated us means, in part, liberty from slavish rules and ethnic laws (5:1), it also means liberty from the enslaving power of our own baser, self-centered, self-gratifying drives and passions (5:13).[4] Christ has given his followers the means to fulfill the righteous demands of the Torah apart from regulating their lives by the Torah. As they allow the Spirit to regulate their lives and empower their service (5:16, 25), they will fulfill the core commandment of the Torah—the command to love one's neighbor as oneself (5:13–14)—in their lives together as Christian communities and in their service beyond the household of faith. The Spirit gives the believer,

---

4. See Philo, *Good Person*, for an informative comparative text on freedom and slavery in terms of the passions and their power over the individual's moral faculty.

as the Torah did *not*, the power to overcome the flesh—to live out his or her mortification (crucifixion) of the flesh (5:24)—and to walk in line with God's righteousness. Although it has been a frequent temptation to read 5:13–26 only as it applies to the individual believer who struggles between the impulsive desires of the flesh and the leading of the Spirit, Paul also has the life of the Christian community and the effects of indulging the flesh or walking in line with the Spirit upon the life of Christians in community in central focus throughout this and the following section (6:1–10).[5]

13 Galatians 5:13 is a well-crafted resumption of 5:1. Both begin from the same premise: "Christ freed us to live in freedom" (5:1); "*you* were called to freedom" (5:13).[6] In 5:1 Paul moved from this premise to the conclusion that the Galatians must not now submit again to any yoke of slavery such as belonged to the pre-Christian revelation (whether the Torah or the gentile *stoicheia*). Now Paul moves forward from the same premise to give them positive instruction on how to live in that freedom so as not to remain in another kind of slavery—slavery to the power of the passions and desires of the flesh.[7] The gift of freedom is not to be misused against the Giver's good intentions, but used fully to accomplish the Giver's intentions, which can be known through the leading of the Spirit.

This freedom is not an opportunity for the flesh to take over, leading a person deeper and deeper into vice, but an occasion for the Spirit to guide the believer into all virtue. The word translated "opportunity" is used in military contexts to denote a "starting-point or base of operations for an expedition,"[8] an appropriate image, given that Paul will go on to describe the campaign of the flesh and the Spirit against one another (5:16–17). Christian freedom is misused if it becomes the occasion to let the flesh launch an offensive against the Spirit.

---

5. So, rightly, Fee, *Empowering Presence*, 425, 470.

6. The explicit nominative pronoun Ὑμεῖς is emphatic. The preposition in the phrase ἐπ᾿ ἐλευθερίᾳ is here a "marker of object or purpose" (so BDAG 366; BDF §235), thus, "you were called *to be free*" (BDAG 316, s.v. ἐλευθερία; so also Bruce, 240; Longenecker, 239; Schreiner, 333). The thought is essentially the same as τῇ ἐλευθερίᾳ in 5:1 (see commentary). Indeed, Lagrange (145) understands the verse as marking a reprise of the subject announced in 5:1, which the vocabulary and syntax of this verse recall.

7. Though Paul has introduced this verse with the conjunction γάρ, it is not clear how this statement is meant to provide support for the preceding material. It may be best to take this word as a marker of clarification (see BDAG 189), particularly introducing clarifications of the ethics of living in the freedom for which Christ freed the believers (5:1) and how such freedom is not truly license for moral abuse. Moo (342) also interprets the γάρ more loosely as "simply introducing the next stage in the argument" (see also Betz, 272; Zerwick, *Biblical Greek*, 159 [§473]).

8. BDAG 158; see also Hays, "Galatians," 321. In Rom 7:8, 11 the commandment similarly gives sin an "opportunity" (ἀφορμήν) to take hold and exert its influence.

By "flesh," Paul does not simply mean the "meat" of our physical person, as Origen thought,[9] and as seems to be true of the word elsewhere in Galatians (e.g., 3:2–5, where it could be read as a cipher for "that which circumcision affects"; 4:21–31, where it refers to the natural, physical power of procreation). The physical body is not in itself evil or any more prone to evil than the mind and affections. Indeed, the "body," unlike "the flesh," is a space that God's Spirit can occupy, an arena in which to glorify God and pursue sanctification (e.g., see 1 Cor 6:13b, 19–20; 7:34; 1 Thess 5:23). While it is capable of being the instrument of sin, it is equally capable of being offered to God in righteousness (Rom 6:12; 12:1). The "flesh" is also not a "lower/sinful nature" that is irrevocably part of our constitution as human beings in contrast to some "higher nature" within us.[10] It is not the whole person, and it is not even the part that is the person in the truest sense (the part that can either assent to the flesh or yield to the Spirit). It is "the influence of an 'era' and its human traditions and assumptions" that has invaded human beings, established a forward command center close to the center of the human will, seeking to claim us as slaves for the powers of this age.[11] It is the sum total of the impulses, urges, and desires that lead human beings away from virtue toward self-promotion and self-gratification, often at the expense of the interests and well-being of others, of the harmony of community, or of the accomplishing of the purposes of God in our lives, communities, and world. It corresponds very closely to what ethical writers named "the passions," over which reason must gain the upper hand if the individual is to live a life of consistent virtue.[12] It is a powerful force at work within human beings that can manifest itself in thought, word, and deed, in the yearnings of mind and soul as well as body.

The power of the flesh is probably what makes the removal of the bridle of law (in some form) all the more frightening and risky. What is to save us from being swallowed up by our own desires, passions, and impulses, if not rules and regulations carefully laid out? Paul's answer will be "the Spirit" (5:16), the divine Spirit poured into our hearts. Regulations could never tame the passions of the flesh, but the Spirit of God can. Yielding to this Spirit in each new moment is now the divinely prescribed path to righteousness. The absence of Torah's restraining rules and discipline does not mean that the flesh will go wild and unchecked, resulting in "ethical chaos," as the rival

---

9. Origen, *First Principles* 1.3.4; 3.2.3; 3.4.1–5; *Against Celsus* 8.23; cited in Longenecker, xlvii. John Chrysostom (41) recognized that what Paul names as "flesh" is "not the natural body but the depraved will."

10. Fung, 244; note the revision to the NIV (1984) in the NIV (2011) in this regard.

11. Barclay, *Obeying*, 213. So also, essentially, Jewett, *Paul's Anthropological Terms*, 113.

12. See, for example, 4 Macc 1:1–3:18. On this Greco-Roman ethical conversation, see deSilva, *4 Maccabees: Introduction and Commentary*, 67–78; and *4 Maccabees*, 51–58.

teachers might well have warned.[13] God's purposes for human community will not fail to be served. Rather,[14] Christians are instructed to use their freedom in service to one another out of love.

Paul now introduces the image of slavery in a startlingly positive sense after passionately urging the hearers to avoid becoming enslaved once again to the *stoicheia* in the form of the Torah (4:8–11; 5:1). Voluntary slavery becomes the genuine expression of Christian freedom: "Through love, make it your habit to serve one another as slaves"; "keep offering one another loving service as people who have bound themselves to one another" (5:13b).[15] Christian freedom in the Spirit means voluntarily offering oneself in service to one's fellow Christians, in opposition to living in line with the self-centered and self-serving orientation of the flesh.[16] Loving action, which always puts the other first and prioritizes the other's good, is the means by which this mutual service comes to expression. Freedom is an opportunity to manifest the mind of the Lord who came to serve (Mark 10:45);[17] used thus, freedom becomes the path to Christ being "fully formed among you" (Gal 4:19).

The community context of this and the following verses is not to be overlooked in favor of an individualistic interpretation of the battle of the flesh and the Spirit. The power of the "flesh" is operative *among* the believers in their divisions, quarrels, and the like; the power of the "Spirit" is operative *among* them where they serve one another in love, bear themselves gently and humbly toward one another, and so forth.[18]

---

13. Martyn, 27.

14. Paul employs ἀλλά here as a marker of strong contrast, introducing a positive command as a counterbalance to the negative instruction to avoid the misuse of freedom.

15. Liberation from one form of slavery for another kind of service recalls the exodus paradigm, where God gives Israel freedom from servitude to the Egyptians so that they might serve God (Exod 4:23; 19:4–6; 20:1–6; see Wilson, "Wilderness Apostasy," 566–68). Many English translations avoid the image of the slave here (e.g., NIV, CEB, ESV; contrast NRSV), no doubt out of sensitivity to the devastating effects of the persistence of slavery as an institution in the United States into the nineteenth century. Nevertheless, Paul has chosen a verb that invokes this particular image rather than a verb like διακονεῖν, "to serve." The form of δουλεύετε is grammatically ambiguous, but the context of giving instructions favors reading this as an imperative rather than an indicative. The present aspect of this imperative suggests persistent activity (see Boyer, "Imperatives," 41).

16. Thus, according to Engberg-Pedersen (*Paul and the Stoics*, 160), the theme of Gal 5:13–14 "is that of other-directedness of the radical kind that Paul formulates in his maxim in Phil 2:4." Barclay (*Obeying*, 109) correctly notices that here, too, is a paradox insofar as "slavery" is generally imposed upon an individual from without that also creates "a hierarchical social structure" rather than a posture voluntarily adopted—and that within a network of "mutual self-sacrifice."

17. Lagrange, 145.

18. Das, 593.

14 Is it really that simple? Does other-centered, loving service really capture adequately God's standards for human behavior in community? Paul claims that it *is* this simple, offering 5:14 as evidence in support of the command issued in 5:13b.[19] By means of such other-centered service, the disciples will *fulfill* the righteous demands of Torah without being obligated to *perform* Torah. Thus Paul asserts that "the whole law"[20] is fulfilled "in a single word," that is, in the living out of a single commandment: "You will love your neighbor as you love yourself" (5:14, reciting Lev 19:18).[21] Paul was likely aware that Jesus himself had identified this commandment alongside the command to "love the Lord your God with all your heart and with all your being and with all your understanding" as the two most important commandments (Mark 12:28–31; Matt 22:34–40; Luke 10:25–28).[22] It was also the basis for Hillel's summary of the Torah: when approached by a gentile who promised to convert if Hillel could teach him the whole Torah while he stood on one foot, Hillel responded "What you hate, do not do to your neighbor; that is the whole Torah, and the rest is commentary" (b. Šabb. 31a).[23] Paul himself

---

19. Paul introduces this verse with the inferential conjunction γάρ.

20. The placement of πᾶς in the expression ὁ . . . πᾶς νόμος is unexpected, and therefore emphatic (it usually appears in predicate position: πᾶς ὁ νόμος). Once again we find Paul conceiving of the Torah as a seamless whole (see commentary on 5:3).

21. The prepositional phrase ἐν ἑνὶ λόγῳ is a brachylogy (a figure of speech whereby a phrase is abbreviated or truncated to the point that more meaning has to be supplied to make sense of the phrase), since the whole Torah cannot be fulfilled "in a single word," but only "in the doing of a single word" (thus Burton, 295: "in [obedience to] one word"; NIV: "in keeping this one command"). The phrase can be understood as instrumental ("by means of performing this single commandment") or simply as presenting a standard, announcing Lev 19:18 as the rule according to which the just demand of the Torah (to borrow a phrase from Rom 8:4) stands either fulfilled or unfulfilled in the individual case. The noun λόγος here refers to an utterance, hence a discrete commandment. The "Ten Commandments" are thus referred to as the "Ten Words" (the "Decalogue," from τοὺς δέκα λόγους, LXX Exod 34:28; Deut 10:4). The prepositional phrase ἐν τῷ Ἀγαπήσεις τὸν πλησίον σου ὡς σεαυτόν provides the textual "location" of the "one word" in which the law is fulfilled (on introducing references to specific texts with the definite article, see BDF §267). It stands, as a whole, in apposition to ἐν ἑνὶ λόγῳ. The future indicative (here, Ἀγαπήσεις) is commonly used to communicate absolute (i.e., divinely given and enforced) imperatives in the LXX (see BDF §362).

22. Schreiner (335) suggests that Paul focuses on only the second of these two commandments because of the particular disruptions in relationships within the Galatian congregations that are underscored throughout this section (see Gal 5:15, 26; also the central eight "works of the flesh" in 5:20).

23. See also Tg. Ps.-J. Lev 19:18, which appends this negative form of the Golden Rule to the commandment, "You will love your neighbor as yourself." Concerning love as a summarizing (and even extending) principle of the Torah, Schreiner (335) insightfully observes that "no rule book could ever summarize all that is involved in loving others, for life is too varied and too complex to codify how love expresses itself."

would provide a more detailed argument in support of the claim that this one commandment encapsulated the intent of the whole Torah in Rom 13:8–10: "Owe no one anything, except to love one another, because the one who loves the other has fulfilled the law.[24] For the commands 'You will not commit adultery,' 'You will not commit murder,' 'You will not steal,' 'You will not covet,' and any other commandment, are summed up in this word: 'You will love your neighbor as yourself.' Love does nothing wrong to the neighbor; therefore love is the fullness of the law."

It might seem strange that Paul would refer positively to a commandment of Torah in Galatians, having gone to such pains to demonstrate that Torah had a limited role for a limited time in God's purposes for God's people. This is a function of the dual nature of Torah for Paul. As a legal code to be followed in all its particulars as a sign that one belongs to God's people, or as a way of trying to align oneself with God's righteous standards, Torah's role is over. To be "under Torah" on this side of the cross is to be in slavery when God's purpose is freedom; it is to reaffirm the special value of being a Jew when God has brought Jew and gentile together in Christ and broken down "the dividing wall of hostility." However, Torah still bears witness to God's purposes, God's plan, and God's standards of righteousness.[25]

Paul observes an important distinction in this regard: Torah is not something to be "done" by Christians (contrast Gal 5:3), but Torah is "fulfilled" by Christians.[26] Jewish authors normally speak of "doing," "keeping," or "guarding" the Torah, having in mind the obligation to perform the various commandments given by Torah. Paul avoids all these verbs when speaking of the Christian's relationship to the Torah, for the *doing* of Torah in all its particulars would build up again the wall that God tore down in Christ and in the distribution of the Holy Spirit to Jew and gentile on the

---

24. Paul's Greek is ambiguous here: ὁ γὰρ ἀγαπῶν τὸν ἕτερον νόμον πεπλήρωκεν. It is tempting to take τὸν ἕτερον νόμον as a single sense unit and translate it as "the one who continues to love has fulfilled the other law," in the sense of "the rest of the law" or "the other law, that is, the Torah (alongside the law of love)," but there is little support for this reading in the history of exegesis (see Dunn, *Romans 9–16*, 776; Jewett, *Romans*, 807–8). Nevertheless, Paul's hearers may well have construed this sentence in different ways on account of his ambiguous construction.

25. It may also be the case, as Francis Watson suggests, that Paul is "arguing that Christians alone possess insight into the true meaning of the law," here expressed in his identification of the true heart and center of the Torah, and are thus the ones who actually fulfill the Torah (*Paul, Judaism, and the Gentiles*, 72). This would be a highly sectarian claim, in keeping with Watson's analysis of the primary issue behind the troubles in Antioch and Galatia: whether the church should be a reform movement within Judaism or a sect outside it (49).

26. Betz, 275; see also Rom 8:4; 13:8; Gal 6:2. The verb πεπλήρωται does not mean "summed up" (NRSV, NJB, NLT), as if Paul were giving a summary of the Torah comparable to Hillel's (although he does use Lev 19:18 to this end in Rom 13:9; see Burton, 295–96).

same basis. Instead, Paul uses the verb "fulfill," a verb that is rarely used in relation to Torah by Jewish authors and *never* in relation to Torah in the Old Testament (either in the Greek Septuagint or in the original Hebrew).[27] Those "under the law" are debtors to *do* the whole law in all its particulars (Gal 5:3); those who walk by the Spirit *fulfill* the whole law in the course of loving service.[28] Paul can thus speak of the Christian realizing in his or her own life all that the Torah sought to bring about in the lives of those who lived under it, without speaking as if the Christian is obliged to "do" Torah in any sense. Insofar as it is the revelation of the righteousness of God, that righteousness emerges in the lives of the believers—but by an entirely different route, namely, "faith working through love" (5:6) or "ordering one's steps in line with Spirit" (5:25).

15 Paul colorfully captures the ugly consequences of failing to focus on "loving service" as the core ethos of Christian community by presenting a contrary scenario:[29] "If you bite and eat one another up, stay on the lookout lest you be gobbled up by one another!" (5:15). The three verbs in this sentence create an image of animals tearing into one another, each action having escalating force.[30] "Serving one another through love" stands at the polar opposite from a dog-eat-dog approach to social, business, and political interactions—an approach that is all too pervasive in any society. The consequence of this common approach is that a lot of people get chewed up in the course of satisfying other people's hunger for power, getting ahead, or gratifying other cravings. Another consequence is the loss of a supportive community ethos, with each individual now standing in need of looking out for the dangers posed by the other members of the community rather than enjoying their protection and support. Paul chooses the Greek form of the imperative that highlights ongoing attention to performing this action: "*keep* on

---

27. Barclay, *Obeying*, 138.

28. See Westerholm, "On Fulfilling the Whole Law," 235; Fung, 247; Engberg-Pedersen, *Paul and the Stoics*, 161; Barclay, *Obeying*, 142. It is important to observe that Paul's statements are descriptive, not prescriptive: he carefully avoids ever telling Christians *to fulfill* the Torah (rightly, Betz, 275; Barclay, *Obeying*, 142). Dunn (290) asserts that Paul does not observe this distinction between "doing the law" and "fulfilling the law," citing Rom 2:14 and Gal 6:9 as evidence that "he can talk of 'doing the law' in a wholly positive sense." Romans 2:14 is at best ambiguous, since Paul speaks of gentiles "doing by nature what the law requires," even though they do not have the law. This does not seem to me to be a commendation of "doing the law," but again of "fulfilling the law" by a means other than strict observance of its particular statutes. Galatians 6:9 does not speak of "doing the law" at all, but rather of "well-doing" in general.

29. The particle δέ introduces this new step in the argument, here essentially an argument from the contrary.

30. Burton, 297.

the lookout." In the merciless, socially cannibalistic environment described in the preceding clause, the converts would need to be continually vigilant in order to survive.

Although the whole ethical section is composed with the Galatians' situation in view, we should not assume that *every* vice Paul names throughout 5:16–26 was rampant in the congregation, nor that every virtue he promotes was missing, nor that every positive command suggests a situation in which that course of action was not being pursued already.[31] Nevertheless, the subject matter of 5:15 is reinforced twice in this section, first in the listing of several overlapping "community" vices among the "works of the flesh" ("enmities, strife, emulation, wrathful outbursts, rivalries, divisions, factions, envying," 5:20–21) and second in the attitudes and behaviors specifically warned against as the opposite of falling in line with the Spirit's leading ("Let us not become conceited, challenging one another, envying one another, 5:26). It is quite plausible that the rival teachers—whom Paul labels "troublemakers" and "agitators"—have stirred up divisions, arguments, and some personal hostilities among the Galatian Christians as a result of their meddling.[32] At the very least, we can say that Paul shows a particular concern throughout this section with promoting the kinds of behaviors that produce harmony, cooperation, and other-centered investment and service among the Christian communities he addresses.

16 Paul now introduces the solution to the problem of the power of the "flesh" over the human being who desires to live a life of righteousness before God, who desires to arrive at the divinely intended consummation of his or her journey (3:3).[33] It is the same Spirit that God gave to the Galatians when they responded with trust to Jesus's giving of himself for them (3:2–5), that bore witness within them that they had entered into a new and intimate relationship with the living God (4:6–7) after their lives of serving things that were not divine by nature.[34] By walking in line with the Holy Spirit, the

---

31. Barclay, *Obeying the Truth*, 217–18.

32. Burton, 297; Lagrange, 146; Hays, "Christology," 289; Moo, 349.

33. The particle δέ indicates that Paul is introducing a new development in the argument, here one that presents a course of action that would avoid the ills named in 5:13, 15 (i.e., allowing freedom to become a beachhead for the "flesh," which would send the community members down mutually destructive paths). It may be appropriately translated "So" or "Now," thus highlighting the new development, or "But," thus highlighting the contrast with 5:15 (Fee, *Empowering Presence*, 428, favors the latter).

34. Paul is not introducing an anthropological dualism between "flesh" as lower nature and "spirit" as higher or rational nature of the individual human being (against, e.g., Lenski, *Galatians, Ephesians, Philippians*, 280–81; rightly, Das, 561). All of Paul's references to πνεῦμα up to this point have been to God's Holy Spirit, given to the believer on the basis of trusting Jesus, and so it is the Holy Spirit who must be in view here as the guiding principle and power that opposes the flesh and that provides the effective alternative to law.

Christian would neither renounce freedom (5:1) nor abuse freedom (5:13). We must remember that, for Paul, the experience of the divine Spirit was unmistakable, a genuine encounter with an Other who was capable of guiding and empowering discernment.

Paul introduces the topic of the mastery of the passions ("you will certainly not fulfill the impulsive desire of the flesh")[35] as if this is an agreed-upon good. Indeed, it was a common topic among ethical philosophers—including those preaching in many marketplaces throughout the Hellenistic world—that "reason" and "the passions" were opposed to one another, and that a person would attain virtue only to the extent that he or she followed "reason" and gained mastery over the "passions," which included desires, emotions, and physical sensations. Where the passions gained the upper hand, however, a person would fall into vice of one kind or another (whether allowing fear or pain to lead to cowardice, or anger or envy to lead to some act of injustice, or sexual cravings to lead a person to immoderate or illicit sexual encounters).[36]

Hellenistic Jewish authors such as Philo or the author of 4 Maccabees would promote close observance of the Torah as the God-given discipline that trained a person to master the passions and walk in line with the dictates of virtue, a line of argumentation that might have played into the preaching of the rival teachers as well. Paul understood, however, that the Torah could not *empower* the individual to consistently resist the flesh and master the force of the "impulsive desire of the flesh." The Holy Spirit, however, could.[37] Paul thus urges the Galatians to "keep walking by the Spirit,"[38] where "walking" is a typical Jewish idiom for "conducting one's life," "living day-to-day."[39] He

---

35. Martyn, 479.

36. For a fuller discussion of this ethical conversation, see deSilva, *4 Maccabees: Introduction and Commentary*, 67–78, and *4 Maccabees*, 51–58; Stowers, "Paul and Self-Mastery." In light of this prominent background, I would not agree with Fung (274) that the "words rendered 'passions' and 'desires' are in themselves neutral."

37. The war between reason and the passions has been significantly transformed by Paul into the war between the Holy Spirit and the power of the flesh (on which, see commentary on 5:13).

38. The present tense of the imperative περιπατεῖτε is appropriate to Paul's conceptualization of such walking as an activity already in progress and one that must be ongoingly in progress (hence, "keep walking"). The dative πνεύματι may be understood to identify the Spirit as the means by which one will live one's life in such a way as to realize the goal articulated in the latter part of the verse (hence, an instrumental dative). We might also understand it as a dative of rule or standard, thus "keep walking *in line with* the Spirit," which would be in keeping with the antithesis between Spirit and Torah, the other standard in regard to which the addressees are considering lining themselves up. Against the latter, however, see Wallace, *Basics*, 158.

39. The Hebrew verb הלך (*hlk*), "to walk," is the root on which the noun "halakah," a legal prescription, is formed. It was the goal of the pious Jew to "walk" in line with the Torah,

has already affirmed that the converts had begun their journey thus (see 3:3), and he now urges them to finish it in the same way.

Paul makes an astounding promise: those who keep themselves centered on the Spirit and allow the Spirit to guide and empower their day-to-day actions "will certainly not bring to completion what flesh desires" (or "will certainly not fulfill the desires that spring from the flesh"). Paul employs here the Greek construction known as an emphatic future negation, reserved for the strongest assertions about consequences that will never, ever come to pass.[40] What "faith" must grasp is that the Spirit is an adequate safeguard against sin and usher to righteous living.[41] Paul realizes that the Spirit's adequacy does not mean that the Christians *cannot* sin; he will immediately make provision for just this possibility in 6:1. But he also promises that the Spirit is more powerful than the flesh and that the Christian who consistently lives from the Spirit will not give himself or herself over to bring the flesh's impulses to their consummation.[42] The challenge lies in *consistently* thus walking.

---

hence the Torah (and further regulations deduced from the Torah) provided the instructions on "how to walk," how to order one's "steps," figuratively speaking. The use of this figure is rooted in the OT (e.g., Exod 18:20; Lev 18:4; 26:3–4; Deut 10:12–13; 11:22; 19:9; 26:17; 28:9; 30:16; Ps 119:1; 128:1). See Longenecker, 244.

40. The RSV and NRSV, which render this clause "do not gratify the desires of the flesh," have missed Paul's meaning by reading the second half of this verse as a command rather than an emphatic statement about future outcomes. It is true that the construction is *occasionally* used in the LXX to issue an implied command, but only when God is represented as personally making the pronouncement (and far more frequently with a future indicative). On the construction here, see Burton, *Syntax*, §172; BDF §365; Burton, 299; Lagrange, 147; Barclay, *Obeying*, 111; Bruce, 243; Betz, 278; Williams, 148; Fee, *Empowering Presence*, 432; Schreiner, 343; Witherington, 393; Dunn, 297. The genitive σαρκός is probably to be understood either as a subjective genitive ("what the flesh desires") or genitive of source ("the desire that springs from the flesh"). On the sense of σάρξ ("flesh") in this passage, see commentary on 5:13.

41. Lagrange (146) helpfully compares Paul's thought here with Rom 6–8: "Before belonging to Christ, the human being is the theater of a battle between the flesh, representing the instincts for gratification and self-centeredness of the person dominated by the action of Sin since Adam's fall, and the human faculty of reason, to which the law cannot give effective aid. All changes with one's union with Christ. The Christian is led by Christ's Spirit and continually possesses within himself or herself a spiritual principle that courageously and victoriously conducts the battle against the flesh. . . . The same battle is described here" (my translation).

42. Bird (*Saving Righteousness*, 173) aptly observes that "Paul's anthropological pessimism about the human inability to keep the law is matched only by his pneumatological optimism that Spirit-empowered persons will be able to fulfill the requirements of the law when they walk in the Spirit (Rom. 8.4; Gal. 5.25) and fulfill the law of Moses and Christ (Rom. 13.8–10; Gal. 6.2)." For this reason, "a pessimistic anthropology," making all "'doing' or 'works' in general problematic," is not the bottom line for Paul (as Moo, "Justification in

17 How can Paul make such a strong claim about the certainty of living beyond the flesh's impulses (5:16)? He himself seems to sense that this assertion requires some explanation:[43] "For the flesh yearns against the Spirit's leanings, and the Spirit against the flesh's leanings, for these stand opposed to one another in order that you may not do whatever you want" (5:17). Paul creates a picture here of the individual person caught in the struggle of two powers as they pull in different directions.[44] This is not, however, a picture of stalemate between two equal forces, nor of the individual's paralysis in the midst of their push and pull.[45] If it were, 5:17 would undermine, rather than provide evidence in support of, the claim made in 5:16. The positive and ab-

---

Galatians," 182, assumes). The Spirit is the answer to the anthropological problem, and as such it also removes the essential obstacle to regarding acquittal on the day of judgment as a response to the righteousness of a life as actually lived, for this righteousness (and thus this acquittal) does not depend on my ability as a human to do what pleases God, but on the Spirit's ability to work within me what is pleasing in God's sight—as I faithfully and gratefully sow to the Spirit rather than to the flesh.

43. Burton, 300; Schlier, 248; Fee, *Empowering Presence*, 434. Paul signals this function by introducing 5:17 with the Greek γάρ.

44. John Chrysostom (42) identifies the "soul" (as the essence of the individual in the truest sense) as the faculty of the individual that may incline to the urges of the flesh or to the prompting and empowering of the Spirit.

45. Several prominent scholars (e.g., Longenecker, 246; Schlier, 249–50; Betz, 279–80; Burton, 300–302; Dunn, 299; George, 387–88) read 5:17 as an admission of a deadlock in which "the human will is disabled from carrying out its intentions" (Betz, 281) or in which "neither the desires of the flesh nor the desires of the Spirit are actualized" (Schreiner, 343). The verse is mistakenly read as a parallel expression of the plight of the person described in Rom 7:13–25. This is especially evident in the NLT's loaded rendering: "so you are not free to carry out your good intentions" (Gal 5:17b).

These two passages, however, do not describe the same state (rightly, Lagrange, 147; Moo, 355). It is also *highly* questionable that Rom 7:13–25 is meant to describe the life of the Christian under the Spirit's influence (in which case it is difficult to see what he or she has gained by trusting in Jesus) rather than the life of the person prior to, or apart from, Christ (see Moo, *Romans*, 442–51). This passage in Romans is spoken "from the viewpoint of unredeemed humanity," even if Christians are all too able, based on their personal experience, to identify with the plight of the "I" in that passage (Klaiber, *Römerbrief*, 131–32).

On the contrary, Paul actually proclaims with great confidence the Spirit's victory over sin, self, and the flesh, such that the person who "walks in step with the Spirit" (Gal 5:25) does, in fact, do what is just and good in God's sight rather than being derailed in his or her attitudes and practice by the clamoring of the flesh. If this is to be equated with any passage in Romans, it would be with Rom 8:2–4, which declares the reversal—or, perhaps better, rectification—of the condition described in 7:7–25. Engberg-Pedersen (*Paul and the Stoics*, 163) captures Paul's confidence well: Paul leaves "it *up to those individuals* whom Paul is addressing whether *they* will let 'the other force' have its way or not. . . . And so, if they will in fact let themselves be led by the spirit, they *will* resist any attacks by the flesh" (see also Barclay, *Obeying*, 115; surprisingly also Betz, 281, on 5:18).

solute declaration of 5:16b is determinative for the interpretation of 5:17: the active presence of the Spirit, if allowed to do its work, defeats the flesh and its impulses.[46] The disciples are not at the whim of the impulses of the flesh (what Paul could elsewhere describe as "the old person" that they were, as in Col 3:9–11; Eph 4:20–24) so as to "do whatever they want"; as they give themselves to the Spirit's guidance, the Spirit will bring to fulfillment in their lives and practice only what the Spirit wants.

The Spirit and the flesh are not equal powers. God has given his Spirit to the believer specifically as a means of keeping the believer from doing whatever it is that he or she might wish *under the influence of the flesh.*[47] The purpose clause here expresses God's intention for the mission of the Spirit in regard to opposing the flesh and the power it exercises in a person's decision-making process (and it is with the Spirit's positive intervention in this process that Paul is primarily concerned here, as the preceding verse makes clear). The Spirit gives the human beings who walk "by the Spirit" the leverage they need against the flesh and its passions and cravings.

It is significant that Paul does not present this struggle as the believer's battle, but rather as the Spirit's war against the "impulsive desire of the flesh." The Spirit is not a resource that can help *us* in *our* battle; rather, we have been drafted to fight in the Spirit's battle, to fall in line with the Spirit as with a commander (Gal 5:25).[48] It is a battle that, as Paul has already assured believers, the *Spirit* cannot lose, if they do thus fall in line.

18 Paul takes another step forward in his argument,[49] here positing the implications of being led by the Spirit for being subordinate to the Torah: "But if you are being led by the Spirit,[50] you are not under the law" (recalling

---

46. Barclay, *Obeying*, 113; Witherington, 394–95. It *would* be possible to read 5:17b as an admission that, given the incompatibility of the two impulses, one will live in line with either the one or the other: one will not "do whatever one might" want, since the struggle between these two more powerful forces will not permit autonomous action (thus Fee, *Empowering Presence*, 435–36; Barclay, *Obeying*, 112; Moo, 356; Dunn, 299; Schnelle, *Apostle Paul*, 296). Paul, however, has already declared the Spirit to be the more powerful determining force.

47. Matera (200) suggests an innovative alternative: the incompatibility (indeed, hostility) of the flesh and the Spirit means that the Galatian Christians must take a decisive stand alongside one or the other force in this war (rather than do "whatever they want," now in line with the flesh, now in line with the Spirit; see, similarly, Dunn, 299–300).

48. Martyn, 530–31, 534–35; Barclay, *Obeying*, 115.

49. Paul signals this progression with the particle δέ.

50. The dative πνεύματι may best be understood as indicating agency. The use of the dative to mark agency is indeed rare, but its usage here would meet all four of Wallace's criteria (*Greek Grammar*, 164): (1) the noun is personal; (2) the person specified displays volition (e.g., in 5:17); (3) the noun is used with a passive verb; (4) the sentence could be rewritten intelligibly with the dative noun as the subject of an active verb (e.g., "If the Spirit

the phrases "under a curse," "under law," and "under a pedagogue" in 3:10, 23, 25, respectively). This liberation can be demonstrated not only by the reasons already given in 3:10–4:11, 21–31, but also because the "Spirit provides all the necessary guidance in the fight against the flesh."[51] Rather than a list of exercises by means of which to get in shape before God, the Christ-follower has a personal Trainer (or, more eloquently, the law written within the heart, as in Jer 31:33–34). The fact that Paul opposes being "led by the Spirit" with being "under law" here also shows that he has the Galatians' situation and the rival teachers' position still very much in view as he composes this ethical section.[52]

As Paul weaves together topics of freedom and slavery, flesh and Spirit, he creates a discourse that is very much at home in Hellenistic Jewish ethics. Philo, for example, also regarded "flesh" and "Spirit" as two guiding principles that competed for the allegiance of human beings: "The race of humankind is twofold, the one being the race of those who live by the divine Spirit and reason; the other of those who exist according to blood and the pleasure of the flesh. The latter species is formed of earth, but the former is an accurate copy of the divine image" (*Who Is the Heir?*, 12.57). Like Paul, Philo understood "freedom" to be realized as one lived according to the divine Spirit and leading of God, which puts "a check upon the authority of the passions," while "slavery" exists wherever "vice and the passions have the dominion" over the person (*That Every Good Person Is Free*, 17). A major difference between the two authors is the role of Torah: for Philo (as also for the author of 4 Maccabees), the study and doing of Torah was the path to freedom; for Paul, the death of Jesus and the gift of the Spirit made this freedom possible apart from Torah.

---

leads you . . ."). Alternatively, the dative could be construed as indicating means, with God being the unexpressed agent doing the leading by means of the Spirit poured into the lives of believers.

51. Barclay, *Obeying*, 116; Schreiner, 345. John Chrysostom (41) comments similarly: "He that hath the Spirit as he ought, quenches thereby every evil desire, and he that is released from these needs no help from the law, but is exalted far above its precepts. He who is never angry, what need has he to hear the command, Thou shalt not kill? He who never casts unchaste looks, what need hath he of the admonition, Thou shalt not commit adultery? Who would discourse about the fruits of wickedness with him who had plucked up the root itself?"

52. Fung, 252. Paul also here clearly aligns "flesh" and "Torah" on the same side of the fence—opposite the Spirit (Fee, *Empowering Presence*, 438; Bruce, 256; Barclay, *Obeying*, 228 on the strategic range of meaning and associations that Paul fixes on σάρξ). Paul's statements about the temporal limits on the validity of the Torah as a body of "law" and about the Christian's removal from the sphere of living "under law" call for considerable nuance in theological traditions that speak of a "third use of the law" or affirm the ongoing validity of the "moral law" contained therein (see also Barclay, *Obeying*, 235). Torah remains *informative* as a collection of divine oracles, but not *prescriptive* as a collection of decrees, as far as Paul is concerned.

19 Paul advances his argument by elaborating first on the activity of the flesh and its consequences (5:19–21), after which he will elaborate on the results of the Spirit's guiding and empowerment (5:22–23).[53] "And the works born of the flesh are clearly evident: sexual immorality, impurity, shameless debauchery, idolatry, drug-induced spells, displays of enmity, strife, fanaticism, angry outbursts, self-promoting acts, dissensions, factions, acts born of envy, drunken bouts, gluttonous parties, and other things like these" (5:19–21a).

Lists of vices and virtues were a common literary form in ethical literature of the Greek, Hellenistic, and Roman periods. The form appears to have been developed by Stoic authors, continuing to appear frequently in the writings of Stoics and of those influenced by Stoic philosophy, for example, Hellenistic Jews like Philo of Alexandria (e.g., *On the Sacrifices of Cain and Abel* 5.32) and the authors of Wisdom of Solomon (e.g., 14:23–26) and 4 Maccabees (e.g., 1:18, 26). It is not surprising also to find lists of vices and virtues commonly in the literature of the early church, as Christian authors were similarly interested in the moral formation of their people.[54]

Paul creates a vice list to illustrate "the works of the flesh," the kinds of attitudes, behaviors, and consequences that result when the flesh directs the lives of human beings.[55] Since Paul has elevated the command to love one's neighbor as oneself as the essence of the ethical demand of the law, and thus elevated acting in love as that which fulfills Torah, it may be appropriate to see in his list of representative "works of the flesh" behaviors that display an absence or perversion of love for the other. The importance of love as an ethical category, reflected in Gal 5:13–14 and in the fact that love heads the list of the Spirit's fruit in Gal 5:22, would incidentally represent one point of differentiation between Paul and the broader Hellenistic-Roman discourse on vices and virtues, as love or failures to love were not focal categories in either Greek or Latin ethics (as were, by contrast, the cardinal virtues of justice, courage, moderation, and prudence and their opposites). It would be misleading to place too much stress on this distinction, however, to the neglect of important points of commonality, such as the shared emphasis on mastery of the passions as prerequisite to living a life of consistent virtue (and thus on the virtues of moderation and self-control) and the typical elevation of justice to the head of the virtues in Greco-Roman ethical discourse. This latter point

---

53. Once again the δέ introduces a new development in the argument ("*Now* the works of the flesh . . .").

54. For a more detailed discussion and extensive references to primary literature, see Longenecker, 249–52; Witherington, 403–6; Betz, 281–83; Charles, "Virtue and Vice Lists."

55. The genitive τῆς σαρκός is best taken as a subjective genitive ("what the flesh does") or genitive of source ("the works that spring from the flesh"; CEB: "the actions that are produced by selfish motives"). On the sense of σάρξ here, see commentary on 5:13.

is important for two reasons: Paul's own awareness that the cultivation of a life of justice, or righteousness (5:6),[56] is the goal of the Spirit's working in the believer and the believing community; and the essentially other-centered, other-focused nature of the virtue of justice as discussed in Greco-Roman ethical works, which is closely akin to Christian definitions of the virtue of love.[57]

Unsanctified sexual indulgence (5:19) objectifies the other, using him or her for self-gratification rather than serving God's desires in one's dealings with the other. Strife and competition (5:20–21a) tear down the other rather than seek the good of the other. Drunken parties and revels (5:21a) stupefy individuals with regard to the needs of the other and anesthetize them to the prompting of the Spirit to build up the other. That Paul understands his list to be representative rather than comprehensive is clear from the way he ends it—"and such things as these" (5:21).[58] His introduction ("the works of the flesh are obvious," 5:19) suggests that this is a matter of common knowledge, and because of the work of popular philosophers, he is no doubt accurate (save for "idolatry," a particularly Jewish innovation on vice catalogs).[59] Greeks, Romans, and Jews all had adequate witness to what kinds of behavior were noble and praiseworthy in the sight of the divine and of people of quality, and what kinds of behavior merited shame.

Paul's sample list begins with "sexual immorality, uncleanness, shameless self-indulgence." "Sexual immorality" seems to have originated as a term for the buying and selling of sexual favors, though it came to be used to refer to a variety of sexual practices outside of marriage.[60] "Uncleanness" is a term originating in the context of the purity codes of ritual and sacred spaces, where special care is shown for approaching the divine in a state of "cleanness" (e.g., by not touching certain things or persons) rather than "uncleanness," bringing some pollution into contact with the holy. The term is frequent in the Greek translation of Leviticus. Here, as frequently in both the LXX and classical Greek authors, it carries a strongly ethical dimension, referring to moral impurity rather than merely outward impurity (e.g., as incurred through touching a corpse).[61] The third term, "shameless self-indulgence,"

---

56. Both are translations of the Greek δικαιοσύνη, a key word in Paul no less than in Greek ethical writings.

57. Engberg-Pederson, "Paul, Virtues, and Vices," 610.

58. Betz, 284; Longenecker, 253; Fung, 260. For a survey of attempts to discern a particular, meaningful ordering or grouping within this vice list, see Tolmie, *Persuading*, 204–8. Tolmie himself helpfully suggests that "the *total effect* . . . is more important than the specific order that one could detect" (*Persuading*, 200).

59. Idolatry is specifically cited as the source of all other vices in Wis 14:12–14, 22–31; Rom 1:18–31.

60. Burton, 305; Jensen, "Does *Porneia* Mean Fornication?"

61. Burton, 305; Das, 570–71.

goes beyond the first two in that it connotes a certain shamelessness in regard to vice or sin. One not only indulges one's flesh, but one does it "without regard for self-respect, for the rights and feelings of others, or for public decency."[62]

20 The list of representative "flesh-driven works" continues with "idolatrous acts." This would not appear in any Greco-Roman authors' vice lists, since worship of the gods was considered an essential facet of justice—giving to each his or her due. The word is of Hellenistic Jewish invention, a combination of the Greek words for "image" and "worship" (or "service"), appearing only in Jewish and Christian literature.[63] It reflects the tendency of Jewish and Christian authors to portray the worship of the Greco-Roman gods in a reductionistic fashion, focusing on the idol itself as the object of worship, and thus something ridiculous.[64] Gentile authors speak of the idol as a means of access to a spiritual reality behind and beyond the image itself, though this distinction may often have been forgotten in the popular mind.[65]

The Greek word here translated "drug-induced spells"[66] gives us our English words "pharmacy" and "pharmaceuticals." The word generally refers to the use of drugs as medicines, with two major negative connotations: poisoning and using drugs in the context of practicing sorcery. Paul probably has the latter in view, as does John the visionary (see Rev 21:8; 22:15).[67] Drugs could be used to manipulate one's state of consciousness, ostensibly opening one up to the spirit world; drugs (or "potions") could be used to manipulate one's situation or other people in one's situation.[68] The modern drug scene is often not far removed from the aims and practices of ancient sorcery in these regards. Paul would regard all such attempts at spiritual manipulation

---

62. Bauernfeind, *"Aselgeia."* See also Barclay, *Flesh and Spirit*, 31; Burton, 305–6; Longenecker, 254.

63. Longenecker, 255; Fung, 256. εἰδωλολατρία = εἴδωλον + λατρεία.

64. See Ps 115:3–8; Isa 44:9–20; Jer 10:2–15; Epistle of Jeremiah; Wis 13:1–15:19; Rev 9:20–21.

65. Plato, for example, recognized that, while the idols "are lifeless, the living gods beyond feel well-disposed and favorable" toward the worshipers (*Laws* 931a). The Latin poet Horace could also mock the practice of making idols: "Long ago, I was a tree trunk. The wood wasn't so good, so the artisan thought about whether I'd make a better stool or a statue of Priapus. So now I'm a god, and I scare thieves and birds out of their wits" (*Satires* 1.8). Varro, a first-century BCE Roman philosopher, was remembered to have approved the Jews' avoidance of images of the divine and to have critiqued contemporary Roman departure from that ancient habit (Augustine, *The City of God* 4.31).

66. Greek, φαρμακεία.

67. The word is used in this sense of Pharaoh's magicians in the LXX (see Exod 7:11, 22; 8:7, 18; Wis 18:13).

68. Drugs were popular throughout Anatolia, as elsewhere in the Greco-Roman Mediterranean basin. See Arnold, "Anatolian Folk Belief," 442.

as antithetical to, and incompatible with, walking by the Spirit, going where the Spirit leads, seeking what the Spirit desires for Christ-followers.

If there is any particular emphasis in Paul's list of vices, it is on those attitudes and behaviors that lead to the disruption and fragmenting of community (see also 5:15, 26): "displays of enmity, strife, fanaticism, angry outbursts, self-promoting acts, dissensions, factions, acts born of envy." Several of these are given in their plural forms, which indicate specific manifestations of the negative qualities, thus "displays of enmity" and so forth.[69] Most of these need little comment, since they—and their liabilities to community—are indeed "evident."

Instances of enmity are the result of two or more parties setting themselves against another in mutual animosity, inclined to work against each other's good in favor of each party's own, competing good, rather than working together for the common good. "Strife" was so prominent a vice as to be personified in Greek mythology as the goddess Eris, who famously began the Trojan War by stirring up a contest between the three goddesses Aphrodite, Athena, and Hera over which would prove the most desirable. The mythic story well captures the essence of the vice: self-centered competition leading to the erosion of community (even the destruction of empires).

The word here translated "fanaticism" can also be translated "zeal," and it can have both positive and negative senses. Positively, it names the feeling of "emulation." Virtuous people feel this emotion when they see someone like themselves achieve great and noble things and want to achieve such things (and their accompanying or resulting goods) for themselves.[70] This was regarded as a constructive character trait, since those who feel it make themselves better people and achieve better things because of it. Paul uses the word here, however, in its negative sense. As a vice, it could name the experience of jealousy, a feeling that divides and creates hostility (rather than friendly competition), supporting enmity and divisions within a community. It could, alternatively, be understood as "'intense devotion' or 'anger' arising out of devotion,"[71] hence fanaticism. "Zeal" in this sense drove Phinehas to murder an Israelite and his foreign lover (Num 25:6–13), Mattathias and his sons to kill apostate Jews and forcibly circumcise their boys (1 Macc 2:23–28), and Paul to persecute the Christian movement (Gal 1:13–14; Phil 3:6). It objectifies and makes an enemy out of those who practice their piety differently, rather than patiently conversing with and perhaps converting them (or perhaps, in humility, even being taught a better way oneself as a result of the conversation). Although seen as a virtue where Phinehas and Mattathias

---

69. Turner, *Syntax*, 27–28; Longenecker, 253; Das, 557.

70. See Aristotle, *Rhetoric* 2.10.

71. Longenecker, 256.

are recollected in Jewish writings, Paul came to view "zeal" quite differently after his own conversion to the faith he once tried to destroy. Paul could have had either of these two senses in mind when he named zeal as a "work of the flesh."

The word translated here "angry outbursts" may also include the floods of misdirected energy that result from getting too caught up in the moment more generally—impassioned responses rather than Spirit-directed ones. The word rendered "acts of self-promotion" was used in civic contexts to talk about gathering support for oneself to get elected or named to an office, or about working for a wage.[72] It names here that attitude of self-seeking and self-promotion that is the opposite of the other-centered, other-serving attitude that the Spirit seeks to bring to life among Christ-followers. In the plural, it names the factions that result from such divisive behavior in one's own or one's group's interests.[73] The following two terms are essentially synonyms of the vices already named. The first denotes dissensions or disagreements that promote division in a social body, while the second (which gives us our loan word "heresies") is also used to speak of different "parties" or "schools" within a larger body. Josephus, for example, uses the term to speak of Pharisees, Sadducees, and Essenes within the larger body of Judaism (*War* 2.118–62). The term in and of itself can be neutral, but it is here used negatively of the splintering of community.

21 Unlike its close relative "zeal," which can manifest itself both constructively and destructively (see commentary on 5:20), the word translated "acts of envying" is always considered to be vicious. Envy is the desire, born of bitterness, to see a person deprived of the rewards his or her virtues and efforts have justly won, whether one wants such for oneself (even if one has no claim to enjoy it) or simply wishes the other to be stripped of them.[74] There is nothing redemptive about envy, since it focuses its energy purely on wishing to see another person deprived of what he or she merits, whereas "zeal," in its positive sense as "emulation," at least motivates a person to go out and do what is necessary to earn those rewards for himself or herself.[75]

---

72. Fung, 258; Longenecker, 256.

73. Burton, 308–9.

74. See Aristotle, *Rhetoric* 2.10.

75. Commentators frequently cite Jas 4:5 as an exception, since there, according to them, "God yearns jealously [πρὸς φθόνον] for the spirit that he has caused to dwell within us" (thus, for example, Longenecker, 257). This highly controverted text is better rendered, "The spirit that he has caused to dwell in us [i.e., the human spirit] inclines toward envy" (cf. McKnight, *James*, 335–42; Johnson, *James*, 281). Martin (*James*, 150) is simply mistaken concerning the semantic overlap between φθόνος and ζῆλος, in regard to which Aristotle had drawn clear and sharp distinctions; the former is also *never* predicated of God in the LXX or NT. James 4:5 would be the sole instance, and therefore a highly unlikely exception.

Paul closes the list of examples with overindulging in drinking wine or eating. "Drunken bouts" denotes the vice of giving oneself over to excessive drinking (esp. in social contexts), such that one loses control of oneself rather than keeping a clear head, thereby handing over the reins of the self to the passions. The Greek word translated "gluttonous parties," Paul's last example, was originally the name for a festive procession in honor of Bacchus, the Greek god of wine. It came to be used of reveling or carousing in general.[76] It could denote excessive feasting, thus eating beyond the needs of the body to the detriment of the body (and to the neglect of those who are hungry and lack even the necessities),[77] but it may not be so clearly distinguishable from its predecessor in Paul's list (see also Rom 13:13, where the two nouns also appear together).

Paul follows this list with a severe admonition: "Concerning such things I warn you, even as I warned you before: those who continue to practice such things as these will not inherit God's kingdom" (5:21). Once again, Paul makes it clear that the preceding list is representative ("such things"), not exhaustive.[78] It is quite reasonable that Paul should have admonished his converts previously, probably during his initial time with them while anchoring them in the new life to which they had committed themselves, about the necessity of leaving behind the "works of the flesh"—or, as he would put it elsewhere, the "works of darkness" (Rom 13:12) or "your earthly aspects" (Col 3:5) or "the old person with its practices" (Col 3:9)—and the consequences of failing to do so.[79] Paul's solemn pronouncement ("I am warning you"), together with this recollection of having spoken along these lines before ("as I warned you previously"), serves to add gravity and emphasis to the statement that follows. He wants to get his hearers' full attention and underline the seriousness of what he is about to say: a transformed life is not optional but *essential!*[80] Paul will underline this point yet again in 6:7–10 when he speaks about sowing and reaping. Investing oneself in fulfilling one's fleshly impulses leads to death; investing oneself in following the Spirit's leading leads to eternal life.

---

76. Burton, 310; Longenecker, 257; Dunn, 306; see 2 Macc 6:4 for one scenario.

77. BDAG 580; Matera, 202.

78. Fee (*Empowering Presence*, 441–42) notices the absence here of vices underscored in other Pauline lists, like covetousness, greed, and wicked speech; also Betz, 284; Longenecker, 253; Fung, 260.

79. Longenecker, 258.

80. Or, as Fung (283) well puts it, "The new life (with the Spirit as its source) must become evident in the new conduct (under the Spirit's direction) and cannot exist without it"; see also Lagrange, 151. Other Pauline texts such as 1 Cor 6:9–10 and Eph 5:5 issue similar warnings about sins, namely, that a person's ongoing commitment to make room for the desires of the flesh and their indulgence leads to exclusion from the eschatological kingdom. See also Fee, *Empowering Presence*, 442; Schreiner, 348; Moo, 362–63.

Paul does not suggest that the occasional failure to walk by the Spirit disqualifies one from inheriting the kingdom; rather, he warns against *persistence* in practicing the works of the flesh as disqualifying.[81] This understanding is borne out in 6:7–10, where he speaks of the one who "keeps sowing to the flesh," as well as in 6:1–2, where he makes provision for the restoration of the person who steps into a snare of the flesh on a particular occasion. Making full use of the gift of the Holy Spirit—or, better, allowing the Holy Spirit to make full use of oneself—is essential to arriving at the goal of God's call in Christ. According to Paul, one's inheritance of God's kingdom, entered at the resurrection of the dead (or the "catching up" of those who are still alive at the time of Christ's return, see 1 Thess 4:16–17), is at stake.[82] Taking part in God's kingdom at the consummation means submitting to God's rule over one's life now (or in the language of Galatians, "walking in step with the Spirit").[83]

22 If the impulses of the flesh direct individual and community life, the result is ugly indeed. The character of the person and the community of persons where the Spirit leads is altogether different:[84] "The fruit produced by the Spirit is love, joy, peace, patience, kindness, goodness, faithfulness, forbearance, self-control" (5:22–23). The contrasting pictures underscore the incompatibility of "what the flesh desires" and "what the Spirit desires" (5:17) and why these two cannot coexist.[85] This list is also illustrative rather than comprehensive, like Paul's list of "flesh-born works," which is suggested by Paul's subsequent claim that "there is no law against *such things*" (5:23; see also 5:21).[86]

These virtuous qualities will naturally result where the person who has received God's Spirit allows the Spirit to control and guide him or her. The Spirit cultivates "certain states *of mind*, namely, *mental attitudes*," with the result that "one will always and everywhere *act* in the proper way," a "genuinely other-directed" way.[87] The "fruit" of the Spirit is the "harvest," not of

---

81. This is the sense of the present tense (continuative aspect) of the participle οἱ ... πράσσοντες. The NIV captures this sense particularly well: "those who *live like this* will not inherit the kingdom of God" (emphasis mine).

82. Burton, 311–12.

83. Fung, 261–62; Matera, 202; Das, 577; see also 1 Cor 6:9–10.

84. Paul marks a new step in the argument here with δέ, appropriately translated "but" as Paul begins to describe the very different qualities infusing the life of the person led by the Spirit rather than the flesh.

85. Fee, *Empowering Presence*, 439.

86. Fee (*Empowering Presence*, 445) again remarks on noteworthy omissions here that feature prominently in other Pauline texts, including gratitude, forgiveness, and humility.

87. Engberg-Pedersen, *Paul and the Stoics*, 160–61; see also Barclay, *Obeying*, 231: by focusing on the fruit of the Spirit as expressed in the character of the Christ-follower, Paul demonstrates that his "concern is for the fundamental direction of a person's life, which may be demonstrated in a plethora of activities but cannot simply be equated with them."

following rules and regulations, but of "the self-forgetfulness that looks away from itself to God."[88] The image of fruit suggests that it is in fact the Spirit who produces this harvest.[89] Here is another significant departure from the Greco-Roman ethical conversations about virtue. The cultivation of character of this kind is, for Paul, not merely or even principally the result of the individual's knowledge of the good or cultivation of the good through habituated practice; it is the result of a power external to and beyond the individual at work within the individual and among the community inhabited by the Spirit. Nevertheless, this fruition calls for conscientious and constant investment on the part of the believers; Paul will soon speak of the disciple investing himself or herself in "sowing" to the Spirit, even as the person who continues in rebellion against God's reign "keeps sowing" to the flesh (6:7–8).[90] The disciple is responsible to keep himself or herself oriented toward God and God's Spirit, so that the Spirit can produce this harvest.

That "love" (the familiar *agapē*) should head the list is no surprise. "Love" is the common element in Jesus's selection of the two most important commandments, as indeed it is Paul's own choice for the most essential virtue (1 Cor 13:13) and the verb that appears in the commandment the doing of which, for Paul, fulfills the whole Torah (Gal 5:14; Lev 19:18; see also Gal 5:6).[91] The Greek noun *agapē* was rarely used by pagan authors, though they did occasionally use the verb form. They preferred to speak of "love" using three other terms: *philia*, often the term of choice for the love that exists between friends; *storgē*, the term for affection, especially as the love that exists between family members; and *erōs*, often, though not exclusively, used to name the attraction between men and women. *Agapē* and its related verb figure prominently in the LXX, particularly in the foundational command to love God with all one's being (LXX Deut 6:4, the opening of the Shema). It is often used to denote the love (as "covenant faithfulness") that the people of Israel are to show one another (Lev 19:18), though not exclusively so.[92] Because

---

88. Barrett, *Freedom and Obligation*, 77; Fung, 262.

89. Reading τοῦ πνεύματος quite naturally as a genitive of source or producer (so also Das, 578). The singular form *"fruit* of the Spirit" (ὁ καρπὸς τοῦ πνεύματος) as opposed to the plural *"works* of the flesh" (ἔργα τῆς σαρκός) is not necessarily significant, as it reflects normal Pauline usage (Moo, 363; see Rom 1:13; 6:21, 22; 15:28; 1 Cor 9:7; Eph 5:9; Phil 1:11, 22; 4:17; the exception in the corpus is 2 Tim 2:6).

90. Longenecker, 259; Betz, 287; Ridderbos, 207; Barclay, *Obeying*, 120. Fee (*Empowering Presence*, 444) observes that "in almost every case these various 'fruit' appear elsewhere in the form of imperatives!"

91. John may be popularly described as the apostle of love, but it is worth noting that Paul uses the noun ἀγάπη seventy-five times and the corresponding verb thirty-four times (Das, 578).

92. The word is also used for sexual desire in LXX 2 Sam 13:15 and frequently in Song of Songs. See Longenecker, 260.

of its connection with the commands to love, and the noun's infrequent use in Greco-Roman authors (thus making the word more semantically available for Christian usage with distinctive content), *agapē* becomes the prominent word for love in early Christian culture, especially the quality of other-centered, self-giving love that Christ demonstrated and disciples are called to imitate.[93] Spirit-empowered love is the antidote to the toxic behaviors (the "works of the flesh") that both poison relationships in this life and disqualify one from entering into the life to come. Such love, it should be emphasized, is a love in action (see 5:6), not merely an internal disposition.

The "joy" of which Paul speaks is rooted in the pleasure of knowing God, of experiencing the friendship of the Holy Spirit, of being assured of one's place in God's people and God's good future. It springs from an awareness of God's love and beneficence toward the believer, and from mindfulness of God's gifts in the midst of all circumstances. Unlike the joys that believers and unbelievers alike experience as a result of good fortune, pleasant circumstances, and other such external goods, this joy is not fragile, liable to being dashed and dispelled by a sorry turn of events. Early Christian leaders often specifically identify the hallmark of this joy to be its persistence under adverse conditions.[94]

"Peace" is not merely the *absence* of strife, and probably more than "tranquility of mind."[95] The Hebrew concept of shalom, the enjoyment of solid and edifying connections with others throughout the community and beyond, cannot be far in the background for Paul. The impulses of the flesh lead to strained or broken relationships; the Spirit, by contrast, leads us to take the initiative in working toward healing and restoration. It moves us to act as peacemakers in a world of bruised relationships and broken communities,[96] even where such action carries a significant cost to our own well-being or security. Thus, "peace" suggests the state that results from enjoying "personal wholeness and beneficial relationships,"[97] in contrast to the "works of the flesh," which disrupt community peace.

---

93. Jesus's self-giving love is explicit in Gal 2:20 and implicit in Gal 1:4 (Fee, *Empowering Presence*, 447). This use of ἀγάπη is a Christian *development*, not an inheritance from the common vocabulary of the Greeks. There is nothing inherent in the word ἀγάπη that denotes selfless love (*pace* Lewis, *Four Loves*, 177); Christian discourse gave it this meaning in particular contexts. It can nevertheless still be used in the NT for love gone wrong, as in John 3:19; 1 John 2:15 (Das, 580).

94. See 2 Cor 7:4; 8:2; Col 1:11–12; 1 Thess 1:6; Heb 10:34; Jas 1:2; 1 Pet 1:6–8.

95. Burton, 314.

96. Fee, *Empowering Presence*, 449; see also Rom 14:19 in the context of Rom 14:1–15:13: doing "what makes for peace" within the larger community of Jewish and gentile Christians.

97. Longenecker, 261; so also Ridderbos, 207; Dunn, 310–11.

The Greek word here rendered "patience" is commonly used to denote one of two qualities. It can name gentleness in the face of others' failures or slights, a slowness to take offense or, especially, vengeance.[98] It is a quality often attributed to God in the Scriptures, beginning with God's self-revelation to Moses on Sinai (LXX Exod 34:6). God's determination not to punish quickly but rather to give those who have offended him time to repent and seek reconciliation, is, for Paul, a manifestation of God's "kindness and . . . patience" (Rom 2:4). The word is also used, however, to speak about perseverance under hardship, as throughout the Testament of Job and in Jas 5:7–11. In this sense, it bespeaks the courage of the disciple, both in the face of the rigors of discipleship (e.g., resisting temptation, seeking steady and sure growth toward the likeness of Jesus) and in the face of the hostility of unbelievers. In the context of a list of relational and "other-centered" virtues that build up community, as here in 5:22–23, the first sense would probably be more readily evoked.[99]

"Kindness" may denote "uprightness in one's relations with others," but also the disposition to treat others well, to help them if possible, to be a harbor for them in the midst of a stormy life.[100] Kindness helps the other person to feel "love's touch," providing a safe haven from interpersonal injury. If "patience" is a passive trait of love, "kindness" is an active counterpart, as in 1 Cor 13:4.[101]

"Goodness," a close synonym of the preceding word, carries overtones of "generosity," as in the contrast between the "good" (generous) landowner and the envious workers in the parable of the laborers (Matt 20:1–16).[102] The disciple's experience of God's goodness and generosity overflows into the lives of others, arousing a genuine benevolence toward others. When we see a need, we must respond to it in the compassion of Christ, uplifting the quality of people's lives around us.

Although Paul often uses the Greek word *pistis* elsewhere throughout Galatians to denote "trust," here in the context of interpersonal virtues it more probably evokes the ethical quality of "faithfulness," "reliability," or "loyalty."[103] It is the quality that leads those around us to feel safe in relying

---

98. Fee, *Empowering Presence*, 450.

99. Louw and Nida distinguish μακροθυμία from ὑπομονή by treating the former as concerned more with inner attitude ("a state of emotional calm in the face of provocation or misfortune and without complaint or irritation," LN 25.167) and the latter as concerned more with actions ("capacity to continue to bear up under difficult circumstances," 25.174).

100. BDAG 1090; LSJ 2007.

101. Fee, *Empowering Presence*, 450.

102. Fung, 268; BDAG 4.

103. Burton, 316; Bruce, 254; Longenecker, 262; Schreiner, 350; Moo, 365. Even if Paul's use of the word to refer to reliability in human relationships is rare, the context would

on us (hence, encouraging others to trust). It is the social counterpart of God's own reliability, bearing each individual believer aloft in the safety net of the community.

23 The Greek word translated here "forbearance" is also often translated "gentleness" (so NRSV, NIV, CEB). It was rendered "meekness" in older translations (such as the KJV), though this word can evoke negative associations (e.g., a failure to be assertive or display appropriate strength). Aristotle defines this virtue as the mean between excessive anger and the inability to get angry (*Nicomachean Ethics* 2.7.10 [1108a]). It speaks of the proper restraint of anger or power, out of consideration for the other person. "Forbearance" may therefore capture its meaning most accurately. Paul will suggest one way in which to put this virtue into action in 6:1, where he urges believers to follow the Spirit in restoring fellow believers "in a spirit of forbearance" rather than in a harsh, judgmental manner. "Forbearance" is able to confront difficult issues or behaviors (see also the use of this word in 1 Cor 4:21 and 2 Tim 2:25), doing so in a way that allows the confrontation to be received as an expression of love, care, and commitment.

"Self-control" closes Paul's list, whereas it would probably open a list of virtues in other authors' discussions of the mastery of desires and passions. Self-control specifically involves such mastery and is often seen as the foundation for all the virtues, since the passions of the flesh are the primary hindrance to every virtue (as in 4 Macc 1:30b–31). Its appearance at the close of Paul's list is probably not an indication of its unimportance, but it may reflect Paul's essential position that being "other-centered" is the ultimate guiding principle of life in the Spirit or of having the mind of Christ (hence "love" and other relational virtues are listed first), whereas "self-control" is focused on "self" (though self-control is a necessary prerequisite to showing genuine love and the other virtues).

This list of nine specifically named virtues, like the list of "works born of the flesh," is representative and not exhaustive, which is clear from Paul's closing declaration that there is no law against "such things as these."[104] Peo-

---

make it unnatural for Paul's readers to leap in this one instance to God as the intended object of the virtue (against Das, 582–83; Fee, *Empowering Presence*, 451).

104. The Greek τῶν τοιούτων could be understood as masculine, referring to a group of people (presumably those manifesting the Spirit's fruit), or as neuter, referring to the virtues that constitute the fruit itself (while singly feminine, these virtues can be referred to collectively with a neuter plural pronoun, incidentally creating an effective contrasting parallel with τὰ τοιαῦτα in 5:21; so Burton, 319; Schlier, 262–63; Barclay, 123; Dunn, 313). The latter is here preferred, particularly as the virtues themselves are the immediately available antecedent for the pronoun (whereas a group of people is not; so also Das, 585). Longenecker (267) observes that, "while we might have expected such items as alms-giving, evangelism, social service, care for the widows and orphans, etc. to appear in the list [of the Spirit's fruit],

ple in whom these kinds of fruit are abundant are people whom the law would never condemn; indeed, *no* law would condemn such people, and where it did, it would reveal a failure in that law itself.[105] The expression "against such things as these there is no law" recalls a statement by Aristotle. Speaking about people who exhibited greater moral excellence than the common lot, Aristotle said that "against such people as these there is no law" (*Politics* 3.13 [1284a]). Aristotle's point, and probably Paul's as well, is that people in whom such virtue is so well formed are exactly the sort of people that a good and just body of laws would have sought to form. Insofar as they are manifesting such virtues, they cannot be running afoul of any law.[106] Paul would add, however, that no external body of laws, however holy and just and good, could effectively *form* such virtuous character within the person. This is the good news about the sending of the Holy Spirit, and why the Spirit is so important a gift that Paul sees it as the inheritance promised to all people in Abraham: the Spirit *can* empower and guide such inner transformation as will make people righteous according to God's standards.[107]

24 Paul advances his argument[108] as he affirms now that those who belong to Christ have taken decisive steps against yielding to the influence of the flesh, with the result that they are available to follow the Spirit (5:25): "And those who are Christ's crucified the flesh along with its passions and desires."[109] Flesh and Spirit are incompatible powers, as Paul has already affirmed by drawing attention to their mutual and perpetual antagonism (5:17). The death of Jesus becomes, by means of the Spirit, something in which the believer can participate. Paul declared that he was "crucified together with

---

Paul enumerates, rather, such items as 'love, joy, peace, patience, kindness,' etc. Again, it appears that Paul is not so concerned with precisely how each of these matters works out in practice, but with the underlying orientation of selfless and outgoing concern for others."

105. Ridderbos, 208; Fung, 273; Garlington, 259; Moo, 367.

106. Paul's presupposition here is that God's driving concern in giving the Torah was forming virtuous people who would exhibit love, generosity, and the like, not creating and reinforcing social boundaries (which, he has argued, was of concern only for a limited time, a time that ended with the coming of Christ). The Torah would not legislate against love, joy, peace, and the rest, but it *would* convict the loving, joyful, peace-nurturing individual who was not also circumcised, avoiding the ingestion of pork and shellfish, and observing the Sabbath day. But—and this seems to be Paul's implication here—it would be wrong, petty, and peevish of the law to do so. Any truly *divine* law would not. See Barclay, *Obeying*, 124–25.

107. So also Moo, 367. Because of the Spirit's active role in the Christian's life, the Christian can escape the fate of the person who, because of imperfect self-control, knows what is good and yet enacts what is vicious against his or her own better judgment (see Engberg-Pedersen, "Paul, Virtues, and Vices," 611–12).

108. Once again signaled by the particle δέ.

109. This death to the flesh, alongside and by means of the empowerment of the Spirit, is essential for realizing the possibility of true obedience (see Fee, *Empowering Presence*, 456).

Christ," with the result that Christ now lived in him (2:19–20). Similarly, the disciple who belongs to Christ voluntarily and actively crucified the power of "the flesh with its passions and desires,"[110] so as to be mastered by them no longer (5:24).[111]

The past tense of "crucified" (5:24) is significant here, something that Paul would affirm again in Romans as he spoke about baptism as a death to sin and a rising to new life in Christ (Rom 6:1–14). Paul calls for a decisive break with the values, thinking, behaviors, and domination systems of this age, all held together as the *kosmos* to which the believer is crucified and which is crucified to the believer. He is well aware, however, that it takes time for that new fact of existence to take shape in the thick of experience, since the new life continues to be lived in the midst of the hostile powers of "this present, evil age."[112] Paul will thus also speak of *continuing* to cooperate with the Spirit (5:16, 25) so that the Spirit can live within him or her—or, to return to Paul's earlier terminology, so that "Christ may be fully formed" in the believer (4:19), or so that the believer's life lived in this mortal flesh may become Christ living in him or her (2:19–20). The infusion of the Spirit into the life of believers brings Christ's life into theirs, which mystically effects their dying to the power of the flesh and their living to God. With Paul, they are crucified to this present, evil age, and the power of the present, evil age is crucified to them (6:14), and they come to life as part of the new creation of God.

Jesus's crucifixion, particularly as crucifixion "for us," releases a new power that allows human beings to rise above the domination of the flesh in favor of giving themselves over to domination by the Spirit. One component of *how* this happens is the relationship of grace, of mutual favor and obligation, into which God invites human beings in Christ. The experience of being loved by the one who "gave himself over for our sins" (1:4; 2:19) weighs in

---

110. The essential elements of the "flesh" to be mortified are represented by the Greek words παθήματα and ἐπιθυμίαι. Although πάθημα frequently means "negative experience endured," hence "suffering" (as in Rom 8:18; 2 Cor 1:5–7; Phil 3:10; Heb 2:9–10; 1 Pet 1:11; 4:13; 5:1, 9), here it carries the more general sense of "feelings, interests" and "affections" (BDAG 748; LSJ 1285).

111. The Christ-follower dies not only to the law (as in Paul's paradigmatic example, 2:19–20) but also to the flesh (Fee, *Empowering Presence*, 455). The active voice of ἐσταύρωσαν "lays the emphasis on the action and responsibility of Christian believers" (Barclay, *Obeying*, 117; so also Dunn, 314–15).

112. Barclay, *Obeying*, 213. Duncan (176) attempts to differentiate between the act of "crucifying" the flesh and "the death to which it is the prelude," drawing attention to the fact that crucifixion is itself a long-drawn-out manner of execution. While this is not likely to have been Paul's intent in his choice of metaphor (determined as it is by the motif of "dying with Christ"), it does align well with the actual experience of the believer.

against our natural (fallen) tendency to live for ourselves, awakening in our hearts the possibility of loving as Jesus loved, of "living no longer for ourselves but for him who died and was raised on our behalf" (2 Cor 5:15), specifically by "looking out not for our own interests, but for the interests of others" in imitation of Jesus's self-giving (Phil 2:3–11). Jesus's death was an act of love that breaks the self-seeking, self-protective, self-reliant power of the flesh, initiating a new cycle of showing love and other-centered concern on the basis of having experienced such amazing love and other-centered concern as Jesus has shown the disciple.[113]

25 There are admittedly good structural indicators for taking 5:25 as the beginning of a new paragraph or subsection. This verse, with its declaration of a condition in which the believers find themselves (a condition that carries some moral obligation), followed by an exhortation to live in line with that condition according to the Giver's intent, resembles the statements in 5:1 and 5:13 and could thus be taken as the third in a series of related opening lines.[114] Galatians 5:26 is also strikingly similar, and thus potentially parallel, to 5:15, potentially reinforcing the impression that 5:25–26 functions as the beginning of a new step in the development of the letter.

Galatians 5:25–26 may also be seen to recall in inverse order, however, the content of 5:16 and 5:15, rounding off (and thus concluding) this section before moving on to more specific and practical guidance (6:1–10). The direct address ("Brothers and sisters," 6:1) would then signal the start of a new step in Paul's exhortation (as it appears to do in 1:11; 3:15; 4:12; 5:13; though not in 4:28, 31; 5:11).[115] The disagreement about where 5:13ff. ends and the next section begins is probably a testimony to Paul's ability to weave together a well-crafted document, in light of which readers who are driven to discover outlines might do well to remain flexible.

Paul's paired pictures of life driven by the flesh and life driven by the Spirit lead Paul to issue a pair of summary exhortations in 5:25–26. Coming to life in the Spirit is the necessary sequel to dying with Christ to the flesh (5:24),[116] that death to who and what we were as "the old person," the person

---

113. See Moule, "Obligation in the Ethic of Paul," 404; Bryant, *Risen Crucified Christ*, 188. Engberg-Pedersen (*Paul and the Stoics*, 165) similarly regards the Christ event as that which "destroys the flesh in believers" and empowers "the completely stable and unalterable set of other-directed attitudes that constitute the fruit of the spirit."

114. Betz, 254–55; Barclay, *Obeying*, 149–50; Dunn, 316–17.

115. Schreiner, 353 (though he opts for a fresh start at 5:25). While the vocative Ἀδελφοί does not signal a new beginning in 4:28, 31; 5:11, the reason is to be found in the connecting particles in those verses that clearly locate them as part of an ongoing discursive block (δέ in 4:28; διό in 4:31; Ἐγὼ δέ in 5:11). Such connectives are absent in 6:1 (as they are in 3:15 and 4:12, where the direct address Ἀδελφοί can add weight to the impression of a new beginning).

116. Fee, *Empowering Presence*, 456.

(mal)formed after Adam's likeness. A similar logic appears in Rom 6 (see esp. vv. 10–13, 16–18, 20–22), where Paul also argues that, since we are dead to one thing and have come alive to another thing, that second thing must be the guiding force and power in this new life: "If[117] we live because of the Spirit, let us also order our steps by the Spirit" (5:25).[118] With the first verb ("if we live"), Paul is again referring to a special quality of life, or kind of life, and not just our physical life as animal beings. Paul speaks here once more of coming alive in a new way in one's relationship to God, with the associated hope of attaining eternal life (see 2:19–20 on the phrase "that I might live"; 3:21 on "to make alive").[119] By living from this new life that the Spirit has given us (5:25), we have the potential to grow fully into "the new person" that is Christ living in us (see 2:19–20), Christ "fully formed" in us (4:19).

Paul carefully chose his second verb as well. The unusual word *stoichōmen* ("let us order our steps," 5:25) cannot fail to recall *ta stoicheia* (4:3, 9), the principles and powers with which the Galatians formerly fell in line before they experienced Christ's liberation. Having been freed from the domination of the *stoicheia*, the believers are now to fall in step with (*stoichōmen*) the Spirit.[120] As they continue walking in step with the Spirit,[121] like soldiers marching according to the orders prescribed by their general, they find the power of the flesh nullified and the fruits of righteousness multiplied in their lives (5:16, 18–23, 25). The Spirit provides the answer to the question raised in 3:3: "Having begun with the Spirit, are you going to reach completion by things that pertain to the flesh?" No, the journey of transformation begun in the Spirit will be completed only in the Spirit, by the Spirit's leading and in the Spirit's power. Just as the cross, not circumcision, is the way to deal with the sinful desires of the flesh (and thus escape the deadly consequences of

---

117. The NIV, NJB, HCSB, and NLT render the εἰ as "since," but this is a mistake that diminishes the rhetorical force of the verse (as it would also in 5:18). The conditional form ("if," as in NRSV, ESV, CEB) impels the reader to ask whether this is true of him or her and to take the steps forward to certify that it is (i.e., by fulfilling the conditions of the apodosis; Schreiner, 345, 356; Moo, 371–72).

118. This brief exhortation provides an excellent example of a genuine chiasm: A—Εἰ ζῶμεν ("If we have life"), B—πνεύματι ("by the Spirit"), B'—πνεύματι ("by the Spirit"), A'—καὶ στοιχῶμεν ("let us also order our steps"; so also Tolmie, *Persuading*, 204). The exhortations in 5:25–26 look back in reverse order to the lists of the works of the flesh in 5:19–21 and the Spirit's fruit in 5:22–23, but this would be an instance of *hysteron proteron* (taking up the last-mentioned issue first, and working backward) rather than of chiasm proper.

119. Schreiner, 356.

120. So also Longenecker, 266; Das, 588.

121. The continuative aspect suggests that the behavior enjoined is to be an ongoing activity, perhaps one that Paul views as already in progress. This verb will be used again in a similarly commended course of action (6:16).

those desires), so the Spirit, not the Torah, is to be the fundamental ordering principle (the *stoicheion*) for the Christian.

26 Just as the "fruit of the Spirit" is both positively defined and defined against its opposite ("the works of the flesh"), so the positive exhortation to fall in line with the Spirit is given additional definition by contrast with its opposite: "Let us not become conceited, challenging one another, envying one another." This exhortation, like the exhortation in 5:15, gives attention particularly to avoiding the "works of the flesh" that threaten the health of interpersonal or community relations within the churches—the vices that dominate the center of that catalog rather than the more obvious vices related to unbridled sex and partying at the beginning and the end. Again, the repetition of these sorts of problems throughout 5:13–26 (and to some extent also in 6:1–6) suggests that they reflect particular issues in the Galatian congregations that Paul sought to remedy. The Spirit's fruit stands in stark contrast to these attitudes and interpersonal behaviors. Where there are envying, provocation, and challenging one another (probably with a view to gaining something at the other's expense, if he or she fails to answer the challenge), there is identifiably greater need to "put to death the leanings of the flesh" and yield further to the Spirit's leading.

EXCURSUS: INDICATIVE AND IMPERATIVE IN PAUL

Galatians 5:13–26, together with the subsequent passage (6:1–10), raises the question of the relationship of Paul's theology to Paul's ethics, of the relationship of Paul's declaration of what God in Christ has accomplished *for* the believer and *in* the believer to Paul's exhortations to the believers still to move forward actively *toward* that which God has, in some fashion, *already* accomplished in them. This has come to be known as the issue of the "indicative and imperative" in Pauline theology and ethics.[122]

This tension emerges in several of Paul's letters. In Romans, Paul says that "we died to sin" (6:2) and that "as many of us as were baptized into

---

122. As Ridderbos (*Paul*, 253) explains: "What is meant is that the new life in its moral manifestation is at one time proclaimed and posited as the fruit of the redemptive work of God in Christ through the Holy Spirit—the indicative; elsewhere, however, it is put with no less force as a categorical demand—the imperative." For a fine review of the development and refinement of this concept, particularly in nineteenth- and twentieth-century German scholarship, see Dennison, "Indicative and Imperative"; Furnish, *Theology and Ethics*, 259–79. Zimmerman has questioned the model's propriety and utility ("Jenseits von Indikativ und Imperativ"; "Implicit Ethics"), though his criticisms are ably answered in Rabens, "Indicative and Imperative," 287–95.

Christ Jesus were baptized into his death. Therefore we were buried with him through baptism into his death" (6:3–4). He claims that "our old person was crucified along with him in order that the body that belongs to sin might be destroyed" (6:6). These are "indicative" statements about a new, allegedly factual state of affairs. Nevertheless, Paul will shortly go on to urge the hearers, "Consider yourselves to be dead to sin," commanding them (the imperative) to embrace a particular stance as if the fact of the indicative is not fully actualized.[123] Are we dead to sin and buried with Christ? Or do we yet need to consider ourselves dead to sin that we might indeed be dead and buried with Christ, and thus hope to share in his resurrection life (6:5, 8)? In 1 Corinthians, Paul says that his converts "*are* unleavened" (an indicative statement), right after telling them to "clean out the old leaven so that you may be a new lump of dough" (5:7, referring to 5:6, where Paul describes their competitive boasting as "leaven" that threatens to work through the whole lump and sour it all and puff it up). Are they "unleavened"? Or do they need to rid themselves of leaven so that they may *be* unleavened?[124]

These statements may appear paradoxical, as if Paul is calling Christ-followers to "become" what they already "are."[125] While Paul's starker—and perhaps therefore more rhetorical than precise—statements may push in this direction, it seems much more to be the case that Paul is urging Christians not to "*become* what you are" but, rather, to "*do* what is appropriate for a creature such as you are" (perhaps adding, "*if* indeed this is what you are," as in Gal 5:16, 25). The indicative statements testify to God's gift to the Christ-follower of a new existence—one that, if real, must and will be lived. There is no experiencing the new life by the Spirit without also walking by the Spirit; at the same time, walking by the Spirit does not come before and lead to experiencing the new life given by the Spirit.[126] The indicative is not the

---

123. Rabens ("Indicative and Imperative," 289, 294) rightly acknowledges the importance of not treating the moods in a literalistic or restrictive way, since there are a good many implicit imperatives in Paul not expressed using the actual imperative mood.

124. Compare also Col 3:3 ("you *died*, and your life has been hidden with Christ in God") with 3:5–11 ("*Put to death*, therefore, the earthly aspects," etc.).

125. This language appears in Bultmann, *Theology*, 332; see also Barclay, *Obeying*, 28–29.

126. Bultmann, *Theology*, 333. Rabens ("Indicative and Imperative," 304–5) helpfully captures the mutually enriching and deepening relationship between what the believer receives/experiences and how the believer responds: "As believers let the Spirit draw them into transforming and empowering relationships with God and the community of faith and then live according to the values set forth by Paul's gospel, the depth of their relationship to God and others will increase. Believers are thus further empowered as they put Paul's (implicit) ethical imperatives (which are, in fact, aimed at deepening their relationships to God and others) into practice. Human 'walking by the Spirit' (Gal. 5:25b) is hence not only a continuation of 'life in the Spirit' but also that which ensures a further unfolding of the divine gift

precursor to or condition for the imperative, but neither is the imperative the prerequisite to the indicative.[127] It is in *doing* what the Spirit moves us to do that we *are* Spirit-driven people; it is because we are Spirit-possessed people that we can do what the Spirit moves us to do.

Paul's careful balancing of indicative and imperative is part of his dynamic portrayal of the dance of grace that God has initiated with human beings. He calls the believers to consistently *live* the new life that God has given them in Christ, or else spoil the gift. The believer who rejects the imperative also defaces the indicative. If those who are led by the Spirit are sons and daughters of God (Rom 8:14), what are they who reject the Spirit's leading in favor of living for the flesh?[128]

In Galatians, the problem is most evident when one compares Paul's statement that "those who belong to Christ Jesus crucified the flesh with its passions and yearnings" (5:24) with his instructions (essentially) not to sow to the flesh, but rather to the Spirit (6:8), or when he urges the Galatian Christians to conduct themselves by the Spirit's direction so that they will not realize the flesh's impulses (5:16).[129] One might compare the first statement with the daughter who says of a father, "He is dead to me." This is a statement of nonrelationship that does not preclude future encounters, future possibilities of influence. The father remains dead to her as long as, in these future encounters, she does not give him a voice or allow him to exert influence afresh. The gravity and ongoing power of the father's offense against this daughter give her the power to continue to resist allowing that relationship to spring to life once again and giving the father any further role in her life. Consider the similar Pauline thought: "You died to sin; how can you keep living in it?" (See Rom 6:2.) The first *remains* true to the extent that the nonrelationship is continually lived out; but that which led to the first statement ("you died to sin") gives the person the power to continue to live out the nonrelationship (e.g., remembering Jesus's death for me as the awful cost of reconciliation, or remembering my baptism as an act in which I embraced the new life God was offering me). The indicative is a

---

of 'life in the Spirit' (5:25a)." This is a good account of the transformative process that results in truly *rectified* relationships with God and neighbor. I would simply add "unto eternal life" (6:7–10) to the final sentence to complete the picture and the process. See further Rabens, *Holy Spirit and Ethics*, 133–38.

127. Furnish, *Theology and Ethics*, 226, adding that "obedience is *constitutive* of the new life."

128. Similarly, Ridderbos (*Paul*, 255) comments on the "if" of Gal 5:25: the opening clause is "a supposition from which the imperative goes out as an accepted fact. But at the same time it emphasizes that if what is demanded in the imperative does not take place, that which is supposed in the first clause would no longer be admissible."

129. Barclay, *Obeying*, 181.

"contingent" indicative: it remains true as it is lived out (i.e., in obedience to the imperative) and to the extent that it is lived out.[130] At the same time, it remains a divine gift that *can* be lived out as the Christ-follower makes "a *deliberate response* to God's claim without which faith forfeits its distinctive character as obedience."[131]

In Gal 5:13–26 Paul seeks to impress upon the Christ-follower that transformation is indeed possible: the power to become righteous is God's gift through the Spirit. At the same time, transformation is necessary and essential, as the consequences of continuing to live for the flesh (5:21; see also 6:8a) are as dire, if not more so, as turning now to the Torah (5:2–4). Whereas some theologians and pastors think it appropriate to reinforce the believer's identity as sinner, Paul seeks to reinforce the believer's identity as one in whom Christ comes fully alive, one to whom the indwelling Spirit has given decisive victory—and one whom the Spirit empowers to live out that victory day by day—over the flesh.[132] Righteousness is an attainable hope (5:5–6) because of the gift of the Spirit, but the believer also has the obligation to become righteous, *since* God has made such a response possible (and since Jesus died in no small part to *make* this possible).[133] The only way to honor the cost of the new life Christ has opened up for us is to *live* this new life so that the Christ who gave himself for the believer may be formed in and live through the believer (4:19; 2:19–20).

Christian freedom is not license, and the consequences of our misuse of this freedom (and thus our neglectful misuse of God's gift of the Spirit) are harsh and inescapable (see 6:7–8). Christian freedom is also not autonomy, the freedom "to do whatever you might wish" (5:17), whether good, bad, or indifferent, because one believes salvation to be a fait accompli. It is not enough to say No to the Torah and its "works"; one *must* also say Yes to the Spirit and the Spirit's power to re-create us (2:19–20; 4:19; 6:15). This new mode of living will feel like "works righteousness" only where Christ-followers lack the vibrant experience of the Spirit that Paul took to be normal and normative for the Christian life.

---

130. See Käsemann, "The Righteousness of God," 175: "Only so long as we keep on the pilgrim way and allow ourselves to be recalled daily to the allegiance of Christ, can we abide in the gift which we have received and can it abide, living and powerful, in us."

131. Furnish, *Theology and Ethics*, 227.

132. Das, 588–89.

133. Or in the words of John Wesley, "First, God works; therefore you *can* work: Secondly, God works, therefore you *must* work" ("On Working Out Your Own Salvation" 3.2, Sermon 90, *Works of John Wesley*, 2:237).

In this section, Paul also provides a sharper image of what "faith working through love" means. Christian freedom is, specifically, the freedom to serve one another as slaves would serve—not as a matter of choice or preference, not only insofar as one's comfort level and sense of pride would permit, but as those put wholly at the disposal of Another, who puts them wholly at the disposal of one another. Here is the essence of Paul's ethic of love as the fulfillment of the law, the kind of love that embodies the paradigm of the Messiah who loved us and gave himself for us. As we give ourselves for one another, we love in the manner of Christ; we fulfill the "law of Christ" (6:2) that is Christ living in, through, and among us. Paul's focus (in line with Jesus's focus) on "love for the neighbor" rather than "love for humanity" prevents Christian love from degenerating into a "vague feeling for humankind stretched so thin as to be non-existent at particular points of need," calling instead for "a practical love, a concentrated love . . . one which utilizes the resources which one actually has in specific 'Jericho-road' situations."[134]

Paul's vision in this and the following section is not just one of transformed individuals but of transformed *community*. Paul's discussion of the works of the flesh and the Spirit's fruit has congregational life as its primary focus. Neither sin nor holiness is just a matter of the individual's heart and practice; they are very much social phenomena as well. A church chooses, by the collective decisions of its members in interaction after interaction, in response after response, what kind of community it will be—and what the health and safety of its individual members will be in such a community (negatively, 5:15, 26; positively, 6:1–2). In this context, Paul's catalogs of "the works of the flesh" and "the Spirit's fruit" serve as diagnostic tools. Are arguments among Christians leading to the division of a group of Christians into factions around some issue? Is the harmony of a Christian body being broken because of some disagreement? This is a sign that "flesh" is at work somewhere in the equation—and more than likely on *both* sides (and flesh is not merely to be resisted or contained; it is to be crucified). It is a sign that all parties need to stop, take a step back, and pray for the Spirit to illumine what is really going on in their situation and in their hearts. It is a call to recommit as a united body to discerning the Spirit's guidance in unity and laying down all personal agendas to that end. Communal harmony cannot be legislated. Rules like "don't argue" or "don't address the difficult issues because it might lead to division" will not achieve God's purposes in the church. Such attitudes are more reflective of fear than faith. Walking together by the Spirit, however, leads to the quality of relationships between people that allows for difficult issues to be addressed in a context of mutual love and commitment. It leads to the quality of relationships that causes outsiders—even those who

---

134. Dunn, 292.

are hostile to the presence of Christianity in their midst—to remark, "Look how they love each other . . . and how they are prepared to die one for the other" (Tertullian, *Apology* 39.7).

Paul's focus on the quality of Christian relations in Gal 5:13–26 suggests that he would take a keen interest in disunity within a church and among churches, calling us to account wherever we act on the basis of competition, rivalry, self-interest, or protecting one's own or one's group's agenda. Even Christian mission and outreach can be driven by the flesh rather than the Spirit. It is not enough to have allowed the Spirit to transform the internal relationships within a particular congregation; the Spirit must also be allowed to transform relationships between individual congregations and between larger Christian bodies (whether we call them denominations or some other term), which are called to reflect the *diversity* of the body of Christ without perpetrating *division* within the body of Christ. Paul's exhortation to put aside relational ugliness (5:26) and instead to learn to bear one another's burdens together (6:2) applies at every level of Christian community.

B. PRACTICAL ADVICE FOR WALKING IN THE SPIRIT (6:1-10)

¹ *Brothers and sisters, even if a person is overtaken in any transgression, you all who are Spirit-led are to restore such a person in a spirit of forbearance, each of you watching yourself lest you also be tempted.* ² *Make it a habit to carry one another's burdens, and in this way you will fulfill*ᵃ *the law of Christ.* ³ *For if anyone thinks himself or herself to be something, when that person is nothing, he or she is deceiving himself or herself.* ⁴ *But let each person*ᵇ *keep testing his or her own work, and then the boast will point to himself or herself alone, and not to the other person.* ⁵ *For each person will carry his or her own load.* ⁶ *Let the one who is instructed in the word continue to share in all good things with the one who gives instruction.* ⁷ *Don't deceive yourselves: God is not mocked. For whatever a person sows, that shall he or she also reap,* ⁸ *because the one who keeps sowing to his or her flesh will harvest destruction from the flesh, but the one who keeps sowing to the Spirit will harvest eternal life from the Spirit.* ⁹ *Let us not grow tired*ᶜ *of doing what is noble, for we will reap the harvest in its own season if we do not give up.* ¹⁰ *As long as we have*ᵈ *a season, then, let us work*ᵉ *what is good toward all, and especially toward those who belong to the household of faith.*

a. Early manuscripts are divided between reading ἀναπληρώσατε ("fulfill," an imperative; ℵ A C D Ψ 33 1739 1881 𝔐) and ἀναπληρώσετε ("you will fulfill," a future indicative; B F G; ἀποπληρώσετε, 𝔓⁴⁶). In the Greek, the difference is a matter of a single letter in the verb ending. Despite the strong external support for the imperative form, it seems more likely that scribes encountering the future indicative ἀποπληρώσετε would change this to an imperative to match the imperatives immediately preceding this verb (καταρτίζετε, 6:1;

βαστάζετε, 6:2) rather than introduce a stray future indicative in place of an imperative (so Metzger, *Textual Commentary*, 530; Comfort, *Text and Translation*, 573).

b. $\mathfrak{P}^{46}$ and B omit ἕκαστος, with the result that the person envisioned in 6:3 remains the subject of the commands in 6:4 (hence, "let such a one test"). This verse becomes, in these manuscripts, even more clearly a prescription against the inflated self-opinion warned against in 6:3. External attestation of the omission beyond these two important witnesses is too slight to overturn the likelihood that ἕκαστος is indeed original to the text.

c. ἐγκακῶμεν is attested by the important trio ℵ A B, as well as D* and the Coptic version. The majority of later witnesses (C D^2 Ψ 1739* 1881 𝔐 *pm*) read ἐκκακῶμεν, which bears a very similar meaning ("let us not grow discouraged") but is probably secondary.

d. Two important manuscripts (ℵ B*) read ἔχωμεν (present subjunctive) rather than ἔχομεν (present indicative). The former is the more difficult reading, as it is rare to find ὡς followed by the subjunctive (without an accompanying ἄν) in the New Testament. Properly, this variant would give to the clause a nuance of purpose ("So, then, that we might have a season"), but it could also simply be a less grammatically adept way of expressing duration of time (as does the indicative ἔχομεν in the better attested reading). Fee (*Empowering Presence*, 464) finds it "too difficult a reading to be original."

e. Some MSS (A B^2 P) read ἐργαζόμεθα, which is likely not original, given both the preponderance of external support for the hortatory subjunctive ἐργαζώμεθα (ℵ B* C D F G; ἐργασώμεθα, $\mathfrak{P}^{46}$) and the greater probability of that form in the context of exhortation. The variant may simply have arisen from an error of hearing.

With the direct prescriptions of Gal 6:1–10, Paul is not beginning to formulate a new legal code. A comprehensive set of rules for Christian conduct at this point would be entirely counter to his vision, painstakingly established in Gal 3–5, for spiritually mature people responsive to the leading of the Holy Spirit. Rather, Paul gives a few specific examples of how the Spirit transforms human community, what the signs are that the Spirit is successfully working to produce a community where the ideal of love is realized, and what the symptoms are when the flesh exerts its power again. Love shows itself where the sinner is gently reclaimed, where believers invest in one another enough to "bear one another's burdens" (6:1–2); love shows itself where believers refuse to regard a sister or brother as a spiritual trophy of any kind, as if the conversion or transformation of another person could become a claim to honor for oneself (as the rival teachers are doing, in Paul's mind; 6:4–5, 13). Love manifests itself in the sharing of resources with believers who dedicate themselves to bringing more of the truth of God to light for the rest (6:6). Where love is made real, God's transforming Spirit is truly at work, bringing believers into conformity with God's righteousness.

The liberty of the Spirit may seem dangerous in the face of a person's ability to fool himself or herself, or a person's ability to try to get away with feeding more of the flesh than he or she might have been able to do under the yoke of Torah. The integrity of the life of the Spirit, however, is guaranteed by the omniscience of God, "unto whom all hearts are open, all desires known, and from whom no secrets are hid" (Book of Common Prayer 1979). There is no fooling God, and thus Christian freedom can never be misused without consequences.

The more practical instructions here are themselves very limited in scope and may be offered because of their direct relevance to the tensions and divisions that have crept up within the Galatian communities.[135] These are not just moral maxims and proverbs strung together without clear connection; they are instructions with direct relevance for the argument and the situation in Galatia, exhibiting a clear logical development.[136] Paul creates here a balance between the individual disciple's responsibility toward other believers (6:1a, 2, 6, 9–10) and the individual disciple's accountability before God (6:1b, 3–5, 7–8).[137] These two fundamental principles function as twin guardrails on the path of true freedom.

1 Addressing the hearers afresh as "brothers and sisters," Paul shifts his focus from the more general pictures of the flesh-led and the Spirit-led life (5:13–26) to some more specific examples.[138] The provision here for the restoration of the transgressor shows that Paul knows that the flesh will not go down without a fight, and that disciples will not always be able to keep in step with the Spirit. There will be occasions of stumbling, of falling back into sinful, self-centered patterns of thought and behavior. The "even if," however, shows that Paul does not regard—or want disciples to regard—such falling back as a normal, even everyday part of Christian experience. The "even if" also shows that Paul is self-consciously continuing the discussion in 5:13–26, particularly responding correctively to the strong claims he has made in 5:16 and 5:24. While 6:1 may be regarded, then, as introducing a fresh topic (namely, specific guidance for Christian practice in community), this material also continues to develop the line of thought begun in 5:13.[139]

What kind of response does the Spirit call for in regard to brothers and sisters who lose a battle with a particular impulse of the flesh? "If a person is

---

135. See discussion of 5:15 and 5:26, as well as the eight central "works of the flesh" that make disturbances in social harmony the most clearly emphasized area of the flesh's operation. "It can be said that all the relevant mirror-reading criteria (tone, frequency, clarity, unfamiliarity) point towards a situation of discord in the Galatian churches" (Barclay, *Obeying*, 153). Such a situation, then, becomes the backdrop for the practical instructions of 6:1–10.

136. Fee, *Empowering Presence*, 459; against Betz, 291–92.

137. Barclay, *Obeying*, 149–50.

138. Longenecker, 265. See commentary on 5:25 on the question of whether to regard that verse or 6:1 as the starting point of a new step in Paul's discussion. The NRSV reads "my friends" rather than "brothers and sisters" (NIV, CEB), an unnecessary elimination of the kinship terms and the ethos those terms evoke.

139. Fee, *Empowering Presence*, 460; see also the use of the phrase "even if" (ἐὰν καί, εἰ καί) in 1 Cor 7:11, 21, 28; 2 Cor 4:16; 5:3, 16; 7:8, 12; 11:15; 12:11; Phil 2:17; 3:12.

overtaken in any transgression, you who are Spirit-led are to restore that person in a spirit of forbearance, each of you keeping an eye on yourself, lest you also be tempted" (6:1). One of the safeguards against the ability of the flesh or "the deceitfulness of sin" (to borrow a phrase from Heb 3:13) to mislead or overpower the individual disciple is the community of faith. In the absence of the road map of a written code like Torah, the community's discernment of what is of the Spirit over against what is of the flesh provides the guardrails to help the individual believer "keep in step with the Spirit."

Being "overtaken" by a sin suggests falling into sin through error, neglect, lack of vigilance, or sheer weakness rather than willful transgression, though it would be artificial to exclude even the last of these, as the goal of intervention is to bring about willful repentance.[140] The Greek verb here can also mean "to be found out" or "to be discovered," thus "caught in the act."[141] This sense cannot be excluded, all the more as discovery is the logical prerequisite to the exhortation itself (only if the transgression has been uncovered can others know to take restorative action).

Those who are themselves led by the Spirit ("you who are in-Spirited") are to invest themselves in restoring the wayward, rather than using it as an opportunity to honor oneself at the other's expense.[142] By "spiritual" or "in-Spirited" people, Paul has in mind the Galatian Christians in general. It is highly unlikely that he uses this term ironically or with any degree of biting sarcasm;[143] it is equally unlikely that he is appealing to some spiritual elite within the congregation.[144] Rather, he is appealing to his audience as broth-

---

140. BDAG 872; Burton, 327; Lagrange, 155; Das, 601. The situation Paul envisions is somewhat different from the case presupposed in Matt 18:15–18, where one party seeks ever wider circles of support in a process of reconciliation/discipline. While Paul elsewhere prescribes shunning as a means of community discipline, presumably *until* the offender repented and returned to an acceptable mode of life (see 1 Cor 5:11; 2 Thess 3:14), this was an extreme step to be taken after other, gentler steps had not produced repentance. In 2 Thess 3:14 shunning explicitly comes only after the offenders had not heeded Paul's (by this point repeated) warning. Mutual correction "in meekness and compassion" was also an important and expected part of community life at Qumran (see 1QS V.24–VI.1).

141. Fee, *Empowering Presence*, 460. See, helpfully, Dunn, 319: "The test of spiritual maturity is dealing kindly not just with the unwitting (and regretted) mistake, but with the fellow Christian whose deliberate unacceptable conduct has come to light despite his or her attempts at concealment."

142. In the context of a body of moral exhortation, the ambiguity of form καταρτίζετε would probably be resolved in favor of the imperative rather than the indicative. The present tense may have been chosen to acknowledge that such restoration involves a *process* of remediation and reincorporation. See Dunn, 321; Das, 604.

143. Against Schlier, 270.

144. Correctly, Fee, *Empowering Presence*, 461. Paul is also not describing people who walk merely according to "a spiritual principle," contra Lagrange, 155.

ers and sisters who are indeed walking in step with the Spirit that they have received as heirs of the promise, as in 3:2–5; 4:6–7; 5:16–25.[145]

They especially have the opportunity to manifest a particular facet of the Spirit's fruit while doing so—"forbearance" or "gentleness" (5:23).[146] They are not to approach the wayward in a spirit that would beat down or alienate or that would bring shame, but with the humility and sympathy that come from each one knowing his or her own equal vulnerability to temptations to sin.[147] There is no room inside the disciple's heart for secretly preening himself or herself on not falling into the sin that has ensnared another believer. There is room only for renewed vigilance, in the face of another's being waylaid by sin, against the inroads that the impulses of the flesh would make into one's own heart.[148]

2 Helping one another discern and stay in step with the Spirit, especially investing in restoring a brother or sister who has strayed back into following the flesh, is one way in which believers must "keep serving one another in love as slaves" (5:13), or as Paul renews that directive here: "Keep carrying one another's burdens, and in this way you will fulfill the law of Christ" (6:2).[149] In the immediate context, "burdens" refers metaphorically to the moral and personal failures from which individual disciples need restoration—the weight of the struggle against falling back under the power of self-centered and self-gratifying impulses (the flesh). Each disciple will at some point rely upon others to help him or her carry this weight in order to remain in the Spirit's path. Paul would no doubt also understand this injunction to extend to include all burdensome experiences of life, all the trials that life sim-

---

145. Burton, 327; Bruce, 260; Barclay, "Mirror-Reading," 82, 92n28; Barclay, *Obeying*, 157; Fung, 285; Longenecker, 273; Martyn, 546; Witherington, 422; Schreiner, 358; Moo, 374; Dunn, 319–20.

146. "In a spirit of forbearance" (ἐν πνεύματι πραΰτητος, Gal 6:1) directly recalls "forbearance" (πραΰτης, Gal 5:23), a fruit of the Spirit. The prepositional phrase indicates manner ("in a spirit of forbearance" = "patiently, gently"). πνεῦμα here probably denotes a human attitude, though clearly one shaped by the Spirit of Christ (i.e., exhibiting the πραΰτης that is a fruit of the Spirit, 5:23). Fee (*Empowering Presence*, 462) stresses the importance of hearing here the overtone of the Holy Spirit, the source of this gentleness in the believer.

147. The explicit use of the nominative singular pronoun σύ is emphatic. Paul has notably individualized the warning ("each one of you watching yourself, lest") attached to the general instruction ("you all who are in-Spirited").

148. Barclay, *Obeying*, 158; Dunn (321) similarly finds Paul affirming "critical self-scrutiny as equally a mark of the Spirit." Since restoration of the wayward will be a process and, no doubt, a habitual practice, such caution in regard to oneself must also be ongoing, hence the continuative aspect (the present tense) of the participle σκοπῶν.

149. Clear connections between 5:13–14 and 6:2 are forged by Paul's "parallel references to mutual obligation" (5:13; 6:2) and verbal repetition involving "fulfilling" a "law" (5:14; 6:2; Barclay, *Obeying*, 131–32).

ply sends each person's way. Believers are to extend love, kindness, support, and, as needed, material help toward those experiencing such burdens so as to make them easier to bear.[150] Carrying another person's burden was the work of a slave, when one was available; voluntarily doing so, particularly in regard to the burdens that make life oppressive or that erode a person's walk in the Spirit, is the work of love—the "working through love" that makes "faith" real and that has value in God's sight (5:6).

Paul claims that such habitual, mutual burden-bearing is the way to "fulfill the law of Christ."[151] The expression cannot help but recall Paul's earlier claim that "the whole law has been fulfilled in one commandment: 'You will love your neighbor as yourself'" (Gal 5:14; Lev 19:18). Mutual burden-bearing is a practical expression of loving one's neighbor as oneself, since one takes up the neighbor's burdens as also one's own. By "the law of Christ," Paul is not referring to the eschatological "Torah of the Messiah" imagined in rabbinic circles, that is, the Torah as it would be interpreted and taught by the Messiah when he comes.[152] Nor would Paul consider the body of Jesus's teachings as a new Torah, a new law, for the Christian disciple.[153] For one thing, Paul at best only alludes to Jesus's teachings (and most rarely in Galatians!) and almost never cites them as warrant for his own or his congregations' practice.[154] For another, the very concept of a body of law is contrary to his prioritization of free, loving response as opposed to compulsory obedience.[155] The closest

---

150. Burton, 329; Betz, 299; Barclay, *Obeying the Truth*, 132; Bruce, 261; Fung, 287; Lagrange, 156; Longenecker, 274–75; Schreiner, 358; Dunn, 321–22. Strelan ("Burden Bearing") is right to *include* financial assistance as an example of helping to bear another's burden, but wrong to focus too narrowly on this one manifestation of burden-bearing. Classical examples similar to this command include Menander, *Sentences* 370, 534; Xenophon, *Memorabilia* 2.7.1–14 (see Betz, 298–99).

151. The continuative aspect of the imperative βαστάζετε suggests that this is to become a habitual practice in the Christian community. The reciprocal pronoun Ἀλλήλων ("one another") is emphatic by virtue of its unusual position (Burton, 329), suggesting an implicit contrast with being concerned only to invest oneself in dealing with one's own burdens (and perhaps also an explicit contrast with tearing one another down in 5:26; Barclay, *Obeying*, 159).

152. Davies, *Sermon on the Mount*, 109–90. The evidence for an eschatological "Torah of the Messiah" consists merely in five possible references, evidence rightly judged to be "extremely thin" (Barclay, *Obedience*, 127; Dunn, 323; Furnish, *Theology and Ethics*, 63).

153. Davies, *Setting*, 341–66; Fung, 288; Dodd, "*Ennomos Christou*," 134–48.

154. On one occasion when Paul clearly cites a dominical saying (1 Cor 9:14), it is in the context of explaining why Paul does not follow or require his converts in Corinth to follow that saying (i.e., by supporting Paul with cash donations). On Paul's citations of Jesus traditions, see Allison, "Pauline Epistles and the Synoptic Gospels"; Thompson, *Clothed with Christ*.

155. See Murphy-O'Connor, "Unwritten Law," 215–20. Murphy-O'Connor points particularly to Paul's refusal to command in Phlm 8–9, 14; 2 Cor 8:7–8; 9:7 so that the response could remain free.

parallel expression in Paul's own writings appears in 1 Corinthians, where Paul speaks of the person who is "within the law of Christ," a person who is neither "under Torah" nor yet "lacking God's law" (1 Cor 9:20–21).[156] Such a person falls into neither category that defined people before and apart from Christ, namely, "Jews" (those "under Torah") and "gentiles" (who are "sinners" by definition, since they are "without Torah," as in Gal 2:15). Instead, they are being normed by Christ, patterned into the mind and example of Christ, by the work of the Spirit within them as this same Christ is "being formed" in them (Gal 4:19).[157]

Paul may have known Jesus's own selection of love for God and love for neighbor as the two most important commandments (Mark 12:31; Matt 22:39; Luke 10:27), which Paul understood not just as Jesus's prioritization of Torah's commands, but as Jesus's selection of the commands that capture the whole essence of Torah, the central direction toward which all of Torah is driving.[158] But "love for neighbor" is also what Jesus himself exemplified to the full when he showed his love for Paul (Gal 2:20) and for all (Gal 1:4) by giving himself on their behalf.[159] Indeed, the example of Jesus's giving of himself for others (in life *and* in death) gives necessary precision to what love means in attitude and action.[160] Jesus is a living law for his followers.[161] The "law of Christ" may certainly call to mind "the law as Christ refocused it," but it may equally well be heard as "the law that *is* Christ."[162] To love one's neighbor as oneself, and thus to fulfill the righteous demand of the law, is to love as Christ has loved,

---

156. Barclay, *Obeying*, 126–27. The Greek here is ἔννομος Χριστοῦ, "normed by Christ." F. W. Danker's paraphrase captures the contrast very well: "I identified as one outside Mosaic jurisdiction with those outside it; not, of course, being outside God's jurisdiction, but inside Christ's" (BDAG 338).

157. Das, 599; Hays, "Christology and Ethics," 273; Schreiner, 360; Fee, *Pauline Christology*, 141. Fee (*Empowering Presence*, 463) sums up Pauline ethics most eloquently: "God's glory is their *purpose*, the Spirit is their *power*, love is the *principle*, and Christ is the *pattern*."

158. Thielman (*Paul and the Law*, 141) regards "Christ's summary of the Mosaic law" as the essence of "the law of Christ"; see Wenham, *Paul: Follower of Jesus*, 256–59.

159. Beker, *Paul the Apostle*, 105; Barclay, *Obeying*, 133; Hays, "Christology and Ethics," 289–90; Schürmann, "Das Gesetz des Christus," 286–88.

160. Hays, "Christology and Ethics," 274.

161. One might compare Philo's presentation of the lives of the patriarchs as "unwritten laws" or as "laws endowed with life and reason," having pursued and embodied virtue in action without following the Torah as legal code (see Philo, *Virtues* 194; *On the Life of Abraham* 5.275–76; *Decalogue* 1; discussed in Murphy-O'Connor, "The Unwritten Law," 220–24), or Cicero's description of the ideal king as one who fully embodies and thus presents the law in his person (*On the Republic* 1.52; Murphy-O'Connor, "The Unwritten Law," 226).

162. Murphy-O'Connor thus resolves the genitive as one of apposition or definition ("The Unwritten Law," 220; BDF §167; Robertson, *Grammar*, 498–99). Christ is a living representation of a norm to embody.

which becomes a real possibility for Christ-followers as Christ comes alive within them (as in Paul, Gal 2:19–20) and lives through them by the power of the Holy Spirit that Christ died to procure for them (3:13–14; 5:16–25).

The phrase "the law of Christ," then, holds together both Jesus's identification of the heart of the historic Torah (Lev 19:18) and Jesus's exemplary and paradigmatic obedience to that one command in which the whole is fulfilled.[163] Christ's other-centered, self-giving love *is* their law, and mutual burden-bearing is a day-to-day expression of living by the norm of Christ. Thus, as Christ takes shape in one by means of the working of the Spirit (2:20; 4:19), one becomes a person who similarly loves and serves as Christ did— and thereby a person against whom the law will lay no blame.

3 Paul supports the command to "carry each other's burdens" with a proverb-like saying presented as a rationale:[164] "For if anyone thinks himself or herself to be something, when that person is nothing, he or she is deceiving himself or herself" (6:3). The proverbial nature of this saying by the first century is evident from the striking parallels in Greek philosophical texts. The late-first-century CE philosopher Epictetus says of the person who lacks knowledge of what is truly noble and what base, and who does not exercise choice and aversion appropriately, that "such a person . . . will go about deaf and blind, thinking that he is somebody, when he really is nobody" (*Discourses* 2.24.19). As early as the fourth century BCE, Plato had similarly pointed out the folly of those who "think themselves to be something, being nothing" (*Apology of Socrates* 41e). Inflated self-esteem was a familiar ethical problem.

This verse supports the preceding statement by providing an argument from the contrary. If other-centered service, seen in the willingness to bow down, figuratively speaking, to help someone shoulder his or her burden is the measure of progress in discipleship, then the conceitedness that makes people think they are more important than, and above, the struggling sister or brother is empty self-deception.[165] The person who is puffed up with self-

---

163. As Martyn (555–56) rightly notes, the previous thirty-one instances of νόμος ("law") have all had some reference to the Mosaic law, and so the thirty-second instance should also be expected to speak to this topic in some way as well.

164. Paul signals this connection by introducing the sentence with the inferential conjunction γάρ.

165. So also Tolmie, *Persuading*, 211. There are other opinions concerning what it means to mistakenly "think oneself to be something" in this context. Burton (330) understands Paul to describe the person who fails to watch his or her own liabilities to temptation and sin, who lacks therefore the healthy self-knowledge that keeps a person humble when dealing with, and inclined to help bear, the failings of another (see also Matera, 214). Lagrange suggests that "the person who refuses to carry the burden of another thinks, no doubt, that he or she will not have need of another's help—and in that he or she errs!" (157,

importance is still just a novice in the faith, whereas the person who thinks his or her struggling sister or brother to "be something," such that that person invests time and self into helping the sister or brother bear some burden, is taking on the shape and role of the Master.[166]

4 The attention given to the practice of one's fellow disciple (6:1) must be matched—indeed outmatched—by the ongoing attention one gives to the critical examination of one's own practice, to make sure it is Spirit-led and affirmed by the presence of the Spirit's fruit: "But let each person keep testing his or her own work,[167] and then he or she will have his or her boast in (or 'to') himself or herself alone, and not in (or 'to') the other person" (6:4). The advice in this verse, namely, to perform honest self-examination, is presented specifically as the alternative to, or remedy for, the state of self-deception depicted in the preceding verse.[168] Paul urges believers to avoid self-deception, whether on the basis of comparing oneself favorably against another who has fallen into some transgression (6:1), or on the basis of comparing oneself competitively with another's positive achievements, as if it was the tally that justified and gave cause for pride and honor, rather than the transforming work of the Spirit.

The cultures found about the Mediterranean basin in the Greek, Hellenistic, and Roman periods can be fairly described as honor and shame cultures. The preservation or advancement of honor was a fundamental good; the avoidance of disgrace, likewise. As Seneca, a first-century CE Stoic philosopher and statesman, observed, "The one firm conviction from which we move to the proof of other points is this: that which is honorable is held dear for no other reason than because it is honorable" (*On Benefits* 4.16.2). People laid claim to honor, often in competitive ways, seeking to establish or advance their own honor at the expense of others.[169] This background explains both the prevalence of the language of "boasting" in Paul's writings *and* Paul's interest in channeling "boasting"—that is, "claiming honor"—in directions that will both uphold the Christian group's distinctive practices and values and also not undermine the Christian group's solidarity through internal competition.[170]

---

my translation). The last-mentioned option seems the least likely, as it requires reading more into the verse than the literary context naturally suggests.

166. Schreiner, 360.

167. The present tense (continuative aspect) of the imperative δοκιμαζέτω suggests that such self-examination is to be an ongoing practice.

168. This connection would be conveyed by the particle δέ, here understood to carry an adversative sense.

169. On honor and shame as foundational values in the ancient Mediterranean basin and their expression, see deSilva, *Honor*, 23–89; Jewett, "Paul, Shame, and Honor."

170. Boasting language (καύχημα, καύχησις, καυχάομαι) appears in the undisputed

Paul allows for the believer to continue to claim honor (to "boast"), but one believer must not use another believer to this end.[171] Paul's precise meaning in the second half of this verse is not immediately clear because of the ambiguity of the preposition (Greek *eis*) translated indecisively above as "in" or "to." The preposition could be understood in the first sense as signifying "with reference/respect to." Read thus, Paul asserts that a disciple would ideally locate the *basis* of his or her claim to honor in himself or herself, that is, in his or her own progress in living by the Spirit, rather than with reference to another person's progress or lack thereof.[172] Paul may be thinking specifically of taking pride in not falling into a particular transgression as another disciple might have done (if 6:1 is still in view here).[173] Alternatively, he might be thinking of comparing one's own progress favorably with that of others, if one considers oneself to have advanced further than other Christians (as Paul himself did in regard to his pre-Christian progress "in Judaism," Gal 1:14). He might already have in mind the rival teachers' alleged desire to boast on account of what they were able to convince gentile converts to do (i.e., accept circumcision, 6:13).[174]

The preposition *eis* could, alternatively, indicate the direction of one's boast, in the sense that one would keep one's claim to honor *to* himself or herself rather than waving it in front of the other person, with the result that Paul's instructions here are geared toward reducing rivalry and competitive boasting.[175] This sense is the more typical for this preposition (see particularly its use in 2 Cor 8:24, where it clearly indicates the direction or audience of Paul's boast about the Corinthians). Moreover, "boasting" language will appear again in the conclusion of Galatians as Paul contrasts the (imputed) motive of the rival teachers to "claim honor on the basis of your flesh" (6:13),

---

Pauline letters fifty-six times, the heaviest concentration being 2 Corinthians—where Paul and certain rival teachers are each asserting the greater honor of their ministries and apostleship over against the other. The early-second-century BCE Jewish sage Ben Sira similarly works to redirect "boasting" in a direction that will sustain the practices of the Jewish minority culture in the face of the growing attraction of Hellenism. He repeatedly urges that one's claim to honor should be "in the fear of the Lord" (e.g., see Sir 1:11; 9:16; 10:22; 25:6; 39:8 ["in the Lord's covenant"]) rather than anchored in any other measurements (which Torah observance might actually impede rather than augment in his setting).

171. Paul famously "excludes" boasting in Rom 3:27, but there he speaks of a very particular type of boasting, namely, the boast of the Jew (Rom 2:17, 23) who possessed, and perhaps has performed, the Torah. This exclusion clearly does not extend to every claim to honor, as attested by dozens of other Pauline passages affirming particular claims to honor (e.g., Rom 5:2, 3, 11; 15:17; 1 Cor 9:15–16; 15:31).

172. Thus Longenecker, 277.

173. Lagrange, 157; Fung, 290; Longenecker, 276; Matera, 215; Moo, 380.

174. Witherington, 428.

175. Barclay, *Obeying*, 160–61; Martyn, 550; Hays, "Galatians," 334.

that is, by figuratively collecting the Galatians' foreskins as trophies by means of which to gain honor in the sight of other Jews, and Paul's own commitment to "claim honor" only "in Christ's cross" (6:14), which has effected a radical reorientation of values and direction in Paul's own life. In these verses, Paul uses a different preposition to identify that *in which* or *with regard to which* one boasts,[176] and not the preposition *eis*, as in 6:4, which *might* give some weight to preferring the second meaning, "to," here.

These observations notwithstanding, almost every major translation renders this verse in a way that reflects the first option for *eis*, "with reference to," taking one's own proven work to be the subject or basis of one's claim to honor (see NRSV, NIV, ESV, NASB, NJB, NLT, CEB).[177] The following verse, offered as a rationale in support of the present one (specifically, the desirability of having a claim to honor in some way attached to oneself rather than to another person, since "each will bear his or her own load," 6:5), would tend to support this option as well.[178] This much is clear: one's fellow disciple is not to serve as the means by which one promotes one's own honor and standing, which is antithetical to serving the other in love (5:13-14). Even though the second sense of the preposition ("to") is the less likely, it is also difficult to imagine Paul countenancing any kind of vocalized boasting within the congregation (whether on the basis of one's own progress in discipleship or Spirit-led works, or on the basis of one's superior achievements in comparison with another's), all of which leads to competitive rivalry, divisiveness, and general conceitedness. The apostle who will claim honor for himself only in connection with the cross of Jesus Christ (6:14) appropriately urges others to find their ground for self-respect in their own rootedness in the Spirit's leading; it may well be that he would counsel each also to exercise self-control by keeping that boast to oneself.[179]

---

176. In Greek, ἐν (Gal 6:13, 14).

177. A further possibility emerges if we understand the subject of the verb "will have" to be "the boast" rather than the person who tests his or her own work. There is an idiomatic usage of this verb along with the preposition εἰς (see LSJ 750) that would yield the following sense: "Then the boast will point toward himself or herself alone, and not toward the other."

178. Although Paul's words about this boast may be understood in the context of self-assessment of one's own claim to honor in the present, Schreiner (362) and Moo (380–81) suggest that the future tense or the verb "he or she will have" points ahead to God's future judgment, rather than the present time of ongoing self-examination, as the time in which this claim to honor will be enjoyed. Paul speaks elsewhere of his own or his congregations' "claim to honor" on that decisive day (2 Cor 1:14; Phil 2:16; 1 Thess 2:19), and the subsequent verse in all probability has the last judgment in prospect, so this must remain a possibility here as well.

179. Barclay, *Obeying*, 161.

5 Paul introduces this brief sentence as a rationale for the statement made in the preceding verse.[180] At first, Paul may appear to be contradicting himself when, after urging disciples to "carry one another's burdens" (6:2), he then declares that "each person will carry his or her own load."[181] Paul strikes a balance between individual responsibility and community support, charging the community with doing all in its power to help each individual member remain within the boundaries of the proper and fruitful exercise of his or her freedom as a Christian (6:1–2)—so that he or she will be best positioned to stand, that is, survive God's judgment, on the last day (6:5). The weight of life's burdens is to be shared among Christians in the assembly as long as life endures (6:1–2); the ultimate responsibility for a life, however, cannot be shared, even if one would wish (6:5).[182]

This principle is true in regard not only to shortcomings, but also to successes. There will be no reward on that day for having done *better* than another believer, only for what one has done oneself in God's sight and God's estimation. In this sense the saying ties in most directly with 6:4. The self-examination that Paul urges is to be done with a view to discovering what, in our own progress and practice, will ultimately have positive value before God when everyone stands in front of Christ's judgment seat, "in order that each may receive the due reward for what was done while in the body, whether good or ill" (2 Cor 5:10).

6 The next exhortation seems to introduce a completely new topic: "Let the one who is instructed in the word share in all good things with

---

180. Once again, Paul signals this connection by introducing the sentence with the inferential conjunction γάρ.

181. Paul uses different terms for "burdens" (βάρη, 6:2) and "load" (φορτίον, 6:5) in the Greek, perhaps to enhance the likelihood that hearers will distinguish between the two. Many English translations introduce the notion of obligation or compulsion (NRSV, "must carry"; NIV, "should carry"; CEB, "will have to carry"), despite Paul's avoidance of the several Greek options for doing so. Here it is a bald statement of fact ("will bear," "will carry").

182. Barclay, *Obeying*, 162; Fung, 291–92. Compare 4 Ezra 7.105: On the day of judgment, "neither shall anyone lay a burden on another; for then all shall bear their own righteousness and unrighteousness." Other scholars who understand here a reference to judgment include Schreiner, 362; Moo, 381; Kuck, "Each Will Bear His Own Burden," 296; Tolmie, *Persuading*, 213. Some scholars argue against such a connection here. See Lagrange, 158; Dunn, 326 (who claims that "it is less likely that the future tense looks to the final judgment," even though he offers no argument concerning the probabilities). Das (616–17) only reluctantly concedes the possibility of an eschatological import. The last judgment, however, is the *consistent* point of reference for individual responsibility for one's action both prior and subsequent to this passage (5:21; 6:7–10). The parallel expression in Gal 5:10—"Whoever is troubling you will bear [*bastasei*, as here] the penalty"—also makes good sense as an invocation of the hovering threat of God's judgment. It seems artificial to eliminate it as a point of reference here, as Paul solemnly asserts that, ultimately, we must carry our own moral weight.

the one who gives instruction" (6:6).[183] The distinction between "the one being instructed" and "the instructor" implies the beginnings of a specialized ministry within the church, with particular individuals entrusted with the instruction and edification of the community and all its members, devoting time to this task that is taken away from other work through which one might provide for oneself (see also Rom 12:7; Eph 4:11).[184] "The word" probably refers generally to Christian instruction, though the basis for such instruction would have been "the word" in the narrower sense of the Jewish Scriptures.

In a spirit of reciprocity, those who benefit from the commitment of the instructors are to share their material resources with them for their sustenance, so that they can continue in their work on behalf of the community. Similar sentiments were expressed in classical culture. The ancient physician taking the Hippocratic Oath promised "to hold him who has taught me this art as equal to my parents and to live my life in partnership with him, and if he is in need of money to give him a share of mine."[185] Paul may be especially concerned that the men and women to whom *he* had entrusted this work among the congregations continue to have the support and allegiance of the communities of faith in South Galatia, as the rival teachers were *their* rivals as well and may well have sought to alienate them and their influence along with Paul's among the Galatian churches.[186] This exhortation also provides a further example of mutual burden-bearing: some within the body bear the burden of equipping the saints for a fully informed faith and effective ministry; others bear the burden of financially supporting these individuals so that they may continue that equipping ministry.[187]

---

183. Dunn (326), however, suggests that Paul added this command as a safeguard against readers/hearers taking the previous verse to relieve them of the responsibility of helping their teachers bear their financial burdens.

184. Bruce, 263; Longenecker, 279; Martyn, 552. Dunn (327) points out that converts to Christianity would need to be exposed to a broad "curriculum"—"the Jesus tradition, the ramifications of the gospel, and Christian interpretation of the Jewish scriptures."

185. Edelstein, *The Hippocratic Oath*, 2–3.

186. Martyn (14) underscored the importance of these "catechetical instructors" as local leaders appointed by Paul to continue the nurture of the congregation(s) in the Pauline gospel (cf. Acts 14:23?), one or more of whom may have been responsible for traveling to Paul with the news of developments in Galatia and then returning to the congregations to read Paul's letter in the assemblies.

187. The present tense (continuative aspect) of the imperative κοινωνείτω suggests that this practice is to be an ongoing mark of community behavior. Duncan (183–85) asserts that "in all good things" refers to "spiritual goods" only (contrast Matt 7:7-11, where "good things" include at least daily sustenance). The context, however, supports no such qualification of the "good things" to be shared. The verb κοινωνέω and its related noun κοινωνία are used specifically of material support in Rom 12:13; 15:26; 2 Cor 8:4; Phil 1:5; 4:15.

7 Galatians 6:7–10 rounds off the discussion begun in earnest in 5:13, namely, the purposes for and safeguard around Christian freedom. If the rival teachers, or perhaps the Galatians themselves, had raised questions about how Paul's version of the gospel ensured that God's righteous standards would not be abused by this newfound freedom that Paul proclaimed, Paul provides a clear and unobjectionable answer: there is no fooling God. If God's gifts are abused or misused, there *will* be consequences; God *will* hold each person accountable. Paul had already moved in this direction in 5:21 as he laid out (and that not for the first time) the eternal consequences for those who continued to put into action the impulses of the flesh.

Christian freedom carries with it substantial responsibility to use that freedom as God intended and as God, through the Spirit, directs and empowers. The absence of law does not mean the absence of consequences or accountability before the One who searches our inmost intentions and thoughts:

> Don't deceive yourselves:[188] God is not mocked. For whatever a person sows, that shall he or she also reap: because the one who keeps sowing to his or her flesh[189] will harvest decay from the flesh, but the one who keeps sowing to the Spirit will harvest eternal life from the Spirit. And let us not grow tired of doing what is noble, for we will reap the harvest in its own season if we do not give up. As long as we have a season, then, let us work what is good toward all, and especially toward those who belong to the household of faith. (6:7–10)

Paul has already spoken about self-deceit in a more limited sense in 6:3; he renews and expands that warning here. The self-deceptive self-talk would be that, somehow, the disciples are protected from the consequences of how they use their freedom in Christ, specifically that there might be more room for them to indulge the impulses that arise from the flesh than for other people who do not have the benefit of the friendship of God's Son. Such a view would make a mockery of God's provisions—the provision of the life of

---

188. The verb πλανᾶσθε could be understood as either a middle or a passive voice. Paul gives no indication here that the danger, however, arises from outside a person (some third party who would be perpetrating the deception) but rather that the danger comes from within. Hence I find the middle, which would no doubt be heard as reflexive ("Don't deceive yourselves"), to be the more likely resolution.

189. The NIV and CEB expand the metaphor interpretatively from "sow to your own flesh" (NRSV) to "sow to please their flesh" (NIV) or "plant only for their own benefit" (CEB). While Dunn (331) chides too harshly the NIV's rendering as "ham-handed," he is correct that these expansions are unnecessary. Indeed, they muddy and perhaps unduly limit the metaphor.

his Son, revealing the heinousness of flesh-driven practices by the cost that they incurred on the cross, and the provision of the Holy Spirit, given to lead the forgiven into, and empower them for, a new life no longer determined by the flesh or the foundational principles of the world's domination systems.

Paul introduces a common maxim as the rationale for his warning.[190] This maxim would be familiar within both Jewish and Greco-Roman discourse. Just within the former, one finds the following examples:

Whoever sows injustice will reap calamity. (Prov 22:8)

Those who plow iniquity and sow trouble reap the same. (Job 4:8)

Sow for yourselves righteousness; reap steadfast love. . . . You have plowed wickedness, you have reaped injustice. (Hos 10:12–13)

Do not sow in the furrows of injustice, and you will not reap a sevenfold crop. (Sir 7:2–3)[191]

It is notably (and appropriately) common in wisdom literature, which is based to a great extent on the observation of the created order and the application of the principles observed therein to the lives and practices of human beings. The maxim captures an undeniable truth of agriculture, proven year after year, crop after crop. The truth of the natural order supports, by analogy, Paul's claim about the moral order of God's economy. The consequences of one's choices (whether to live for the impulses of the flesh or to live for the cultivation of the Spirit's fruit) will prove that mortals cannot outwit God. To live now in service to the flesh is to forfeit any future rewards of virtue.[192]

---

190. Paul uses the familiar conjunction γάρ to signal that 6:7b provides argumentative support for 6:7a.

191. See also T. Levi 13.6; Plato, *Phaedrus* 260c; Aristotle, *Rhetoric* 3.3.4; Cicero, *Orator* 2.65; Philo, *On the Confusion of Tongues* 21; *Names* 268–69, mostly cited in Longenecker, 280. The universal currency of this metaphor is demonstrated from its appearance also, for example, in Buddhist texts of the pre-Christian era (e.g., see *Dhammapada* 66–69, 119–20, 127).

192. So, rightly, Lagrange, 159: "The person who professes Christianity and lives in line with the flesh mocks God, but God will have his hour, and one will reap what one has sown!" (my translation). Witherington (431) suggests that 6:7–8 be read as an argument specifically supporting the course of action urged in 6:6: "The sowing unto the Spirit that Paul has in mind is the supporting of proper teachers, materially and otherwise." While Witherington is correct that the use of the metaphor of sowing and reaping occurs elsewhere in Paul in regard to finances (1 Cor 9:10–11; 2 Cor 9:6), this fact has no bearing on the application of the metaphor here, where Paul is not using the metaphor to promote reciprocity (as in 1 Cor 9:10–11) or to encourage generosity by suggestively promising incremental returns (2 Cor 9:6), but rather is using the metaphor to draw a sharp contrast between the consequences of

8 As Paul moves forward to provide an explanation of the rationale (6:7b) that he had offered in support of the affirmation that "God is not mocked" (6:7a), he shifts his metaphor ever so slightly from the essential identity of the plant sown and the plant reaped to the kind of soil to which one commits one's efforts at sowing or the direction in which one casts the seed (itself an image of one's orientation, alignment, investment of effort and resources), applying this to the flesh-versus-Spirit antithesis that has dominated this final section (especially 5:16–25).

Paul urges his converts to take the long view in regard to the gratification of the impulses of the flesh over against devoting oneself to following, in a disciplined and consistent fashion, where the Spirit leads. Giving oneself over to the impulses of the flesh (as the bundle of self-centered, self-gratifying drives that are inimical to loving the neighbor as oneself and destructive of community) results in "decay," by which Paul means quite literally the death and the decay of one's body, the rotting of one's flesh as the meat in which we live.[193] It is the antithesis of "eternal life," the crop that sowing to the Spirit yields.[194] Ultimately, the flesh in the first sense (as a power working upon us) offers no power to escape the fate of the flesh in the second sense (so much meat destined for rotting), so that self-seeking drives and impulses turn out, ironically, to be the most self-destructive drives and impulses. This is a warning comparable to Paul's warning about exclusion from the kingdom of God (5:21), and "sowing to the flesh" is no doubt meant to recall the ongoing practice of those "flesh-driven works" (5:19–21) that lead to such exclusion.[195] Paul is here talking about habitual action, the ongoing trajectory of the Christian's

---

two basic life-orientations. After the broad portraits of the flesh's crop (and its consequences) in 5:19–21 and the Spirit's fruit in 5:22–23, it is difficult to see how the hearer would suddenly limit "sowing to the Spirit" to "supporting local teachers" and "sowing to the flesh" to "withholding aid" or "supporting the rival teachers" rather than hearing both in terms of the full range of flesh-driven works and Spirit-produced fruit.

193. On the meaning of "flesh" in this section, see commentary on 5:13. It is not here limited to "gratifying one's own physical desires" (contra Burton, 341). Much is made of the alleged distance between Paul and James, but it is noteworthy that Paul and James see the desires of the flesh moving in a very similar direction. The desires of the flesh lead to sin (Jas 1:15), expressed in Galatians as "works of the flesh" that exclude a person from the kingdom of God. The full crop of sowing to the flesh is "death" (Jas 1:15), expressed in Galatians as "corruption" (i.e., decaying as a corpse in the grave) as opposed to "eternal life" (6:8).

194. Lagrange, 160; Fung, 295; Longenecker, 281.

195. Thus, rightly, Fee, *Empowering Presence*, 466: "To live out of selfish ambition, to give way to outbursts of rage, to sow discord and provoke hostility, to give way to sexual indulgence or excesses like drunkenness—this is to 'sow unto *one's own* flesh.'" There is a notable tension between Paul's warning here and his earlier, confident declaration that "those who belong to Christ crucified the flesh with its passions and yearnings" (5:24). See excursus "Indicative and Imperative in Paul" on pp. 473–76 for further discussion.

life, not about sporadic deviations from the Spirit-driven life (in which case the instructions of 6:1 would apply).[196]

Those who "keep sowing to the Spirit," conversely, enjoy eternal life as the consequence of their investment.[197] The Spirit of God, who currently works to transform us into the likeness of Jesus, also has the power to "transform the bodies of our humiliation into the likeness of his glorified body" through resurrection from the dead (Phil 3:21). Sowing to the Spirit (or walking by the Spirit, or falling in step with the Spirit; 5:16, 25) by giving oneself over more and more to the other-centered, self-giving love that characterized Jesus and that fulfills the righteous demands of the law becomes, then, the way to secure one's own life for eternity and to arrive at the full possession of one's inheritance in God's kingdom.[198] Reaping in this instance would seem to be connected with the last judgment or an eschatological harvest, a perspective that the following verse will affirm.[199]

We recognize here a basic and inescapable fact of Pauline theology and ethics: a person's actions (still) have eternal consequences. The Christ event has not changed this reality (indeed, see 2 Cor 5:10).[200] Whether or not we arrive at God's goal for us—let us call it "salvation"—is directly impacted by the orientation of our lives, characterized by our serving (or sowing to) either the impulses and goals of the flesh or those of the Spirit.[201] What *is* qualitatively different on this side of the Christ event is the availability of the Spirit as divine gift and empowerment for a God-ward life that results in a blessed eternity. This provision does not diminish human responsibility to invest in that for which God has empowered us.[202]

---

196. This is the sense of the present tense (the continuative aspect) of the participle ὁ σπείρων ("the one who keeps sowing," 6:8), as also the present tense of the participle οἱ . . . πράσσοντες ("those who keep practicing") in 5:21.

197. Paul has not shifted focus to the human spirit in this passage (contra Burton, 342–43). He speaks clearly of sowing to "*one's own* flesh" but then speaks of sowing to "the Spirit" (not "*one's own* spirit"). So, rightly, Dunn, 330.

198. So, rightly, Fee, *Empowering Presence*, 466–67: "To perform the tasks of a slave for one another, to restore the fallen, to bear the burdens of another, to have a proper estimation of one's own worth, to bear with those who are hostile or slow to come along—this is to 'sow unto the Spirit.'"

199. Schreiner, 369; Moo, 386–87.

200. Thus, rightly, Yinger, *New Perspective*, 31–32: "Paul did not break with his Jewish convictions regarding the role of works, or obedience, in final salvation. His insistence that Christ-believers would be judged according to their deeds (for salvation) reiterates both the language and the concepts he had earlier learned." See also the more complete investigation of this topic in Yinger, *Paul, Judaism, and Judgment*.

201. See also Moo, 387: "We must be careful lest our insistence on 'faith alone' leave insufficient space for responsible human activity."

202. Barclay, *Obeying*, 226–30; Das, 620.

9 The farmer sows knowing that he or she will have to invest a lot of work and care into the crop over a lengthy period of time before enjoying the fruits thereof. The person who wants instant gratification for his or her labors cannot be a farmer. Similarly, the Christian journey calls for ongoing investment of oneself, one's resources, one's energies, promising its most significant rewards at a distant, future time. It calls for the manifestation of another variety of the Spirit's fruit, namely, patience.[203] The parallelism between this and the preceding verse clearly shows that, by "sowing to the Spirit," Paul means (at least) "doing what is noble" or "good."

the one habitually sowing to the Spirit / will reap . . . eternal life. (6:8)

doing what is noble / in due season we will reap. (6:9)

We thus note once again Paul's positive support for our doing good works.[204]

The second part of the verse offers a rationale in support of Paul's encouragement not to grow weary or lose heart.[205] Paul speaks with certainty about the harvest time of the last judgment. The word "season" is especially appropriate to the metaphor of sowing, reaping, and the need for perseverance in tending the crop. The proper time for the harvest of the rewards of one's moral and spiritual investments is the time following the judgment, or at least following this mortal life. The exhortation and the rationale both depend upon the fundamental conviction that continued investment and labor are required to reach the end of many pursuits.[206] This principle is particularly true in regard to agricultural endeavors, which strengthens the (transferred) sense that it must be expected to be true of discipleship as well. Paul urges Christians to keep on living, as he does, for *that* day and the honor and joy it will bring to those who have taken the long view on reaping the benefits of faithful, Spirit-led action—"doing what is good" or "virtuous" (6:9)—in the here and now.

This paragraph is not about "earning" eternal life, any more than sowing "earns" a harvest, which depends on so many factors beyond human control. But sowing *is* prerequisite to enjoying a harvest, and a harvest *is* a natural consequence of sowing. Paul is not crossing a line into "justification on the

---

203. Barclay, *Obeying*, 166.

204. Dunn, 333. The author of Titus can even go so far as to present Paul calling his converts to be "zealots for good works" (2:14), which must be adjudicated as fairly representing the Paul of Galatians, at least. See further Lappenga, *Paul's Language*, 205–8.

205. Paul introduces 6:9b with the inferential conjunction γάρ, presenting it as evidence in support of 6:9a.

206. The adverbial participle ἐκλυόμενοι may be taken to communicate the conditions under which the action of the main verb will take place.

basis of works [of the law]" or "earning salvation," but he is also not shying away from warning us that our sowing now has eternal consequences.[207] God has graciously given us the opportunity and the privilege even of sowing to the Spirit, giving our lives over more and more to the Spirit's promptings and guidance. Doing so, then, more and more—giving God's gift to us of the Spirit the proper attention and esteem—connects us to the promise of eternal life as surely as sowing is connected to harvest.

10 Paul now presents the conclusion that he would draw from the foregoing.[208] Now (as long as there is a "now") is the time, the "season," for sowing; believers are well advised therefore to make the best use of the opportunity they have during this mortal life to "work what is good" on behalf of every person,[209] paying special attention to the "members of the household of faith." The word "season," repeated from the preceding verse, refers here to a period of time with certain constraints or duress (namely, that the time will extend only so far, after which people will face God's judgment).[210]

Paul draws two concentric circles of care and benevolence. Christians are to reflect God's love in this world, thus offering loving care and assistance to all people, even as God gives the gifts of sun and rain to all (Matt 5:44–48). They need, however, to take special care to extend support to fellow Christians, since the latter would now largely lack the support of non-Christian networks.[211] These fellow believers are here, as so frequently throughout the

---

207. Das (622) well captures the relationship between good works and eternal life or salvation: "Christians are not saved *by* good works, but they certainly will not be saved without them," insofar as we have opportunity but do not heed the Spirit's promptings to "do good to everyone, especially to those of the household of faith." This summary is also in keeping with Paul's description of the "faith" that has power to accomplish what neither circumcision nor uncircumcision had power to accomplish as "faith working through love" or "faith investing itself through love" (5:6). Thus, "Paul is not contradicting himself when he makes salvation dependent here on one's behaviour and elsewhere on one's faith, for Christian conduct is a vital constituent element of faith" (Watson, *Paul, Judaism, and the Gentiles*, 65).

208. The verse opens with ἄρα οὖν, two inferential particles that, used together, strengthen the sense of logical connection between the preceding statement and the present exhortation.

209. The NRSV and CEB render this command as "work for the good of all," thus effectively reconstruing the relationships between the verb ἐργαζώμεθα, the substantive τὸ ἀγαθόν (which now becomes an indirect object of the verb), and the substantive πάντας (which now becomes a qualifier of τὸ ἀγαθόν). The original grammatical relationships do not need to be sacrificed for the sake of natural expression (e.g., "Let us do good things for everyone"). As they stand, the NRSV and CEB could be read to encourage working for "the common good" rather than doing specific good things for each specific person whom one encounters or has opportunity to help.

210. Furnish, *Love Command*, 101.

211. See Paul's very similar exhortations in 1 Thess 3:12; 5:15b.

New Testament epistles (following the precedent of Jesus himself; see Mark 3:31–35; 10:29–30), described as *family*, consisting of those who have been adopted together into God's household as God's sons and daughters (4:5–7), who are children by virtue of trusting (exhibiting "faith" toward) God's promise.[212] In connection with this identification, early Christian leaders sought also to shape the ethos of the church (a group of largely unrelated people) after the ethos of family. For example, family members (at their best) seek to cooperate with one another and avoid competition. They seek to advance one another's honor and interests, not competing for honor at one another's expense, as is typical among nonkin. They more readily hide one another's shame from public view rather than parade it. Because of this mutual commitment to each other's interests, kin can share a deep level of trust in one another. They also share resources freely, seek to maintain harmony and unity, and work attentively toward forgiveness and reconciliation.[213] Many facets of this ethos are apparent behind Paul's exhortations to his "sisters and brothers" in Galatia.[214]

Alongside other early Christian leaders, Paul recognizes that the steady progress of the individual disciple moving out from being driven by the flesh toward being fully Spirit-led requires the investment, intervention, and support of other disciples.[215] As individuals, we are easily prone to deceive ourselves concerning what comes from the Spirit and what comes from the flesh. We are easily prone to our own weakness and to being "overtaken" by some sin (6:1). Paul commissions all the members of the Christian community to

---

212. The ultimate precedent for conceptualizing the Christian movement as family is the conception of "the house of Israel" as an extended kinship group and the ongoing attempt on the part of prophets and teachers to nurture an inner-Jewish ethic based on the premise that all Israelites are kin and obliged to extend to one another what is due kin. Dunn (333) reads this as a phrase composed on the model of, and in distinction from, "the house of Israel" (referring to Num 20:29; 2 Sam 1:12; Ezek 3:4; etc.), "in which case it will be significant once again that the bonding characteristic of this household is faith, and not membership of ethnic Israel, and not the Torah."

213. See further deSilva, *Honor*, 165–73, 194–239. Dunn (333) rightly observes that "the sense of mutual obligation and responsibility is certainly heightened by depicting the Christian community as a family."

214. The warnings against divisiveness ("enmities, strife, jealousy, . . . acts of self-promotion, divisions, factions, envy," 5:20–21; "provoking and envying one another," 5:26) and antagonistic behavior ("if you bite and devour one another," 5;15) and the injunctions to invest one's energies in lifting up the other rather than promoting oneself at another's expense (5:13; 6:1–3) and to show generous kindness indiscriminately toward fellow Christians (6:9–10) all reflect this attempt to replace the competitive ethos of strangers/nonkin with the cooperative ethos of family within the church.

215. See also 1 Thess 5:14; Heb 3:12–13; 10:24–25, 32–34; 12:15–17; 13:1–3; Jas 5:19–20; Jude 22–23.

help any individual member recognize when he or she is not speaking the truth to himself or herself about some direction or practice he or she has embraced.

Paul calls for a level of mutual involvement and investment that is rare, particularly in the Western world. In the West, the values (one might even say, the "foundational principles") of individualism and of the boundary between private and public are so strong that it is highly countercultural for believers now to practice Paul's exhortations. Nonetheless, we *need* the intervention of fellow Christians who will confront sin in our lives and who will do it gently and with forbearance. We need the support, encouragement, and admonition of other Christians in order to maintain our resolve to resist the enticements of sin and to give ourselves fully to the Spirit's victory over our fleshly impulses. Paul's directions are salutary in another important regard here, as they direct speech *about* a sister or brother who has fallen afoul of the Spirit-led life *to* that sister or brother, where it may do some good, as opposed to the common but toxic practice of speaking *about* that sister or brother to others for no edifying purpose.

Paul seeks to nurture a church culture of mutual burden bearing, rather than one in which we neglect or even add to the burdens of our sisters and brothers. Indeed, the degree to which a church community is committed and effective in regard to such burden-bearing (and not just among its own congregation, but cooperatively with other local and global churches as well) may be one of the more important metrics of its spiritual health and maturity.

Throughout this commentary, we have tried to do justice to justification as "gift and task."[216] It is "gift" insofar as Christ gave himself on our behalf, as an expression of God's love and generosity toward us, to reconcile us to God and to redeem us from this present, evil age. It is "gift" insofar as God pours his Holy Spirit out upon all who are joined in trust to Jesus, the Seed. It is "gift" insofar as this Holy Spirit, freely lavished upon us, is sufficient to guide us into and empower us for living righteously before God, specifically by living fully in line with the commandment to love our neighbor with the care, investment, and commitment that the fleshly person reserves for himself or herself *above* the neighbor. It is "task," however, insofar as we must "walk by the Spirit" (5:16), "fall in line with the Spirit" (5:25), "serve one another as slaves through love" (5:13), "stand fast," not submitting again to the powers and principles that formerly enslaved us, from which Christ freed us at such cost to himself (5:1) and, here, "sow to the Spirit" by "working what is good toward all" (6:7–10), fulfilling the command to "love one's neighbor as oneself" in concrete, practical, beneficent, helpful, needful ways. Participating in this process of transformation that God has opened up for believers in

---

216. Käsemann, "Righteousness of God," 170.

Christ through the power of the Spirit leads to "the final fulfillment of that which began in justification, namely, the gift of salvation to be consummated at the last day."[217]

Paul closes his exhortations to the Christians in Galatia by reminding them—and us—of our ultimate responsibility before God to use God's gifts well, to submit our lives fully to the Spirit who came upon us only because Jesus bore the cost of submitting his life fully to God's good will for us. Paul concludes with the solemn warning that we cannot fool God. No theology of justification or eternal security or other conceptual construct that we espouse will pull the wool over God's eyes as he peers into our hearts and minds to learn: did we spend our lives sowing to the flesh or sowing to the Spirit? Did we dedicate ourselves to making the best use of the gifts God gave us to bring us fully in line with his righteousness, to bring Christ to life within us and, through us, ongoingly to life throughout the world? Did we resist the Spirit in order to protect some areas of fleshly indulgence? Does God recognize his Son in the people we came to be? The good news is that God lavishly supplies all that is needed for us to walk in righteousness and enjoy the consequences of living righteous lives.[218] What is required of us is, essentially, to cultivate awareness (including honesty with ourselves before God and one another) and steady commitment as we consistently invest ourselves and our resources as the Spirit directs and empowers.

---

217. Donfried, "Justification and Last Judgment," 99. It is important to note that Donfried, in his brilliant study, follows the definition of "justification" in Romans (rather than Galatians) as that which occurs at "the beginning of the Christian life" (99) and, also following Romans, uses "salvation" to speak of final deliverance/acquittal.

218. See also Barclay, *Obeying*, 227: "By describing Christian ethics in terms of 'walking in/by the Spirit' Paul could convey this sense of *constant* divine power and direction without, however, diminishing the urgency of his moral imperatives. It is this *constant interplay* between the grace of God and the work of the believer (outside Gal, cf. Phil 2.12–13; 1 Cor 15.9–10 etc.) which . . . accords with his complex understanding of faith as response, reception, trust, decision, *and* obedience (cf. Rom 1.5; 10.16 etc.)."

IX. PAUL'S PARTING SHOTS AND AFFIRMATIONS (6:11–18)

11 *Look at what large letters I made as I wrote to you with my own hand!* 12 *As many as wish to make a good showing in the flesh, these are the people who are pressuring you to get circumcised, only so that they may[a] not undergo persecution for the cross of Christ.[b] 13 For those who are circumcised[c] don't keep the Torah themselves, but they want you to get circumcised in order that they may make a boast in your flesh. 14 But may it not be for me to boast, except in the cross of our Lord Jesus Christ, through which the world has been crucified to me and I to the world. 15 For[d] neither circumcision nor uncircumcision is[e] anything, but a new creation—now that's something! 16 And as many as line up[f] with this measuring stick, peace and mercy be upon them—even upon the Israel of God. 17 For the rest, let no one lay any further burdens on me, for I myself carry the brand marks of Jesus[g] in my body. 18 The generous kindness of our[h] Lord Jesus Christ be with your spirit, brothers and sisters. Amen.*

a. A good number of early witnesses read διώκονται (present indicative; $\mathfrak{P}^{46}$ A C F G K L P) in place of διώκωνται (present subjunctive). The former would be grammatically incorrect, which might suggest its originality (with later scribes introducing the correction); alternatively, the incorrect form could have been introduced through errors in hearing. The sense would remain essentially the same on either reading.

b. Some MSS (including $\mathfrak{P}^{46}$ B) add Ἰησοῦ, in keeping with the tendency to expand references to Jesus (see 5:24 on οἱ . . . τοῦ Χριστοῦ; 6:17 on Ἰησοῦ).

c. A few early MSS ($\mathfrak{P}^{46}$ B L Ψ *al*) read περιτετμημένοι (a perfect middle or passive participle) instead of οἱ περιτεμνόμενοι (a present middle or passive participle). The former reading is probably the result of scribes trying to solve the problem of applying the present participle to the expected party (the rival teachers). If the perfect passive were the original, no explanation could be given for the tidal wave of changes to the present middle/passive in the majority of manuscripts, early and late. Most English translations and commentators, reading the participle as referring to the circumcised condition of the rival teachers, treat it effectively as if it were an aorist or perfect passive participle (e.g., see NIV, CEB, and ESV).

d. Many MSS bear witness to a tendency to harmonize this verse to the earlier and very similar statement in 5:6. ℵ A C D F G 1739^c 1881 𝔐 *pm* add ἐν γὰρ Χριστῷ Ἰησοῦ to the beginning of this verse (omitting the γάρ following οὔτε) in imitation of the opening of 5:6 (*"For in Christ Jesus* neither circumcision nor uncircumcision avails anything"; see the KJV, which follows this harmonized reading). The shorter and more fully differentiated reading, "For neither circumcision nor uncircumcision is anything" ($\mathfrak{P}^{46}$ B Ψ 33), is more likely to stand closer to Paul's original at this point.

e. Again under the influence of Gal 5:6, many witnesses substitute ἰσχύει for ἐστιν (ℵ^2 D^2 Ψ 1881 𝔐 *pm*). Aside from the fact that this substitution is an obvious harmonization (see previous note), external evidence strongly favors ἐστιν ($\mathfrak{P}^{46}$ ℵ* A B C D* F G 33 1739).

f. There is some variation on the form of the verb here. ℵ B C^2 Ψ 𝔐 read στοιχήσουσιν ("as many as *will* fall in line," future indicative); several manuscripts (A C* D F G) read στοιχοῦσιν ("as many as fall in line," present indicative). $\mathfrak{P}^{46}$ reads στοιχήσωσιν (an aorist subjunctive).

g. A few MSS (P Ψ 81 *al*) read Χριστοῦ in place of Ἰησοῦ, but the early evidence in favor of the latter as the original is overwhelming (𝔓⁴⁶ A B C* 33). Predictably, expansions also occur in the manuscript tradition (κυρίου Ἰησοῦ Χριστοῦ, ℵ; κυρίου ἡμῶν Ἰησοῦ Χριστοῦ, D* F G 𝔐; cf. Gal 6:18).

h. Although most manuscripts, early and late, read κυρίου ἡμῶν Ἰησοῦ Χριστοῦ (𝔓⁴⁶ A B C D F G K L etc.), a few omit ἡμῶν (ℵ 69 1739 1881). Though the addition of the pronoun is easier to explain as an intentional scribal alteration (its omission would simply be a mistake), the weight of external evidence favors taking the pronoun as original (against Fee, *Empowering Presence*, 468).

The peroration (or conclusion) of an address could be expected to attend to a number of goals. It might provide a closing summary of the position advanced or course of action urged in the address. It might seek to arouse strategic emotions among the audience, to leave them in a frame of mind especially well suited to adopt the speaker's agenda for their situation. It might give some parting attention to issues of credibility, both affirming the speaker's own credibility and taking parting shots at the credibility of rival speakers or opponents, thus "disposing the hearer favourably towards oneself and unfavourably towards the adversary" (Aristotle, *Rhetoric* 3.19.1).[1] Paul's closing lines in Galatians admirably and succinctly achieve all of these purposes for his own communiqué to his converts as they stand poised to make a decision about what course of action they will take (individually or collectively).[2] Paul reaffirms his own credibility and his investment in his hearers (6:11, 14, 17–18), suggests two self-centered motives driving the rival teachers and calling their reliability and good will into question (6:12–13), and reminds the hearers of the major issues at stake here (6:15–16).

Galatians 6:11–18 is especially reminiscent of 5:7–12 in its attention to undermining the rivals' credibility and affirming Paul's credibility (in part against the assertions that rivals have made about him). It is also reminiscent of 5:2–6 in terms of theological and ethical content. Indeed, were it not for the need to address the pressing question concerning the sufficiency of the Spirit to empower and lead one to the completion of the journey begun in Christ by trust (see 3:3), Paul could well have ended his letter at 5:12 (though perhaps a wish for grace to be with the audience might be a bit jarring after such a wish in regard to the rival teachers). Having addressed the question of how "walking in the Spirit" would better equip the disciples for victory over the power of the flesh than the Torah ever could have done (5:13–6:10), Paul

---

1. For an extensive discussion of the purposes typical of perorations of speeches, see Aristotle, *Rhetoric* 3.19.

2. For my purposes, it is more important to consider how Paul's letter-closing *accomplishes* the rhetorical goals typical of perorations than to claim that his letter-closing *is* a peroration.

wants to leave the hearers where he had brought them in 5:1–12. To this end, Paul delivers what he hopes will be a series of knockout punches to the rival teachers and their position.

11 Paul begins his peroration by drawing attention to his handwriting: "Look at[3] what large letters I made as I wrote to you with my own hand!" (6:11). A principal question that arises in the interpretation of this verse is whether it reveals something about the mechanics of how Galatians was written. Galatians 6:11 is often read as a signal that Paul used a secretary in the process of composing Galatians.[4] Paul's command to the readers, "See with what large-sized letters I wrote to you" (6:11), is understood to signal a *change* in handwriting at that point, the implication being that Gal 1:1–6:10 was dictated by Paul to a coworker or even to a hired scribe functioning as a secretary. The size of the characters underscores the importance of the closing words.[5]

It was indeed typical for people to use a professional scribe or secretary when writing letters or business documents like bills of sale. There is clear evidence in several of Paul's letters that Paul himself involved someone else—most likely a fellow Christian on his missionary team—in the writing of those letters. In many cases, he names members of his team as coauthors or cosenders (Sosthenes in 1 Cor 1:1; Timothy in 2 Cor 1:1, Phil 1:1, Col 1:1, and Phlm 1; Silvanus and Timothy in 1 Thess 1:1 and 2 Thess 1:1), though the precise nature of their contribution to the letters remains unknown. In some cases, Paul explicitly draws attention to a change of handwriting near the end of a letter as a way of providing a more personal touch and authenticating the letter as genuinely his own when the actual writing of the whole was otherwise done by someone other than Paul. In 1 Corinthians there are a clear transition to a new hand and an explicit reference to the same: "This greeting is in my own hand, that of Paul" (1 Cor 16:21). This personally written postscript presumably extends to 16:24. *Exactly* the same six Greek words appear at the close of Colossians (4:18) and 2 Thessalonians (3:17), introducing shorter postscripts written (presumably) in Paul's own hand.[6] It is also clear that Paul had secretarial support in the composition of Romans. Tertius, a fellow disciple functioning as a secretary, adds personal greetings of his own

---

3. While imperatival forms of this verb are often used as interjections (see Gal 1:20), Ἴδετε issues a genuine invitation to the readers to examine the script.

4. Longenecker, lix–lxi; Betz, 1; Richards, *Paul and First-Century Letter Writing*, 81; Das, 67, 630–33; Schreiner, 374, 376; Moo, 392; Dunn, 334 (presenting this position as the "more likely," without offering any supporting argumentation).

5. Betz, 314; Schreiner, 376; Lagrange, 162. Lagrange compares Paul's larger letters in the peroration (vis-à-vis the smaller, professional script of the scribe) to the practice in inscriptions and some papyri of "underlining the important passages by using larger letters."

6. Ὁ ἀσπασμὸς τῇ ἐμῇ χειρὶ Παύλου (= 1 Cor 16:21; Col 4:18; 2 Thess 3:17).

toward the close of this letter (Rom 16:22), though with no corresponding greeting from Paul explicitly in Paul's own hand.

In these four instances, for the moment accepting 2 Thessalonians and Colossians as genuine, Paul's use of a secretary (amanuensis) is certain. However, 2 Corinthians, Ephesians, Philippians, 1 Thessalonians, and the Pastoral Epistles give no indication of a closing change of handwriting as a means of authentication (unless in 2 Corinthians this happens as early as 10:1), nor do they give any other explicit indications of a secretary's involvement (e.g., in the manner of Romans). We could assume that they were written either entirely in Paul's own hand or entirely in the hand of a secretary or coauthor without Paul caring to add a closing greeting in his own handwriting. It is against this range of Pauline practice (and not simply the practice of 1 Cor 16:21; Col 4:18; 2 Thess 3:17) that the evidence of both Phlm 19 and Gal 6:11, the two other places where Paul refers to his own handwriting, ought to be weighed before assuming that these texts also bear witness to a *change* in hand in the writing of the respective letters.

In Phlm 19 Paul emphasizes the fact that he is writing in his own hand in order to give weight to the IOU he is rhetorically providing Philemon on behalf of Onesimus: "I, Paul, wrote with my own hand: 'I will pay you back.'" Paul's reference to employing his own handwriting here has nothing to do with the convention of closing a scribed letter with one's own handwriting, but with the convention of giving writs of debt (which Paul uses to shame Philemon into granting his request, for Paul goes on immediately in the remainder of the verse to remind Philemon of the far greater debt he owes Paul), which have force only when written or somehow identified with the handwriting or seal of the debtor. One cannot infer from Paul's emphatic (and rhetorical) affirmation in Phlm 19 that Phlm 1–18 (or 20–25) was written in a hand other than Paul's own.

Galatians 6:11 also differs significantly from the formula of writing a closing greeting in one's own handwriting: "Look at the large letters I used as I wrote with my own hand." Paul is calling attention to the *size* of the letters, perhaps as a way of highlighting his agitation as he writes. The amplitude of the characters signals the urgency of the matters he raises and his own investment in the outcome. Paul looks back over what he has already written (i.e., Gal 1:1–6:10) as he begins his closing appeal to the congregation, reflecting on the nature of his own handwriting and inviting his converts to do the same with the document before them.[7] John Chrysostom read the form as such and

---

7. I read ἔγραψα as an ordinary aorist verb. Reading it as an "epistolary" aorist ("Look at the large letters I am using as I *write* to you with my own hand") does not add force to the case for reading 6:11 as a sign that Paul has used a secretary to write the bulk of the letter (e.g., against Matera, 224). The comment could still be inclusive of 1:1–6:10, giving no clear

took the verse to imply that Paul had written this particular letter entirely in his own hand (though he was well aware of Paul's practice elsewhere).[8]

The syntactically awkward start-and-stop style of passages like Gal 2:3–5, rife with anacolutha, further suggests the lack of secretarial mediation between Paul, his agitated thoughts, and the parchment or papyrus before him. Galatians certainly shows care in terms of argumentative composition, but not care in terms of syntactic polish, such as might suggest the use of a skilled secretary.[9] The fact that Paul undeniably used secretaries in the composition and transcription of other letters (a fact that is established only in regard to four, with the authenticity of two, ironically, debated) is no argument that he did so here.[10] That Paul is so clear elsewhere (1 Cor 16:21; Col 4:18; 2 Thess 3:17) when he is adding his authenticating signature, marking a change of handwriting, argues *against* a change of hand in Gal 6:11.

At the letter's close (as he looks back at what he has written himself), Paul draws attention to the unusually large size of his handwriting.[11] It has not been the professional, precise, economically sized lettering of a professional scribe, but rather the oversized scrawl of a writer who was emotionally agitated and personally invested in the communication and its outcome. Paul subtly draws attention once again to his emotional and personal investment in the Galatian believers, as it is a consequence of their close bond, Paul's

---

indication that the stylus has changed hands at 6:11 (as the addition of a "now" or "here" would have supplied). On the epistolary aorist, see Smyth, *Greek Grammar*, 433 (§1942); BDF §334; Wallace, *Greek Grammar*, 562–63. BDF (§334) rightly notes that, as an example of an epistolary aorist, this instance is disputed. Such specialized categories seem to me to be invoked too easily.

8. "By this he signifies that he had written the whole letter himself, which was a proof of great sincerity. In his other Epistles he himself only dictated, another wrote, as is plain from the Epistle to the Romans . . . but in this instance he wrote the whole himself" (45–46). Indeed, "the vast majority of the Church Fathers, whether Greek or Latin, were of the opinion that Paul wrote the whole letter to the Galatians in his own hand" (Lagrange, 162).

9. Contrary to the judgment of Betz, 312; Witherington, 442.

10. Contra Witherington, 439.

11. Das (632) objects, following Burton (349; see also Lagrange, 162): "If Paul had been writing by his own hand with such conspicuous letters from the very beginning, why would he call attention to it only here at the *end* of the letter?" This is a strange objection, as there are no rules for when an author ought to call attention to the agitation evident in his or her handwriting. It makes sense to me, however, that this would strike Paul as he came to the conclusion of the body of his letter and he looked back at what he had composed (as authors often do) before writing the closing, parting paragraphs. Burton's own objection (349), namely, that Paul would have had to decide at the outset to write in large letters and sustain this through to the end, also lacks argumentative force. Such "intent" is not at all necessary; all that is necessary is for Paul to notice as he closes his letter how his agitation has shown through his handwriting from the outset, and then decide to use this to his advantage.

personal love for and commitment to them, and the great danger of their situation.

12 The source of Paul's agitation is the topic of the following two verses: "As many as wish to make a good showing in the flesh, *these* are the people who are pressuring you to get circumcised,[12] only so that they will not be persecuted for the cross of Christ. For those who are circumcised don't keep the Torah themselves, but they want you to get circumcised in order that they may make a boast in your flesh" (6:12–13).

Paul accuses the rival teachers of operating out of selfish and cowardly motives, not because they are well disposed toward the Galatians. They are conforming the gospel to what will look good (or, better, to what will make *them* look good or gain face)[13] to the people for whom they have regard, even fear, namely, non-Christian Jews. These fellow Jews would be readier to accept Christianity if they began to see it as a movement that kept Jews in line with the Torah while bringing gentiles in line with the same, rather than a movement that encouraged Jews to be looser in their obedience to Torah for the sake of accommodating the gentiles in their midst.

"Making a good showing *in the flesh*" retains the very negative associations of "flesh" developed throughout the letter. In a context dealing with circumcision, the resonances of "flesh" as physical matter return. As the realm of what is weak, slavish, opposed to promise (e.g., see 4:21–31), "flesh" would have negative connotations on its own, but these connotations are amplified by the repetitive use of "flesh" in 5:16–24 and 6:7–10 to denote the self-centered cravings and inclinations that are hostile to the leading of the Spirit. The verb "make a good showing" also suggests hearing "flesh" here as the realm merely of appearances.[14] The area of central concern to the rival teachers is thus unambiguously presented as negative

---

12. The present tense of the verb ἀναγκάζουσιν implies that an effort to compel is currently (at the time of writing) being made, not necessarily that it is successful, hence the translation "they are pressuring you." See BDF §319; Turner, *Syntax*, 63; Burton, 351. The parallel expression in 6:13 (θέλουσιν ὑμᾶς περιτέμνεσθαι, "they want you to get circumcised") also shows this to remain an unrealized goal as of the time of writing. There is little difference in meaning whether the infinitive περιτέμνεσθαι is understood as "receive/accept circumcision" (middle) or as "be circumcised" (passive).

13. LSJ 728; BDAG 411. The word εὐπροσωπῆσαι appears to be Paul's invention, based on attested adjectival forms. Winter ("Imperial Cult," 73–75) argues that "making a good showing" (6:12) has the more technical sense of "securing a good [legal] face/standing" as part of his argument in favor of seeing the imperial cult in the background here, but aside from the problems establishing this as a legal term (that is also used in its technical, legal sense by Paul in his invented form), this sense is highly unlikely. See excursus "Galatians and the Imperial Cult" on pp. 368–75; also Das, *Stories of Israel*, 210–15.

14. BDAG 916: "the outward side of life."

and inferior to the realm of concern for Paul (namely, the Spirit and the Spirit-led life).

In the end, the rival teachers are motivated by their own cowardice, trying to avoid the kind of persecution that Paul formerly *inflicted* upon Christian Jews and that Paul now *suffers* as a preacher of the Torah-free gospel (see 5:11; 6:17).[15] This motivation represents essentially the flip side of their desire to "make a good showing." The "cross of Christ" is an abbreviated expression for the offense caused by the cross where, in Paul's view, the "truth of the gospel" is lived out in the mixed community of Jewish and gentile Christians, no longer regulated by the purity and pollution taboos of the Torah. Non-Christian Jews would be motivated to take action against Jews preaching this gospel not merely because of the idea of a crucified Messiah, but because of the specific implications of the crucified Messiah, as Paul spells them out, for the role of the Torah on this side of the Messiah's coming and for the basis of the gentiles' acceptance into the people of God.[16]

To the extent that Paul can convince his congregation that the rivals are acting from selfish motives, their character will be diminished in his converts' eyes. This rhetorical goal may account for Paul's reductionistic representation of his rival's motives ("*only* so that they may not be persecuted").[17] Paul did not have direct access to all the motives of the rival teachers, which probably included some good motives as well. They no doubt believed that they were pursuing a pious course of action, preserving and extending faithfulness to the Torah.[18] Paul was in a position, however, to see the larger picture of the dynamics within which he and the rivals were operating. He knew—and sometimes felt firsthand in the form of a lashing or stoning—the pressures that were put on the Jewish Christian community, and he asserts that such pressures cannot be ignored when assessing the motives of Jewish Christian teachers who come around trying to turn gentile Christians into Christian Jews and to keep at least the appearance of loyalty to the Torah among the Christian groups spreading through the diaspora. Their cowardice and their desire to be accepted by their fellow Jews, Paul would assert, would not permit them to think otherwise than they do about the continuing role of the Torah. Social engineering within the Jewish community had done its work upon them.

13 In support of his claim that the rival teachers ultimately pursue their work on the basis of self-serving motives,[19] Paul appears to accuse the rival

---

15. Paul's endurance of hardships, many of them inflicted by people who disapproved of his mission and message, is well documented (see 2 Cor 1:8–9; 6:3–10; 11:23–33; Acts 13:50–51; 14:5–7, 19–20; 16:19–24; etc.).

16. Rightly, Dunn, 337. See also commentary here on 5:11.

17. Dunn, 336.

18. Lagrange, 164.

19. Paul once again uses the inferential conjunction γάρ to present 6:13 as evidence

teachers of being themselves insincere, failing to keep the Torah themselves, even as they attempt to fasten this yoke upon the Galatian converts. Their own performance of the Torah, he asserts, demonstrates their lack of investment in the gospel they are peddling.

There are a number of significant questions pertinent to the interpretation of this verse. First, about whom exactly is Paul speaking in the opening part of the verse? The context virtually demands that Paul is speaking here still of the rival teachers. Paul has just spoken of them in 6:12, clearly has them in mind again in 6:13b, and gives no indication that the people described in 6:13a are a different group. The Greek participle Paul uses to identify the subject, however, is painfully ambiguous. It could be read as "those who are circumcising [others] in their own interest" or "those who are getting themselves circumcised." It is thus not entirely clear from the verb form whether Paul indicates the rival teachers or the gentile Christians persuaded by them. It is, moreover, an awkward way of describing the rival teachers, unless he is thinking of them as a smaller, representative group from a much larger population, namely, the Jewish people—"those who habitually get themselves circumcised."[20] This is an instance where the context makes clear whom Paul *means* (i.e., the rival teachers), though his precise word choice is odd.

How do these rival teachers fail to keep the Torah, as Paul alleges? Paul may be judging the performance of the rival teachers by his own exacting, pre-Christian standards of faithful Torah observance as a member of the Pharisees, the "strictest sect" of the Jewish way of life.[21] Paul might have in mind what would presumably have been his rivals' opinion, as was common among early Christians, that Christ had fulfilled the cultic facets of the Torah. Such a view would remove any impetus to continue to observe the large body of regulations concerned with the sacrificial system of the temple. Paul might more simply intend to suggest that the rival teachers' self-interested action, pressuring the Galatian gentile Christians to do what was against the Galatians' best interests in Christ, revealed their failure even to keep the commandment to

---

in support of the claims made in 6:12, specifically his claims there concerning the limited, self-serving motives of the rival teachers.

20. Thus Lagrange, 163. The present tense of οἱ περιτεμνόμενοι is an odd choice to describe specific people who had already been circumcised decades before. An aorist or perfect form would have been more natural. Thus, rightly, Burton (353–54), who therefore suggests that Paul is referring to gentile Christians who have been persuaded (perhaps elsewhere) by the rival teachers and their ilk. A few early MSS ($\mathfrak{P}^{46}$ B L Ψ *al*) bear witness to the problem of applying the present participle to the expected party (the rival teachers): certain of this intended identification, the scribes of these manuscripts write περιτετμημένοι (a perfect passive participle) to make the connection clearer for their readers.

21. Thus Acts 26:4, though I think the Qumran community has the stronger claim to the title.

love one's neighbor as oneself.[22] Whatever Paul might have thought in regard to these specifics, he is clear on one point: the rival teachers are promoting circumcision, not because they are wholeheartedly devoted to the whole of the Torah, but because their success among gentile Christians will enhance their prestige in the eyes of (and reduce negative attention from) their significant others, the larger Jewish population.

Paul puts his criticism even more crassly: "They want to claim honor for themselves (in the eyes of other Jews) on the basis of your flesh (your circumcised penis)."[23] They want to make personal trophies out of the Galatian converts.[24] The rival teachers are thus examples of people who seek their "boast," their claim to honor, in what they can impose on someone else (cf. 6:4b).

14 In stark and emphatic contrast to the opposition,[25] Paul claims to be free from such selfish motives as trying to make the Galatians into trophies for himself or statistics of ministry success. The only thing on the basis of which he is willing to claim honor (to "boast") is "the cross of our Lord Jesus Christ, through which the cosmos was being crucified to me, and I to the cosmos" (6:14).[26] Paul also speaks about the locus of his claim to honor in 2 Cor 11:21b–29 and Phil 3:4–14.[27] In both passages, as here, Paul renounces finding and promoting his own honor and worth in his Israelite pedigree and

---

22. Nanos, *Irony of Galatians*, 227–28. Dunn (338) suggests that their insistence on the Torah as the only path to alignment with God's righteousness was "itself a sign of the pride and presumption which the law was meant to undermine (Rom iii.9–20)."

23. The CEB "about your physical body" seems a less helpful circumlocution for "about your flesh" (NRSV) than the NIV "about your circumcision in the flesh," since it is clear from the context that Paul is talking about a very particular part of said flesh here. Paul's rhetorical impact here might have been better captured, if some more accessible replacement for the term "flesh" is deemed necessary, by the coarser "about your penis."

24. Note David's collection of Philistines' foreskins as trophies in connection with his attempt to satisfy Saul and win Saul's daughter in marriage (1 Sam 18:25, 27).

25. The forward placement of the dative pronoun ἐμοί is emphatic, contrasting Paul with the rival teachers, whose boast (Paul avers) is in something far less noble than Paul's (so also Tolmie, *Persuading*, 223). The conjunction δέ would carry an adversative force, as Paul contrasts his boast with what he alleges to be the concern of his rivals.

26. The relative pronoun in the prepositional phrase δι' οὗ could grammatically refer to the cross (as in NRSV, NIV) or to Christ (as in CEB), as both are masculine singular nouns in Greek. It seems more likely, almost by definition, that Paul has in mind the "cross" as the instrument by which anything is "crucified" (ἐσταύρωται). "Cross," as the "head noun" (*nomen regens*) in the phrase "cross of Christ," also recommends itself as the intended antecedent on this basis (Lagrange, 165). Had Paul intended to indicate "Christ," it would have been more in keeping with his expressions elsewhere to write "with whom" (σὺν ᾧ) rather than "through whom" (δι' οὗ) here (see esp. 2:19: "I have been crucified together with Christ," συνεσταύρωμαι, and this in close proximity to his naming of the agent/instrument of his death, namely, the "law," διὰ νόμου, 2:19).

27. Longenecker, 293–94.

his record of Torah observance in favor of finding that claim to honor in what Jesus's death on the cross on his behalf has done to him and for him, turning the world's systems of value on their heads and revealing what really matters in God's sight. In these other passages, as here, Paul is also contrasting quite explicitly his own approach to boasting with the approach of rival Jewish Christian missionary teachers.

Paul revels in the stark juxtaposition of the concept of "claiming honor" and the image of a cross with a victim hanging upon it. After centuries of venerating the cross and seeing it presented in myriad decorated and beautified forms, Christians can hardly imagine the revulsion witnesses felt at the long, agonizing, messy, degrading death of a condemned criminal writhing in pain fixed to two pieces of wood. But because God's own Son hung on such a cross to accomplish God's beneficent purposes *for us*, the cross becomes the perfect symbol for how completely upside-down the world's values and operating principles are (e.g., see 1 Cor 1:17–31). Serving one another is the path to distinction. Obedience to God, even when it leads to utter disgrace, is the path to eternal honor. Giving oneself away is the path to securing oneself for eternity. The cross that was meant to be a judgment upon Jesus becomes instead a judgment upon the world that placed him there.

Because he is united with Jesus, Paul finds that Jesus's death on the cross becomes Paul's crucifixion to the "world" and the crucifixion of the "world" to Paul. Paul is not speaking of detachment from the world of people, human needs, and beneficent relationships; on the contrary, the cross compels us to invest ourselves more and more fully in the world thus defined.[28] By "world" here, Paul denotes specifically the ordering of life by the "foundational principles" of human societies with their divisive categories—the ethnic, class/caste, and gender divisions and related valuations that have been transcended in Christ (3:28)—and their other operating principles that perpetuate this world order's unjust, violent, subjugating practices. The "world" here is the present, evil age with its guiding principles and powers (1:4; 4:3); it is the distorted, fallen, old creation.[29] It is "the sphere of the enjoyments and ambitions that Paul characterizes as life 'in the flesh.'"[30] The formulation "the world was crucified to me, and I to the world" signifies an end of the power of these structures and their logic over Paul and an end to Paul's subordination to these structures and their logic. This is a death that all disciples are to share, as they crucify the "flesh with its impulses and desires" (5:24) in union with Christ, and live in the freedom beyond the old codes of the present, evil age that honor the boundaries between Jew and gentile, between person and person.

---

28. Longenecker, 295.
29. Dunn, 341.
30. Lagrange, 165 (translation mine).

The cross "of our Lord Jesus Christ" is the instrument of this death to the rules and regulations of this present world order and its structures because the cross of Jesus summons the "new creation" (6:16) into being.[31] It is, for Paul, a legitimate ground for boasting precisely because it is the instrument of deliverance from the power of this present, evil age and its constraints upon human life and community. It is also the means by which the Holy Spirit, the agent of our transformation into "new creation," has gone forth into and among those who trust in Jesus, bringing the Righteous One to life within and among them and thus fitting them for final justification.

15 Paul's declaration of death to the structures and rules of this fallen creation gives him the opportunity to give a summation of his position: "For neither circumcision nor uncircumcision is anything, but a new creation— now that's worth something" (6:15).[32] Circumcision and uncircumcision establish a dividing line of importance within this present, evil age, a dividing line upheld by the Torah and other "foundational principles" (*ta stoicheia,* 4:3, 9) that place value on the Jew over the gentile (or the gentile over the Jew!). This is one of many dividing lines that God has abolished in Jesus Christ and in the community that is formed around him—or, better, that is formed as individuals join themselves to Jesus in baptism (3:27). There is no place for valuing circumcision or lack of circumcision now that "there is no longer Jew nor Greek" (3:28).[33] The boundaries of Israel, the people of God, have been redrawn by the decisive act of God in Christ at the close of this present, evil age. Inclusion in the household of God, among the children of Abraham, is not effected through circumcision, nor does uncircumcision exclude one.

Paul names that which matters—"a new creation"—in such a brief and formulaic fashion that it appears to be a catch phrase with which the Galatians may have been familiar from Paul's earlier instruction (see 2 Cor 5:16–17, another passage where this concept emerges, and in somewhat more detail).[34] "New creation" is what comes about by the Spirit's indwelling in each Christian and thus in Christian community. "New creation" takes shape as Christ, the New Adam, is fully formed in the believers (2:20; 4:19), who thus come to bear the image of the New Adam rather than the Old Adam, who was crucified in them in their union with Christ. This statement directly recalls Paul's earlier, similar formulation: "In Christ Jesus neither circumcision nor

---

31. Burton (354) suggests that the fullness of the reference to Jesus as "our Lord Jesus Christ" gives added weight to Paul's statement.

32. Paul has omitted any verb in the second half of this declaration. Based on the contrast he is creating between "new creation" and the two nouns in the first half of the declaration, one can complete the phrase assuming the simple elision of a second τί ἐστιν: "but a new creation *is indeed something.*"

33. Bruce, 29.

34. Betz, 319.

uncircumcision has any force, but rather faith working through love" (5:6). The parallelism suggests that "faith working through love" is integral to the emergence of the new creation and thus, by implication, is the "walking in the Spirit" or the "falling in step with the Spirit" that is of focal concern for Paul as he explicates what it means for faith to become effective through love in 5:13–6:10. [35] These are the new ordering principles that have taken the place of the "foundational principles," by which the world is presently governed and ordered, in the lives of believers and in the believing community.

Paul offers this verse explicitly as a rationale for the validity of his claim to honor on the basis of the cross of Christ, since the metaphorical crucifixion of which he speaks in 6:14 effects the death that makes room for the new life in God, the "new creation" that comes into being as Christ comes to life in the believer. This verse also, less directly, provides the premise that leads to the inference that the rival teachers' (alleged) claim to honor (their "boast in your flesh," 6:13) is empty, since that of which they allegedly boast (circumcising gentile Christians, as well as valuing their own circumcision as a sign of inclusion in the covenant people) is now nothing in God's sight.[36]

16 The principle articulated in 6:15 becomes a yardstick, a "rule" in the sense of a straightedge instrument for drawing a straight line.[37] Paul invokes God's blessings of peace and mercy upon those who "line up with this yardstick," an image that recalls the language of "walking straight toward the truth of the gospel" in 2:14.[38] The *conditional* blessing encourages the hearers to

---

35. Paul would return to this formulation once again when writing to the believers in Corinth: "Neither circumcision nor uncircumcision matters, but keeping God's commandments" (1 Cor 7:19). The irony of Paul's position is most evident here: circumcision (a "commandment of Torah") is no longer within the sphere of "God's commandments." Snodgrass ("Justification by Grace," 78) finds here, in conjunction with the similar formulaic statement in Gal 5:6, a summary of what really matters for Paul and what he understood the gospel to accomplish in the lives of the faithful: "Being a new creation for Paul meant a life of faith working through love, and outside the context of the debate over 'works righteousness', this could even be described as a life of keeping the commandments of God."

36. Lagrange, 165.

37. Lagrange, 166. The dative case (τῷ κανόνι τούτῳ) is typically used in connection with στοιχέω to denote that to which the subject is conforming or with which he or she is walking in line (BDAG 946).

38. The sentence lacks a verb in Greek, in keeping with the tendency to omit forms of the verb "to be." It is most likely that an optative ("may peace and mercy be") is implied. The phrase ὅσοι τῷ κανόνι τούτῳ στοιχήσουσιν creates a contrast with ὅσοι θέλουσιν εὐπροσωπῆσαι ἐν σαρκί (Gal 6:12). People-pleasing and seeking honor from worldly-minded people, such as Paul alleges to motivate the rival teachers, will draw one away from lining up with the truth of the gospel. Those who resist the rival teachers' message, however, and continue in obedience to the gospel Paul proclaimed and to the community arrangements that Paul's gospel seeks to nurture are commended, by implication, as genuine disciples who place truth above social acceptance.

align with Paul's yardstick while also implicitly warning them that to fail to do so means falling outside the lines of blessing (and under curse, Gal 3:10–12).[39] In both passages, walking in line with the new reality that God was bringing about in Christ meant leaving behind the boundary-making codes and principles of the old creation—most particularly those that distinguished Jew ("circumcision") from gentile ("uncircumcision"). The verb here rendered "fall in line" (*stoichēsousin*) recalls the similarly commended action of "walking in step with [*stoichōmen*] the Spirit" (5:25), as well as the "foundational principles of the world" (*ta stoicheia tou kosmou*, 4:3, 9), which notably uphold the value of the distinction between circumcision and uncircumcision. The wish for peace upon Israel (Ps 125:5; 128:6) or mercy upon Israel (Ezek 39:25; Pss. Sol. 13.12; 16.6; 17.45; 18.5) is common in Jewish literature.[40] It is striking that Paul invokes this wish over those who agree that Israel's most distinctive identity marker is no longer significant.[41]

Does Paul pronounce this blessing of "peace and mercy" upon two different groups or only upon a single group described in two different ways? Should we understand "the Israel of God" as literally "Israel" or metaphorically as "the people of God who have, in some sense, inherited the title 'Israel'"? Connected with this question is that of how to understand the Greek word *kai*—as a simple connective ("and") or as an adverb ("even, indeed")? If the former, Paul invokes peace upon those who line up with the "rule" of 6:15 *and* mercy upon "the Israel of God" (so NRSV, CEB).[42] If the latter, Paul

---

39. Tolmie, *Persuading*, 224.

40. Dunn, 344.

41. Having made this observation, it is surprising to find Dunn nevertheless preferring the reading that adds a reference to ethnic Israel here (345). Similarly, Davies ("People of Israel") can acknowledge that "the meaning of 'descent' from Abraham" is "radically reconsidered" in Galatians, with the result that "it no longer has a 'physical' connotation" (9) and that "in Galatians Paul is uncompromising, radically insisting on a parting of the ways: as in his discussion of the law, so in his treatment of Israel" (10), and yet still posit that 6:16 "may refer to the Jewish people as a whole." Unpopular as it may be in a post-Holocaust environment, we have to reckon with the possibility, indeed the probability (for the reasons given in the main text), that Paul is here continuing rather than backing away from his reconfiguration of "God's Israel" throughout the letter.

42. See Dunn, 345; Davies, "People of Israel," 10. Paul may indeed elsewhere express a hope that "all Israel" inclusive of ethnic Israel may be saved in God's future (Rom 11:25–32). However, that position (itself a point of dispute) is not determinative for how we should read Gal 6:16. A letter written potentially a decade later (Romans) does not negate or replace the thought of a letter written a decade before, though it can show its author plumbing the depths of new questions and issues.

Burton (357–58) argues in favor of reading "the Israel of God" as a reference to the remnant within Israel that believed in Jesus, even if they did not yet see things Paul's way in regard to circumcision. While a generous position, this does not seem to square with

invokes peace and mercy upon those who walk in line with the "rule" of 6:15, whom he renames the "Israel of God" (so NIV). In this reading, "Israel of God" is a title bestowed by Paul upon the Christian movement, particularly upon the portion of the Christian movement that has embraced the same conclusion that he has concerning the value of ethnicity on this side of Christ's coming (i.e., who walk by the "rule" of 6:15).

The latter solution seems the more probable for a number of reasons. First, Paul's qualification of "Israel" here as "*God's* Israel" would seem to distinguish this group from "Israel according to the flesh," to use a phrase from Paul's later work (1 Cor 10:18), in a manner similar to his distinction between the "children born in line with the flesh" (non-Christian Jews and Judaizers) and "children born in line with the promise" (Jewish and gentile Christians together) in Gal 4:21–31.[43] Second, Paul has also been arguing most forcefully in this epistle for the identity of all Christians (specifically, those who rely on Jesus and the Spirit and *not* on Torah observance in order to be brought into line with God's righteousness) as the true heirs of the promise (3:6–9, 14, 26–29), the true heirs of Abraham (through *Isaac*, technically the progenitor of Israel "according to the flesh"; 4:21–31; see also Rom 9:8), and thus could very well declare, climactically, that they are the true "Israel," namely, "God's Israel." Third, after taking such pains to demonstrate the equality and unity of Jews and gentiles in Christ throughout the letter, Paul would hardly reintroduce the divisions between the church of Jews and gentiles, on the one hand, and, on the other, "Israel" as an ethnic entity defined by Torah, with the special blessing of the latter based on their ethnic identity (and thus its ongoing value in God's sight!), in his closing benediction.[44]

17 Paul points to his own scars as proof of his sincerity and reliability: "For the rest, let no one lay any further burdens on me, for I myself carry the brand marks of Jesus in my body" (6:17). By the time Paul had written 2 Corinthians, he had amassed quite a catalog of beatings and hardships endured

---

1:8–9, where Paul unequivocally and unhesitatingly calls down God's curse upon the Jewish Christians who are energetically promoting their different understanding in Galatia at the time of Paul's writing. Lagrange (166) reads this verse as referring to two separate groups, but he takes "the Israel of God" to refer to the global church, which is not so functionally different from reading the two terms as referring to the same group (i.e., the church of Jewish and gentile Christians).

43. Schreiner (382) also suggests that "Israel according to the flesh" (1 Cor 10:18) has a counterpart in Paul's mind, such as "Israel according to the Spirit" (see his claims about lineage in Gal 4:21–31) or "Israel of God."

44. Longenecker, 298; Martyn, 571–77; Köstenberger, "Identity," 13. For other discussions in support of this reading, see Schlier, 283; Ridderbos, 227; Fung, 311; Luz, *Das Geschichtsverständnis bei Paulus*, 269; Barclay, *Obeying*, 98; Schreiner, 382–83; Moo, 403; Dahl, "Der Name Israel"; Tolmie, *Persuading*, 224–26.

because of the unpopularity of his message with both Jewish and Roman officials. Compared with other traveling Christian teachers, Paul could lay claim to being more fully Christ's servant on the basis of having endured "labors more abundantly, imprisonments more abundantly, and beatings surpassing abundantly, often in danger of death: five times I received the forty stripes minus one from the Jews, three times I was beaten [by Roman authorities] with rods, once I was stoned" (2 Cor 11:23–25).

Paul wrote this catalog sometime between 54 and 57 CE. There would have been considerably fewer items on it at the time he wrote Galatians in 49 or early 50 CE. Nevertheless, Paul's South Galatian mission gave ample opportunity for scars (Acts 13–14; 2 Tim 3:11). Far from being signs of disgrace, Paul pointed to his scars as "brand marks" (*stigmata*). The term may refer to the custom of fugitives taking refuge in a temple and receiving the marks of the local god (and with these marks of belonging, amnesty from further molestation); it may also refer to the custom of branding slaves with the mark of their owner or (less frequently) soldiers with the mark of their general.[45] While each option is attractive, Paul speaks of himself as Christ's slave with some regularity (Gal 1:10; Rom 1:1; Phil 1:1; Titus 1:1; cf. also 2 Cor 4:5), and this is therefore the likeliest frame of reference. The pragmatic effect of this self-identification would be to claim Christ's protection and authorization (in effect, "if anyone has a problem with me or my gospel, let them take it up with Christ").

Paul's scars are the marks that show whose he is, in whose service he labors. They are also the marks of his sincerity in his preaching. Despite the opposition he encountered and the physical pains he endured, Paul had not altered the message that God had entrusted to him, but rather had proven himself a loyal messenger. He was not a coward, nor was he an opportunist. Unlike the rival teachers (6:12–13), he has been willing to suffer beatings and whippings for telling the truth about what God has done in Jesus, however unpopular this stance has made him with those same people whom the rivals fear.[46] These same scars are also proof that Paul has not "preached circumcision" where it suited him (5:11); he has preached the Torah-free gospel wherever he has gone, even when it meant being whipped for it. The absence of such marks on the bodies of the rival teachers becomes, at the same time, a stroke against them. Their smooth skin proves that they are unwilling to face the hostility that the "truth of the gospel" arouses (6:12). Paul thus asserts here at the end the physical evidence of his unassailable

---

45. Burton, 360–61; Lagrange, 167, citing Herodotus 2.113.

46. Paul points to himself emphatically, using the (redundant) nominative pronoun ἐγώ. This emphasis underscores further the contrast between Paul and the rival teachers (6:12).

credibility.[47] On this basis he commands that "no one keep making trouble for me" by calling his gospel or apostleship into question, as the rival teachers have done.[48]

18 Paul normally closes his letters with a prayer for "the favor of the Lord Jesus Christ" to be with the addressees (Rom 16:20b; 1 Cor 16:23; 2 Cor 13:14; Gal 6:18; Eph 6:24; Phil 4:23; Col 4:18b; 1 Thess 5:28; 2 Thess 3:18; Phlm 25). "Favor" (or "grace") is used here in the sense of a benefactor's disposition to do good for, or provide assistance to, another. Paul's closing prayer is that the Lord Jesus Christ will continue to make his favor known to and experienced among the Galatians converts.[49] This, however, will be the only letter in which Paul also addresses the hearers as "brothers and sisters" in his closing wish for grace to be with the addressees. Indeed, "brothers and sisters" (in Greek, the single word *adelphoi*) is the last word of the letter itself, apart from the formulaic "Amen." This closing invocation of kinship may reflect Paul's desire to affirm connection with his converts at the end of a challenging communication.[50]

Appropriately, grace and kinship sound the last note of the letter. Paul has argued at length that what the Galatians have received through the generous favor of Christ, who redeemed them, and of God, who poured out the Spirit upon them, is sufficient to bring them into the unending life of God's kingdom. He has warned them of the dangers of responding inappropriately to such favor, such that they might "fall from grace" (5:4), breaking off the grace relationship they enjoy with God through God's Son. Now at the letter's

---

47. An instructive comparative text is found in Josephus, *War* 1.193. Antipater, the father of Herod the Great, is described as a person whose every body part bore scars from battles received in Caesar's service and who can offer these scars as ample proof of his loyalty. John Chrysostom (47) intuits a connection between the scars of battle and the proof of sincerity Paul offers here: "For no one who saw a soldier retiring from the battle bathed in blood and with a thousand wounds, would dare to accuse him of cowardice and treachery, seeing that he bears on his body the proofs of his valor, and so ought ye, he says, to judge of me."

48. Paul explicitly introduces the second half of the verse as a rationale (γάρ) for the action urged in the first half of the verse. He uses more figurative language here than the translation indicates, commanding that no one "continue to lay any further burdens [κόπους]" upon him. Imposing "burdens" is used metaphorically for "giving or causing trouble." The present tense (continuative aspect) of the imperative here suggests a command that detractors *desist* from such activity, already begun, hence "any *further* burden."

49. Specifically, Paul prays that this favor will be "with your [pl.] spirit," where πνεῦμα represents the immaterial, internal part of the human being, that which animates and directs the σῶμα, the corporeal part. Paul employs a distributive singular, as in Rom 1:21; 6:12; 8:23; 1 Cor 6:19, 20; 2 Cor 3:15; 4:10; 6:11; Eph 1:18; 4:18; 5:19; 6:5; Phil 1:7 and frequently beyond Paul (as in Heb 10:22). This is a grammatical commonplace and not a statement about the supposed oneness of the members of the congregation.

50. Burton, 362.

end he directs their hearts and minds to Christ's favor, in order that they may continue to rely upon it and walk in it.

Paul has also directed a substantial portion of his argument toward establishing that they have been made one family in Christ, having been joined to the family of Abraham by virtue of being united with the Seed that is Christ, and by virtue of having been adopted as God's own sons and daughters, as the Spirit testifies. He has also sought to orient them to one another as kin, so that they would banish rivalry, competition, and all that is divisive from their midst, and invest in one another's successful walk in the Spirit through the trials of the present, evil age. Now at the end, he reminds them again of their kinship with each other and with Paul, so that they will remember to treat one another as family.

As Paul criticizes the motives of his rivals and clarifies his own, he brings the topic of integrity, both as Christian leaders and as Christian disciples, to the fore. In particular, he contributes three considerations to a process of examining one's own integrity:

1. Am I adapting the message to what will make me personally more popular or the message more palatable?
2. Am I guided in this ministry or mission by a desire to build up my own reputation or approval ratings?
3. Am I taking this ministry or mission in a particular direction, and avoiding other directions, out of a concern to avoid opposition, criticism, or even persecution?

These become essential points for self-examination for Christian leaders and disciples alike.

Paul has from the beginning affirmed that he is not a people-pleaser and that, indeed, the drive to please people only undermines one's ability to be a servant of Christ (1:10–11). Integrity increases as people-pleasing and its converse, cowardice (i.e., the unwillingness to pay the cost of letting the stumbling block of the cross remain evident and poignant), are diminished and eliminated. A side benefit of such a commitment would be the elimination of a great deal of competition between churches and other Christian organizations, since this behavior is driven by a commitment not to the work of God but to establishing one's own reputation and that of one's own ministry or organization.

For Paul, suffering for Christ was proof of his genuineness (6:17). The marks on his body were a testimony to his faithfulness to his commission and his Commissioner, communicating that he was obedient first to the latter and that he was faithful to preach and practice the truth of the gospel, when it would have been far easier and more comfortable to alter it here and there so as to avoid opposition and hostility. The marks of a Christian are not the wearing of a cross on a chain or the carrying of a Bible. The marks involve developing Christ-like character and cultivating the fruit of the Spirit (5:22–23), showing Jesus himself branded in our lives so that, in any situation, we can be only what Jesus would have us be. It leaves marks in other ways as well—on how we spend our time and energies, investing perhaps in a homeless man to teach him new skills or help reconnect him with family. It leaves marks on how we use our homes, as when perhaps a family takes in a young girl from the street to give her an option other than a life of prostitution. In many regions of the world, it still leaves marks on our bodies, as others express their rage and prejudice against Christianity through violence.

Christian integrity also requires ministering or otherwise living in line with Paul's rule that, through the cross, "the world was crucified to me and I to the world" (6:14). The minister and the disciple have been crucified to the world's lines of divisions between ethnic groups, castes, socioeconomic strata, and the like. As Christians bear witness to this transformation in their own relationships and practice, their neighbors, for whom these lines are still often vitally important to their own identity and sense of order, may react with scorn or worse. It is a matter of integrity, however, not to accommodate one's practice to the demands of worldly thinkers, but always to the demands of the Spirit and the rule of the new creation. Only by such a path can the Christian community also preserve their witness to the new creation and call others to join them in moving "toward the truth of the gospel" (2:14).

Paul challenges us to embrace the freedom and the challenge of living by the Spirit, trusting this gift of God to bring us fully in line with the character and standards of God and to transform us into the likeness of Jesus, the image of the Father. He challenges us to use this freedom responsibly, as spiritual adults. Christian freedom is never an occasion for self-serving, but always an occasion to serve and to love beyond the limits set on us by our upbringing, our socialization, our customs—in short, by the "world" (6:14). The righteousness that God seeks to impart will be manifested in the character of our Christian community. Are we other-centered or self-centered? Are we marked by cooperation or by competition? Do we live out the vision where, indeed, ethnic, social, and gender distinctions—and the hierarchical evaluations, limitations, abuses, or avoidances that are fostered by such distinctions—are transcended in the one family of God's children and heirs? Only by following the Spirit will we, as a Christian community, arrive at the full freedom and glorious inheritance of the sons and daughters of God.

Index of Subjects

anathema, 127–28, 129, 131, 139
apostolic decree, 52–53, 56, 58, 114, 193

baptism, 134, 191, 205, 244, 304, 306, 325, 335–39, 359, 424, 470, 473–74, 510
Barnabas, 32, 35–58, 170–72, 180–84, 203–6
boasting, 374–75, 474, 485–88, 508–10, 511

chiasm, 93, 238, 273, 472
circumcision, 17–19, 174–76, 226, 273–74, 279–80, 338, 392, 414–18, 423–24, 426, 437–40, 472, 505–8, 510, 514
collection, the, 55, 107–8, 174, 187–90, 257

epistolography: in antiquity, 71–74; and Galatians, 74–81, 91–94, 111–12, 123–24, 136
ethos, appeals to, 9–10, 22–25, 68, 98–99, 112–14, 123, 127, 129–33, 136–37, 138, 194, 267, 376–77, 382–85, 387–88, 431–41, 501–2, 505–8, 513–17
exordium, 70, 71, 103–4, 112, 117, 122–23, 133

faith: as basis for inclusion, 278–84; as message and way of life, 168, 325–27; "of Jesus Christ," 229–37, 323–24; as response to patron, 6, 124, 183, 248; as salvific response, 5–6, 237, 248–53, 323–24, 326, 377–78, 409, 423–25, 428–32, 477–78, 483, 510–11
flesh, 21–22, 149, 273–75, 396–97, 443–72, 493–94, 505–6

freedom, 24, 105–6, 120, 176–78, 222, 247, 259, 268, 291, 304–5, 333, 338–39, 346, 363, 365, 368, 391, 396, 398, 407, 410–14, 445–48, 450, 453, 457, 476–77, 480, 491, 517

Galatia: North or South, 28–48; Paul's ministry in, 3–7, 41–48, 379–82; presenting situation in, 7–16
Galatians (audience): ethnicity of, 26–28; location, 28–48
Galatians (document): and ancient epistolography, 91–94; authorship of, 1–2; and classical rhetoric, 74–80, 94–106; date of, 58–62; efficacy of, 107–8; involvement of secretary, 2, 502–5; Paul's goals for, 94–97; rhetorical arrangement of, 103–6
Gallio, 58–60
Gentiles: and Abraham's family, 278–84, 303, 333–41, 358–59, 377–78, 392–406, 510, 512–13, 516; acceptance in Christ, 210, 215, 227, 246–47, 272–73, 333–41, 355–59, 440–41, 510; eating with, 196–97, 198–203, 242–45, 377–78; ingathering, 154–56
grace and reciprocity, 117, 118–19, 124–25, 147, 228, 245–52, 254–62, 412, 414–20, 428–32, 475, 476, 490, 498–99, 515

Holy Spirit: and adoption, 355–59, 396, 398–99; as agent of transformation, 205, 222–23, 248–49, 252–53, 263, 275, 304, 353, 368, 385–87, 409, 420–23, 429–31, 452–72, 476–78, 479–82, 493–94; experience of, 263, 265, 269–70,

519

275–76, 344, 356–57, 364, 380–81, 434, 453; as promised gift, 7, 248, 272, 302–4, 305–6, 313, 416, 452, 469, 476

hypocrisy, 203–4

imperial cult, 368–75
indicative and imperative, 410–11, 473–76

James, 24, 31–32, 35, 36, 38, 49, 114, 160–64, 173, 174, 181, 183–86, 191, 194, 195, 196, 197, 210, 493
Jesus: "Christ," 115; "Christ crucified," 4–5, 268–69, 439–506; death for others, 118–19, 152, 223–24, 237, 246–50, 259–60, 293–96, 326, 401–2, 412, 416, 418, 470–71, 509; resurrection of, 120, 152–54; as "Son," 354–55
justification. See righteousness

kinship, 116, 496–97

law: as boundary, 327–29; as path to righteousness, 19–22; purpose, 314–24; role in Christian life, 10–12, 186, 208–9, 218, 239–41, 243, 246–47, 250–51, 269, 287–88, 293, 332–33, 366–68, 377–79, 391–406, 414–20, 426–27, 449–51, 456–57; role in God's plan, 289–91, 305–13, 324–33; and slavery, 412–14; "works of," 224–29, 270–73
law of Christ, 483–85
logos: appeals to, 69–70, 100–102, 263–64, 409; arguments from analogy, 305–13 (testamentary law), 324–33, 343–46 (coming of age); arguments from consequences, 27, 100, 101, 287, 296, 363, 407, 415, 416, 420–21, 451, 454, 458, 463, 476, 491–93, 494, 496; arguments from contrary, 101, 263, 286, 312, 313, 320, 420, 431, 451, 485; confirmation of the rationale, 245, 336, 423; deliberative topics, 64, 68, 70, 96, 407–9, 412, 418; enthymemes, 69, 70, 100–101, 181, 411–12, 415, 420; historical example (Abraham), 277–304; maxims, 434–35, 485, 492; rationales, 100, 101, 105, 179, 240, 245, 261, 286, 301, 334, 336, 339, 392, 398, 400, 411, 420, 421, 485, 488, 489, 492, 493, 495, 511, 515; scriptural interpretation, 285–304, 390–406; syllogisms, 69, 288, 411, 412

ministry reflections, 133–35, 190–92, 211–12, 253–54, 278, 304–5, 340–43, 359–62, 388–89, 400, 426–31, 441–42, 476–78, 497–99, 516–17

narratio, 71, 104–5, 136–37, 170, 174
new creation, 27, 120, 135, 205, 223, 249, 293, 338, 341–43, 352, 354, 359, 424, 441, 472, 510–11, 517

passions, 17, 19, 21–22, 222, 249, 330, 408, 414, 438, 443, 445–47, 453–54, 456–58, 468, 469–71, 475, 493
pathos, appeals to, 68–69, 99–100, 125, 376, 386, 432, 433, 436, 437, 441, 501
Paul: apostleship, 113–14, 182–83; and confrontation in Antioch, 192–212, 378, 432; conversion and commission, 113–14, 129–33, 138–40, 145–48, 149–56, 164–65; experience of persecution, 14–15, 403–4, 439–40, 506, 514–17; life under Torah, 144–45, 287–90; ministry in Galatia, 3–7, 379–82; name, 113; opposition to Jesus, 150–52; persecution of Christians, 14, 140–43, 167; training in rhetoric, 85–91; visits to Jerusalem, 48–58, 158–61, 169–92
promise (Abrahamic), 8, 18, 119, 145, 156, 194, 215, 223, 227, 230, 241, 248, 251–52, 263–64, 266, 269, 271–72, 277–84, 287, 290–95, 297–99, 303–15, 318–23, 325–26, 340, 355, 377, 390–402, 404–6, 469, 482, 513
propositio, 71, 105, 123, 214–15, 265, 391, 407–10

Res Gestae, 117–18
rhetoric: classical, 63–71; and New Testament interpretation, 81–84; Paul's training in, 85–91; relevance for Galatians, 74–80, 94–106
righteousness, 216–24, 243–44, 252, 259–60, 322–23, 385–87, 420–23, 428–31, 463–64, 476–78, 491–94, 499
rival teachers: activity, 7–10, 124; identity and motivation, 10–16, 23–25; message, 16–26, 126; and persecution, 14–16

salvation: from curse of the Law, 293–96, 300–302; as "life," 207–8, 293, 319–20, 419, 493–94; from present, evil age,

5, 112, 119–20, 338–39, 372, 417; from
slavery, 354–55, 446–48; as Spirit-empowered transformation, 6–7, 96–97,
246–53, 337–38, 385–87, 389, 420–33,
445–46, 463, 476–78, 491–94, 499
Shema, 155–56, 319, 339, 465
slavery, 105, 130, 178, 259, 268, 291, 293,
295, 302, 346, 347, 348, 356, 357,
359–60, 363, 365–66, 391–99, 410–14,
426, 435, 445, 446, 448, 457
stoicheia, 115, 332, 339, 344, 346–53, 355,
359–62, 363–68, 378, 391, 419, 442,
448, 472–73, 508–10, 511–12, 517

text-critical issues, 111, 122, 138, 159,

169–70, 193, 212–13, 265, 285, 305, 314,
343, 362, 390–91, 408, 431, 444–45,
478–79, 500–501
Titus, 24, 32, 35, 49, 53, 55, 57, 137,
170–71, 174–78, 190, 193, 194
Torah. *See* law
"truth of the gospel," 178–79, 195–96,
205, 210–11, 432, 441–42

works: good, 6, 224–25, 235–36, 409,
424–25, 491–96; "of the Law," 224–29,
270–73 (*see also* law)

zeal, 13–15, 31, 50, 87, 140–44, 158, 290,
385, 438, 461–62

Index of Authors

Alexander, L., 61
Allison, D. C., 160, 483
Anderson, R. D., 78, 97
Armitage, D. J., 128
Arnold, C. E., 460
Aune, D. E., 69, 81, 411
Aus, R. D., 184

Banks, R., 117
Barclay, J. M. G., 7, 10, 18, 22, 97, 115, 137, 225, 226, 244, 246, 255, 275, 354, 393, 425, 438, 443, 447, 451, 452, 454, 455, 456, 457, 460, 464, 465, 468, 469, 470, 471, 474, 475, 480, 482, 483, 484, 487, 488, 489, 494, 495, 499, 513
Barrett, C. K., 59, 184, 259, 393, 410, 465
Bauckham, R., 46, 162, 163
Bauernfeind, O., 460
Becker, J., 61
Beker, J. C., 153, 484
Belleville, L. L., 298, 316, 320, 329, 332, 346, 350
Berger, P. L., 359
Betz, H. D., 1, 2, 8, 10, 22, 54, 62, 94, 95, 112, 115, 123, 132, 133, 140, 148, 158, 169, 171, 176, 180, 181, 182, 203, 214, 215, 245, 267, 269, 272, 275, 277, 292, 298, 307, 315, 316, 318, 326, 329, 331, 332, 334, 336, 337, 345, 346, 349, 363, 382, 384, 407, 408, 410, 413, 415, 421, 434, 440, 441, 443, 446, 450, 451, 454, 455, 458, 459, 463, 465, 471, 480, 483, 502, 504, 510
Biguzzi, G., 370
Bird, M. F., 87, 90, 91, 216, 221, 222, 424
Blanton, T., 254
Bligh, J., 10, 93, 194, 355

Blinzler, J., 348, 349
Boers, H., 176, 225
Bonner, S. F., 329
Borgen, P., 15, 19
Bornkamm, G., 144, 172
Boyer, J. L., 448
Bray, G. L., 429, 430
Breytenbach, C., 44
Brinsmead, B. H., 8
Briones, D., 254
Bruce, F. F., 10, 11, 29, 31, 33, 44, 50, 52, 61, 116, 128, 140, 147, 158, 159, 166, 168, 171, 173, 174, 187, 198, 208, 226, 242, 246, 248, 266, 271, 275, 283, 287, 290, 291, 298, 303, 307, 315, 347, 348, 349, 357, 365, 366, 382, 384, 407, 436, 446, 454, 457, 467, 482, 483, 490, 510
Bryant, R. A., 120, 471
Bultmann, R., 474
Burkitt, F. C., 50, 176
Burton, E., 1, 10, 31, 40, 42, 52, 114, 121, 126, 128, 130, 131, 132, 135, 139, 140, 141, 147, 149, 158, 164, 165, 171, 173, 175, 176, 178, 180, 182, 184, 185, 197, 239, 242, 251, 266, 269, 275, 276, 279, 288, 296, 298, 303, 308, 315, 318, 322, 326, 332, 345, 346, 348, 350, 351, 352, 356, 367, 382, 383, 384, 396, 398, 407, 410, 416, 420, 422, 423, 434, 435, 436, 438, 439, 440, 444, 449, 450, 451, 452, 454, 455, 459, 460, 462, 463, 464, 466, 467, 468, 481, 482, 483, 494, 505, 514, 515
Byrne, B., 334

Callan, T., 318
Callaway, M. C., 403

Calvin, J., 333, 428
Campbell, D. A., 223, 230, 231, 232, 239, 248, 326, 437
Campbell, T. H., 34
Caneday, A., 236, 239, 296
Charles, J. D., 458
Choi, H.-S., 231, 326, 421, 431
Cimok, F., 267
Classen, C. J., 82, 86, 98, 103, 105, 136
Collins, A. Y., 162
Comfort, P. W., 193, 343, 376, 479
Conzelman, H., 17
Cook, D., 112
Cosgrove, C. H., 307, 312
Cranford, M., 289, 418
Crossan, J. D., 369
Cullmann, O., 182
Cuss, D., 370

Dahl, N. A., 97, 106, 124, 319, 407, 410, 513
Danker, F. W., 5, 118, 125, 254, 371, 372, 484
Das, A. A., 2, 10, 11, 14, 20, 25, 31, 41, 44, 45, 50, 51, 52, 53, 54, 55, 60, 74, 75, 77, 78, 79, 84, 93, 96, 111, 115, 120, 121, 124, 125, 128, 132, 138, 144, 146, 158, 160, 161, 167, 168, 171, 172, 173, 176, 177, 178, 183, 194, 196, 197, 200, 204, 209, 215, 239, 240, 244, 245, 246, 247, 248, 279, 283, 285, 288, 292, 295, 301, 310, 318, 329, 331, 344, 345, 355, 356, 357, 358, 364, 382, 393, 415, 420, 421, 422, 437, 444, 448, 452, 459, 461, 464, 465, 466, 468, 472, 476, 481, 484, 494, 502, 505
Daube, D., 88, 89
Davies, W. D., 483, 512
Davis, B. S., 268
deBoer, M. C., 10, 108, 120, 131, 132, 235, 250, 346, 348, 349, 357, 365, 410, 413, 414, 415, 416, 417, 421, 425
Deissmann, A., 410
Dennison, W. D., 473
deSilva, D. A., 2, 5, 7, 14, 17, 20, 21, 53, 56, 66, 86, 88, 93, 99, 116, 117, 119, 121, 135, 141, 142, 151, 153, 161, 162, 186, 187, 196, 197, 200, 207, 221, 225, 228, 238, 254, 257, 258, 279, 328, 337, 342, 349, 355, 369, 370, 381, 386, 416, 419, 447, 453, 486, 497
Dibelius, M., 164, 443

Di Mattei, S., 393, 394, 397, 398, 399, 400, 402, 405
Dodd, B. J., 23
Dodd, C. H., 483
Donaldson, T. L., 144, 146, 151, 152, 155, 156, 297, 298, 299, 301, 302, 335, 347, 355, 438
Donfried, K. P., 260, 499
Drane, J., 62, 269
Duncan, G. S., 176, 470, 490
Dunn, J. D. G., 10, 11, 20, 29, 45, 46, 54, 57, 107, 115, 132, 141, 142, 149, 150, 151, 153, 158, 161, 166, 170, 171, 172, 173, 175, 176, 178, 180, 181, 182, 183, 184, 186, 188, 194, 199, 200, 204, 205, 206, 209, 210, 215, 216, 224, 226, 227, 228, 230, 231, 233, 235, 238, 239, 240, 245, 246, 247, 248, 249, 250, 251, 258, 269, 277, 283, 288, 290, 306, 307, 311, 315, 316, 329, 330, 331, 335, 355, 367, 395, 407, 410, 413, 417, 418, 422, 423, 432, 436, 438, 440, 441, 443, 450, 451, 454, 455, 456, 463, 466, 468, 470, 471, 477, 481, 482, 483, 489, 490, 491, 494, 495, 497, 502, 506, 508, 509, 512
Dupont, J., 144, 146, 152
Dzino, D., 40

Eastman, S. G., 398
Eckstein, H.-J., 246
Eddy, P. R., 216
Edelstein, L., 490
Ehrman, B. D., 16
Eisenbaum, P., 236
Elliott, S., 397, 440
Engberg-Pedersen, T., 222, 223, 248, 252, 254, 256, 258, 316, 321, 329, 330, 339, 410, 429, 443, 448, 451, 455, 464, 469, 471
Esler, P. F., 202, 206, 312

Fairweather, J., 63, 87, 88, 90, 215
Fee, G. D., xvii, 97, 130, 131, 133, 147, 158, 168, 177, 178, 193, 203, 234, 235, 248, 249, 267, 270, 276, 278, 303, 356, 403, 425, 443, 446, 452, 454, 455, 456, 457, 463, 464, 466, 467, 468, 469, 470, 471, 480, 481, 484, 493, 494, 501
Feldman, L. H., 17
Fitzmyer, J. A., 294
Foakes-Jackson, F. J., 11, 50, 52
Forbes, C., 348

Frey, J., 370
Friesen, S., 369, 370
Fuller, D. P., 228
Fung, R. Y. K., xvii, 10, 48, 50, 52, 53, 55,
    61, 116, 128, 140, 158, 160, 164, 168, 172,
    173, 186, 187, 195, 198, 207, 215, 242, 251,
    252, 268, 271, 276, 288, 292, 298, 308,
    320, 321, 322, 327, 336, 345, 358, 366,
    380, 381, 382, 385, 399, 401, 403, 404,
    407, 409, 410, 416, 417, 419, 420, 423,
    424, 438, 439, 441, 447, 451, 453, 457,
    459, 460, 462, 463, 464, 465, 467, 469,
    482, 483, 487, 489, 493, 513
Furnish, V. P., 259, 473, 475, 476, 483, 496

Gardiner, E. N., 432
Garlington, D., 223, 469
Gathercole, S. J., 221, 222
Gaventa, B. R., 137, 142, 148, 167, 339, 386
George, T., 357
Georgi, D., 172, 173, 177, 184, 186, 188, 189
Gese, H., 397
Gill, C., 254
Goldin, J., 318
Gombis, T. B., 245
Gordon, T. D., 236
Gorman, M. J., 216, 223, 224, 237, 248,
    422
Greeven, H., 164
Griffin, M., 254
Gundry, R. H., 418
Guthrie, D., 10
Guthrie, W. C. K., 348

Haenchen, E., 50, 52, 166, 195
Hafemann, S., 379, 380
Hagner, D. A., 145
Hall, R. G., 95
Hansen, G. W., 91, 92, 93, 124, 214, 245
Hanson, R. P. C., 395
Hardin, J. K., 368, 372, 374
Harnack, A. von, 34
Harrison, J. R., 254, 255, 257, 260
Harrisville, R. A., 232, 234
Hartman, L., 331
Hays, R. B., 158, 203, 230, 231, 235, 245,
    270, 297, 298, 302, 395, 396, 399, 401,
    404, 446, 452, 484, 487
Hemer, C. J., 44, 60
Hengel, M., 87, 88, 142, 144, 153, 294
Henten, J. W. van, 118, 119

Hietanen, M., 105, 214, 215, 276, 308, 392,
    407
Hoenig, S. B., 19
Hofius, O., 160
Holmberg, B., 136, 257
Hooker, M. D., 224, 230, 235, 236
Howard, G., 298, 336
Hübner, H., 315, 318
Hultgren, A. J., 143, 152, 168, 234, 235
Hurtado, L. W., 153

Jayakumar, S., 342
Jensen, J., 459
Jeremias, J., 356, 357
Jervis, A. B., 197, 420
Jewett, R., 198, 259, 260, 357, 447, 450,
    486
John Chrysostom, 2, 23, 63, 128, 129, 130,
    145, 147, 158, 160, 174, 182, 233, 245,
    246, 280, 307, 308, 317, 320, 330, 333,
    364, 366, 382, 387, 401, 412, 416, 433,
    434, 436, 447, 455, 457, 503, 515
Johnson, H. W., 231
Johnson, L. T., 462
Joubert, S., 246, 254
Judge, E. A., 88
Jüngel, E., 223

Kahl, B., 338, 351
Käsemann, E., 262, 476, 498
Keck, L., 316
Keener, C., 34, 36, 40, 41, 43, 53, 54, 59,
    60, 140, 166, 276
Kennedy, G., 64, 86, 95, 101, 393
Kern, P. H., 65, 215
Kim, S., 149, 288
Klaiber, W., 455
Klauck, H.-J., 82, 86
Knox, J., 51
Köstenberger, A., 513
Kraftchick, S., 85, 94
Kraybill, N., 370
Kuck, D. W., 489

Lagrange, M.-J., 114, 131, 298, 407, 412,
    416, 423, 425, 432, 434, 436, 438, 440,
    443, 448, 452, 454, 455, 463, 481, 483,
    487, 489, 492, 493, 502, 504, 506, 507,
    508, 511, 514
Lake, K., 11, 52, 160
Lambrecht, J., 242, 245, 319
Lappenga, B., 384, 385, 495

Lategan, B., 23, 137
Leithart, P., 223
Lemmer, H. R., 270
Lenski, R. C. H., 452
Lewis, C. S., 466
Lichtenberger, H., 20
Lightfoot, J. B., 10, 29, 39, 44, 50, 54, 55, 61, 62, 180, 277, 306, 438, 440
Longenecker, B. W., 188
Longenecker, R. N., 2, 10, 12, 27, 45, 46, 50, 51, 52, 53, 58, 60, 86, 91, 92, 93, 97, 106, 124, 128, 131, 136, 140, 158, 160, 161, 164, 165, 166, 168, 170, 171, 172, 173, 176, 178, 181, 183, 184, 185, 187, 193, 198, 206, 207, 213, 215, 219, 244, 245, 247, 251, 265, 266, 267, 268, 271, 276, 287, 288, 293, 295, 308, 315, 316, 318, 322, 329, 330, 333, 336, 339, 345, 346, 347, 350, 354, 355, 358, 365, 367, 382, 383, 384, 386, 391, 392, 393, 395, 403, 407, 410, 411, 413, 414, 415, 416, 421, 423, 433, 434, 435, 436, 438, 439, 444, 446, 447, 454, 455, 458, 459, 460, 461, 462, 463, 465, 466, 467, 468, 472, 480, 482, 483, 487, 490, 492, 493, 502, 508, 509, 513
Lüdemann, G., 194
Lührmann, D., 158
Lull, D. J., 315, 316, 330
Lütgert, W., 12, 443
Luther, M., 177, 249
Luz, U., 513
Lyons, G., 137, 147

Malherbe, A. J., 71, 73, 74, 75, 76, 78, 79, 80, 91
Marrou, H. I., 87
Martin, R. P., 462
Martin, T. W., 368
Martyn, J. L., 9, 10, 16, 26, 27, 30, 45, 46, 60, 83, 107, 120, 124, 126, 130, 131, 147, 171, 173, 177, 181, 185, 186, 188, 189, 197, 206, 209, 215, 236, 243, 244, 245, 246, 271, 277, 279, 291, 293, 296, 298, 301, 303, 316, 326, 344, 346, 347, 348, 349, 350, 351, 365, 367, 380, 381, 382, 383, 384, 385, 386, 390, 392, 393, 397, 398, 399, 403, 407, 448, 453, 465, 482, 485, 487, 490, 513
Matera, F. J., 10, 115, 140, 147, 158, 159, 160, 171, 173, 180, 182, 184, 185, 196, 205, 212, 213, 244, 251, 266, 268, 269, 272, 276, 298, 308, 315, 316, 332, 350, 379,

385, 402, 405, 410, 416, 419, 432, 438, 443, 456, 463, 464, 485, 487, 503
Mathew, S., 255
Matlock, R. B., 232, 233, 234, 235, 236, 270
McKnight, S., 249, 462
McNamara, M., 397
Meeks, W. A., 29, 94, 257
Meier, J. P., 162, 356
Mellor, R., 369
Metzger, B. M., 2, 111, 138, 170, 193, 213, 285, 390, 391, 455, 479
Milligan, G., 379
Mitchell, S., 28, 43, 44, 45
Moffatt, J., 28, 29, 39, 41, 44, 46, 47
Mommsen, T., 30, 165
Moo, D. J., 10, 131, 132, 147, 221, 224, 225, 407, 413, 416, 422, 436, 438, 439, 452, 454, 455, 456, 463, 465, 467, 469, 472, 482, 487, 489, 494, 502, 513
Moore-Crispin, D. R., 348
Morland, K. A., 127
Moule, C. F. D., 224, 235, 435, 440, 471
Moulton, J. H., 379
Moxnes, H., 254
Mullins, T. Y., 92
Munck, J., 10
Murphy-O'Connor, J., 59, 156, 158, 173, 268, 483, 484
Mussner, F., 54, 142, 287, 319, 379, 425

Nanos, M., 11, 199, 200, 203, 205, 208, 508
Nock, A. D., 289

Oakes, P., 28, 116, 117
O'Brien, K. S., 294
O'Brien, P. T., 223, 289
Olbricht, T. H., 86
Olson, S. N., 435
O'Neill, J. C., 443
Oropeza, B. J., 255, 258

Painter, J., 164, 196, 208
Perelman, C., 411
Pervo, R., 54
Phillips, T. E., 56
Pitts, A. W., 232
Porter, S. E., 63, 77, 81, 82, 83, 86, 89, 90, 99, 100, 103, 166, 232
Price, S. R. F., 369
Przybylski, B., 220

Qimron, E., 226

Rabens, V., 270, 473, 474, 475
Räisänen, H., 144, 155, 246
Ramachandra, V., 362
Ramsay, W., 30, 31, 40, 45, 50, 345
Reed, J. T., 74, 78, 83, 104, 105
Reinhold, M., 17
Richards, E. R., 2, 502
Ridderbos, H. N., 10, 44, 45, 52, 54, 248,
    465, 466, 469, 473, 475, 513
Riddle, D. W., 160
Riesner, R., 31, 34, 41, 44, 45, 60
Robbins, V. K., 85, 100
Robertson, A. T., 484
Robertson, C. K., 204, 205, 210
Robinson, D. W. B., 174, 175, 176, 193, 194
Robinson, J. A. T., 60, 171
Ropes, J. H., 443
Rowlingson, D. T., 38
Rusam, D., 348

Saller, R. P., 254
Sampley, P., 164
Sanders, E. P., 200, 225, 291, 298, 316, 330
Savage, T. B., 380
Schechter, S., 224
Schellenberg, R., 86
Schlier, H., 54, 125, 128, 139, 158, 160, 165,
    171, 178, 180, 184, 246, 251, 275, 276,
    281, 289, 292, 298, 307, 315, 322, 330,
    337, 344, 345, 386, 404, 407, 410, 413,
    414, 415, 416, 419, 425, 429, 455, 468,
    481, 513
Schmithals, W., 12
Schnabel, E. J., 50, 55
Schnelle, U., 29, 54, 143, 149, 174, 178, 183,
    185, 194, 196, 209, 249, 317, 318, 321,
    418, 456
Schreiner, T., 10, 131, 132, 159, 160, 161,
    165, 168, 178, 180, 198, 234, 239, 240,
    244, 246, 250, 252, 271, 293, 303, 315,
    379, 380, 384, 405, 410, 422, 446, 449,
    454, 455, 457, 463, 467, 471, 472, 482,
    483, 484, 486, 488, 489, 494, 502, 513
Schrenk, G., 217, 218, 220, 221, 423
Schürmann, H., 484
Schüssler-Fiorenza, E., 341, 342
Schütz, J. H., 25
Schweizer, E., 348
Schwemer, A. M., 158
Scott, K., 369

Segal, A., 10, 19, 146, 335
Seifrid, M. A., 216, 218, 221, 239, 243, 321
Silva, M., 44, 126, 138, 140, 141, 234, 266,
    277, 285, 286, 287, 311, 312, 313, 319, 320,
    423
Smit, J., 95
Snodgrass, K., 511
Spicq, C., 220, 224
Sprinkle, P., 229, 272, 292, 327
Stamps, D. L., 79
Stanley, C. D., 287, 405
Stanton, G., 93
Stein, R. H., 51, 54
Stendahl, K., 145
Stowers, S. K., 231, 453
Strelan, J., 483
Stuhlmacher, P., 217
Sumney, J. L., 8

Tabor, J. D., 162
Talbert, C. H., 34
Tannehill, R., 246, 247
Taubenschlag, R., 345
Taylor, L. R., 369, 372
Theissen, G., 29, 257
Thielman, F., 282, 288, 289, 291, 303, 314,
    414, 484
Thompson, M., 483
Tolmie, D. F., 63, 115, 116, 126, 128, 129,
    130, 132, 136, 139, 148, 157, 158, 165, 166,
    176, 177, 178, 179, 182, 194, 195, 196, 197,
    205, 213, 234, 238, 242, 243, 251, 266,
    267, 269, 273, 276, 277, 279, 281, 283,
    287, 292, 296, 298, 300, 303, 306, 307,
    312, 314, 316, 319, 329, 331, 334, 344,
    345, 346, 356, 366, 384, 399, 403, 405,
    407, 410, 415, 416, 421, 423, 435, 459,
    472, 485, 489, 508, 512, 513
Tomson, P. J., 199, 200
Turner, N., 397, 420, 461, 505
Tyson, J. B., 255, 252

Vainio, O.-P., 222
Vermes, G., 225, 226
Vielhauer, P., 365
Vos, J. S., 23, 115, 123, 131, 132, 136, 167, 214

Walker, W. O., 239
Wallace, D. B., 315, 418, 435, 453, 504
Wallace-Hadrill, A., 254, 257
Wallis, I. G., 326
Watson, D. F., 63

Watson, F., 25, 107, 128, 137, 154, 177, 178, 184, 208, 225, 228, 236, 287, 292, 293, 418, 425, 438, 450, 496
Weima, J. A. D., 79, 83, 87
Wengst, K., 369
Wenham, D., 484
Wesley, J., 476
Westerholm, S., 217, 220, 261, 333, 451
White, C. D., 362
Wilckens, U., 155, 244
Wilcox, M., 295, 309
Williams, D., 54
Williams, J. J., 5, 119,
Williams, S. K., 203, 243, 248, 271, 272, 287, 298, 301, 303, 320, 323, 355, 410, 419, 454
Wilson, T. A., 327, 346, 365, 448
Wink, W., 348, 352, 362
Winter, B. W., 90, 363, 364, 370, 373, 374, 375, 505
Wisdom, J. R., 283, 286, 289
Witherington, B., 9, 10, 23, 25, 31, 42, 44, 50, 59, 61, 93, 95, 97, 106, 137, 158, 160, 162, 164, 173, 176, 187, 188, 198, 203, 204, 206, 210, 246, 267, 277, 287, 298, 307, 308, 315, 316, 346, 357, 368, 382, 384, 396, 407, 408, 410, 414, 415, 416, 420, 421, 434, 437, 438, 441, 454, 456, 458, 482, 487, 492, 504
Wright, B. G., 21, 201
Wright, N. T., 126, 144, 148, 149, 152, 153, 154, 155, 156, 158, 173, 183, 213, 216, 217, 220, 221, 222, 223, 226, 231, 249, 278, 284, 303, 311, 326, 332, 340, 346, 416, 422

Yinger, K. L., 227, 494
Young, N. H., 289, 329, 335, 350

Zahn, T., 42
Zanker, P., 369
Zerwick, M., 240, 420, 446
Ziesler, J. A., 248
Zimmerman, C., 264, 380
Zimmerman, R., 473
Zuntz, G., 390

Index of Scripture and Other Ancient Texts

OLD TESTAMENT

Genesis

1:4	119, 359
1:10	119, 359
1:12	119
1:14	366, 367, 368, 373
1:27	338, 342
3	119
3:16c	342
6:1–4	119
11:30 (LXX)	401
12:3	232, 282, 283, 284, 303
13:15	18, 309
13:16	309, 310
15:1–6	393
15:5	282, 309, 310
15:6	231, 277, 281, 282, 291
15:13	309, 310
16:1–6	90
16:1–16	393
16:10	310
17:8	18, 309
17:9–14	279, 281
17:10	18
17:11	273
17:13	273
17:14	18
17:19–21	402
18:15	367
18:18	282, 283, 284
21:1–14	393
21:6–7	401
21:9–10	403

21:10	404
21:12	404
21:14–21	403
22:17	309
22:17–18	310
22:18	309
24:7	18, 309

Exodus

4:22–23	334
4:23	448
12:40	310
12:43–51	367
12:48–49	18
19:4–6	448
20:1–6	448
20:2–3	258
20:8–11	366
20:18–22a	317
29:38–42	418
31:16–17	366
34:6 (LXX)	467
34:28 (LXX)	449
34:29	318

Leviticus

2:13	14
11	200
11:44–45	197
17:10–14	209
18:5	20, 289, 292, 293
18:6–18	209
18:26	209
19:2	197
19:18	449, 465, 483, 485

20:22–26	203, 226, 240, 242, 290, 328
26:46	318

Numbers

4:37	318
4:41	318
4:45	318
4:49	318
10:10	366
18:9	258
25:1–13	15, 142
25:6–13	461
28:1–8	418
28:11–15	366

Deuteronomy

5:6–7	258
5:12–15	366
6:4	155, 319, 339
6:4 (LXX)	465
7:26	127
10:4	449
13:18 (LXX)	127
14	200
14:1–2	334
15:4–11	192
15:11	187
18:18	290
21:22–23	151, 293, 294
21:23	295
24:10–22	187
27–28	14
27:11–26	286, 287
27:11–30:20	143

27:26	20, 151, 286, 290, 295, 322, 416	115:3–8	460	36:26–27	269, 303
28:1–14	287	115:7 (LXX)	394	37:1–14	303
28:15–68	287	116:12–19	258	39:25	512
28:58	286, 290	116:16	394		
30:10	286	117:1	154	**Daniel**	
30:11	288	125:5	512	1:8–16	202
30:15–16	20	128:6	512	12:1–3	153
30:15–20	287	142:3 (LXX)	240		
30:19–20	20	143:2	217, 218, 224, 240	**Hosea**	
32:43	154			10:12–13	492
		Proverbs		11:1	334
Joshua		22:8	492	11:3	334
6:17–18	127				
7:11–13 (LXX)	127	**Isaiah**		**Habakkuk**	
		11:10	154	2:4	291, 292
1 Samuel		14:30	188		
9:1–2	113	14:32	188	**Zephaniah**	
16:7	180	40:9 (LXX)	125	3:9	188
18:25	508	44:3	303	3:12	188
18:27	508	44:8–21	6		
		44:9	18	**Zechariah**	
2 Samuel		44:9–20	460	9:9	151
1:12	497	49:1	147		
7:14	153	49:5–6	147		
13:15 (LXX)	465	49:6	154	**NEW TESTAMENT**	
		51:1–3	401		
1 Kings		52:1	18	**Matthew**	
18:40	142	52:7 (LXX)	125	1:25	161–62
19:10	142	52:19–53:12	401	3:7–9	232
19:14	158	53:1	271	5:44–48	496
19:15	158	53:10–11	401	11:29	413
		54:1	310, 401	13:33	434
Job		54:1–2	400	13:55	161
4:8	492	58:3	192	15:2	144
		58:5–7	192	19:17	20
Psalms		61:1 (LXX)	125	20:1–16	467
2:7	153			22:34–40	449
2:7–8	156	**Jeremiah**		22:39	484
9:17	215	1:5	146	24:15–21	38
18:49	154	10:1–12	6	26:42	121
32:1	281	10:2–15	460	26:61	151
67:12 (LXX)	125	31	24	27:40	151
68:17	318	31:33–34	457		
72:8	156			**Mark**	
85:16 (LXX)	394	**Ezekiel**		1:19–20	183
86:16	394	3:4	497	1:29–31	150
89:27	156	11:19	303	2:1–12	150
95:2 (LXX)	125	11:19–20	269	2:15–17	150
110:1	153	18:31	303	2:23–28	150
115:1–8	6	20:11	292	3:1–6	150
		20:13	292	3:20–21	162

3:31–35	162, 497	7–8	404	12:25	48, 50, 51, 54
6:3	161	7:38	318	13:1–3	114, 172
7:1–13	150	7:53	318	13:1–14:28	46, 47, 51, 514
7:3–5	144	7:58	15	13:6–12	58
7:14–23	150	7:58–8:3	166	13:9	113
9:37	355	8:1–4	15	13:13–52	42
10:1–12	151	8:3	36	13:13–14:23	39, 44
10:19	20	9	147	13:13–14:28	379
10:29–30	497	9:1	143	13:14–14:23	28
10:45	152, 448	9:1–2	36, 403	13:29	294
11:1–10	151	9:1–6	15	13:42–43	300
11:15–18	151	9:1–19	36	13:43	28, 334
12:6	355	9:10–26	35	13:46	154
12:28–31	449	9:11	87	13:47	155
12:31	484	9:21	15	13:48	300
13:1–2	151	9:22–25	157, 158	13:50	439
13:14–19	38	9:23	35	14:1	28, 300, 334
14:24	152	9:26–27	50	14:2	439
14:36	356	9:26–30	35, 48, 50, 166	14:12	47
14:58	151	9:30	36	14:19–20	439
15:29	151	10–11	202	14:21–23	9
		10:1–11:18	195, 272	15	44, 47, 48, 52, 56
Luke		10:9–16	37	15:1	47
1:4	36	10:15	207	15:1–2	24, 178
2:32	155	10:17–48	37	15:1–4	11
2:42	49	10:28	202	15:1–5	48, 169
2:52	144	10:28–29	37	15:1–29	35
10:25–28	449	10:34–35	37	15:1–30	50
10:27	484	10:39	294	15:5	196
12:33	192	10:45–48	53	15:5–7	55
13:21	434	10:48	37, 202	15:6–21	54
18:22	192	11:1–18	37	15:6–35	48
21:20–24	38	11:1–26	165	15:7	37
22:42	121	11:2–3	37	15:8–11	53
		11:3	182, 197, 202	15:11	37, 53
John		11:12	53	15:12	182
2:19–20	151	11:15	37	15:12–13	55
3:19	466	11:15–18	182	15:12–21	163
7:1–8	162	11:17–18	53	15:19–20	52, 186
7:8	49	11:19–20	195	15:20	48
7:10	49	11:19–26	51	15:22	46, 55
19:31	294	11:25–26	36	15:22–27	114
		11:27–30	35, 48, 51, 53, 54, 61, 188	15:22–29	56
Acts				15:23–29	52
1–8	60	11:27–12:25	53	15:28–29	186
1:14	163	11:28–30	50, 51, 57, 60, 171, 187	15:29	48
2:46	116			15:35–41	46
3:22–23	290	11:29–30	48	15:36	42
4:32–35	192	12:2	183	15:36–16:5	43
5:30	294	12:12	54	15:41	42
5:38–39	144	12:17	163	16–18	46
5:42	116	12:20–23	54	16:1	43, 108

16:1–3	438	2:23	226, 487	7:13–25	455
16:1–4	46	2:25	415	7:14–25	144
16:1–5	42	2:25–29	416	8:1–4	6
16:4	43, 108	2:28–29	335	8:2–4	455
16:6	29, 39–43, 44,	3:1–3	233	8:4	454
	46, 379	3:3	231, 233	8:9	358
16:6–9	43	3:9	322	8:10	249
16:7	40	3:9–20	508	8:11	314
16:15	117	3:10–18	322	8:13	222
16:37–38	113	3:20	316	8:13–14	260
17:1–18:5	34	3:21	392	8:14	358, 475
18:7	116	3:22	229, 233, 236	8:14–17	357
18:12–17	58	3:22–26	230, 231	8:15	356
18:22	49, 50	3:26	229, 233	8:15–16	358
18:23	29, 39–41, 43, 44,	3:27	487	8:20	411
	46, 108, 379	3:27–28	319	8:24	411
18:25–26	140	3:27–30	226	8:29	389
20:4	39, 46	3:29	251	9–11	332
20:20	116	3:29–30	156, 319	10:2–4	290
21:17	49	4:3–8	218, 281	10:3	221
21:17–18	163	4:9–11	281	10:16	499
21:20–21	15, 143	4:12	231, 233	10:16–17	271
21:39	87	4:16	231, 233	11:25	184
22:3	87	5:2	423	11:25–32	512
22:6–21	36	5:10–11	218	11:28	290
22:25–29	113	5:12–21	320–22	11:31	290
23:23–26:32	58	5:15	125	11:35	261, 430
23:26	111	5:18–19	230	11:36	121, 261
25:14–22	38	5:20	316	12:1	447
26:4	507	5:21	219	12:1–13:14	6
26:12–20	36	6–8	454	12:2	389
26:18	155	6:1	259	12:7	490
26:19–20	166	6:1–14	247, 337, 389, 470	13:8–10	454
26:20	36	6:1–23	258, 472	13:9	450
28:17–29	154	6:1–7:6	6	13:11–14	120
		6:2	475	13:12	463
Romans		6:4–5	259	13:13	463
1:3–4	153	6:12	447	14:1–6	13
1:5	183, 499	6:12–13	225, 252	14:1–12	427
1:7	112	6:12–23	220	14:1–15:7	333
1:18–21	258	6:13	259	14:3–4	58
1:18–32	215	6:15	259	14:5–6	47, 134
1:25	258	6:15–23	262	14:13–23	134
2:4	467	6:20–22	260	14:14	58
2:6–11	217, 225, 252	6:23	260	15:7	13
2:11	221	7:1	247	15:9–12	154
2:12–14	298	7:1–6	419	15:15–16	183
2:13	237	7:7–8	316	15:25–28	55
2:13–16	222	7:7–24	289	15:25–31	187
2:14	355, 451	7:7–25	144	15:26	107, 189, 190
2:16	429	7:8	446	15:27–29	189
2:17	487	7:11	446	15:30–32	174, 190

16:4–5	117	11:1	137, 377	5:17	205
16:22	2, 503	11:2	139, 149	5:21	295
16:23	117	11:23	139	6:3	135
16:27	121	11:23–26	149	6:3–10	506
		11:25	396	8:1–9:15	187
1 Corinthians		12:1–14:40	270	8:9	192, 295
1:12	185	12:3	136	8:18	107
1:14	161	12:13	336, 337, 338	8:23	107, 114
1:17	90	13:12	191	8:24	487
1:17–31	509	13:13	465	9:3	107
1:18	120	14:6	172, 415	9:6	492
1:18–20	351	14:26	172	10:1	414, 503
1:21	112	14:30	172	10:3	248
1:23	268, 439	15:1	139	11:4	182
2:1–5	7, 90, 270, 381	15:3	152	11:21b–29	508
2:2	4, 268	15:3–8	149	11:21b–33	253
3:4–15	385	15:3–9	161	11:23–24	143
3:19	351	15:7	163	11:23–25	514
3:22	185	15:9–10	499	11:23–33	506
4:14–15	26	15:20–22	120	11:24	403, 439
4:15	386	15:22	321	11:32–33	157
4:21	468	15:35–58	274	13:5	249
5:6	435, 474	15:45	321		
5:7	474	16:1	107	**Galatians**	
5:9–11	79	16:1–4	187, 189	1–2	38, 51, 54, 60
5:11	481	16:19	117	1:1	25, 114, 139
5:13	405	16:21	2, 502, 503, 504	1:1–3	92
6:9–10	463	16:22	357	1:1–5	91, 92, 104
6:13b	447	16:24	502	1:1–6	2
6:19–20	262, 447			1:1–2:14	25, 98
6:20	259	**2 Corinthians**		1:2	28, 30, 39, 48
7:34	447	1:8–9	506	1:3–4	117
8:1–9	58	1:14	488	1:4	5, 121, 223,
8:1–13	200	1:15–2:11	66		236, 248, 350, 352,
8:6	354	2:1–4	79		354, 359, 412, 415,
9:5	185	2:14–7:4	135		417, 418, 419, 466,
9:6	46, 204	2:15	120		470, 484, 509
9:9–10	395	3:6	396	1:6	7, 8, 26, 32, 52, 104,
9:10–11	492	3:9	219		105, 387, 433
9:19–23	13, 47	3:18	386, 389	1:6–9	93, 112, 132, 138,
9:20	148, 185	4:3	120		139, 182, 214,
9:20–21	298, 355, 377,	4:5–7	381		432, 436
	438, 484	4:6	148	1:6–13	92
9:24–25	222	4:10	135	1:6–4:11	92
9:24–26	432	5:1–4	274	1:7	8, 9, 99, 104, 441
9:26–27	222	5:9–10	217	1:8–9	32, 99, 190
10:1–11	392	5:10	489, 494	1:8–10	104
10:4	354	5:14	230, 246	1:10	23, 25, 101
10:11	333	5:14–15	249, 262	1:10–11	516
10:14–33	200	5:15	135, 259, 299, 471	1:10–2:21	26, 93
10:18	513	5:16–17	510	1:10b	138
10:25–30	13, 58	5:16–18	249	1:11	91

1:11–12	25, 115, 129, 140, 156		2:6	149, 164, 186		3:1	4, 9, 28, 30, 39, 91, 433
1:11–17	437		2:6–10	32		3:1–5	3, 7, 53, 93, 125, 128, 335, 340, 344, 356, 362, 381, 383, 387, 406, 416
1:11–20	112		2:7–9	49			
1:11–2:14	94, 104		2:7–10	166, 194			
1:12	149, 190		2:9	46, 164			
1:13	92, 167, 289, 403		2:10	32, 49, 53, 55		3:1–6	281
1:13–14	14, 31, 57, 145, 150, 246, 247, 414, 461		2:11	193		3:1–7	92
			2:11–13	57		3:1–4:7	410
			2:11–14	13, 24, 27, 32, 36, 37, 52, 53, 170, 189, 190, 224, 244, 266, 333		3:1–4:11	105
1:13–16	155, 167					3:1–4:21	26
1:13–2:14	51					3:1–5:12	96
1:13–2:21	129		2:12	36, 202		3:2	32, 92, 320, 428
1:14	87, 289, 487		2:13	46		3:2–5	182, 227, 262, 303, 409, 419, 429, 434, 447, 452, 482
1:15	155, 193		2:14	2, 27, 105, 213, 214, 383, 432, 517			
1:15–16	31, 140, 144, 149						
1:15–17	171		2:14–18	377			
1:16	153, 158, 248		2:14–21	265		3:3	8, 12, 25, 219, 243, 244, 304, 443, 454, 472, 501
1:16–17	274		2:14–4:11	376			
1:16–22	35		2:14–5:12	126			
1:17	31, 35		2:15	207, 242, 484		3:5	32, 172, 428
1:17–18	35		2:15–16	11, 27, 37, 53, 146, 152, 197, 229, 298, 299, 300, 313, 332, 421		3:6	231, 284, 434
1:17–19	25					3:6–9	101, 230, 291, 513
1:18	51, 60, 193					3:6–14	307
1:18–19	31, 35, 165, 172					3:6–29	8
1:18–20	49, 50, 55, 148, 171		2:15–21	105, 196, 208, 266, 281, 408		3:6–4:7	93
						3:6–4:31	278
1:19	162		2:15–3:14	327		3:7	340, 391, 405
1:19–20	50		2:16	105, 217, 218, 230, 232, 235, 236, 273, 275, 282, 285, 323		3:7–9	266, 271, 277, 286
1:20	35, 51, 92					3:8	232, 303, 304, 396
1:21	32, 36, 48, 51, 157, 193					3:9	231, 340
			2:16–21	271		3:10	20, 282, 284, 329, 353
1:21–23	140		2:17	218, 222			
1:21–24	170		2:18	227, 251		3:10–12	280, 301, 512
1:22	31, 36		2:19	293, 358, 378, 470, 508		3:10–14	227, 236, 237, 240, 421
1:23	14, 157, 403						
1:23–24	32, 165		2:19–20	207, 221, 222, 259, 262, 293, 321, 339, 359, 419, 470, 472, 476, 485		3:11	207, 396
1:24	31					3:12	20
2:1	46, 50, 51, 60, 193					3:13	298, 301, 412
2:1–2	32, 49, 148					3:13–14	208, 281, 296, 297, 300, 355, 396, 406, 409, 429, 430, 485
2:1–10	25, 35, 37, 44, 47, 48, 50, 51, 52, 53, 54, 55, 56, 57, 60, 61, 194		2:19–21	119, 244, 377, 412			
			2:20	5, 148, 223, 224, 237, 275, 288, 320, 337, 386, 387, 412, 423, 424, 425, 466, 484, 510			
						3:14	248, 272, 278, 335, 353, 356, 513
2:1–14	133, 160, 439						
2:2	432					3:15–16	327
2:2b	49, 55		2:20–21	13, 236		3:15–18	101, 282, 304, 325, 326, 340, 345, 402, 419
2:3	194		2:21	101, 105, 117, 219, 220, 240, 246, 260, 268, 273, 293, 296, 300, 415, 417			
2:3–5	24, 32, 49, 196, 206, 224, 403						
2:4–5	211, 268, 411					3:15–19	325
2:5	2, 383					3:15–21	396
						3:15–22	283

3:15–25   14, 285, 290
3:15–4:7   241
3:16   315
3:18   320
3:19   326, 329, 332
3:19–22   240
3:19–25   283, 299, 306, 402
3:19–28   156
3:19–4:7   313
3:20   251, 339, 423
3:21   101, 207, 220, 221, 240, 248, 291, 312, 419, 472
3:22   229, 230, 233, 243, 325, 329, 353
3:23   298, 322, 421
3:23–25   101, 120, 247, 295, 300, 301, 317, 320, 343, 344, 347, 365, 411, 416
3:23–26   27, 296, 297
3:23–29   301, 362
3:23–4:2   349
3:23–4:11   178, 245
3:25   345, 353
3:26–27   424
3:26–28   120, 186, 196, 205, 243, 244, 419
3:26–29   32, 166, 277, 303, 304, 310, 346, 356, 367, 513
3:27   244, 510
3:28   173, 227, 251, 319, 320, 347, 350, 358, 359, 423, 509, 510
3:29   283, 302
4   47
4:1   302
4:1–2   329
4:1–4   295
4:1–5   120
4:1–7   14, 101, 247, 285, 362, 365, 419
4:1–11   115, 325, 335, 411, 416
4:1–5:13   178
4:2   120, 302, 329, 353
4:2–3   332
4:3   329, 346, 348, 353, 391, 472, 509, 510, 512

4:3–5   344, 350, 399
4:3–7   296, 298, 300
4:4   120, 306, 315, 326, 329, 353
4:4–5   237, 365
4:4–7   27
4:5   329, 353
4:5–7   367, 497
4:6–7   53, 250, 272, 303, 381, 383, 406, 434, 452, 482
4:7   329
4:8–9   27, 329, 346, 419
4:8–11   8, 93, 120, 237, 265, 347, 383, 413, 448
4:9   302, 348, 351, 391, 472, 510, 512
4:9–10   349
4:10   8, 226
4:10–11   346, 377
4:11   91, 387
4:11–20   92
4:12   92, 93, 106, 137
4:12–15   26
4:12–20   25, 106, 391
4:12–6:10   92
4:13   39
4:13–14   3, 32, 36
4:14   47
4:15   32
4:16   98
4:17   9, 12, 99, 378
4:17–18   127
4:19   26, 98, 224, 249, 250, 273, 321, 337, 358, 389, 423, 424, 436, 448, 470, 472, 476, 484, 485, 510
4:19–20   78, 91
4:20   339, 377, 385
4:21   12, 22, 333, 443
4:21–28   303
4:21–31   105, 106, 275, 277, 290, 329, 335, 377, 407, 410, 411, 447, 505, 513
4:21–5:1   295
4:28–5:13   92
4:30   10
4:31   408

5:1   8, 10, 22, 94, 96, 105, 106, 123, 265, 300, 329, 392, 432, 445, 446, 448, 453, 498
5:1–4   47, 95, 97
5:1–6   226, 260
5:1–12   106, 502
5:1–6:10   391
5:1b   346
5:2   8, 12, 13, 47
5:2–4   13, 27, 117, 119, 214, 240, 251, 261, 263, 273, 287, 293, 300, 476
5:2–6   105, 106, 392, 501
5:2–12   106
5:3   12, 227, 450, 451
5:4   8, 218, 219, 515
5:5   218, 221, 252, 320, 433
5:5–6   27, 237, 263, 277, 278, 284, 285, 287, 445
5:6   27, 120, 146, 225, 252, 451, 459, 465, 466, 474, 483, 496
5:7   9, 127, 474
5:7–9   93
5:7–12   25, 32, 106, 127, 377, 501
5:8–9   10
5:9   101
5:10   127, 489
5:10b–12   9
5:11   23, 25, 48, 98, 101, 130, 143, 403, 506, 514
5:11–12   8
5:11b   135
5:13   94, 106, 482, 498
5:13–14   260, 458, 488
5:13–15   287
5:13–25   225, 227, 240, 247, 273, 278, 285, 346, 425
5:13–26   407, 473, 480
5:13–6:10   8, 22, 26, 96, 97, 103, 106, 126, 244, 248, 249, 252, 269, 274, 275,

	305, 316, 321, 349,
	359, 396, 411, 422,
	423, 424, 501, 511
5:14	483
5:15	477, 497
5:16	94, 95, 96, 429, 474,
	475, 494, 498
5:16–24	505
5:16–25	222, 237, 250,
	262, 277, 482,
	485, 493
5:16–6:10	304, 330, 421
5:17	469
5:19–21	6, 225, 260, 431
5:20–21	497
5:21	91, 128, 222, 252,
	400, 494
5:22	458
5:22–23	223, 517
5:24	222, 237, 249,
	475, 509
5:25	94, 207, 320, 352,
	429, 451, 456,
	474, 475, 494,
	498, 512
5:26	452, 477, 497
6:1	206, 454, 468,
	482, 486
6:1–2	464, 477
6:1–6	473
6:1–10	471, 473
6:2	454, 478, 482
6:3	180
6:3–4	474
6:4b	508
6:5	474
6:6	9, 124, 474
6:7	101
6:7–8	252, 321, 465, 476
6:7–9	260
6:7–10	222, 225, 250, 273,
	431, 463, 464, 505
6:8	429, 474, 475
6:8b–9	247
6:9	451
6:9–10	287
6:10	106, 192, 293, 408
6:11	2, 92
6:11–17	25
6:11–18	92, 98, 377
6:12	9, 45, 48, 99,

	176, 198, 374, 403,
	436, 440, 507, 511
6:12–13	8, 9, 12, 32, 106,
	127, 133, 143, 268,
	438, 439, 514
6:12–15	226
6:12–16	410
6:13	9, 99, 374, 418, 487
6:14	99, 106, 237, 249,
	470, 488, 517
6:14–15	352
6:15	25, 27, 120, 146,
	205, 341, 354, 423,
	424, 476
6:15–16	27, 106
6:16	352, 472
6:17	32, 48, 106, 130,
	268, 440, 506,
	516
6:18	92, 117

Ephesians

2:8–10	234
2:10	225, 252
2:11	243, 490
2:11–16	205, 227
2:11–22	27
2:14–15	155
2:14–16	339
2:18	234
3:8	183
3:12	234
3:17	249
4:20–24	456
5:5	463
5:21	342

Philippians

1:12–14	379
1:15–18	385
1:22	248
1:24	248
2:3–11	471
2:5–8	323, 354
2:12–13	222, 499
2:16	488
3:2	440
3:2–21	11
3:3–6	226
3:4–14	508
3:4b–8	180
3:5	31, 113

3:5–8	145, 253
3:5–11	155
3:6	14, 87, 141, 144,
	228, 241, 289, 461
3:7–11	253
3:8–11	386
3:8–14	243
3:9	221, 229
3:10	389
3:11–14	222
3:17	137, 377
3:20	400
3:21	389, 494
4:9	139
4:20	121

Colossians

1:15–17	354
1:27	249, 423
2:4	90
2:8	350
2:16	349, 428
2:20	348, 349, 350
2:20–22	428
2:20–23	349
3:1–17	247, 389
3:3	474
3:5	463
3:5–11	474
3:5–17	337
3:9	463
3:9–11	337, 456
3:11	338
3:16	125
4:6	125
4:10	204
4:14	37
4:15	117
4:16	79
4:18	2, 502, 503, 504

1 Thessalonians

1:7–8	34
1:9	258, 364, 425
1:9–10	6, 15, 118, 200, 369
2:7–8	26
2:11–12	26
2:13	139, 272
2:13–16	403, 404
2:14–16	15
2:17–3:6	34
2:19	488

4:1	139
4:1–7	6
4:16–17	464
5:3	118
5:8	423
5:23	447

2 Thessalonians

1:5–12	217
2:1–2	79
2:16	125
3:6	139
3:14	481
3:17	2, 502, 503, 504

1 Timothy

1:2a	112
4:3–5	58

2 Timothy

2:1	125
2:25	468
3:11	47, 514
3:14	140
4:7	327, 432
4:11	37

Titus

1:4a	112
2:14	495

Philemon

10	386
19	503
24	37

Hebrews

1:1–4	354
2:1–4	7
2:2	318
2:3–4	270
5:7–10	253
5:12	350
9:15–17	307
11:11–16	400
12:5–11	253
12:26–28	400
13:2	117
13:13–14	400
13:23	7

James

1:1	111
1:15	493
1:27	192
2:10	416
2:14–16	234
2:15–17	192
2:19	244
4:5	462
5:7–11	467

1 Peter

3:7	342
3:18	295
4:9	117

2 Peter

3:5–6	400
3:10	348, 400
3:12	348

1 John

2:15	466
3:16–18	192

3 John

5–10	117

Jude

3	190

Revelation

2:14–15	200
2:20	200
9:20–21	460
21:1	120
21:1–22:5	400
21:4	120
21:8	460
22:15	460

OLD TESTAMENT APOCRYPHA

Tobit

1:3	187
1:7–8	187
1:10–13	202
2:2–23	187
4:7–11	187

12:6–7	256
12:8–9	187
12:12–14	187
13:3–6	288
13:6	215
13:11	298
14:2	187
14:4–7	288
14:5–7	298

Judith

9:2–4	142
10:5	202
12:1–20	202

Additions to Esther

C 28	202
6:3	255

Wisdom of Solomon

3:1–9	153
3:14	255
7:17	348
8:7	219
8:21	255
9:4–5	394
13:1	258, 363
13:1–2	348
13:1–15:19	460
13:2	349
13:5–9	258
13:10	364
14:12–14	459
14:22–31	215, 459
14:23–26	458
18:13	460
19:18	348

Sirach

1:11	487
3:31	255, 257
4:10	187
4:22	179
4:27	179
7:2–3	492
7:8	416
7:10	187
7:32–35	187
9:16	487
10:22	487
12:1	256
24:1–23	228, 413

24:7–12	20
24:23	20
25:6	487
29:9–13	187
35:2	256
35:12–13	179
36:13–17	288
39:8	487
42:1	179
44:20	274
45:23–24	142
51:26	413

Baruch

3:23–4:1	20
4:1	311
4:4	20, 311
4:5–16	288
4:8–37	398
4:21–23	288
4:28–29	288
4:36–37	288
5:5–6	288, 398

1 Maccabees

1:15	175
1:18	458
1:26	458
1:48	175
1:60–61	175
1:60–63	16
2:15–18	15
2:23–28	461
2:26–27	142
2:42–48	15
2:44–47	142
2:46	175
2:54	142
2:58	142
3:6	15
3:8	15, 142
4:36–58	54
6:1–16	54
6:58	184
10:18	111
12:6	111
15:2	111

2 Maccabees

1:1–9	89
1:10–2:18	89
2:21	141

3:33	255
4:7–17	87
4:16–17	14
5:17–20	14
6–7	153
6:4	463
6:8–10	175
6:10–11	16
6:12–17	14
6:18–31	204
6:18–7:42	16
6:18–8:5	4
6:21	204
6:24–25	204
7:1–8:5	119
7:24	124
7:30–38	14
7:37–38	4
9:1–10:9	54
14:38	141

3 Maccabees

1:9	255
2:31–33	15
3:3–4	201, 207, 226
3:4	328
6:28	334
7:10–15	15

2 Esdras (4 Ezra)

3.20–27	288
7.20–25	258
7.37	258
7.45–60	289
7.70–73	289
7.77	228
7.105	489
7.127–29	288
7.127–31	289
8.33	228
8.59–60	258
9.18–20	258
9.37	311
10.6–10	398
13.12–13	288
13.39–50	288
14.29–34	288

4 Maccabees

1:1	21, 65
1:1–3:18	447
1:2	65

1:13–17	21
1:18	219
1:30–31	468
1:31–2:9	22
2:5–6	288
2:14	22
2:21–23	20, 288
3:19	65
4:11	151
4:23	141
4:26	141
5:1–6:30	204
5:1–17:1	16
5:9	255
5:20–21	416
5:22–26	228
5:23–24	22
5:24	219
5:25–26	288
6:20	384
6:27–29	5
6:28–30	119
7:19	247
11:4	141
11:12	255
12:13	348
15:1	386
16:2	65
16:13	386
16:17	384
16:25	247
17:21–22	5, 119
18:1–2	65

PSEUDEPIGRAPHA

Apocalypse of Abraham

1–8	18

1 Enoch

6–36	119
82.9	367
90.30	298
90.33	298

Joseph and Aseneth

2.1	380
7.1	202

Jubilees

1.22–25	334
1.27–29	318
1.29–2.1	318
2.8–10	367
6.17	14
6.19	14
11.15–17	18
15.25–26	19
16.20–29	367
16.27–29	14
16.30	14
21.5–18	14
22.16–17	200–201, 226
22.20–23	201
30.17–20	142
33.23–24	215

Letter of Aristeas

128–69	21
134–35	201
139	201, 226, 328
139–42	290
142	226, 328
221–22	21
256	21

Psalms of Solomon

2.1–2	215
13.12	512
16.6	512
17.26–31	288
17.27	334
17.45	512
18.5	512

Sibylline Oracles

3.710–23	298
3.772–76	298

Testament of Dan

5.8	288
5.9	288
5.13	288

Testament of Judah

23.3	288
23.5	288

Testament of Levi

9.6–7	14

9.9–14	14
13.6	492
15.1–2	288
16.5	288

Testament of Moses

6.9	294
8.1	294

Testament of Naphtali

5.8	288

Testament of Zebulon

9.6–9	288

OTHER JEWISH WRITINGS

Dead Sea Scrolls

Rule of the Community (1QS)

XI.16	394

4Q381	394
4QMMT	225–26
4QpNahum	294
11QTemple 64.6–13	294

Josephus

Against Apion

2.137	17
2.174–75	330
2.293	220

Jewish Antiquities

1.192	175
1.215	403
6.165	220
8.208	220
12.241	175
13.257–58	18, 175
13.297	144
13.318	18, 175
13.379–83	151
13.380–81	294
15.136	318
18.65	375
18.81–85	375

18.328–29	184
20.38	124
20.51–53	54
20.197–203	164

Jewish War

1.96–98	151
1.159	173
1.193	515
2.118–62	462
2.420	11
3.453	173
4.141	173
4.656	125, 372
5.449–51	294

The Life

2.8	144

Philo

Against Flaccus

72	293
83	293
96	16

Embassy to Gaius

36	288
118	258
149–50	370
281–83	288

On Dreams

1.140–44	318

On Planting

126–31	258

On the Change of Names

39.217	329
268–69	492

On the Confusion of Tongues

21	492

On the Contemplative Life

3–4	348

On the Creation of the World

169	258

On the Decalogue

1	484
53–54	258

On the Eternity of the World
109   258

On the Life of Abraham
5.275–76   484

On the Life of Moses
2.166   318

On the Migration of Abraham
86–93   21
89   19
89–94   274
92   19

On the Preliminary Studies
9–10   395
14   395

On the Sacrifices of Cain and Abel
4.15   329
5.32   458

On the Special Laws
1.1.1–2   17
1.2.9–11   19
1.71   219
1.293   434
2.184–85   434
2.253   143

On the Virtues
194   484
212–16   18

Questions and Answers on Genesis
3.48   19

That Every Good Person Is Free
17   457

Who Is the Heir?
5.19   318
12.57   457
134   348

Rabbinic Literature

'Abot de Rabbi Nathan
2   318
25.1   184

b. Berakot
28b   184

b. Menaḥot
43b   339

b. Pesaḥim
54a   311

b. Sanhedrin
56b   19

b. Šabbat
31a   449

Genesis Rabbah
1:4   311
53:11   403

m. 'Abot
2.1   416
3.5   413
4.2   416
6.7   293, 321

m. Berakot
2.2   412

m. Nedarim
3.11   19

Sipre Deuteronomy
42 [11:14]   318
325 [32:35]   318

Targum Onqelos
Gen 16:7   397
Gen 21:9   403
Lev 18:5   293

Targum Pseudo-Jonathan
Gen 16:7   397
Gen 21:10   403
Lev 18:5   293
Lev 19:18   449

t. Berakot
6.18a   339

GRECO-ROMAN LITERATURE

Aeschylus

Prometheus Bound   4

Anaximenes

Rhetoric to Alexander
1420a1–3   77
1421b8–12   65, 80
1421b18–20   65
1421b21–27   64
1421b21–1423a12   96
1421b23–30   412
1421b38–40   412
1422a5–7   412
1427b31–35   66
1428b12–17   70
1429a25–28   70
1430a27–34   69
1430a40–47   70
1432a33   165
1436a33–37   117

Aristotle

Metaphysics
982a1–2   291
986a22–27   351

Nicomachean Ethics
2.7.10   468
5.1–11   219
5.5.7   256
8.14.2   256, 260
8.14.3   256
8.14.4   257

Politics
1.2   342
1.4   130
3.13   469

Rhetoric
1.2.3   68, 98
1.2.4   68
1.2.5   69
1.3.5   66, 96
1.4–2.26   67
1.8.6   435
1.9.34   381
1.9.40   70

2.1–11	99
2.1.2	69
2.1.3	68, 435
2.1.4	69
2.1.5	68, 435
2.1.8	69
2.2–11	69
2.2.8	257
2.5.1	420
2.7.1	255
2.10	461, 462
2.11.1–7	383
2.18–19	70
2.21	70
2.21.2	69, 411
2.22	69
2.23–26	70
3.3.4	492
3.11.2	268
3.14	71
3.14.6–7	117
3.15.3	66
3.19	71
3.19.1	501

Caesar

Gallic War
2.1	39
4.5	39
6.16	39

Cicero

Invention
1.5.6	77
1.9	67

Letters to Atticus
8.14.1	75, 76
9.10.1	75, 76
12.53	75, 76

Letters to Friends
4.13.1	76
9.21.1 [188]	74
10.33.2 [409]	74
12.30.1	75
15.21.4	75

On Divination
1.5	39
2.36–37	39

On Duties
1.47	256

On the Republic
1.52	484

Orator
1.142	67
2.65	492

Pro Flacco
16.37	75

Tusculan Disputations
3.22	21
4.38	21
4.57	21

Demosthenes

Epistles
1.2–4	77
3.1–35	77

On the Crown
131	255

Dio Cassius
79.11	440

Dio Chrysostom

Discourses
14.3–6	413
14.18	413
29.21	65
31.7	257
31.37	257
32.11	132
32.39	90
33.1–16	132
73	183
74	183
80.5–7	413–14

Diodorus Siculus

Library of History
3.31	440
17.116.4	149
34/35.1.1	201
40.3.4	201

Diogenes Laertius

Lives of Eminent Philosophers
1.33	339
7.166	124

Epictetus

Discourses
2.9.20	204
2.14.28	160
2.22.26	329
2.24.19	485
3.7.1	160
3.19.5–6	329
4.1	130

Euripides

Helen
1234	256

Iphigenia in Tauris
57	184

Heraclitus

Homeric Allegories
5.2	394

Hermogenes

Preliminary Exercises
3.7–8	101

Hesiod

Works and Days
342–51	257
401–4	257

Homer

Iliad
20.67	348

Isocrates

To Demonicus
24	257
26	256
29	256, 257

Julius Victor

Art of Rhetoric
27   75, 77

Juvenal

Satires
14.98–106   17

Lucian

Toxaris
40–41   382

Menander

Sentences
370   483
534   483

Nicolaus of Damascus

Life of Augustus
1   369

Philostratos of Lemnos

On Letters
2.257   75

Plato

Apology
21b–e   173
22a–b   173
29a   173
36d   173
41e   173, 485

Gorgias
452e   131
462b–466a   131
500c–503d   131
521a–b   131

Laws
7.790c   350
7.808–809   329
7.931a   460

Letters
7   93

Lysis
208c   329

Phaedo
93–94   21

Phaedrus
260c   492

Protagoras
352e   131

Republic
364c   132

Theaetetus
162e   90

Pliny the Elder

Natural History
5.10 §58   54
18.46 §46   54
28.7 §36   380
28.7 §39   380

Plutarch

How to Tell a Flatterer
1–2   383
5   383

On Moral Virtue
1   21
3   21
8   384

On the Education of Children
6–7   329

Roman Questions
289f   434

Polybius

Histories
3.48.12   160

Pseudo-Callisthenes

Alexander Romance
1.1   348

Pseudo-Cicero

Rhetorica ad Herennium
1.4.7   70
1.5.8   433, 435
1.9   68

1.24–25   66
3.2.2–3.4.9   64
3.2.3–3.3.5   219
3.3.4   412
3.8.15   66
3.10.18   67

Pseudo-Demetrius

De elocutione
17   72

Epistolary Types
Prol.   71, 80
11   73
14–16   80
18   80
25–30   71

On Style
229   75
231   78

Pseudo-Libanius

Epistolary Styles
2   75
5   96
6   72
46   66
51   91
92   66

Quintilian

Education of the Orator
2.15.19–33   77
3.4.1–4   72
3.8.12–13   68
3.8.36   70
5.10.1–3   411, 415
6.2.29–32   268
9.2.51   174
9.4.19–20   80

Seneca

Moral Epistles
75.1–2   74, 75
81.9–10   256
81.27   256
81.29   350
90.5–14   317

On Benefits

1.1.9	257
1.3.3–5	255
1.4.2	255
1.4.3	256
1.4.4	257
1.10.5	257
2.18.5	256
2.22.1	256
2.24.4	260
2.25.3	256
2.30.1–2	257
2.30.2	260
2.33.3	256
2.35.1	256
3.1.1	257
3.15.4	256
4.10.4	256
4.16.2	486
4.18.1	257
4.20.2	256
4.24.2	256
4.26.1	258
4.28.1	258
5.3.3	260
5.4.1	260
5.11.5	256
6.18.2	246
6.19.2–5	246
6.41.1–2	256
7.14.4	260
7.14.6	260
7.31.1–7.32.1	258

Sophocles

Ajax

522	256

Strabo

Geography

14.5.13	87
16.760–61	17

Suetonius

Tiberius

36	375

Tacitus

Annals

2.85	375

Histories

5.5.1–2	17, 201
5.5.2	175

Theocritus

Idyll

6.39	267, 380

Theon

Progymnasmata

3	393
15	393

Thucydides

History

2.44	65

Tryphon

De tropis

1.1	394

Virgil

Aeneid

6.792–93	120
6.851–53	118

Xenophon

Constitution

3.1	329

Memorabilia

2.1.1	350
2.7.1–14	483

EARLY CHRISTIAN LITERATURE

Augustine

City of God

4.31	460

De Doctrina

4.3.4–5	86

Didache

10.6	357

Epiphanius

Panarion

1.29.3–4	162
2.66.19	162
3.78.7–13	162

Refutation

30.21.2	434

Eusebius

Ecclesiastical History

3.11	163
3.32.6	163
4.22.42	163

Justin Martyr

Apology

2.5.2	349

Dialogue

10.3	294
23.3	349
32.1	294
38.1	294
89.2	294
90.1	294

Origen

Against Celsus

8.23	447

First Principles

1.3.4	447
3.2.3	447
3.4.1–5	447

Second Apocalypse of James

50.15–22	162

Tertullian

Apology

39.7	478